Social Science Text=Books
EDITED BY RICHARD T. ELY

COMPARATIVE FREE GOVERNMENT

SOCIAL SCIENCE TEXT-BOOKS

OUTLINES OF ECONOMICS
> By RICHARD T. ELY, PH.D., LL.D., Revised and enlarged by the Author and THOMAS S. ADAMS, PH.D., MAX O. LORENZ, PH.D., ALLYN A. YOUNG, PH.D.

HISTORY OF ECONOMIC THOUGHT
> By LEWIS H. HANEY, PH.D.

BUSINESS ORGANIZATION AND COMBINATION
> By LEWIS H. HANEY.

PROBLEMS OF CHILD WELFARE
> By GEORGE B. MANGOLD, PH.D.

THE NEW AMERICAN GOVERNMENT
> By JAMES T. YOUNG.

OUTLINES OF SOCIOLOGY
> By FRANK W. BLACKMAR, PH.D., and JOHN LEWIS GILLIN, PH.D.

COMPARATIVE FREE GOVERNMENT
> By JESSE MACY and JOHN W. GANNAWAY.

AMERICAN MUNICIPAL PROGRESS
> By CHARLES ZUEBLIN.

COMPARATIVE FREE GOVERNMENT

BY

JESSE MACY

PROFESSOR EMERITUS OF POLITICAL SCIENCE
IN GRINNELL COLLEGE

AND

JOHN W. GANNAWAY

PROFESSOR OF POLITICAL SCIENCE
IN GRINNELL COLLEGE

New York
THE MACMILLAN COMPANY
1915

All rights reserved

COPYRIGHT, 1915,
BY THE MACMILLAN COMPANY.

Set up and electrotyped. Published December, 1915.

Norwood Press
J. S. Cushing Co. — Berwick & Smith Co.
Norwood, Mass., U.S.A.

PREFACE

WITH the advent of a world movement toward democracy has come a comparative study of government. Already a large body of literature, based on such study, has appeared. The fact is gaining recognition that to understand clearly the problems of democracy, and to solve them adequately, world experience with free institutions must be drawn upon. Democracy is not the exclusive possession of any people; nor is it dependent upon any particular form or method. Every nation, whether it is far advanced on the path of freedom or is only beginning the slow journey toward liberty, has its lesson for the whole world. It is of high value to have the important contributions of the various states analyzed and compared for the purpose of throwing light upon the problems and processes of free government. No nation is so far advanced that it cannot learn from the experience of others.

The comparative study of government is particularly valuable for the student just beginning his work in Political Science. It not only brings knowledge of fundamental principles, but gives breadth of view and develops sympathetic appreciation of what peoples of other races and nationalities are doing to meet the demands of modern society. It is the most effective safeguard against the narrow, intolerant provincialism and the cheap chauvinism which characterize the attitude of so many persons and which are so great an obstacle in the path of genuine political progress. The authors of this book are firm in the belief that the basic course in Political Science should be comparative in nature. It is a profound pity that so many men and women enter upon the duties of citizenship in complete ignorance of what the nations of the world are doing to achieve self-government.

A word concerning the plan and purpose of the chapters that follow should be given. The purpose is not primarily a comparative study of existing governments, but a study of the various processes and institutions by which free government is being attained. In this is found one of the book's distinctive features. The aim is not to give a mass of detail concerning each of the governments considered, but to treat of the rise and present status of democracy by means of the most important contributing types, emphasizing those aspects which throw light on the main theme. In this way the student is made acquainted with the essential features of the world's free governments as they are now constituted.

Since all governments are manifestly affected by the struggle for freedom, none can be omitted from the final comparison. Yet as an introduction to the study some governments are clearly more important than others and may be used to illustrate the political organizations of the less conspicuous members of their own class. In this respect the United States holds first place because it was the first great state distinctly founded upon the theory of popular control, and because of its influence, both direct and indirect, upon all other states. It forms, especially for the American student, a natural basis for a comparative study of government throughout the world. The institutions of the United States are therefore described with considerable detail, fully half of the book being devoted to their consideration. This part is not primarily comparative, but descriptive.

A knowledge of free government in America involves an understanding of the rise of democracy in England; and therefore England, for distinctively comparative study, holds the next place. The United States is itself a product of England. Together the two great Anglo-Saxon states furnish the two leading types of free government, — the Presidential and the Cabinet. The one has been copied with many variations by the Republics of the New World and the other by the states in which free governments have developed out of monarchies. The treatment of the English government is not intended to be exhaustive, but is sufficiently full to show England's great contributions to democracy and to make clear the important contrasts between English practices and those of other states.

With equal definiteness the third place is assigned to France, whose relation to Anglo-Saxon history has been intimate and significant. France, unlike England and the United States, is developing a democracy under the normal condition of close proximity to rival states. Moreover, the French democracy is conspicuous because of the high centralization that prevails. It involves a governmental organization that differs fundamentally from those of England and America. Furthermore, it is through France that modern free governments are most notably linked to the ancient Roman Republic through the system of Roman law. French experience, therefore, is of peculiar interest and value in the comparative study of political institutions.

Germany and Switzerland are selected for study because the one government exhibits the early stages of transition from autocracy to democracy and the other an advanced stage of assured democracy. Switzerland is also of especial interest because it furnishes a type of free government which is neither Cabinet nor Presidential, yet is completely democratic. The comparison is still further extended by chapters on the small states of Europe and the leading states of South America, and a final chapter on the relation of federation to democracy.

In the treatment of the various governments special attention is given to the federal system as an agency of free government; to the development and position of the executive authority; to political parties as a universal phenomenon in the transition from despotism to democracy; and to the judiciary because of its close relation to partisan politics in America and to the conflict between autocracy and democracy in all the great states. The judiciary is of peculiar interest, also, because of the two competing systems of English and Roman law, involving distinctly different governmental organizations and different means of access to the people as the source of authority.

In the preparation of the book the authors have incurred many obligations. They are especially indebted to Professor Ely, Editor of the Series, who read the entire manuscript and made many helpful suggestions. They are also under obligation to Professors F. A. Ogg, of the University of Wisconsin, and P. F. Peck and C. E. Payne, of Grinnell College, who read parts of the manuscript and gave valuable assistance through both suggestions and corrections. A part of the manuscript on England was read by Sir Frederick Pollock. Numerous friends in the various states described have been most helpful in supplying material for the book. Of these special mention should be made of Professeur C. Cestre, of the University of Bordeaux, and Professeur Emile Saillens, of the University of Toulouse.

GRINNELL, IOWA,
    October 20, 1915.

TABLE OF CONTENTS

		PAGE
INTRODUCTION.	THE NATURE OF FREE GOVERNMENT	xiii

PART I

THE UNITED STATES OF AMERICA

CHAPTER		
I.	THE STATES AND THE NATION	3
II.	SOURCES OF THE CONSTITUTION	14
III.	PRINCIPLES OF THE CONSTITUTION	22
IV.	THE PRESIDENCY	31
V.	THE ELECTION OF THE PRESIDENT	38
VI.	THE PRESIDENT AS AN EXECUTIVE	55
VII.	THE PRESIDENT AND LEGISLATION	70
VIII.	THE PRESIDENT'S CABINET	81
IX.	NATIONAL ADMINISTRATION	96
X.	THE CONGRESS — GENERAL OBSERVATIONS	116
XI.	THE SENATE	127
XII.	THE HOUSE OF REPRESENTATIVES — COMPOSITION AND ORGANIZATION	145
XIII.	THE HOUSE OF REPRESENTATIVES — COMMITTEES AND PROCEDURE	158
XIV.	THE PARTY SYSTEM	177
XV.	THE NATIONAL CONVENTION	190
XVI.	PARTY MACHINERY AND METHODS — NATIONAL	205

CHAPTER		PAGE
XVII.	PARTY MACHINERY AND METHODS — STATE AND LOCAL	219
XVIII.	THE FEDERAL COURTS — CONSTITUTIONAL STATUS AND DEVELOPMENT	231
XIX.	THE FEDERAL COURTS — PRESENT ORGANIZATION	241
XX.	JURISDICTION OF THE FEDERAL COURTS	250
XXI.	THE COURTS AND LEGISLATION	266
XXII.	CONSTITUTIONAL READJUSTMENT BY AMENDMENT	281
XXIII.	CONSTITUTIONAL READJUSTMENT THROUGH LAW, CUSTOM, AND JUDICIAL CONSTRUCTION	295
XXIV.	THE STATES — CONSTITUTIONAL POSITION AND POWERS	307
XXV.	THE STATES — SUFFRAGE AND CITIZENSHIP	319
XXVI.	THE STATES — POLICE POWER AND CONTROL OVER LOCAL GOVERNMENTS	329
XXVII.	STATE LEGISLATION	340
XXVIII.	STATE ADMINISTRATION	361
XXIX.	THE STATE JUDICIARY	379

PART II

ENGLAND

XXX.	THE CABINET SYSTEM	395
XXXI.	NATURE OF THE ENGLISH CONSTITUTION	403
XXXII.	SOURCES OF THE ENGLISH CONSTITUTION FOUND IN LOCAL GOVERNMENT	412
XXXIII.	THE RISE OF THE CABINET	421
XXXIV.	THE RELATION OF THE CABINET TO THE EXECUTIVE AND TO THE JUDICIARY	435
XXXV.	THE HOUSE OF COMMONS	447
XXXVI.	THE HOUSE OF LORDS	459
XXXVII.	THE MINISTRY IN PARLIAMENT	466
XXXVIII.	THE CROWN	478
XXXIX.	THE ORIGIN OF PARTIES	491
XL.	THE PARTIES IN PARLIAMENT	498
XLI.	LOCAL PARTY ORGANIZATION	505

TABLE OF CONTENTS

CHAPTER		PAGE
XLII.	Religion and the Church	516
XLIII.	The Courts and Local Government	523
XLIV.	Wales, Scotland, and Ireland	533
XLV.	The Self-governing Dominions	540

FRANCE

XLVI.	Origin and Nature of the French Constitution	550
XLVII.	The Executive in France	562
XLVIII.	The Legislature and Political Parties	572
XLIX.	The Roman Legal System and Modern Government	582

GERMANY

L.	The Origin of the German Empire	592
LI.	The Present Constitution and Government	602

SWITZERLAND

LII.	Origin of the Swiss Government	614
LIII.	The Frame of Government	621
LIV.	The Working of the System	632
LV.	Switzerland Compared with the United States and England	639

PART III

DEMOCRACY IN OTHER STATES

LVI.	The Small States of Europe	649
LVII.	South America and Free Government	656
LVIII.	Cabinet and Unitary Government in Chile	663
LIX.	Federal and Presidential Government in Argentina	672
LX.	Federation and Democracy	689

BOOK LIST	701
CASES IN AMERICAN CONSTITUTIONAL LAW	719
INDEX	725

INTRODUCTION

The Nature of Free Government

ARISTOTLE and Plato in their descriptions of the ideal city-state elaborated principles which are being incarnated in modern free states. In such a state the citizen realized himself through his conscious participation in the life of the city. There could be no conflict between the man and the state because man was a political animal and he became a man by participation in the body politic. There could be no perfect man until the body politic was perfected. Perfection in the city implied perfection in the citizenship. Education and training were the chief means for making known to each member his place in the service of the city. Aristotle described two sorts of government, one of which was in harmony with the true interests of the state, while the other introduced an alien element which tended to destroy the state. The officers in the good government retained their place as conscious members of the body politic. They sought in all ways to serve the state; they were the willing agents for the self-expression of the city; they had no will of their own apart from the interests of the city. These were the characteristics of the true government. The bad government was one in which the rulers separated themselves from the normal life of the citizen. They made use of office for self-aggrandisement. They relied upon force in matters of government and thus introduced a state of war between the city and its rulers. The triumph of a bad government meant the destruction of the body politic and the substitution of a state composed of rulers and their subjects, in which the rulers command and the subjects are forced to obey.

Each of these two kinds of government might have any one of three forms, — monarchy, aristocracy, or polity for the good; tyranny, oligarchy, or democracy for the bad. The form, according to Aristotle, was of minor importance as compared with the fundamental question whether the government was in harmony with the life of the city or was imposed upon the city by force.[1]

In his view, the body politic included only a small fraction of the people, while some nine tenths of them were consigned to perpetual slavery, and were entirely subject to the will of their masters. Where slavery prevailed in the household it was natural that the relation of master to slave should be carried into that of rulers to subjects in the state, rulers commanding and subjects obeying. Whether the rulers were one, few, or many, the tendency was to force their will upon the city, and in practice every form of government became bad. The citizens became divided into rulers and subjects and the true ideal of the city vanished. That which the Greeks described as a degenerate government became the accepted definition of all government.[2] Not until the abolition of slavery in very recent times has it been possible to revert to the Greek conception of a good government. A citizenship composed of those who believe in slavery will naturally have a government which is imposed by force upon the masses of the people. The disappearance of slavery clears the field for a real body politic composed of the entire people. It becomes possible for the first time in human history to fulfill the Greek ideal of a state whose rulers are at the same time subjects of the people.

The new order requires a new literature, the use of new words and phrases, or, what is more difficult, the use of old words with different and often contradictory meanings. For instance, the term " government " in the modern state is coming to involve a flat contradiction of its former usage. In the literature of the past, the term, in its various uses, carries with it the idea of compulsion, the forcing of men to do things which they do not wish to do.[3] It implies a separation of the people into two classes, rulers and subjects, self-government being a contradiction in terms. The new order in a free state reverses the former relation of officers and people. The officers, as the servants of the people, have no authority not conferred upon them by the

---

[1] Aristotle's "Politics," Book III.
[2] *Ibid.*, Book I.
[3] Austin, "Lectures on Jurisprudence, the Philosophy of Positive Law," Part I, § 1, Lecture VI, p. 111.

people. In an ideal democracy neither officers nor people would be under command, but the good government described by Aristotle would be realized. Officers, in common with all citizens, would be servants of the state, all working to a common end, government being the chief agency for the self-realization of the citizens.

The word " Democracy " has had a most remarkable history. Aristotle's three terms to designate the forms of good government were " Monarchy," " Aristocracy," and " Polity "; Democracy does not appear in the list. The Monarch became a tyrant when he ceased to rule as a servant of the body politic. The Aristocracy became an oligarchy or a plutocracy when public officers ceased to be servants of the city and entered into a conspiracy for its destruction. The Polity is in itself an ideal government in which the entire citizenship has become so trained that each man finds his place in the service of the city by mutual agreement. The degenerate Polity becomes a " democracy," a government by violence and brute force directed by demagogues, — in all respects a bad government. Yet this same word, used by Aristotle to designate a vitiated government, which never had any support or approval, is now taken up and applied to every movement in modern society which tends to fulfill the Greek ideal of a polity, or a form of government suited to the perfect state. Democracy now includes all that Aristotle describes in his three forms of good government. In place of the autocrat it would substitute the democratic monarch, a willing servant of the people, as has been done in Norway. Oligarchs and plutocrats who have been in conspiracy against the people give place to families who have won reputation for superior service, as is the case in some of the Swiss communes and cantons. The ideal democracy, as the term is now used, is a state in which all are equally bound to render service and all freely observe the rules of the service, the necessity for the use of force being a mark of failure in government. This ideal is not confined to institutions of the state; it is carried into the industrial world where it would abolish industrial wars and establish agreement among all industrial classes. It pervades schools and churches, where it is working a revolution no less significant. Every form of association is being democratized.

Between the extreme and contradictory definitions of the term political literature furnishes illustration of numerous intermediate uses.[1] Democracy is often described as government by majorities. As thus used the word denotes a mere form of government without any implication as to whether it is good or bad. Such a definition is natural to those who define all government in terms of force. Majorities compel minorities to obey. The modern democrat, while maintaining the ideal of government by common agreement, admits that majorities are of immense use in the transition from despotism to true democracy. It is better to have free and fair discussion of the few issues in which common consent cannot be otherwise reached and then to accept for the time a majority vote, than to adopt the old method of force. As one has said: "It is better to count heads than to break heads." But the ideal democracy is not a government by majorities, it is a government by common consent in which majorities serve as one of the means for reaching agreement.

The transition from government imposed by the strong upon the weak to government achieved by the willing coöperation of citizens involves a great revolution. That revolution is yet in its early beginnings. Democracy will not have had a fair trial until its principles have become generally understood and accepted. It calls for a new type of statesman, a new standard for the superior man. The old order called for the man who could break the wills of the multitude and render them submissive. The new order calls for the man of insight, of sympathy and discernment, who perceives most clearly the needs and aspirations of the people. It will require many generations fairly to test the merits of the new order.

The new era involves a new interpretation of history. So long as the relation of master and slave served as a model for the organization of the state it was impossible to gain a hearing for the teachings of the Greek philosophers on the real nature of the true state. That teaching lay dormant for two thousand years. The contradictory interpretations of Hebrew history are likewise significant. The divine right of kings and every other form of despotism have been upheld by appeals to Jewish and

[1] Aristotle and other Greek writers gave a variety of meanings to the term. "What Aristotle calls πολιτεία (polity) Polybios calls δημοκρατία (democracy); what Aristotle calls δημοκρατία Polybios calls ὀχλοκρατία." — Freeman, "Growth of the English Constitution," p. 167, London, 1884.

early Christian literature. Effective use is now made of the same literature in support of the modern free state. The free state calls for no new principles; all needful principles are clearly stated in Greek and Hebrew and other ancient literature; the application alone is new. As the upholders of the former order have sought to monopolize the interpretation of history, advocates of free government are now disposed to be equally monopolistic. No past human experience is foreign to their needs; the entire course of evolution is interpreted as contributory to the one end of producing the free man in a congenial environment. Slavery and despotism have themselves been cardinal agencies in making men free. They have compelled their victims to combine for self-protection and thus to gain experience for the future democracy. The revolution now in progress arises from the conviction that all human beings may become free without the use of the brutal agencies of the past.

Western civilization has always meant a freer civilization. Innumerable communities have been organized during the migrations of races westward, each of them a new experiment in government. The movement falls into two divisions. For many centuries after the nations had crossed the Eastern continents the Atlantic Ocean served as a barrier to their further progress. Then free communities were organized on its western shore and the migration went on across another great continent.

Modern democracy is thus rooted and grounded in the past. Its teachers have been states rather than individuals. All states contribute, but some much more than others. In the Old World the great contributors have been Palestine, Greece, Rome, France, and England; in the New the United States. Free states assume innumerable forms and modifications, but a few leading types serve as a basis for classification. It is customary to classify nearly all free governments as of Cabinet form after the English model or of Presidential form after the model of the United States. Cabinet governments appear in the states in which free governments have been derived from monarchy, and are mainly confined to the Old World, while the United States is accepted as a model for the organization of American Republics. The Old World form is the result of evolution; the New World form is characterized by artificial construction.

Another classification is based upon principles even more

fundamental. Except in the United States and in the British Empire free governments are founded upon the principles of law and government developed by the Roman Republic and perfected by the Roman Empire. The Roman system involves radical differences in the allotment of powers to the legislature and to the executive, and a still greater distinction in the place assigned to the judiciary. France holds a leading place in the adaptation of the Roman system to the needs of modern democracy.

PART I
THE UNITED STATES

COMPARATIVE FREE GOVERNMENT

CHAPTER I

THE STATES AND THE NATION

THE term "free government" implies no particular form of government. Such a government may be of the unitary type and be a monarchy, as in England, or a republic, as in France. It may be of the federated type and be republican, as in the United States, or monarchic, as in the German Empire. It may be presidential in form or of the cabinet type. It is not the form that makes a government free, but the fact that it is dependent upon the people whom it governs. A free government is a popular government, and any government that is based upon the will of the people and is controlled by that will is to be classed as free.

The United States has a government whose powers are divided between the Nation and the States. But it is a government of the federal type and not a mere confederation. There is a vital difference, as the history of the United States has revealed. A confederation involves a union of independent, sovereign states for some common purpose. Sovereignty continues in each of the states. The union is essentially temporary in its nature, a kind of treaty alliance, and each state is free to withdraw at any time it chooses. Federal government implies a union of states or commonwealths to form a single state whose governmental authority is divided between a central organization and the various commonwealth organizations. Sovereignty resides in the state as a whole and not in the commonwealths that compose it. Each of the component units is an integral part of the larger state and cannot withdraw from it. Each of the commonwealths has its own government which exercises full control over its own local affairs. It is independent of all the other commonwealths and to a large extent independent of the central authority, but not entirely so, as in the case of a confederation. The central government cannot interfere with the commonwealth in its own sphere and the commonwealth cannot interfere with the central government. The authority has been divided between them and each is supposed to go its own way in regard to the matters that have been assigned to it.

Federation Inevitable in the United States. — Political and economic conditions existing at the time the Constitution of the United States was framed determined the form of government that was to be established. A federal government was not only logical but inevitable. A unitary government was impossible. The agencies of the central government under the Articles of Confederation were powerless and the Confederation was a failure. Each of the thirteen States was a law unto itself and could obey or ignore the commands of the Congress as it pleased. To remedy the weaknesses of the Confederation the new government must possess wide powers, must be supreme, indeed, with respect to a good many things, but, under the conditions that prevailed, no constitution could be adopted which did not recognize the equality of the States and their independence of one another and, to a large extent, of the central government itself.

The principle of federalism alone could meet the requirements. The States, though united by a common interest in the prosecution of the war against England, were jealous and suspicious of one another after their independence had been gained. Their commercial and industrial interests were in conflict, and distrust prevailed on every side. Particularly were the small States distrustful of the large States and fearful lest their rights and equality might be destroyed under the new government through the latter's preponderating influence. Moreover, the predominant sentiment in all of the States was opposed to any unnecessary centralization of power. It was recognized that there must be some centralization, but this should be held to the lowest limit possible and still give the central government sufficient power to do its work effectively. A government of a unitary character, therefore, or one based upon the monarchic principle, was out of the question. It was to free themselves from this principle that the people had fought and suffered, and the liberties thus gained must not be endangered by setting up a new master which might in time become as objectionable as the old one had been.

The real problem confronting the framers of the Constitution, therefore, was not that of determining the form of government; that was settled by the very conditions which gave rise to the need for a new government. Their great problem was the extremely difficult one of setting up a federal government in which there should be a proper balance of powers between the States and the central government. The futile, even farcical attempts of the Congress to control matters of common interest under the Articles of Confederation made it plain that the new central government must be strong; but not too strong. All possible danger of a monarchy must be averted. On the other hand, the States must retain all of the power that was necessary for the protection of their own independence and rights and for the solution of their own local problems; but not too much power should be retained. The weakness and the inefficiency of the old Confederation must be avoided. But how should this nice balancing of functions and powers be brought about? Just how much power should be retained by the States and how much should be given to the central government? In what sphere of activity should the latter be supreme and in what the former? Exactly what limitations should be imposed upon each? Just how should the adjustment of powers be made? This was the problem which faced the men of the constitutional convention. Its right solution demanded the most consummate statecraft; and it is not to the discredit of the men who framed the Constitution that their work was deficient in some respects. A perfect adjustment of the relations between the States and the central government was impossible.

This problem would not have been so difficult had the States not existed as independent commonwealths, each with its own fully developed government. If the task had been merely to create a new government of a unitary type, or even of a federal type, parceling out the powers between the States and the

Nation, it would have been much more simple. The Constitution would then have been the source of all powers for States and Nation alike, and it would not have been impossible to distribute these powers in such a way as to eliminate all cause of friction and discord. But such was not the case. The States existed. In theory, at least, each was an independent state, possessing all the powers that any independent commonwealth could possess. Practically, of course, none of the States was able to maintain its sovereign supremacy. Nevertheless, all jealously and insistently asserted their independence, and the practical difficulty of placing over them an effective central authority was one of vast proportions. This could be done only by inducing the States to surrender certain definite powers to the Nation and to impose certain definite restrictions upon themselves. Without the latter the former would be worthless.

Distribution of Powers. — It should be clear that the central government is one of conferred or limited powers. These are sometimes spoken of as enumerated powers. The Nation can exercise only those powers that are specifically delegated to it by the Constitution or are necessarily implied either by the definite grants or by the Constitution as a whole. Obviously the grant of power to do a certain thing carries with it the power to provide the necessary means to make that power effective.[1] The definite recognition of the doctrine of implied powers was made by the Supreme Court early in the national history. The central government can do nothing that it is not permitted to do by the Constitution, either directly or by implication. Over the powers that have been granted to it, however, its control is absolute.

The States, on the other hand, are not governments with conferred or delegated powers, but with reserved or inherent powers. All powers belong to the States which have not been specifically denied to them by the Constitution or granted to the central government. In the case of the central government it must be shown affirmatively that a power has been granted, either expressly or impliedly, before its exercise can be valid.

---

[1] "Let the end be legitimate, let it be within the scope of the constitution, and all means which are appropriate, which are plainly adapted to that end, which are not prohibited, but consist with the letter and spirit of the constitution, are constitutional." — *McCulloch* v. *Maryland*, 4 Wheaton 316 (1819).

In the case of the States the denial of the power must be affirmatively shown before its exercise can be considered invalid. The States were antecedent to the Nation and originally possessed all power.

The principle which controlled in the distribution of powers was a simple one. Questions that were national in their scope or that affected more than one of the States were placed under the control of the central authority. The control of questions that were local or intrastate in their character was left to the States. Expressed in this general way the principle which guided the Constitution makers is simple and easily understood; but in the actual practice of determining what is intrastate and what interstate in its reach, difficulties of the most intricate nature are frequently encountered. The great crises of the Nation's history, indeed, have centered around the question of whether certain powers had been granted to the Nation or reserved to the States.

According to the division of powers effected there was lodged in the federal government control over foreign relations, interstate and foreign commerce, questions of war and peace, army and navy, post office, coinage, currency, and other matters that are of concern to all of the States. The taxing power, of course, was given to the central government, for without that it would be as helpless as the Congress had been under the Articles of Confederation.

The States retained control over all local questions and institutions, education, the care of the poor, private law, both civil and criminal. They possess "all the ordinary legal choices that shape a people's life. Theirs is the whole of the ordinary field of law; the regulation of domestic relations and of the relations between employer and employee, the determination of property rights and of the validity and enforcement of contracts, the definition of crimes and their punishment, the definition of the many and subtle rights and obligations which lie outside the fields of property and contract, the establishment of the laws of incorporation and of the rules governing the conduct of every kind of business."[1] It is plain that the great bulk of governmental activity rests with the States. The central government

---

[1] Wilson, "Constitutional Government in the United States," p. 183.

may do comparatively few things, whereas the States may exercise authority in a multitude of things.

In the case of both Nation and States a number of definite prohibitions were established by the Constitution. These are contained for the most part in sections 9 and 10 of Article I and in the first ten amendments to the Constitution, known as the Bill of Rights. By these provisions Congress and the States alike are prohibited from passing bills of attainder or ex post facto laws, from suspending the writ of habeas corpus, and from granting titles of nobility. Congress is also forbidden to place duties upon articles exported from the States or by its regulation of commerce give preference to any State; it cannot pass laws restricting freedom of religion or of speech or of the press or of public meeting; it cannot deny trial by jury or establish a religious test for the holding of public office.

The States, in turn, are forbidden to enter into any treaty or alliance, coin money, make anything but gold and silver coin a legal tender, or pass any law impairing the obligation of contracts. No State can, without the consent of Congress, levy any import or export duties or enter into any compact with another State or with a foreign nation. No State shall maintain any but a republican form of government, or abridge the privileges or immunities of citizens of the United States, or deprive any person of life, liberty, or property without due process of law, or deny to any person the equal protection of the laws. In the case of both States and Nation other restrictions are imposed, in addition to those mentioned.

With regard to a number of subjects there is a concurrent jurisdiction. Bankruptcy, for instance, is a subject upon which both the States and the Nation may legislate. The rule governing this point, as determined by the courts, is to the effect that the States may exercise concurrent power in all cases with the exception of three; first, where the power is lodged exclusively in the federal Constitution; second, where it is given to the United States and prohibited to the States; and, third, where from the very nature and subjects of the power, it must necessarily be exclusively exercised by the United States government.[1]

[1] *Gilman* v. *Philadelphia*, 3 Wallace 713 (1866); *Sturges* v. *Crowninshield*, 4 Wheaton 122 (1819).

In case of conflict between the law of a State and the law of the Nation upon any subject over which there is concurrent power, the law of the State must give way. Of course if Congress does not pass any law at all, the States are free to act as they please. Most important of these concurrent powers is the taxing power, for neither the Nation nor the States could survive without the power to raise revenue.

It is obvious that although the principle upon which the division of powers was based is simple, the actual division was not absolute, that there is a good deal of overlapping of the two authorities, and that friction can easily arise. This has occurred, indeed, again and again. There is not and cannot well be an exact delimitation of authority. Moreover, the new economic and political problems that result from constantly changing industrial and economic conditions make it inevitable that conflicts shall continue to arise from time to time. As the relations of life become more complex the difficulty of determining exactly what belongs to the States and what to the Nation becomes greater. Particularly troublesome in this connection have been the questions of industry and commerce. Authority claimed and in various ways exercised by the Nation over interstate commerce has repeatedly been denied by the States. And notwithstanding all of the controversies that have arisen since the Constitution was adopted, the precise amount of power which the Nation has is still unknown. There can be no doubt that the tendency has been for it to exercise more and more control. The relation existing at present between the States and the Nation is by no means what it was at the beginning. There has been beyond question a shifting of powers from the States to the national authority. Centralization has taken place far beyond the thought of the framers of the Constitution. To what extent this centralizing process should continue is one of the great and apparently abiding problems before the American people.

Growth of National Power. — Centralization was feared by many of the men who helped to frame the Constitution and every effort was made to protect the rights and powers of the States. One group in the convention favored a strongly centralized government even at the expense of the States; another group sought to hold the power of the central government to the lowest limit possible. The former emphasized national interests and the latter local and State interests. These two views later were championed by the political parties that first sprang into existence after the adoption of the Constitution, the Federalist party, under the lead of Alexander Hamilton, standing for the power of the Nation, and the Democratic-Republican party, under the lead of Thomas Jefferson, standing for the powers and rights of the States. There has been incessant dispute over the line of separation of the two authorities ever since, and the end is not yet.

One of the first instances of the denial of federal authority on the part of the States was in connection with the establishment of the second United States Bank in 1816. Two years later Maryland imposed a tax upon the circulating notes issued by the branches of the bank and circulating within the limits of that State. The famous case of McCulloch *v.* Maryland was the result.[1] Maryland denied the power of Congress to establish the bank because there was no express grant of power for that purpose. Chief Justice Marshall held, however, speaking for the Supreme Court, that the bank was constitutional notwithstanding the absence of a specific grant of power, and so definitely established the principle of implied powers. By this decision the national power was greatly strengthened.

The Nullification Act of South Carolina in 1832 brought on a real crisis over the rights of the States as against the rights of the Nation. Congress had passed a tariff law to which a number of the States objected. South Carolina through a convention passed an ordinance of nullification and thus defied the national authority. But under the vigorous leadership of President Jackson, Congress adhered to its policy and nullification failed. Again the supremacy of the federal government was maintained in the face of bitter opposition by the States, and a " critical matter, of lasting importance, was decided. The federal government was conceded the power to determine the economic opportunities of the States."[2]

But the climax of the struggle over States' rights was reached in the great Civil War which grew out of the long and bitter slavery controversy. Whatever may have been the constitu-

[1] 4 Wheaton 316 (1819).
[2] Wilson, "Constitutional Government in the United States," p. 175.

tional right of Congress with respect to slavery in the Territories or the constitutional right of a State to secede, the outcome of the struggle was the absolute supremacy of the Union. By the arbitrament of war the relation of the States to the Union, as far as secession is concerned, was settled for all time. The United States is not merely a confederation.

The controversies that have arisen since the Civil War and the reconstruction period have centered about the control of commerce and the great corporations. A new industrial order, involving vast economic interests and tremendously difficult problems, has developed which was not and could not be foreseen when the Constitution was adopted. The control of commerce among the States, which was given to the national government by the Constitution, was a simple thing at the beginning. It involved no great centralization of power in the Nation. But the rapid and unforeseen development of industry, the growth of great railway systems and huge industrial corporations doing business in all of the States of the Union have transformed the life of America and have, under the interstate commerce clause of the Constitution, brought about a vast centralization of power in the national government. The States have not kept pace with the Nation in this development and more and more the people look to the central government for protection and relief from corporate and monopolistic oppression. In the changed and changing attitude of the people there is perhaps grave danger for the States. It is possible that the readjustment which seems inevitable may involve some kind of reorganization of the State governments and a renewed activity and control on their part in the field of corporate industry, but the trend for years has been decidedly in the other direction, and the outcome seems certain to be another recognition of the supremacy of the national authority concerning vital public problems which are now the subject of dispute. The tendency from the beginning has been toward a larger and more effective national control. It is not unreasonable to assume that the centralizing process will continue.

Supreme Court's Control over Division of Powers. — It is important to note that the ultimate authority to determine whether a question comes within the power of the States or of the Nation rests with the national government. It is the Supreme Court of the United States that interprets the Constitution, and by constitutional interpretation the powers of the Nation may be extended far beyond their present limits. Experience has shown repeatedly that this may be done. The Constitution is constantly being altered by the interpretation process. Some changes have been accomplished by the formal process of amendment, but many of the most significant modifications have been brought about through judicial construction. The fame of Chief Justice Marshall largely rests upon decisions which contributed to the development of the national authority. There is no reason to think that changes in the meaning of the Constitution by this method will cease; indeed, such changes are necessary in order that the Constitution may be adapted to new needs and new problems. It may well be expected, if past and present tendencies are indicative of future development, that the Nation will acquire by the interpretative process a larger control than it now has, unless the people place an arbitrary limit upon its powers by the formal amendment of the Constitution.

Some friction between the States and the national government was unavoidable. The framers of the Constitution endeavored to reduce the chance of conflict to the lowest limit possible, but its entire elimination was not to be expected. On the whole, the complex governmental machine has worked with wonderful smoothness. The student may well wonder why more friction has not occurred. The explanation, in large part, is found in one very important fact. The central government is not dependent upon the States as such for the powers it exercises or for the accomplishment of its purposes. It acts directly upon the people. It has its own governmental machinery which is entirely separate from the governments of the States. Its laws are passed and enforced by its own agents. It performs its functions as if the States did not exist. In its own sphere of action it is supreme.[1]

The States, on the other hand, are beyond the control of the Nation in the exercise of the powers that belong to them. As long as they keep within the limits set by the federal Constitution they are free to act as they please. The national authority can in no way interfere. Each State may go its own way as

[1] For a radically different policy see chapters which follow on Germany and Switzerland.

long as it does not violate the fundamental law as contained in the Constitution. This freedom from dependence upon each other in the discharge of the functions which each must perform accounts in large measure for the orderliness and smoothness with which the whole complex system has worked. The citizen owes allegiance to both governments, but this double allegiance involves no practical conflict of duty.

REFERENCES

BEARD. *American Government and Politics*, Edition 1914, Chaps. III, VIII.
BRYCE. *The American Commonwealth*, Edition 1910, Vol. I, Chaps. II, XXVII, XXVIII.
WILLOUGHBY. *The American Constitutional System*, Chaps. I, II, VII, VIII.
WILSON. *Constitutional Government in the United States*, Chap. VII.
WOODBURN. *The American Republic*, Chap. II.

CHAPTER II

SOURCES OF THE CONSTITUTION

THE Constitution of the United States is the product of both evolution and conscious effort. It is not the invention of the men who composed the Constitutional Convention of 1787, although some of its features were worked out by them without experience as their guide. In most of its essentials, however, it is the result of experience and not of theory, as is true of nearly all of the important, vital political institutions of the world. Its roots are in the past and an adequate comprehension of its principles and of the scheme of government which it established cannot be obtained without an understanding of the essential facts in the previous history of the States and the Colonies. It is a mistaken view which holds that it was cut out of whole cloth, so to speak, by the convention that framed it. Gladstone's famous assertion that it is " the most wonderful work ever struck off at a given time by the brain and purpose of man," though in a sense true, is quite as noteworthy for the false understanding it is likely to cause as for the unstinted admiration it expresses.

Nevertheless, the Constitution is not an unconscious growth like the unwritten Constitution of England. As it stood at the beginning it was, in an important sense, the result of deliberate effort, of conscious analysis. Some of its features, particularly the method of choosing a President, were essentially the inventions of the men who framed it. The materials of which it is made, however, the principles which it embodies, even the form of government which it outlines, were furnished and determined by the experience of the colonists and the economic and political conditions that led to its adoption. Its framers took these materials and principles and shaped them to their purpose. It is this conscious action of the people through their representatives and the sanction which they gave to the Constitution through the process of ratification, that differentiates it so fundamentally from the Constitution of England. The latter was never framed or adopted, but is entirely the product of English political history and experience. This fundamental fact must never be lost sight of in the comparative study of the political life and institutions of the two countries. It is one of those basic things, to overlook which means confusion and inadequate understanding.

Colonial Experience. — What were the materials that were at hand with which to build the new government? First of all there was the experience of the colonists with their colonial governments. The people had chief executives in the form of governors. They had legislatures for the enactment of laws and courts for their interpretation. They were familiar with the processes and principles of representative government. They were devoted to political liberty. In short, the people had worked out, and in the school of experience had learned how to use, the basic principles of the Constitution.

In its broad outlines the form of government that prevailed in the different Colonies was similar to that which was established by the federal Constitution. There were the three departments of government, — legislative, executive, and judicial, more or less definitely separated in their functions. The executive authority was largely in the hands of the governor who attended to the enforcement of the laws, made appointments to office, granted pardons, commanded the military forces, recommended legislation to the assembly, exercised the veto power, and performed many other functions similar to those conferred upon the President by the Constitution. In the colonial governor and the governor of the States after independence from Great Britain was declared, the Constitution makers found the prototype of the President and in the creation of the presidency, were guided by the experience which the people had had with these colonial and State executives.

The legislatures in all of the Colonies except Pennsylvania were composed of two houses. The upper house, usually called a council, was an appointive body except in Massachusetts, Rhode Island, and Connecticut. It took part in all legislative matters along with the assembly, but in addition had certain executive and judicial duties as well. In this combining of the different functions of government the colonial council was not unlike the Senate provided for in the Constitution, so that the positions of the council and the Senate in their respective governments are not dissimilar. In each Colony, also, there was an assembly which was elective. This body was an important part of the colonial legislature and in its manner of selection suggests the House of Representatives under the Constitution. The assemblies usually had broad legislative powers and repeatedly claimed exclusive rights over certain functions of primary importance like that of taxation. The colonial legislature as a whole was suggestive of a form of organization for the national congress.

In each of the Colonies there was a system of courts. The lowest courts were the justice courts, ruled over by justices of the peace. Next above these were usually county courts that had a wider jurisdiction and exercised larger powers than the justice courts. At the head of the system in each Colony there was a high or supreme court that settled the most important controversies and heard appeals from the lower courts. Above these, of course, was the Privy Council in England to which appeals in some instances might be taken. So there was in the Colonies a series or gradation of courts which contained a definite suggestion for a system of courts in the Nation. The analogy between these colonial institutions and those provided for in the federal Constitution must not be carried too far; but it is plain that in setting up the three great departments of the federal government the framers of the Constitution had a definite body of experience, in which they had their own personal share and to which they could look for guidance in their action.

Individual and Collective Experience of the States. — The colonial experience with the different departments of government was merged in that of the States after their independence was declared. Some of the States went right on with little or no change in their governmental organizations. Of course there was a great deal of confusion in setting up the new State governments to take the place of the old colonial organizations; that was inevitable. Most of the States adopted new constitutions, but the outlines of the governments thus set up were essentially the same as under the colonial charters. Connecticut and Rhode Island did not even find it necessary to change their charters at all, but simply renounced their allegiance to the English authority and went on with their accustomed agencies of government. The experience of the States, then, is to be taken simply as a continuation of that of the Colonies and in this combined experience is found the chief source of the federal Constitution. The men who framed that document had shared in this experience and had contributed to it. So in organizing the new federal government they drew upon their personal knowledge of institutions which they had helped to operate in the Colonies and in the States.

In addition to the experience of the States considered separately, as a factor in determining the form and powers of the central government under the Constitution, is that of the States collectively under the Articles of Confederation. This was largely negative in its influence. It revealed clearly what the new government ought not to be. Reference has already been made to the jealousies and conflicts among the States and to the weakness of the Congress under the Confederation. Practically the power of Congress amounted simply to the power to advise or request the States to act in accord with its plans. They could grant or refuse the request as they pleased. Congress could not deal with the people of the States directly and so compel obedience to its commands; it could deal only with the States as such and had no power whatever to force them to do its will. Congress could not even force the levy and collection of taxes with which to meet the necessary expenses of government. The States were sovereign. The Congress was without authority. The government of the Confederation was a failure and every passing day made it more and more plain that if peace was to continue and trade and commerce thrive, there must be an effectual readjustment of the powers of the central government.[1]

It was this weakness on the part of the Congress and the increasing hostility among the States that led directly to the calling of the constitutional convention of 1787. Particularly was it felt that the commercial relations of the States would have to be harmonized and controlled by some effective central

[1] For a good brief statement of the defects of the government under the Articles of Confederation, see article by Professor Max Farrand in *The American Political Science Review*, Vol. 2, p. 532.

authority. Several ineffectual attempts had been made before 1787 to accomplish this result. The last effort of this kind, immediately preceding the convention of 1787, was made by a convention which met at Annapolis in 1786. All of the States had been asked to send delegates, but only five responded. The object of the convention was to seek a remedy for the commercial troubles of the States, and to consider particularly the question of import duties. Realizing its own helplessness, the convention voted to recommend to Congress the calling of another convention which should meet in Philadelphia the next year to revise the Articles of Confederation in such a way as would, when adopted by the States, " render the Federal Constitution adequate to the exigencies of government and the preservation of the Union." Congress acted upon the recommendation and called the convention which framed the present federal Constitution.

This convention, which assembled in Philadelphia on the 14th of May, 1787, recognizing the futility of attempting to repair the broken-down governmental machine of the Confederation, ignored the instructions of the Congress to revise the Articles and framed an entirely new constitution. So the immediate cause of the framing and adoption of the present federal Constitution was the wretched weakness and inefficiency of the Confederation. The Articles provided for neither a central executive nor a central judiciary, and Congress, as has already been said, was helpless as against the States. This failure of the Confederation, with its disastrous effects upon the relations of the States, particularly their commercial relations, had a profound influence upon the work of the convention of 1787. The men of that convention had before their minds an object lesson of what the new government ought not to be. This object lesson had a positive as well as a negative influence, however. It made the fact perfectly plain that the new central government must be one of real powers and that it must be free from dependence upon the States in the discharge of its functions. Its powers must be its own and rest upon a foundation that could not be questioned or overthrown by the States. There can be no doubt that in this collective experience of the States under the Confederation, so disastrous in its consequences, is found one of the chief sources of the federal Constitution.

English Institutions and the Common Law. — Although the influences already described were the chief ones in determining the fundamentals of the new Constitution, there were others of considerable importance which should be noted. The English Parliament, while by no means a model for the federal Congress, was without doubt before the minds of the men who drafted the Constitution. There were many things about the English Constitution, as it then was, that appealed strongly to the men of the convention and to the people of the States generally, for after all they were true Englishmen, devoted, as were the people of England, to those fundamental human rights and liberties which are the basis of the English Constitution. Those great historic guaranties of liberty like Magna Charta and the Habeas Corpus Act belonged to them as well as to the people of England. They cherished the rights that had been won through the long course of English history and intended to preserve them; that is why they rebelled against the oppression of George the Third. It is indisputable that they admired the spirit of the English Constitution even though they exaggerated the importance of its monarchic features. The men in the constitutional convention were thoroughly familiar with the working of English political institutions and, determined as they were to avoid the risks and dangers of monarchy, it is certain that they were influenced in their work by the underlying principles of the Constitution upon which those institutions were based.

Likewise the English Common Law was an important factor. This system of law had been transplanted to America when the Colonies were first established and in it were grounded those fundamental rights which the people sought to preserve. Its influence upon the men who drafted the Constitution is clearly discernible. One principle of the Common Law in particular is basic in the Constitution. It is the principle, as Bryce points out, " that an act done by any official person or law-making body beyond his or its legal competence is simply void." By the application of this principle the framers of the Constitution were able to divide rather definitely the powers of government between the States and the central government, and to separate the powers of the three great departments of the central government as established by the Constitution. As Bryce puts it, they had in this principle " a key to the difficulties involved in the establishment of a variety of authorities not subordinate to one another, but each supreme in its own sphere. The application of this principle made it possible not only to create a National government which should leave free scope for the working of the State governments, but also so to divide the powers of the National government among various persons and bodies as that none should absorb or overbear the others."[1] In the practical working of the entire federal system this principle has been of great value. Upon it is based one of the fundamental doctrines of the Constitution, the doctrine of the separation of powers. Manifestly the Common Law must not be overlooked in listing the sources of the Constitution.

Political Philosophy. — The political philosophy of certain seventeenth- and eighteenth-century writers should also be mentioned as an influence that contributed something to the constitutional system of the United States. But this influence was slight and it is easy to overemphasize its significance. It must be remembered that the builders of the Constitution used experience and not theory as the foundation of their structure. Notable among the philosophers who have been credited with having profoundly influenced political evolution in America are Harrington, Locke, Montesquieu, and Rousseau. The statesmen who drafted the Constitution were certainly familiar with the writings of these men, and no doubt were influenced by them, but there is little, if anything, in the Constitution itself to indicate that fact. In this respect the Constitution is very different from the Declaration of Independence.[2] In the latter there is abundant evidence of the influence of eighteenth-century philosophy. The personal views of the men who framed the Constitution were without doubt affected more or less by the writings of the philosophers mentioned, but it was not to these writings but to the political experience of their own people that they turned for the fundamental facts upon which to erect the new governmental organization. It would be wrong to say that these writers had no influence at all upon the result, but that influence was very slight as compared with the experience of the colonists

---

[1] Bryce, "The American Commonwealth," New and Revised Edition, Vol. 1, p. 30.

[2] Below, Chap. XLVI.

in working out the problems of free government with their own colonial and State institutions.

REFERENCES

BEARD. *American Government and Politics*, Edition 1914, Chaps. I, II.
BEARD. *Readings in American Government and Politics*, pp. 25-34. (The Articles of Confederation.)
BRYCE. *The American Commonwealth*, Edition 1910, Vol. I, Chap. III.
FARRAND. "The Federal Constitution and the Defects of the Confederation," *The American Political Science Review*, Vol. II, p. 532 (Nov., 1908).
HART. *Actual Government*, pp. 39-53.

CHAPTER III

Principles of the Constitution

A POLITICAL constitution may be defined as "that whereby the instrumentalities and powers of government are distributed and harmonized."[1] It may be written and contained in a single document as in the United States; or it may be written and be embodied in a number of constitutional acts as in France; or it may be unwritten, being made up of a number of customs, understandings, precedents, legislative acts, as in England. It is important, particularly for the American student, to grasp the full significance of the definition given. The natural tendency of the American is to assume that a true constitution must be in a definite written form. Nothing could be farther from the truth, for a living constitution cannot be confined to a written document. Anything, written or unwritten, that creates or establishes the instrumentalities of government and gives to each its powers and harmonizes these agencies in the exercise of their powers is a constitution. Whether a written constitution is more sacred or more binding upon the people than is an unwritten constitution depends altogether upon the people's state of mind and attitude towards it. The Constitution of England is no less venerated by the people of England than is the federal Constitution by the people of the United States.

The statement was just made that a living constitution cannot be confined to a written document. This is a fact of profound importance in the study of government, for no one can obtain an adequate understanding of the working of a government who confines his effort to a study of its structure as outlined in the written constitution. The actual working constitution of the United States, for instance, is not at all the same as the written Constitution framed by the convention of 1787. It has been

[1] Macy, "The English Constitution," p. 6.

changed in many vital respects by court interpretations, by custom, and by the development of extra-constitutional institutions. Government must be studied in operation, as a " going concern," to be understood. The constitution is and must ever be, — to use President Wilson's apt phrase — a " vehicle of life." The functioning of the organs of government set up by the written Constitution, as well as their structure, must be comprehended before one can lay claim to anything that approaches an understanding of the real constitution of a country. Constitutions, governments, are living, changing things. They must adjust themselves to the ever shifting conditions of life if they are to be truly effective instruments of political and social progress.

The United States a Federal Republic. — The constitutional system of the United States is built upon a number of fundamental principles, as contained in the written Constitution, which it is necessary for the student to understand.

In the first place the government of the United States is a republic. The " fathers " of the Constitution did not intend it to be a democracy. They were determined not to have a monarchy; but in avoiding the dangers of monarchy they did not intend to run into the pitfalls of democracy. However democratic may be the tendencies of the present day, the intention of the framers of the Constitution is plain. They were not thoroughgoing democrats by any means. They wanted a republic and that is what they established. A republic is a government in which the power is exercised by the people through chosen representatives. The people are the source of power, but they do not rule directly. They and their representatives alike are restrained by constitutional provisions. This was the only kind of government which the framers of the Constitution believed to be safe. Their view was well expressed by James Madison: " We may define a republic to be a government which derives all its power directly or indirectly from the great body of the people; and is administered by persons holding their offices during pleasure, for a limited period, or during good behavior. It is essential to such a government that it be derived from the great body of the society, not from an inconsiderable proportion, or a favored class of it. It is sufficient for such a government that the persons administering it be appointed, either directly or indirectly, by the people; and that they hold their appointments by either of the tenures just specified."[1] The government which Madison described, and which he and his associates established, is thus a republic of the democratic type. It rests upon the will of the people, but the people can express their will only through regularly chosen representatives who are subject to constitutional restrictions. In the course of the years the democratic element in the control of the government has undoubtedly become stronger. Particularly in recent years has the movement toward direct democracy within the States made rapid progress. The tendency at present is clearly in the direction of a larger direct participation of the people in the control of both State and National governments.

Not only is the government of the United States a republic, but it is a federal republic. It is not a centralized republic like France, in which all powers are lodged in the national authority, but it is a federation of States in which the powers of government are divided between the central organization and the organizations of the States that form the federation. Reference has already been made to the fact that the federal form was determined by conditions. No other form was possible and no other was seriously thought of by the constitutional convention. The absolutely underlying principle of the constitutional system of the United States is the principle of federalism. The great contribution which the United States has made and is making to the political experience of the world is its demonstration of the fact that federalism can be successful, both from the standpoint of state autonomy and national efficiency. It is, indeed, furnishing to the world a model, perhaps the model, for the great world state of the future.[2]

Separation of Powers. — Probably no theory of government was more widely accepted by the people of the States at the time the Constitution was adopted than the theory of the separation of powers. Naturally, then, this theory is one of the fundamentals of the Constitution. It was impossible to organize the central government on any other basis. The general belief was that the separation of powers is essential to liberty. That individual liberty could be preserved under a government in which the legislative and executive powers were lodged in

---

[1] *The Federalist*, No. 39.   [2] Below, Chap. LX.

the same hands is a theory of government which the constitution makers and the people generally did not believe. It must be remembered that the English Constitution as it is to-day, with its guaranties of individual liberty, had not then developed.

The theory of the separation of powers is easily stated. There are three great functions of government, — legislative, executive, and judicial. The powers to discharge these functions should be lodged in different departments. Each department should be supreme in its own sphere of action. Each is coordinate with the others and as far as practicable should be independent of them. Each, therefore, is confined in its work to the exercise of the powers that have been specifically given to it. If it steps beyond the limit set by the constitution into the field of another department, its acts are void. Only by separating the powers of government in this way, and as far as possible keeping them separate, can the liberties of the people be adequately protected. To keep the departments separate each must be hedged about with definite constitutional restrictions. The more completely this separation can be maintained, the safer will be the people in the enjoyment of their civil and political rights.

The wide acceptance of this theory is generally ascribed to the influence of the great French writer, Montesquieu. He was by no means the first to differentiate the functions of government, but he expressed the theory of the separation of powers in its modern form and insisted strongly that there can be no liberty if the legislative and executive powers are united in the same person. The judicial power, also, must be separated from the other two. "There would be an end of everything," Montesquieu says, if the same person or the same body were to exercise the three powers of government.[1] The book in which he formulated his theory was widely read in America as well as in Europe, and, there can be no doubt, had influence upon the thought of the colonists. This influence was doubly great because of the frequent conflicts which had arisen in the Colonies between the legislative and executive authorities, and because the powers of the colonial governments were more or less definitely separated in accordance with this theory. Thus Montesquieu's influence was reënforced by that of actual colonial

[1] Montesquieu, "The Spirit of the Laws," Book XI, Chap. 6.

practices. To this combined influence of colonial experience and of Montesquieu's philosophy was added, when the time came for the establishment of the new federal government, the fear of monarchy. The framers of the Constitution believed, as did their fellow citizens, that the danger of monarchy would be lessened by a clean-cut separation of the departments and by keeping them separated by rigid constitutional provisions.

It is plain that the theory in its full, extreme form is an unworkable theory. It cannot be put into operation. There can be no complete separation of the departments. They must come together at certain points or the governmental machine will not work. There is bound to be more or less overlapping in their functions. Indeed, no attempt is made in the Constitution to carry out the theory in its extreme form. Some of its limitations were recognized by the men who drafted the Constitution and, although in the main the theory was applied, a number of exceptions to it were made. A careful reading of the Constitution will reveal how greatly the theory was modified as it was actually applied. Each department shares more or less the powers that belong to the others. The President, to whom is given the executive power, shares in the exercise of legislative power through his right to recommend and to veto legislation and through his power to establish regulations by executive order that have the force of law. Congress, through its power over revenue and expenditures and through its power to create new administrative departments and to reorganize or destroy existing departments, exercises large control over the executive. Through its absolute control over the federal courts below the Supreme Court and through its right to pass upon the qualifications of judges, Congress exercises a vital influence upon the work of the courts. The Senate, particularly, breaks over into the fields of the executive and judicial authorities. In the confirmation of appointments and the ratification of treaties it shares directly in the executive power. In hearing impeachment cases it sits as a court and exercises directly the judicial function. The courts, in turn, control in a direct way the work of Congress through their right to interpret the laws and the Constitution and to declare acts of Congress invalid. The latter really amounts to a judicial veto. So it is clear that the separation of the departments by the Constitution is by no means complete. A study of the national history will reveal, also, that that separation has grown less distinct with the development of the years.

The separation theory has been subjected to a good deal of adverse criticism from time to time, particularly in recent years. It is charged against it that it divides the responsibility for the conduct of the government to such an extent that inefficiency and corruption result; that it causes lack of harmony and unnecessary friction in the working of the government; that it frequently causes costly delay when prompt action is desirable; that it is primarily responsible for the development of the vast and complex party organizations with all of the attendant evils; that it is not essential to a free government and that it "altogether works for confusion and obscurity instead of simplicity and efficiency."[1]

There is a good deal in these criticisms. Most assuredly the theory breaks down completely in its assumption that without a separation of powers liberty cannot exist. One need take only a glance at the working of the English government to see how fallacious the theory is in this respect. Moreover, it has been the cause of a great deal of friction between the legislative and executive departments in the course of the years, to the sacrifice of the highest efficiency in the government. The Supreme Court, through its interpretations of the Constitution, has sometimes overthrown acts of Congress which the Congress and the people generally have thought desirable; as, for instance, the decision upon the income tax law of 1894. Because of the divided responsibility it has frequently been impossible to fix the blame definitely for objectionable acts as well as for failure to act; and definiteness of responsibility is essential in a free government. The relation of the separation of powers to the party system will be discussed in a later chapter, but note should be taken here of the dangers and difficulties which are attendant upon a deadlock between the executive and legislative departments when the President is controlled by one party and Congress by the other. Under those conditions no advance can be made so far as progressive, constructive legislation upon controversial questions is concerned. Such delay

[1] Beard, "American Government and Politics," New and Revised Edition, p. 155.

may mean serious loss to the nation. Hence it is plain that there are valid criticisms to be made of the separation theory.

But there are some things to be said for the separation of powers as well; it is by no means all bad. There are some solid virtues in an executive that is independent of the legislature. In fact, in the government of a people with the political traditions, training, and habits of the American people, an executive under the control of the legislature, as in the cabinet system of government, would probably be impossible. Particularly important is it to have the judicial authority beyond the absolute control of the legislature. Courts that are subservient to any particular interest within the state are contrary to American traditions, if not actually opposed to the spirit of American institutions. And the form of any government or of any part of it must be judged in connection with the spirit and traditions of the people over whom it rules. Moreover, there are practical reasons why the doctrine of the separation of powers is not to be rejected entirely. It has within it sound principles. "In government, as in all highly developed organizations, differentiation of function and division of labor are essential. Different requisites are demanded for different duties, and efficiency is secured by specialization. It is therefore desirable that legislative, executive, and judicial functions should in general be exercised by separate organs, and that within these further subdivisions be made."[1] But the primary reason, of course, why the separated departments are better for the United States is found in the accumulated political experience and the state of mind of the American people. An executive that is responsible to the legislature epitomizes English political history; but in America separation of the departments in the main is of the very stuff of free government. An increasing dissatisfaction with the working of the theory is to be noted, however, and it may well be that still further modifications will occur; but its abandonment is not to be anticipated, notwithstanding the growing influence of the executive in legislation.

Checks and Balances. — The separation of the departments of government involves necessarily a complicated system of checks and balances. The intention was not simply to separate the departments, but to keep them separated in their functions

[1] Gettell, "Introduction to Political Science," pp. 227–228.

as far as possible. This means that not only were limits established beyond which the departments should not go, but that each has been given certain powers by which it is definitely to restrain the others from exceeding their constitutional authority. Congress has the power of impeachment and may withhold supplies from the executive. The Senate may check the President in the matter of appointments and in the exercise of the treaty-making power. The President has the veto power over acts of Congress and appoints the judges. The courts may pass upon the validity of acts of Congress and by interpretation of the Constitution and the laws restrain both the legislature and the executive. The departments are independent in the main, but are nevertheless dove-tailed together in such a way as to make each dependent on the others in vital respects. The Constitution establishes a balance of powers and makes it the duty of each department to help maintain that balance. This constitutional provision is of course reënforced by the natural desire of each department to prevent encroachment upon its powers. Thus self-interest combines with moral and legal obligations to maintain the constitutional adjustment.

Some kind of system of checks and balances is inevitable in every free government. Indeed, it may be said to be a *sine qua non* of free government. Restraints of some kind there must be upon governmental authority. The peculiarity of the system of checks and balances in the United States which differentiates it so fundamentally from the system provided by the English Constitution is that the former is a vast system of legally established checks which may be enforced by the courts, while the latter is a limited system of checks and balances which rests partly upon legal provisions and partly upon traditions, habits, and understandings which can only be enforced by an appeal to public opinion.[1] The results are the same, but the methods are vitally different. In each country there is a harmonizing and balancing of powers. In the one this is accomplished chiefly by the provisions of the written Constitution; in the other by the understandings of the unwritten Constitution. It should be noted, however, that not all of the checks that are operative in the United States are contained in the Constitution. The party system furnishes a positive

[1] Macy, "The English Constitution," p. 35.

check of great potency, but the party system is entirely outside the Constitution. This influence is seen particularly when the executive and legislative branches are controlled by opposing parties. Public opinion is likewise, as in England, a powerful restraining influence, but public opinion is not the creation of the Constitution.

REFERENCES

BRYCE. *The American Commonwealth*, Edition 1910, Vol. I, Chaps. IV, XXIX, XXX.
FORD. *The Rise and Growth of American Politics*, Chaps. II, III, IV.
GOODNOW. *The Principles of the Administrative Law of the United States*, Book I, Chaps. III, IV.
MERRIAM. *American Political Theories*, Chaps. II, III, IV.
SMITH. *The Spirit of American Government*, Chaps. II, III.
WOODBURN. *The American Republic*, Chap. I.

CHAPTER IV

The Presidency

The presidency is one of the greatest political offices in the world. No official in any of the other free governments has so much power as the occupant of the presidency in the United States. The English prime minister alone, perhaps, is to be compared with him. In the great dignity, power, and influence of the presidency is found one of the striking features of the American constitutional system. Its place in the government, under the political party régime that has developed, is not exactly what the framers of the Constitution intended it should be; its occupant does not bear the precise relationship to the legislative department that was expected, nor does he show that independence of popular control which was thought so necessary; it has not always been held by men who, in point of ability or temperament, have measured up to the high requirements set by its creators for such an exalted position; but, notwithstanding the valid criticisms that may be made of it or of the men who have held it, the presidency has proven a notable success as an institution of government. It has stood the test of experience and is stronger to-day than at any previous time in the Nation's history, with the exception of the Civil War period when the normal balance of the government was destroyed. No other part of the governmental system is looked upon by the common people with more satisfaction than the presidency. Fearful concerning it as the people generally were in the beginning, it now belongs to them and to it they look more and more as a means of accomplishing their purposes in the field of national politics.

Fluctuations in the Presidency's Influence. — The presidency, as a determining force in the Nation's politics, has had its ups and downs. Its influence has varied from time to time, sometimes greater, sometimes less, depending upon the characters and personalities of the men who have held it, and the political conditions and problems that confronted it. The history of the presidency naturally breaks up into a number of distinct periods, of which separate accounts should be taken, as President Woodrow Wilson suggests. The thought of this eminent writer, partly in his own words, is here given.[1]

The first period extends from 1789 to 1825 during which the government was establishing itself at home and gaining recognition abroad. In this period men were chosen to the presidency who were trained to an unusual degree for the leadership of the Nation. The second period is that in which the headstrong, imperious Jackson forced his will upon the Nation, regardless of legal or constitutional refinements. The third period may be said to date from 1836 to 1861, during which great questions of domestic policy were fought out and Congress assumed the dominant place. In this period the Presidents " lacked the personal force and initiative to make for themselves a leading place in counsel." The fourth period is the time of the Civil War in which for a time under Lincoln the presidency became almost a dictatorship, " Congress merely voting supplies and assenting to necessary laws, as Parliament did in the time of the Tudors." The fifth period extends from 1865 to 1898, during which domestic questions were again to the front and Congress was in the ascendancy, President Cleveland alone among the Presidents of this period taking any " leading and decisive part in the drama of national life." The war with Spain in 1898 marked the beginning of the sixth and present period in which there has been a shifting of positions and powers and the President again has become the national leader. In recent years the presidency has been the most conspicuous part of the government and its occupant has had centered upon him the attention of the entire nation. It is not at all unlikely that the presidency will continue to hold permanently a relatively larger place in the government than it formerly did. The exigencies of party politics seem to demand aggressive leadership on the part of the President.

The Constitution Makers and the Presidency. — The organization of the executive department of the government furnished one of the most puzzling problems which the makers of the

[1] Wilson, " Constitutional Government in the United States," pp. 57–59.

Constitution had to solve. No other part of their work gave them more concern than this, and no other was considered with greater care. Widely different views as to the character of the executive and the extent of its powers were held and expressed, and it was only after many concessions had been made by the opposing elements in the convention that the plan for the presidency, as contained in the Constitution, was agreed upon. Like all of the other important features of the Constitution, the executive organization which was finally accepted was the product of compromise.

On one thing, however, the constitutional convention was unanimous from the start. The executive must have sufficient power to make it an effective agency of government. The impotency of the Congress under the Articles of Confederation must be avoided. On the other hand, the power of the executive must be so limited and its exercise so hedged about by restrictions that all danger of monarchy would be averted. But just how should this be accomplished? Should the executive power be lodged with one person or with several; should there be a single or a plural executive? Should the person or persons exercising the executive powers be dependent directly upon the people for the commission of authority or should the executive be chosen by indirect methods? Should Congress, the legislative branch of the government, be given the power to choose the executive and thus make the executive dependent upon the legislature? If a single executive were established, should there be provided a privy council in addition to act as an advisory and restraining body? These were questions of vital importance and were considered with care and debated with vigor.

An early agreement was reached in favor of a single executive in place of the plural executive which was urged so strongly by some members of the convention. There were historical precedents for the plural form and plausible arguments were advanced in support of it, but the majority of the convention felt that unity and promptness of action, and therefore effectiveness, might be destroyed if the executive powers were divided among the members of a council. The dangers of too great centralization of power in one individual might better be risked than impotency and indecisiveness at critical times through too much diffusion of power. So the single executive was decided upon. In reaching this conclusion the men of the convention were chiefly influenced by the experience of the States with their governors, some of whom bore the title of president. The people were accustomed to the exercise of the chief executive power by a single individual. Thus the establishment of the presidency to be held by one man was quite in accord with American experience and seemed to involve no inherent risk of executive usurpation which would result in monarchy.

The amount of power that the executive should have was a different matter, however, and gave cause for a great deal of vigorous discussion. Should the executive be independent of the legislature or not? If independent, should it have power to negative or veto acts of the legislature? Should power over the questions of peace and war be lodged with the executive? Would the exercise of such power be likely to lead to the overthrow of the republic and the establishment of monarchy? How much control over the judiciary should the executive have? Should it have the power of appointment and removal of officers? What control should the executive have over legislation? Should it be confined entirely to the work of executing the laws passed by the legislature? These and many other questions of similar import were asked and thoroughly discussed by the convention. The answer to them was the creation of an office that had no counterpart in any of the then existing nations of the world. This is not the place to give in detail the powers that were conferred upon the President; the present purpose is simply to indicate the nature of the problem with which the convention wrestled in determining the organization and authority of the executive department. The decision of the convention was that the executive should have large powers over both domestic and foreign affairs and that in the exercise of its powers it should be independent of both the legislative and judicial departments. It was made coördinate with the other departments and was not to be bound by the restraining influence of an advisory council, except with regard to treaties and appointments to office, in which the Senate was to have its share.

The Presidency a Democratic Institution. — The ever present fear in the minds of great numbers of people at the time the Constitution was being formulated by the convention and later when it was presented to the States for ratification, was the fear of monarchy. The establishment of a monarchic government was the one thing of all things to be prevented. Any feature of the new government, therefore, that might appear to be in contravention of the prevailing antimonarchic sentiment was certain to be the subject of bitter, denunciatory criticisms. The presidency came in for its full share of this hostile comment. It was suggested in the constitutional convention that the executive department, as finally established by the constitution, savored of monarchy and that the President, through his power of appointment and his control of the army and navy and his independence of the legislative department, might be able to subvert the republic and turn himself into a king. This view was repeated again and again when the Constitution was submitted for ratification. It is very questionable, indeed, whether ratification could ever have been obtained if the people had voted upon the Constitution directly. Even as it was, with the ratification left to conventions within the States, almost a year passed before favorable action by nine States, necessary to put the Constitution into force, could be brought about. There can be no doubt that much of the hesitancy was due to the dissatisfaction that was felt concerning the organization and the powers of the presidency. And yet this widely prevalent fear as to the dangers inherent in the presidency was groundless, as the whole history of the United States under the Constitution has so clearly shown.

Instead of becoming monarchic in character the presidency has become more democratic with the passing of the years, far more democratic, in fact, than the framers of the Constitution ever intended that it should be. Under the party system it has become the chief agency for the execution of the popular will. Although it was not intended to be so, the President's responsibility is now directly to the people, and it is to him that they look, more than to any other officer or department of the government, as the champion of their rights and interests. It is the President, more than any other, who is the spokesman of the people. Democracy is stronger, not weaker, because of the presidency. Curiously enough, however, it was not the intention of the framers of the Constitution to promote democracy through the presidency. They did not believe very much in democracy, even the most democratic of them. They were almost as anxious to prevent the President from becoming too dependent on the masses as they were to prevent him from transforming himself into a monarch. That is why they rejected the plan to have him chosen directly by the people and provided for his indirect election by presidential electors. Contrary to the commonly expressed fear the presidency has never endangered the Republic; and contrary to the intention of the fathers it has become directly dependent upon and responsible to the people themselves.

The presidency is the distinctive feature of the United States government. It gives name, indeed, to that type of free government of which the United States is the most notable example, differentiating it from the cabinet or parliamentary type. It stands as one of the great, vital contributions of the United States to the science of government. Its occupant does not hold merely an ornamental position, useful only in a social way, but is the real head of the Nation with powers and responsibilities greater than are those of monarchs in the Old-World countries. The way in which he is elevated to his high position by the votes of his fellow citizens, and the way in which, after his term of office has expired and his successor has been chosen, he retires to the seclusion of private life, shorn of his power and on a perfect legal equality with all those whom he has served, furnish striking evidence of the strength and merit of the presidency as an instrument of democracy. The President in office is simply the servant of the people; the President retired from office is simply one of the people. His usefulness to the State after retirement, however, is by no means at an end if he chooses to interest himself actively in public affairs, but his work is that of a private citizen unless by the action of his fellows he is again called to the public service.

Of course the presidency is not a perfect institution of government. Valid criticisms may be made of it and of the way in which it often works. It is possible that the details of its organization as worked out in the Constitution might be improved. It is, indeed, a great prize which stirs the ambitions of men and often leads them to sacrifice convictions and consistent conduct in order to obtain an election or a reëlection. It does offer opportunities for the corrupt use of power. The four years' term is possibly too short and the reëligibility of the President may invite and sometimes does lead to manipulation and scheming, to obtain a reëlection, which are seriously detrimental to the public interest.[1] But perfect political institutions are not found in this world of imperfect men, and, in spite of all the criticisms that have been made against it, the presidency has been a conspicuously successful part of the federal government. Its merits are by no means offset by its demerits; its strength by its weakness. Although in operation it differs radically in some respects from the original intention, the presidency stands as a monument to the wisdom and statesmanship of the men who planned it and established it. And its success has been so marked that it has been taken as a model for the executive organizations in most of the other Republican states of the New World.

REFERENCES

(For References, see the following chapter.)

[1] Bryce, "The American Commonwealth," New and Revised Edition, Vol. I, pp. 69–71.

CHAPTER V

The Election of the President

THE evidence that the working constitution of the United States is radically different from the written document upon which its governmental institutions are based, is perhaps clearer in connection with the presidential office than with any other part of the government. In form the presidency is still what it was planned to be; in spirit it is not. The intention of its originators with regard to the manner of election, dependence upon the people, and freedom from partisanship has not been followed. With the exception of George Washington no President has been chosen in the spirit and according to the real intention of the men who drafted the Constitution. Moreover, Washington alone of the Presidents conducted the office in the way originally planned. In a sense the office was created for Washington; that is, he was the man whom the great majority of people considered almost ideally fitted for the place and whom they expected to see made the first President. It seems to be clear that the men of the convention were influenced in working out the organization of the executive by the belief that Washington was the man who would be given the leadership in the actual work of setting up the new government. He presided over the convention and thoroughly understood and approved the convention's intention concerning the purpose of the presidential office. But the advent of political parties and the development of the party system changed the very character of the office, and some of the things that the men of the convention dreaded and hoped to prevent are now expected and held to be essential.

The purpose of the convention is clear. The President was to be the best fitted man for the place in the entire Nation, from the standpoints of ability, character, temperament, and training. He was to be free from partisanship, impartial, of national vision, loyal to all of the States alike, devoted to the highest interests of the Nation. He was not to be the representative of a group or a faction, or a party, but the leader and representative of the whole people. By his very qualities of character he was to be above factional strife and above participation in political intrigues of any kind. His one, undivided aim would be, without thought of himself or of any State or of any class, to promote the welfare of all the people.

In order to insure the choice of such a man for the presidency a special plan for his election was devised. The choice of the President, as Alexander Hamilton argued in *The Federalist*, was not made to " depend on pre-existing bodies of men, who might be tampered with beforehand to prostitute their votes," but was referred " in the first instance to an immediate act of the people of America, to be exerted in the choice of persons for the temporary and sole purpose of making the appointment." [1] That is, provision was made for a special body, which has come to be known as the electoral college, whose sole duty it should be to select the President. To make sure that no one should take part in this selection who might have a personal interest in the choice, it was provided that no Senator, Representative, or other person holding a place of trust or profit under the United States should serve as a presidential elector. " Thus, without corrupting the body of the people, the immediate agents in the election will at least enter upon the task, free from any sinister bias."

Constitutional Plan of Choosing the President. — Thus the choice of a President, according to the Constitution, is made only indirectly by the people. Each State is required to choose a number of electors equal to the number of its Senators and Representatives in the national Congress. These electors meet in their respective States, at the time prescribed by Congress, and vote by ballot for President and Vice President. Under the original provision they were to vote for two persons and the one receiving the highest number of votes, provided he had a majority of the whole number of electors, was elected President, and the one having the next highest number of votes was elected Vice President. But experience, after the political parties sprang up, showed that this provision would not work

[1] *The Federalist*, No. 68.

because the party controlling the majority in the electoral college would cast the same number of votes for its two candidates and neither could be declared elected President or Vice President, as was the case in the election of 1800 in which Thomas Jefferson and Aaron Burr were candidates. This provision of the Constitution was changed by the twelfth amendment by which the electors vote definitely for a President and a Vice President. The record of the vote in each State is certified in the proper way and sent to Washington, addressed to the president of the Senate. In the presence of both houses of Congress the votes are counted and the candidate for President and the candidate for Vice President having the highest number of votes are declared elected, if in each case this number is a majority of the whole number of electors. If no candidate for President has a majority, the choice goes to the House of Representatives, where the candidates having the highest votes, not exceeding three in number, are balloted upon, the vote being taken by States. Each State has one vote and a majority of all of the States is necessary for an election. In case no candidate for Vice President receives a majority of all the electors the choice goes to the Senate where from the two highest candidates the selection is made, a majority of the whole number of Senators being necessary for a choice.

The method of choosing the presidential electors is left to the States, acting through their legislatures. The selection may be made by the State legislatures themselves, by popular vote, or by any other method which the legislatures may prescribe. The time of the election is fixed by Congress. But, regardless of the way in which they are chosen, the whole legal, constitutional power to elect the President rests with the college of electors. Each elector is free, as far as the written Constitution is concerned, to vote for whomsoever he pleases. Indeed, that is what he is expected to do according to the plan of the fathers. It was by means of this picked body of presidential electors that they hoped to obtain the one man in the entire nation best fitted for the office of President. It was the intention that these men should meet at designated places in their respective States and there, free from personal considerations, factional strifes, party influence, and popular clamor pick out the man most perfectly equipped in every way for the high office of

President. The framers of the Constitution felt certain that with this system of indirect election in operation no unfit person would ever become the head of the Nation. Hamilton, arguing for the ratification of the Constitution, expressed his opinion in this way: " This process of election affords a moral certainty, that the office of President will seldom fall to the lot of any man who is not in an eminent degree endowed with the requisite qualifications. Talents for low intrigue, and the little arts of popularity, may alone suffice to elevate a man to the first honors of a single State; but it will require other talents, and a different kind of merit, to establish him in the esteem and confidence of the whole Union, or of so considerable a portion of it, as would be necessary to make him a successful candidate for the distinguished office of President of the United States. It will not be too strong to say, that there will be a constant probability of seeing the station filled by characters pre-eminent for ability and virtue." [1]

Hamilton in this statement expressed the view of the majority of his associates in the constitutional convention. They were not all of one opinion as to the wisdom of having a single executive with such great powers as were given to the President, but they finally agreed that if there was to be such a President, the method prescribed for his election was the very best that could be devised. The dangers that might lurk in the organization of the presidency would be minimized by the manner of electing those who were to hold it. Particularly would it be impossible for men to get into the presidency by currying favor with the masses. The danger of too much democracy in the selection of the President would be averted.

Failure of the Electoral Plan. — But how has the plan worked? How successful has it been? How accurately did its sponsors foresee the developments of American politics? Except in the case of Washington it has not worked at all as it was intended. It was the first part of the Constitution to break down; and the collapse was strikingly complete. It is significant in this connection that the plan of electing the President was one of the few features of the Constitution that was practically original with the constitutional convention. In almost all respects the Constitution is built on solid experience, but the electoral

[1] *The Federalist*, No. 68.

college was an experiment. That this experimental feature of the Constitution was the first to fall is illustrative of the dangers that confront any people who seek to erect their governmental system upon untried theories.

The reason for the failure of the electoral college to work according to design is easy to find. The strange thing is that the men who planned it did not foresee the inevitable result. The development of political parties made the plan impossible. When Washington retired at the end of his second term the party spirit blazed out and the Federalist and Democratic-Republican parties were formed. Each party had its candidates for President and Vice President and expected its representatives in the electoral college to vote for their party nominees. The moment it was settled that Washington would not consent to a third election it was plain that his successor would not be chosen by the electors in that calm, dispassionate manner contemplated by the framers of the Constitution because of his special fitness for the presidential office, but that he would be chosen as a party man because his party controlled a majority of the electoral votes. The organization of parties, for reasons that will be considered later, was inevitable. All through the eight years of Washington's administration the division of the people into two opposing parties was taking place. As the years passed, the line of separation became more marked, one side tending more and more to favor the exercise of wide powers by the central or national government, and the other side standing out as the champion of the States and local governments as against the Nation. This division of opinion upon the interpretation of the Constitution began, indeed, in the constitutional convention itself. It seems now that it should have been clear to the men of the convention that political parties would inevitably result from the differences of opinion manifested in the constitutional debates; but this was not the case and it clearly was their hope that the President would never be selected as a result of a party struggle. Equally clear was their intention to prevent such a struggle, if possible, by the establishment of the electoral college. But their plan broke down almost at the start and from the time of the election of John Adams, in 1796, to the present the Presidents, almost without exception, have been chosen as party men and the presidential electors have simply registered the will of their respective parties. The real selection of the President, therefore, is made by the people of the States at the election when they vote for electors, now called the presidential election.

Actual Method of Choosing the President. — It is plain that the method of choosing a President that has prevailed almost from the beginning is not a part of the written Constitution. It is one of the many extra-constitutional features of the United States government. The important steps in the procedure that is followed should be noted.

First of all is the selection of the party candidate, for no one will receive electoral votes who is not the candidate of a party with sufficient strength to elect some of the presidential electors. The choice of the presidential candidate of each party, under the practice that has prevailed during the greater part of the Nation's life, is made by a national convention composed of delegates from all of the States and Territories. These conventions are usually held in June or July of the year of the presidential election. For months preceding, the chief political interest of the nation centers upon the work of the nominating conventions, and the selection of delegates by the different States is followed with the closest attention. Sometimes there may be only one leading candidate and he will receive the nomination by acclamation, or if the opposition is strong enough to prevent a nomination by acclamation, he may have sufficient strength to be nominated upon the first ballot. Sometimes the nomination is hotly contested by two or more candidates and the nomination may come only after many ballots are taken by the convention. And then it may go to some one who has not been a leading aspirant; indeed, it may go to some one who has not been looked upon as a candidate at all, a so-called "dark horse."

The national conventions of the leading parties are rightly looked upon by the people generally as of vital concern. It is there that the choice of the people, to be determined later at the November election, is narrowed to two men, the candidates of the two leading parties. One or the other, under the normal working of the party system, unless removed by death, will become President and will have it in his power to influence profoundly the course of the Nation's history.

As soon as the conventions have made their nominations, the presidential election campaign begins. From the time the conventions adjourn until the election in November the fight is waged in all of the States, usually with increasing intensity as the day of the election approaches. In all of the States presidential electors must be chosen. As already indicated, the method of choosing the electors is left to each State. The regular rule now is for each political party by a party primary or convention to nominate in each State candidates for all of the electors to which that State is entitled. The voter at the general election votes for those electors who represent the party whose presidential candidate he favors. Under the prevailing practice the voter does not vote for one elector only, but for the entire number to which his State is entitled. The electors are thus usually chosen by the general ticket system and not by the district system, though this is a matter for the States to determine. The voter does not vote directly for the presidential candidate, of course; he votes for one set of electors and thus indicates his preference as to presidential candidates. As soon as the results of the November election in the different States are ascertained the people know who is to be their next President. Of course no legal election of a President has occurred; the voters of each State have simply declared their preference. But the contest is at an end, although the legal election is still to come, for the presidential electors will merely carry out the instructions given to them by the voters of their respective States. The electors observe the strict letter of the Constitution and of the law as prescribed by Congress, but their work is entirely perfunctory and without special interest to the general public, for every one knows in advance what the vote in the electoral college will be. No elector would think of voting against the candidate of his party.

The general procedure which must be observed by the electors is prescribed by the Constitution, as already indicated. Details have been left to Congress and the State legislatures to work out. By an act of Congress the electors of each State are required to meet on the second Monday of January next following their election at whatever place has been designated by the State legislature — always the State capital — for the purpose of casting their ballots for President and Vice President.

The manner in which the vote is to be certified and sent to the president of the Senate at Washington, to be counted in the presence of both houses of Congress has already been described. This count takes place on the second Wednesday in February. The significant thing to note is that the method of electing a President contained in the Constitution has become, because of the party system, a mere formality, the observance of which is important only because such observance is necessary in order to make the election legal.

Consequences and Dangers of the Electoral System. — The working of the electoral college scheme in connection with the prevailing party system has a number of important consequences. The plan of the constitution makers has been set aside and there has been substituted for it a general election in which all of the voters of the country may take part, but this election is not a truly popular election, although it is frequently referred to as such. The election is really by States and the outcome of the election is not determined by the result of the popular election in the Nation as a whole; that is to say, the success of a candidate is not dependent upon his receiving a majority of the total vote in the Nation. His success depends upon his carrying enough States to give him a majority of the presidential electors. But a candidate may receive a majority of the electoral votes and have only a minority of the popular vote. This has happened upon several occasions. Abraham Lincoln, for instance, in 1860, received only 1,866,452 votes, while the combined vote of his opponents numbered 2,815,617. Yet in the electoral college Lincoln had 57 more votes than all of his opponents. In this case the votes opposed to Lincoln were divided among a number of candidates. But even when there are only two candidates it may happen that the one receiving a minority of the popular vote will obtain a majority of the electoral votes because of the particular combination of States that he carries. In 1888 Harrison received a hundred thousand fewer votes than Cleveland, but had a majority of sixty-five in the electoral college. This result springs from the fact that the presidential electors are chosen on a general ticket, and the total vote of a State in the electoral college goes to the candidate that carries the State in the general election, no matter how small may be his majority over his competitor.

Indeed, he may have only a plurality if there is a third candidate with any considerable strength. In 1884 Cleveland carried the State of New York over Blaine by a margin of only 1149 votes. A change of only 575 votes from the Democratic to the Republican candidate would have elected the latter. But the entire electoral vote of the State went to Cleveland, giving him the necessary majority. Majorities for Blaine in other States, however large, could have no effect upon this result. A small majority in a State at the presidential election is just as effective in controlling the electoral vote of that State as is a large majority.

Another result of very great significance comes from this system. Since the election is really by States, the chief interest in the presidential election centers in the "close" or "doubtful" States. The decision in these States is likely to determine the result in the Nation. The party that can carry the doubtful States will probably win. The effect of this is not only to center popular interest upon the struggle in these States, but to concentrate the efforts of the party managers. The States that are " safe " or " sure," that is, the States that can be depended upon to give their accustomed majority for the one party or the other, receive comparatively little attention from the campaign managers. In the doubtful States, however, the campaign is waged with the greatest intensity, each party struggling to the utmost of its power to carry enough of these to insure the election of its candidate. They are invaded by an army of speakers and deluged by a flood of campaign " literature." Large sums of money are spent to " organize " the voters and get out the vote. In short, the real fighting in the presidential campaign takes place in these pivotal States. The influence of this is by no means salutary. In fact, it is just the opposite. The prize at stake is so great that campaign managers and party workers often make use of corrupt means to accomplish their purposes. The use of so much money, particularly, is objectionable. It leads to bribery and other disreputable practices. The influence of it all is anything but good upon the life and citizenship of the State. This practice of making the close States bear the brunt of the campaign is inevitable, however, as long as the present method of electing the President prevails. A truly popular election would of course remedy the difficulty in large measure.

That there are possible dangers to the country in connection with the constitutional method of choosing the President is clearly shown by the Hayes-Tilden controversy growing out of the presidential election of 1876. Neither candidate had a majority of the electoral votes unless votes from States in which the charge of fraud was made were counted for him. In each of the States in which fraud was charged there were two sets of electors, each claiming to be the properly chosen electors.[1] The difficult problem was to decide which votes should be counted, a problem concerning which the Constitution is silent. Yet some method for the settlement of the controversy had to be discovered or serious danger to the Nation, perhaps war, might ensue. The device hit upon by Congress which assumed jurisdiction over the problem was a special electoral commission which finally, by a strict party vote, recognized the claims of the Republican electors and thus gave the presidency to Hayes. The crisis passed and the danger to the Union was averted, but the experience revealed some of the serious defects of the electoral plan. Ten years later, in 1887, Congress attempted to remedy the difficulty by passing a statute which requires that each State, through tribunals established for that purpose, shall pass upon the legality of its electoral votes. If a State fails to provide for this special court, then the decision rests with Congress, and, if the two houses cannot agree, the vote of the State concerned is lost. This is doubtless better than no remedy at all for the Constitution's omission, but it is plain that the remedy itself is not free from defects and objections. The decisions of the States might be anything but fair. Fraud can easily enter in and determine the choice of the President. It is quite possible under the law of 1887 for Congress to override the will of a State or shut it out completely from participation in the electoral college vote, and thus practically dictate the selection of a President. The point would seem to be well taken that the Constitution itself must be changed before the dangers inherent in the present system will be removed.

Another omission of the Constitution in this connection is deserving of notice. No way is provided for the selection of a President in case the President-elect and the Vice President-

---

[1] The States involved were South Carolina, Florida, Louisiana, and Oregon. In the case of Oregon the charge of fraud was not made.

elect should die during the time that intervenes between the second Monday in January when the electors meet and the fourth of March when the President is inaugurated, a possibility that is not at all fanciful. Of course if the successful candidates should die at any time preceding the second Monday in January, the electors could proceed to select a President and Vice President according to the design of the Constitution. But if that should happen after the electors have assembled and voted, the problem is a very different one. Opinions differ as to what could be done, but the belief seems to be growing that here is a case of a real omission of the Constitution upon a vital point which can be remedied only by a constitutional amendment. Manifestly serious consequences may arise under the Constitution as it is at present.[1]

Suggested Reforms. — Various reforms in the method of choosing the President have been suggested from time to time. The most important seeks to abolish the electoral college and leave the election of the President to the people. It has been a useless part of the governmental machine almost from the beginning. Moreover, danger lurks within it. It was established largely as a check upon the people, but the rising tide of democracy has swept it aside in spite of the Constitution, although it still stands in the way of a genuine popular election. As long as the college of electors is retained, its members, under the present party system, will probably be chosen according to the general-ticket plan. This means the continuation of a practice which permits the election of a President by a minority of the people and makes possible his election by actually fraudulent votes. This is not only undemocratic, but unsafe. In the interest of democracy, therefore, as well as to avoid unnecessary risks, the college of electors should be eliminated by constitutional amendment and there should be substituted in

---

[1] In case both the President and the Vice President should die, it is provided in the Presidential Succession Law, enacted by Congress in 1886, that members of the cabinet shall succeed to the presidency in the order prescribed. The order of succession is as follows: Secretary of State; Secretary of the Treasury; Secretary of War; Attorney-General; Postmaster-General; Secretary of the Navy; Secretary of the Interior. At the time the Succession law was passed, these were the only departments existing. The Secretaries of the departments created since that time — Agriculture, Commerce, and Labor — have not been authorized to succeed to the presidency.

its place a genuine popular election of the Preside[nt]
enable the majority of the voters to carry out their [will.]

There can be no question that the spirit and the [purpose of]
this reform are in accord with the sentiment of the p[eople.]
There is a marked desire on the part of the people to [democra-]
tize all of the undemocratic features of the governm[ent.] The
whole of the government must be brought closer to the source
of its power. The presidency, in particular, is so powerful a
political office and holds so strategic a position in the governmental structure that the people should control it directly by
voting directly for those who are to occupy it. Effective popular
control, moreover, should not be confined to the formal voting
process of the general presidential election, but should be extended so as to include the whole nominating process as well.
The mere opportunity to choose between two candidates who
have been nominated by small groups of men who are not
definitely, legally representative of the voters and who may be
dominated by political bosses and controlled by political machines, is not sufficient to satisfy the demands of democracy nor
insure the election of a President who will truly represent the
will of the entire people as expressed by the electorate at the
polls. The whole nominating process, therefore, must also be
democratized.

The sentiment in favor of this reform has developed rapidly
in recent years and has assumed the form of a demand for a
presidential primary. The national conventions have never in
their entire membership been truly representative of the voters.
Some of the delegates, chosen at direct primaries or by representative conventions in the States, have given true expression
to the will of their constituents, but many others have not
because they have been under the domination of political
bosses or party machines or some special business interests, or,
as has so frequently been the case, have been controlled by the
President in office through the use of patronage. The federal
office holders have been always much in evidence in the national
convention of the party in power. That this is not only unfair
but dangerous is a feeling that has been growing stronger year
by year. The result is the demand for a presidential primary
at which the voters, with all of the safeguards of a formal election, shall determine what candidates their respective parties

shall put forward. This particular method of nomination may prove to be unsatisfactory, if it is adopted, but the demand for it is significant. It is only a part of the broader movement which seeks to place the presidency under genuine popular control. It is as vital to this purpose to have popular control over the nomination of candidates as to have popular election after the nominations are made. As the indirect election of the President, by means of a college of electors, has been swept aside by the rising tide of democracy, so the present methods of nominating presidential candidates, by means of which the party leaders and organizations are enabled to maintain their control, must give way to other methods by which the power over nominations is placed in the hands of the people. The spirit of democracy is abroad in the land and will not now be denied, even as it would not be denied in the beginning. In the United States, as in England, the conviction grows stronger year by year that the will of the people must prevail. In order to make that will effective, readjustment in both constitutional and extra-constitutional features of the government is necessary, and is slowly taking place.

Attention should be called at this point to the constitutional qualifications for an election to the presidency. Limitations were placed upon the presidential electors so that their freedom of choice is not absolute. No person except a natural-born citizen is now eligible to the office of President. Nor is any one eligible who has not attained the age of thirty-five years and been for fourteen years a resident within the United States. One of the purposes of these restrictions was manifestly to minimize the dangers of foreign influence and aggression. Men born in the United States would be more likely to be free from the taint of monarchy and therefore more devoted to republican institutions.

Presidential Term and Compensation. — The President's term of office is four years, with no constitutional provision whatever touching the question of reëligibility. This unusually short term for so important an office has been the subject of a great deal of severe criticism. Bryce's adverse comment is particularly pointed, but he is by no means alone in this; many of the ablest American publicists find the provision equally objectionable. They hold with Bryce that the presidential election, coming so frequently, throws the country into a state of turmoil and uncertainty for which there is often no real occasion; that this frequency of elections causes a discontinuity of policy which is not only unnecessary, but often seriously detrimental to the nation's interests. It is held also that the fact that a President is eligible for reëlection often has an unfavorable influence upon him; he is tempted to "play politics" in order to obtain a renomination and thus sacrifice the good of the Nation to his selfish ambitions.[1] That there is merit in these criticisms cannot well be questioned. There is good argument in support of the theory that the term should be increased to six or seven years and that the President should be ineligible for reelection. It must be remembered, however, that there are great benefits, from the standpoint of patriotism and citizenship, which spring from these frequently recurring presidential elections. There can be no doubt that they have profound educational results. They give to the voters the opportunity to take stock of what their representatives in office have done, and force them to pass judgment upon the Nation's policies. The value of this in any democratic government is not to be questioned, although it is easy to place too much emphasis upon it. Moreover, it should be added, a term of four years is more than enough in the case of an inefficient or otherwise objectionable President.

The Constitution places no limit upon the number of times a President may be reëlected. Tradition or custom, however, fixes the limit at one reëlection. Washington was importuned to accept a third term, but refused, and from that time on the two-term precedent has been observed, although there have been attempts to break it, notably that in the case of General Grant whose supporters made a vigorous and almost successful effort to force his nomination for a third time. Thus far the "no third term" tradition has held, even when the terms are not successive, but it can hardly be said to be an absolutely settled policy. It is doubtful, in fact, if the opposition to a third term is as pronounced and widespread now as in former years. The large vote cast for Theodore Roosevelt in 1912 suggests a radical change in the popular mind with respect to this.

The compensation of the President, by the terms of the Con-

[1] Bryce, "The American Commonwealth," New and Revised Edition, Vol. I, pp. 69-72.

stitution, is fixed by the Congress. His formal salary was made $25,000 a year at the beginning. In 1871 this was increased to $50,000 and remained at that figure until 1909, when it was made $75,000. This is simply the personal salary of the President and by no means represents the total expense incurred in support of the presidency. The maintenance of the executive offices with their large clerical force, the upkeep of the White House and its grounds, the traveling expenses of the President and various other items, bring the total expenditure up to $300,000 or more.[1]

The Vice Presidency. — A word concerning the vice presidency may be added here as appropriately as anywhere. It is difficult, as a matter of fact, to find a logical place for a discussion of the Vice President and his functions for the reason that the constitutional position of the vice presidency is illogical. It is, indeed, a misfit in the national governmental structure. It is a practically useless office.

The Vice President is chosen for a term of four years in the same manner as the President. He receives a salary of $12,000. His part in the operation of the government consists in presiding over the Senate, where he sits as a parliamentary official, exercising no control over the deliberations of the Senate except in the case of a tie vote, when the decision of the question rests with him. The Constitution provides that in case of the removal of the President from office, or of his death, resignation, or inability to discharge his functions, his powers and duties shall devolve upon the Vice President. That this is an important provision of the Constitution is abundantly proven by the number of instances in which Vice Presidents have succeeded to the presidency due to the death of the Presidents. The Vice President as such does nothing but preside in the Senate and has no official relation whatever to the President. The President may consult with him if he wishes to, but apparently this practice has never been followed to any marked degree.

The vice presidency should be treated with more respect than it has received, because of the fact that its incumbent may suddenly succeed to the presidency. That fact ought to insure the utmost care in the selection of the Vice President, but that it has

[1] Beard, "American Government and Politics," New and Revised Edition, p. 205.

not done so, under the working of the party system, is a certainty beyond all question. The vice presidency has, indeed, been only a tail to the presidential kite. In selecting their candidates for Vice President the national party conventions have been actuated by a variety of motives. Sometimes the nomination has gone to a leading competitor of the successful candidate for the presidential nomination. Sometimes it has gone to the favorite son of some doubtful State in order to help hold that State in line at the election. At other times it has gone to the representative of some faction in order to insure harmony within the party. And at still other times it has gone to the man who could make the largest contribution to the party's campaign fund. The merits of the candidate, as a possible President, usually receive very slight consideration. The essential thing, from the standpoint of the party managers, seems to be the availability and financial strength of the candidate. The result is that men have often been elected to the vice presidency who were very far from being satisfactorily equipped for the duties of the presidency which they might have been called upon to assume.

There is clear need for greater care in the selection of the Vice President. And there is clear need, also, for bringing the Vice President into reasonably close relations with the administrative work of the government, so that if he is called upon to succeed the President, he will be somewhat familiar with the work that must be done. The suggestion that the Vice President should have a seat at the cabinet table and take part in formulating the policies which he not improbably may be compelled to execute, is one of real merit. Under the constitutional plan he is merely a highly ornamental officer with high social standing and no political power. By the accident of death or from some other cause, he may become the most powerful political officer in the Nation, if not the world. As Bryce so aptly puts it, he is *aut nullus aut Cæsar*.[1]

REFERENCES

BEARD. *American Government and Politics*, Edition 1914, Chap. IX.
BRYCE. *The American Commonwealth*, Edition 1910, Vol. I, Chap. V.

[1] Bryce, "The American Commonwealth," New and Revised Edition, Vol. I, p. 300.

DOUGHERTY. *The Electoral System of the United States.*
The Federalist, Nos. 67 to 72 inclusive.
FORD. *The Rise and Growth of American Politics*, Chaps. XV, XXII.
HART. *Actual Government*, Chap. XV.
STANWOOD. *A History of the Presidency.*
WILSON. *Constitutional Government in the United States*, Chap. III.
WOODBURN. *The American Republic*, Chap. III, pp. 94-142.

CHAPTER VI

THE PRESIDENT AS AN EXECUTIVE

THE powers of the President cover a wide range of governmental activities. They relate to both foreign and domestic affairs and involve legislative as well as executive functions. These powers are so vast that the President who is strong in mind and will, and aggressive in character, can make himself the dominant force in the government. Before taking up in detail, however, the discussion of the President's powers and duties, it is well to have in mind the essential provisions of the Constitution.

The whole executive power of the national government is vested in the President, and he is required to take care that the laws are properly executed. He is made commander in chief of the army and navy and of the militia of the States when called into the service of the United States. He is given power to grant reprieves and pardons for offenses against the United States, except in cases of impeachment. With the advice and consent of the Senate he is given power to make treaties and to appoint ambassadors, consuls, judges of the Supreme Court, and all other officers of the United States whose appointment is not provided for in the Constitution or by acts of Congress. He may veto bills and resolutions passed by Congress and may convene both houses, or either of them, in special session, when in his judgment occasion demands. In case they cannot agree as to the time of adjournment, the President may adjourn them to whatever time he thinks proper. It is also his right and duty, under the Constitution, to give to Congress, from time to time, information concerning the state of the Union and recommend whatever legislation he may think necessary and expedient. Upon him is imposed the duty of receiving foreign ambassadors and other public ministers, and of commissioning all the officers of the United States.

The President as Chief Executive. — It will be noticed that the functions of the President, as listed in the Constitution, naturally divide into two main classes, those relating to domestic affairs and those dealing with foreign affairs. It will also be noticed that, despite the theory of the separation of powers which underlies the main structure of the government, the President has been charged with the exercise of legislative as well as executive powers. It was plain to the men who drafted the Constitution that, if the central government was to be effective in its work, the President could not be confined exclusively to executive duties. It is desirable to take up each of his important functions for separate discussion.

First of all should be considered the President's position as the Nation's chief executive. It is the primary duty of the President under the powers granted to him to see to the faithful enforcement of the laws of the United States. In doing this he has the authority of the Nation behind him. He must see that violations of the laws are prosecuted in the courts and that the dignity and authority of the Nation are maintained. He is responsible for the execution of the policies determined upon by Congress, a duty that becomes more difficult to perform with the increasing complexity of industrial and political life. It is his duty to see that the treaty obligations of the United States are observed. In the discharge of these duties he has a large power of direction over the work of administrative officials. He is chiefly responsible for the manner in which the administrative departments are conducted, and may remove officials who refuse or fail to carry out his orders. He cannot, of course, have personal knowledge of all that transpires, but in him the executive power is vested and to him the Nation looks for administrative direction and efficiency.

In the performance of his administrative duties the President exercises a large ordinance power. Under this power he may supplement the acts of Congress concerning administrative activities with detailed executive rules or regulations. Some of the systems of rules which he has established in this way, acting with the heads of the executive departments, assume the proportions of codes of regulations, such as those which apply to the army and navy, and to the postal service. Among other branches of the government in which there are elaborate systems of executive regulations may be mentioned the patent, pension, and land offices and the Indian, consular, customs, and internal revenue services. Many of these regulations are established in response to definite instructions by Congress, but others are put in operation without special authorization by reason of the general executive power vested in the President. It should be noted that this is closely akin to the legislative or law-making function.[1]

The President's Military Powers. — The military powers of the President, though great at all times, are especially so in times of war. Then they expand rapidly and tend to overshadow the powers of other branches of the government. The President is at all times in control of the army and navy and appoints all military and naval officers with the advice and consent of the Senate. If, because of rioting or violence, he considers it impossible to enforce the laws of the United States by the ordinary judicial processes, he may call upon the military to uphold and enforce the national authority, as President Cleveland did at the time of the great Chicago railway strike in 1894. In times of peace the President's military powers are under rather definite restrictions, but when the Nation is at war these powers become far-reaching in their magnitude. Practically there are no limitations upon the President as far as the direction of the war is concerned. It is for him to decide how it is to be conducted. He directs the campaigns, establishes blockades when he wishes, and is responsible for the way in which the army and navy are managed. " The President is not limited in the conduct of war to the direction of the armed forces; he may do whatever a commander-in-chief is warranted in doing under the laws of war to weaken and overcome the enemy. It was under this general authority, inherent in his office, that President Lincoln, during the Civil War, suspended the writ of habeas corpus in the states that were not within the theatre of the armed conflict. It was under this authority that he abolished slavery in many of the states; arrested and imprisoned arbitrarily those charged with giving aid and comfort to the Confederacy; established a blockade of southern ports; and, in short, brought the whole weight of the North, material and moral, to bear in the contest. Greater

[1] See powers of French executive, below, Chap. XLVII.

military power than was exercised by President Lincoln in the conduct of that war it would be difficult to imagine." [1]

If, as a result of a war, as was the case in the war with Spain, territory is acquired, the President may assume control and through his military power set up a military government which will continue in force until provision is made by Congress. The President may, indeed, under these conditions, appoint a provisional civil government with power to levy taxes and establish courts and administrative departments. The war powers of the President, it is thus seen, are capable of vast expansion when the need arises.

Power of Appointment. — The power of appointment which the President has under the Constitution and the laws of Congress is one of the most important powers that he must exercise. This is true from the standpoint of administration because the efficiency of the whole government machine will depend in large measure upon the character of the appointments made by the President. He is the head of the administrative system and it lies with him through his appointments to determine in large measure how that system shall work. But this power is of great consequence also from the standpoint of party politics. The distribution of public offices has been from the beginning a matter of vital concern to the party organizations. The party to which the President belongs expects him to use the appointing power so as to strengthen and help it in its contests with the opposing party. This is usually done by the President, though perhaps not so much now as formerly. It must be kept in mind, in this connection, that the President is, first of all, the leader of his party, for the time being, and it cannot reasonably be expected that he will entirely ignore his own political fortunes and the interests of his party in making appointments. Probably no other part of his work has given the average President more anxiety than this question of appointments.

There are two classes of appointments, recognized by the Constitution, which the President is required to make. One has to do with the chief federal officers provided for in the Constitution or by the laws of Congress whose appointment requires confirmation by the Senate, and the other relates to inferior

[1] Beard, "American Government and Politics," New and Revised Edition, pp. 194-195.

officers provided for by acts of Congress whose appointment has been given to the President alone. The first class is, of course, by far the more important. It includes justices of the Supreme Court, judges of the lower federal courts, ambassadors, members of the cabinet, consular officers, members of important commissions, like the interstate commerce commission, postmasters in the larger cities, and many other high officials whose work is vital to the welfare of the nation. The number of these officials is, of course, large, and, since many of them under the prevailing practice hold office for a four-year term, each President is sure to be called upon to make a great many appointments. The minor appointments, which by act of Congress the President is required to make without consulting the Senate, are not so numerous as the others and as a rule give no special trouble. Some of the minor appointments, by direction of Congress, are made by heads of departments. But, as a matter of fact, most of the offices created by Congress and filled by appointment by the President require confirmation by the Senate. There are more than 6000 of these presidential offices, carrying with them an aggregate salary of over $12,000,000.[1] It is easily seen, from the mere number of offices, how great the President's appointing power is and how burdensome its exercise is certain to be to the conscientious President.

The requirement of the Constitution that the President shall appoint a large number of officers " with the advice and consent of the Senate " has been the cause of a great many conflicts between the President and the Senate and has had serious consequences to the Nation. The intention of the constitution makers seems to be clear enough. Their fear of a possible monarchy was too keen to permit them to give the power of appointment to the President alone. He might use that power to further his own ambitions and be able to subvert the republican form of government. Some check upon him, therefore, was considered imperative. This power to check the President was given to the Senate, which, representing all the States as it does, would be on the alert to prevent him from making appointments which were in his own interests and against the interests of the Union. With regard to both appointments and treaties with other countries, the Senate was to be an advisory

[1] Fairlie, " The National Administration of the United States," p. 4.

body to the President, but with power to defeat absolutely his wishes if it considered that he was acting contrary to the public interest. It was obviously not the intention that the Senate should dictate to the President in the matter of appointments, as it has done so frequently in the past, but that it should simply see that he does not use the appointing power to the injury of the Nation by putting objectionable men into office. In the words of Jefferson, " the Senate is only to see that no unfit person is appointed."

The part which the Senate has played with regard to appointments, however, has been very different from what was intended. Here again the development of political parties has wrought havoc with the design of the Constitution. In large measure the discretion of the President in the making of appointments has been eliminated by the aggressions of the Senate. In the case of many offices he is compelled to appoint men who are acceptable, as party men, to the Senators from the States in which the offices are located if those States are represented by Senators of the President's own party. If he does not do this, his appointments will not be confirmed by the Senate. The practice which the Senate has come to follow with respect to such appointments is known as " senatorial courtesy." The majority of the Senators yield to the Senators most concerned and if the appointment is disapproved by them, confirmation is withheld, and the President is forced to submit the name of some one who is acceptable or, at any rate, who is less objectionable to the protesting Senators than his first appointee. The result of this practice is that, in the case of those offices to which it applies, the appointments are really made by the Senators. Thus the President has practically surrendered some of his constitutional rights to the Senate. In order to avoid opposition to his appointments, he must consult certain Senators in advance. This rule of courtesy, so called, is not an iron-clad rule, however. Whether the President submits to the demands of the Senate depends largely upon his character and temperament. His action is also sometimes influenced a good deal by the interests of his party.

The senatorial courtesy practice does not apply, however, to all appointments made by the President. In general, Senators claim privileges under it only in connection with federal offices which may be considered local in their jurisdiction, such as postmasters, district attorneys, marshals, judges of the lower courts, customs officers, and the like. The most important appointments, as a rule, are exempt from this obstructive senatorial interference. Usually appointments to fill vacancies on the Supreme Court are confirmed without open opposition, although this is not always so. During President Cleveland's second administration the Senate twice rejected his nominee for a place on the court. Mr. Cleveland very neatly solved the difficulty by sending in the name of Mr. White, one of the Senators from Louisiana, and, of course, "senatorial courtesy" demanded immediate confirmation of the appointment. The President is also comparatively free in the selection of ambassadors and other high diplomatic officers. In the case of cabinet officers he is entirely free to make whatever appointments he pleases. The Senate makes no attempt to control these appointments. The attitude of the Senate is that since the President is responsible for the acts of his cabinet associates in the conduct of their offices, and since collectively the cabinet is a body of confidential advisors to the President, he should have the right to select whomsoever he pleases. Of course, if the President were to make a really disreputable or ineligible appointment, the Senate would undoubtedly interfere.

Although the members of the House of Representatives have no constitutional control over appointments, the Senators, in general, accord to the members of the House the right to pass upon appointments which affect their own districts, if the districts in question are represented by members of the President's own party. If they are controlled by the opposing party, then the appointments are determined by the Senators of the State if they are of the same party as the President. When both Senators and Representatives are of the opposite party, the President is expected to consult with the leaders of his own party and make appointments that will strengthen the party organization. It is a common practice for the entire congressional delegation of a State, Senators and Representatives, to confer upon questions of patronage within their State, the President being expected to make the appointments that are decided upon. This is done because the political interests of those members of the delegation who are of the same political party are for the most part identical. Moreover, the Senators are vitally interested in the appointments that are made in the various congressional districts by the Representatives. They must see that these appointments are not opposed to their own personal interests. But it should be noted again that the extent to which the Senate goes in its attempts to control appointments depends a good deal upon the kind of man who is President.

This whole question of patronage is one that is very vital both to the political parties and to the nation at large. The doctrine that " to the victors belong the spoils " is deeply rooted in the national life, although in recent years, under the operations of the civil service law, noteworthy progress toward its overthrow has been made. The tendency to emphasize merit rather than party or personal considerations is steadily growing, to the great benefit of the government service. It is hardly to be expected, however, that the spoils system will ever be completely destroyed.

The Removal of Officers. — The President's power of removal is also a matter of vital concern. The Constitution itself gives no power of removal specifically to the President. The only provision of the Constitution for the removal of officers is that which establishes the process of impeachment, and in this the President has no part. But very early it was agreed that this is an unsatisfactory way of removing officers, particularly those of minor importance. The question came up for detailed discussion during the session of the first Congress and after careful debate the right of the President to remove officers that he had appointed was recognized. In general the view was accepted that the right to remove is inherent in the right to appoint, and that, notwithstanding the failure of the Constitution to make specific mention of it, the right of removal is a constitutional right which belongs to the President. The power of the President to remove officers whom he has appointed is practically absolute, except, of course, in the case of judges who hold office for life under the Constitution and can be removed only by impeachment.

The understanding reached in 1789 as to the President's right of removal continued without change until 1867 when Congress, in the course of its quarrel with President Johnson, passed the Tenure of Office Act which provided that the President must obtain the consent of the Senate before removals could be made. The right of the President to suspend officers, during the recess of the Senate, was conceded, but this must be done only for good cause. Two years later, after General Grant had become President, the law was modified so as to recognize the right of the President to suspend officers "in his discretion." But nowhere in this law, either in its original or amended form, was there a definite statement or indication of just where the power of removal is lodged. In 1885, after President Cleveland came into office, difficulties again arose between the Republican Senate and the Democratic President, the Senate still claiming that its assent had to be obtained before removals could be made. The President stood firm, however, and the Senate finally yielded. In 1887 an act was passed which repealed the law of 1867 and thus recognized again the full right of the President. No other attempt has been made by Congress to question the authority of the President and it seems to be a settled policy that he can remove at will any officers whom he appoints except judges, and without giving causes for his action. The constitutional question involved has not been definitely settled by the Supreme Court, but the power of the President, by common acceptance, is beyond question. The opinion prevails that since the President is responsible for the faithful enforcement of the laws and for the manner in which the vast administrative work of the government is performed, he must be free to discharge faithless or incompetent officials without interference.

It is to be understood that what has been said concerning the President's power of removal has no reference to officers holding positions under the protection of the civil service law. There is a large number of civil service employees who hold their positions as the result of competitive examinations prescribed by the Civil Service Commission, acting under authority conferred by Congress, and who cannot be removed without adequate cause.[1] It is in the case of officers appointed directly by the President, that his power of removal is without restriction.

The Granting of Pardons. — The President's pardoning power is given to him by the Constitution. "He shall have power to grant reprieves and pardons for offences against the United States, except in cases of impeachment." It will be

[1] Below, p. 113.

noted that this is a very broad grant of power. In fact, in the cases in which the President may act at all, his power is unlimited. His pardoning power does not reach to the States, but is confined to crimes against the United States. With respect to these, however, the President is free to act as he pleases. There are no restrictions as to how or when the power of pardon shall be used. At any time after an offense has been committed, whether legal proceedings have been started or not, the President may act. The only way that he may be called to question for an abuse of the pardoning power is through impeachment proceedings. Congress has attempted by legislative enactment to restrict the President in regard to general amnesties, but the Supreme Court has held that this is an invasion of the President's rights. During the Civil War it was demonstrated that the power to grant reprieves to soldiers convicted by court martials is a power of vast importance.

The President and Foreign Relations. — One of the greatest of the powers possessed by the President is that which gives him practical control over the foreign relations of the United States. He is not absolute in this control, by any means, because the power to declare war has been given to Congress and his treaty-making power is checked by the requirement that treaties must be ratified by the Senate. But aside from these important restrictions he has a free hand and practically determines the Nation's foreign policy. The peace and prosperity of the Nation are therefore largely in his charge. It is a heavy responsibility that is imposed upon the President by this vast power.

The President's authority under the Constitution is not contained in a single provision but is found in several. He is charged with the duty of receiving ambassadors and other public ministers from foreign countries; he is given power to appoint, with the advice and consent of the Senate, the ambassadors, other public ministers, and consuls of the United States; and he is given the power to make treaties, with the advice and consent of the Senate, provided two thirds of the Senators present concur. Moreover, the control of foreign relations is looked upon as an executive function and since in the President has been lodged the executive power of the Nation, his absolute control over foreign affairs must be recognized, except as definite limitations have been prescribed by the Constitution. The control of foreign relations is thus inherent in the executive office.

It is convenient, for purposes of discussion, to divide the President's powers in this regard into two classes, those which relate to the general intercourse of the United States with other countries, and those which relate to the formal enactment of treaties, in which the Senate has a share. Under the first come all communication and negotiation with other nations. In this the President is absolutely supreme. Neither the Senate nor Congress as a whole has any restraint upon him. He is the sole organ of communication between the United States and other countries. He alone receives foreign ministers and passes upon their credentials. With him alone, strictly speaking, do they have official relations. They have official intercourse, to be sure, with the Secretary of State, but the latter is the direct and personal organ of the President.

The diplomatic representatives of the United States are directly responsible to the President and he stands responsible for their acts. Their instructions are from him and all of their dealings are really with him, through the Department of State. All the correspondence and negotiations between the President, or the State department, and the diplomatic representatives of the United States or of other countries are usually conducted in secret and may indefinitely be kept secret if the President considers such action necessary in the public interest. In carrying on these negotiations any kind of policy may be pursued that he may wish to adopt. Congress cannot control him in any way. The President does not have the power to declare war, but by the policy he pursues he may force the Nation into such a position that war is the only way out, and thus practically compel Congress to make the formal declaration. Or in his dealings with another nation he may assume a position which will compel that nation to take the initiative in declaring war and thus leave Congress no choice but to accept the challenge. The President by his foreign policy may easily entangle the Nation so that war is inevitable. President Polk in 1846, just preceding the Mexican War, ordered the United States troops into disputed territory where they were fired upon by the Mexicans; Congress acted immediately, saying merely that " war existed by the act of the Republic of Mexico."

Another important power belongs to the President under the provision of the Constitution which confers upon him the sole right to receive foreign ministers. That is the power to give or withhold official recognition of other governments; and that means not merely governments that are firmly established, but also new governments that are trying to obtain a recognized standing among the governments of the world. This means that to the President has been given the power to pass upon the independence of states, a power whose exercise may influence profoundly the developments of world history. In this, as in regard to communications and intercourse with other nations, Congress has no part. The President has " the absolute and uncontrolled and uncontrollable authority." [1]

The Treaty Making Function. — In the making of treaties the President is restrained by the Senate which must give its approval, by a two-thirds vote of the Senators present, before a treaty may be put into force. The peculiar wording of the constitutional provision which gives to the Senate its right, " by and with the advice and consent of the Senate," has given rise to a great deal of discussion as to the relative parts of the Senate and the President in the treaty-making function. Respectable argument may be and has been advanced in support of the theory that the Senate shares equally with the President in this important power and that the Senate is not confined simply to a decision as to whether it will ratify a treaty that has been presented to it by the President, merely altering it more or less by way of amendment, but that it has the right also to participate with the President in the formulation of the treaty. This view denies the right of the President to negotiate or formulate treaties as he pleases without consultation with the Senate. He must seek the advice of the Senate in the framing of a treaty as well as its consent to the treaty's adoption.

But this is not the view of the ablest constitutional lawyers and publicists. The theory that has the greatest weight of authority is that the President is absolutely without restriction in the negotiation of treaties with respect to all questions which may properly become the subject matter of treaty agreements. He may frame a treaty with any other nation upon any proper subject that strikes his fancy, in any way he pleases, and for

[1] Reinsch, " Readings on American Federal Government," p. 84.

any proper purpose, without consulting the Senate or any other branch of the government. He may negotiate as many of these treaties as he may want to, if he can persuade other nations to join with him. After they are framed, he may submit them to the Senate or not, just as he pleases. They cannot be put into operation and become law, of course, without the approval of the Senate, but as to what treaties shall be made and what their purposes shall be, the President alone has the authority to decide. Neither the Senate alone nor Congress as a whole can control him in this function. The President must take the initiative. Congress, or either house acting separately, may pass resolutions concerning international relations containing suggestions as to the need of treaties for certain purposes and what their content should be, but such acts are only gratuitous advice and are in no way binding upon the President. He can accept or ignore them as he wishes. The negotiation of a treaty belongs exclusively to him because he alone has the constitutional right to communicate with foreign countries. "He must negotiate the treaty, make all the stipulations, determine all the subject-matter, and then submit the perfected convention to the Senate for ratification or rejection. They must take his finished work and approve or disapprove."[1]

The right of the Senate to amend treaties, however, is recognized. It may give its advice in the form of amendments or it may reject the treaty entirely. It is not confined to a vote of Yes or No. The amendments may be of such a character as to make the treaty fundamentally different from the one submitted by the President. The President, however, is under no obligation to accept these amendments. He is free to accept them or not. Even if the Senate ratifies the treaty without alteration, the President may pocket it if he pleases and refuse an exchange of ratifications with the other country. This power does not belong to the President by an express grant of the Constitution, but it inheres in his executive authority to conduct foreign relations.

The power of the Senate to thwart the will of the President with regard to treaties is clear. It may defeat them by refusing ratification, or it may amend them so that in their amended forms they are objectionable to the President. Both actions

[1] Pomeroy, "Constitutional Law," Sec. 673, Third Edition.

have repeatedly been taken. It is obvious, therefore, that the President, in the negotiation of a treaty, may find it desirable to inform the Senate as to what he intends and keep it informed as to what is being done. He is entirely free to ask for the advice of the Senate while negotiations are pending if he wishes so to do. This is often done in order to obtain the coöperation of the Senate and lessen the chances of a rejection of the treaty when it is submitted in formal manner for ratification. It is good policy for the President to keep in the good graces of the Senate in order to minimize the latter's hostility to his treaty projects. This is usually done through the Senate's Committee on Foreign Relations, whose chairman, at least, is frequently consulted about treaty negotiations and kept informed as to the progress of events. With the coöperation of this important committee the chances of ratification are greatly improved. A good illustration of the way in which a President may obtain this coöperation was furnished by President McKinley when he appointed Senator Davis, chairman of the Committee on Foreign Relations, a member of the commission to negotiate the treaty of peace with Spain in 1898. Senator Davis, having helped to prepare the treaty, would of course defend it in the Senate and because of his influence as chairman of the Committee on Foreign Relations would be able to render valuable assistance in obtaining its ratification.

At times the House of Representatives may have a part to play in connection with treaties. It has nothing to say concerning either the negotiation of treaties or their ratification, but sometimes treaties contain provisions that involve legislation on the part of Congress in order to make them effective. In such case the House is free to exercise its discretion with regard to this necessary legislation. The treaty may involve the appropriation of money, for instance, and the right of the House to withhold the appropriation, if it disapproves of the purpose for which the money is to be spent, seems to be fairly well established. The House as a political branch of the government may exercise its discretion upon matters of legislation that come before it. The Supreme Court has recognized this right, as is shown by the following excerpt from an opinion by Chief Justice Marshall: " Our Constitution declares a treaty to be the law of the land. It is consequently to be regarded in courts of justice as equivalent to an act of the legislature, whenever it operates of itself without the aid of any legislative provision. But when the terms of the stipulation import a contract, when either of the parties engages to perform a particular act, the treaty addresses itself to the political, not the judicial department, and the legislature must execute the contract before it can become a rule for the court."[1]

The execution of treaties is left to the President, unless they involve acts of legislation of the character referred to by the Supreme Court. They are laws just like the acts of Congress, and the President is charged with the enforcement of the laws. If treaties are in conflict with the acts of Congress, the rule of the court seems to be that 'the one last in date will control, providing always the stipulation of the treaty is self-executing."[2] A treaty and an act of Congress stand on the same footing.

REFERENCES

(For References, see the following chapter.)

[1] *Foster* v. *Neilson*, 2 Peters 253 (1829).
[2] *Whitney* v. *Robertson*, 124 U. S. 190 (1888).

CHAPTER VII

THE PRESIDENT AND LEGISLATION

THE President is a legislator as well as an executive; that is, he participates in the legislative function in a number of ways and often to such an extent that he becomes the controlling force in determining the legislative policy. A part of the President's power in legislation is his by constitutional provision, but a notable part of it is of the extra-constitutional type which has come to him as the result of two great facts or developments.

The first of these is the fact that, though not intended by the framers of the Constitution, the President has become directly responsible to the people, who look to him, not simply as an executive, but as leader of the Nation whose duty it is to see that the popular will is carried out in the work of legislation as well as in that of administration. The President is the only officer in the government who is directly responsible to the whole people. He is the only one who may be looked upon as the representative of the entire Nation. He alone may be considered as the spokesman of all the people, and, therefore, he is expected to be active in seeing that the popular will is embodied in the laws of the land.

The second fact which helps explain the President's share in the legislative function is that he is for the time being the leader of his party and is pledged to see that the party promises, as contained in the platform upon which he was elected, are carried out. This almost always means legislation of some kind. If his party in Congress fails to act in accord with the party pledges, the President himself is discredited. He in part is held responsible for the failure. In considering the legislative activities of the President this dual capacity in which he acts, as leader of the Nation and as leader of his party, must be kept in mind.

The constitutional provisions covering the President's legislative functions are brief. He is required to give to Congress from time to time information of the state of the Union and to recommend to the consideration of Congress whatever measures he thinks necessary and expedient. He is also given the right to call Congress in special session to consider legislation that he holds to be imperative. He is also required to pass upon every bill enacted by Congress before it shall become a law and is given power to veto bills which he disapproves. His constitutional powers may be considered, then, under the two heads, the power to recommend and the power to veto.

Recommendations to Congress. — Two methods have been used by the Presidents in making recommendations to Congress. According to one, the President in person attends a joint meeting of the two houses of Congress and reads an address containing the suggestions he wishes to make. According to the other, he sends to each house of Congress a written message, containing his recommendations, which is read by Senate and House clerks to those members who are willing to hear it. Presidents Washington and John Adams delivered their messages in person, but Jefferson refused to follow their example and transmitted to Congress a written message. From 1801 until 1913 the practice begun by Jefferson was observed without a break. But President Wilson in the latter year set aside the tradition of over a century, and followed the rule begun by Washington and Adams.

At the assembling of Congress in December of each year the President, in one of the ways indicated, submits what is known as his annual message. When delivered by the President in person this is likely to be rather brief and to deal with the subjects of legislation suggested in rather general terms. The written message, however, as it usually appears, is a long document, carefully prepared, which is based on information that comes from the various departments and which reviews the governmental conditions in the Nation, and the relations which exist with other countries. It contains, as a rule, many suggestions as to needed legislation for the improvement of the government service, and usually a somewhat detailed discussion of the one or more pressing political problems of the day upon which the President and his party are pledged to act. This message is usually sent to Congress upon the second day of its session and is read to both houses. The reading is a perfunctory proceeding, as a rule, members giving it only slight attention and preferring to study it at their leisure, if they study it at all. The message is the subject of more or less discussion in the newspapers of the country and serves to give the people information concerning governmental affairs and the policies for which the President intends to stand. The usefulness of the message now is not so great as in the early years of the Republic when the means of transport and communication were so crude, but its usefulness is by no means gone. It is still of distinct educational value. Congress, of course, is not obliged to give heed to what the President suggests, but when Congress is controlled by the President's party it is usually inexpedient, not "good politics," to ignore his recommendations.

The President's opportunity to suggest legislation is not confined, however, to the regular annual message. Special messages dealing with one or more topics are frequently sent to Congress or delivered personally by the President. Those relating to the formulation and ratification of treaties are sent to the Senate alone. The special message really gives the President a better chance to discuss in detail specific legislative policies, and thus to influence Congress, than does the annual message which usually, and with apparent necessity, is much taken up with administrative matters. But whether the recommendations contained in the messages are adopted by Congress and embodied in laws, depends upon a number of things. "The treatment which the President's recommendations receive, of course, varies according to circumstances. They may be accepted because Congress feels that they are sound in principle or because there is an effective demand for them in the country; or they may be accepted because the President by his party leadership or personal favors or use of patronage can bring the requisite pressure to bear on Senators and Representatives to secure their passage."[1] But whether accepted immediately by Congress or not, they serve as a means of communication between the President and the people, and through them he may lead in the formation of a public opinion that will demand definite action at the hands of Congress. President Roosevelt, particularly, was skillful in the use of his messages to stir up

[1] Beard, "American Government and Politics," New and Revised Edition, p. 201.

public sentiment. Likewise, President Wilson, delivering his messages in person, has been effective in developing widespread popular support.

The President's recommendations occasionally take a more definite form than that of a mere suggestion in a message. Occasionally bills are prepared under his general direction to be presented to Congress. This does not happen often because Congress is likely to resent the action of the President as being outside his powers and therefore an unwarranted interference with the legislative department. There is no provision in the Constitution definitely conferring upon the President the right to prepare bills and have them introduced into Congress. But on the other hand, there is no provision that denies him that right. So it may be assumed that he is not transgressing the Constitution in having bills drafted with a view to their introduction into Congress. He cannot introduce them directly, but it is not at all difficult for him to find some Senator or Representative who will stand sponsor for his bill and seek to force it through Congress. There are objections to this practice on the part of the President, but it has been done a number of times and very probably will become more common in the future. It is certain that the points of contact between the executive and legislative departments are much more numerous now than in the beginning, and it is reasonable to assume that executive leadership in the field of legislation will become more potent in the course of the years than it is now. It is natural for the executive to take the leadership in government, for it is in the executive that such leadership naturally rests. The unusual success of President Wilson in directing legislative reform in connection with such great acts as the tariff and currency laws of 1913 has centered attention not only upon the President's legislative powers, but also upon the need for efficient leadership such as only a strong President can provide.

The Veto Power and Its Use. — The veto power gives to the President an effective legislative weapon. It is an instrument by which, at times, he can force his will upon Congress. The constitutional provision by which this power is conferred upon the President is a part of the broader provision which prescribes the procedure upon bills after they have been passed by both houses of Congress. No bill can become a law unless it has been presented to the President for his signature.[1] If he signs it, it becomes a law. If he disapproves of the bill and refuses to sign it, he must return it, together with a statement of his objections, to the house in which it originated, where, after the objections have been entered upon the house journal, it may be reconsidered. If after reconsideration two thirds of that house agree to pass the bill again, notwithstanding the President's objections, it is sent, together with the President's statement, to the other house where it is likewise reconsidered and, if approved by two thirds of that house, it becomes a law. The Constitution requires that in both houses the vote to pass a bill over the President's veto must be by yeas and nays and the names of the persons voting for and against the bill must be recorded in the journal of each house respectively. If a bill is not returned by the President within ten days (Sundays excepted) after it is presented to him, it becomes a law just as if he had signed it. If, however, Congress adjourns before ten days have passed, it does not become a law.

Since the time of Andrew Jackson the use of the veto by the Presidents has differed radically from the original intention. The plan of the constitution makers did not contemplate the use of the veto to defeat bills whose purpose the President merely disapproved of, but which otherwise were unobjectionable. The primary purpose of the veto was to protect the Constitution and the executive authority against inroads on the part of Congress. In the words of Hamilton, writing in *The Federalist*,[2] the grant of the veto power to the President was due to "the propensity of the legislative department to intrude upon the rights, and to absorb the powers of the other departments," and to the "insufficiency of a mere parchment delineation of the boundaries" of the authority of the departments. Without

---

[1] This applies also to joint resolutions, but concurrent resolutions and constitutional amendments need not be presented to the President for his signature. Concurrent resolutions are not used for purposes of legislation, but as a means of expressing fact, principles, or the opinions and purposes of the two houses. The appointment of joint committees, for instance, is authorized by resolutions of this form. Joint resolutions, however, are used for minor legislative purposes and are looked upon as bills so far as procedural requirements are concerned. Special appropriations for minor and incidental purposes are sometimes made in this way. Formerly the joint resolution was used for the enactment of general legislation, but this practice has been abandoned. See House Manual, paragraphs 389, 390.

[2] No. 73.

a negative or veto of some kind, either absolute or qualified, the executive " would be absolutely unable to defend himself against the depredations " of the legislative branch of the government. Therefore " the primary inducement to conferring the power in question upon the Executive, is to enable him to defend himself; the secondary, is to increase the chances in favor of the community against the passing of bad laws, through haste, inadvertence, or design."

The early Presidents followed the constitutional intention and used the veto sparingly. Washington vetoed only two bills during his two terms in the presidency. Down to 1830 only seven more were vetoed by his successors. The attitude of the early Presidents was that the policy-determining function had been given by the Constitution to Congress and the President was not to interfere with this congressional function except for clearly defined constitutional reasons. But President Jackson held an entirely different view of the use of the veto.[1] His theory was that the President must share the responsibility for legislation with Congress and that, therefore, he is free to veto bills that seem to him of doubtful wisdom. Jackson used the veto freely to defeat measures that were contrary to his personal views or his party's policy as he understood it. His position was bitterly denounced by his political opponents, but from that time on the Presidents have uniformly followed the Jacksonian theory. The extent to which the veto has been used is indicated in the following passage: " From the organization of the government under the constitution to the end of President Cleveland's second term, the number of bills vetoed was about five hundred. Authorities differ slightly. The figures, including pocket vetoes upon which messages were written and bills informally or irregularly presented, seem to be four hundred and ninety-seven, of which the number regularly vetoed appears to be four hundred and eighty. Two hundred and sixty-five of these were private pension bills, of which five were vetoed by President Grant and the remainder by President Cleveland. Of private bills, other than pension bills, seventy were vetoed; of local or special bills, eighty-seven. The remainder, seventy-five in number, including bills for the admission of states into the union, are classified as general bills. Of these seventy-five, President Washington

[1] Woodburn. "The American Republic," p. 149.

vetoed two, Madison three, Jackson six, Tyler five, Polk one, Pierce three, Buchanan three, Lincoln two, Johnson eighteen, Grant nine, Hayes ten, Arthur three, Cleveland eight, Benjamin Harrison two. Of Presidents who served full terms, John Adams, Jefferson and John Quincy Adams did not use the veto, nor did W. H. Harrison, Taylor, Fillmore or Garfield."[1] The veto has been freely used by all of the Presidents, since Cleveland's second administration, McKinley, Roosevelt, Taft, and Wilson. McKinley is credited with at least fourteen vetoes, and Roosevelt with forty-two.

It is important to note that public opinion supports the Presidents in this free use of the veto. The people look upon the President, regardless of constitutional theories, as in large measure directly responsible for the legislative policy. They place him in his high position to see that their will is made effective. If the acts of Congress are contrary to that will or express it inadequately, it is his business to interpose the veto to prevent those acts from becoming laws. In the public mind the President is a definite, vital part of the lawmaking department. He is, moreover, the one direct representative of all the people and his veto power is simply looked upon as an instrument for the execution of the popular will.[2]

Experience shows that the veto is an effective instrument in the hands of the President. It is a check upon Congress which is hard to overcome. It has not often been possible to pass bills over the President's veto, notwithstanding the fact that the

[1] Finley and Sanderson, "The American Executive and Executive Methods," p. 211.

[2] "While the veto power has had an astonishing development in this country, the kingly prerogative upon which it was modelled has disappeared. Neither George III nor any of his successors ever used it. There is no instance of a veto from the crown upon a law of Parliament since Queen Anne's reign. In the hands of the President, who, in the estimate of 'The Federalist,' would have to be even more cautious in exercising this power than the British king, it is in robust operation. Either monarchical prerogative has found a more congenial soil in the republic than in the kingdom whose sovereignty was thrown off, or else a remarkable transformation has taken place in the constitution of the presidency, and instead of an embodiment of prerogative, it has become a representative institution. The history of the phases of the development of the veto power shows that the latter view of the case is certainly the true one. Jackson's democratic instinct correctly informed him of the source of his power when he told the Senate that it was 'a body not directly amenable to the people,' while the President 'is the direct representative of the people, elected by the people, and responsible to them.'" — Ford, "Rise and Growth of American Politics," p. 186.

two-thirds vote that is required to overcome a veto has been construed to mean simply a vote of two thirds of the members present and not two thirds of the entire membership. No bill was passed over the President's veto until the time of President Tyler and no really important measure was thus passed before the controversy arose between Congress and President Johnson.[1] The influence of the President due to the fact that he is the party leader is an important factor in this connection. There must be a wide split between the President and the representatives of his party in Congress before a sufficient number of them will oppose him so actively as to force a measure through in the face of his veto. And Congress is not likely to be so overwhelmingly of the opposite party as to be able to overcome the veto by a strict party vote.

The "pocket veto," of which mention has been made, is deserving of brief consideration. This grows out of the provision of the Constitution to the effect that if Congress adjourns before the ten days allotted to the President for passing upon a bill have expired, the unsigned bill shall not become a law. Thus the pocket veto can occur only in the case of bills that are sent to the President in the closing days of a session of Congress. If more than ten days intervene between the time he receives the bill and the time Congress adjourns, he must either sign it or return it to Congress with his objections. But if the time is less than ten days, he can simply fail to sign, if the measure is one that he wishes to defeat, and this is called the "pocket veto." No reason for his failure to sign need be given. Congress cannot criticize him for his inaction because it did not give him the full constitutional period of ten days in which to consider the measure. It is clear that the pocket veto is a convenient device for the President when he wishes to defeat measures that are presented to him during the closing days of a session without taking an open stand against them. Many bills have met their death in this way.

Extra-legal Methods of Influencing Legislation. — Much of the President's activity in a legislative way, under present practices, does not lie within the bounds of the Constitution. He has extra-constitutional methods of influencing the course of legislation which, from the standpoint of practical results, are

---

[1] Finley and Sanderson, "The American Executive and Executive Methods," p. 212.

quite as important as those provided for him in the Constitution. As leader of the dominant party, for the time being, he holds a strategic position. If he is so fortunate as to have the rank and file of his party a unit behind him, he is able frequently to force Congress to do his bidding. He may accomplish this by making direct appeals to the people and thus bring the full force of public opinion to bear upon Congress. He may do it by convincing members of Congress who oppose him that their opposition, if continued, will mean their own political ruin. He may obtain the legislation he wants through persuasion, holding conferences with the leaders and other members of Congress for the purpose of bringing them into line. He may succeed through a threat of veto. Or, if his sense of propriety permits, he may accomplish his purpose by the use of patronage, a method which has been found to be at times extremely efficacious. Rewarding friends and punishing enemies by the bestowal or the withholding of federal patronage has been a somewhat common practice, although the Presidents have been unwilling to admit it. The number of offices that every President must fill by appointment is so large, and the need, according to accepted standards, for every Senator and Representative to control his proper share of the appointments is so great, that the President is often able to obtain public support of his policies from men who, in private, bitterly denounce him, and seek his undoing.

Some of these extra-legal methods of influencing Congress are plainly inconsistent with the spirit of the Constitution and the spirit of free government. It is proper for the President to concern himself actively with questions of legislation, but to make bargains with Senators and Representatives that involve the distribution of patronage and promises of preferment, is not a legitimate means of influencing congressional action. Its usual potency only emphasizes its objectionable features. Some of the methods suggested, however, may fittingly be used. Direct appeals to public opinion are salutary and, if the President's position is reasonable, are likely to be effective. A well-developed public opinion is, after all, the most potent force in the politics of a free state.

The position which the President holds with regard to legislation is not a definitely fixed position. His activity and his influence will depend in large part upon his own personality, and his convictions as to his constitutional authority. The President who believes that he has the right, and that it is his duty, to take the lead in the formulation of legislative policies will find abundant means, both constitutional and extra-constitutional, to make his leadership effective. And in doing this he need not violate the proprieties nor transgress the spirit of the Constitution. The following from Woodrow Wilson, written before he could have had much thought of ever being President, states the point clearly: " Some of our Presidents have deliberately held themselves off from using the full power they might legitimately have used, because of conscientious scruples, because they were more theorists than statesmen. They have held the strict literary theory of the Constitution, the Whig theory, the Newtonian theory, and have acted as if they thought that Pennsylvania Avenue should have been even longer than it is; that there should be no intimate communication of any kind between the Capitol and the White House; that the President as a man was no more at liberty to lead the houses of Congress by persuasion than he was at liberty as President to dominate them by authority, — supposing that he had, what he has not, authority enough to dominate them. But the makers of the Constitution were not enacting Whig theory, they were not making laws with the expectation that, not the laws themselves, but their opinions, known by future historians to lie back of them, should govern the constitutional action of the country. They were statesmen, not pedants, and their laws are sufficient to keep us to the paths they set us upon. The President is at liberty, both in law and conscience, to be as big a man as he can. His capacity will set the limit; and if Congress be overborne by him, it will be no fault of the makers of the Constitution, — it will be from no lack of constitutional powers on its part, but only because the President has the nation behind him, and Congress has not. He has no means of compelling Congress except through public opinion. . . . The personal force of the President is perfectly constitutional to any extent to which he chooses to exercise it, and it is by the clear logic of our constitutional practice that he has become alike the leader of his party and the leader of the nation." [1]

[1] Wilson, " Constitutional Government in the United States," pp. 70–72.

REFERENCES

BEARD. *American Government and Politics*, Edition 1914, Chap. X.
BEARD. *Readings on American Government and Politics*, Chap. X.
BRYCE. *The American Commonwealth*, Edition 1910, Vol. I, Chaps. VI, VII, VIII.
FAIRLIE. *National Administration of the United States*, Chaps. I, II.
FINLEY and SANDERSON. *The American Executive and Executive Methods*, Chaps. XV, XVII, XIX.
REINSCH. *Readings on American Federal Government*, Chaps. I, II, III, IV.
The Federalist, Nos. 73 to 77 inclusive.
WILSON. *Constitutional Government in the United States*, Chap. III.
WOODBURN. *The American Republic*, Chap. III, pp. 142–194.
YOUNG. *The New American Government and Its Work*, Chap. II.

CHAPTER VIII

THE PRESIDENT'S CABINET

THE President's cabinet is composed of the heads of the great executive departments. Its members, as heads of departments, have both a constitutional and a legal status, but the cabinet, as a collective body, has neither. The term cabinet is not used in the Constitution. There are only two references in the Constitution to the officers who are members of the cabinet. The first is the provision which gives the President the power to require the opinion in writing of the heads of executive departments upon any subject relating to their respective offices; and the second is that which gives to Congress the right to vest in the heads of departments the power to appoint inferior officers. Nothing is said in the Constitution as to where the power to create the executive departments shall rest, but this power has always been claimed and exercised by Congress. So each of the executive departments is the result of an act of Congress. No one of them is definitely the creation of the Constitution itself. The Constitution seems merely to take it for granted that executive departments would be established, for it was manifest that the President himself could not administer the national government in all of its details.

As to the collective character of the present-day cabinet, there was apparently no thought whatever in the minds of the men who drafted the Constitution.[1] It was recognized that the President would need advisers, but it was generally felt that the Senate, which by the Constitution was brought into intimate relations with the President, would meet that need adequately. The implied duty of the heads of the executive departments was simply to administer their departments under the President's direction and control. The cabinet as a col-

[1] Perhaps Charles Pinckney is to be excepted. See Learned, "The President's Cabinet," pp. 90 ff.

lective body, therefore, is simply the product of custom. It is another of the important extra-legal institutions of the United States.

The practice, on the part of the President, of seeking advice from the heads of departments was begun very early. Washington, indeed, from the very start, looked upon these officers as his confidential advisers. In the beginning he advised with them individually, and not collectively, as if they constituted a real privy council to the President. Soon, however, he began to invite some or all of them to somewhat formal meetings to consider governmental problems. Before 1793 these meetings were irregular in point of time and procedure, but by the beginning of 1793 the formal cabinet meeting was pretty well established.[1] The name cabinet was not at first applied to the President's advisory council, but soon came into general use, although it remained unknown to the formal law until 1907.[2]

The Cabinet's Relation to the President. — The relation which the cabinet members bear to the President should be clearly understood. It is this relation, in fact, which differentiates the President's cabinet from the cabinets of the parliamentary governments of the Old World. Cabinet officers in the United States are responsible to the President and not primarily to Congress, notwithstanding the fact that the powers they exercise are determined by Congress, and that by the same authority may be fixed in the minutest detail the organization of their departments and the procedure that must be followed.

---

[1] See article by Henry Barrett Learned, in *The American Political Science Review*, Vol. 3, p. 329.

[2] "Not only was a definite Council now set apart by the President's repeated summonses; but it began to be called by a particular name. Madison, Jefferson, and Randolph were among the first to refer to the President's council as the Cabinet. Washington did not employ the term, his customary phrase being 'the Secretaries and the Attorney-General,' or 'The Heads of Departments and the Attorney-General,' with such variations as 'the Confidential officers of Government,' and 'the gentlemen with whom I usually advise on these occasions.' Neither did Hamilton adopt the name Cabinet, though he freely employed the term Ministers. In Congressional usage we have not noted the name earlier than the spring of 1806, when the changes were rung on it in a caustic debate in which John Randolph figured. It appears in a resolution in the house of representatives, for the first time, we believe, so late as July, 1867. And it remained unknown to the statutes, until it appeared in the General Appropriation Act of February 26, 1907." — Hinsdale, "A History of the President's Cabinet," p. 15.

The cabinet officers are not responsible in any way for the acts of the chief executive, the President. In this respect they hold a fundamentally different position from that of the cabinet ministers in England where each is responsible for the acts of the nominal executive, the king or queen. The President is charged by the Constitution with the executive function and is responsible for the manner in which that function is discharged. But he must act through the heads of the departments. Therefore their acts are his acts. He profits from their successes and must assume the responsibility for their failures. They are appointed by him and because of his responsibility for what they do, the Senate does not interfere with the appointments that he makes. It is held that he is entitled to have whomsoever he pleases as his confidential advisers and as heads of departments through whom he must act. The President has full practical authority over them, regardless of restrictions which Congress may seek to establish. This authority is shown by his unquestioned right to remove them whenever he pleases and for reasons of his own. This power to dismiss cabinet officers from the government service has been used with the utmost freedom, although only in a few instances have the dismissals been technically removals. " But virtual removals, couched in the polite phrases of resignation and acceptance, are numerous, probably more so than anybody knows, since there may well be cases, in which retiring Cabinet officers have succeeded to second or third class diplomatic posts, or to inferior judgeships, without knowledge on the part of the public as to whether the change was more desired by Secretary or President." [1] This power of removal assures to the President the power of direction. This is true practically, regardless of the fact that from the standpoint of theory there is no clear understanding as to just what the President's power of direction over administrative officials actually is. Attempts have been made at times by Congress to interfere with the power of removal, but without success.

The work of the members of the cabinet must be considered from two points of view; first, as that of individual executive officers charged with the administration of the departments over which they have been placed, and, second, as that of a col-

[1] Hinsdale, "A History of the President's Cabinet," p. 317.

lective body of advisers to the President. In their individual capacity they are the direct agents of the President through whom he acts in the discharge of his executive function. In their collective capacity they assist the President in the formulation of governmental and party policies. The relation they bear to the President in this advisory capacity is a personal one, recognized neither by the Constitution nor by the laws. Moreover, this relation is entirely dependent upon the President's will. He need not seek the advice of his cabinet, individually or collectively, if he does not wish to do so. Also, he need not accept their advice if he prefers some other course of action. The responsibility is his and his freedom to act according to his judgment is unquestioned. It is expected, however, that the President will consult with the cabinet, and it is likely that he will be influenced materially by the opinion of his cabinet associates. He has chosen them for their positions because he has confidence in their judgment upon questions of policy as well as in their ability to discharge their administrative duties efficiently. It would hardly be expedient for him, as a rule, to ignore their advice. The questions upon which the opinion of the cabinet as a whole is sought are naturally questions of general policy, the special problems of each department being considered separately by the President and the head of the department.

Regular hours are set by the White House rules for the cabinet meetings, although special meetings may be called, of course, whenever the President pleases. These meetings are formal, in a sense, although they concern no one but the President and the members of the cabinet. They are usually secret meetings and no formal records are kept of what is done. This fact illustrates the personal, unofficial character of the relationship of the cabinet in its collective or political capacity to the President.

In a very real sense the cabinet collectively is a party body, assisting the President as party leader, although the cabinet is not a part of the formal party organization. The President must at all times consider the influence of his acts and of his policies upon the interests of his party and it is the business of his cabinet advisers to help him steer clear of party entanglements and mistakes which may lead to party disaster. It is not possible to obtain an adequate understanding of the President's work without keeping in mind constantly his relation to his party. As party leader it is necessary for him not only to keep in touch with public sentiment throughout the Nation, but also, by one means or another, to appeal frequently to the people in order to promote public opinion favorable to him and his policies. Many of these appeals are made through his messages to Congress and his own public addresses. Cabinet members, however, frequently appear before the public as the spokesmen of the President, outlining administration policies and arguing for particular measures which the President wishes to induce Congress to pass. When appearing in this way they are looked upon as the personal agents of the President in his rôle as leader of his party and political leader of the Nation. The responsibility for what they say concerning controversial subjects in reality belongs to him.

Principles Governing the Selection of a Cabinet. — The relation that exists between the President and the cabinet and the nature of its function as a political body are clearly indicated by the principles which usually control in the selection of cabinet members. There is always a mixture of motives revealed in the selection, sometimes one being more prominent and sometimes another, depending largely upon the President's own purposes and the political conditions of the country.

In the beginning Washington recognized the opposing parties in his appointment of the heads of departments. Hamilton, the real leader of the Federalists, was made Secretary of the Treasury, and Jefferson, the leader of the Democratic-Republicans, was placed at the head of the State department. Washington seemed to feel that the conflicting interests of the Nation, as indicated by the opposing political parties, should be represented and balanced in the new government. This experiment was far from successful, however, and in the later years of his administration, Washington definitely committed himself to the policy of selecting cabinet members who were of the same party faith, and who would consequently be likely to work together harmoniously. Since that time the cabinet has been essentially a party body. The regular rule is to have the cabinet made up of men of the same political faith as the President, although the exigencies of politics sometimes demand that factions within the President's party that are really not in sympathy with him be given representation. The result of this is a coalition cabinet made up of men representing more or less antagonistic elements within the party. Lincoln, in the formation of his first cabinet, furnishes a noteworthy illustration of this factional representation. His chief competitors for the presidential nomination, and therefore the leaders of the various factions within the then new Republican party were given seats at the cabinet table. This policy, on the part of Lincoln, was necessary in order to promote harmony among the supporters of the Union, but it was a difficult policy, and it was only Lincoln's tactful ability to handle men that made it successful. Other Presidents have fallen far short of Lincoln's achievement. It is usually the President's purpose to find men who are not only members of his own party, but who are also, in most respects, in complete accord with his own policies. The result of this practice has usually been the selection of men who have attained recognized standing as party leaders in the Nation. There is a tendency in recent years, however, to break away to some degree from this rule. The Presidents now appear to feel more free to appoint men to the cabinet in whom they have personal confidence, whether these men have been considered party leaders or not. In other words, a greater emphasis is now placed upon the function of the cabinet as a body of personal advisers to the President than was formerly the case when the cabinet was more distinctively a body of party leaders brought together for the purpose of administering the government according to the party program. Also there is discernible a tendency to place increasing emphasis upon the function of cabinet members as administrative officers and minimize their function as purely political officers. The character of the cabinet as a party body is not likely to disappear, however, although its relationship to the President may possibly become even more personal than it is now.

In the formation of a cabinet, geographical considerations are usually given great weight. The President, as a rule, attempts to balance State and sectional interests so that no one State or section will have a preponderating influence in the administration. But here again the rule is by no means absolute. The practice of balancing the sections is rather carefully observed, but in recent years it has been not infrequent for a single State to have two representatives in the cabinet. Under President Roosevelt, indeed, New York for a time had three representatives as well as the presidency itself. Since the time of President Cleveland's first cabinet it has been common for the Presidents to give two cabinet appointments to a single State. The President is, of course, after the man whom he considers best fitted for the particular work in mind and it is not always possible to find the right man in the State which he might wish to recognize by a cabinet appointment. Sectional considerations, however, are never overlooked. There is too much at stake, in a personal and party way, for the President to ignore the conflicting interests, fancied or real, between East and West, North and South. He must have a following in all sections and in all States if his administration is to be of the highest success. The practice of giving consideration to the geographical distribution of cabinet members began with Washington and has been more or less strictly adhered to by all of the Presidents since. The nation expects this, and trouble would certainly follow for the President who ignored it completely and picked his cabinet associates from a single section.

Another question of great practical importance which the President must take note of in the formation of his cabinet is whether or not he shall give any of the places to members of Congress. The President must work with and through Congress for the accomplishment of his purposes, and his chances of success are much improved if he has in his cabinet men who have been leaders in Congress. This is particularly true in case the President himself has not had congressional experience. If he has among his advisers men who understand thoroughly the intricacies of congressional procedure and the influences which are effective in the work of legislation, he is much more likely to obtain from Congress what he wants than he otherwise would be. Consequently there will usually be found in the cabinet men who have had congressional experience. Particularly are Senators likely to be called upon to accept positions in the cabinet; members of the House of Representatives are less frequently taken into the President's official family. This is doubtless due to a number of reasons. Senators are usually men of larger abilities and longer political experience than are members of the lower house, although this is by no means always the case. Moreover, the President is more directly dependent upon the Senate because of the latter's control over appointments and its share in the treaty-making power. If the Senate is antagonistic to the President, he may be defeated in the attainment of his most cherished purposes. With men in the cabinet, however, who have been prominent in the work of the Senate, he is in a much more favorable position for bringing influences to bear which will induce the Senate to yield to his desires. Presidents have not always been successful in persuading Senators to give up their places in the Senate for positions in the cabinet. Many men prefer the legislative work of the Senate to the administrative duties of the cabinet. But it is worth while to remember that even the offer of a cabinet position to a Senator is conducive to friendly relations between him, and consequently his associates in the Senate, and the President. The value of such friendly relations is obvious.

Sources of Cabinet Material. — There is no one special branch of the government service which may be looked upon as a training school for cabinet positions. Congress usually furnishes one or more of the cabinet members, but the President must find the men whom he considers suitable where he can. From the very start, as already shown, the leaders of the President's party who are of national standing have frequently been drafted for cabinet service. The appointment of such leaders may or may not tend toward real harmony within the administration and the party. The outcome depends largely upon the characters and ambitions of these leaders and upon the President's hold upon the public confidence. The President who has the people back of him can usually force his will upon his associates and at least maintain the appearance of harmony. Many of the cabinet members, however, do not come from the active party leaders, but from the ranks of successful business and professional men who, because of their training and experience, are considered fitted for these high governmental positions.

The President is under no restraints whatever in making his selection, and the appointments of recent years show that there is a tendency to look for cabinet material among men who have had a successful experience in the conduct of large business undertakings. In the legal profession, also, many cabinet members have been found. A knowledge of the principles and the technique of the law, though not in itself sufficient to insure efficiency in administration, manifestly may be of great help to those who must execute the laws. The legal profession has always been liberally represented in the cabinet. The diplomatic service, also, has furnished a number of cabinet appointees. The training gained in this service is particularly important for the work of the State department. Of equal importance with these others as a source of cabinet material must be mentioned the governorships of the States. The administrative experience of the governors is often of such a character as to fit them admirably for service as heads of the great executive departments. Moreover, their successful careers in the practical politics of their States give them an understanding of party problems and methods which may prove of very great benefit to the President. The result is that ex-governors are frequently found in cabinet positions. Sometimes, also, appointment to specific places comes by way of promotion within the cabinet itself. Some of the departments, such as the State and Treasury departments, are considered of higher rank than others, and it not infrequently happens that Secretaries are transferred from some of the lower to higher positions, the ranking or gradation of the departments in the main being determined by the order of their establishment.

It is clear from this brief enumeration of the chief sources from which cabinet members are drawn that the President is not limited in his selection to any one class or profession. He has all of his fellow-citizens from whom to choose. He is free, if he wishes, to be guided by his own judgment. His motives are known to himself alone. He has the interests of his party and the interests of the nation, as well as his own personal fortunes to conserve. Just how he shall do this, as far as cabinet appointments are concerned, is for him alone to say.

The Cabinet's Relation to Congress. — Notwithstanding the direct responsibility of the department heads to the President, they hold a close and somewhat peculiar relation to Congress. Their right to be is casually recognized by the Constitution, as before stated, but they do not hold office by reason of a specific constitutional provision.[1] The departments over which they

[1] Above, p. 81.

preside have been created by acts of Congress, and it was from Congress that the authority they exercise was derived.[1] The control of Congress over the organization of the departments is complete. New departments may be created, old departments may be reorganized or abolished, their powers may be increased or diminished, as Congress sees fit. The detailed procedure to be followed by the departments may be fixed by statute. Of course the President might intervene with his veto if the proposals of Congress were objectionable to him, but the veto could be overcome if Congress were determined to enforce its will. According to the theory of the Constitution, the legislature is not to control the executive, but it should be noted that the power of Congress over the executive departments, and therefore over the agencies through which the President must work, is so great that the actual exercise of the executive authority may in large measure be regulated by legislative action. This power of regulation is not confined, however, to a control over the organization and procedure of the departments. Congress has other means of exerting influence upon the activities of the executive branch, the use of which brings it into close relationship with the departments.

Full power of direction by the President over the departments has never been conceded by Congress and frequently attempts are made, by one process or another, to control the executive heads in some of their activities. This is done in spite of the fact that Congress has definitely recognized the President's power of removal in which the power to direct is inherent. That Congress can effectively restrain executive action is unquestioned. One of the important means of accomplishing this is through its control over appropriations. The President and all branches of the executive authority are dependent upon Congress for the funds with which to do their work. The executive is thus helpless without the aid of Congress. The work of all of the departments, or of any particular department, may be curtailed and limited by the refusal of Congress to grant the needed supplies. In this way Congress may, if it wishes to assert itself, practically dictate the policy of a department. Technically the President is responsible for the work of each department, but his hands may be so tied by congressional

[1] Contrast with French cabinet, Chap. XLVII.

action that there is only one course of action open to him. Congress does not attempt in this extreme manner to dictate executive action, but that it may do so, if it wishes, is a fact of vital significance. The departments are regularly consulted about appropriations for their support, but the estimates submitted by the departments are in no way binding upon Congress; they may or may not be followed. Items may be included in the appropriation acts, indeed, which are openly disapproved of by the department heads, as, for instance, in connection with river and harbor improvements and the free distribution of seeds by the Department of Agriculture. Attention has already been called to the fact that the House of Representatives, by refusing to appropriate the necessary funds, may prevent the execution of a treaty which has been negotiated by the President and formally ratified by the Senate.

Another means by which Congress influences the conduct of the departments is by requiring departmental reports which are submitted each year at the opening of Congress. These reports are provided for by the statutes and contain detailed information concerning the working of the departments. Moreover, frequent requests are made by one or both houses of Congress for additional or special information upon questions in which Congress is interested. These communications are sometimes in the form of requests and sometimes in the form of demands. The President, or the Secretary immediately concerned, under direction of the President, need not comply with the request if he does not wish to do so; Congress has no way to compel him to furnish the desired data. But through these requests Congress obtains a great deal of information concerning both policies and methods of administration which is of material assistance in enacting legislation for the departments. These requests are not always prompted by disinterested motives; they are frequently designed to promote the interests of the party opposed to the President by forcing him to reveal facts which are considered detrimental to the administration. Usually, however, they are the result of a desire for information which is thought to be important and which it is the right of Congress to have. The resultant publicity is often salutary in its effects.

Formal investigations furnish another method by which

Congress may bring pressure to bear upon the President or upon any particular administrative officer. The conduct of a department may be examined critically in this way by an investigating committee of Congress that has power to summon witnesses, take testimony, collect documents and obtain all of the information that it can. Heads of departments cannot be compelled to appear and give testimony, but they usually do appear in response to the committee's invitation and give the information that is sought, if it seems proper for them to do so. Investigations of this kind sometimes have a far-reaching effect upon the policies of the nation, as was the case in the investigation into the conduct of the Interior Department under Secretary Ballinger in 1910, concerning the administration of the public land laws and the government's conservation policy. Wide publicity is naturally given to the results of such investigations and not only the attitude of Congress, but also the opinion of the people at large may be determined by them. The possibility of an investigation of this kind beyond doubt has a decided restraining influence upon administrative officers. It tends to make them attentive to the demands of Congress, and so strengthens the directive power of Congress over them.

The power of impeachment gives to Congress an additional means of control, but not a very satisfactory one as far as the ordinary working of the departments is concerned. This power belongs to Congress by constitutional grant. Impeachment proceedings may be brought against the President, Vice President, and all civil officers of the United States on charges of "treason, bribery, or other high crimes and misdemeanors." It is plain that the impeachment process can be employed only in case of serious misconduct on the part of the accused officer and that it does not furnish to Congress a serviceable agency for the control of ordinary administrative activities. Bryce aptly says that it is the "heaviest piece of artillery in the congressional arsenal, but because it is so heavy it is unfit for ordinary use. It is like a hundred-ton gun which needs complex machinery to bring it into position, an enormous charge of powder to fire it, and a large mark to aim at."[1] Although it is a powerful check upon the executive power and may at times be

[1] Bryce, "The American Commonwealth," New and Revised Edition, Vol. I, p. 212.

employed, it is practically worthless as a means of directing administrative policies. Without its mention, however, any statement concerning congressional control over executive officers would be incomplete.

Under the practice that has grown up members of the cabinet do not speak in Congress or take direct part in any way in its sessions. This is a matter of custom and not of constitutional provision. According to the Constitution, no person holding any office under the United States may be a member of Congress during his continuance in office, but this provision does not forbid the heads of departments to appear in Congress and speak upon questions under consideration. Whether they shall have this privilege rests with Congress, and Congress has not chosen to grant it to them. Several attempts have been made, at different times, to induce Congress to admit cabinet officers to debates upon questions relating to their respective departments, but without success. In the beginning, when this custom could easily have been established, Congress was too fearful of executive encroachments upon its power to permit the heads of departments to appear in either house for the purpose of taking part in the discussions. It has not seen fit to change its attitude, notwithstanding the rather widespread belief that benefits would accrue to the Nation from a closer relation between Congress and the executive departments in matters of legislation. There is no present indication that Congress is likely to change its attitude, although it is plainly manifest that executive leadership is rapidly gaining in influence and recognition in the determination of legislative policies. If the actual participation of cabinet officers in the debates of Congress were the only means of making this executive leadership effective, it is not improbable that Congress would be forced to modify its practice, but other ways of influencing legislative action are open to the executive authorities.

The Cabinet and Legislation. — The various ways in which the President may affect legislation have already been described. It remains to note that cabinet officers are in rather close relation to legislative work through their dealings with members of Congress and with the congressional committees. All members of Congress have a good deal to do with the different departments in looking after the interests of their constituents and in the discharge of their legislative duties, and it is usually desirable, from their point of view, to be on friendly terms with the department heads. They may wish, for instance, to obtain information from the departments in preparation for their speeches before Congress or the committees, or they may seek political appointments for their friends; and so, for these and other reasons, are likely to give heed to cabinet suggestions. Cabinet members are men of both political and social influence, and members of Congress frequently have need of their help. With the committees, or at any rate the chairmen of committees, that have to do with problems relating to their respective departments, cabinet officers are in frequent consultation. They have no right to demand a hearing before the committees, and their appearance is always by invitation, but it is hardly probable that a request for a hearing would be denied. Information which they have is needed by the committees. Their judgment concerning legislation affecting the departments is usually desired and sought by the committees. So that, notwithstanding the apparent resentment of Congress as a whole and of its committees individually, with regard to what is called executive interference, there is recognition that to a considerable extent the committees are dependent upon the department officials. The real significance of this is understood all the more clearly when it is remembered that the bulk of the work of Congress is done in the committee rooms. The denial by Congress of the privilege of appearing on the floor of the houses and of sharing in the formal discussions by no means deprives the Secretaries of effective contact with the legislative process. Through their influence with the committees they play a valuable part in shaping legislation. Their relation to the committees is entirely unofficial, but it takes the place, in no small degree, of that official ministerial leadership which characterizes the parliamentary governments, and is a vital factor in the harmonization of the legislative and executive departments.

In the discharge of their duties as heads of departments cabinet officers are called upon to establish many departmental rules and regulations that have the force of law. The power they exercise in this is a delegated power. By statute the head of each department is authorized to " prescribe regulations, not inconsistent with law, for the government of his department, the conduct of its officers and clerks, the distribution and performance of its business, and the custody, use, and preservation of the records, papers, and property appertaining to it." This is an important power, particularly in certain departments, to which special ordinance powers have been given, as, for instance, the Treasury and Post Office departments, in which a vast system of regulations must be provided. In making these regulations the department heads cannot go beyond the power delegated to them. Within the limits set, the rules thus prescribed have the full force of law and will be enforced by the courts. Closely allied to this power to prescribe regulations is the power to hear cases on appeal from lower administrative officers and to render final decision.

REFERENCES

BRYCE. *The American Commonwealth*, Edition 1910, Vol. I, Chap. IX.
FINLEY and SANDERSON. *The American Executive and Executive Methods*, Chap. XVI.
HINSDALE. *A History of the President's Cabinet*, pp. 1-16, 283-328.
LEARNED. *The President's Cabinet*, Chaps. II, III, IV, V, VI, XIII.

CHAPTER IX

THE NATIONAL ADMINISTRATION

THE Nation's administrative work is, for the most part, under the control of the executive departments, of which there are ten. Those in charge, usually called Secretaries, are appointed by the President, and are, as already shown, members of the President's unofficial cabinet. Each receives an annual salary of $12,000. In addition to the regular departments there are several commissions, to be described later in this chapter, which are of the very highest importance and whose work rivals in its magnitude that of the departments themselves.

The department is the largest unit of administration in the national government and is thoroughly centralized in its organization. It is divided into a number of smaller administrative units known as bureaus, which, in turn, are frequently subdivided into still smaller parts known as divisions. In charge of these divisions are officers known as chiefs of divisions who are responsible to their respective bureau chiefs, who, in turn, are responsible to the Secretary of the department. Bureaus are established by act of Congress just as are the departments; divisions and the smaller units may be established by executive order. Various names are applied to those in charge of the bureaus, the heads of the most important bureaus being usually called commissioners, and the heads of the less important ones being designated simply chiefs of bureaus. Each Secretary or head of the department has one or more assistants usually called assistant secretaries. These officers are the ones with whom the Secretary has direct dealings and to whom he looks for the execution of his orders. They in turn act through the bureau chiefs. There is thus a gradation or hierarchy of officials corresponding to the units of administration into which the department is divided. Many minor differences exist with regard to the details of organization in the various departments, but, in the main, the outline suggested holds true for all. The authority of the department centers in the Secretary who is directly responsible to the President.

At the beginning Congress established only three regular departments, — State, Treasury, and War. These were created in 1789, but not by the same act of Congress. The State department, then known as the Department of Foreign Affairs, was the first to be established. Then followed the War and Treasury departments, and soon after the office of Attorney-General was created. The latter was not at first looked upon as a department; in fact, it was not so recognized until 1870 when the Department of Justice was established, although almost from the beginning it took rank with the departments, and the Attorney-General was considered a member of the President's cabinet. The other departments, established as the need demanded, came in the following order: Navy in 1798, Post Office in 1829, Interior in 1849, Agriculture in 1889, and Commerce and Labor in 1903. In 1913 the last was divided by act of Congress, and a separate Department of Labor was created. The Post Office service, with a Postmaster-General at the head, was established by the first Congress in 1789, but it was not an independent department, and for forty years remained as a branch of the Treasury department. The rapid development of the Nation, with the resultant enormous increase in administrative activities by the government, made the establishment of new departments vitally necessary. In fact, the general development of the national life is indicated rather clearly by the formation of the executive departments. In the beginning the pressing problems for the new government were those of establishing satisfactory relations with the Old World countries, protecting itself against outside aggressions, maintaining law and order at home, and placing the Nation's finances upon a sound basis. The first three departments were charged with these duties, while those established later have been the logical results of different phases of the national development.

The State Department. — The Department of State traditionally has been considered the most important of the departments, and the Secretary of State has from the beginning taken first rank among the members of the cabinet. He is sometimes spoken of as the premier of the cabinet, but this is wholly inaccurate and implies a position on the part of the Secretary of State which he does not have. His relationship to his associates in the cabinet is in no sense that of a prime minister to his colleagues. They are in no way officially dependent upon him either for their positions or their influence. Like him they hold office at the will of the President. The relation of the Secretary of State to the President, however, ordinarily has been somewhat different from that of other cabinet members. He has had greater freedom usually in the control of his department than any of his associates. This is due to the nature of the State department's work in connection with foreign relations. This work requires for its efficient performance the highest ability, and thorough understanding of international law and the problems of world politics. It requires familiarity with the ways of diplomacy and great tact and skill in handling the many delicate questions of foreign policy that constantly arise. By no means all of the Presidents have been fitted by training and character to direct personally the Nation's foreign policy. Moreover, the pressure of duties in connection with the domestic administration is usually so great that the average President cannot give detailed attention to foreign affairs. The President, of course, may interfere with the plans of the Secretary, or take personal charge of the matter under consideration if he wishes to do so, for the responsibility is his and cannot be shifted to any one else. Frequently this is done, and at times of real crisis in international relations, the strong President will assume personal direction of the nation's foreign policy.

The most important duties of the Secretary of State are those in regard to foreign affairs, although other duties are imposed by law. The negotiation of treaties of all kinds is carried on through his office. Under his direction is conducted all correspondence with the public ministers and consuls of the United States and with the representatives of foreign powers accredited to the United States. He signs extradition papers for the return of fugitives from justice, issues passports to citizens of the United States, and, in general, looks after American interests in foreign countries. He is assisted in his work by three assistant secretaries and a large clerical force. The work of his department is classified and is conducted by a number of separate bureaus, the two dealing with foreign affairs being the diplomatic and consular bureaus. The former has charge of correspondence with the diplomatic representatives of the government and the latter of correspondence with the consular officers. The diplomatic service concerns itself with the relations of the government of the United States to other governments, while the consular service gives its chief attention to the personal and commercial interests of American citizens. All of this work is under the general supervision of the Secretary of State, who thus has direction over a large number of officials located in all of the countries of the world. It is unnecessary to elaborate here the functions of the State department with reference to foreign affairs since the control of foreign relations was discussed somewhat in detail in connection with the work of the President.[1]

The minor duties which the Secretary of State performs are those which come to him as the medium of correspondence between the President and the governors of the States and as the keeper of the seals and the archives of the national government. He affixes the Great Seal to the President's proclamations and to important commissions, and to warrants for the extradition of fugitives from justice. He publishes the laws and resolutions of Congress, amendments to the Constitution, and proclamations declaring the admission of new States into the Union. He is custodian of the laws and treaties of the United States and is charged with the preservation of the government archives. These duties are, for the most part, merely formal. They add little to the influence of the State department. That which gives it primacy among the executive departments is the vital importance of the Nation's foreign relations. The issue of peace or war may hinge upon the judgment of the Secretary of State and the work of his subordinates.

Financial Administration. — General control of the Nation's finances is lodged in the Department of the Treasury. Naturally, then, this department is looked upon as one of the most important. In rank it is accorded a place next to the State department. The age-long belief that the liberties of the people are involved in the control of the public purse has lost none of its vitality. Because of this belief Congress has sought to retain

[1] Above, p. 64.

power over the Treasury department to a degree not attempted in connection with the other departments. The relation of this department to Congress is, therefore, somewhat different from that of the other departments. The attitude of Congress is shown by the acts passed in 1789 creating the State, War, and Treasury departments. The Secretaries of State and War were ordered to " perform and execute such duties as shall from time to time be enjoined on or entrusted to them by the President of the United States." Upon the Secretary of the Treasury, however, were imposed certain duties enumerated in the statute, and, in addition, that of performing " all such services relative to the finances, as he shall be directed to perform." But the law does not intimate whether this direction shall come from the President or from Congress. Moreover, the Secretary was ordered " to make report and give information to either branch of the Legislature, in person or in writing, as he may be required."[1] By reason of this last provision Congress need not address its request to the President, but may send it directly to the head of the Treasury department.

The general management of the department rests with the Secretary who has under him three assistant secretaries and a large number of other departmental officers and employees. The assistant secretaries are of the same rank and to each is given supervision of certain divisions in the Secretary's office and other somewhat independent bureaus. The duties of the department cover a wide range, some of them being unrelated to fiscal affairs. Discussion here will be confined substantially to the collection of revenue, a function of the highest importance in every State.

The collection of revenue involves two important services, namely, the customs service and the internal revenue service. The first has to do with the collection of duties imposed by law upon imported goods. Such duties have been one of the chief sources of the government's income. Necessarily, therefore, all branches of the government and the people generally are keenly interested in the customs administration. A somewhat complex administrative organization has been evolved, by congressional acts and executive orders, for the discharge of this function. The country is divided into collection districts, with designated ports of entry, at which goods shipped from

[1] Hinsdale, " A History of the President's Cabinet," p. 8.

abroad are received. At each port of entry government officers are stationed, the most important of whom is the collector. At the larger ports, such as New York or Philadelphia, there are a collector, surveyor, and naval officer, with a large number of subordinate employees such as appraisers, inspectors, gaugers, and clerks. It is the business of these officers to watch the unloading of goods, check up the invoices, pass judgment on quantity and values, and see that the customs laws are enforced. This is a task of great difficulty, and smuggling is not infrequent. General supervision of the customs administration is intrusted to one of the assistant secretaries who is, of course, under the direction of the Secretary of the Treasury.

The second branch of the revenue administration is known as the internal revenue service. This is a regular bureau in the Treasury department, although its head, known as Commissioner of Internal Revenue, is to a large degree independent of control by the Secretary of the Treasury. The function of the Commissioner is to enforce the excise or internal revenue laws as enacted by Congress, the chief taxes collected being those upon liquors, tobacco, corporations, and incomes. Other taxes, however, such as stamp taxes of various kinds, are levied at times to meet a need for greater revenue. To facilitate the enforcement of the laws the country is divided into internal revenue districts, but this is done by order of the President and not by act of Congress, as is the case with the customs districts. In each district there is a collector, appointed by the President, and whatever subordinate officers are necessary, the latter being appointed by the Secretary of the Treasury. To insure adequate enforcement of the laws it is necessary to employ a corps of internal revenue agents who are directly responsible to the Commissioner of Internal Revenue and whose duty it is, in the capacity of detectives, to ferret out and prevent frauds. The taxes are not levied upon the value of the product, but upon the amount, and the collection procedure is therefore more simple than that in connection with customs duties. Manufacturers must purchase government stamps which cover the amount of the tax. Heavy penalties are imposed upon those found guilty of selling goods upon which the tax has not been paid.

In addition to the work of collecting revenue, the Treasury

department has important duties in connection with the supervision of national banks, the issuance of paper currency, the coinage of gold and silver, the custody of public moneys, the auditing of governmental accounts, the administration of the public debt, and other matters not related to fiscal affairs, such as the promotion and protection of public health, the construction of public buildings, and the management of the life-saving service. These non-fiscal activities may properly be transferred to other departments at any time if Congress so wishes.

Departments of War and the Navy. — The problem of national defense, by authority of Congress and under the direct control of the President, is intrusted to the Department of War and to the Department of the Navy. The policy to be pursued with respect to the strength of the military and naval forces is exclusively within the control of Congress. The War and Navy departments can have nothing to say concerning that except by way of recommendations. Their function is exclusively administrative and is discharged under the direct supervision of the President, who, by the Constitution, is made the commander in chief of all the armed forces. This authority he holds in times of peace as well as in times of war. He is likewise the head of the militia of the States when called into the service of the Nation. It is for him to say what disposition shall be made of both land and sea forces. The department heads through whom he acts are the Secretary of War and the Secretary of the Navy. The chief function of each is to see that the service under his control is well equipped, well trained, and efficient, to the extent possible under the regulations and the grants of money made by Congress. The organization of each department is complex, involving many bureaus and divisions, and the employment of a large number of officers.

The duties of the Secretary of War are such as are imposed upon him by law or by order of the President. By law he is required to prepare estimates of appropriations needed by the War department and to look after all expenditures for the maintenance and operations of the army. Under his supervision is the United States Military Academy at West Point, the various army posts throughout the country, and all the military bureaus into which the War department is divided for administrative purposes. The Secretary of War is usually a civilian, but the heads of the military bureaus are officers of the regular army. The preparation of plans for the national defense and the mobilization of the army for peaceful maneuvers as well as for operations in time of war is in the hands of the General Staff Corps, at the head of which is the chief military officer known as the Chief of Staff. There is one assistant secretary to whom the Secretary of War delegates important functions and upon whom heavy responsibilities are imposed by law.

The bulk of the work of the War department is naturally concerned with the administration of the army, but other functions of very great value to the nation have been given it by law. One of these, involving the expenditure of very large sums of money, is the construction of river and harbor improvements that have been authorized by Congress. The duty of examining and passing upon surveys and plans and making recommendations for improvements is placed upon the Board of Engineers for Rivers and Harbors, but the actual work of construction is in the hands of the Corps of Engineers of the army, at the head of which is the Chief of Engineers. The primary function of the engineering corps is, of course, to solve engineering problems which confront the army in time of war, but to the great advantage and profit of the Nation the skill of the engineers has been used in the construction of important public improvements. A striking illustration of this is seen in the construction of the Panama Canal, one of the world's greatest engineering achievements. It was only after this huge undertaking was placed in the charge of the army engineers that satisfactory progress was made. Splendid results have also been achieved by the Corps of Engineers in the Philippine Islands in the construction of roads, bridges, and other public works.

The Department of the Navy, like the other departments, is divided into a number of bureaus, each with its special field of work. General control over the department rests with the Secretary who acts under the direction of the President. There is one assistant secretary, who, like the Secretary, is a civilian. The different bureaus are in charge of officers who understand the technical problems of naval administration.

Administration of Justice. — In a country as large as the United States, with a government in which the courts hold so central a place and legal checks are so prominent, the department which has in charge the administration of justice is certain to be of high rank and great practical value. Law is exalted to a high place in America, as an agency for reform, and is resorted to for all kinds of purposes; yet, singularly, respect for the law on the part of the average citizen is far below what it ought to be. In fact, the positive disrespect for law which is so prevalent in the United States constitutes one of the Nation's serious problems. Because of it the administration of justice is difficult, whether national, State, or local, and the officers in charge carry a heavy burden of responsibility.

The branch of the national administration which is immediately responsible for this work is the Department of Justice. At the head of this department is the Attorney-General who is the chief law officer of the government. He is legal adviser to the President and the other heads of departments, and upon request gives his advice and opinion upon questions of law that arise in connection with administrative activities. It is his duty to enforce the laws of the United States, under the direction of the President, and to represent the government, either in person or through subordinate officers, in all legal controversies to which the government is a party. He has general supervision over the United States attorneys and marshals in the States and Territories. He is, in short, responsible, under the President's direction, for the administration of the Nation's laws as far as court proceedings are essential. His work has steadily increased in importance with the growth of the Nation. In view of the complex industrial life that has developed and the resultant difficulties with respect to the enforcement of the corporation laws, no other officer in the administrative departments holds a position of more vital consequence. It is plain, at a glance, that the Attorney-General must have a great deal of help.

First in rank among the Attorney-General's assistants is the Solicitor-General. Under the regular practice the chief duty of the Solicitor-General is to look after the government's business before the Supreme Court of the United States. The Attorney-General may appear in person in such cases, and sometimes in the more important cases does so, but as a rule arguments before the Supreme Court on behalf of the government are made by the Solicitor-General, with the help of Assistant Attorneys-General. He is under the direction of the Attorney-General and may be sent to represent the government in cases pending in the lower federal courts or even in State courts in which the interests of the United States are involved. He may also be called upon by the President and the heads of departments for legal advice, subject to the approval of the Attorney-General.

Next below the Solicitor-General is an officer known as Assistant to the Attorney-General, who for the most part has charge of special cases arising under the antitrust and interstate commerce laws. He is under the direction of the Attorney-General, however, and other duties may be assigned to him as the latter may desire.

There are, besides, a number of Assistant Attorneys-General who have important duties to discharge in connection with the preparation of legal opinions and the presentation of cases before the Supreme Court and the Court of Claims. It is the function of these officers to assist the Attorney-General in whatever ways may be prescribed by him, and hence they may be called on to help represent the government in any of the courts. In addition there are assistants known as Solicitors who are assigned to different executive departments to look after legal questions that arise. These Solicitors are the chief law officers of their respective departments, but are under the supervision and control of the Attorney-General.

To obtain efficiency in its work, the Department of Justice is divided into a number of smaller administrative units. Of the officers in charge of these, mention may be made of the Superintendent of Prisons and Prisoners, to whom is given supervision of all United States prisons, and the Attorney in charge of pardons who receives and looks after all applications for pardon except in military and naval cases. These officers, of course, are under the direction of the Attorney-General who is responsible to the President for all that is done.

Department of the Interior. — A branch of the national administration which deserves special emphasis, because of the magnitude of its work, is the Department of the Interior. Its activities cover a wide range and, as is true of some of the other departments, deal with a number of wholly unrelated subjects. The head of the department is known as Secretary of the Interior and has the help of two assistant secretaries and various commissioners and directors who are in charge of the different bureaus into which the department is divided. The number of employees is necessarily very large.

One of the leading functions of the Department of the Interior is in connection with the general policy, so vital to the Nation's welfare, known as the conservation of natural resources. Immensely difficult problems are involved and the Secretary of the Interior is necessarily a big factor in their solution. It is one of his chief duties to help devise methods for the rational development and use of the Nation's natural resources, and for the prevention of the exploitation and needless waste which have been permitted in years past. Much of this work now centers in the Territory of Alaska, with its wonderful deposits of coal and the precious metals, and almost limitless possibilities of development. At least three of the bureaus of the department are directly related to this conservation work, — the General Land Office, the Reclamation Service, and the Geological Survey.

The first of these, under the supervision of an officer known as the Commissioner of the General Land Office, is charged with the management and disposition of public lands. This involves a number of duties, such as the issuance of patents for lands, adjudicating conflicting claims, keeping full records of all transactions touching public lands, and the general administration of the land laws. Branches of this office are maintained in different States, with agents in charge. Owing to the vast amount of land which the United States has had in its possession, and its rapid development under the homestead laws and other statutes providing for its utilization, the Land Office has always been of great importance. Though the public domain is by no means what it used to be, it is still immensely valuable. Fully a million and a half square miles of public lands are still held by the government. All of this is under the supervision of the Land Office except the administration of the national forests, which is lodged in the Department of Agriculture.

The Reclamation Service, under the supervision of a Director, has charge of all the government's work in reclaiming arid lands through the construction and operation of irrigation works. Numerous projects of this kind, involving difficult engineering problems and the expenditure of large sums of money, have been undertaken. The satisfactory results attained point to still larger achievements in the years to come.

Upon the Geological Survey is imposed the duty of classifying the public lands, analyzing their geologic structure, and determining their mineral deposits. Careful surveys are made, both topographic and geologic, and detailed statistical information is collected and published. This work is considered of high value, and upon it depends to a considerable degree the policies of the government concerning the development and conservation of the public domain.

Among the other untreated branches of the Interior department mention should be made of the Patent Office, the Pension Office or Bureau, the Office of the Commissioner of Indian Affairs, and the Bureau of Education. The Indians are the wards of the Nation and the enforcement of the laws for their protection and for the promotion of their welfare is in the hands of the Commissioner, who acts under the supervision of the Secretary of the Interior. The Pension Office passes upon claims made under the laws enacted by Congress by those who have served in the army or navy. The work of this bureau is heavy, though to a large extent ministerial in character. The amount of money expended for pensions is enormous. In the fifty years following the Civil War at least four billions of dollars were paid out in this way. The Patent Office is under the direction of a Commissioner who is in full control of the issuance of patents and the administration of the patent laws. The work of this office in the examination of applications for patents is very heavy. More than 50,000 applications are filed each year.[1] The relation of patented inventions to the industrial development of the Nation and the growth of industrial monopolies need only be mentioned to indicate the value of good patent laws and efficient patent administration. The settlement of infringement suits is in the hands of the federal courts, the Circuit Court of Appeals having final judgment. The function of the Bureau of Education is largely informational. It has no administrative authority over school management; that lies with the State. Its duty is mainly that of collecting

[1] Fairlie, "National Administration of the United States," p. 211.

and disseminating information for the purpose of promoting the cause of education.

The Remaining Departments. — The four remaining departments are those of the Post Office, Agriculture, Commerce, and Labor. The name of each suggests rather definitely the nature of its work. The Post Office department is one of the largest of all and is noteworthy for the manner in which its administration has been sacrificed to the interests of the political parties and the demands of partisan office-seekers. It is in that department more than in any of the others that the patronage evil has been most deeply rooted and has shown its largest fruitage. For a long time post office positions, however small, were looked upon as spoils to be awarded to workers in the victorious party in return for partisan services. In recent years this evil has been greatly reduced by the extension of the civil service regulations so as to protect a large number of postal employees; but the appointment of postmasters in the larger, more important offices in all the States is still a partisan matter. That the postal service has suffered greatly from this abuse goes without saying. Elimination of partisan administration of this service is one of the reforms most needed in the United States and for which a public demand is steadily developing. The establishment of the parcels post and the possibility of the government's taking over ultimately the telegraph and telephone services of the Nation only emphasize the need for thoroughly efficient administration, free from partisan politics and party control.

The underlying purposes of the other departments mentioned are the development and conservation of the great agricultural resources of the United States; the promotion of her industries and expansion of her commerce; and the protection and advancement of her industrial workers. Within the province of these departments are found some of the greatest problems confronting the American people. These include problems of both wealth production and wealth distribution; they involve vital questions of social economy as well as questions of industrial economy. To the solution of these the Nation is devoting earnest thought, and the departments named give evidence of the national desire to have the government respond to the real needs of the people. These departments, particularly those of Agriculture and Labor, as they are organized and actually operate, illustrate well the fact that the functions of government in a modern democracy multiply rapidly in number and expand widely in scope, if the common life of the people, in all of its aspects, receives adequate consideration. Democracy is social, and the general social welfare is its one great aim.

Interstate Commerce Commission. — In addition to the regular executive departments, the national administration includes several independent bureaus or commissions which play a big part in national affairs. Among these are the Interstate Commerce Commission, the Civil Service Commission, and the Federal Trade Commission. Only brief, general comment upon the work of these bodies may be given here.

The Interstate Commerce Commission was established by Congress in 1887, after many years of agitation for national regulation of railway rates and service. The action of Congress was taken under its constitutional grant of power to regulate commerce among the States and with foreign nations. Before the Civil War, very little use of this power was made, but following the war, when the United States entered upon a period of great industrial development and trade expansion, the demand arose and became insistent that the transport companies engaged in interstate commerce be placed under adequate national control. This demand was caused by widespread and flagrant abuses on the part of the railways in granting rebates and special privileges to favored shippers, in discriminating among communities and sections, and in charging unreasonably high rates for transportation service. Congress was slow to respond to public sentiment, but finally yielded, and the interstate commerce act of 1887 was the result. This law has been amended several times, under pressure of public opinion, with the result that the powers of the Interstate Commerce Commission are far more extensive than they were at first. Its authority over railways and other common carriers is very great and involves a burden of responsibility such as few of the other branches of the national administration are forced to bear.

The Interstate Commerce Commission is composed of seven members, appointed by the President and confirmed by the

Senate. Each commissioner receives a salary of $10,000 a year. The law which the Commission administers applies to all corporations and persons engaged in the transportation of passengers or property by railway, or by rail and water, from State to State or to a foreign country, — and to all common carriers transporting oil or other commodities, except water and gas, by means of pipe lines, or by means of pipe lines and rail or water combined. Of course the transportation must be interstate in character to bring it under the Commission's control; intrastate commerce lies within the authority of the States. By law many restrictions are imposed upon carriers. Rebates and discriminatory rates among shippers are forbidden; all charges for carrying passengers and freight must be reasonable; schedules of rates must be kept open to the public; changes in rates can be made only after proper notice to the Commission, which is empowered to suspend increases in charges pending investigation and to determine whether the changes shall be made; granting free transportation, except as specified by the law, is forbidden; giving preference to one locality over another, through discriminatory charges, is prohibited; detailed annual reports must be made to the Commission according to forms which the Commission prescribes; and railway engines and cars must be equipped with certain safety appliances specified in the law. The enforcement of these regulations, and others not enumerated, is in the hands of the Commission. In addition, certain powers are given to the Commission, and specific duties are imposed upon it. It may begin the prosecution of carriers which violate the law, by requesting the Department of Justice to bring suit. It may investigate fully the management of carriers coming under the law, and in doing this may summon witnesses, take testimony under oath, and compel the production of all books and papers needed in the investigation. It is also authorized to hear complaints either by or against any carrier engaged in interstate commerce, to fix reasonable charges in accordance with the facts revealed, and to award damages to shippers or other persons injured by unlawful acts on the part of carriers. In the performance of its work, covering so wide a field, the Commission requires the services of a trained force of investigators, engineers, and accountants.

In view of the very large railway mileage in the United States and the enormous volume of interstate commerce transported every year, it needs no comment to make plain the high importance of the Interstate Commerce Commission and its work. The business of transportation is fundamental and the general industrial prosperity of the Nation is inextricably bound up with it. The judgments of the Commission are therefore of far-reaching influence.

Federal Trade Commission. — The Federal Trade Commission, established by act of Congress, began its work in 1915. It is composed of five members, appointed by the President with the approval of the Senate. It is an outgrowth of a nation-wide demand for effective regulation of corporations engaged in interstate business, and for stringent control of trusts and monopolies. According to the act creating it, the purpose of the Federal Trade Commission is to prevent persons, partnerships, and corporations engaged in interstate trade from using unfair methods of competition. If the Commission suspects that unfair methods are being employed, it may issue a complaint against the person or corporation under suspicion and hold a formal hearing for the determination of the facts. It is empowered to issue orders forbidding the practices complained of unless proper showing is made that the complaint is not well founded. If an order of this kind is issued and the offender does not cease the objectionable practices, application may be made by the Commission to the Circuit Court of Appeals for the order's enforcement, the judgment of this court being subject to review by the Supreme Court of the United States. The Commission, which is a quasi-judicial, quasi-administrative body, is also empowered to investigate the organization, methods, and management of corporations and their relations to other corporations and business institutions; to require the filing of information concerning their affairs by all such firms and corporations; and to investigate trade relations with foreign countries, and make reports to Congress, together with recommendations for new and supplementary legislation.

It is plain at a glance that Congress has imposed a heavy task upon the Federal Trade Commission, — a task which will grow increasingly difficult with the continued industrial development of the United States. At the time the Commission was organized there were considerably more than 300,000 corporations, in more than 300 different industries, doing business in the United States. This number will grow larger, of course, with the passing of the years, and to prevent " unfair methods of competition," to say nothing of the other duties imposed, is a work of enormous difficulty as well as of gigantic proportions. The Commission represents one part of the Nation's antitrust policy and of its attempt to maintain competition as an active force in industry and interstate trade. Its work is closely related to that of the Department of Justice in the administration of the antitrust laws. As to the wisdom of Congress in establishing the Commission, judgment must await future developments.

The Civil Service. — The third of the independent commissions named above, as deserving special mention, is the Civil Service Commission, which aids the President in the administration of the civil service laws. The act creating the Commission was passed by Congress in 1883, after several earlier but futile attempts at civil service reform and long-continued agitation. By the terms of the law the Commission has three members, appointed by the President and confirmed by the Senate. It is provided that not more than two of these may be adherents of the same political party. The chief function of the Commission is the preparation of rules, as the President may request, for carrying the civil service requirements into effect, and exercising general supervision over the work of examining applicants for office.

The law requires open competitive examinations for testing the fitness of applicants for positions in the classified service. This involves the preparation of many different kinds of examinations in order to supply all the administrative offices with adequately trained employees. Any citizen of the United States may try for a position in the federal service. Examinations, of various kinds and covering a wide range of subjects, are held in each State and Territory at least twice a year. These are in charge of local boards of examiners, of which there is a large number throughout the Nation. A chief examiner has his office at Washington.

The appointments are made from those receiving the highest grades in the examinations. According to the rules in

THE NATIONAL ADMINISTRATION

force, the Civil Service Commission, when called upon, sends to the department which is seeking a new employee the names of the three highest on the list of applicants for the positions in the service where the vacancy exists, and from these the appointment is made. The two remaining names are returned to the Commission and replaced on its register of candidates. Before absolute appointment is made, the successful candidate must serve a probationary period of six months. This procedure is the one usually observed, but there are provisions which modify it a good deal at times. For instance, persons honorably discharged from the military and naval services are given preference over those who have not served in the army or navy. Also, positions in the departments at Washington are to be apportioned among the States and Territories according to population. Such special rules prevent the strict application of the merit principle.

Persons holding office under the civil service law are not exempt from removal. The rule governing removals is rather vague and capable of abuse. It is that no one may be removed from a position gained through a competitive examination "except for such causes as will promote the efficiency of the service." This means that the President or the head of a department, as the appointing officer, may remove any civil service employee on grounds of incompetency.

The number of positions in the federal executive service is very large. On June 30, 1914, there were more than 482,000 of these, of which more than 292,000 were in the classified service, subject to competitive examinations. The number of positions protected by the merit rule has increased rapidly in recent years. The act of 1883 by its own terms placed only a few offices in the classified service, but provided for its extension by executive order. Of course Congress may extend the scope of the law — or limit it — as it sees fit. It is largely through executive orders, however, that the development has occurred. It can hardly be said that Congress has at any time been zealous in its advocacy of civil service reform.

It requires no very intensive study of the civil service system in the United States to see that it is a far from perfect system. The spoils idea is still rather deeply rooted in American politics. The claims of party workers are frequently given recognition at the expense of administrative efficiency. Yet improvement in the personnel of the administrative departments, as well as in administrative organization and methods, is slowly taking place; and it may be assumed that, as the citizenship of the Nation becomes more enlightened and more alive to the responsibilities involved in democracy, great advance will be made toward the goal of administrative efficiency. It may not be too much, perhaps, to anticipate the time when there will be full protection of the administration against the spoilsman and the office-seeking politician who subordinate the public interest to private gain.

That this condition, greatly to be desired, does not exist, however, is a fact too plain to be overlooked by even the superficial student of American government. The work of administration has not been taken seriously by the people generally; its high importance has not been understood. The need for trained, efficient administrators, free from partisan selection and partisan control, has been only slightly felt. Indeed, the very idea of a permanent, expert service is abhorrent to the minds of many Americans. The traditional view has been that any person who can win an election or obtain an appointment to a public office is as good as another for the discharge of its duties. Proven ability to do the work demanded has not been considered essential. Success and zeal as a party worker have been placed before fitness and capacity. The general results have been weakness in administrative organization, inferior administrative methods, and low standards of public service. Because of the failure to emphasize the high value of efficient administration by trained officers, the Nation finds itself unable, as yet, to cope with some of the great social and industrial questions which face it. The consequence is that the cause of real democracy suffers and the Nation's progress is retarded. One of the fundamental needs in the United States, perhaps the greatest need, is a realization of the weakness of the government from the standpoint of administration, and the attainment of genuine efficiency through thorough administrative reorganization and reform.

REFERENCES

BEARD. *American Government and Politics*, Edition 1914, Chaps. XI, XVI, XVII, XVIII, XIX.

FAIRLIE. *National Administration of the United States.*

FINLEY and SANDERSON. *The American Executive and Executive Methods*, Chap. XX.

HART. *Actual Government*, Chap. XVI.

REINSCH. *Readings on American Federal Government*, Chap. IX.

YOUNG. *The New American Government and its Work.*

CHAPTER X

The Congress — General Observations

The legislative power of the Nation is vested in the Congress, composed of two houses, the Senate and the House of Representatives. This power is limited; that is to say, the field of action belonging to Congress is limited to those powers which are specifically conferred by the Constitution or are necessarily implied. But as previously pointed out, in discussing the relation of the States to the Nation, the power of Congress within the sphere assigned to it is absolute. Its powers are found within the four corners of the Constitution as interpreted by the Supreme Court, but in the use of the powers thus derived it is without restraint, except as restrictions may be imposed by the Constitution itself. The most fundamental fact, however, is not the plenary character of the powers which have been granted to Congress, but the definite limitation of its jurisdiction. It is in no sense a sovereign body, and is therefore radically different from the English Parliament upon which it was, in part, modeled. It may act only when the right to act has been conferred upon it by the Constitution, and if it goes outside the limitations prescribed, its act is without validity. The legislative department is not superior to the executive and judicial departments, but is in theory coördinate with them. The extent to which Congress is in practice subject to the judiciary will be discussed later in connection with the power of the courts.

The Powers of Congress. — Notwithstanding the constitutional limitations upon Congress, its authority is very great and extends to a number of questions that are of supreme consequence to the entire Nation. The Constitution confers upon Congress the power to lay and collect taxes and uniform duties, imposts and excises; to pay the debts of the Nation and provide for its common defense and general welfare; to borrow money; to regulate commerce among the States and with foreign nations; to establish uniform bankruptcy and naturalization laws; to coin money and regulate its value; to protect the Nation against the counterfeiting of its coin and securities; to fix the standard of weights and measures; to establish post offices and post roads; to enact patent and copyright laws; to constitute courts inferior to the Supreme Court; to define and punish piracies and felonies committed on the high seas, and offenses against the law of nations; to declare war; to provide and maintain an army and a navy and to make rules for their government; and to make all laws necessary and proper for carrying into execution the enumerated powers and all other powers vested by the Constitution in the United States or in any of its officers or departments.

In exercising some of its powers Congress is subject to certain limitations, as, for instance, duties and excises must be uniform throughout the United States; and in regulating interstate commerce preference shall not be given to one State over another. Moreover, as stated in Chapter I, Congress is subject to a number of absolute prohibitions. The powers granted to Congress are far-reaching, however, and have become increasingly so with the rapid development of the United States in an industrial and commercial way. National authority touches the individual citizen far more frequently now than when the government was established. Yet it is to be remembered that Congress has very little to do with the general civil law of the land. That is almost wholly under the control of the States. "While Congress, in the exercise of such powers as that to regulate interstate commerce, may originate rules by which people in general are bound in their business relations, such action does not constitute a large part of its work, and its legislation is ordinarily regulative of governmental agencies, or in other words, administrative."[1] That is to say, questions of administrative organization and policies chiefly occupy the attention of Congress. "The chief business of Congress is the appropriation of money for the work of the various departments of government, the providing of ways and means to meet this expenditure, the creation of new administrative agencies, the maintenance of the national defense on land and sea,

[1] Reinsch, "American Legislatures and Legislative Methods," p. 33.

the control of the various wards of the nation — the Indians and the people of the territories and dependencies — the regulation of economic activities as far as they form part of interstate commerce, and the administration of what remains to the United States government of natural wealth in forests and other public lands." [1]

The Sessions of Congress. — Congress must assemble at least once each year, the time of the meeting, as prescribed in the Constitution, being the first Monday in December. Congress may appoint another day, however, if it wishes to do so. During the two-year life period of each Congress, therefore, there will be held at least two sessions. One is known as the long session and the other as the short session. The long session is the first regular session of a new Congress and begins at noon on the first Monday in December of each odd-numbered year and continues until well along in the year following. No definite time is prescribed for the adjournment of this session. Congress may bring it to an end at any time which the two houses may agree upon. Usually adjournment takes place about the middle of the year. It is possible, however, for the long session to continue a full year; that is, until the first Monday in December of the even-numbered year when the short session begins. The latter has a definite life period. It must close at noon on the fourth of the following March, when the two-year period which constitutes the full life of a Congress comes to an end.

Special or extraordinary sessions of Congress, or of either house, may be called by the President at his discretion. Special sessions of the Senate have frequently been held. The purpose of such sessions is to pass upon appointments to office or treaties submitted by the President. The House of Representatives has never been called in extraordinary session. There is no reason why it should be, since there is nothing that the House, acting alone, can do, except vote impeachments.

All bills and resolutions pending at the close of a short session, that is, at the close of a Congress, lapse or die. The legislative slate is wiped clean, and if these measures are to receive further consideration, they must be reintroduced into the next Congress and started along the regular course prescribed by

[1] Reinsch, "American Legislatures and Legislative Methods," p. 34.

the rules. In the case of the long session, or a special session, pending measures do not lapse, but retain their legislative status in the session following. The slaughter of unpassed measures caused by the expiration of a Congress is sometimes very great. Owing to the large number of bills and resolutions introduced during the two-year life of a Congress, running from twenty to thirty thousand, there is always a great congestion of work in the closing days. As a natural result, oftentimes, measures of much concern to the Nation are lost in this way, with a resultant delay that may be not only objectionable but costly as well. And measures that are passed in the rush of the last days, it should be noted, are likely to prove defective both with respect to content and form. One of the serious problems always confronting Congress is found in the huge mass of proposed legislation that is always pending.

Election and Qualifications of Members. — The control over the election of members of Congress is in practice divided between Congress and the State legislatures, though the ultimate authority rests with the former if it chooses to use its power. The provision of the Constitution is to the effect that the times, places, and manner of electing members of Congress shall be prescribed by the legislatures of the States, but that Congress may alter such regulations or make rules of its own, except as to the places of choosing Senators. The restriction contained in the last clause was made necessary by reason of the fact that Senators were to be elected by the State legislatures which would always meet at their respective State capitals. Now that Senators are chosen by popular vote, this restriction is without force. By act of Congress the election of Representatives for many years has occurred on the first Tuesday after the first Monday in November of the even-numbered years, except where a different date has been fixed by a State law enacted prior to the law of Congress. Since the adoption of the seventeenth amendment Senators are elected at the same time as Representatives, whenever vacancies in the Senate are to be filled. It will be noted that in presidential years, the time of election of members of Congress coincides with that of the President. As illustrations of the general supervision Congress exercises over the election of its members may be cited the act of 1842, by which single-member districts are required for the election of Representatives, and the act of 1872, by which written or printed ballots must be used in these elections. The granting of suffrage rests with the States, as, for the most part, does the regulation of voting. With respect to the latter, however, Congress may have a good deal to do through its power to provide for the purity of congressional elections. The right of Congress to impose and enforce penalties for fraud and delinquency in such elections has been clearly upheld by the Supreme Court.[1]

By the Constitution each house is made the judge of the "elections, returns, and qualifications of its own members." It is for each house to say whether its members are rightfully entitled to their seats. Charges of corruption or ineligibility are sometimes made against persons claiming seats in one house or the other, and are considered at great length. In the Senate, two of the best known recent instances are the cases of Reed Smoot of Utah and William Lorimer of Illinois. Attempt was made to prevent Smoot, an apostle of the Mormon church, from taking his seat on the ground that he was a polygamist. After a long investigation, the Senate recognized his right to membership. In the case of Lorimer grave charges of corruption were made in connection with his election by the Illinois legislature, and finally substantiated to the satisfaction of the necessary majority of Senators. By formal vote he was expelled from the Senate and his place declared vacant.

Likewise, in the lower house the validity of the election of members is frequently questioned for one reason or another. Contests by rival claimants to positions are common. The charge may be fraudulent voting, error in counting the ballots, or other delinquency on the part of election officials. In such case one of the House committees on elections makes the necessary investigation, reports its findings, and by vote of the House the dispute is settled. Inasmuch as the contestants are always party opponents, there is good opportunity for party spirit to show itself. It is interesting, at least, to note how frequently contests are decided by a substantially strict party vote.

In 1900 a case arose similar to that of Smoot in the Senate. The right of Brigham H. Roberts of Utah to sit in the House was challenged on the ground that he was a polygamist. After

[1] *Ex parte* Siebold, 100 U. S. 371 (1880).

a long and bitter controversy he was excluded by vote of the House, upon the recommendation of the majority of the committee to which the matter had been referred for investigation. The constitutionality of such action, however, is doubted by many. The question involved is as to the right of either house to add to the qualifications for membership which have been fixed in the Constitution. In the Roberts case the House of Representatives did this, whereas in the Smoot case the Senate refused to do so. Professor Beard says that the correct answer to this constitutional question seems to have been made by Senator Hopkins in his discussion of the Smoot case. " Mr. Hopkins says that neither the Senate, Congress, nor a state can add to the qualifications prescribed by the constitution; that the power given to the Senate is not to create Senators, but to judge whether they have the qualifications prescribed by the constitution; that the Senate has no constitutional authority to inquire into the antecedents and early career and character of a Senator who applies for admission with the proper credentials of his state; that no Senator has ever been denied a seat in the Senate of the United States because of any lapse of career prior to his election by the state; and that the Senate should content itself with the exercise of its power to expel a member for disorderly behavior whenever his conduct is such as to lower the standard of that body or bring it into disrepute."[1]

Control over Rules of Procedure. — Each house has authority to determine its own rules of procedure, except with respect to a few things. By provision of the Constitution a majority in each house is constituted a quorum to do business, although a smaller number may adjourn from day to day and may be authorized to compel attendance of absent members. Each house is required to keep a journal of its proceedings, which shall be published from time to time. Publication is not required, however, of those parts which in the judgment of the house require secrecy. At the request of one fifth of those present, the yeas and nays of the members of either house on any question shall be entered on the journal. This is an important rule, particularly from the standpoint of those who are in the minority upon any question. Neither house, during a session of Congress, can adjourn for more than three days with-

[1] Beard, "American Government and Politics," New and Revised Edition, p. 240.

out the consent of the other, nor can it adjourn to any other place than that in which the two houses are sitting.

Under this authority to determine in general their own procedure, complicated systems of rules have been established in both the Senate and the House of Representatives. In each the rules as they are to-day have been slowly evolved. They have been added to, and modified from time to time, to meet new needs and changed conditions. As the business of Congress has increased in bulk and in difficulty, the rules have grown in number and in complexity. They are a logical outgrowth of legislative conditions. In the Senate the rules continue in force until changed, inasmuch as the Senate is a continuous or permanent body. But in the House of Representatives a body of rules is adopted at the beginning of each new Congress. It will be understood that the entire membership of the House changes every two years and therefore a new House must adopt its own set of rules. The usual thing is for the House, when it assembles, to adopt the rules of the last one, and continue them in force with few, if any, changes. Some of the chief differences between the procedure in the Senate and that in the House will be noted later in the detailed discussion of the two houses.

Compensation and Privileges of Members. — The compensation of its members is fixed by Congress itself. There is no constitutional limitation upon its power in this regard. Public opinion, however, is a powerful restraining influence in keeping congressional salaries at a reasonably low sum. Before 1855 members were given a per diem allowance. By an act of that year a salary system was established, the sum allowed being $3000 per year. In 1865 this was increased to $5000, which continued to be the sum paid until 1873, when it was raised to $7500. The terrific public protest which followed the enactment of this "salary grab" measure, as it was called, caused its repeal at the next session of Congress.[1] The $5000 salary was restored and continued in force until 1907 when it was again increased to $7500, which is the sum at present received by both Senators and Representatives. In addition there is

[1] The measure was thus characterized because by its terms the increased compensation was given to the members of the Congress which enacted it; whereas, the law of 1907 was made to apply only to future Congresses.

an allowance for mileage, of twenty cents per mile, clerk hire, and stationery.

In accord with the practice of the English Parliament and other legislative bodies members of Congress enjoy certain personal privileges. By provision of the Constitution they are in all cases, except treason, felony, and breach of the peace, exempt from arrest while attending sessions of their respective houses and in going to and returning from the sessions; and cannot be questioned for any speech or debate in either house, except by the authority of the house itself. This exemption from arrest, however, does not confer as great a privilege as might appear at first glance. Freedom from criminal law processes is really not granted. " The object of the privilege from arrest is to exempt members from being interfered with by judicial procedure while in the discharge of their duties. At other times and in other respects they are subject to the jurisdiction of the courts as fully as private persons. Indeed, the exemption is of little practical value, as arrest or seizure of the person is no longer generally authorized except for crime, and all crimes of a serious nature are included within the description of treason, felony and breach of the peace." [1]

The other privilege, which carries freedom from legal accountability for what members say and do in the discharge of their legitimate duties, is of more obvious value. Action for libel or slander cannot be brought for anything said in Congress. This privilege extends to the committee rooms and all official publications, as well as to the proceedings of the Senate or House. Undoubtedly its influence is wholesome, although at times the privilege may be abused. It is clearly based upon the English practice, whose original purpose was to protect members of Parliament against arrest for criticism of the monarch. The protection afforded Senators and Representatives, however, is not against monarchs, but constituents.

One important restriction is imposed by the Constitution upon members of Congress in the provision that " no Senator or Representative shall, during the time for which he was elected, be appointed to any civil office under the authority of the United States, which shall have been created, or the emoluments whereof

---

[1] McClain, "Constitutional Law in the United States," Second Edition, pp. 69–70. See also *Williamson* v. *United States*, 207 U. S. 425 (1908).

shall have been increased during such time; and no person holding any office under the United States shall be a member of either house during his continuance in office." A recent illustration of the effect of the first part of this provision is found in the case of Senator Knox of Pennsylvania who, when he became Secretary of State under President Taft in 1909, could not receive the regular compensation of cabinet officers because only a short time before, as a member of the Senate, he had voted to increase the salaries of heads of departments from $8000 to $12,000. After the term for which Mr. Knox had been elected to the Senate had expired, he came in for the higher salary. It is to be noted that this restriction applies only to appointments to "civil" offices. It does not prevent the appointment of a Senator or a Representative to a position in the military or naval service which was created or whose salary was increased while he was a member of Congress. Of course, by the second part of the provision quoted, he is barred from holding both offices at the same time. An interesting instance of an attempt to hold two offices is cited by Professor Beard. A Representative from New York " was appointed major of the militia under the authority of the United States in the District of Columbia, and the committee on elections in the House declared by unanimous vote that by his acceptance he had forfeited his seat." [1]

It has been held that this constitutional restriction does not apply to members of commissions appointed to make investigations and negotiate treaties, as, for illustration, was done in connection with the treaty of peace with Spain in 1898. The practice of appointing members of Congress to commissions created for various purposes has become common, and the question has frequently arisen whether such appointments are permissible under the Constitution. The answer of Congress, which by common consent is to be taken as correct, is that they are permissible. The judiciary committee of the Senate in passing upon the point decided that " a member of a commission created by law to investigate and report but having no legislative, judicial, or executive powers, was not an officer within the meaning of the constitutional inhibition." [2]

[1] Beard, "American Government and Politics," New and Revised Edition, p. 233.
[2] Hinds, " Precedents," Vol. I, p. 604. Quoted in Beard, "American Government and Politics," p. 234.

Theory of Representation. — It is essential to note the character of the representation afforded by Congress. As far as the theory of the written Constitution is concerned, members of Congress are in no sense to be looked upon as delegates of the people. They are representatives, charged with the legislative function. The Senators are elected by the voters of the States and the Representatives by the voters of districts within the States, but there is no constitutional method by which their constituents can give them instructions and see that these instructions are carried out. The voters have no grip upon them after they are once elected. As far as their constituents are concerned, members of Congress, during their term of office, may do as they please. It is only in case they seek reëlection that the voters have the chance to punish or reward. They possess unlimited power of representation. As Professor Ford puts it, for the purposes of government they are the people themselves and it was to " protect them in the complete exercise of this representative capacity " that the Constitution provided that " for any speech or debate in either house they shall not be questioned in any other place." [1]

It was not a government by the people, therefore, that was set up by the Constitution. Government controlled by public opinion was far from the original intention. Democracy was not a favored type of government at the time the Constitution was formed. " The desire was not to enable the people to control the government, but to enable the government to control the people." [2]

Here again, however, the working constitution of the present day differs a good deal from the written document. Members of Congress now, under the party system, are not representatives in the strict sense planned for by the constitution makers. They bear the character of delegates to a greater or less degree. They are, in fact, more or less definitely restrained and controlled by public opinion. Legally they are independent of such control; actually they are held in check by it. In the Nation, as well as in the States, democracy has gone forward with tremendous strides since 1787. Particularly in recent years has the advance been rapid. The actual constitution is clearly undergoing important changes. Whatever the legal authority of

[1] Ford, "Rise and Growth of American Politics," p. 63.   [2] *Ibid.*, p. 64.

Senators and Representatives may be, the will of the people, the power of public opinion, can no longer be ignored. There is slowly being evolved an unwritten constitutional requirement which imposes upon members of Congress a direct responsibility to the people and which binds them by unseen, intangible bonds to carry out the public will. Constitutional forms are the same, but the spirit is changing. For good or for ill, the Nation is moving on toward a larger and ever larger democracy.

REFERENCES

(For References, see Chaps. XI and XIII.)

CHAPTER XI

THE SENATE

THE Senate is the smaller and in many respects the more interesting as well as the more powerful of the two houses of Congress. In organization and procedure it differs radically from the House of Representatives. Moreover, its constitutional position is somewhat peculiar inasmuch as it exercises executive and judical functions as well as legislative, notwithstanding the general acceptance and application of the separation of powers theory. It has, perhaps, maintained the position and powers assigned to it by the Constitution more successfully than has any other branch of the government. Beyond doubt, in spite of many shortcomings, it has proven itself one of the most efficient parts of the governmental machine.

The Senate consists of two Senators from each of the States, its membership numbering ninety-six. To be eligible for the Senate a person must be thirty years of age, an inhabitant of the State from which he is chosen, and have been a citizen of the United States for at least nine years. The term of office is six years, one third of the Senators being chosen every two years, thus making the Senate essentially a permanent body. The salary is $7500 per year. In addition each member is given mileage and an allowance for clerk hire and for stationery.

The method of choosing Senators prescribed by the Constitution and followed without change until the adoption of the seventeenth amendment in 1913 was election by the legislatures of the various States. Under the seventeenth amendment election is by direct vote of the people of the States. The framers of the Constitution were unwilling to have both branches of the national legislature chosen by popular vote, just as they were unwilling to provide for the popular election of the President. It was their belief that one branch of Congress, at least, should be elected by an indirect method so that it would not be subject to popular clamor and violent changes of public sentiment, and thus would be free to stand out against hasty and ill-advised action by the direct representatives of the people in the other house. The Senate was to be the conservative element in legislative action. It was designed to be, in part, a check upon the House and serve as a sort of balance wheel to keep the legislative machine running smoothly and at a reasonable speed. It was designed, also, to be a check upon the President, and thus help protect the government from executive encroachments. By giving to the State legislatures the right to select the Senators it was believed that the Senate would be composed of men who were carefully chosen with respect to their ability, patriotism, property, and freedom from radicalism and dangerous popular control. With men of this character in the Senate the danger of excessive democracy, anticipated in connection with the House of Representatives, and the danger of monarchic power, feared in connection with the presidency, would alike be minimized.[1]

Furthermore, it should be kept in mind that the whole plan of the Congress, as it was finally worked out, was the result of a compromise between antagonistic elements in the constitutional convention. There was a great deal of jealousy among the States. Particularly was this shown in the constant bickering between the small and the large States. The former sought to have all the States equally represented in both houses of Congress, regardless of size and population. The latter sought to have the representation in both houses based on population, thus giving absolute popular control of Congress. The question was debated at great length, but neither side would yield its position entirely, and a compromise was the result. Equal representation of the States in the Senate, without respect to population, and unequal representation in the House based on population, were provided for. Thus each of the States was given two Senators, but their representation in the lower house in the first Congress varied from one to ten. With the great increase in population since that time the variation has become much larger, ranging from one to thirty-seven in 1912.

[1] For a discussion of the aims of the Senate as intended by the framers of the Constitution, see *The Federalist*, Nos. 62–66.

Representation of States and Sections. — One other fact of great significance should be noted in connection with the composition of the Senate. It was designed to represent, not the people of the States, but the States as such, that is, as political entities. It was intended to be a kind of Council of States, whose members should owe their election to the controlling element in the State governments, namely, the legislatures and not directly to those exercising the right of suffrage. This was the constitutional theory upon which the Senate was based until the adoption of the amendment providing for the popular election of Senators. In the actual work of the Senate the theory has been of little consequence, since the voting in the Senate has not been by States. By the Constitution each Senator is given one vote and it not infrequently happens that the Senators from a State vote on opposite sides of a question, thus canceling their votes and, as far as the voting itself is concerned, depriving their State of any real part in the determination of the question in hand. To a large extent this is due to the conflicting interests of the political parties. A State is likely to be controlled by one party at one senatorial election and by another party at the next; hence upon almost all party questions the votes of the Senators from that State would cancel each other. Upon a great many questions, however, party lines are not followed, and it frequently happens that Senators of the same party vote against each other. It is clear, therefore, that this theory of the Constitution — that the Senate represents the States as governmental organizations and not the people of the States — has little practical effect. Moreover, experience has shown that the jealousy of the small States against the large, as revealed in the constitutional convention, was really without foundation. They have not at any time been in danger. Sectional interests have frequently caused the Senators from a number of States to act together, but in this large and small States have been influenced alike; in no instance have the former combined against the latter. With the adoption of the seventeenth amendment this old theory was in effect abandoned.

Of greater interest and importance than this theory of the representation of States is the fact which President Wilson so forcefully points out, that the thing which gives the Senate "its real character and significance as an organ of constitutional government is the fact that it does not represent population, but the regions of the country, the political units into which it has, by our singular constitutional process, been cut up. The Senate, therefore, represents the variety of the nation as the House does not. It does not draw its membership chiefly from those parts of the country where population is most dense, but draws it in equal parts from every state and section."[1] The artificial character of many of the States, says this eminent authority, the fact that they are not "real communities, with distinct historical characteristics, a distinct social and economic character of their own, as most of the older states are," is not of material consequence.[2] The principle which is of really great importance is that "regions must be represented, irrespective of population, in a country physically as various as ours and therefore certain to exhibit a great variety of social and economic and even political conditions. It is of the utmost importance that its parts as well as its people should be represented; and there can be no doubt in the mind of any one who really sees the Senate of the United States as it is that it represents the country, as distinct from the accumulated population of the country, much more fully and much more truly than the House of Representatives does."[3] Due to the concentration of population in certain sections, the House of Representatives does not represent the Nation as satisfactorily as it once did. It tends to represent "particular interests and points of view, to be less catholic and more and more specialized in its view of national affairs. It represents chiefly the East and the North. The Senate is its indispensable offset, and speaks always in its make-up of the size, the variety, the heterogeneity, the range and breadth of the country, which no community or group of communities can adequately represent. It cannot be represented by one sample or by a few samples; it can be represented only by many, — as many as it has parts."[4]

Results of Indirect Election. — The hopes of the constitution makers with respect to the method of choosing Senators have by no means been realized. The State legislatures have not acted from the motives and in the manner anticipated. The

---

[1] Wilson, "Constitutional Government in the United States," p. 114.
[2] *Ibid.*, p. 115.   [3] *Ibid.*, p. 116.   [4] *Ibid.*, p. 117.

personnel of the Senate has by no means been always of the character desired by the framers of the Constitution. For the most part this has been due to party interests and influence. Places in the Senate, next to the presidency itself, became the great prizes for which party leaders struggled. The control of the Senate has almost from the beginning been one of the great objectives of the leading parties. The result has been that usually the election of a Senator was the occasion for a bitter party struggle over the choice of members of the State legislature, in which the function of the legislature as a department of the State government was lost sight of and the local interests of the State were sacrificed. Very frequently the contests over the senatorship were long drawn out, lasting many weeks, to the serious detriment of the regular work of the legislature. Sometimes deadlocks occurred and the legislatures were unable to elect. The results of these long-continued contests were naturally bad. Not only were the States in which they occurred for the time deprived of their full representation in the Senate, but abundant opportunity was afforded for corrupt practices on the part of dishonest party leaders and the representatives of big business interests seeking control over congressional legislation. Some of the most notorious political scandals in the country's history have grown out of deadlocks in senatorial elections. As a consequence of this system of election, as might be expected, men have sometimes acquired places in the Senate who were unworthy of positions of such high honor and vast influence. Inevitably the Senate lost standing in the eyes of the people and the belief grew strong that a change in the method of choosing Senators was necessary. The outcome of the agitation, which continued through many years, was the seventeenth amendment. Whether the general character of the Senate as a legislative body will be improved by the system of popular election, time alone can tell. The growing spirit of democracy made the change inevitable, sooner or later. But whatever the ultimate effect may be upon the Senate, senatorial deadlocks with their peculiar evils and dangers are things of the past. And perhaps more important still, the legislatures of the States are now free from any official connection with national politics and may, if they choose, devote themselves exclusively to State affairs.

The point of the last statement deserves special emphasis for the method of electing Senators by State legislatures has tended, under the party system, to paralyze the political life of the States. That is, it has not been possible for the people of the various States to divide upon local and State questions and settle them upon their merits, because all the time the partisan demands of national politics interfered. In choosing members of the State legislatures, the voters almost always had to keep in mind the choice of United States Senators. As a result, not infrequently there was a conflict of interest under which the voter must sacrifice his convictions either upon vital questions of State policy or upon the election of Senators. Moreover, in order to maintain the vast party organizations and keep them in good running order, practically all local and State offices, however insignificant, have been made the objects of partisan contests. Thus the control of town, township, county, city, and State governments alike have been hopelessly bound up with the control of national politics. This was not what the framers of the Constitution either desired or expected; quite the contrary, in fact. But it was inevitable under the constitutional requirement that Senators be chosen by the State legislatures. The breaking of this tie between the State and national governments by the seventeenth amendment makes possible the growth of State political parties and the development of real State politics. The ultimate effect should be wholesome. It has opened the way for real progress by the States.

The Senate's Organization and Committees. — In a general way the organization of the Senate is similar to that of the House of Representatives, although there are points of difference which are of great importance. By provision of the Constitution the Vice President of the United States is the Senate's presiding officer, bearing the title, President of the Senate. He has no vote upon pending questions except in case of a tie, when he may cast the deciding vote. Now and then this constitutional privilege has been of real consequence and has enabled the Vice President to have an important part in the action of the Senate. Ordinarily, however, he has little to do with the course of legislation except as he may have personal influence with individual Senators. As presiding officer of the Senate he is purely a parliamentary officer and is supposed to be entirely impartial. His position is one of great dignity and high social standing, but of insignificant powers.

All the other officers are chosen by the Senate. These include the president pro tempore who presides in the absence of the Vice President, the secretary, chief clerk, legislative and reading clerks, sergeant-at-arms, doorkeeper, and all the many assistants to these officers whose employment is made necessary by the pressure of the Senate's work. In the appointment of these officers party lines are observed. All the higher positions are held by men who are members of the party that is dominant in the Senate; many of the less important places are by common practice given to the minority party. Some of them pay rather large salaries and are vigorously sought by faithful party workers who feel that the time for their reward has come.

A large part of the Senate's most important work is done through its standing committees of which sixty-five or more are regularly maintained. All matters of legislation are referred to appropriate committees for investigation and report before they are given consideration on the floor of the Senate. It is in the committees, in fact, that usually the real work of legislation is done, although the Senate is not so completely dominated by the committee system as is the House of Representatives. The committees have no constitutional basis, but are provided for simply by the rules of the Senate. Among those commonly considered of most consequence may be mentioned the committees on Finance, Appropriations, Judiciary, Interstate Commerce, Foreign Relations, and Military Affairs. A number of the committees are of very slight, if any, importance and are maintained for the purpose, apparently, of providing as many chairmanships and committee clerks as possible, together with adequate office accommodations for their members. The power of the leading committees is very great under the Senate's rules of procedure and the fate of important legislative proposals is usually determined by committee action. Some of the gravest criticisms of both houses of Congress are to be made in connection with the committee system, but discussion of the general effects of that system will be deferred until after the organization of the House of Representatives has been considered. It is sufficient here to note the central position of the committees in the work of the Senate.

The appointment of committees in the Senate is nominally made by the Senate itself; actually it is made by the party caucuses through a committee on committees chosen by the caucuses for the purpose of assigning Senators to the various committees. The recommendations of this committee are almost always approved by the Senate, although the Senate, of course, could reject such recommendations if it should desire to do so. The majority party always controls each committee by a safe margin. The committees vary in size from three to seventeen members. The most important ones have usually fourteen or fifteen members. The powerful committees on Finance and Foreign Relations each have fourteen members, nine from the majority party and five from the minority. In the case of committees whose work is non-partisan in character the minority party has a larger proportionate representation. In selecting both the majority and the minority members the rule of seniority is observed; that is, the chairmanships and ranking positions on all committees are usually given to those Senators who have served longest in the Senate, and the ranking of the members of any particular committee is determined by the period of their service on that committee. Occasionally there is some variation from this rule, but not often. It is plain that this practice is not always in the interest of the best legislative work. It by no means follows that the man who has served longest on a committee is the best man for the position of chairman. Moreover, the rule tends strongly to place the control over all important legislation in the hands of a small number of Senators and makes possible the building up of an organization or machine among the majority leaders which is all but invincible. The wisdom which comes from experience in legislative work is to be cherished and utilized to the utmost, but mere length of service is not necessarily a true measure of either experience or ability. There can be little doubt that greater freedom in the selection of committee members than the seniority rule permits would be in the interest of better legislation.

The Party Caucus. — A vital part of the Senate organization whose work may at times be of supreme concern to the nation is the party caucus, to which reference has already been made. The minority party, as well as the majority party, has its caucus in which frequently its position upon important projects of legislation is determined. But it is the caucus of the majority party whose action is of chief interest to the nation. It is through the caucus that the majority leaders seek to line up their party associates in support of party measures so that there may be no question as to the passage of these measures when they come up for action in the Senate. The caucus is a voluntary, unofficial body, and its action is without legal force. The obligation of its members to abide by the decisions reached is wholly moral. The Senator who refuses to enter the caucus, or having entered reserves the right to act independently, is in no way bound by its action. The meetings of the caucus are secret. The great importance which at times attaches to it is easily comprehended when it is noted that the actual determination of the content of legislative measures may be transferred from the Senate to the party caucus. A good illustration of this is found in the action of the Democratic caucus upon the Underwood-Simmons tariff bill at the special session of Congress called by President Wilson in April, 1913. After the measure had been received from the House of Representatives and had been considered in detail by the majority members of the Finance Committee of the Senate, it was submitted to the Democratic caucus. There it was taken up section by section, discussed at length, modified in minor ways, voted upon, and approved. All this was done to assure for it, if possible, the solid Democratic support. After it had been approved by the caucus it was submitted to the entire Finance Committee where, by a strict party vote, it was recommended to the Senate for passage. Of course this committee action was a mere formality, made necessary by the Senate rules which require that all bills be considered in committee. A long debate in the Senate ensued, but to no purpose whatever, except to give the minority members the opportunity to express their opposition. With the exception of two or three Senators who refused to be bound by the caucus with respect to particular items in the bill, the entire Democratic vote was pledged in advance and the leaders in charge of the measure were reasonably sure of its passage. The action of the Senate was essentially a formality; the vital decision was reached in the caucus.

Objections to the caucus method of legislation are obvious and need not be discussed at length. The substitution of irresponsible group action in a secret caucus for public personal responsibility on the floor of the Senate is of doubtful wisdom. Publicity with respect to all the processes of legislation is desirable. It is true that the action of the caucus fixes rather definitely the responsibility of the dominant party, a fact of real significance, but regardless of this the caucus is not an institution that is popular either in or out of Congress.

Freedom of Debate. — With respect to its rules of procedure the Senate, though similar in the main to the House of Representatives and other legislative assemblies, is exceptional in one important thing. There is unlimited freedom of debate. No closure rule exists. Each Senator is free to debate a measure as long as he wishes. In this is found the greatest contrast between the Senate and the House of Representatives in which a rigid control over debate is exercised. The Senate is almost alone among the great legislative bodies of the world in its refusal to provide some system of closure. In most countries it has been found necessary to limit debate both for the purpose of expediting business and preventing obstructive practices on the part of the minorities.[1] It is comparatively easy in the Senate for a filibuster to be effective. This is particularly true in the closing days of the life of a Congress. Undoubtedly the nation suffers at times from the unrestricted discussion. This procedure has been subjected to very severe criticism. It is frequently referred to as "legislation by unanimous consent," manifestly a difficult kind to obtain. But one exceedingly valuable result of this freedom is to be noted. There is real debate in the Senate, and at times debate of very high character. In the House of Representatives, for the most part, there is no debate worthy of the name. It is in the Senate ordinarily that the publicity which comes from exhaustive discussion is given to pending legislation. Delays, of course, are frequent; and sometimes delays which are wearisome to the Nation. But the delays in the Senate tend to counteract the haste and carelessness which only too frequently characterize the actions of the lower house.

Moreover, the Senate's practice gives opportunity to individual Senators to show the stuff that is in them and to develop into effective debaters. Undoubtedly it helps to make service

[1] Lowell, "The Government of England," Vol. I, p. 292.

in the Senate attractive to men of ability, although it is everywhere recognized that a Senator's influence upon the work of the Senate is by no manner of means dependent upon his oratorical powers. Many of the strongest, most influential men in the Senate have been men without forensic ability; indeed, some of them seldom, if ever, took part in the general discussion of measures on the open floor of the Senate. Yet it cannot be denied that the ability to take care of one's self in the rough and tumble of debate is a thing of great value and under the Senate's rules abundant opportunity is afforded for its display. In the House of Representatives this opportunity is for the most part lacking. This fact undoubtedly explains in part why service in the Senate is generally looked upon with greater favor by public men than service in the lower house. There is freedom to grow in the Senate and the man with the capacity for statesmanship is sure of his chance.

The Senate's Legislative Position. — As a legislative body the Senate has no peculiar constitutional position or powers. It is coördinate with the House of Representatives. It is simply the second chamber of the national legislature and, with one exception, has exactly the same legislative powers as the other chamber. That exception is in connection with bills for raising revenue which, by constitutional provision, must originate in the House of Representatives. In giving the lower house this special power the constitution makers were clearly following English experience. The struggle for political liberty in England centered around the struggle for the control of the public purse, and one of the fundamentals of the English Constitution is that this control shall be exercised by the representatives of the people in the House of Commons. In the American colonies, likewise, the struggle for the control of taxation by the representatives of the people was long and bitter. Hence it was natural that the principle of popular control over national taxation should be embodied in the Constitution. The House of Representatives was made elective by the people directly, or rather by that portion of the people upon whom the right of suffrage was conferred by the States. The Senate was made elective by the State legislatures, thus being only indirectly representative of the people. Therefore the House of Representatives should have the initiative in the raising of revenue as a safeguard of the people's liberties and rights of property. But this constitutional provision is of only nominal significance in actual practice, for in passing upon revenue bills the Senate, by provision of the Constitution, may "propose or concur with amendments as on other bills." This right of amendment gives to the Senate practical equality with the House, for by amendment a bill expressing the desires of the Senate may be substituted for one passed and submitted to it by the House. The House must take the lead, nominally, in drafting revenue legislation, for the letter of the Constitution must be observed; but that does not prevent the Senate, if it wishes, from framing through its Finance committee a measure of its own and by "amendment" substituting it for the House bill at the proper time. Hence this apparent privilege of the House of Representatives amounts to little or nothing in actual practice and the powers of the two houses with respect to legislation are in reality equal. No bill can become a law without the approval of both. This equality, it should be noted, is theoretical rather than actual, for the Senate not infrequently is able to force its will upon the lower house. The reasons for this will be suggested in the discussion of the general character and success of the Senate.

It is a significant fact that at first the Senate did not make use of its constitutional privileges with respect to legislation. Its consent was necessary, of course, for the enactment of laws, but the task of originating and framing the measures which came before Congress was left for the most part to the House of Representatives. The Senate looked upon itself as a kind of executive council whose function was to give advice to the President, and for a number of years after the government was established gave its chief attention to questions of treaties and appointments laid before it by the President. As already pointed out, the theory of the constitution makers was that the Senate should be a body of dignity, conservatism, and impartiality which would keep itself free from partisan strife. This point of view was quite generally accepted and as a consequence the Senate sat in secluded dignity behind closed doors, deliberating upon the executive business that was submitted to it by the President. It was not for some years that the Senate seemed to awaken to its opportunity in connection with legislation and began to make use of its constitutional powers. Very rapidly, after the start was once made, the Senate asserted its rights under the Constitution and at all times since has shown a very jealous concern for what is called its "prerogatives." Frequent controversies have arisen between the two houses of Congress over their respective rights and between the Senate and the President. In the main, it is generally conceded, the results of these controversies have strengthened the Senate. Always ready to resent any invasion of its own rights, real or apparent, the Senate has not always been very scrupulous about observing the rights of the House of Representatives and of the President. Much has been said in the Senate about "executive usurpation" of powers that belong to the Senate alone or to Congress as a whole. Of "usurpation" on the part of the Senate, not so much has been heard; yet clearly the Senate has asserted powers in connection with revenue legislation and acquired a dominance in connection with appointments to office by the President, which lie outside its province as measured by the intentions of the constitution makers.[1] It has grown in influence and power, both as a legislative body and as an advisory council to the President.

Executive and Judicial Functions. — It has already been made clear that the Senate exercises executive as well as legislative powers, in this respect differing radically from the House of Representatives. Its executive functions are two: the confirmation of appointments, and the ratification of treaties. The part which it plays in these two very important matters has previously been discussed in connection with the powers of the President and does not again need detailed treatment. It should be kept in mind that the Constitution requires the confirmation of appointments to certain offices enumerated in the Constitution itself, and the ratification of all treaties. In the case of other offices, created by act of Congress and to be filled by appointment of the President, confirmation may be required or not as the Congress sees fit to direct. Usually it is required. The Senate is thus a powerful check upon the President and is in a position to influence very directly the work of the executive branch of the government. In fact, through its "Senatorial

---

[1] See article by A. Maurice Low, "The Usurped Powers of the Senate," *The American Political Science Review*, Vol. I, p. 1.

Courtesy" system, already described, it has to a high degree practically supplanted the President in the matter of appointments; although the extent to which this is true depends a good deal upon the character of the man who is President.

With respect to treaties, although its consent is necessary for their validity, the Senate has not been so successful in forcing the President to do its will. It may prevent him from carrying out his own policy, but it cannot compel him to accept the policy which the Senate itself favors. It needs no argument to make clear that these executive functions give to the Senate an influence in the government which the House of Representatives does not have and cannot have under the Constitution. Moreover, because the members of the lower house have a keen personal and political interest in the appointment of public officers, the Senate is in a position to affect seriously at times the course of legislation in the House of Representatives, a fact which helps to explain in part the frequent successes of the Senate in the controversies which arise between the two houses.

The Senate has also a judicial function to discharge. It is given by the Constitution the "sole power to try all impeachments." In exercising this power the Senate sits as a court, hears the evidence submitted and passes upon its admissibility, listens to the arguments for and against the accused, and, by formal vote upon each of the specific charges in the impeachment, determines his guilt or innocence. The members of the Senate are on oath or affirmation. The Vice President presides except when the President of the United States is on trial, when the Chief Justice of the Supreme Court is the presiding officer. The vote of two thirds of the members present is necessary for conviction. By constitutional provision, judgment in impeachment cases cannot extend further than to "removal from office, and disqualification to hold and enjoy any office of honour, trust, or profit under the United States." This provision, however, does not exempt the convicted officer from indictment, trial, and punishment according to existing law. The grounds for impeachment are "treason, bribery, or other high crimes and misdemeanors," — a statement somewhat vague and indefinite. The Senate has nothing to do with the voting of impeachments; that is the exclusive function of the House of Representatives. The President, Vice President, and all civil officers of the United States are subject to impeachment.

Valid criticisms may be made of the impeachment process. It is, as suggested in a previous chapter, a slow and ponderous procedure, not well adapted to a large number of cases of minor importance; it is only in connection with the gravest offenses committed by the highest officials that its use seems to be justified. Moreover, some of the constitutional provisions relating to it are hardly satisfactory. The expression "other high crimes and misdemeanors" is not sufficiently explicit as a definition of crimes. It leaves the way open for personal and party prejudices to work their will. Also there have been serious differences of opinion as to the meaning of the term "civil officers of the United States." Senators and Representatives, for instance, are not civil officers, as was decided in 1789, in the first impeachment case tried by the Senate, that of Senator William Blount of Tennessee. However serious might be the offense of a member of Congress during his term of office, the only penalty that can be imposed is expulsion from the house to which he belongs. Furthermore, there is a difference of opinion as to whether a person may be impeached after he has retired from office for acts which he committed while holding his official position, and as to whether the accused may escape from trial and punishment by resigning from office.[1] In spite of its faults, however, the existence of the impeachment process is undoubtedly a powerful restraining influence upon the conduct of public officers.[2]

General Character of the Senate. — Reference has been made to the Senate's efficiency and success as an instrument of government, notwithstanding its obvious shortcomings. The reason for this success is not found in any one specific phase of the Senate's organization, but in a number of things which make clear its general character.

[1] Woodburn, "The American Republic," pp. 231–239.
[2] Notwithstanding the large number of persons who have held civil office under the United States since the government was established, there have been only nine cases of impeachment. Of the accused there was one President, one cabinet officer, one Senator, and six judges. Only three of the nine — all judges — were convicted. For an excellent brief review of the impeachment process, see article on "The Law of Impeachment in the United States," by Professor David Y. Thomas, *Political Science Review* for May, 1908, pp. 378 ff. Consult also, *The Federalist*, Nos. 65 and 66.

1. The Senate, comparatively speaking, is a small legislative body; much smaller than the corresponding houses of leading European legislatures. The advantages of this are plain. The small size of the Senate makes unity of purpose and collective action more easily attainable; increases the dignity and influence of the individual member; makes it possible for each Senator to keep intimately in touch with all of the Senate's work; fixes more definitely the responsibility for what is done; permits greater freedom in procedure; and assures general and thorough debate upon pending measures. In the matter of size the Senate is much more fortunate than is the House of Representatives.

2. As a consequence of its small size and the complete freedom of debate allowed by its rules, the Senate is a real deliberative assembly; too much so, in the view of a great many people. In this respect it differs vitally from the House of Representatives where deliberation and debate, as far as the House as a whole is concerned, are farcical rather than real. The value of this characteristic of the Senate is beyond question, though there are abuses in connection with it which should be prevented. The problems of free government are not to be solved without full and adequate discussion.

3. For the most part the Senate is composed of men who are experienced in public life. Always many of its members have had previous experience in the House of Representatives, where they learned the ins and outs of congressional procedure and the difficulties in the way of legislative action. Many others pass from the governorships of States where they have had excellent experience in both the formulation and the administration of public policies. Of course not all Senators have had these opportunities for training in public service, but almost always the men who go to the Senate have been leaders in their States, either in politics, professional life, or in business. The result is an average of ability distinctly higher than that in the House of Representatives.

4. The term of office, — six years, — unlike the two-year term in the lower house, is sufficiently long to enable the new member to acquire experience and develop such latent powers of statesmanship as he may possess. It takes some time to "get on to the ropes" of the Senate's procedure. Moreover,

the longer term tends to make the Senators a little more independent in their judgments and actions than are the Representatives. They may, if they choose, ignore with greater safety to their political fortunes the demands of extreme partisanship and sudden changes in public opinion. The all-absorbing, if not all-important, problem of a reëlection is not quite so central and dominating in the thought of a Senator as in that of a Representative.

5. The Senate is what may be called a continuous or permanent body. Its members are not all chosen at the same time, as is the case with the House of Representatives. One third are chosen every two years, thus insuring to the majority at least two years of experience with the business of the Senate. This makes possible a continuity of purpose and policy, — a fact of real importance. In addition, Senators are frequently reëlected again and again, so that there is always an accumulated experience on the part of the Senate, taken as a whole, which adds greatly to the dignity and influence which belong to it by reason of its constitutional position and powers. As a consequence service in the Senate is usually attractive to men of superior abilities, and it is doubtless true, as Bryce suggests, that "the position of a senator, who can count on reëlection, is the most desirable in the political world of America."[1] The rules of procedure, to which the Senate has adhered in the face of sharp criticism, give to its members the chance to "make good," to develop their talents for statesmanship and to leave the imprint of their characters upon the national life. The unrestrained freedom of debate which prevails, though it places a powerful weapon in the hands of those who may be more concerned with private than with public interests, tends to encourage individual initiative and to strengthen the feeling of individual responsibility. The individual looms large, a fact of great significance which in no way destroys for the average person the attractiveness of service in the Senate. Indeed, it accounts for much of the Senate's success.

Judgments differ as to the value of the Senate, as is the case with all agencies of government. Praise and blame alike have been heaped upon it. Perhaps there can be no full unanimity of opinion concerning it, for, as President Wilson

[1] Bryce, "The American Commonwealth," New and Revised Edition, Vol. I, p. 121.

points out, it is exceedingly difficult to form a just estimate of it. " No body has been more discussed; no body has been more misunderstood and traduced. There was a time when we were lavish in spending our praises upon it. We joined with our foreign critics and appreciators in speaking of the Senate as one of the most admirable, as it is certainly one of the most original, of our political institutions. In our day we have been equally lavish of hostile criticism. We have suspected it of every malign purpose, fixed every unhandsome motive upon it, and at times almost cast it out of our confidence altogether.

" The fact is that it is possible in your thought to make almost anything you please out of the Senate. It is a body variously compounded, made many-sided by containing many elements, and a critic may concentrate his attention upon one element at a time if he chooses, make the most of what is good and put the rest out of sight, or make more than the most of what is bad and ignore everything that does not chime with his thesis of evil. The Senate has, in fact, many contrasted characteristics, shows many faces, lends itself easily to no confident generalization. It differs very radically from the House of Representatives. The House is an organic unit; it has been at great pains to make itself so, and to become a working body under a single unifying discipline; while the Senate is not so much an organization as a body of individuals, retaining with singularly little modification the character it was originally intended to have." [1]

With respect to one general fact, however, there will be few to disagree, namely, that the Senate has played a conspicuous rôle in the nation's history, that it is a vital part of the national government, and that it has fully held its own in competition with the House of Representatives and the presidency.

REFERENCES

BRYCE. *The American Commonwealth*, Edition 1910, Vol. I, Chaps. X, XI, XII.
FORD. *The Rise and Growth of American Politics*, Chap. XXI.
REINSCH. *American Legislatures and Legislative Methods*, Chap. III.
REINSCH. *Readings on American Federal Government*, Chaps. V, VI.
WILSON. *Constitutional Government in the United States*, Chap. V.
WOODBURN. *The American Republic*, Chap. IV.
YOUNG. *The New American Government and its Work*, Chap. IV.

[1] Wilson, " Constitutional Government in the United States," p. 112.

CHAPTER XII

THE HOUSE OF REPRESENTATIVES — COMPOSITION AND ORGANIZATION

THE House of Representatives is very different from the Senate, both with respect to what it was intended to be and what it actually is. It differs in manner of selection, in organization, in purpose, and in procedure. Some of the most interesting phases of government in the United States are revealed by the contrasts between the two houses of Congress.

The House was designed by the Constitution makers to be the popular branch of the national legislature. It was to stand for the people's share in the new government The men chosen to the lower house were to be representatives, however, not delegates. They were to owe their positions to the people, or rather to the voters of their respective States, but they were not to be under popular control. The Senate was to represent the States as political organizations and its members were to be chosen by the State legislatures. The House was to represent the people of the States directly, its members being chosen by popular election. Receiving their commissions of authority in this way, the Representatives could, if they wished, give full expression to the will of their constituents, and, subject to the check of an indirectly elected Senate and an indirectly elected President, could seek to make that will effective in the enactment of laws and the determination of national policies. It was taken for granted that radicalism and excessive democracy would characterize the work of the House, as, in all likelihood, would hasty and ill-advised action, but in the Senate and the presidency adequate safeguards were provided. Democracy might run rampant in the House without danger to the Republic. It was expected that the House would indulge in long, passionate, turbulent discussions in which the whims, prejudices, and follies of the masses would find free expression. It would be the center of continuous partisan strife. But no serious harm could ensue because a conservative Senate and a disinterested President would always be on guard. It was never supposed in the beginning that the membership of the House could be brought under a rigid party discipline, such as has prevailed for so long, and made subject to a system of rules which reduces debate almost to the vanishing point and makes a free general expression of opinion practically impossible. A House chained by rules of procedure, at its own volition, and in subjection to leaders of its own selection, was not anticipated. As it is to-day, the House of Representatives is quite essentially different from what it was expected to be. The transformation that has taken place will be indicated in the discussion that follows.

Basis of Representation. — Since the House was to represent the people directly, it was natural, in order to have the people of the various States on the same footing, that population should be made the basis of representation. Also, the acceptance of this plan was made necessary by the compromise reached by the large and small States with respect to the composition of the two houses. The former would not consent to equal representation of the States in the Senate unless population was made the basis of representation in the House; and the small States would not consent to the latter arrangement, unless the former were provided for. The number of Representatives which each of the original States was to have, at first, was fixed in the Constitution, the total membership of the first House being sixty-five. The authority to determine the population unit upon which Representatives should be apportioned among the States was lodged in Congress. This means that the number of members of the lower house is fixed by Congress. Two limitations upon this power are imposed. First, that each State shall have at least one Representative, and, second, that the total number of Representatives shall not exceed one for every thirty thousand of population. A census must be taken every ten years for the purpose of apportioning Representatives in accord with changes in population. If the unit of representation remains the same — and Congress may do as it pleases about that — the number of members must increase as the population grows larger. If the membership is to remain the same or be reduced, of course the unit of representation must be increased accordingly.

The great growth in population, from 5,000,000, in round numbers, in 1800, to 92,000,000 in 1910, has naturally resulted in a marked increase in the House membership, notwithstanding the fact that the unit of representation is more than six times as large as the minimum set in the Constitution. At the present time, based on the 1910 census and with a population of about 200,000 for each congressional district, the number is 435. With the exception of the reapportionment of 1842, the membership has been increased as the result of each decennial census.

This is a large membership for any legislative assembly; too large, in fact, for the highest efficiency. The size of a legislature always materially affects its organization and methods. The rules of procedure are necessarily numerous and complicated in a body of such size. General debate is practically impossible. Some satisfactory system of obtaining efficient and responsible leadership is imperative, as the history of the House of Representatives so clearly shows. The vast power which the Speaker of the House came to have and the rigid requirements of its committee system are due in no small degree to its cumbersome size. One of the significant contrasts between the Senate and the House lies in the size of the two bodies. Whether the House will become larger in the future is doubtful. There is a fair probability that Congress will decline to add new members at the next apportionment, regardless of population growth. At the apportionment following the census of 1910, there was strong and general objection to further increase.

The qualifications of a Representative, as prescribed by the Constitution, relate to age, citizenship, and inhabitancy of the State represented. No person can serve as Representative who has not attained the age of twenty-five years, and been for seven years a citizen of the United States, and who is not at the time of his election an inhabitant of the State in which he is chosen. Whether or not these requirements have been satisfactorily met rests with the House to say. Question has sometimes arisen as to both citizenship and inhabitancy, particularly the latter, and a number of rulings have been made. The right of the House to add to the constitutional qualifications has been the subject of a great deal of discussion and the question must be looked upon as undecided, although in one instance, as pointed out in a previous chapter, the House excluded a member-elect chiefly for reasons not provided for in the Constitution.[1] The States, however, clearly have no power to impose additional requirements. With respect to the election of Representatives, the Constitution prescribes that the voters participating in each State " shall have the qualifications requisite for electors of the most numerous branch of the state legislature," — the suffrage qualifications being left to the State to determine.

The Congressional Districts. — Members of the House of Representatives are chosen from districts, known as congressional districts, into which the various States are divided, except in the case of States that are entitled to only one Representative. In such instances, of course, the State itself is the congressional district and the Representative is elected from the State at large. The district plan is not based upon any constitutional provision, but was first required by act of Congress, passed in 1842. The Constitution simply says that Representatives shall be chosen " by the people of the several states." For more than half a century the States were permitted by Congress to use their own discretion with respect to methods of electing Representatives. Election upon a general ticket was common. In the apportionment act of 1842, however, Congress provided that " in every case where a State is entitled to more than one Representative, the number to which each State shall be entitled under this apportionment shall be elected by districts composed of contiguous territory, equal in number to the number of Representatives to which said State may be entitled, no one district electing more than one Representative." In later acts the requirement concerning the territory of the district has been made somewhat more stringent. The regular rule is that the districts shall be composed of " contiguous and compact territory containing as nearly as practicable an equal number of inhabitants." Under certain conditions Congress permits the election of members at large. In case a new apportionment gives to any State an increase in the number of Representatives, the additional members thus authorized are elected at large until the State is redistricted so that the number of districts corresponds to the number of

[1] Hinds, " Precedents," Vol. I, p. 477.

Representatives to which the State is entitled. If the representation of a State is reduced as a result of a new apportionment, and at the time of the election the number of districts has not been reduced accordingly, all of that State's Representatives are elected at large and will continue to be so chosen until the State is redistricted in harmony with the requirements of the law.

The division of the States into congressional districts is in the hands of the State legislatures. Except for the restriction that the districts shall be composed of contiguous and compact territory, — a restriction which proves very elastic in practice, — the legislatures are free to arrange the districts pretty much as they please. County boundaries, and, in the cities entitled to more than one Representative, ward boundaries, are usually observed in the formation of districts. The purpose of Congress in adopting the district system was to have the districts fairly equal with respect to population. Great inequality exists, however, some districts having from two to three times the population of others. With respect to the number of votes cast at congressional elections, the variation is even greater.[1] It should be remembered, however, that representation is based on population and not on the number of voters or the number of votes cast at election.

Some inequality among the districts is unavoidable, but much of that which exists and gives rise to justifiable criticism is clearly by design. The dominant parties in the legislatures have in many instances purposely arranged the districts so that they would have a marked advantage over their opponents, regardless alike of an equitable distribution of population and the geographical formation of the districts. By a careful grouping of the counties of a State, for illustration, the strength of the minority party may be so concentrated in a small number of districts that the majority of the districts will be safely controlled by the party in power. Or, counties which are strongly of the minority faith and so situated that they naturally constitute a district of "contiguous and compact territory," may be separated in forming the districts and joined with counties controlled by the majority party so that the latter will easily maintain its supremacy. This practice of arranging

[1] Beard, "American Government and Politics," New and Revised Edition, p. 235.

districts for the sake of party advantage is known as gerrymandering, a political term which came into early use.[1] As a result of it many curiously shaped districts have been formed, as is indicated by the names by which they are popularly characterized, — "shoestring," "monkey wrench," "belt line," and "saddle bag" being among the most suggestive. The latter term was applied to an Illinois district comprised of "two groups of counties at different sides of the state, so connected as to crowd as many Democratic counties as possible into one district and thus secure Republican seats in near-by districts by eliminating the vote of hostile localities."[2]

A striking example of the advantage which is sometimes obtained by the dominant party through "scientific gerrymandering" is found in the arrangement of districts made by the Democrats in Indiana by which, in 1892, they succeeded in electing eleven Representatives with a vote of 259,190, while the Republicans with a vote of 253,668 were able to elect only two.[3] It should be noted, however, that the advantage gained by the party making the gerrymander is often short-lived. Not infrequently, through a sudden change in public opinion, the arrangement so carefully made proves the undoing of the party responsible for it and gives ascendancy to the party against which it was directed. The gerrymander is a weapon which the parties have been willing to use, but sometimes it has proven itself to be of the boomerang type.

The Residence Rule. — In connection with the discussion of district representation, the question of residence within the district should be noted. Either by custom or by the laws of the States such residence is almost an absolute requirement. It is practically not possible as it is in England for any man, however experienced and influential, to obtain an election in a

---

[1] "So called from Elbridge Gerry, a leading Democratic politician in Massachusetts (a member of the Constitutional Conventions of 1787, and in 1812 elected Vice-President of the United States), who when Massachusetts was being re-districted contrived a scheme which gave one of the districts a shape like that of a lizard. Stuart, the well known artist, entering the room of an editor who had a map of the new districts hanging on the wall over his desk observed, 'Why, this district looks like a salamander,' and put in the claws and eyes of the creature with his pencil. 'Say rather a Gerrymander,' replied the editor; and the name stuck."
Bryce, "The American Commonwealth," New and Revised Edition, Vol. I, p. 126.

[2] Reinsch, "American Legislatures and Legislative Methods," p. 202.

[3] Commons, "Proportional Representation," Second Edition, p. 61.

district in which he does not reside. This is in accord with the general practice in the United States where by law the residence rule is almost always required with respect to elective offices of all kinds. In the election of Representatives, however, it is not required either by the federal Constitution or by the law of Congress. The former simply says that Representatives shall be inhabitants of the States in which they are elected, and the latter, in substance, that they shall be regularly elected by districts instead of by the State at large upon a general ticket. As suggested, the observance of the rule is due either to the force of a long-standing tradition or to the authority of State law. Only rarely is the rule not observed. In the city of New York, there have been instances of representation of downtown districts by men who were not resident within them; but aside from these, the rule has almost never been violated. The constitutionality of the practice, however, is exceedingly doubtful. In fact, it is freely held to be invalid inasmuch as it adds to the qualifications for membership in the House as prescribed in the Constitution. The assumption may be safely made, though, that it is in no immediate danger of being set aside, since it is so generally approved by the people and is so fully in harmony with their political habits.

The Time of Meeting. — The time of meeting of a new Congress, as prescribed by the Constitution, is open to criticism and has been made the subject of frequent discussion. As already stated, the election of Representatives takes place every two years, and by act of Congress occurs on the first Tuesday after the first Monday in November of the even-numbered years. Their term of office begins on the fourth of March following their election. But unless called into special session by the President at an earlier time, or a different date for the meeting of Congress is set by law, Congress will not assemble until the first Monday in the following December, — about thirteen months after the congressional election. Of course Congress can fix a different time for the first regular session to begin, and has often been urged to shorten the period elapsing between the election and the time of its assembling, but there is little to indicate any change in the practice within the near future, although the advantages of such a change are obvious.

There are at least two unfortunate results which come from

this long delay to which a newly elected Congress must submit before it normally begins its work. One is that after the new Congress has been chosen, the closing or short session of the old Congress is still to be held, beginning on the first Monday in December immediately following the congressional election and continuing until the fourth of March. Many members of this old Congress may have been defeated for reelection and the work of Congress discredited in the eyes of the people. Yet, however strong may have been the protest registered by the voters at the polls, the existing Congress still has three months to serve and may proceed in its own way to carry out its own will. The very policies condemned by the voters may be enacted into law during this time. It may easily happen in a presidential year that the party in power, controlling the presidency and both houses of Congress, will be routed at the election, and a President and Congress of the opposite party chosen. Nevertheless, the President and Congress thus discredited have a free hand with respect to legislation until their terms of office expire. During this time many things may be done, or left undone, contrary to the wishes of the people, for the purpose of embarrassing the incoming administration. Enormous appropriations of money are sometimes carried through by men who within a few weeks or a few days will pass from power. There is almost certain to be extravagance and carelessness, if nothing worse, under such conditions. It can hardly be expected that the same degree of responsibility will be felt by men who have been rejected by the voters and are giving up their official positions as will characterize the attitude of men who are just entering upon their duties.

The second result to be noted is that in less than a year after a new Congress begins its work, the next one must be elected. That means that members of the House of Representatives, at the very beginning of their terms, must give thought to the problem of reëlection if they wish to continue their congressional service. Indeed, before the end of the first session, barely more than six months after taking their seats, many Representatives must make the fight for renomination at the party primaries. This is a very distracting proceeding and diverts their attention from legislative duties, and tempts them to courses of conduct that are not consistent with disinterested public service. In such circumstances "playing politics" is inevitable. The man who wishes to make a career for himself in the lower house is under the necessity of constantly giving heed to the political conditions and movements in the district he represents. If he does not do so, his power at home is likely to be undermined, either by party opponents or by rivals within his own party, and he be retired to the gloom of private life. A high degree of efficiency in legislation is not possible under such conditions. The necessity of "playing politics" during the session of Congress would be lessened, although it would not be removed, by having a new Congress assemble soon after its election.

This evil — for it is truly an evil — is intensified by the short term of office for Representatives. If this were longer, say four years, instead of two as prescribed by the Constitution, members of the House could devote some of their time exclusively to legislative work without incurring so much risk of defeat and political oblivion. Less attention to personal advancement, on the part of Representatives, and more to serious consideration of the problems of government are greatly needed in the House. The opportunity for this, at least, would be afforded by a longer term. Real statesmanship can hardly be expected of the man whose thought is chiefly occupied with the question of reëlection. Moreover, the short term practically insures the presence of a large number of Representatives who are lacking in the experience necessary for efficient legislative service. Many fail of reëlection and are retired to private life after only a term or two, and this is not sufficient to enable the average member to become thoroughly familiar with the work of the House and acquire real influence in its deliberations. Just when many Representatives have completed their apprenticeship, so to speak, and have become equipped by experience for the difficult work of legislation, they are driven from office, and untried men take their places. As a consequence, there is a great loss to the nation. Those who become the real leaders of the House, almost without exception, are men who have been repeatedly reëlected. The speakership and the important committee assignments are almost certain to go to men of long experience. The seniority rule, it is true, is not so stringently observed in the House as in the Senate, but it is nevertheless of very great consequence. And as a result of it, in part, legislative power is centered in the few, while the great majority of members, possessing equal constitutional privileges and powers with the leaders, hold places of comparative insignificance.

The House Organization. — With the expiration of the two-year term, as previously pointed out, the entire membership of the House ceases, and the House organization disappears. "The moment after the expiration of a Congress, the House has no Speaker, no committees, no rules, no sworn membership, and no actual existence as an organized body."[1] Of course when the new Congress assembles, a new organization must be effected. This involves the taking of the oath by the members-elect, the choosing of the Speaker, and the other House officers, the adoption of rules, and the appointment of committees. In accomplishing this a regular procedure is observed. The members-elect are called to order by the Clerk of the preceding House who, until the Speaker is elected, serves as the presiding officer. The roll is called of those whose credentials show that they have been properly elected. In this way the presence of the constitutional quorum is ascertained and the way prepared for the election of a Speaker. The roll is again called and each member in turn states his choice for Speaker. When the report of the tellers, appointed by the Clerk and representing the different political parties, shows that any candidate has a majority of all the votes cast, he is declared elected, and is escorted to the chair by a committee of members, where the oath of office is administered. The Speaker then takes charge of the proceedings and gives the oath to the members-elect. Following this comes the election of the Clerk, Sergeant-at-Arms, and other House officers, and the adoption of a set of rules. With respect to the latter, usually the rules of the preceding House are adopted, to remain in force until otherwise ordered. Upon the completion of these steps, the House is said to be organized and ready to do business. However, it has no committees, and without committees practically no legislative work can be accomplished.

The most notable of the House officers is the Speaker. In fact, he is one of the most notable officers in the entire government, although his power is not so great under the rules now

[1] McCall, "The Business of Congress," p. 34.

in force as it formerly was. The position of speaker has constitutional recognition in the provision which declares that "the House of Representatives shall choose their speaker and other officers." No other reference to the speakership is contained in the Constitution. It will be noted that nothing is said as to his powers and duties. The determination of these is left to the House through its own rules. His power and influence are very great, however, arising first from the fact that he is the presiding officer, charged with the enforcement of the House rules, and, second, from the fact that he is the leader of the dominant party in the House. He is always chosen as a party man and is expected, therefore, not only to discharge the duties of a parliamentary presiding officer, but also to guide his party in the legislative and parliamentary controversies which arise. In this latter respect he differs very radically from the Speaker of the English House of Commons, who is expected to be entirely free from all partisan bias and activity. His parliamentary duties are such as usually pertain to the presiding officer of legislative bodies and are clearly set forth in the rules. He is a member of the House, with all the rights of the ordinary member in addition to those of the presiding officer. He may vote upon all questions if he chooses, although by the House rule he is not required to vote in ordinary legislative proceedings, "except where his vote would be decisive or where the House is engaged in voting by ballot." The Speaker's name is not on the roll used in calling the yeas and nays and is not called except upon his request. Usually he does not vote when not required to do so.

Formerly, that is, prior to the Sixty-second Congress, the Speaker, acting for his party, appointed all standing committees. This privilege gave him commanding power, for through his control over the personnel of the committees, he was in a position practically to control the actual work of the House. Naturally he would not appoint men to important committee positions who stood for legislative policies to which he was opposed. This, coupled with his parliamentary power to grant or withhold recognition to those seeking opportunity to address the House and his dominance in the small committee on rules, as it then existed, made the Speaker almost a dictator in the affairs of the House. In point of actual influence he became second only to the President. The growth of the Speaker's power is one of the most interesting and most significant developments that have occurred in connection with the United States government. It has not been due either to constitutional provision or to legal requirement, but, fostered by the House rules and by long-standing custom, is the result of a slow evolution in response to one of the vital needs of the House, — the need of leadership and centralized control.

For many years the House, under the decentralizing influence of democratic theories, was loosely organized and without adequate discipline; hence it was frequently subject to the demoralization that comes from obstructionist and dilatory practices, to the sacrifice of power and efficient action. It became clear in time that leadership and effective organization must be provided. This was done through the extension of the Speaker's power and the development of the committee system. But, as frequently happens in governmental reforms, the movement went too far, and ultimately there developed an autocratic régime, which made the House subject to the will of the Speaker and a few of his chief lieutenants who were at the head of the leading committees. It became possible for the Speaker practically to determine what the House should and what it should not do. The hands of the ordinary member were tied and he could get nothing through the House that did not meet with approval from the leaders. Of course, this situation could be changed whenever the majority wished to change it, for the Speaker's power was not personal. He occupied the position he held because his followers preferred that he should. He was "the instrument, as well as the leader of the majority in controlling the processes of the House."[1]

Though opposition to such centralized power was always existent, it was many years, because of personal and party considerations, before a majority of the members could be induced to take a stand for a change in the House rules, looking to the curtailment of the Speaker's powers. This was accomplished finally in 1910, after a spectacular parliamentary struggle, and nominally, at least, the Speaker was deprived of certain privileges. Two changes of consequence to the Speaker were made. His power of appointing all standing committees was

[1] Wilson, "Constitutional Government in the United States," p. 95.

taken from him, and these were made elective by the House itself. Also the very important committee on Rules was increased in membership from five to eleven and the Speaker was debarred from membership upon it. With respect to the first, the appointment of committees, the change made is perhaps not so significant as appears at first thought, for the party caucuses have always had a leading part in the selection of committees, and continue to have under the new rule. Professor Beard says: "Since the beginning of the party system in the United States, the selection of the members of committees has been in the hands of the caucus of each party, under the leadership and perhaps dominance of a few men experienced in the arts of management. To borrow a term from economics, we may say that the committee assignments in the House and in the Senate are determined by a 'higgling in the market' and that the various posts fall to members roughly according to their abilities, their actual power as leaders, their skill in management. This 'higgling' begins long before a new Congress meets; most of the important assignments are determined probably before the party caucuses assemble, and the caucuses only ratify the work of the pre-caucuses, while the houses ratify the work of the caucuses."[1] So the Speaker's position, though somewhat different under the present rule, is only a little less powerful than under the older order. Inasmuch as he is the leader of the dominant party of the House, he is certain to have a good deal to say about committee assignments and House procedure, whatever the formal requirements may be as set up by the rules. His only rival in influence is the chairman of the Ways and Means Committee, who is the floor leader of the majority and consequently, from the standpoint of party success, is in a position of the greatest responsibility. It is possible that the future may see the Speaker transformed into an exclusively impartial parliamentary officer and the burden of party leadership in the lower House transferred to the floor leader.[2]

REFERENCES

(For References, see the following chapter.)

[1] Beard, "American Government and Politics," New and Revised Edition, p. 277.
[2] The other chief officers of the House are the Clerk, the Sergeant-at-Arms, the Doorkeeper, the Postmaster, and the Chaplain. In addition, there are many assistants to these officers, committee clerks, secretaries, messengers, and other employees.

CHAPTER XIII

THE HOUSE OF REPRESENTATIVES — COMMITTEES AND PROCEDURE

FREQUENT reference has been made to the House committee system. This must be considered still further and somewhat in detail, for no proper understanding of the organization and work of the House can be obtained without full knowledge of the part which the committees play in congressional legislation. Though they have no constitutional foundation, without its committees the House would be utterly helpless. The volume of business each session is so vast that the House as a whole could do nothing with it. With all of their faults the committees are necessary.

The rules provide for a large number of standing committees, almost sixty, in fact. All proposed legislation must be referred to appropriate committees for investigation and report before being acted upon by the House. For each important subject there is a standing committee. The reference of measures and the jurisdiction of committees are governed by the rules. To illustrate, all legislation relating to the revenue and the bonded debt of the United States must be referred to the Committee on Ways and Means; that relating to judicial proceedings, civil and criminal law, to the Committee on the Judiciary; that relating to banking and currency, to the Committee on Banking and Currency; and so on through the list. Naturally the committees vary a good deal in importance, some of them having little to do, and that little of slight consequence. Likewise the size of the committees varies a good deal, the most important having twenty-one members. Those named above and some dozen others have this number. There are a good many with a membership of from thirteen to sixteen. The smallest committee has only two members. The committee of highest rank is that on Ways and Means, places on which are eagerly sought by leading members of the House. In addition to this and the committees on Judiciary, and Banking and Currency, previously referred to, the list of leading committees includes those on Appropriations, Interstate and Foreign Commerce, Rivers and Harbors, Merchant Marine and Fisheries, Agriculture, Foreign Affairs, Military Affairs, Naval Affairs, Post Office and Post Roads, Education, Labor, Reform in the Civil Service, District of Columbia, and Rules.

The chairman and the other members of each committee are formally elected by the House, the real selection, however, being made by the party leaders and the party caucuses. The plan followed since the change in the rules in 1910 is for the Committee on Ways and Means, whose members are selected by the party caucuses, to act as a committee on committees, and recommend to the House the committee assignments. The House then makes the selection official by giving formal approval. The minority party is represented upon all committees, its members being selected by the party caucus. The majority, therefore, permits the minority to name its own committee representatives, but sees to it that practically all committees, particularly those that have to do with contentious questions, are under its own control by a safe margin. For instance, the Committee on Rules has seven members from the majority party and four from the minority; that on Ways and Means has fourteen from the majority and seven from the minority. Other committees are divided in about the same proportion.

Power of the Committees. — Though the committees are the creatures of the House, established for the purpose of enabling it to do its work, yet their position in the House organization is so central that they exercise at times tremendous power of themselves. Practically no action is taken upon a legislative proposal that has not been under consideration by a committee. As President Wilson says, " the business of the House is what the committees choose to make it." As a rule, they formulate the measures reported to the House.[1] It is true that a

---

[1] The actual work of drafting a committee measure is usually assigned to a sub-committee. If the bill is partisan in character, the sub-committee is composed entirely of members of the majority party. In the preparation of committee reports, also, the sub-committee is used. For a discussion of the sub-committees and their work, see article by Burton L. French, *American Political Science Review*, Vol. IX, p. 68.

bill introduced by a member and referred to a committee may be accepted by the latter as satisfactory with respect to both form and substance, and be reported to the House practically without change. On the other hand, they may "pull it about and alter it, or they may throw it aside altogether and frame a measure of their own, or they may do nothing, make no report at all. Few bills ever see the light again after being referred to a committee." [1]

This power of the committees to "pigeonhole" proposed legislation, and thus kill it, is very great, although their jurisdiction in this regard is not quite so wide as it formerly was. By a rule adopted in 1910 it is possible for any member, under decidedly rigid restrictions, however, to move for the discharge of a committee from "further consideration of any public bill or joint resolution which may have been referred to such committee fifteen days prior thereto." [2] This opens the way for interference on the part of the House when committees fail to report upon matters referred to them, but this action would hardly be taken except where a committee was dilatory in connection with some measure that was of general interest and upon which the House desired action. In that case the committee would hardly seek to defeat the House in its purpose, although that is not unknown. The rule may afford relief at times, but it will not prevent the continued wholesale slaughter of measures through committee inaction. It is inevitable, indeed, that this slaughter shall go on by one process or another, because otherwise the House would be swamped by the veritable deluge of measures at each session. A large proportion of these bills would doubtless be killed by the House if they were submitted for its action. Killing them in committee is a more expeditious method. The unfortunate thing, however, is that now and then really worthy and desirable measures are dispatched in this way, to the serious loss of the Nation.

Committee Meetings and Proceedings. — It should be noted, also, in this connection, that the meetings of the committees are secret unless the committees wish to have them open to the public. All their work can be done behind closed doors if they so wish. No one has a right to appear before a committee

[1] Wilson, "Constitutional Government in the United States," p. 90.
[2] House Rule, No. XXVII, paragraph 4.

and express his views as to pending legislation. A committee may invite particular individuals, or extend a general invitation to all interested persons to appear and give testimony either for or against the proposed measures; but if this is done, it is because the committee wishes to do so of its own accord or feels that it must in deference to public opinion. The public cannot demand admission.

Moreover, the proceedings of committee meetings are not ordinarily officially reported and published as are those of the House and of the Senate. Therefore, no publicity is given to committee work except as the newspapers, in response to public interest, may uncover and publish what was done. Even then, however, the reports are very meager as a rule, and the mass of the people is usually in profound ignorance of what transpires in the committee rooms. This is all the more remarkable when it is recalled that the real work of legislation takes place in the committees. It is there that the real debating of measures occurs, for the House itself does not debate; it has not the time. It is by the committees that the information is gathered which determines the character of the legislation that is enacted, and it is by the committees that the bills are either drafted or scrutinized carefully and put in form for submission to the House. In most instances the latter does little more than give official sanction to what the committees recommend. Yet, for the most part, the committees act in secret and their members are without that acute sense of personal responsibility attendant upon wide and full publicity of official acts. That this is a dangerous practice and lends itself to the uses of the evil forces of politics, which love the darkness rather than the light, cannot be questioned. One of the big reforms yet to be accomplished is in connection with committee procedure.

One practice, however, should be mentioned here, which is frequently observed and is of great significance, — the practice of holding public hearings upon pending legislation. This has become more common in recent years and may be taken as presaging the time when what is a mere privilege now on the part of the public may become a right, — the right to be heard by the committees of Congress upon any measure that is under consideration. In fact, the public hearing may mark a most important development in free government. It is really a unique practice and is the product of American experience, existing in no other country. It is freely used by both houses of Congress and by the legislatures of the various States. Its influence is wholesome and its use should be extended. Speaking of public hearings, President Lowell says: "They are, indeed, a highly valuable element in popular government; and this is the more true because with the elimination of thorough discussion from our representative bodies, due partly to the increase of legislative business, partly to the cutting down of time, and partly to the large proportion of new members, most of the real work must be done through public opinion by sample in the form of committees, and committees without public hearings are cut off from their best source of light."[1]

Influence of Committee System. — That the committees are essential to the House and have a vital place in its organization, is obvious at a glance. They make it possible for the House to do its work. Yet their results are not all beneficent. One of the points most worthy of emphasis is the degree to which the unity of the House is broken up by the committee system. The House is dependent upon its committees. Each of the committees is a sort of miniature legislature in itself. Each has its own work to do, and does it with little or no regard to what the others are doing. They are under no responsibility or obligation to one another, and go on with their work, regardless of whether the results harmonize or not. This unfortunate consequence is particularly noticeable in connection with financial legislation. Income, in the form of revenue, and outgo, in the form of expenditures, are wholly unrelated as far as the House committees are concerned. The Committee on Ways and Means has nothing at all to do with the various appropriation committees. The former may favor a policy of niggardly economy, and the latter one of wasteful extravagance, but there is no way of bringing them as committees into harmonious relations in support of a common policy. And not only is there this complete separation between the revenue-raising and the revenue-spending committees, but the authority to prepare appropriation bills is diffused among a number of committees, each independent of the others in all respects. There are, in fact, not fewer than nine committees in the House that have

[1] Lowell, "Public Opinion and Popular Government," p. 256.

to do with the framing of appropriation measures. Unity under such conditions, of course, is impossible. It not infrequently happens that measures involving fundamental conflicts are reported to the House by different committees, and sometimes such measures become laws. The efficiency that comes to the House through its committee system is acquired at high cost. The quality of its work is not always such as to be a source of pride.

Other unfortunate results of the system are equally clear, two of which may be stated in the well-known words of Bryce. " It gives facilities for the exercise of underhand and even corrupt influence. In a small committee the voice of each member is well worth securing, and may be secured with little danger of a public scandal. The press cannot, even when the doors of committee rooms stand open, report the proceedings of sixty bodies; the eye of the nation cannot follow and mark what goes on within them; while the subsequent proceedings in the House are too hurried to permit a ripping up there of suspicious bargains struck in the purlieus of the Capitol, and fulfilled by votes given in a committee. . . .

" It reduces responsibility. In England, if a bad act is passed or a good bill rejected, the blame falls primarily upon the ministry in power whose command of the majority would have enabled them to defeat it, next upon the party which supported the ministry, then upon the individual members who are officially recorded to have 'backed it' and voted for it in the House. The fact that a select committee recommended it — and comparatively few bills pass through a select committee — would not be held to excuse the default of the ministry and the majority. But in the United States the ministry cannot be blamed, for the cabinet officers do not sit in Congress; the House cannot be blamed because it has only followed the decision of its committee; the committee may be an obscure body, whose members are too insignificant to be worth blaming. The chairman is possibly a man of note, but the people have no leisure to watch sixty chairmen: they know Congress and Congress only; they cannot follow the acts of those to whom Congress chooses to delegate its functions. No discredit attaches to the dominant party, because they could not control the acts of the eleven men in the committee room. This public displeasure rarely finds a victim, and everybody concerned is relieved from the wholesome dread of damaging himself and his party by negligence, perversity, or dishonesty. Only when a scandal has arisen so serious as to demand investigation is the responsibility of the member to his constituents and to the country brought duly home."[1]

The House Rules. — In the House, as in the Senate, an elaborate system of rules has been found necessary. With so large a membership and so much business to be attended to each session, the House would be in a state of hopeless confusion if every step in its procedure were not under strict control. The organization of the House, the duties of its officers, the work of the committees, the conduct of members, the procedure on bills and resolutions, the order of business, and other things as well, are all provided for in minute detail. The rules of procedure include the principles of parliamentary law found in Jefferson's "Manual of Parliamentary Practice," based on the practice of the English House of Commons, and the standing rules of the House, adopted from time to time to meet its own special needs. In addition there is the large number of precedents which have grown up since Congress first assembled in 1789.

The rules now in force are at base substantially the same as those adopted in the early years of Congress, modified and extended as occasion demanded. The chief objects sought by the extension of the rules have been to expedite business, to centralize control in the House so as to insure orderly, systematic procedure, and to prevent the minority, through filibustering and other obstructionist practices, from defeating the will of the majority. As expressed by the House, the purposes in view have been: "Economy of time, order, and the right of a majority to control and dispose of the business for which it is held responsible." Before 1890, the minority would frequently block the way to action on the part of the majority by breaking a quorum through refusal to vote, by demanding the yeas and nays, and by the use of certain privileged motions such as "to take a recess," and "to adjourn to a day certain," upon the amendments to which, as well as to the original motion, the call of the roll could be demanded. As the rules then stood,

[1] Bryce, "The American Commonwealth," New and Revised Edition, pp. 162-163.

these motions could be made again and again, without limit, to the utter confusion of the House. At one time during the Fiftieth Congress, the House was in continuous session for eight days and nights. More than a hundred useless roll calls were taken upon privileged motions at the demand of the minority for the sole purpose of delay. The House had completely broken down as a legislative body, and, to its complete demoralization, had become the plaything of an obstructionist minority. Immediate and drastic reform was needed. This came in the following Congress, under the leadership of one of the greatest Speakers the House has ever had, the brilliant Thomas B. Reed, who, in the face of tremendous opposition, put an end to one of the worst abuses by counting as present for the purpose of a quorum all members who were in the chamber, whether they responded to the roll call or not. In Mr. Reed's opinion the constitutional quorum was not a voting quorum and "physical presence and constructive absence" were impossible. The principle he acted on is now embodied in the House rules and is regularly followed. Another reform of equal importance was made during the same session when the Speaker was given power to refuse to entertain motions which he looked upon as dilatory. The exception to this, of course, is the call for the yeas and nays, which members have a constitutional right to make, and which must be ordered upon the demand of one fifth of the members present, no matter what the purpose may be. The rule makes it possible, however, to prevent a great deal of needless delay, and has accomplished much in the way of expediting business.

One of the rules deserving of special mention is that which restricts debate in the House. Under a provision adopted in 1841, " no member shall occupy more than one hour in debate on any question in the House or in Committee." By the rules the discussion of certain motions is limited to a specified number of minutes. The five-minute rule is frequently observed when the House sits as a Committee of the Whole. Under special rules brought in by the Committee on Rules as occasion may demand, the time to be devoted to the discussion of particular bills may be fixed, and a definite hour set for taking the vote. No matter how important the measure may be, this time is always short, possibly only a few hours. This is divided between the leaders on each side of the question and by them is parceled out to their respective followers. The demand for chances to speak is always very great, while the time is very short. The result is that many of the speeches in the open House upon questions of the highest importance are only of five or perhaps ten minutes' length. Thorough debate is hardly possible under such conditions.

Because of the very limited debate that occurs the House has been subjected to a great deal of criticism. The value of free debate is everywhere recognized, yet it is hard to see how the House, with its 435 members, could possibly do its work without limiting the time of speakers. If debate is to be at all general, individual members must be restrained. Moreover, unlimited debate is not without its faults as the experience of the Senate clearly shows. One of the striking contrasts between the two houses — and one which is by no means wholly in the Senate's favor — lies at this point. In this connection the words of President Wilson are, as usual, suggestive and interesting:

" Perhaps the contrast between them is in certain respects even sharper and clearer now than in the earlier days of our history, when the House was smaller and its functions simpler. The House once debated; now it does not debate. It has not the time. There would be too many debaters and there are too many subjects of debate. It is a business body, and it must get its business done. When the late Mr. Reed once, upon a well-known occasion, thanked God that the House was not a deliberate assembly, there was no doubt a dash of half-cynical humor in the remark, such as so often gave spice and biting force to what he said, but there was the sober earnest of a serious man of affairs, too. He knew the vast mass of business the House undertook to transact: that it had made itself a great organ of direction, and that it would be impossible for it to get through its calendars if it were to attempt to discuss in open house, instead of in its committee rooms, the measures it acted upon. The Senate has retained its early rules of procedure without material alteration. It is still a place of free and prolonged debate. It will not curtail the privilege of its members to say what they please, at whatever length. But the Senators are comparatively few in number; they can afford the indulgence. The House cannot. The Senate may remain individualistic, atomistic, but the House must be organic, — an efficient instrument, not a talkative assembly.'[1]

Bill Procedure. — The procedure upon bills and resolutions is practically identical with that in the Senate. Bills may be introduced by any member without restriction by depositing them with the Clerk. If a member desires legislation upon some subject, but prefers not to draft the measure himself, he may introduce a petition for a bill of the kind in mind, which will be referred to the proper committee for drafting. The committee, of course, is under no obligation to prepare such a bill; no more so than it is to report to the House bills that have been referred to it. Technically the committees do not have the right to initiate measures, but this is of little moment because if a committee desires to bring in a bill upon a question which is within its jurisdiction, any of its members may introduce a measure of the kind contemplated and have it referred; then the committee can proceed to prepare its own draft and report it to the House. Also the House may instruct any of its committees, if it wishes, to prepare and report bills or resolutions. Messages from the President and communications from the executive departments when referred to the committees give them authority to originate bills.

Upon introduction, a bill is immediately referred to a committee, numbered, and printed. As already noted, the committee may or may not report it to the House. If it is reported, the recommendation of the committee may be that it pass as introduced, or that it be amended in certain ways, or that it be indefinitely postponed. If the latter be the opinion of the committee, however, the likelihood is that the measure would not be reported at all, unless the report was forced under pressure from the House. Not infrequently measures are reported without recommendation. After a bill is reported to the House, it is placed on the particular Calendar where it belongs, from which it will be taken in the regular order. Occasionally a privileged bill is considered by the House when it is reported by the committee, but not often. If the bill is a revenue or an appropriation bill, it is considered in Committee of the Whole, where it is first subjected to general debate and then to

[1] Wilson, "Constitutional Government in the United States" p. 88.

reading for amendment under the five-minute rule. It is finally reported to the House for formal action. If it does not require consideration in Committee of the Whole, it is read a second time, upon report to the House from the committee, and is open to debate and amendment. Following this step in the procedure it is up for engrossment and third reading. The question is on ordering engrossment and third reading at one vote. If the vote is in the affirmative, the third reading, by title, usually occurs at once. But objection to this may be made by any member who may demand a reading in full of the engrossed copy. If this is done, the bill must be laid aside, of course, for engrossment, and the vote deferred. A negative vote on the question of engrossment and third reading defeats the measure. The final step is the passage of the bill, the question on this being put by the Speaker at once, without waiting for a motion from the floor.

After the House has passed the measure and it has been properly authenticated, it is transmitted to the Senate by message, where it is referred to a committee and subjected to practically the same treatment that it received in the House. If the Senate passes the bill without amendment, it is returned to the House where it goes into the possession of the Clerk and is immediately enrolled for signature. If the Senate amends the bill, upon return to the House it goes to the Speaker's table and at the proper time is laid before the House. Each amendment is taken up in turn and voted upon. If the amendments are accepted, the amended bill is at once enrolled. If they are not accepted, the House may either ask for a conference with the Senate or merely send notice of its disagreement, leaving it to the Senate to take the next step, by receding from its amendments or asking for a conference.

When a conference is decided upon, each house appoints its representatives, usually three in number and known as managers. The House managers are appointed by the Speaker, who selects them so as to represent both the majority and minority positions upon the points in issue, if disagreement exists. Usually, also, they represent the different political parties. The managers of the two houses really constitute two distinct committees. The questions they may consider are only those upon which the houses are in disagreement. The conference may be either " free " or " simple." A free conference is one in which the managers may act as they please upon the questions in controversy, while a simple conference is one which confines the managers to specific instructions from the house they represent.

With respect to the instruction of managers the Senate and the House of Representatives do not agree in their practices. The former insists on free conferences and only rarely has given instructions; it has, in fact, sometimes declined to participate in the conference when the House has instructed its managers. The latter, however, insists upon its right to instruct, and usually does so. It is the business of the conference committees to reach an agreement, if possible, by which the differences between the houses may be settled. Sometimes this can be done without serious difficulty, one house receding from its position or a compromise being agreed upon which both houses can accept. Occasionally, however, neither house will yield, and the bill over which the contention has arisen is lost. If a compromise agreement is reached, the committees report to their respective houses which proceed to approve or disapprove of the action taken. If disapproval is given in either house, the measure is lost unless through further conference some other solution of the difficulty may be found. If approval is voted by both houses, the measure goes to the house in which it originated for enrollment. It is carefully examined by the Committee on Enrolled Bills, which is really a joint committee, though each branch acts independently. After the enrollment is completed, the bill is ready for the signatures of the Speaker and the President of the Senate. The Speaker always signs first, whether it be a House or a Senate bill, after which it is presented to the President of the Senate. It is then ready for transmission to the President for executive approval or disapproval. If the President approves, he simply signs the measure and it becomes a law to take effect at the time designated by Congress. It is then deposited in the office of the Secretary of State, who is the custodian of the laws of the United States. If the President disapproves of the bill, he returns it to the House in which it originated, with a message stating his reasons for withholding his signature. It is then for Congress to determine whether the bill shall become law, notwithstanding the President's veto. If both houses pass it by the necessary two-thirds vote, it becomes a law and is transmitted to the Secretary of State by the presiding officer of the house which acted on it last.

This brief statement describes, in the main, the stages through which a bill passes in the process of becoming a law. There is, of course, a multitude of intricate details of procedure which cannot be given here. Before leaving the subject, however, attention should be directed to at least two things. The first is that the procedure outlined is used for public and private bills alike. There is no special private bill procedure such as is used in the British House of Commons.[1] This is an unfortunate fact because of the very large number of private bills introduced and acted upon each session. Both houses of Congress could greatly increase their efficiency and improve the character of their legislation by providing a suitable, more stringent procedure for private bills. The second point to be mentioned is that there is no legislative draftsman or drafting bureau whose duty it is to put bills into the best possible form. Each member may not only introduce as many bills as he pleases, but may draft them in any way that suits his fancy. The result is a vast amount of legislation that is very faulty in its construction. Congress has been slow to see the value of expert draftsmanship, such as that afforded by the English Parliamentary Counsel and by the drafting bureaus in a number of the American States. The interest in scientific legislation has increased rapidly in recent years, and it is safe to say that the near future will witness the establishment of a congressional drafting bureau of some kind. The volume of business confronting the House of Representatives each session is so great, and is increasing so rapidly, that greater care and accuracy in the drafting of measures are absolutely necessary. As an illustration of the amount of work the House must look after, Professor Beard says that there were introduced into the House during the Fifty-ninth Congress 26,154 bills, 257 joint resolutions, 62 concurrent resolutions, 898 simple resolutions, and 8174 reports. Of these, 692 public bills and 6940 private bills, mostly pension measures, were passed.[2] The

[1] Below, Chap. XXXV.
[2] Beard, "American Government and Politics," New and Revised Edition, p. 271.

difficulty of legislating wisely, under such conditions, with proper regard to form as well as substance, is superlatively great.

Political Parties in the House. — As has been suggested repeatedly in the foregoing discussion, the political parties are vital factors in the organization and activities of the House of Representatives. Some further comment as to their place and influence is necessary.

Attention has been called to the tendency of the committee system to destroy the unity of the House of Representatives. This tendency is a very real one, whose significance is not to be underestimated. Yet there is a degree of unity which should not be overlooked, for without it the House would be hopelessly inefficient. This unity comes from the fact that the party controlling the House makes itself accountable for the conduct, not only of the House as a whole, but also of the committees. The House is always organized on party lines. The Speaker, the House officers, the chairmen, and majority of the members of each committee are all members of the dominant party. The House is organized so as to permit the majority party to carry out its will. And, as we have seen, the rules of the House have been modified from time to time so as to insure this result against attempts at obstruction on the part of the minority. The responsibility of the party in control, it is true, is not so direct and inescapable as it ought to be, but by no means can it be said to be non-existent. Particularly is this responsibility forced upon the majority party for its action upon questions arising in the field of contentious politics. Again and again the voters at the polls have given rebuke to those in control of Congress for failure to carry out their mandates upon partisan, controversial questions, such as, for example, the tariff. However, questions of this kind are few in number. It is only on comparatively rare occasions that either of the houses divides on strict party lines. Upon most questions the lines of cleavage cut across party divisions. This is an important fact. Yet the party lines exist, and party responsibility at times is keenly felt. Moreover, the parties, through their leaders, are constantly maneuvering for position in order to have the advantage in the congressional and presidential elections. The minority party, particularly, is alert and active in its efforts to discredit the majority, to "put it in a hole," as the saying is. This critical, at times even hypercritical, attitude of opposition is directed most frequently towards the President and those in control of the administration of government. In fact, the executive is never free from this, whether he is the leader of the party which is in the majority or in the minority in the houses of Congress. It is the business of the members of the President's party to defend the administration, to answer the charges made against it by the opposition, whether unjust or just. The discussions in both houses are filled with this sort of thing. As a result the issues to be fought out in the elections are for the most part formulated in Congress, and the leadership of the parties determined. This fact, regardless of whether or not strict party votes are few or many, gives to Congress a central place and influence in the organized party life of both the Nation and the States. The leadership of Congress and its influence upon party organization and activity cannot be measured, indeed are not even suggested, by the degree of partisanship and party strife to be found in the legislative work of the Senate and the House.[1]

The Party Caucus and House Leadership. — The distinctive party organization in Congress is the caucus. This is found in each house and is maintained by each of the parties. The function of the caucus with respect to the determination of legislative policies has already been described in the chapter on the Senate.[2] Where caucus action is taken by the majority party upon a pending measure, the real decision of the matter is transferred from the properly constituted legislative body, established by the Constitution, to an unofficial, voluntary group, which acts without the slightest legal responsibility. This is no less true of the House caucus than of the Senate. All members of a party are members of that party's caucus. Participation in the caucus is voluntary, however; any one may refuse to take part if he wishes, although the recalcitrant member is usually subjected to a good deal of pressure from his party associates. The caucus is strictly a party institution and its sole purpose is to look after party interests.

[1] For a discussion of congressional leadership and the relation of Congress to the political parties, see Macy, "Party Organization and Machinery," Chap. IV.
[2] Above, p. 134.

THE HOUSE OF REPRESENTATIVES — PROCEDURE

Aside from the part the caucus frequently plays in determining the party attitude upon pending legislation, it is an institution of real significance, for it is in the caucus that to a large degree the selection of party leaders in Congress actually takes place. It is in the caucus of the majority party that the choice of a Speaker is really made. The formal election in the House is merely a ratification of the caucus action. It is in the caucus also that the committee on committees is appointed. It is here that the party's floor leader is named and the chairmen of the leading committees practically agreed upon. It is here that the party whips are chosen, and the members of the Congressional Campaign Committee, an important branch of the national party organization.[1] The caucus is governed by rules of its own adoption, and may be called for any proper purpose upon the request of a sufficient number of its members. Its meetings are behind closed doors, although the general public is usually informed by the newspapers as to what transpires.

The minority caucus, in its organization and functions, is identical with that of the majority. It differs from the latter only in the fact that it does not have the votes to control the action of the House. It selects the minority floor leader who is always given the complimentary vote of his party associates for the position of Speaker. It looks after the committee assignments of the minority, chooses the whips,[2] names the members of its party's Congressional Campaign Committee, and frequently determines the party position upon the legislative proposals of the majority. It is its business to make all the trouble it can for the majority through criticism and opposition.

Lack of leadership is one of the leading criticisms brought against the House of Representatives by many writers upon American government. There is merit in the criticism. Responsible leadership of the type that characterizes parliamentary or cabinet government certainly does not exist. To say, however, that there is no leadership at all, even that there is no effective leadership in the House, is very far from correct. One of the prime functions of the party caucuses which lie back of the formal, official House organization, is to provide

---

[1] Below, Chap. XVII.   [2] Below, Chap. XL.

capable leaders and maintain party discipline. The men who stand out conspicuously as leaders are the Speaker, the floor leader of the majority, who is always the chairman of the Ways and Means Committee, and the floor leader of the minority. These men are all selected by their respective party caucuses and are chosen because of their ability, gained through long experience in the House, to guide their parties in the parliamentary and legislative controversies that arise. Under the older rules the Speaker was preëminent in his position as majority leader, and had as his chief lieutenant the majority floor leader. Under the rules in force since 1910 the Speaker has lost and the floor leader has gained in power and prestige. It is the latter who is now most active, and if he does not surpass the Speaker in actual power, he is at least the Speaker's equal. The developments of recent years seem to indicate a still larger sphere for him, and make him comparable in some respects to the Old World prime ministers so far as they are engaged in legislative work. He has nothing to do, of course, with administrative or executive activities. Any fair, adequate discussion of the House of Representatives, it is clear, must give recognition to the commanding position of the majority floor leader, and accord to the House a leadership that is clearly defined and highly efficient. As a matter of fact the House could not do its work without such leadership.

General Observations. — In concluding this discussion of the House of Representatives several significant facts should be noted.

1. The House is materially different from what it was expected to be by the framers of the Constitution. It is in no sense the uncontrolled, turbulent body that was anticipated. Quite the contrary, in fact, is true. No other branch of the government is under more rigid discipline.

2. Traditionally, the House is the popular branch of the national legislature. Yet in practice it is no more so than is the Senate. In fact, it may be doubted whether oftentimes it is as directly responsive to public opinion as is the Senate.

3. There is great inequality among members of the House with respect to power and influence, aside from that which is due to difference in natural abilities. There are always a few in any legislative body who are bound to be more influential

than their associates; these are the leaders. But the House organization is such that, as a rule, a comparatively few control the House's action. They are in a position to thwart the wishes of members who are their equals under the Constitution.

4. As a legislative body the House has not held its own with the Senate. Unquestionably the Senate is a more vital factor in legislation than is the House. Even the exclusive power to originate revenue legislation, given to the House by the Constitution, was not sufficient to keep it in the ascendancy. As we have seen, the Senate has been able practically to nullify that constitutional prerogative through its right of amendment. The other exclusive powers of the House, — to vote impeachments and choose the President in case of failure to elect on the part of the electoral college, — though at times of very great importance, are not of a nature to strengthen it in legislative controversies with the Senate.

5. The House, to a notable degree, has become subject to the influence of the President. Executive leadership in legislation has been much more successful in the lower house than in the upper. By establishing proper relations with those who are at the head of the House organization, a strong President can force through the legislative projects that he favors.

6. The House does not have the weight with the general public that it once had, although it has gained materially in mere efficiency as a legislative machine. By giving so much power to its leaders, by establishing such effective discipline, by dividing up the work among so many committees, and by practically eliminating debate, the House has cut itself off from the means of influencing in any profound way the thought of the Nation. The discussions in the Senate are of much more significance in this respect than anything that is done in the House. And most powerful of all is the influence of the President.

REFERENCES

BEARD. *American Government and Politics*, Edition 1910, Chaps. XII, XIII, XIV.
BRYCE. *The American Commonwealth*, Edition 1910, Vol. I, Chaps. XIII to XXI inclusive.
FOLLETT. *The Speaker of the House of Representatives*.

FORD. *The Rise and Growth of American Politics*, Chaps. XIX, XX.
HART. *Actual Government*, Chaps. XIII, XIV.
McCALL. *The Business of Congress.*
McCONACHIE. *Congressional Committees.*
REINSCH. *American Legislatures and Legislative Methods*, Chaps. I, II.
REINSCH. *Readings on American Federal Government*, Chaps. VII, VIII.
WILSON. *Constitutional Government in the United States*, Chap. IV.
WOODBURN. *The American Republic*, Chap. V.
YOUNG. *The New American Government and its Work*, Chap. III.

CHAPTER XIV

The Party System

One of the most interesting, even phenomenal developments in the political life of the United States, is the rise and growth of political parties. There is nothing in the experiences of other nations, not even England, that is comparable with it. Particularly is this true with respect to the growth of party organization, for in no other country of the world has the machinery of party life and activity been developed to so high a degree of perfection and efficiency as in the United States. This is, indeed, one of the marvels of American politics, and no student can understand the operation of government, in Nation, States, and minor political divisions as well, unless he is familiar with the purposes, organization, and methods of the political parties.

As in England, the parties hold a central place in the government, although the government of the United States is not a true party government, as is the case with the government of England.[1] The principle of the separation of powers, fundamental in the United States Constitution, makes genuine party government impossible. Yet usually the United States is spoken of as being governed by parties; and to a very considerable degree this is true in fact as well as in appearance. It is the parties that furnish the motive power for running the government machine. It is the parties that control the nomination and election of the President and the members of Congress. It is the parties, to a large degree, that determine national policies. The great political struggles that stir the Nation to the depths are party struggles. If the parties were suddenly to cease to exist, the operations of government would be most seriously affected.

Yet the political parties are wholly without constitutional status, and only in a minor way have they received formal legal

[1] Below, Chaps. XXX, XXXVII.

recognition from the national government. They are voluntary, extra-constitutional bodies. They are a vital part of the working constitution, but have no place in the written Constitution. They are the product of custom and tradition, the outgrowth of the Nation's own experience, and not the result of formal action by any legally constituted authority.

Constitution Makers and Political Parties. — The framers of the Constitution did not believe in political parties. In fact, they vigorously opposed party struggles and feared for the existence of the Republic if parties should spring up. They desired a government that would be free from party or " factional " strife, and thought that with the constitutional system finally agreed upon their hopes, in the main, would be realized. This attitude was given frequent expression in the constitutional convention and in the discussions that ensued when the Constitution was submitted for ratification. James Madison was representative of his associates when he said that among the many advantages " promised by a well constructed Union, none deserves to be more accurately developed than its tendency to break and control the violence of faction. The friend of popular governments never finds himself so much alarmed for their character and fate, as when he contemplates their propensity to this dangerous vice." [1] Washington, also, in his famous Farewell Address solemnly warns the people against the " baneful effects of the Spirit of Party." This, because of its " continual mischiefs," it is the duty of a wise people to discourage and restrain. " It serves always to distract the Public Councils, and enfeeble the Public administration. It agitates the community with ill-founded jealousies and false alarms, kindles the animosity of one part against another, foments occasionally riot and insurrection. It opens the doors to foreign influence and corruption, which find a facilitated access to the Government itself through the channels of party passions. Thus the policy and the will of one country are subjected to the policy and the will of another.

" There is an opinion that parties in free countries are useful checks upon the administration of the Government and serve to keep alive the Spirit of Liberty. This within certain limits is probably true — and in Governments of a Monarchical cast,

[1] *The Federalist*, No 10.

Patriotism may look with indulgence, if not with favour, upon the spirit of party. But in those of the popular character, in Governments purely elective, it is a spirit not to be encouraged. From their natural tendency, it is certain there will always be enough of that spirit for every salutary purpose, — and there being constant danger of excess, the effort ought to be, by force of public opinion, to mitigate and assuage it. A fire not to be quenched, it demands a uniform vigilance to prevent its bursting into a flame, lest, instead of warming, it should consume."

That this was the attitude of the constitution makers is beyond question, and yet it is a bit hard to see how they could have failed to comprehend the inevitableness of party activity. Party spirit was even then becoming active and parties were forming. Indeed, the constitution makers themselves, at first unconsciously but later with full recognition of what they were doing, contributed to the upbuilding of those very agencies which, in their former opinion, endangered the Republic. Washington's address was hardly finished before party spirit blazed forth and the lines began to form for the contest over the selection of his successor.

Origin of Parties in America. — The origin of the parties is not hard to discover, although the exact moment when parties became a reality, of course, cannot be fixed. Certainly it is true that prior to the Revolution there were no real parties in the American colonies. Indeed, the same may be said of the period of the Revolution. During the Colonial era the people were divided into two groups or factions corresponding to the factional or party divisions in England. Accepting the English terminology, one was called Whig, and the other Tory, and each sympathized in general with the views of the party of its own name in the mother country. In the period of the Revolution, also, there were two factions. The Whigs supported the Revolution and were sometimes called Patriots; the Tories opposed the Revolution and were known as Loyalists. But it is far from correct to consider these groups true political parties. They were merely factions, and the distinction between political factions and political parties is clear and unmistakable. The party may come into existence through the faction, may grow out of it, but the two are fundamentally different in their nature.

The party is characteristic of free government, while the faction is characteristic of despotism.[1]

It was not until the time of the constitutional convention, 1787, that there sprang up certain fundamental differences of opinion which resulted in the organization of political parties. In the debates of the convention and the discussions which occurred in all the States upon the question of ratifying the Constitution, there developed one great, fundamental issue with respect to the nature of the government. This issue involved the powers of the States as against those of the new national government provided for in the Constitution. Those upon one side sought a strong and virile central government, placing emphasis upon the elements of unity and efficiency; those on the other wished to limit the national authority to the lowest point possible, placing emphasis upon individual liberty and the rights of the States. In the vigorous discussion which followed the submission of the proposed Constitution to the people of the States for their action, the prominent, immediate issue was, of course, whether or not the Constitution should be ratified. Many and varied were the arguments advanced for and against ratification; and many and varied were the principles and issues dragged into the debate. But back of all these lay the supremely important issue, just referred to, involving the relationship between States and Nation; and it was because of this that the first political parties came into existence, — the one, standing for national power, with Alexander Hamilton as its most active leader, and the other, standing for the States, under the leadership of Thomas Jefferson. There were, in addition to this underlying issue, involving the interpretation of the Constitution, specific questions of policy brought forward during Washington's administrations, about which radically differing opinions were held, and which accentuated the development of party spirit and party activity. Although forming, it cannot be said that the parties actually existed until it became plain that Washington would not accept a third term as President. When that fact was made known, the party alignment speedily followed and the Nation was soon in the throes of a bitter partisan struggle

[1] For a discussion of the nature of the modern political party and the distinction between party and faction, see Macy, "Political Parties in the United States," Chap. I.

of the kind Washington condemned with such solemn earnestness in his farewell address.

The party of Hamilton was called the Federalist party, and that of Jefferson the Democratic-Republican party. The latter was sometimes called Anti-Federalist. It should be noted, however, that the use of these names did not identify the two parties with the groups which were contending over the ratification of the Constitution and which made use of these terms. Those who were in favor of the ratification were called Federalists and those who opposed ratification were called Anti-Federalists. In the main the party of Hamilton, which bore the name of Federalist, was made up of those who worked for ratification, but not exclusively so. Some of those most active at first in opposition to the Constitution, joined with Hamilton. Likewise, the party of Jefferson, though in the main composed of those who opposed the acceptance of the Constitution, was not exclusively so, for many of those who worked untiringly for the ratification of the Constitution, joined with Jefferson in promoting the Democratic-Republican party.[1] Jefferson himself, though not a member of the convention which framed the Constitution, was favorable to its acceptance and helped set the new government on its feet. The Jefferson party, however, was the party of strict construction and was opposed to the extension of national power through the interpretation of the Constitution by the courts. The Federalists, on the other hand, desired a broad, liberal interpretation and full recognition of national authority.

It is not the purpose here to give, even in brief, the history of the political parties. All that is desired is to make plain the fact that the origin of the parties is to be traced to this fundamental issue involving the extent of the national power and its enlargement through constitutional interpretation. The antagonistic views that prevailed with respect to this question made it inevitable that differences of opinion would arise over specific questions of national policy; and out of these differences grew the political parties.

Separation of Powers and Party Development. — One other exceedingly significant point must be considered in accounting for the swift development of the parties; and that is the inevi-

[1] Woodburn, "Political Parties and Party Problems in the United States," p. 13.

table lack of harmony between the legislative and executive branches of the government under the separation of powers provided for by the Constitution. These departments were not only separated, but were to be kept so through a specific definition of the powers and duties of each. Moreover, each was to spy on the other, as it were, and both were to be held in their proper places by an elaborate system of checks and balances. Antagonism, friction, conflict are unavoidable under such an arrangement. Yet harmony, good will, and coöperation between these departments are essential in any smoothly working, efficient government. Without a reasonable amount of coöperation between these branches the machinery of government will not run. The need and value of this were not adequately comprehended by the framers of the Constitution, while the dangers were greatly exaggerated. Only one result could ensue. The gap, wide and deep, between the executive and legislative departments must be bridged over in some way or other. Some agency must be brought into being to establish a workable relationship between them. If this could not be done in a formal, constitutional manner, then some informal, extra-constitutional device must be discovered. This unifying, harmonizing function must be performed.

It happens that this gap is bridged, this unifying function is performed, by the political parties; and in doing this the parties render to the Nation one of their greatest services. It is the function which the cabinet performs in a parliamentary system of government, and without which ceaseless confusion and discord would prevail. The parties fill out with flesh and blood, so to speak, the skeleton organization of government set up by the Constitution. " Party organization acts as a connective tissue, enfolding the separate organs of government, and tending to establish a unity of control which shall adapt the government to the uses of popular sovereignty." [1]

It cannot be said that the parties actually grew out of this sharp separation of governmental departments, which, from the very nature of things, must be in close and harmonious relations; as we have seen, parties were forming even before the new government was set in motion. But it can be said that the development of the parties was greatly accentuated by this separation.

[1] Ford, "The Rise and Growth of American Politics," p. 215.

Moreover, the conclusion must be that, even though there had been in the beginning no clash of opinions over the interpretation of the Constitution and the powers of the States and of the Nation, sooner or later the political party or some agency similar to it would have been devised to discharge this unifying, co-ordinating function. It is, therefore, well within reason to assert that the American party system is the resultant of the peculiar constitutional organization of the legislative and executive departments, and it is proper to emphasize this particular unifying function of the parties in connection with a discussion of their origin and early development. In spite of the hopes and beliefs of the constitution makers to the contrary, parties were inevitable; the very structure of the government made them so.

Character of the Party System. — The American party system, like the English, is of the dual party type, and is fundamentally different in its nature from the group system that prevails in the countries of Continental Europe, where, in a single legislative assembly, there may be a dozen or more political parties. With the exception of a short period of transition following the break-up of the Federalist party, there have always been in the United States two leading parties which struggled for the control of the government. Many so-called third parties have appeared and disappeared in the course of the Nation's history, but the two-party character of the system has been consistently maintained.

The theory of the system is easily stated; and the mere statement of it makes plain the fact that it has never been in perfect operation. That could not reasonably be expected, indeed, since the system has never been fully understood nor fully approved by the American people. Until this is so, the system cannot be said to have had a fair trial. It is possible that it never will have a fair trial since, although the typical American view is that the government of the United States is a government by parties, there is a large and perhaps increasing number of people who profess not to believe in parties and seek to thwart the development of a thorough-going party system. The theory involves the division of the voters into two groups and the maintenance of two great organizations, evenly balanced as to numbers, under the guidance of experienced, capable leaders, and with local organizations sustained in every part of the Union. The two parties include all the voters and each must be effectively organized, from the Nation on down to the smallest political subdivision. These parties are like huge armies, trained and ready for battle. The object of their struggles is the control of the government, not for the purpose of destroying it, or undermining it, or subverting its constitutional structure, but for the purpose of using its power and its agencies for putting into effect certain public policies which the majority of the voters demand and for which the winning party stands. Each of the parties seeks to serve the whole Nation and therefore represents the whole Nation. The American party, according to the theory on which it rests, cannot represent a locality or a section, but must represent the whole country; it cannot represent a particular class, but must represent all classes; it cannot represent a special interest, but must stand for the totality of interests. If a party becomes the champion of any particular policy, like tariff protection, or free trade, it must rest its claims to preference and its advocacy of the policy for which it stands upon the benefits and advantages that will come to all classes and interests, and not upon those that will come to a particular class, or group, or section. Each party contends that the welfare of the whole Nation is best promoted and protected when it is in control of all the departments of government and its policies are being carried out. And because each party must stand for the whole State, representing all sections and all interests with equal fidelity, each must take side upon a large number of questions, involving many unrelated subjects. A party of a single issue cannot be a true national party, because the interests of the Nation are never bounded by the limits of a single problem. Back of each party's position upon questions of national policy, however, there is a more or less vague, indefinite political philosophy for which each has come to stand. Each becomes traditionally associated with certain tendencies, the champion of a few underlying principles, which are involved, sometimes directly and sometimes remotely, in the political controversies which arise. Thus, by way of illustration, the Democratic Party, which is the only one that has been in existence during the whole of the Nation's life, is traditionally the champion of individual or "personal" liberty and of the rights of the States against the Nation. The Federalist traditions concerning nationalism and a strong central government were inherited by the Republicans, through the Whigs.

As suggested, this theory of the party system has never been put into full practice. The parties have always fallen far short of what the theory demands. The system in practice bristles with imperfections. The parties have not always been truly national; indeed, the Democratic party is the only one that may be said to have met this requirement. They have not always been evenly balanced and fully organized in all localities. They have not always been actuated by a truly national spirit and free from the influence of special interests. Moreover, third parties have sprung up from time to time, and have interfered seriously at times with the normal working of the party system. Yet with all its imperfections and failures, and notwithstanding the obvious evils and difficult political problems to which it has given rise, the American party system has been a most useful agency in the development of the American democracy. It has been a help and not a hindrance. Because of it democracy is farther along the path of achievement, free government rests on a more solid foundation.[1]

Beginnings of Party Organization. — What has been said thus far has had to do in a general way with the political parties as agencies of government. It remains to treat in detail of the development and present status of party organization, and analyze and describe party methods, activities, and problems. The parties are dependent upon their organization. The character, success, and power of a party rest upon its organization. Party practices are evolved by it and party problems spring from it. It is, therefore, in the organization and machinery of the parties that the greatest interest lies for any one who wishes to comprehend clearly the real function and service of the party system.

Party organization in the United States is a highly developed, complicated thing. Like government it has evolved from the simple to the complex. Beginning with small, voluntary, isolated political clubs, it has grown into a huge political institution, nation-wide in its reach, with ramifications into every nook and

---

[1] For a fuller discussion of the theory and nature of the American party system and the influence of third parties, see Macy, "Political Parties in the United States," Chap. XII.

corner of the land and essential to the orderly on-going of governmental processes. Without their organizations the parties would fall to pieces; and without the parties the government would practically cease to operate.

It is difficult, without going into a lengthy historical dissertation, to make clear the real beginning of organized party activity. The subject may be approached from the top or from the bottom; from the manifestations of party life in national affairs, particularly as related to the nomination of candidates for the presidency and vice presidency, or from the evidences of a developing party spirit in the local communities revealed by the organization of voluntary societies or clubs for the propagation of specific governmental policies. The Congressional Caucus, the first device for the selection of party candidates for the presidency proved weak and did not long survive, however, while the local organizations grew strong and possessed elements of permanent value. While proper enough, therefore, to begin with a description of the Congressional Caucus, it is better to put the emphasis of first mention upon the voluntary local club. It is, indeed, out of the habit of association on the part of the common people as shown in these local societies that the enduring party organization has grown. The fact is that this permanent party organization grew from the local community on up to the central government. Even before the Revolution the local caucus was known and its value proven. Hence, when the time came for real party life and party struggles, the agency for effective action was at hand.

To Thomas Jefferson, skilled in the art of political management, belongs the credit of first discerning clearly the value of the local association as an instrument of party activity. When, as Secretary of State, he found himself in serious controversy with the Washington administration, he began to organize his followers in opposition. An ardent advocate of individual liberty and local self-government, he encouraged the formation of local Democratic Clubs to resist what he considered the central government's encroachments. This work went quietly on until the Jeffersonian or Democratic-Republican party was locally organized, to a greater or less degree, in all the States. The administration party, the followers of Washington and Hamilton, made little effort to organize local societies in support of their policies. In fact, the Federalists never were thus locally organized. They developed and used the Congressional Caucus at the top, but they apparently cared nothing for the local caucus at the bottom. The result was vigor and permanency for the party of Jefferson, which still lives in the Democratic party, while the Federalist party soon became extinct. The American political party is institutional in character; it fulfils local as well as general needs. And it is the local organizations of the kind Jefferson encouraged which afford proof of this and give to the parties enduring vitality.

The Congressional Caucus. — In its national aspect, party organization has always centered around the nomination and election of candidates for the presidency and vice presidency. Various nomination methods were used before the well-known convention system was established. A word about these is desirable.

The first agency set up for the selection of party candidates for these high offices was the Congressional Caucus to which reference has already been made. As the name implies it was an institution that grew up within the national legislature. It was first used as a nominating agency by the Federalists in connection with the presidential election of 1800. Its meeting was secret and was attended only by Federalist members of Congress. A candidate for the presidency and one for the vice presidency were nominated and the members of the caucus were pledged to try to obtain the electoral votes of their respective States for these candidates. News of the caucus leaked out, however, and soon after the Republican members of Congress held a similar meeting in secret and nominated candidates. At the next presidential election, in 1804, the Congressional Caucus again appeared, but this time its meeting was not secret. The Federalists did not hold a caucus because of their demoralized condition as a party. The Republicans, however, used it openly and continued to use it as the regular method of selecting candidates until its final overthrow. The last Caucus held was that of 1824.

To understand the Congressional Caucus it is necessary to recall the constitutional provision relating to the choice of President and Vice President as it was before the twelfth amendment was adopted.[1] The presidential electors, chosen by the States,

[1] Above, p. 39.

were to vote for two persons, — the one having the highest number of votes, provided this was a majority of the whole number of electors, to become President, and the one receiving the next highest number to become Vice President. This might have been a satisfactory arrangement if the political parties had not appeared on the scene. Each of the parties was eager to control both offices; yet there was no assurance that this result could be attained unless there was agreement upon candidates. The majority party might divide its vote among several candidates and so throw away its opportunity. To prevent this, if possible, the Federalists made use of the Congressional Caucus, and the Republicans, seeing the value of the scheme, also took it up. The candidates went before the voters with increased prestige because of the caucus indorsement.

The caucus was never popular. It was constantly under suspicion and, in fact, met with decided opposition from the beginning. There were several reasons for this. For one thing, the people did not approve of the secrecy that surrounded its meetings. It appeared to be an attempt on the part of a few leaders to gain control of the new government, possibly to subvert it. Again, the Caucus was clearly in violation of the spirit and purpose of the Constitution. The presidency was not to be a prize for party contests. To accept the Caucus plan was, in substance, simply to set aside the constitutional method of choosing the President. Furthermore, and perhaps most important of all, the Caucus endangered the independent relationship between the legislative and executive departments. On the one hand it threatened the subjection of the President to Congress which might give its indorsement to a subservient weakling, and on the other, the submission of Congress to a powerful President who might curry favor with its members and either perpetuate himself in office or dictate his successor. Either was dangerous and subversive of the Constitution. The separation of the departments was a safeguard of the people's liberties and was to be scrupulously maintained. For these and other reasons, the Caucus became an object of increasingly bitter opposition until its abandonment was forced upon Congress.

Yet, beyond question, the Caucus served a highly useful purpose. It furnished leadership for the parties at a time when capable leadership was of vast importance. At that time modern means of communication and transmission of intelligence were entirely lacking. It was difficult for the people throughout the States to keep in touch with national affairs. Under the circumstances the natural leaders were those who were at the national capital in charge of the government. Members of Congress understood both the needs and problems of the Nation and the desires and demands of their constituents. No other group of citizens was in a position to render so large a service in the way of crystallizing party sentiment in support of party policies and candidates. Through the Caucus, members of Congress exerted a powerful unifying influence, and in this way did a necessary work. The consciousness of party life was not keen, at first, and not generally diffused. The Congressional Caucus, therefore, was an agency that was suited to the time in which it originated. Within Congress, party lines were sharply drawn; without, they were not. It was natural, therefore, for its members to seek to direct their respective parties in the selection of candidates as well as in the formulation of policies. Moreover, the Caucus tended to establish that coöperation between the legislative and executive departments which experience has shown to be so essential. It was a step, the first step, toward party solidarity and party responsibility for the conduct of the national government. Valuable as it was, however, for the time being, the Congressional Caucus was not suitable as a permanent system of nominating presidential candidates and soon outlived its usefulness.

REFERENCES

BEARD. *American Government and Politics*, Edition 1914, Chap. VI.
FORD. *The Rise and Growth of American Politics*, Chaps. VII, XII, XXIII, XXIV, XXV.
GOODNOW. *Politics and Administration*, Chaps. VII, VIII, IX.
JONES. *Readings on Parties and Elections*, pp. 28–46.
MACY. *Party Organization and Machinery*, Chaps. I, II, XXII, XXIII.
MACY. *Political Parties in the United States*, Chaps. I, II, XII.
MEYER. *Nominating Systems*, Chap. I.
OSTROGORSKI. *Democracy and the Party System in the United States*, Chap. I.
SMITH. *The Spirit of American Government*, Chap. VIII.
WILSON. *Constitutional Government in the United States*, Chap. VIII.
WOODBURN. *Political Parties and Party Problems in the United States*, Chaps. I, II.

CHAPTER XV

THE NATIONAL CONVENTION

THE passing of the nominating caucus left the parties without a regular, official way of selecting candidates. A period of confusion in party organization ensued. No systematic procedure was observed. Miscellaneous methods of making nominations were everywhere used. Sometimes presidential candidates were brought forward by State legislatures, acting formally and officially. Sometimes nominations were made by caucuses in the State legislatures, acting in a spirit and manner similar to those of the old Congressional Caucus. Again, candidates were placed in nomination by local and State conventions, by mass meetings, by newspapers, by individuals.[1] One or all of these methods, indeed, might be employed in a single State. The period between the decline of the Congressional Caucus and the establishment of the convention system was one of transition and the nomination processes were informal, unauthoritative, and inconclusive. There was a spirit of revolt against dictation by party leaders and a demand for a thorough democratization of party organization. The ultimate outcome was the nominating convention which has played so big and vital a part in American politics. This from the beginning was fundamentally different from the nominating caucus, which was an unauthorized body. The convention was made the authorized agent of the party and received its power from the members of the party acting through their local organizations. The rise of the convention, in fact, is one of the evidences of the rising tide of democracy which characterize the "Jacksonian period" of American history.

The first national party convention was held in 1831 by the Anti-Masons, a third party. This was a new thing in national politics, but the convention as a nominating agency had already been used in the States. In 1832 both of the leading parties, the

[1] Dallinger, "Nominations for Elective Office," p. 29.

National Republicans and the Democrats, called conventions. From that time until the present, with the single exception of the Whigs in 1836, the candidates of all parties for the presidency and vice presidency have been nominated by conventions. The convention system, therefore, has been in use during the greater part of the Nation's history, and until very recent days remained essentially what it was in the beginning, although necessarily it has been modified somewhat to meet the needs of party growth. What the future has in store for it, future events must reveal. It has been an institution of such vital significance and interest and has influenced so profoundly the development of American democracy, that further treatment of it is necessary. It is the apex of a huge system of party machinery which involves all the States of the Union and all their multitudinous political subdivisions. In no other country of the world is there anything like the American national convention.[1]

The Convention's Functions and Composition. — The functions of the convention are threefold. First, to formulate and officially adopt for each presidential election the party platform, the principles and policies for which the party stands; second, to nominate its candidates for the presidency and the vice presidency; and, third, to choose a National Committee which will direct the campaign for the election of the party ticket and take the necessary steps for calling the next convention. The convention is the supreme party authority, and in discharging these functions, its action is, in theory, the action of the party itself. It is the party's legislature to which has been delegated the supreme power of determining party policies and choosing the highest party officers. Inasmuch as the candidate of the successful party becomes President, and the policies of that party may be embodied in the law of the land, these functions of the national convention are of transcendent importance. Yet its work is by no means always done with wisdom and scrupulous regard for the Nation's best interests. It is usually, in fact, the scene of astute, if not astounding, political manipulation. Nowhere else has the "game of politics" been played more zealously and, at times, more recklessly.

The national convention is composed of delegates representing the States and Territories, and is governed by rules of its own

[1] Below, p. 498.

making. The practices of the leading parties have differed somewhat with respect to the manner of choosing delegates and the representation of the Territories. By a long-standing rule each State is entitled to twice as many delegates as it has Senators and Representatives in Congress. Each Territory and dependency and the District of Columbia are given representation as provided for in the rules under which the convention has been called. Thus in the Democratic convention of 1912 each of these had six delegates, while in the Republican convention of that year there were six delegates from Hawaii and two each from the District of Columbia, Alaska, Porto Rico, and the Philippines. The total number of Democratic delegates was 1094 and of Republican delegates 1078. In addition to the regular delegates there is an equal number of alternates who do not participate in the proceedings of the convention except in the absence of regular delegates. It is seen that the convention is a large body, entirely too large for a deliberative assembly. It should be stated, however, that though there is abundant need, the conventions as such seldom deliberate. That function is usually attended to by the convention's leaders and managers in secret conferences held whenever and wherever occasion demands.

Selection of Delegates. — Reference was just made to the fact that the Democratic and Republican practices differ somewhat in the manner of choosing delegates. The method to be pursued by the Republicans is always stated in the official call for the convention issued by the National Committee. With the Democrats this is left to the States and Territories to decide for themselves. The Republican practice is to hold a convention in each State, for the purpose of choosing the four delegates-at-large, and their alternates, who correspond to the United States Senators, and a district convention in each congressional district to choose the two delegates and their alternates, who correspond to the Representative of the district in the lower house of Congress. Where direct primary laws have been made to apply to convention delegates, the selection is made by the members of the party at the polls, and conventions are not held. The congressional district has long been recognized by the Republicans as the unit of representation. The territorial delegates are chosen at conventions. This same general practice is now observed by the Democratic party, though not in all of the States.

The Democrats are traditionally the champions of the States as against any other political authority, and formerly assigned to the State convention the task of selecting the entire delegation to the national convention. This is still done in a number of the States. A common practice with the Democrats is for the entire State convention to choose the delegates-at-large, just as the Republican conventions do, and for the delegation to the State convention from each congressional district to name the national delegates to which the district is entitled. This selection by the district delegations is then ratified by the State convention. In this way the congressional districts are recognized and at the same time the character of State delegations is maintained. This makes it possible for the State convention to instruct the entire delegation to the national convention, — a practice common with the Democrats and entirely in harmony with Democratic traditions which look to the State as the important unit in party action.[1] These instructions may be made under the unit rule, recognized by the Democrats, by which the entire vote of a State delegation in the national convention is cast according to the wishes of a majority of its members; the individual delegate cannot vote as he pleases, but must vote as the majority of the delegation direct. The Republican State conventions have no authority to impose the unit rule and may give instructions only to the delegates-at-large chosen by them. The district delegates receive their whole authority from their respective district conventions and are subject to instructions only from them. In either party, when no instructions are given, each delegate is free to act as he pleases.

This, in a few words, is a statement of the convention method of choosing the national delegates, — a method that has been in use from the very beginning. It is based wholly on the representative principle and has been accepted by all parties. In times past it has been the only method of choosing the delegates, but that is not true to-day. To a marked degree the representative principle as applied to party activities has been pushed aside in recent years and that of direct action by party members has been substituted for it. To a large extent the convention method of nominating candidates for public office has been supplanted by the direct primary, under which the nominations are made

[1] Woodburn, "Political Parties and Party Problems in the United States," p. 158.

directly by the members of the party, without the aid of intermediary bodies of any kind. Practically all the States have adopted the direct primary in one form or another. In a number of them it has been made to include the selection of delegates to the national convention. The primary plan has proven very popular and it may be assumed with some assurance, it would seem, that, if the convention system of nominating presidential candidates is retained, all delegates to the conventions, in time, will be chosen directly by the party voters, and be instructed by them as to their preferences with respect to presidential candidates. In a number of States this is now done. The question of whether the convention system of nomination will be retained is problematical, however. In the last few years an insistent, nation-wide demand has arisen for the nomination of candidates for the presidency and the vice-presidency at direct primaries. The enactment of a national law by Congress to provide for this seems probable. It has already been recommended to Congress by President Wilson. If a law of this kind is not enacted, the result will be attained substantially through presidential preference primaries established by State authority.

It is proper to note here that for some years fundamental readjustments have been taking place in party life. Under the powerful pressure of an aroused democracy, with clearer conceptions of its privileges and its obligations, old issues and methods and forms are giving way, wholly or in part, to new ones. What the ultimate outcome will be, no one can tell. It is certain, however, that the national convention, if retained at all, will be radically different from what it has been for three quarters of a century.

Convention Organization and Procedure. — The manner in which the national convention assembles, organizes, and does its work is full of interest and deserves some attention. All arrangements for the convention are made by the National Committee, which at the proper time sets the whole intricate system of party machinery in motion in preparation for this great quadrennial party assembly. Some six months before the accustomed time for the convention, which usually is held in the June or July preceding the presidential election, the National Committee issues the official call. Although there is always more or less activity before this in connection with the approaching election, particularly among the candidates for the party nomination, the call represents the real beginning of the party's campaign. The Democratic call is much briefer than the Republican. It states the time and place of holding the convention, the number of delegates to which each State, Territory, and dependency is entitled, and invites, in general terms, those who are in sympathy with the party's principles to participate in the selection of delegates. The Republican call not only provides for these points, but also specifies the manner and time in which the delegates are to be chosen and their credentials sent to the secretary of the National Committee. It also states what must be done in case there are contesting delegations from any State or district.[1] A copy of the call is sent to each of the State central committees which, in turn, prepare and issue the summons for the necessary State and district conventions. The process of choosing the delegates then begins.

When the convention assembles it is under the direction of the National Committee, which, through its subcommittees, has made detailed arrangements. A large hall is provided and profusely decorated, officers and their assistants are appointed, the seating of the State delegations arranged for, and everything done that can be done to make the convention pass off smoothly and expeditiously.

At the time designated the convention is called to order by the chairman of the National Committee. After a prayer, with which the proceedings are always opened, the official call for the convention is read. Then the chairman announces the name of the man whom the committee has selected for temporary chairman of the convention and also the other temporary officers. The committee's choice for chairman is usually approved by the convention without division, although sometimes opposition has arisen and occasionally the committee's nomination has been rejected. After his election by the convention the temporary chairman proceeds to deliver a carefully prepared speech, — a " key note " speech, as it is called, — the purpose of which is to arouse enthusiasm and to help keep the party harmonious and in condition for the coming struggle. At the close of this address, the convention, upon motion made and carried, pro-

[1] Ray, "An Introduction to Political Parties and Practical Politics," p. 146; Jones, " Readings on Parties and Elections," p. 86.

ceeds to appoint its committees. There are four of these, — the committees on credentials, permanent organization, rules and order of business, and resolutions. The appointment is made in this manner. The roll of the States is called in alphabetical order, and in turn the chairmen of the delegations either arise and announce the names of the members chosen by the delegations to represent them upon the committees, or send the names to the secretary who reads them to the convention. Each State has one representative on each committee. With the naming of the committees the first session of the convention normally comes to a close, and adjournment is taken to await the reports of the committees which begin their labors at once.

The first report due in the regular order is that of the committee on credentials, whose duty it is to determine those who have right to seats in the convention and make up the permanent roll. The temporary roll has been made prior to the meeting of the convention by the National Committee. Sometimes there are few and sometimes there are many contesting delegations. The National Committee must pass upon the claims of each and decide the question as to who shall take part in the preliminary proceedings of the convention. This is at times a very difficult task and in connection with it sometimes serious abuses have arisen. Delegations claiming seats and dissatisfied with the decision of the National Committee may take the matter before the credentials committee and seek recognition of their claims, for the work of the National Committee cannot stand as conclusive. The convention itself must determine its own membership, and it does this largely through its committee on credentials. It may be that there are no contests at all. In that case the committee reports at once when the convention assembles for its second session, and its report is speedily adopted. It may be, on the other hand, that there are serious contests which are difficult of solution. In that case, many hours, perhaps even several days, may be required for the committee to go over the evidence and formulate its report. The convention cannot go on with important work, however, until it has decided who have the right to participate in its proceedings. When the committee finally reports, the convention must take action upon its findings. A unanimous report is almost certain to be approved. If the committee is divided, usually the majority report is accepted, although sometimes the minority report is substituted for it.

After the credentials of its members have been passed upon and approved, the convention is ready to effect a permanent organization. The committee reports the names of a permanent chairman, the secretaries and vice presidents. Usually there is no opposition to the committee's recommendations and its report is promptly approved. The permanent chairman takes his place, makes a brief address, and calls for the report of the committee on rules and order of business. Ordinarily there is no controversy over the rules, those of the preceding convention being adopted without opposition. Now and then, however, spectacular convention fights occur over this question, as was the case in the Republican convention of 1912. With the adoption of the rules which are to govern the proceedings, the convention is fully organized and ready for the work for which it assembled. All that is done up to this point is merely preliminary in character, and yet it may be of the profoundest significance because the real nature of the platform and the actual choice of the presidential candidate may have been determined in making up the convention's permanent roll.

The next order of business is the report of the committee on resolutions, whose duty it is to frame the party platform. " The platform is an address to the people, consisting sometimes of various 'planks,' or a series of resolutions, sometimes of an address without division into numbered sections, containing the principles and program of the party. It arraigns the opposing party for its errors, criticises it for its course, joins issue with it on prominent policies before the public, and gives promise as to what the party will do if it is elected to or retained in power. In the platform the managers usually try to conciliate every section of conflicting party opinion, and they frequently produce a document which treats with 'prudent ambiguity' the questions on which there is division within the party."[1] The adoption of the platform may be the occasion of a bitter struggle in the open convention between party factions which are fighting for ascendancy, as was the case in the famous Democratic " free silver " convention of 1896. On the other hand, it may be adopted without division. Unfailingly, however, sharp con-

[1] Woodburn, "Political Parties and Party Problems in the United States," p. 181.

troversies occur in the committee on resolutions over what shall be included in the platform. Many of these are settled by compromise or in other ways, so as to enable the committee to bring in a unanimous report, but sometimes the issue is so acute that agreement is impossible, and majority and minority reports are made to the convention where the controversy is finally settled.

Nomination of Candidates. — Following the adoption of the platform, the next order of business is the selection of the party's nominee for the presidency. This is the big event of the convention, the thing to which the delegates have been looking eagerly forward and upon which the attention of the whole Nation is centered. It is always a moment of intense interest when the convention takes up the task of nominating its candidate. It usually marks the culmination of a long period of excitement and suspense, during which the claims of rival aspirants for the nomination have been before the country, and the delegates to the convention have been selected. It may be that the contest is exceedingly close between two candidates and the outcome will depend upon the votes of a few uninstructed delegates. It may be, again, that there are several candidates, evenly balanced in strength, and a long deadlock is in prospect. The nomination may be made on the first ballot, or the second, or the third; and then again, it may not be made until the twentieth, or the thirtieth, or the fortieth. It depends upon a number of things, — the availability and strength of the candidates, the skill of their managers, the fidelity of delegates to their instructions, the temper of the convention, the state of the public mind. The prize at stake is leadership of the party for the time being and perhaps the attainment of the highest office and greatest honor possible to an American citizen. The intense interest of the convention and of the Nation as a whole is fully warranted.

The formal nomination procedure is simple. The roll of the States is called in alphabetical order and each is given a chance to name a candidate. One near the head of the roll which has no candidate of its own, but favors the candidate of another which comes farther down in the list, may yield to the latter, in order that its favorite may be placed in nomination early in the proceedings. A candidate from one State may be placed in nomination by another State. This is frequently done for the sake of the influence it may have upon delegates who may be wavering or in doubt as to what they should do. The nominations are accompanied by speeches which have been carefully prepared and which are characterized by fervid, white-hot oratory, and sometimes by genuine eloquence. These are the occasions for wild and stormy demonstrations for the rival candidates. As the calling of the roll proceeds, speeches seconding the various nominations are made. These are shorter than the main speeches, but vie with them in eulogistic oratory.

After the speech-making is concluded, balloting upon the names presented begins at once. The roll of the States is called again and the chairman of each delegation in turn announces its vote. If no candidate has the necessary number of votes at the conclusion of the first ballot, another ballot is ordered and the roll is called again just as before. This continues until some candidate receives the necessary majority. If a large number of ballots is required, the convention may adjourn from time to time to give opportunity for rest and for conferences among the leaders. These intermissions are periods of manipulation, intrigue, and feverish excitement. At last, perhaps as the result of deals and combinations, some candidate receives the required vote and is declared nominated. With respect to the vote required the leading parties differ. The Republicans nominate by a simple majority, while the Democrats require a two-thirds vote. This "two-thirds rule" and the "unit rule," to which reference has been previously made, are the two important points of difference between the practices of the two parties.

The naming of the party's candidate for the vice presidency is the convention's next work. The same procedure is observed as for the nomination of the presidential candidate. The interest in the vice presidential nomination is usually slight, and the convention's proceeding is perfunctory. Occasionally, however, it is the real center of interest, as was the case with the Republican convention of 1900 which nominated Theodore Roosevelt for the vice presidency and renominated William McKinley for the presidency by acclamation.

There remains to the convention the appointment of the National Committee, to be described in the next chapter, and two special committees to notify officially the candidates of their nomination, a ceremony that takes place some weeks later and at which the candidates make elaborate speeches of acceptance. The convention then adjourns *sine die*.

Controlling Forces and Environment. — It should be clearly understood that what has been said in this brief sketch of the national convention has to do almost entirely with its formal structure and routine procedure. And this by no means is always the most important. By itself it is insufficient; for the national convention, like the government itself, cannot be understood from a mere study of its structure and outward appearance. Back of these lie the informal, unauthorized processes of practical politics; the play of all those hidden forces, — personal, factional, economic, social, — which control the affairs of men and nations and which converge and clash with one another under cover of the convention's formal procedure. The outward action may be, very likely is, the result of secret manipulation and bargains. What takes place behind the scenes may be, very probably is, much more significant than that which takes place on the stage in front. It is therefore supremely essential in trying to comprehend the full significance of the national convention, that judgment of *what* was done be tempered with knowledge of *why* it was done; that the work of the open session be studied in relation to the unrevealed actions of the secret caucuses and other midnight gatherings which seek to control the convention's proceedings. Only in this way can a perverted view of what the convention is be avoided.

Moreover, the work of the convention must be considered in the light of its surroundings, of its environment. The huge convention hall, seating ten or twelve thousand spectators, crowded to the limits with the adherents of the aspiring candidates; the terrific noise; the loudly playing bands; the tremendous enthusiasm, genuine and otherwise; the fervid oratory; the processions; the songs; the banners; the vociferous and long demonstrations; the cheering; the stamping of feet; the waving of flags; the carefully and shrewdly planned appeals to partisan spirit; all these are parts of the national convention and give it character. Their influence upon its actions cannot be ignored. All the elements in the picture must be observed and understood if the right perspective is to be obtained. It is not possible to elaborate them here, through want of space; only a warning can be given that they be not overlooked.[1]

The Convention in Theory and Practice. — In theory the convention is a most admirable institution. It is built wholly on the principle of representation. It stands for the millions of party members, owes its authority to them, and assembles to carry out their will in the formulation of a platform and the selection of candidates. It is the only body that can speak authoritatively for the whole party. It is composed of delegates chosen at State and district conventions, and these are made up of delegates elected at county conventions, held in each county of the State or district. The county conventions are composed of delegates from the various townships, and wards — or other election units — into which each county is divided. And the township and ward delegates are chosen at township and ward caucuses, which are primary assemblies, composed in theory of the entire party membership within them. So the authority of the national convention is clearly derived from the party voters. The convention represents all interests and all factions within the party. Its sole purpose is to give expression to the party will. It is, in short, a theoretically perfect representative body. "It passes the highest test of a political institution in a democratic community. It admits of the purest application of the principle of representation or delegated authority. Step by step the voice of each individual voter can, in theory, be transmitted from delegate to delegate, until finally it finds its perfect expression in the legislature, the executive, or the judiciary." [2]

That the convention system has been of very great value to the parties and at times has rendered high service to the Nation cannot be questioned. It has been a tremendously powerful unifying force. In the party convention all phases of the party's problems are considered. One of its chief functions is the conciliation of antagonistic elements within the party and the harmonizing of opposing forces. "The convention thus, in theory, lies at the foundation of party success. It perfects

---

[1] For brief though excellent descriptions of the national convention, see Bryce, "The American Commonwealth," Chap. LXX, Vol. II, p. 186, New and Revised Edition; Ostrogorski, "Democracy and the Party System," Chap. VIII, p. 133; Jones, "Readings on Parties and Elections," pp. 80-106.

[2] Meyer, "Nominating Systems," p. 49.

party organization, measures its strength, conciliates its factions, defines its issues, selects its candidates, and arouses enthusiasm."[1] These are all exceedingly important things; they must be done and done effectively if party government is to be successful. In so far as the convention has accomplished them it has been an agency of the highest value.

The convention in practice, however, has not always proven to be the admirable institution which the theory calls for. It has been far from perfect; its representation of the party voters far from ideal. The system, of which the national convention is the apex, is too complex. The convention is too far removed from the voters. Their voice becomes too much weakened, their authority and control too much diffused, before the national convention is reached. The sense of personal responsibility to the voters on the part of delegates becomes less and less keen the farther they are removed from the original local primary. The result frequently is gross misrepresentation of the true party opinion.

Moreover, the convention system has lent itself to the uses of the political bosses and machines, and has shielded corrupt practices. The nomination of candidates has too frequently been merely the ratification of a " slate " arranged in advance by the party leaders. This has been true particularly of State and local conventions. The framing of the platform has too often been under the skillful direction of the agents of special interests which seek legislation in their own favor, at the expense of the general public, or oppose legislation which is designed to prevent them from doing things that are detrimental to the public. The packing of caucuses, the bribery of delegates, the objectionable use of proxies, the fake contests among delegations, the manipulation of credentials, the log-rolling, the disorderly proceedings, the unfair rulings from the chair, — these are all familiar things in connection with the convention system. It is not to be understood of course that all conventions are characterized by these objectionable practices; far from it. It is the purpose here merely to suggest some of the serious evils which have grown up and which have made the convention system so imperfect in operation. And because of these things nomination by delegate conventions has become

[1] Meyer, "Nominating Systems," p. 53.

discredited. Under the malign influence of machine politics the conventions have increasingly misrepresented the popular will.

The result is the almost startling development of the direct primary, by which nominations are made directly by the voters. The convention as a nominating agency for local and State officers is rapidly giving place to the primary. A State-wide compulsory primary, applying to all State officers, including United States Senators, is the prevailing system of nomination. Everywhere there are the same secrecy, the same legal protection, and the same safeguards against corrupt practices as are afforded for the regular elections. The general acceptance and approval of direct nominations mark a big step forward in the movement for democracy, — and, as previously suggested, it was inevitable that sooner or later the suggestion be made that the principle be applied to the selection of presidential and vice presidential candidates. The presidency has become the one truly representative national office and the chief weapon in the hands of the people for accomplishing their will. It has already been democratized to a large degree, as compared with what the framers of the Constitution intended, but by no means to the extent that the people desire. It is therefore natural that the wide acceptance of the direct primary in nominating State officers and members of Congress should cause a demand for it for the nomination of Presidents. No one can say what the result of this demand will be. It may be the complete elimination of the national convention, the most interesting and most spectacular feature of American party organization.

It should be borne in mind, however, that the system of direct nominations has not proven in practice to be entirely satisfactory. Its results, in fact, have fallen far short of what many of its sponsors expected from it. It cannot be said, as yet, that it has acquired a permanent status as an institution of government. In some of the States, as in Wisconsin, which was a pioneer in the adoption of the primary plan, a distinct reaction has set in against it. Many progressive thinkers who helped establish the system, and whose belief in fundamental democracy cannot be questioned, have grave doubts as to its permanent value and its efficacy in preventing boss domination and the selection of unfit candidates for office. What the future will bring forth with respect to nomination procedure, the future must reveal. The primary may remain as it has been, or a regenerated, reconstructed convention system may take its place. The one fact which seems to be beyond question is that the people are determined to control their government in all of its phases; if not by one process, then by another. The government is to be democratic in more than name.

REFERENCES

BRYCE. *The American Commonwealth*, Edition 1910, Vol. II, Chaps. LXIX, LXX.
FORD. *The Rise and Growth of American Politics*, Chap. XVI.
MEYER. *Nominating Systems*, Chaps. IV, V.
OSTROGORSKI. *Democracy and the Party System in the United States*, Chaps. II, III, IV, V, VIII.
RAY. *An Introduction to Political Parties and Practical Politics*, Chap. VIII.
REINSCH. *Readings on American Federal Government*, Chap. XVI.
WOODBURN. *Political Parties and Party Problems in the United States*, Chaps. X, XI, XII.

CHAPTER XVI

Party Machinery and Methods — National.

There are two parts to the organization of the political parties. One is temporary, transitory, in character, and the other is permanent. The conventions constitute the one and the party committees the other. The conventions are called into existence at stated times for specific purposes, — the nomination of candidates and the adoption of party platforms. In States where nominations are made at direct primaries, the State conventions have only the platform function to discharge. But even where the convention system remains intact, the convention is in existence for only a very short time. In a single day, perhaps, or two or three days, its work is completed, and the convention ceases to be. For a few brief hours it embodies the whole party and exercises the highest party power; then it is gone, — a mere incident in history.

The committees, however, are enduring, permanent institutions. As is the case with the House of Representatives, the committees in existence at any particular time have definite life periods, say, two or four years. Their members hold office for definite terms. At the end of the periods the old committees pass from power and new ones take their places. The personnel of the new committees may be different, wholly or in part, from that of the old, yet as party institutions the committees are continuous bodies. The old committees do not disappear, until the new ones take charge. The result in each party is a great, complicated system of machinery that is constantly in operation for the promotion of the party's interests. Upon the efficient working of this machinery, made up of the various committees, the party is largely dependent for its success. A knowledge of the committees, and their work and methods, is essential, therefore, to a proper understanding of the party system.

The permanent committees constitute the administrative branch of the party's organization. There are two main functions that must be performed. One is to formulate and give expression to the party will, and the other is to execute that will, to carry it into effect. The first is legislative in nature and is performed by the party conventions, which may be called the party's legislatures. The second is administrative in nature and is performed by the permanent committees, which, taken together, may be called the party's executive. It is the supreme business of the party committees, or executive, to win elections for the party so that its agents may control the government and its will be embodied in public policies. The object of all party activities is the control of the government, and the function of the committees is to make this possible. In theory the convention and the primary represent the direct authority of the party members. The committees, however, are not so directly popular in their origin, but represent the convention or the primary. They are the agents for executing the will of these popular bodies.

Each convention or primary district has its own committee. These districts in the main correspond to the various governmental units. There are as many party committees, therefore, as there are important governmental areas for which public officers must be elected. It is obvious that there is in the whole Nation an enormous number of party officials. It may be said with assurance that there are more persons holding official positions in the two leading party organizations than there are in all the elective civil offices in the entire country above those of the township and the ward. This means that there is a veritable army of workers who are constantly active in an official way in support of each party. They foster and promote the party's interests not only during the heat and struggle of election campaigns, but also during the quieter periods between elections when party enthusiasm runs low and party spirit becomes sluggish. It is the mission of party committeemen not only to lead in and direct the party's contests, but also, at all times, to nourish and encourage party sentiment and build up the party organization so that it will be always in good fighting condition. The duties of committeemen, particularly of members of the more important committees, are sometimes arduous, but as a rule are performed with a fidelity which excites admiration; and particularly so in view of the fact that they serve without compensation. It is true that many of them receive appointments to offices as rewards for party service, and no doubt pull the wires to obtain these honors. But a great many committeemen, as well as other party workers, give to their parties faithful and effective service in unheralded manner without thought of recognition or reward of any kind. This is particularly the case in the rural districts. The real strength of the parties, as a matter of fact, lies in the devotion and activity of men of this type. Considering the selfishness and crookedness which so frequently characterize party struggles, it is astonishing to one unfamiliar with conditions to discover in America so large an amount of genuinely disinterested party activity as is to be found in all of the parties.

The National Committee. — The committee of highest authority, standing at the head of the permanent party machinery, is the National Committee, to which frequent reference has been made in connection with the national convention. Its place is one of the highest importance and responsibility, for upon its work depends, in large degree, the party's chances of controlling the presidency, and through it the whole executive branch of the national government. Its field of operation is the Nation itself. It is the one permanent party institution which stands for the unity of the whole party. It represents all the States and Territories and is concerned with the party fortunes in all parts of the Nation.

The National Committee owes its authority to the national convention by which it is chosen every four years when the convention assembles to nominate the national ticket. Each State and each Territory has one representative. Though the formal election is by the national convention, the actual selection of its members is made by the various State and Territorial delegations to the convention. Each delegation is free to make its own choice, designating one of its own members or some other active and influential party leader in the State or Territory it represents. Strictly speaking, this choice is a mere nomination to the convention, which makes the official appointment of the committee. However, the convention always accepts the recommendations which the delegations make.

The new committee thus chosen takes charge of the party's affairs immediately upon the adjournment of the convention and continues in power for four years until the next national convention is organized. During the short time that the convention is in existence it embodies the supreme party power and takes back to itself the power delegated to the National Committee by the last convention. Before it adjourns the convention confers some of its powers upon the new National Committee, which begins at once to plan for the presidential campaign which the party has just started.

The first thing the committee must do is to effect its own organization by the election of its chairman, vice chairman, secretary, and treasurer, and the appointment of the necessary subcommittees. The election of the chairman is a merely formal procedure notwithstanding the fact that he is by long odds the most important member of the committee. The real selection of the chairman is made by the party's candidate for the presidency. The relationship between the chairman and the candidate is so close, and the latter has so much at stake in the election, that the propriety of his naming the chairman is everywhere conceded. He may select some one from within the committee or some one from without. The committee then takes formal action and the candidate's nominee becomes the committee's chairman and as such the head of the entire national party organization. His position is one of great power and responsibility, and upon his understanding of practical politics, his capacity for leadership, and his initiative and skill in managing the campaign, the fortunes of the party largely depend.

Aside from the chairman, the most important official is perhaps the secretary, who becomes the executive officer of the committee. He has charge of the committee's headquarters and is called upon to do a vast amount of detailed work and keep intimately in touch with every phase of the committee's activities. He is not so much in the lime light as is the chairman, but upon him in high degree the chairman and the committee are dependent for the success of their plans. The treasurer is also a very responsible and important officer, for to him chiefly falls the duty of raising the funds necessary for the campaign. Without adequate funds the committee is seriously handicapped and a successful campaign can hardly be waged. The nature of his duties gives to the treasurer a pivotal place in the committee's organization. In his selection, also, the presidential candidate is likely to have some voice, for the outcome of the election may be materially influenced by the sources of the party funds and the manner in which they are solicited and collected. Many grave political scandals have arisen in connection with campaign contributions.

National Committee and National Convention. — The work of the National Committee naturally divides into three rather unrelated parts; first, its duties in connection with the national convention; second, its management of the presidential election campaign; and, third, its activities during the quiescent period between elections. With respect to the order of their occurrence, the committee's convention work comes last; in fact, just at the end of the four-year term. The first work of a new National Committee is to direct the campaign for the election of its presidential candidate.

All arrangements for the national convention are made by the committee. The first step is taken when the chairman summons the committee for the purpose of preparing the official call for the convention, and determining the time and place at which it shall be held. This meeting is usually held in December or January, some six months prior to the time of the national convention. The content of the official call has been given in the last chapter.[1] Nothing more need be said about it here, except to call attention to the fact that the Republican practice of specifying the manner in which delegates to the convention should be chosen has at times given rise to serious trouble. The committee establishes the official party rule covering the selection of delegates unless the convention itself chooses to say what the rule shall be. Any deviation, then, from the procedure determined upon by the committee will cause contests and disputes within the party which may lead to party disruption. This, in fact, was one of the difficulties confronting the Republican convention in 1912 and which led to the split that resulted in the organization of the Progressive party. Some of the delegates had been elected under State primary laws that were at variance with the official call. The National

[1] Above, p. 195.

Committee, in passing upon the claims of contesting delegations caused by this conflict, chose to stand by its own rule, even in the face of party disaster. This action met with such condemnation, however, that the committee has been forced to propose radical changes in the rules by which the rights of delegates chosen at primaries are fully protected. The Democratic practice has been to leave the selection of delegates wholly to the States, and so in Democratic conventions this difficulty has not arisen.

The selection of the place at which the convention is to be held is by no means an unimportant detail. It is sometimes the cause of sharp controversy in the committee. Always there is keen rivalry among a number of cities which seek to entertain the convention and are willing to pledge large sums of money for the privilege. The successful city must have, of course, a large convention hall and adequate hotel and railway accommodations. The decision which the committee finally makes may have a direct effect upon the convention's choice of a presidential candidate and, therefore, will likely be in accord with the preference of the majority of the committee among the aspirants for the nomination. The convention is affected more or less by its surroundings. A striking example of the influence which the place of meeting may have upon the convention's work is found in the Republican convention held in Chicago in 1860. Abraham Lincoln's chances for the nomination were greatly improved by the fact that the convention was held in his own State. It is generally believed that William H. Seward would have been nominated over Lincoln if the convention had been held in New York or some other eastern city.

Prior to the time set for the convention to assemble, the committee makes all the needed arrangements for its accommodation. Committee headquarters are opened; the convention hall is obtained, decorated, and made ready in all respects; tickets of admission are printed and circulated; the official delegate badges are prepared; accommodations for the newspaper representatives are provided for; the temporary chairman and the other convention officers are selected; arrangements are made with the local police for the maintenance of order; contests between rival delegations claiming seats in the convention are decided, and the temporary roll of the convention is made up. Nothing is overlooked that seems necessary or desirable for the convenience of the convention and the satisfactory performance of its duties. The last week before the convention is likely to be a laborious time for the National Committee.

Among the duties suggested, the naming of the temporary chairman and the hearing of contests among delegates are the most important. The temporary chairman delivers the "key note" speech, and through this, as well as through his power as presiding officer, may have marked influence upon the outcome of the convention's deliberations, particularly upon the platform adopted. By deciding contests among delegates the National Committee determines who have the right to participate in the preliminary proceedings of the convention. This may not only influence, but may practically determine the result of a close fight for the presidential nomination. Where serious factional troubles exist this function of the committee acquires additional significance. A marked preference for one faction or the other may tend to wreck the party by intensifying personal and group antagonisms. The possibility of thus promoting unfortunate dissensions within the party is increased by reason of the fact that the committee has been in power for four years and is about to give way to a new one. During this time party sentiment may have changed radically from what it was when the committee was appointed and, as a result, the majority of the committee may at the time of the convention stand for policies and practices which the party condemns. The committee is supposed to be merely the agent of the party and to do its will, but under such conditions it may seek to become the master of the party and to defeat its will. The seriousness of a situation of this kind needs no comment. Since the Republican convention of 1912, where this antagonism was sharply revealed, the demand has developed for the election of the new committee in time for it to arrange for the convention and to pass upon the merits of the claims put forward by contesting delegations. Under such a plan the committee would be representative, presumably, of the actual party sentiment and would be in harmony with the majority in the convention. Some such reform as this is very likely to occur, unless, indeed, the convention system itself is subjected to still more radical changes. It is only very recently that the popular mind has come to comprehend the great power, — a power amounting almost to dictation, at times, — which the National Committee has taken to itself in the last thirty years or so. Limitation of this power, at least with respect to the committee's control over the national convention, is inevitable. The nation-wide movement for the democratization of government in all its phases will not pass the National Committee untouched.

The Committee and the Election Campaign. — The most important work of the National Committee from the standpoint of the party is the management of the presidential election campaign. It is in this that the skill and astuteness of the chairman, and the zeal and capacity of his committee associates, are tested to the utmost. Their one supreme duty is to win the election and by so doing place or retain their party in power. They are the head of the great army of party workers in all the States, organized into multitudes of State and local committees, and it is their business to see that the whole organization is working smoothly and effectively. To do this they must keep in intimate touch with the political developments and party activities in all parts of the country. Where the organization is weak, it must be strengthened; where party spirit is lax, enthusiasm must be aroused; where party funds are inadequate, money must be supplied; where factional differences are rife, harmony must be restored. The period of the campaign is filled with intensive, systematic, strenuous labor which goes on without let-up until the hour of the election has arrived.

All the States receive attention from the committee, although not in equal degree. The States that are "solid" or "safe" for the party are left largely to their State and local committees. The struggles in the States that are "doubtful" or "pivotal," however, are under the constant supervision of the National Committee. There the most effective party workers and speakers are sent, the money poured in, and everything done that can be devised by experienced party leaders to help carry the day; for upon the outcome of a single one of these States the winning of the presidency may depend. With such a prize at stake, no chances can be taken; every possible move must be made that gives promise of increasing the party's vote.

PARTY MACHINERY AND METHODS — NATIONAL 213

Above all, the party's organization in these States must be perfected. " Every experienced political manager knows that the first essential to the successful conduct of a campaign is *organization*. The next important essential, it has been said, is *organization*; a third is *organization*. The organization must be thorough and complete. The National Committee, the State committees, the county committees, the township committees, and the appointed party agents and workers in the city precincts and wards, must all be in close articulation and coöperation with one another." [1]

To enable the committee to do its work more successfully, a number of subcommittees are appointed, each with its own special duties. These usually consist of an executive committee, a finance committee, a committee in charge of the bureau of speakers, a committee in charge of literary and press matters, and a committee in charge of the distribution of public documents.[2] All of these subcommittees are essential parts of the National Committee's organization. The most important, however, are the executive and finance committees. The former, with the chairman of the National Committee at its head, has general charge of the campaign, and is sometimes called the "campaign committee." Its members are carefully chosen from the shrewdest political managers available. It is in immediate contact with the campaign activities in all the States. The finance committee, as its name implies, is charged with the task of raising funds for the prosecution of the campaign, — of supplying the party with the "sinews of war." The treasurer of the National Committee is its chairman and together with the national chairman, bears the brunt of the work of obtaining campaign contributions. The difficulties involved in this task are sometimes very great. Until a few years ago, large contributions from corporations and wealthy men, who for business reasons were interested in the party's success, were looked upon with general complacence, if not approval. The special interests were willing to pay, in the form of campaign contributions, either for the enactment of legislation that was favorable to them or for the defeat of legislation that was objectionable; and the party managers

---

[1] Woodburn, "Political Parties and Party Problems in the United States," p. 202.   [2] *Ibid.*, p. 202.

were willing to have them pay. The general public was ignorant of what transpired, since no publicity was given to party finances, and the public conscience was not aroused. Under those conditions money was easily obtained for campaign purposes. But the situation now is very different. Campaign contributions are now strictly regulated by State and national statutes, and publicity is given to the source and expenditure of party funds. Corporation contributions are forbidden. This has been a most wholesome reform, but it has increased considerably the difficulties in the way of the National Committee's treasurer and finance committee. These difficulties must be overcome, however, for without plentiful funds the campaign cannot be carried on successfully. Each party spends an enormous sum of money in conducting the presidential contest in ways that are both legally and morally proper, such as, the maintenance of committee headquarters, printing, postage, transportation, renting of halls, sending out speakers, and distributing campaign literature. With the most economical management the expense will approximate a million dollars for each of the leading parties; and in some campaigns it has been several times this amount. It is obvious that the financial side of the National Committee's work must always be an object of great concern.

The remaining subcommittees have to do with the work of placing the party's claims before the voters, developing party sentiment and arousing enthusiasm for the ticket. The committee in charge of the speakers' bureau is responsible for providing and sending out speakers wherever they are needed. It may have on its list several hundred of the best available speakers, some of whom receive compensation for their efforts. It is the business of the committee to send these men where they will accomplish the most good. This means that the committee must understand thoroughly the local conditions in the various States. The speaker must fit the conditions. An extreme radical is not the man for a community of extreme conservatism. All phases of party opinion must be given respectful consideration, racial and religious prejudices heeded, and antagonisms avoided wherever possible. To manage the speakers' bureau successfully requires thorough understanding of all the cross currents, the conflicting forces, of party life, and of the "inside" things of practical politics. Not all the speakers, of course, are under the control of this bureau. There are thousands of them at work under the direction of State and local committees.

The committee in charge of literary and press matters and the committee in charge of the distribution of documents look after the publicity side of the campaign. Instruction must be given the voters and their reason and intelligence appealed to through printed matter. This takes the form of newspaper and magazine articles and advertisements, and campaign documents of various kinds. A great many special articles designed for newspaper use are prepared under the direct supervision of the literary bureau, and, without charge, sent to the newspapers for publication. The country weeklies, particularly, are solicited to publish these. A press agent, skilled in journalistic work, is regularly employed by the bureau. Campaign documents are multitudinous in number and vary greatly in form. Cards, posters, pamphlets, speeches, and books are prepared and distributed, some free and others at low charges. The campaign textbook should receive special mention. This is a volume of three hundred pages or so, carefully prepared, and containing information of all kinds for the use of campaign speakers and party workers. Campaign biographies of the presidential and vice presidential candidates are also prepared and sold at popular prices. Pamphlets and posters of various kinds and speeches of the candidates and leading members of Congress are distributed in enormous numbers. Great use is made of partisan speeches delivered in Congress because many of these may be sent out under the congressional franking privilege, without expense for postage. Much of this literature, however, is not mailed directly to the voters, by the literary bureau, but is shipped in bulk to State and local committees and by them distributed where the need is greatest. With respect to the output of campaign documents in a presidential year, the following is suggestive: "In the campaign of 1900, for example, the Democrats published 158 different documents and distributed over twenty-five million copies, and the Republican party probably surpassed this record. In that year eight million copies of one of Mr. Bryan's speeches were printed in eleven different languages, and seven million copies of Mr.

McKinley's letter of acceptance were distributed. In one day four and a half million copies of a single speech were sent out from the Republican headquarters in Chicago, and over three tons of other documents were shipped on the same day."[1]

This brief statement of the campaign duties of the National Committee gives only in a general way a glimpse of the work which must be done by the parties in connection with the presidential election. It is not designed to be exhaustive, but merely to suggest the usual plan of campaign. To describe this in detail would require a volume. All that is desired is to bring out clearly the huge proportions of the task with which the National Committee is charged, and to outline the manner in which it organizes for this and the methods it pursues.

Committee Activities between Elections. — The third part of the National Committee's work, — that which it does during the three years intervening before the next campaign opens, — is very different in character from that which it does with reference to the presidential election. The circumstances surrounding the committee during the two periods are radically dissimilar. While the election campaign is on, the National Committee is decidedly in the foreground. Its plans and actions are chronicled in the daily press. The eye of the public is upon it. But when the election is over, it almost immediately drops into the background, if not out of sight. Its name appears only infrequently in the newspapers, and the general public ceases to give attention to it. This is only a little less true of the committee that was successful in the election than of the one that was defeated. Does this mean, however, that the National Committee has become unimportant and negligible as a party institution until the time comes round for the next national convention? To some extent, there is ground for this belief. The committee, as a committee, has no formal duties to discharge during this time. It holds no meetings and seldom maintains even the semblance of headquarters. Yet the committee is hardly in the comatose condition which the casual observer might ascribe to it. Information concerning its functions during this period of lapse is not easily obtained, but there is good evidence that its members continue to serve the party in an effective, though quiet manner. It was made a part of the

[1] Ray, "Introduction to Political Parties and Practical Politics," p. 200.

duty of the first Democratic National Committee, established in 1848, to "promote the Democratic Cause." This work of "promoting the party cause" is the real work of every National Committee and the opportunities for doing it are obviously not confined to the period of the presidential campaign. The party machinery must not be neglected and allowed to deteriorate or the party will suffer seriously in the next election. Factional differences within the party must be held in check and obliterated, if possible, and dissensions healed. The National Committee, through tactful efforts, is in a position to serve the party in a most practical and highly beneficial way by harmonizing discordant and antagonistic elements within it.

Moreover, the success of a party depends in no small degree upon a clear understanding, on the part of its leaders, of the significance of political developments from day to day. It is no less essential for the party in opposition than for the party in power to gauge accurately the state of the public mind. The effect of policies proposed, as well as policies enacted, must be measured so as to guard against a loss of popular confidence. It is necessary, therefore, for both those who are in control of the government and those who are leading the opposition, to be intimately familiar with what is going on among the masses of the people. In this work of analyzing public opinion and studying the trend of political sentiment with a view to preventing party blunders, members of the National Committee have one of their largest opportunities for "promoting the party cause."

In one other way, also, members of the committee representing the party in power are of assistance both to the party and to the administration. This is in connection with the distribution of patronage. The chairman of the committee, who is a close personal adviser of the President, is particularly influential in this respect. His indorsement of a candidate for an appointment to office is certain to carry great weight with the President. This, indeed, is one of the sources of the chairman's power over his associates in the party organization, many of whom look upon him as the dispenser of party patronage. This has, in fact, been literally true with some chairmen. Two notable examples are found in Senator A. P. Gorman, who led the Democrats to victory in 1884, and Senator Marcus Hanna, who managed the Republican campaigns of 1896 and 1900.[1] Both of these men wielded tremendous influence over appointments to office and greatly increased the prestige of the national chairman. Particularly was this true of Senator Hanna who was given substantially a free hand in apportioning party patronage in the Southern States. His indorsement, in fact, at any time practically insured an appointment. Chairman Hanna is not to be taken as typical, however, for in him the national chairman reached the high tide of influence. At all times, it is to be remembered, the Senators and Representatives have a great deal to say about federal appointments.

In States in which the President's party has no representatives in either house of Congress, the members of the National Committee from those States become influential factors in the distribution of patronage. This is also true where the party controls only a part of the congressional delegation. The committeeman becomes a referee for settling disputes as to preference, and the President looks to him for guidance. It is his business in all this to look after the interests of the organization and to see that appointments are not made which will tend toward party disruption. One of his prime functions always is to prevent party divisions and factional strife. And no other thing is so fruitful of these as is the dispensing of the spoils of office.

REFERENCES

BRYCE. *The American Commonwealth*, Edition 1910, Vol. II, Chaps. LXXI, LXXII, LXXIII.
MACY. *Party Organization and Machinery*, Chap. VI.
OSTROGORSKI. *Democracy and the Party System in the United States*, Chaps. IX, X.
RAY. *An Introduction to Political Parties and Practical Politics*, Chaps. IX, pp. 172-179, X, XI.
WOODBURN. *Political Parties and Party Problems in the United States*, Chap. XIII.

[1] Jones, "Readings on Parties and Elections," pp. 199-205.

CHAPTER XVII

Party Machinery and Methods — State and Local

It has been made clear in the preceding chapter that the organization of each party consists, in addition to the National Committee, of a large number of State and local committees. Each of these has its own set of officers, its own field of action, and its own work to do. Each is an important part of the party machine. In fact, it is to the fidelity, enthusiasm, and efficiency of these local and State committees that the National Committee must look for the success of its plans. Without all this subordinate organization the National Committee would be helpless.

Each State has its own organization which is entirely separate from those of other States. It must be remembered that the presidential election, though first in importance, is only one of many elections which the parties seek to carry. There is a vast number of elective local and State offices which each party is eager to control. The successful party has a tremendous advantage over its opponent. It is through this control, to a large extent, that the organization is kept intact. The elective offices carry with them a large number of appointive positions, and these, except where civil service laws prevent, are given to party men. It is easily seen, therefore, that it is necessary for the party in each State to maintain an efficient organization to look after its interests in all these elections. Even in the year of the great presidential election, the national ticket is not the only one that is of concern to national as well as State party managers. There must also be chosen Senators and Representatives in Congress, Governors, and other State officers, members of the State legislatures, officers for counties, cities, towns and townships, wards and villages. The lists of offices to be filled in the various States are not identical, of course, but in each there is a large number of local contests to be decided at the same time the presidential battle is determined. Sometimes it happens that local contests are the cause of even keener excitement and enthusiasm than is the presidential election. In fact, the party managers depend in no small degree upon these local fights to arouse party spirit and help bring the voters to the polls. It is for this reason that the managers are so desirous of having full party tickets nominated in all the governmental divisions where elections are to occur. The State and national tickets are certain to profit from the activity caused by the local contests. Party committees in the various districts to look after these local elections are essential, therefore, to the party's success in States and Nation.

The State Central Committee. — At the head of the State organization stands the State committee, usually called the State Central Committee. This committee bears the same relation to the State organization that the National Committee does to the national organization. It is chosen, as a rule, in much the same manner as the National Committee, is organized in a similar way, and, within its more limited district, has the same work to do. In the election of the President, the State committee, though organically independent of the National Committee, comes under the direction of the latter and becomes an effective part of the national organization. With respect to the State elections, however, it is an independent agency, and works out its own plans and is responsible for the outcome. Inevitably, though, the fortunes of the State and national tickets are bound together. So the State and National Committees work in harmony, as a usual thing, to their mutual benefit.

There is a good deal of variation in the composition and powers of the State committees in the different States. In apportioning membership on the committee, different practices are observed. Various units of representation are used, the congressional district, the county, the legislative district, the judicial district, and the town. In some cases a mixed basis is used.[1] In most cases the committees are made up of representatives from either the congressional districts or the counties. As a rule the apportionment of members is based on geographical considerations and not on the number of party adherents within

[1] Merriam, C. E., *Political Science Quarterly*, XIX, p. 224.

a district. In size, also, there is great lack of uniformity. At least five State committees have a hundred or more members, while two have only eleven. They serve for limited terms, in most cases two years. The variation ranges, however, from one to four years. The terms coincide, as a rule, with those of the State officers. In general the members of the State committee are chosen according to the plan followed in the election of the National Committee. In the case of the latter the delegates to the national convention from the various States choose their respective committeemen; in the case of the former, the delegates to the State convention from the various districts or areas to be represented choose their respective committeemen. At a separate caucus of the delegates from each district the selection is made and reported to the State convention at the proper time. A different practice must be observed, of course, if through direct primary legislation the State convention is abolished. In Wisconsin, where this has been done, party committeemen are chosen at a meeting of the party nominees for the various State offices and for seats in the State legislature. The prevailing practice in the States with direct primaries, however, is to retain the State convention, though with greatly limited powers, and at this the party committee is chosen in the manner outlined. In some States where the county is the unit of representation, the central committee is chosen by the local county authorities. Vacancies in the State committee are usually filled by the remaining members, although there are several States where this is not true.

The powers and duties of the State committee are similar to those of the National Committee, though in a much more limited field. They have to do with the holding of the State convention, with the management of the election campaign, and the building up and nurturing of the party's strength in all parts of the State. In the matter of the convention, the committee decides upon the time and place, issues the formal call, fixes the ratio of representation among the districts from which delegates are to be chosen, selects the convention's temporary officers, passes upon contests among rival delegations in making up the temporary roll, and makes all necessary arrangements for the convention's needs and convenience. As with the national organization, this is all done by the committee which is about to retire from power. During the time the convention is in session the committee's powers are suspended. This convention's organization and procedure is practically identical with that of the national convention already described.

The new State committee, upon its election, organizes at once by choosing its officers. There are always a chairman, a secretary, and a treasurer; sometimes other officers are appointed, such as vice chairman and sergeant-at-arms. The chairman is general director of the committee and its work, and, as with the national chairman, a great deal depends upon his skill, executive ability, and understanding of political conditions and forces. The work of planning for the election campaign that is just opening begins at once. To enable the committee to conduct the campaign more effectually, various subcommittees are appointed. These usually include an executive or campaign committee of which the State chairman is the head, a finance committee whose duty it is to raise money for the campaign, a committee in charge of the speakers' bureau, and a committee in charge of the literary or publicity bureau. Sometimes the latter two are combined. Frequently an auditing committee is appointed to check up all financial transactions. The most important officers, of course, are the chairman and the secretary. The campaign duties of the committee are similar to those of the National Committee. It raises funds for its own use and the use of local committees where most needed, prepares and sends out campaign literature of all kinds, including that received from the National Committee, arranges for political meetings and assigns the speakers, holds conferences with candidates and party workers, and does whatever it thinks will contribute to a party victory. At all times it must keep in close touch with the local committees and party workers. Without the aid of these its plans could not be carried out. After all, it is only a kind of general staff directing the State party army. Without the subordinate officers and organizations it is helpless.

The County Central Committee. — Below the State committee, and giving the latter its chief support, stands the County Central Committee — one of the most useful parts of the whole party organization. In size and manner of election the county committees vary greatly in different States. A typical county committee in a rural county is one made up of one representative from each township into which the county is divided. Where the county contains a city of the lower rank, yet large enough to be divided into wards, a representative from each ward is also upon the committee. In the large cities where the wards are divided into precincts, each precinct has its committeeman. In some States members of the county committee are chosen at a county convention composed of delegates from the townships and other election precincts of the county. In others the committeemen are chosen at the township, ward, or precinct caucuses. And in still others, where the direct primary has been adopted, members of the county committee are elected at the polls by the party members, at the time party candidates are nominated for the various public offices. So there is great variety in the manner of its election.

The powers of the county committees are also lacking in uniformity. In some States their powers have never been defined by party authority and are therefore vague and indefinite. In other States, specific rules have been adopted in which the powers of the committee are clearly stated and their exact relationship to the State organization established. In some instances the county committee becomes the "ring" in control of the local party and practically dictates what it shall do. With respect to the duties of county committees there is rather widespread agreement. Their general purpose — to quote from the rules governing the Democratic county committee in the County of New York — is to "have the care of the interests and be charged with the administration of the affairs of the party in the County, and with the promotion of measures for the harmony, efficiency and success of the party." The county committee is supposed never to become inactive; it is always to be on the alert for chances to strengthen its party for the struggles that are always coming. Of course, in the heat of a campaign, its work is more urgent and more laborious than during the periods intervening between elections. It is then that the efficiency and zeal of its members are put to the test. It is through them that the individual voter comes in contact with the party organization. Each member is usually expected to poll his precinct — that is, ascertain the sentiment of each voter — at least once during the campaign. Sometimes in doubtful States and districts this is done several times in the course of the campaign to enable the party leaders to plan and work to the best purpose. The county committee carries out the instructions of the State committee, and attends to many details intrusted to it. It is expected to raise money for use in its own county, to employ speakers and arrange for political meetings or "rallies," to distribute the campaign literature sent to it by the State committee, to stir party workers who are not on committees to activity, to confer with candidates and help them come in contact with local leaders and the voters, to see that all the party members are properly registered, where registration is required, to appoint watchers at the polls where this is necessary, and do many other things to promote the party's success. Above all, it is the business of the committee to see that the full party vote is polled on election day. Each committeeman is responsible for his own precinct and to "get out the vote" is one of his chief aims as well as, oftentimes, one of his most difficult tasks. The work of the county committee, in all of its phases, is vital to the success of the party, and must be clearly understood in order to comprehend fully the part which organization plays in party politics.

There are still other committees in this complex system which have not been mentioned as yet. There is likely to be a committee or committeeman, in fact, in each election district, no matter how small it may be. The committees in mind here, though, are the congressional, judicial, and senatorial district committees which are found in most States. Though serving larger districts than the county, these committees are ordinarily of less importance, however, than the county committees. They are often more nominal than real. The effective campaign work is done by the county committees. In fact, these other committees are frequently made up of county committeemen, — one member from each county committee in the district. The committees which carry the burden of a presidential campaign are the National, State, and county committees. In a strictly State campaign it is the State and the county committees alone which wage the fight.

Congressional Campaign Committee. — There remains to be described one other party committee which is of unusual interest. This is the Congressional Campaign Committee. Since its work is national in scope, having to do with the election of members of Congress, it might properly have been described in connection with the National Committee, whose ally it is. But there is a difference between the Congressional Committee and the National Committee as well as the others which have been mentioned, which warranted passing it over for the moment. The National, State, and county committees are official party institutions, created by proper party authority and maintained according to established party usages. They are officially recognized as the party's agents. The Congressional Campaign Committee, on the other hand, is not an official party committee. The party never established it and does not maintain it, although, for the most part, it meets with cordial party approval. It is simply an organization set up and maintained by party members who have seats in Congress; and, it might be added, who want to retain those seats. The nature of its work and the place it holds in the party organization are better understood by noting the manner in which it came into being and how it is perpetuated.

The Congressional Committee is not an old institution, as political institutions go, although it has been in existence for a number of years, and both parties have adopted it. The first one came into existence in 1866 and was the direct product of the sharp controversy that was on at that time between the Republicans in Congress and President Johnson. The National Committee was under the domination of the President, as it usually, though not always, is. The Republican congressmen were unwilling to trust their political fortunes, when they came up for reëlection, to the National Committee. As a resultant of this state of mind they formed a committee of their own, made up from their own number, to take charge of the congressional campaign of 1866. The results were entirely satisfactory. The Republicans retained control of the House of Representatives, in spite of the President's efforts to oust them through the use of patronage.

It was seen at once that the Republicans had brought into service a highly useful party agency. It became a regular part of the Republican organization and was soon after adopted

Q

by the Democrats. Since that time both parties have kept their Congressional Committees organized and have looked to them for direction in the congressional contests. There can be no doubt that the parties have been wise in maintaining these committees, although they are not free from valid criticisms. There is need for an agency of this kind, particularly in the so-called " off-year " elections, when the regular National Committee, as has been pointed out, is in a state of comparative inaction. The National Committee, as a campaign committee, is concerned with presidential elections. Yet the election of a new House of Representatives midway in the presidential term is a matter of vital concern to both parties, and particularly to the party in power. The need for a vigorous, well-planned, well-conducted campaign is apparent. The Congressional Committee supplies this need, and is without doubt a valuable adjunct to the regular party organization. Only a little less important, however, is its work in the presidential years. The congressional elections must be looked after as in the off years, the only difference being that in the presidential years the Congressional Committee acts as the ally of the National Committee and in general does its work under the latter's supervision.

The methods of the Congressional Committee are similar to those employed by the National Committee in the presidential campaigns. It prepares a campaign textbook for the use of its speakers; sends out immense quantities of printed matter — a good deal of this at government expense, under the franking privilege enjoyed by congressmen; raises money necessary for the maintenance of committee headquarters, the payment of bills for printing and transportation, the hiring of speakers, and the discharge of all the many other financial obligations incurred during a campaign; and like all campaign committees performs a multitude of exacting duties. It concentrates its work in the doubtful districts, just as the National Committee centers its attention upon the doubtful States. It works in conjunction with the various local committees in the different States and seeks in every way possible to strengthen the local organizations and hold the party's forces in line for its candidates. To do this work successfully, the committee must necessarily closely study local conditions and keep in touch with local party leaders. The opportunity of the committee thus to influence party conduct is very great.

The Republican and Democratic committees differ somewhat in their organization. Each committee is reorganized every two years, at the beginning of a new Congress. The Republican committee is chosen at a joint caucus of the members of both houses. Each State and Territory that is represented in Congress by Republicans has one representative on the committee. States that have no representatives in Congress are deprived of committee representation. If a State has only one Republican congressman, he serves upon the Congressional Committee. Senators may be members, although there is no requirement that they shall be. The practice, however, is to have the Senate represented.

Upon the Democratic committee each State and Territory is represented whether it has representation in Congress or not. If a State has no Democratic Representative, some well-known party worker in that State is selected to serve on the committee. The Democratic committee is not chosen at a joint caucus, as is the Republican committee, but the Democratic members of each house hold their own caucus and appoint their representatives. The Senate always has nine members on the committee.

The efficiency of the Congressional Committee as a strict campaign agency is beyond dispute; it challenges admiration, in fact. Yet it is not looked upon with absolute approval. Some of its methods, in fact, have been subjected to the strongest criticism. Particularly has criticism been directed to its practice of raising large campaign funds from individuals who have or may have a special interest in legislation that is to come before Congress. The charge is made that members of Congress in this way place themselves under such obligation to the financial backers of their campaigns that they cannot pass unbiased judgments upon questions of legislation which affect the interests of their benefactors. This feeling has grown so strong in recent years that a demand has sprung up for the abolition of the Congressional Committee, — the view being taken that the regular party committees are fully capable of directing all party campaigns. That there is merit in the criticism noted must be granted by any one familiar with American politics.

The big business interests of the country have been strongly represented in the Congress and there is abundant reason to believe that financial contributions to the Congressional Campaign Committees have had somewhat to do with that fact. It seems reasonably safe to believe that some of the committee's methods will be altered. The public welfare demands that the Congressional Committees, if they are retained at all, shall not place the members of Congress under obligations to business and corporate interests which may be the subject of congressional legislation.

Another comment upon the Congressional Committee which should be made involves its relation to the policy or platform of its party. This is especially pertinent at times when factional differences are rife. Is the work of the committee to be affected in any way by these factional troubles? Is it, as a committee, permitted to take sides? Does it have the right to pass judgment upon, or help determine in an official way, what the party policy or platform shall be? A case in point was the attitude of the Republican committee in 1910, when the insurgent movement among Republicans in Congress was at its height. The Congressional Committee was controlled by the stalwarts or regulars, and its influence was turned against the insurgents. Refusal of aid to insurgent nominees was threatened. Was the committee acting within its powers?

There is no doubt that this attitude was contrary to the accepted understanding. Traditionally the Congressional Committee has nothing to do with the formulation of the party platform, not even so much as has the National Committee. Both of these committees are executive party institutions. It is their business to manage election campaigns and leave to the regular party conventions the task of adopting platforms and labeling candidates. It is to be remembered that the Congressional Committee was not created by, and is not representative of the party voters, but is the creation and agent of representatives of the party voters in the national legislature. The interests of the voters and their representatives are not necessarily identical. Moreover, if representative government is to be more than a mere name, it is the business of the representatives to carry out the public or the party will. It is not a part of their function to say what that will shall be. The

Congressional Committee, therefore, is without authority to say what is and what is not the party faith. In its own proper sphere of action, it is a useful, efficient party instrument. But that sphere is limited to the work of conducting congressional election campaigns; it does not include the power to originate party policies or to judge of party orthodoxy.

Party System Far from Perfect. — Any attempt to describe the American party organization would be very incomplete and give a decidedly erroneous impression, which did not make it clear that the system in practice is full of defects and gives rise to many serious problems. The desire of party managers to win elections leads to many questionable practices and frequently to flagrant corruption. Falsification of the registration lists, bribery of voters, repeating, " stuffing " the ballot box, tampering with the election returns, and other corrupt acts are things of rather frequent occurrence. This is especially the case in some of the large cities where the legitimate party organization has degenerated into a corrupt political ring. It would be far from the truth, however, to conclude that such evil practices characterize the work of all the party committees. It is probably true that in no other country has there been a state of political corruption and viciousness that measures down to the outrageous conditions which have at times been exposed in certain American cities; but, without doubt, it is equally true that in no other country is there more of partisan struggle and political strife that is free from improper and illegitimate conduct. Political conditions found in some cities are not typical of the whole country, — a fact which all students of American politics, and foreign students especially, should keep clearly in mind. The great bulk of the activity of party committees is not subject to criticism from the standpoint of dishonesty and corruption. It is partisan, of course, but not crooked.

It remains true, however, that the party system is far from perfect. The complicated party machinery has made it easy for the political boss and the political ring to develop. The delegate conventions, particularly, have furnished opportunity for boss manipulation. The control of the party machinery has too often meant the control of the party itself. The party committees are supposed to be the agents, the servants, of the party and to be responsible to the party voters from whom their power comes; but too frequently they have tried to be the masters of the party and have ignored their responsibility to the voters. As a consequence the party will has often been thwarted. In so far as this is a fact, true party government does not exist, for the true political party is merely an organ for the expression of public opinion. The boss and the ring have no place in the true political party. This fact is coming to be understood by the American people, in whom the spirit of genuine self-government is more alive to-day than ever before. A new, regenerated, democratized party system is being developed.

REFERENCES

BEARD. *American Government and Politics*, Edition 1914, Chap. XXX.
BRYCE. *The American Commonwealth*, Edition 1910, Vol. II, Chaps. LIX to LXIII inclusive.
MACY. *Party Organization and Machinery*, Chaps. VIII to XVII inclusive.
MERRIAM. *Primary Elections*.
MERRIAM. "State Central Committees," *Political Science Quarterly*, XIX, 224 (1904).
OSTROGORSKI. *Democracy and the Party System in the United States*, Chaps. XI, XII.
RAY. *An Introduction to Political Parties and Practical Politics*, Chaps. IV, V, VI, VII, XVI.
WOODBURN. *Political Parties and Party Problems in the United States*, Chaps. XVI, XVII, XVIII.

CHAPTER XVIII

THE FEDERAL COURTS — CONSTITUTIONAL STATUS AND DEVELOPMENT

A FACT to be kept constantly in mind in the study of American government is that to a large extent the government is the result of conscious action, of deliberate choice. This involved, on the part of its founders, not only the sifting of the experience of the Old and New Worlds, but the creation of some new institutions of government, — institutions that had no counterpart in any other nation, either contemporaneous or of the past. The presidency is one of these. Another is the federal judiciary, in which is to be found one of America's most significant contributions to world experience with free government. The organization of the courts created under the Constitution and the Judiciary Act of 1789, their development, work, and status in the government system are the subjects for discussion in this chapter.

The provision of the Constitution with reference to the organization of federal courts is very meager and indefinite. The sole authorization of a court system is contained in a single sentence, found in Section 1, Article III: "The judicial power of the United States shall be vested in one Supreme Court and in such inferior courts as the Congress may from time to time ordain and establish." The other sentence in Section 1 relates to the term of office and compensation of the judges, and the remaining parts of the Article, with great brevity, deal with the jurisdiction of the courts, trial by jury, and the definition and punishment of the crime of treason. A considerably smaller proportion of the Constitution is devoted to the judiciary than to either of the other coördinate branches of the government. This does not mean, however, that there was less of forethought and careful consideration concerning the judiciary than the other departments. The fact is that the organization of the courts, and particularly the question of their jurisdiction, and their relation to the other departments and to the States of the Union, constituted one of the hardest and most baffling problems which the constitutional convention had to meet. The brevity and indefiniteness of the constitutional provisions are not to be taken as indicative of indifference on the part of the constitution makers, or of failure to appreciate the vital significance of the judicial function; the exact opposite, in fact, would be more nearly the truth. The provisions are brief, the terms general, by design. Setting up a new judicial organization in addition to those in existence in the various States, with jurisdiction over the same persons and the same territory as the latter, was a decidedly difficult undertaking. Too much of detail upon so delicate a matter, in view of prevailing popular opinions, might prove disastrous rather than helpful. The men of the convention themselves were far from being unanimous in their views as to the courts, and in their differences accurately reflected the state of the public mind.

Need for Federal Judiciary. — It was plain enough to all that some kind of federal judicial system was needed and must be provided for. Under the Articles of Confederation there were no courts to give force to the orders of Congress in case of disobedience by either individuals or States. The State courts were under no obligation whatever to do this, and would not do it unless it happened to be their wish to aid Congress. This unsatisfactory condition was generally conceded to be one of the grave weaknesses of the Confederation. But without some kind of national courts the situation would be very much worse under the new Constitution than under the Confederation. A national legislature was to be established with wide powers and authority to make its laws apply directly to the individual citizen, and not merely to the States as was the arrangement under the Articles. Moreover, a strong executive branch was to be set up, charged with the enforcement through its own officers of the law of Congress. In order to protect the rights of individuals and of the States, a judiciary with ample power to interpret these laws and apply them to the ends of justice was therefore imperatively necessary. One of two things could be done. Either the State courts, already in existence, could be required to discharge this duty, or a new system of federal courts could be established. Plainly it would not do to impose this function upon the State courts, for reasons that were at once apparent. These reasons are succinctly given by Bryce. "State courts were not fitted to deal with matters of a quasi-international character, such as admiralty jurisdiction and rights arising under treaties. They supplied no means for deciding questions between different States. They could not be trusted to do complete justice between their own citizens and those of another State. Being under the control of their own State governments, they might be forced to disregard any Federal law which the State disapproved; or even if they admitted its authority, might fail in the zeal or the power to give due effect to it. And being authorities coördinate with and independent of one another, with no common court of appeal placed over them to correct their errors or harmonize their views, they would be likely to interpret the Federal Constitution and statutes in different senses and make the law uncertain by the variety of their conclusions. These reasons pointed imperatively to the establishment of a new tribunal or set of tribunals, altogether detached from the States, as part of the machinery of the new government."[1]

However, notwithstanding the obvious necessity of setting up federal courts, there was a good deal of uncertainty and hesitancy in deciding just what these courts should be and do. As we have seen, the final conclusion as formally stated in the Constitution is by no means specific. A good deal is left to legislative action and the unknown forces of tradition and custom. Out of that simple constitutional authorization has been erected a judicial organization which doubtless far transcends in size and complexity anything the constitution makers anticipated, and which exercises powers such as the courts of European nations never possessed.

Relation of Congress to the Courts. — It will be noticed that the only court specifically created by the Constitution is the Supreme Court. The establishment of other courts of inferior rank is left wholly to Congress. As to the details of the Supreme Court's organization and work the Constitution makes only partial provisions. It is declared that the judges of the court,

[1] Bryce, "The American Commonwealth," New and Revised Edition, Vol. I, p. 229.

as of any inferior courts that might be established, shall hold office during good behavior, and that they shall receive compensation for their services which shall not be diminished during their continuance in office. It is given original jurisdiction in a few cases, and appellate jurisdiction in all others that may come before the federal courts, subject to the regulations that may be made by Congress. It is also provided that the members of the court shall be appointed by the President with the approval of the Senate, and like other civil officers are subject to impeachment. Nothing is said about the number of Supreme Court judges, the time of the court's sessions, or the rules that shall govern it. These matters are left to Congress to determine, as is the question of setting up other judicial tribunals.

It is plain at a glance that in spite of the separation of powers doctrine which is so fundamental in the United States Constitution, Congress has a good deal to say about the judiciary. Exactly how much power Congress has over the court organization is a subject of some dispute. Clearly it cannot destroy the Supreme Court, but unquestionably it could so injure the court by legislation as to render it useless by making it hopelessly inefficient. For example, in deciding upon the number of judges, which is always subject to congressional control, Congress might make the membership so large as to interfere seriously with its capacity for judicial work. Again, while Congress cannot reduce the number of judges by removing them, except through impeachment, it can provide that as vacancies occur through death or resignation or removal after impeachment, such vacancies shall not be filled and the judgeships involved be abolished. This was done in 1866 when the number of judges was reduced from ten to seven. This could be continued until only one judge remained, and still the constitutional requirement be fully met. But one judge could not by any means do the work which devolves upon the Supreme Court. Again, while Congress cannot diminish the salary of a judge during his continuance in office, it clearly could provide that as a vacancy in the Supreme Court occurs, the salary for that particular judgeship should be reduced to so low a sum as to cause service on the supreme bench to appear ridiculous and thus make jurists of standing unwilling to accept appointment. This might be continued until the character of the whole court would be changed. As to the inferior courts, the power of Congress would seem to be even greater. While the lower judges, like the Supreme Court justices, are secure in their positions except in cases of impeachment, the lower courts themselves can be abolished. In fact this was done once, though under rather exceptional conditions, and opinions differ as to the validity of the act.[1] In 1801, just before the close of President John Adams's administration, the Federalists provided for the reduction of the Supreme Court membership from six to five, in order to prevent the in-coming President, Thomas Jefferson, from filling the vacancy, and created sixteen new circuit judgeships. On the last night of his term, President Adams filled these positions with partisan adherents. One of the first things done by the new Congress at the beginning of Jefferson's administration was to repeal the law creating these "midnight judges," and the act never went into effect. The constitutionality of this may be questioned, but the repealing law was never tested in the courts and therefore stands as valid. It needs no further comment to make plain that by this power to abolish the inferior courts, Congress could practically destroy the whole judicial system. That there is any danger of this, however, is of course an absurdity. Congress has in a few instances interfered with the courts for partisan reasons, and may possibly do so again, but that it will seek to abolish the lower courts without providing for other tribunals to take their place, is a supposition beyond all reason. The purpose of the foregoing statements is merely to suggest the very close relationship between the legislative and judicial departments and some of the things it would be possible for Congress to do under the formal Constitution. The independent judiciary, however, is a thing of fact, notwithstanding the possibilities of congressional interference, and its influence was never greater than at the present time.

Development of the Court System. — Understanding of the relation of the judiciary to Congress, as well as of the actual court organization, will be promoted by a brief review of the development of the various courts in the federal system. As already pointed out, action by Congress was necessary before

[1] Beard, "American Government and Politics," New and Revised Edition, p. 224.

the judicial machinery could be set in motion. Even the Supreme Court, required by the Constitution, could be nothing more than a name until Congress took the steps necessary to make it a reality. As for the inferior courts, they had not even a nominal existence.

The act by which Congress did its part in establishing the judicial organization is known as the Judiciary Act of 1789. This became a law on September 24 of that year and remained operative until January 1, 1912, when it was superseded by a new judicial code. Provision was made for the organization of the Supreme Court which was to consist of one Chief Justice and five Associate Justices. The jurisdiction of the court was regulated by extending its original jurisdiction beyond that provided for in the Constitution to two classes of cases, and giving it final appellate jurisdiction in all cases. By this act the country was divided into thirteen districts, and in each of these a District Court was established with one judge, known as district judge. The jurisdiction of this court was determined by giving it certain powers in both civil and criminal cases. By further provisions of the act these districts were grouped into three larger districts known as circuits. In each of these circuits a court was created with original jurisdiction in both civil and criminal causes, and with appellate jurisdiction in a number of cases arising in the District Courts below. Separate Circuit Court judges, however, were not authorized. It was provided that each of these Circuit Courts should be composed of two Supreme Court justices and the district judge of the district in which the case at issue originated. The Supreme Court justices were required to go from district to district within their respective Circuits and hold court at stated times in conjunction with the various district judges. Appeal, where it was allowed, would be from the Circuit Court to the Supreme Court.

This, in brief, gives the organization of the federal judiciary as it was established in the beginning and as it has continued in its fundamentals to the present time. The basic idea with respect to the inferior courts is the division of the country into districts, each with a court of its own, and the grouping of the districts into a number of circuits, whose courts stand midway between the District and Supreme Courts. The real unit of the system of lower courts is the district, and has been from the first. The District Court is the only federal court whose jurisdiction is exclusively original.

The task of getting this judicial machinery in motion and winning for it a position of favor in the public mind, was naturally a difficult one which required both patience and tact. There was a vast amount of suspicion among the people concerning the whole system, and particularly the Supreme Court. They feared it and were resentful toward it. Considerable time elapsed before popular confidence in the federal courts became a fact. The story of the growth of the Supreme Court from an institution that was surrounded by fear and distrust, and without work to do, to one with the vast power and prestige which it has now long had, is a story of entrancing interest, and reveals one of the most notable developments in the history of free government. The court held its first meeting on the first Monday in February, 1790, appointed a clerk, and then adjourned because there was nothing for it to do. The situation at the moment and the striking change that has occurred since then are graphically indicated by an American lawyer: " Not a single litigant had appeared at their bar. Silence had been unbroken by the voice of counsel in argument. The table was unburdened by the weight of learned briefs. No papers were on file with the clerk. Not a single decision, even in embryo, existed. The judges were there; but of business there was none. Not one of the spectators of that hour, though gifted with the eagle eye of prophecy, could have foreseen that out of that modest assemblage of gentlemen, unheard of and unthought of among the tribunals of the earth, a court without a docket, without a record, without a writ, of unknown and untried powers, and of undetermined jurisdiction, there would be developed within the space of a single century a court of which the ancient world could present no model and the modern boast no parallel; a court whose decrees, woven like threads of gold into the priceless and imperishable fabric of our constitutional jurisprudence, would bind in the bonds of love, liberty, and law the members of our great Republic. Nor could they have foreseen that the tables of Congress would groan beneath the weight of petitions from all parts of the country, inviting that body to devise some means for the relief of that over-burdened tribunal whose litigants are now doomed to stand in line for a space of more than three years before they have a chance to be heard."[1]

The author of these words does not, in his eloquence, exaggerate the facts of the case. It was a most inauspicious beginning for one of the world's greatest political institutions. The court was almost exclusively an appellate court, and its work for some time was far from heavy. Its members traveling on circuit, however, were confronted by laborious and exacting duties. Transport facilities were meager at that time, and the work of the judges was physically hard. Within four or five years the Supreme Court's docket filled up to such an extent that its members had to be relieved of some of their responsibilities in connection with the Circuit Courts. In 1793, Congress provided that only one Supreme Court justice should be assigned to each circuit.

The judicial organization as outlined here continued in force until the reorganization act of 1869 was passed by Congress. Minor changes, of course, were made in the meantime, — the number of Supreme Court justices being increased, and additional District Courts authorized as new States were admitted to the Union and the work of the courts grew heavier. Under this new law the number of Circuit Courts was increased to nine and a circuit judge in each circuit provided for. By the act of 1789 there were Circuit Courts, but no circuit judges. As previously stated, the law of 1801 creating sixteen circuit judgeships was repealed the next year before it went into effect. By the law of 1869 the new circuit judge was given practically the same power as that held by the Supreme Court justice assigned to the circuit. It was provided that the Circuit Court might be held by the Supreme Court justice, by the circuit judge, or by the district judge sitting alone; two or all three of these might sit together, of course. The Supreme Court justice, however, was not required to attend the Circuit Court more than once in two years, and even then might be present for only a day or two. This was because the Supreme Court

[1] Carson, Hampton L., "A History of the Supreme Court of the United States." Quoted by Representative Reuben O. Moon, "The Reorganization of the Federal System." Case and Comment, Vol. 18, June, 1911. Because of the relief that has come from the establishment of the Circuit Courts of Appeals, the Supreme Court is not now so far behind with its work.

itself was so burdened with work that its members could not be spared much of the time to go on circuit. The Circuit Court had both appellate and original jurisdiction, but on account of the volume of business before it, gave most of its time to cases on appeal from the District Courts. The district judge might be called on to hold Circuit Court, and often did so, but the district judges had their time well filled, as a rule, with the work of their own District Courts, whose field steadily grew larger as the country developed and laws became more restrictive. The system thus organized was continued until 1891, when further modification was made in connection with the Circuit Courts.

By the act of 1891 Circuit Courts of Appeals were created. This was done to relieve the Supreme Court, which by this time was swamped by the mass of work devolving upon it. It was hopelessly behind with its docket, to the serious loss of all who might have business before it. The law of 1891 provided a Circuit Court of Appeals for each of the nine circuits and to these courts was given final jurisdiction over a large number of cases which formerly went to the Supreme Court on appeal from the lower courts. This relieved the pressure of business on the Supreme Court and added much to its efficiency. New judges were not provided for the Circuit Courts of Appeals, however, the work of these courts devolving upon the judges of the various Circuit Courts, which were continued as courts of original jurisdiction, their appellate powers being transferred to the new courts. So, under the law of 1891, the federal court system consisted of the Supreme Court, nine Circuit Courts of Appeals, nine Circuit Courts, and the District Courts, seventy-seven in number. The work of the Supreme Court was entirely appellate, except in the few cases where original jurisdiction was imposed on it by the Constitution; that of the Circuit Courts of Appeals was wholly appellate, its jurisdiction being final in a large number of cases; and that of the Circuit and District Courts was exclusively original.

The anomalous element in this arrangement was the situation of the Circuit and District Courts. Both were courts of original jurisdiction, and to a large extent this was concurrent. Each had exclusive jurisdiction in a few cases, but these were comparatively unimportant, and for the most part the two courts paralleled each other. In fact, as has already been stated, the district judge alone could hold the Circuit Court. Moreover, the circuit judges were required to do the work of the Circuit Courts of Appeals. There was thus, not only an overlapping of jurisdiction, but serious interference with the work of each. The result naturally was that the Circuit Court was held more and more by the district judges, while the circuit judges gave more and more attention to their duties on the Circuit Courts of Appeals. Clearly further change was necessary; and the logical thing was to eliminate the Circuit Court, which, though an historic court with an honorable record, had outlived its usefulness as an independent tribunal.

This reform was accomplished when the so-called Judicial Code, under which the federal courts are now organized, was passed by Congress on March 3, 1911, and went into effect January 1, 1912. This act is a thorough revision and codification of the laws relating to the judiciary and provides in minute detail for the entire judicial department of the government.[1] By the terms of this law there are three grades of courts in the regular system, — the Supreme Court, the Circuit Courts of Appeals, and the District Courts. Two special courts are maintained to handle special cases, the Court of Claims and the Court of Customs Appeals. These are courts of limited jurisdiction and are not looked upon as parts of the regular system. There is also a complete judicial organization in the District of Columbia, but its courts are essentially local courts, whose jurisdiction is almost entirely confined to cases arising within the District. The regular hierarchy of courts consists of the three great courts that have been named. Further description of the judicial organization is necessary.

REFERENCES

(For References, see Chap. XXI.)

[1] United States Statutes at Large, Vol. 36, Part I, p. 1087.

CHAPTER XIX

THE FEDERAL COURTS — PRESENT ORGANIZATION

THE Supreme Court, with its foundation resting upon the solid rock of constitutional authorization, stands at the head of the judicial system. It now has nine members, one of whom is designated Chief Justice, and presides over the court's deliberations. The presence of six justices is necessary for a quorum. Members are appointed by the President, subject to confirmation by the Senate, and hold office during good behavior. They receive compensation as fixed by Congress. The Chief Justice now receives $15,000 a year and each Associate Justice, $14,500. The Court is required to hold, at the seat of government, at least one term annually, beginning on the second Monday in October. This usually continues until May or June. Adjourned or special sessions may be held whenever the Court considers it necessary. It is authorized to appoint a clerk, a marshal, and a reporter of its decisions and whatever deputies are necessary for looking after its business. It also establishes the rules which govern its procedure.

Work and Procedure of Supreme Court. — A large number of cases is always before the Supreme Court. These are almost exclusively cases from the lower federal courts or from the State courts on appeal or by writ of error. It is only rarely that the Supreme Court is called upon to exercise its original powers. A good deal of its attention is occupied with questions of constitutional law and passing upon the validity of legislative acts, either of Congress or of the State legislatures. Naturally this is considered its most important work. No case will be considered by the Supreme Court which does not come to it in the regular way. It will express no opinion about cases that are not before it, and in deciding those that are before it, the Court will regularly confine itself to ruling upon those points in controversy which are essential to a determination of the specific cases at issue. Sometimes this rule has not been observed and the Court has given expression to *obiter dicta*, but not often. It is unwilling to decide more than is absolutely necessary to dispose of the case at hand. Upon political questions, also, the Supreme Court refuses to give any opinion. It is a court of law and confines itself to applying the Constitution and the laws to specific legal controversies which are brought to its attention by the regular legal processes.

The work of the Supreme Court is very heavy. On an average, more than five hundred cases come to it every year. For many years its docket has never been clear, in spite of the fact that from four to five hundred decisions may be handed down each year in a term of eight months. The immense amount of labor involved in this is more clearly comprehended when the procedure of the Court is kept in mind. Briefs are submitted by the opposing counsel in every case. Oral argument in open court is allowed unless the counsel waive the privilege. The time allotted to each side is usually one and one half hours, but in the more important cases this may be extended by the Court. When the arguments are completed, each of the judges is required to read the record of the case as it has been developed in the courts below. This may in some instances involve the careful reading of several thousand pages. After this task has been completed by each member of the Court, a conference is called at which the various points of the case are talked over for the purpose of reaching a common opinion and determining the principles of law that apply. If the judges are agreed as to the decision in the case, or if five of them, constituting a majority of the Court, are agreed, one of them is designated by the Chief Justice to prepare the Court's opinion. If the Chief Justice is of the minority, however, the designation of a justice to prepare the majority opinion is left to one of the majority, usually the senior member. When this is done by the member so charged, the opinion is submitted to each of the judges for careful study and revision. If the opinion is approved by the majority, the decision of the Court is announced at the proper time and the opinion is placed on record and printed. It may be, however, that some member of the Court does not approve of the reasoning upon which the opinion is based, although agreeing with the conclusion that is reached.

In that case he may feel called on to prepare an opinion of his own, a " concurring opinion " in which he reasons out the conclusion in the way he thinks is right. It may happen, indeed, that several of the justices feel impelled to give concurring opinions. On the other hand, one or more of the judges may not agree with the majority in the decision of the case and prepare what is called a " dissenting opinion " in which the minority view and the reasoning on which it is based, are given expression. Possibly there may be two or more dissenting opinions. A good many cases are settled by a divided court and not infrequently by a bare majority, as was true of the famous income tax case of 1895 when the Court stood five to four. The various dissenting and concurring opinions are printed in the official reports together with the majority opinion.

It is plain that this careful consideration of the hundreds of cases that are disposed of every year involves a vast amount of work. Yet it does not exhaust the duties of Supreme Court justices. Applications are numerous for various writs which the Court may issue, particularly for writs of error, a process by which the Supreme Court orders cases brought before it for a review of the proceedings and findings of lower courts. These consume time and energy and add not a little to the load which the Supreme Court must carry. Sometimes, in addition, special duties must be attended to by the Court, such as revising the rules of procedure which are observed not only in the Supreme Court itself, but also in all of the federal courts. For example, there went into effect February 1, 1913, a complete new set of equity rules which had been carefully prepared by three of the justices to whom the work had been delegated.

The Supreme Court is a very dignified body, and its sessions are characterized by much formality and impressiveness. Judicial robes are worn while the Court is in session. In solemn manner, with the Chief Justice leading, the members of the Court in the order of seniority pass from the gowning room to the court chamber, and with court attendants, members of the bar, and spectators standing, ascend the bench just as the clock strikes the hour of noon, bow with dignity to the attorneys present, and take their seats. The court crier then announces the sitting and the work of the session begins. Not only is the Court a body of great dignity, but it is a most honorable body, having the highest respect and confidence of the Nation it serves. Where, in the beginning, it was an object of fear and distrust, it is now, and long has been, an object of veneration and highest esteem. Its influence, at first *nil*, is now immeasurable. Why this is so great is made plain in the next chapter, which deals with the powers and jurisdiction of the federal judiciary.

Circuit Court of Appeals. — The court next below the Supreme Court is the Circuit Court of Appeals. There is one of these courts in each of the nine circuits into which the United States is divided.[1] The number of judges in the different circuits varies from two to four, according to the business which has to be done. One circuit has two judges, five circuits have three judges, and three have four judges. Each judge is required to reside in his own circuit and receives a salary of seven thousand dollars a year. One member of the Supreme Court is allotted to each circuit. The Supreme Court justices and the various district judges are competent to sit as judges of the Circuit Court of Appeals within their respective circuits. In practice, the Supreme Court justices do not take part in the work of this court, their time being more than filled with their duties on the higher court. In case the full membership of a Circuit Court of Appeals is not present at any term, the law requires that one or more of the district judges within the circuit shall be called in to make up a full bench. The district judges, however, are not permitted to sit in cases which they have previously tried, or heard in the District Court. These courts are required to hold several terms annually, sitting in different cities of the circuits, some of which are specifically provided for in the Judicial Code. Each court appoints a clerk whose duty it is to keep a proper record of its proceedings. The United States marshals in the several districts where the court is held are the marshals of the Circuit Court of Appeals. It is their duty to attend the sessions of the court, serve and

---

[1] The circuits are made up as follows: The first circuit, with three judges, includes the States of Rhode Island, Massachusetts, New Hampshire, and Maine; the second circuit with four judges, Vermont, Connecticut, and New York; the third with three judges, Pennsylvania, New Jersey, and Delaware; the fourth, with two judges, Maryland, Virginia, West Virginia, North Carolina, and South Carolina; the fifth, with three judges, Georgia, Florida, Alabama, Mississippi, Louisiana, and Texas; the sixth, with three judges, Ohio, Michigan, Kentucky, and Tennessee; the seventh, with four judges, Indiana, Wisconsin, and Illinois; the eighth, with four judges, Nebraska, Minnesota, Iowa, Missouri, Kansas, Arkansas, Colorado, Wyo-

execute its orders, and have charge of the property of the United States used by the court. As previously stated, the purpose in view in establishing the Circuit Courts of Appeals was to relieve the Supreme Court of a part of its excessively heavy labors as an appellate court of highest authority. They were therefore given final jurisdiction in a large number of cases. This has worked to the advantage of the higher court, but because the Supreme Court is made the final arbiter in all cases involving the constitutionality of laws, both State and national, and because of the ease with which the question of constitutionality may be raised, the relief afforded has not been as great as was desired.[1] Notwithstanding this fact, however, the Circuit Courts of Appeals are tribunals of very high standing and great powers, as is shown later in the discussion of their jurisdiction.

The District Court. — Below the Circuit Court of Appeals, and at the bottom of the list, stands the District Court. This court was established by the Judiciary Act of 1789 and has held its position without a break, steadily gaining in influence and power. The country is divided into eighty districts and in each of these there is a District Court. Each State constitutes at least one district. Some of the larger and more populous States are divided into two or more districts, Texas and New York each having four. As a rule, each district has at least one judge, though in a few instances one judge serves two districts. In several of the districts an additional judge is provided for in the law, the southern district of New York being allowed three additional judges. Each one is required by law to reside in the district or in one of the districts for which he is appointed. Failure to comply with this provision is made a high misdemeanor, an offense which subjects the offending judge to impeachment. The salary of district judges is fixed by statute at six thousand dollars a year.

Several terms of the District Court are held each year. The time when the term shall begin and the place where the court

ming, North Dakota, South Dakota, Utah, and Oklahoma; the ninth, with three judges, California, Oregon, Nevada, Washington, Idaho, Montana, the Territory of Hawaii, and the Territory of Alaska. The Circuit Court of Appeals in the ninth circuit is also empowered to review upon appeal or writ of error the decisions of the United States Court for China, established in 1906 under treaty agreement.

[1] Beard, "American Government and Politics," New and Revised Edition, p. 298.

shall sit are in each instance specified in the law. A good many of the districts are divided into smaller districts known as "divisions," provision being made for holding court in each division at stated times. To illustrate the arrangement, take the provisions of the law that apply to Iowa, a typical State. Iowa is divided into two districts, known as the northern and southern districts, in each of which there is a District Court. Each of these courts has its own judge and staff of court officers. The northern district contains four divisions and the southern district six divisions, in each of which the court convenes twice a year. The time for holding court in each division is fixed by law. Similar provision is made for each of the divisions and districts, where the latter are divided, in the entire country. District Court is held in some two hundred and seventy-six places.

Special terms may be held at any time when the district judge feels that there is need. These may convene at the same places as the regular terms, or elsewhere as the judge may direct. Any business may be transacted at a special term which may be transacted at a regular term. For equity and admiralty business, the District Courts are always open, whether in term time or in vacation.

In case a district judge is prevented, by any disability, from holding court at the stated time, some other district judge, under a procedure provided by law, may be called in to take his place and perform all his duties while the disability continues. Ordinarily the judge called upon in this way will be the judge of some other district in the same circuit, but if no other district judge of the same circuit is available, a judge of some other circuit may be designated, in the manner provided by law, for the performance of this duty. Or, if no district judge can be found for the assignment, one of the circuit judges may be named and he will proceed to hold District Court until the disabled judge returns or other provision is made for supplying the temporary vacancy.

The District Court is a court of exclusively original jurisdiction. Its powers are wide and cover both civil and criminal matters. Its criminal jurisdiction, however, is limited to offenses made criminal by federal law, and is therefore very different from that of the courts of the several States. The federal courts are not concerned with crimes under State statutes

THE FEDERAL COURTS — PRESENT ORGANIZATION 247

or the common law, but only with offenses against the Nation which have been made crimes by the law of Congress. In the trial of criminal cases the jury is always used. This is required by the Constitution which guarantees to the accused in all criminal prosecutions except impeachment cases, the right to a speedy and public trial by an impartial jury. In some civil matters, also, the jury is used. The District Court thus is the one jury court in the federal system. Indictments are voted by the grand jury which is summoned by the district judge at the time of the court's regular sessions. The grand jury indictment is required by the Constitution before any person may be tried on a criminal charge. The federal grand jury consists of not less than sixteen nor more than twenty-three persons. It is not summoned to attend the District Court unless the judge considers that there is need for its services. The selection of jurors and service upon both the grand and petit juries are minutely regulated by law.

In connection with the District Court some reference should be made to the representatives of the Department of Justice in the different judicial districts. These are the United States district attorneys and marshals. There are a district attorney and a marshal in each district, and where there is need, assistants and deputies are appointed. These officers are appointed by the President, with the Senate's approval, and are under the direction of the Attorney-General of the United States, who is responsible to the President for the administration of the Department of Justice. It is through the district attorneys that prosecutions for the violation of federal laws are begun and carried on in the District Courts. In the summoning of grand juries, the district judges are guided largely by their wishes. The efficient enforcement of the laws, in fact, depends a good deal upon the integrity, zeal, and skill of these officers. The duty of the marshals is to arrest offenders against federal laws, serve official papers, enforce the orders of the court, and help see that the laws are obeyed. The district marshals are not confined in their work to the jurisdiction of their respective District Courts, but serve also the Circuit Courts of Appeals.

Special Courts. — In addition to the courts in the regular system, the United States maintains two special courts, as previously noted. The older of these is the Court of Claims, established in 1855. It consists of a chief justice and four judges, who are appointed in the same manner as other judges and hold office during good behavior. The chief justice receives an annual salary of $6500, and the other judges, $6000. The court is required to hold one annual session at the city of Washington, beginning on the first Monday in December and continuing as long as the court considers necessary. Three of the judges may hold court and transact any business that may properly come before it; but the concurrence of three judges is necessary to decide any case. In general the work of the Court of Claims, as its name indicates, is concerned with claims against the government of the United States. It is very much more than an auditing body, however, and its power and dignity as a court of high rank should not be underestimated. Its jurisdiction has been extended from time to time by act of Congress. Its judgments are final in many cases, but where the amount in controversy exceeds $3000, the claimant, if the judgment is against him, may appeal to the Supreme Court, providing the appeal is taken within ninety days after judgment is rendered. The government is given the right of appeal in all adverse judgments, regardless of the sum involved. Many important cases, involving large sums of money, oftentimes millions of dollars, are brought before the Court of Claims. Cases may be referred to it, also, by Congress or by the executive departments. This court, aside from expediting the settlement of claims against the government, has served two good purposes; it has lightened the load upon the Supreme Court, and it has relieved Congress from a good deal of annoyance at the hands of those having private claims, who use political influence to obtain congressional action. Such cases are simply referred to the Court of Claims, and Congress acts according to the court's findings.

The other special court is the Court of Customs Appeals. This court was established by the tariff act of 1909, and was made necessary by the multitude of controversies arising out of the administration of the tariff laws. It consists of a presiding judge and four associate judges, appointed by the President in the usual way. The salary is seven thousand dollars a year. Any three members constitute a quorum, and the concurrence of three members is necessary for the decision of any case. The court is always open for the transaction of business, and its sessions may be held in the several judicial circuits, at its own discretion. It is made by law the court of final appeal in all cases arising out of controversies over the classification of imported goods which involve questions of jurisdiction and law. In the words of the law creating the court, it shall exercise " exclusive appellate jurisdiction to review by appeal, as herein provided, final decisions by a Board of General Appraisers in all cases as to the construction of the law and the facts respecting the classification of merchandise and the rate of duty imposed thereon under such classification, and the fees and charges connected therewith, and all appealable questions as to the jurisdiction of said board, and all appealable questions as to the laws and regulations governing the collection of customs revenues; and the judgments of said Court of Customs Appeals shall be final in all such cases."

The courts of the District of Columbia are federal courts inasmuch as the District is federal territory and is wholly under the authority of Congress, but they are not parts of the regular court system. They are local courts that correspond in their nature and functions to the courts of one of the States, although cases sometimes are instituted in them which are of importance to the whole Nation. A complete system of courts has been established. This includes a Court of Appeals, a Supreme Court, a Municipal Court, a Police Court, and a Juvenile Court. The Court of Appeals, consisting of three judges, is the highest in rank, hearing cases on appeal from the District Supreme Court and the other lower courts. It also hears appeals from the decisions of the Commissioner of Patents. Its judgments are reviewable, under the conditions prescribed by law, by the Supreme Court of the United States.

In the foregoing discussion of the federal courts, attention has been given only to their organization and relations to one another from the standpoint of structure. But this, of itself, gives only an imperfect understanding of the courts and their working. To complete the picture, consideration must be given to the vital question of powers and jurisdiction, the subject of the next chapter.

REFERENCES

(For References, see Chap. XXI.)

CHAPTER XX

JURISDICTION OF THE FEDERAL COURTS

THE jurisdiction of the federal judiciary is a subject that is likely to be somewhat confusing to persons untrained in the law, and yet a fairly accurate knowledge of its intricacies is essential to a clear understanding of the administration of justice in the United States. Indeed, more than that is dependent on this knowledge. The very powers of government — of the States, of the Nation, of governmental departments — may be involved in the action of the federal judicial authority. Constitutional readjustments and changes in legislative and administrative policies may follow its decisions. The question of the right of the judiciary to act, therefore, becomes one of supreme consequence, and an understanding of the relation of the States to one another and to the Nation, and of the status and powers of the governmental departments, involves some knowledge of what the judiciary may and may not do.

The confusion which seems to inhere in the subject is reduced somewhat if the fact is grasped that there are two kinds of jurisdiction to be kept in mind. There is the jurisdiction of the federal court system, taken as a whole, as distinguished from that of the State courts, and there is the specific jurisdiction of each of the courts in the federal system. The one is conferred on the courts by the Constitution, which enumerates the kinds of cases they may hear, and the other by act of Congress, except in the case of the Supreme Court, a part of whose jurisdiction is specifically provided for in the Constitution. These are not in conflict in any way, for Congress cannot give jurisdiction to a court involving powers that are not recognized by the Constitution. All that Congress can do, subject to the limitation with respect to the Supreme Court, is to parcel out the judicial powers enumerated in the Constitution among the courts that are established, and provide regulations for their exercise. The totality of judicial power cannot be increased or diminished by act of Congress. In apportioning the jurisdiction of the inferior courts, Congress is free to do what it pleases. It may happen, therefore, that some of the judicial power recognized by the Constitution is not actually exercised by any court, because Congress has not provided for its exercise.

Constitutional Jurisdiction. — First, then, let the constitutional jurisdiction of the federal judiciary be considered. This is not a general jurisdiction, in the legal sense, but a limited jurisdiction. That is, the federal courts cannot hear any and all cases that may arise, but only those over which jurisdiction is given by the Constitution. The judiciary, like the legislative and executive departments, exercises delegated, limited powers. It can do only what it is expressly or by implication permitted to do by the Constitution. In the use of the powers granted, however, it is without restriction. It is this limitation of their powers, it should be noted, which differentiates fundamentally the federal courts from the courts of a State the latter being courts of general jurisdiction. The principle involved is the same as that which is in mind when it is said that the federal government has delegated powers, while the States have the inherent or original powers of government. The States can act in all matters that have not been denied to them by the Constitution, but the federal government can act only in those things that have been delegated to it by the same supreme authority. So it is with the courts.

The provisions of the Constitution giving the totality of judicial power lodged in the Nation are contained in one short paragraph, which reads: " The judicial power shall extend to all cases, in law and equity, arising under this constitution, the laws of the United States, and treaties made, or which shall be made, under their authority; to all cases affecting ambassadors, and other public ministers, and consuls; to all cases of admiralty and maritime jurisdiction; to controversies to which the United States shall be a party; to controversies between two or more States; between citizens of different States, between citizens of the same State claiming lands under grants of different States, and between a State, or the citizens thereof, and foreign states, citizens, or subjects."

It is helpful to note, what a careful study of these provisions makes clear, that the causes which may come before the federal courts are of two classes: those that relate to certain questions or matters, regardless of the persons who are litigants, and those that involve certain persons or parties, regardless of the questions that are in controversy.[1] Let us take up in order the various cases in each of these classes, beginning with the first one mentioned, cases that depend upon the questions in litigation.

Jurisdiction Dependent upon Questions Involved. — I. There are two general kinds of questions that carry with them federal jurisdiction: cases in law and equity arising under the federal Constitution, statutes, or treaties; and cases of admiralty and maritime jurisdiction.

1. The first of these is the most extensive class of cases assigned to the federal courts and gives to them the authority to hear and decide any case which involves the interpretation of the federal Constitution, of federal laws, or of treaties. It gives to either party to a suit who claims protection under any of these the right to have his case adjudicated by the federal courts, subject to the regulations provided by Congress. It does not require, however, that all cases arising under the federal Constitution, laws, or treaties shall be heard by the federal tribunals. The purpose of the provision is to give the federal government, through its own courts, full authority to pass upon all controversies involving its own powers. This was necessary in order to maintain its supremacy in the field assigned to it by the Constitution. Action involving rights under federal law may be brought in State courts, and if the law is upheld and enforced, the national authority has no further concern in the matter. But if the rights claimed under federal law are denied by the State court, then the way must be open for the case to be determined by the federal court of proper jurisdiction, either upon the initiative of the party asserting the authority of the federal law, or that of the federal court itself. Likewise, if action is brought under State law, and the issue is made that this law is repugnant to the federal Constitution, laws, or treaties, the final determination of the matter must rest with the federal judiciary, if the State court upholds the validity of the law in

[1] *Cohens* v. *The State of Virginia*, 6 Wheaton 264 (1821).

question. But if this validity is denied, the national authority is fully recognized and there is no need for an appeal to the federal courts.[1] The principle involved in this is the supremacy of the national authority in its own sphere. The only way to make this sure was to give to the Nation the unquestioned right to decide for itself by means of its own properly constituted agencies whether it has or has not the powers that are called in question.

It is to be noted that the phrase, "in law and equity," in the constitutional provision is without particular significance as far as distinction between the federal and the State judicial authority is concerned. It simply means that whether the cases are in law or in equity, they may be heard by the federal judiciary, if they come within its constitutional jurisdiction.[2]

2. The other kind of cases in which the jurisdiction turns upon the character of the question involved, are "cases of admiralty and maritime jurisdiction." This jurisdiction is not limited to the high seas, but has been extended by judicial construction to include all navigable waters within the United States. Also, the cases within this jurisdiction are not confined to prize cases, but cover all transactions in connection with navigation and the control of the great lakes and navigable rivers. With the great commercial development of the United States this branch of the judiciary's power has become increasingly important. The meaning of admiralty and maritime jurisdiction as developed in the United States is given thus by Professor Willoughby:

"Admiralty jurisdiction refers to that class of cases which are cognizable in courts established by an admiral, in that officer being vested, according to English law, the government

---

[1] Bryce, "The American Commonwealth," New and Revised Edition, pp. 233–234.

[2] "In the jurisprudence of England, there were at the time our Constitution was framed, and until recently, distinct courts of law and of equity. Law and equity in this sense are simply different divisions of jurisprudence; the distinction between them depends on the nature of the case, or the nature of the relief which the court may grant. Such distinction is still recognized in some of the states, although in many states the same courts administer both law and equity. By the use of these two terms in the federal constitution, it was only intended to indicate that both law and equity may be administered in the federal courts, if the case is one otherwise coming within jurisdiction of those courts." — McClain, "Constitutional Law in the United States," Second Edition, p. 230.

of the King's navy and the authority to hear all causes connected with the sea.

"Maritime jurisdiction, as the name itself indicates, is the jurisdiction over matters relating to the sea. To a very considerable extent, then, admiralty jurisdiction and maritime jurisdiction are of like meaning. The terms are not, however, synonymous. Admiralty now has reference, primarily, to the tribunals in which the causes are tried; maritime to the nature of the causes tried. The admiralty and maritime jurisdiction of the United States is then of a double nature; that over cases depending upon acts committed upon navigable waters; and that over contracts, and other transactions connected with such navigable waters. In the former class of cases the jurisdiction is given by the locality of the act; in the latter class by the character of the act or transaction."[1]

Jurisdiction Determined by Parties Involved. — II. The second class of cases within the control of the federal judiciary, those in which the jurisdiction is determined by the parties to the suits, without regard to the question at issue, is not so extensive as the one just considered, though itemized at greater length in the Constitution. It includes controversies, however, of the very highest importance. The cases are as follows:

1. When ambassadors, public ministers, or consuls are parties to the suit.

The control of foreign relations rests exclusively in the federal government. The representatives of foreign nations are accredited to the United States and have no dealings with any of the State governments. They are the representatives of independent sovereign States, and in any court proceedings in which they might be involved are entitled to a settlement by the tribunals of the national government. It would be considered highly improper to subject them to action by the State courts, and any attempt to do so doubtless would be resented by their respective governments. So the Constitution provides that cases affecting ambassadors, public ministers, or consuls come within the control of the federal courts; and not only that, but also, that over such cases the Supreme Court has original jurisdiction. This, however, is not made an exclusive jurisdiction. Hence, Congress may confer original jurisdiction

[1] Willoughby, "The Constitutional Law of the United States," Vol. II, p. 1107.

upon the inferior federal courts in cases involving foreign representatives, if it wishes to do so. This has been done in the case of consuls who, according to the usages of international law, hold a position somewhat different from that of ambassadors and ministers. The right of such officers to bring suit in the Supreme Court continues, however; Congress cannot set aside or qualify in any way the constitutional provision. With respect to wrongs committed by ambassadors and public ministers, redress, under the rules of international law recognized by civilized nations, is not sought in the courts but through an appeal to the State Department and diplomatic intercourse and agreement. Such officers are looked upon as exempt from court control. The consul, however, being a mere agent and not the personal representative of a foreign sovereignty, holds a different status and is within the courts' jurisdiction.

2. When the United States is a party.

This provision merely gives to Congress the power to provide for the trial in the federal courts of cases in which the United States is a party, either as plaintiff or defendant. It does not, of course, confer upon any person the right to bring suit against the United States, or imply that such right exists. The national government, the same as a State government, cannot be sued by individuals without its own consent. The provision simply makes clear that, if suits against the Nation are to be permitted, they shall be heard in the federal and not in the State courts. No other plan was possible, in the light of the experience of the Congress under the Articles of Confederation. The Nation's supremacy in its own constitutional sphere could not be maintained, if it were subject to the authority of the State courts. Only by its own courts can the Nation have its powers determined. By act of Congress individuals are permitted to bring suit against the national government whenever, as provided by law, there is ground for action. The Court of Claims was established for the particular purpose of hearing cases for recovery against the United States. This court, however, can decide only the validity of the claim; the payment of the judgment must be authorized and provided for by Congress.

3. When two or more States are parties to the suit.

Obviously the settlement of a controversy between two or more States could not safely be left to the courts of one of the interested parties. The fundamental idea which lies back of every judicial body is its impartiality. There can be no satisfactory administration of justice on any other basis. To insure proper protection of the States in their relations to one another, jurisdiction over disputes arising among them was given by the Constitution to the federal judiciary, which is independent of all the States alike. Disputes over State boundaries constitute the most important cases that have arisen among the States. At the time of the adoption of the Constitution there were existing controversies involving eleven States over the question of boundaries, and the constitutional provision under discussion was unquestionably inserted by the constitution makers with these disputes in mind. It was clearly impossible to leave the decision of these controversies, which were of long standing, to the courts of the States whose claims were in dispute.

Moreover, some such arrangement as this was made necessary by the constitutional provision which forbids the States to negotiate agreements with one another. By such agreements or by permitting the States to settle their differences in their own way through their own agencies, the Union itself might be seriously endangered. Here again the maintenance of the national authority made the use of the federal courts a necessity.

It is to be noted that cases of this kind are placed by the Constitution within the original jurisdiction of the Supreme Court, on the same plane with cases affecting ambassadors, public ministers, and consuls. These are the only kinds of cases thus set apart. It should be added, however, that cases brought by the United States against individual States, and by States against the United States, have been entertained and decided by the Supreme Court.

4. When a State and citizens of another State are parties to the suit.

As the Constitution was in the beginning, two kinds of cases were possible under this provision: those brought by a State against the citizens of another State, and those brought by the citizens of a State against another State. The first is possible now, but the second is not. By the eleventh amendment which became a part of the Constitution in 1798, only nine years after the Constitution itself became operative, the right of citizens of one State to bring suit against another State was abolished. It was held to reflect upon the dignity and to be a denial of the independence of the States to compel them to submit to suits against their will.[1] The result of this amendment was to make it impossible for the federal courts to claim jurisdiction in any case brought against a State, unless the case were instituted by another State, or by a foreign state, or by the United States.

Good reasons existed for placing the cases that may arise under this clause within the jurisdiction of the federal courts. For one thing, justice demands that they be heard by courts entirely free from the charge or even the suspicion of partiality. A State appearing as plaintiff in a suit against a citizen of another State could not reasonably expect to have the cause determined by its own courts; neither could the defendant in the case reasonably expect to have the courts of his own State adjudicate the matter. The latter not only might result in injustice to the plaintiff State, but would compel it to submit to a course that was not consistent with its dignity as a State. Moreover, there is a practical difficulty in the way of having the case determined by the courts of the State bringing the suit. The jurisdiction of a State's courts is limited absolutely to the territory and persons within its own boundaries; a non-resident, therefore, cannot be brought within their control unless he appears voluntarily. This of itself made it necessary to give the federal courts jurisdiction; otherwise no decision could be obtained and the ends of justice would be denied.

5. When citizens of different States are parties to the suit.

This is one of the most important of the classes of cases assigned to the federal judiciary. Most of the civil business coming before the inferior federal courts involves controversies between citizens of different States. The object of the constitutional provision is the same as of others previously considered, — to make available for the litigants a court that is free from prejudice, or the possibility of prejudice on account of their citizenship. The law applied need not be federal law;

[1] Great indignation prevailed among the people of all the States when the Supreme Court in 1793, in the case of *Chisholm* v. *Georgia* (2 Dallas 419) held that a suit of this kind was permissible under the Constitution. In this case Georgia refused to appear, and judgment was given against her by default. The agitation which this case aroused resulted in the eleventh amendment.

it may be State law, — the law of one of the States of which parties to the suit are citizens, or even of a third State in which, for instance, the property involved in the controversy is located.

In these cases the question of citizenship is fundamental, and sometimes must be determined by the court before which the suit is brought in deciding whether or not it has jurisdiction under this clause of the Constitution. Citizenship of a State and citizenship of the United States are not identical. One may be a citizen of the latter without being a citizen of the former. Therefore for a suit to be brought under this constitutional provision, the State citizenship of each party must be definitely established; and this citizenship must be of different States. A controversy between a citizen of a State and a citizen of the United States residing in one of the Territories of the United States or in the District of Columbia, could not be brought to trial under this clause of the Constitution. It has been held, however, by the Supreme Court, that within the meaning of this clause any person who is a citizen of the United States, whether native born or naturalized, is a citizen of the State in which he has his domicile.[1]

It is important to note that corporations, though they are not citizens in the strict sense of the term and cannot have citizenship such as belongs to natural persons, are conceded the right, by ruling of the Supreme Court, to bring suits under the clause in question. The Court's position on this has been changed from time to time, however. In the beginning it was held that a corporation is not a citizen within the meaning of the diverse citizenship clause. This is still the theory of the law, but by a fiction the Court practically concedes citizenship to corporations for the purpose of this clause. For many years the Court held that, since a corporation is an artificial legal entity, it " would look behind its corporate personality to see whether the individuals of which it was composed were, each and every one of them, citizens of a State different from that of each of the parties sued." Later, however, this position was yielded and the Court asserted that it would presume the citizenship of the persons composing the corporation to be that of the State in which the corporation was chartered. And still

[1] Willoughby, " The Constitutional Law of the United States," Vol. II, p. 984.

later it was held that this presumption could not be rebutted.[1] The ruling which the court made and which holds may be stated in its own words: "Where a corporation is created by the laws of a State, the legal presumption is, that its members are citizens of the State in which alone the corporate body has a legal existence; and that a suit by or against a corporation, in its corporate name, must be presumed to be a suit by or against citizens of the State which created the corporate body; and that no averment or evidence to the contrary is admissible, for the purpose of withdrawing the suit from the jurisdiction of a court of the United States."[2] That the actual citizenship of the stockholders is not of the State in which the corporation is chartered seems to be of no importance. The practical effect of the Court's position is to make corporations citizens as far as the diverse citizenship clause is concerned.

6. When citizens of the same State are parties to a suit involving lands claimed under grants of different States.

Practically this class has not given rise to serious difficulties in its application, though under it cases involving large financial interests may arise. The necessity for a provision of this character is clear enough. The laws that are applicable are not those of the State of which the parties to the suit are citizens. And the laws of one State cannot be administered by the courts of another State. Cases of this kind are clearly cases for the federal courts and were so regarded by the framers of the Constitution.

7. When a State or its citizens and a foreign state or its citizens or subjects are parties to a suit.

This clause, though far less important than the others that have been considered, is interesting for different reasons. Several kinds of cases are possible under it, at least theoretically. The suit may be one between a State and a foreign state; between a State and the citizens of a foreign state; between the citizens of a State and a foreign state; or, between the citizens of a State and aliens, that is, citizens or subjects of foreign states. With the exception of the last kind, no cases under this clause have ever arisen, and it is difficult to see how they could arise. The Constitution, of course, cannot give a State the

[1] Willoughby, "The Constitutional Law of the United States," Vol. II, p. 985.
[2] *Ohio & Mississippi R.R. Co* v. *Wheeler*, 1 Black 286 (1862).

right to sue a foreign state; in no way could such foreign state be compelled to appear as defendant. Since the States can have no dealings with foreign states, except with the consent of Congress, it is hard to imagine a situation in which a foreign state would seek redress from a State through the courts. If such should happen, it is presumed the jurisdiction would lie with the federal courts, although it is by no means sure. It would lie there if anywhere, but it is not at all certain that this jurisdiction could be asserted, even if both parties were to consent to the suit.[1] Even the theoretical right of aliens to bring suit against a State, as provided for in the original Constitution, was destroyed by the eleventh amendment, and for the same reasons that the citizens of one State were deprived of the right to sue another State. It was inconsistent with the dignity and independence of the States of the Union. Suits between citizens of a State and aliens, however, are of frequent occurrence. That these should be decided by the federal judiciary and not by that of the State whose citizens are parties to the litigation is obviously the only proper procedure possible.

Jurisdiction of Particular Courts. — In the discussion thus far the only jurisdiction considered is that which, by constitutional grant, is possible to the federal judiciary as a whole, as distinguished from that of the State courts. No account has been taken of the special jurisdiction of particular courts. It remains to take up in turn each of the courts in the regular system and see in a general way what part of the constitutional jurisdiction has been apportioned to it by Congress, which, with the exception of two instances in connection with the Supreme Court, has full authority to say what powers each court shall exercise. It is logical to begin with the Supreme Court which, in part, has its jurisdiction defined in the Constitution.

I. The only reference in the Constitution to the powers of particular courts is found in the short paragraph: " In all cases affecting ambassadors, other public ministers and consuls, and those in which a State shall be a party, the Supreme Court shall have original jurisdiction. In all the other cases before mentioned, the Supreme Court shall have appellate jurisdiction, both as to law and fact, with such exceptions, and under such regulations as the Congress shall make."

[1] Willoughby, " The Constitutional Law of the United States," Vol. II, p. 1060.

It will be noticed that the Supreme Court's original jurisdiction in the two cases mentioned is not, as has been pointed out previously, an exclusive jurisdiction. The inferior courts may be made courts of first instance in the same kinds of cases by act of Congress. Of course, the Supreme Court cannot be deprived by law of its original jurisdiction, and parties to suits in the cases mentioned cannot be denied the right of beginning action in the Supreme Court, but they may be given the opportunity to start proceedings in the lower courts if they wish. By law, however, the Supreme Court is given exclusive jurisdiction in all cases where two or more States are parties, and in all suits or proceedings against ambassadors or other public ministers, or their domestic servants; in cases brought by ambassadors or public ministers it has original but not exclusive jurisdiction.

It is to be noticed, also, that practically all of the Supreme Court's work is appellate in character, extending to all cases that may come before the federal judiciary, with the exception of the two cases in which it is a court of first instance. Full authority to regulate this appellate jurisdiction, however, is conferred upon Congress, the constitutional provision not guaranteeing in any manner an appeal to the Supreme Court. It is under this authorization that Congress has conferred upon the Circuit Courts of Appeals final jurisdiction in a large number of cases, and has regulated minutely the conditions of appeal from the different lower courts. Congress could prevent appeals entirely by making no provision for them.

Attention should be directed at this point, also, to the fact that the Constitution does not confer upon the federal courts absolutely exclusive jurisdiction in any kind of cases. As far as the language of the Constitution is concerned, the State courts may exercise a concurrent jurisdiction with respect to all of the cases enumerated as being within the scope of the judicial power of the Nation. It is left with Congress to say what the apportionment of jurisdiction shall be. This the Congress has done and has given exclusive jurisdiction to the federal courts in a number of things, such as federal crimes, admiralty cases, patent right and copyright cases, suits in which the United States is a party, suits between two or more States, and many other matters. A good many cases under the regulations of Congress may be brought in either the federal or State courts;

and in a few instances the State courts are permitted to have exclusive jurisdiction. In thus distributing court jurisdiction, Congress does not and cannot delegate judicial power to the State courts. Congress has no power over the State courts or any other branch of the State governments. Whatever concurrent jurisdiction the State courts have is theirs of their own right. No powers of any kind have been given the States by the federal Constitution or by any of the agencies created by it. This concurrent judicial power, as is true of any of the concurrent legislative powers, must be looked upon as a part of the inherent powers of the States. The Constitution gives to Congress authority to confer exclusive jurisdiction in certain cases upon the federal courts. If it does not do this, the State courts are free to act of their own right.

The appellate jurisdiction of the Supreme Court, under the regulations prescribed by Congress, is extensive, and relates to questions of fundamental importance. To make clear the Court's powers in this regard, the cases in which it is permitted to review the judgments of the lower courts, either on appeals or writs of error, may be grouped under several heads, according to the courts whose judgments are under review.

1. Appeals and writs of error may be taken from the District Courts direct to the Supreme Court in cases involving the District Courts' jurisdiction, — in such cases the question of jurisdiction alone being certified to the Supreme Court for decision; from final sentences and decrees in prize cases; in any case that involves the construction or application of the federal Constitution; in any case in which the constitutionality of any law of the United States, or the validity or construction of any treaty made under its authority is drawn in question; and in any case in which the constitution or law of a State is claimed to be in contravention of the Constitution of the United States.

2. Appeals and writs of error may be taken from the Circuit Court of Appeals in any case in which the decision of the lower court is not made final by law, provided the matter in controversy exceeds one thousand dollars, besides the costs. In any case, civil or criminal, in which the decision of the Circuit Court of Appeals is made final, the Supreme Court may by the proper writ, upon petition from any party to the suit, order the case before it for review and determination; in this, the Court has

the same power it would have if the case were before it on appeal or writ of error. In any case within its appellate jurisdiction, as defined by law, the Circuit Court of Appeals may certify to the Supreme Court any questions of law upon which it desires the higher court's instruction; and the Supreme Court may then give instructions which will be binding upon the lower court, or call for the whole record of the case and proceed to decide it just as it would if the matter were before it for review by writ of error or on appeal.

3. Writ of error may be taken from any State court of last resort in any case in which is involved the validity of a federal statute, or treaty or authority exercised under the United States, and the decision is against such validity; in any case where is drawn in question the validity of State laws or of an authority exercised under them on the ground of their being repugnant to the Constitution, treaties, or laws of the United States, and the decision is in favor of their validity; and in any case where the decision is against any title, right, privilege, or immunity claimed under the Constitution, laws, treaties, or authority of the United States. In these cases the writ of error has the same effect as if the action complained of had been taken by a federal court, and the Supreme Court may reverse, modify, or affirm the judgment of the State court as it sees fit.

4. Appeals may be taken from the Court of Claims to the Supreme Court, both by the United States, which may appeal from all adverse judgments, and by the plaintiff, who can appeal when the amount in controversy exceeds three thousand dollars, or when his claim has been declared forfeited to the United States on the charge of fraud.

5. Writs of error or appeal may also be taken from the Court of Appeals of the District of Columbia, the supreme courts of the Territories, Alaska and Hawaii, and from the courts of last resort in Porto Rico and the Philippine Islands.

6. Appellate jurisdiction is given to the Supreme Court, under conditions prescribed by law, in controversies arising in bankruptcy proceedings.

This brief statement of the conditions under which the judgments of lower courts may be reviewed, though incomplete as to details, makes plain the wide extent of the Supreme Court's appellate jurisdiction. With these facts in mind it is easy to understand why the work of the Court each year is so heavy. This is especially the case when the number of courts from which appeals may be taken is recalled, — nine Circuit Courts of Appeals, about eighty District Courts, forty-eight State courts, and in addition the various special courts and the courts of the Territories and Dependencies.

II. Next in order comes the jurisdiction of the Circuit Courts of Appeals as established by Congress. These courts have no original jurisdiction. Their appellate power, though limited, is extensive and in a good many important cases is final. The essential provisions of the law may be given in a few words. It is stated that the Circuit Courts of Appeals shall have power to review by appeal or by writ of error the final decisions of the District Courts in all cases except those in which appeals may be taken direct from the District Court to the Supreme Court. The cases in which this direct appeal may be made have already been given. It is provided, also, that except when the Supreme Court shall be asked for instructions or shall order a case to be sent up by the Circuit Court of Appeals for determination by the high court, as previously outlined, " the judgments and decrees of the Circuit Court of Appeals shall be final in all cases in which the jurisdiction is dependent entirely upon the opposite parties to the suit or controversy being aliens and citizens of the United States, or citizens of different States; also in all cases arising under the patent laws, under the copyright laws, under the revenue laws, and under the criminal laws, and in admiralty cases." It is further provided that under the conditions prescribed by law, this court may entertain appeals in bankruptcy cases and from the decrees or orders of the District Courts in certain equity proceedings, such as the appointment of receivers and the granting or dissolving of injunctions.

III. The District Court is the court of first instance, and as such has jurisdiction over an exceedingly large number of cases. In fact, almost all of the cases recognized as coming within the scope of the federal judiciary are heard in the District Courts. An entire chapter of the Judicial Code is devoted to its jurisdiction. In this there are listed, in detail, twenty-five kinds or groups of cases that may come before the District Court. Only the more important of these can be given here. The District Court is given original jurisdiction of all crimes and offenses cognizable under federal laws; of all civil or equity cases brought by the United States; of cases between citizens of different States; of cases arising under the Constitution, laws, or treaties of the United States; of all admiralty cases, seizures, and prizes; of cases arising under the postal laws; of suits under the patent, copyright, and trade-mark laws; of suits for violation of interstate commerce laws; of suits relating to civil rights; of suits against consuls; of all proceedings in bankruptcy; of suits under the immigration and contract labor laws; of all suits against trusts, monopolies, and combinations in restraint of trade.

This list of cases is not exhaustive, but it is sufficiently complete to indicate the great importance of the District Courts and to suggest the vast amount of litigation that comes before them. Special attention, perhaps, should be called to their criminal jurisdiction. This has always been considered the most important part of their jurisdiction, but it is greater now than it used to be. The jurisdiction which formerly belonged to the Circuit Courts was, upon their abolition, transferred to the District Courts. The crimes of which these courts may take cognizance under federal law are, of course, wholly statutory in character. There is no federal common law jurisdiction. For an act to be a crime against the United States it must be declared to be such by law of Congress or by constitutional provision. Among the federal laws under which criminal proceedings are especially frequent are the internal revenue, tariff, and postal laws, and laws relating to industrial combinations, public lands, and national banks. As the Nation has developed the criminal jurisdiction of its courts has become wider.

REFERENCES

(For References, see Chap. XXI.)

CHAPTER XXI

THE COURTS AND LEGISLATION

OF the various powers possessed by the federal judiciary, one stands out with striking clearness as preëminent. This is the power of the Supreme Court to declare acts of both the State legislatures and of the Congress unconstitutional. The tremendous significance of this prerogative is manifest. It gives to the Supreme Court of the United States a position that is really unique among the judicial tribunals of the world. In none of the countries of Europe is there a court with authority to set aside an act of the legislature on the ground that it is not in harmony with the constitution. It is true that in some of the newer states in other parts of the world, this American practice has been adopted to a greater or less degree.[1] Nevertheless, the principle back of it is a singularly American principle; it represents one of America's most vital contributions to the science of government. Perhaps no other feature of the government of the United States has excited such deep interest among students of politics. It is universally admitted to be of profound importance.

The peculiar position which the Supreme Court holds in American government, as a result of this power, is also a matter of lively interest and, to a good many persons, one of grave concern. By the theory of the Constitution, the judiciary, of which the Supreme Court is the head, is a coördinate branch of the government. It is neither inferior nor superior to the legislative and executive departments. Yet it is, in fact, the authoritative judge of their powers, as it is also of its own. European courts have no such supreme function as this. In England, for example, the courts are bound by any act of Parliament. They cannot question the Parliament's authority.[2] If the interpretation of a law by the English judiciary is not what

[1] Below, p. 547.   [2] Below, p. 398.

Parliament intended or desires, it may alter the law as it sees fit; the courts will be bound by what it does. But in the United States, the power of Congress is what the Supreme Court says it is. The validity of any act may be passed upon by the Court. This will not be done, of course, unless a " case " arises in which the constitutionality of the act is drawn in question. The Supreme Court on its own initiative will not call in question a legislative enactment, but it will not hesitate to nullify any act that is brought before it in the prescribed manner, when it is convinced that the act is repugnant to the Constitution, whose final, authoritative interpreter the Supreme Court is.

Constitution Makers and the Courts. — It is a fact of great interest that the Constitution does not expressly confer upon the Supreme Court this remarkable power. There is in it no reference whatever to the constitutionality of laws. As previously indicated, the language of the Constitution is somewhat vague with respect to the judiciary. The precise intention of the constitution makers is not clear. That some of this vagueness was intentional is beyond dispute. At least some of the men who helped frame the Constitution were unwilling to have the powers of the judiciary minutely defined. In this connection Professor Beard quotes Gouverneur Morris, one of the leaders of the convention, who, in speaking of the language of the Constitution, used these words: " Having rejected redundant and equivocal terms, I believed it as clear as our language would permit, excepting, nevertheless, a part of what relates to the judiciary. On that subject conflicting opinions had been maintained with so much professional astuteness that it became necessary to select phrases which expressing my own notions would not alarm others nor shock their self-love." [1] This statement makes it clear that some members of the convention had in mind judicial activity which is not specifically mentioned in the Constitution.

Opinions differ, however, whether there was an intention to give the federal judiciary power to pass upon the constitu-

---

[1] Beard, "American Government and Politics," New and Revised Edition, p. 307. For an interesting study of the intentions of the constitution makers with respect to the power of the Supreme Court to pass upon the constitutionality of statutes, see Professor Beard's "The Supreme Court and the constitution." An equally interesting article in answer to Professor Beard's argument, by Horace A. Davis, is given in *The American Political Science Review*, Vol. VII, p. 541 (November, 1913).

tionality of laws. It is held by some that the exercise of this power is "usurpation" on the part of the courts.[1] By others it is asserted that the courts are clearly within their constitutional rights. The controversy over the original intention can never be settled, but that some of the men who helped to draft the Constitution expected the courts to exercise the power in question cannot be doubted. Alexander Hamilton, for instance, brought out this fact clearly in his arguments for the ratification of the Constitution. In *The Federalist* he discusses the question at some length and asserts squarely that the limitations of the Constitution upon legislative authority can be preserved only through the courts of justice, "whose duty it must be to declare all acts contrary to the manifest tenor of the Constitution void."[2] His views are clearly stated in these words: "There is no position which depends on clearer principles, than that every act of delegated authority, contrary to the tenor of the commission under which it is exercised, is void. No legislative act, therefore, contrary to the constitution, can be valid. To deny this would be to affirm, that the deputy is greater than his principal; that the servant is above his master; that the representatives of the people are superior to the people themselves; that men acting by virtue of powers, may do not only what their powers do not authorize, but what they forbid. . . . The interpretation of the laws is the proper and peculiar province of the courts. A constitution is, in fact, and must be regarded by the judges as a fundamental law. It must therefore belong to them to ascertain its meaning, as well as the meaning of any particular act proceeding from the legislative body. If there should happen to be an irreconcilable variance between the two, that which has the superior obligation and validity ought, of course, to be preferred; in other words the constitution ought to be preferred to the statute, the intention of the people to the intention of their agents. . . . Nor does the conclusion by any means suppose a superiority of the judicial to the legislative power. It only supposes that the power of the people is superior to both; and that where the will of the legislature declared in its statutes, stands in opposition to that of the people declared

[1] Judge Walter Clark in *The Independent*, Sept. 26, 1907; *Political Science Quarterly*, Vol. XXVI, p. 238. Other magazine articles may readily be found.
[2] No. 78.

in the constitution, the judges ought to be governed by the latter rather than the former. They ought to regulate their decisions by the fundamental laws, rather than by those which are not fundamental."

The opinion of Hamilton is quoted here at such length for the reason that it not only shows what was intended and publicly discussed by one of the ablest members of the constitutional convention, but also gives in essence the argument upon which the Supreme Court based the exercise of its power in the beginning and by which it has been constantly justified. Moreover, to give expression to the views of a man who was so influential as Hamilton is all the more permissible inasmuch as the power of the courts, and particularly this power to nullify legislative acts, has become an issue in the practical politics of the present day. From one standpoint it is a matter of little or no importance what the framers of the Constitution intended; the *fact* is that the Supreme Court for more than a century has claimed and exercised the right to set aside legislative acts which it considered to be contrary to the Constitution. And the wisdom of permitting the Court to exercise the power now and in the future cannot rationally depend upon the original intention. However, the popular judgment as to the wisdom of the Court's possessing this power may be materially influenced by the manner in which it was acquired. If the general public were convinced that the Supreme Court has usurped this great power, its judgment would certainly be different from what it would be if the opinion prevailed that the Court was clearly acting within its constitutional rights. So the question of whether or not the Court was intended to have this power becomes one of some practical significance.

Supreme Court's Power to Nullify Legislation. — As stated before, the Supreme Court's power to nullify legislation is not the result of an express grant in the Constitution. It is an implied power, derived by "necessary implication." The case in which the Supreme Court asserted the power and developed the principles on which it is based, is the famous case of Marbury *v.* Madison.[1] The opinion in this case, given by Chief Justice Marshall, is one of the most important that has ever been handed down. The position taken by the Court is somewhat similar to

[1] 1 Cranch 137 (1803).

that of Hamilton. It asserts that the basic fact on which the American government rests is the original right of the people to establish whatever kind of government they think will serve them best. The principles thus set up are deemed fundamental. Since they proceed from the supreme authority, which can seldom act, they are intended to be permanent. The Constitution embodies these principles. The will of the people, through the Constitution, organizes the government and assigns to each department its particular powers. In addition to this, limitations may be set for each department which are not to be disregarded. The United States is a government of this kind. The powers of the legislature are limited, and that the limitations may not be mistaken or forgotten, they are written in the Constitution.

This Constitution either controls any legislative act that is repugnant to it, or any ordinary legislative act may work a change in the Constitution. There is no middle ground between these two alternatives. The Constitution is either the supreme law, unchangeable by ordinary means, or it is on the same plane with ordinary acts and may be changed whenever the legislature wishes to change it. But it was clearly the intention of the people to make the Constitution the fundamental and paramount law of the land, and therefore an act of the legislature repugnant to the Constitution must be void. It is the function of the judiciary to say what the law is, both the fundamental law and the act of the legislature. In the words of Marshall: "So if a law be in opposition to the Constitution; if both the law and the Constitution apply to a particular case, so that the court must either decide that case conformably to the law, disregarding the Constitution; or conformably to the Constitution, disregarding the law; the court must determine which of these conflicting rules governs the case. This is of the very essence of judicial duty. If, then, the courts are to regard the Constitution, and the Constitution is superior to any ordinary act of the legislature, the Constitution, and not such ordinary act, must govern the case to which they both apply." Moreover, the judges have taken a solemn oath to support the Constitution, and they would fail in this and break faith with the people, if they should give effect to a law that is not in harmony with it.

The reasoning of the Court, thus briefly outlined still stands; it has not been modified by later decisions. However, it is not free from criticism. Many able expositors of the Constitution believe that it is inconclusive. For example, the solemn oath to support the Constitution, of which the Court makes so much, of itself does not single out the judiciary as the only department that might pass upon the constitutionality of laws. The President takes an equally solemn oath, yet it is not asserted by any one that this function therefore belongs to him. Neither does it necessarily belong to the courts merely because of the oath. That the Constitution should be maintained supreme is not questioned; the criticism is directed to the contention that the judiciary is a sort of divinely ordained agency to which alone could the power of testing the constitutionality of laws be intrusted. Even the expediency of having the courts exercise this power is not doubted by many who question the soundness of the logic upon which the Supreme Court rests its authority. Professor Willoughby states well a matured judgment, held by many others, when he says: "That organ or body which has the final power to interpret the Constitution has necessarily the power to give to that instrument what meaning it will. It thus becomes, in a sense, supreme over all the other organs of government. Unless, therefore, the body from whose action the Constitution itself derived its force is to be resorted to in every case of doubtful construction (and this, of course, is impracticable) the only alternative is to delegate this supreme power to some one of the permanent organs of government. But it does not necessarily follow, as the reasoning of Marshall, Webster, and Kent would seem to indicate, that, as an abstract proposition, this power must always be possessed by the judiciary. Indeed, in all other countries except the United States, this power is vested in the legislature. These other written constitutions did not, indeed, exist at the time that Marshall rendered his opinion, but their present existence shows that under a written instrument of government it does not necessarily follow that the courts should have a power to hold void legislative acts contrary to its provisions."[1] This writer goes on to show that in his opinion the Supreme Court has authority under the Constitution to disregard legislative acts which it considers

[1] Willoughby, "The Constitutional Law of the United States," Vol. I, p. 4.

unconstitutional. But this power comes from the fact that the Constitution and the laws of the United States made under its authority are declared to be the "supreme law of the land" and that the judicial power is extended to "all cases, in law and equity, arising under the Constitution." Judge Marshall recognized the force of this in his opinion in Marbury *v.* Madison, but, it is asserted, he did not make it, as he should have done, the foundation of his argument. The words of Marshall are given to show his thought: "The judicial power of the United States is extended to all cases arising under the Constitution. Could it be the intention of those who gave this power, to say that in using it the Constitution should not be looked into? That a case arising under the Constitution should be decided without examining the instrument under which it arises? This is too extravagant to be maintained." [1]

Popular Criticism of the Courts. — It is to be noted that the general criticism of the Court for exercising this power is confined to its use in nullifying acts of Congress; it does not extend to the setting aside of State laws because they are inconsistent with the federal Constitution. The latter is conceded by almost every one to be a proper function of the Court. The perpetuity of the Union is dependent upon a full observance of the limitations imposed on the States by the Constitution; and whether or not these limitations are observed must be determined by national authority. In no other way could the national supremacy in its own field be maintained. The nullifying of State statutes by a State's own judiciary, on the ground that they are not in harmony with the State constitution, is a different matter. The federal courts have nothing to do with this. The widespread dissatisfaction over the voiding of legislative acts by the courts is largely due to the action of the State courts. Although a discussion of the State judiciary does not properly belong here and is given in a later chapter, it may be said that this dissatisfaction has grown rapidly in recent years, both in extent and intensity, and a strong demand has sprung up in many of the States for thoroughgoing court reform. The recall of judges by popular vote, already provided for in the constitutions of some of the States, the recall of judicial decisions, a proposed reform which has become an issue in practical politics,

[1] Willoughby, "The Constitutional Law of the United States," Vol. I, p. 6.

and the vast amount of criticism of the courts found in magazines and books of recent years, all give evidence of the awakening that is taking place among the people with respect to the judiciary and its functions. The movement for a greater democracy, which is getting well under way in the United States, will not overlook the courts. The position they hold in America is too central, too political, for them to be ignored. They must be the servants, not the masters of the people. Although, as stated before, the shortcomings of the State courts have been chiefly in mind in the agitation for reform, the national judiciary has come in for its share of adverse criticism. The belief is widespread that the federal courts have been too much under the influence of the big business interests of the country and that they have often failed to dispense even-handed justice. The will of the people has sometimes been thwarted by their decisions and popular reforms blocked. The inevitable result of this is to bring the courts into the field of partisan political discussion and to arouse a demand for the curtailment of judicial powers.

Rules Governing the Courts. — The attitude of the federal courts in passing upon the constitutionality of laws should be kept clearly in mind. Unless this is done, unfair judgment of them is probable. Their position is definitely stated in the rules of construction which have been set up for their guidance in constitutional cases. These rules are not required by the Constitution or by law, but are established by the courts voluntarily and are strictly adhered to. A somewhat full statement of the more important of these principles of construction is well worth while.[1]

1. Courts of first instance will not hold an act unconstitutional except in clear cases, but will leave this to the final judgment of the Supreme Court. The lower courts are bound by the prior decisions of the higher courts as to the validity of an act, even though new arguments against it are advanced. The presumption is that the superior courts considered all phases of the question.

2. The regular rule of the Supreme Court is that no law will be held void except by majority of the full bench.

---

[1] The formulation of these rules is based on that of Willoughby in his "Constitutional Law of the United States," Vol. I, p. 12.

T

3. The courts will not pass on the constitutionality of laws except in suits brought before them in the manner prescribed by law by parties whose material interests are involved. They will not of their own accord raise the question of constitutionality. That must be a point in controversy in the suit. Neither will the Supreme Court express opinions as to the constitutionality of proposed acts upon request.

4. The Supreme Court will not deny validity to an act of Congress unless that is absolutely necessary to decide the case before it. It will not only not go out of its way to declare the law invalid, but will go as far as possible to uphold the law.

5. If it is possible without doing too great violence to the language used in the statute, it will be construed so as to hold the law constitutional. The presumption of the Court is always that Congress intended to act, and did act, within its powers, until the contrary is affirmatively shown. On the other hand, if the purpose of the act is clearly unconstitutional, the Court will not make a strained or arbitrary interpretation of the language used in order to give validity to the law.

6. When only a part of a law is held to be unconstitutional, the Court will not permit this to invalidate the entire act, if the invalid part can be separated from the remainder so as to leave the latter complete, and the Court is convinced that Congress or the legislature would have enacted the remaining portion without that which is set aside. If the Court feels that the part held void is essential to the accomplishment of the legislative intent, the whole act will be nullified.

These are in substance the leading rules which govern the courts in dealing with the question of constitutionality. In addition, it is to be emphasized that the courts are not concerned with the motives that actuated the legislature in passing the law whose validity is in dispute, or with the wisdom or expediency of its enactment. It is also to be emphasized that the presumption, as before stated, is always in favor of the constitutionality of an act of Congress. For this presumption to be overthrown, it must be shown positively to the Court's satisfaction that Congress has exceeded its powers. In the words of the Court: " A decent respect for a coördinate branch of the federal government demands that the judiciary should presume, until the contrary is clearly shown, that there has been no transgression of power by Congress, all the members of which act under the obligation of an oath of fidelity to the Constitution."[1]

Peculiar Function of American Courts. — It is in the action of the courts in setting aside unconstitutional legislative acts that the one unique function of the American judiciary finds its most striking expression. This function is fundamental and is peculiar to the American system. It goes to the very root of constitutional government in the United States and differentiates it sharply and fundamentally from those of other countries. This underlying function of the courts is to protect the individual citizen in the enjoyment of his rights against the government, which have been created by the fundamental law, and at the same time preserve the powers of government in all of their fullness. It is the function of the balance-wheel, as President Wilson describes it. In no other country is the constitutional system balanced in this way. In the courts of no other country may the rights of individuals be asserted and protected against all governmental interference and the powers of government in all its departments be authoritatively defined. In no other country is the judiciary " means to maintain that nice adjustment between individual rights and governmental powers which constitutes political liberty."[2] In the courts of other nations, individuals, as against one another, may have their rights adjudicated and fully protected; but as against the government this may not be done.[3] This is a fact whose vital significance must not be overlooked in the comparative study of free governments. That the action of government may be blocked by an individual citizen, through an appeal to the courts, is a stupendous fact.

President Wilson puts the matter this way: " Constitutional government exists in its completeness and full reality only when the individual, only when every individual, is regarded as a partner of the government in the conduct of the nation's life. The citizen is not individually represented in any assembly or in any regularly constituted part of the government itself. He cannot, except in the most extraordinary cases and

---

[1] *Knox* v. *Lee*, 12 Wallace 457 (1871).
[2] Wilson, " Constitutional Government in the United States," p. 143.
[3] Below, Chap. XLIX.

with the utmost difficulty, bring his individual private affairs to the attention of Congress or of his state legislature, to the attention of the President of the United states or of the executive officer of his state; he would find himself balked of relief if he did by the laws under which they act and exercise their clearly specified powers. It is only in the courts that men are individuals in respect of their rights. Only in them can the individual citizen set up his private right and interest against the government by an appeal to the fundamental understandings upon which the government rests. In no other government but our own can he set them up even there against the government. He can everywhere set them up against other individuals who would invade his rights or who have imposed upon him, but not against the government. The government under every other constitutional system but our own is sovereign, unquestionable, to be restrained not by the courts, but only by public opinion, only by the opinion of the nation acting through the representative chamber. We alone have given our courts power to restrain the government under which they themselves act and from which they themselves derive their authority."[1]

That this is a profoundly significant principle of government needs no proof. It accords to the citizen of the United States a prerogative such as the citizen of no other country enjoys, — that of holding in check the various agencies of government if they seek to invade the inviolable sphere of liberty which is recognized as his by the Constitution. The manner in which this is done is most spectacularly shown by the judicial nullification of legislative acts, — an action which, as has been pointed out, the courts never take except upon the initiative of an individual or of a group of individuals whose interests are identical.

Yet, there is grave criticism of the principle among Americans. The opinion prevails among a good many persons, and is becoming more prevalent, that the liberty of the citizen is being jeopardized by the exercise of the very power, which, under the principle stated, is designed for his protection. The danger, it is said, comes not from the executive or legislative departments, but from the courts themselves. It is by the courts that the will of the people, as expressed by the legislature, is frequently

[1] Wilson, "Constitutional Government in the United States," pp. 143–144.

defeated and the pathway to important political and economic reforms blocked. Through their power to interpret the laws and the Constitution, the function of the legislature is invaded by the courts, and judicial legislation takes place. This is contrary not only to the spirit and letter of the Constitution, but also to the spirit of genuine free government. The legislative function, that of determining national policies, must either be in the hands of the people themselves or of direct representatives of the people who are chosen for this particular purpose and who may be held personally accountable for their actions. To permit the judges, who are appointive officers and therefore are without direct responsibility to the people, to have it in their power to say whether or not the public will can be made effective in the form of law, is to permit a form of oligarchy to govern in a nation where the people are by theory supposed to rule themselves. Curtailment of judicial power, particularly with respect to the constitutionality of laws, is therefore necessary in the interest not only of individual liberty, but of free government.

Such, in brief, is the attitude of a great many Americans toward the courts. They are zealous in their desire for a genuinely popular government, and they do not want it possible for five men, a majority of the Supreme Court, to stand in the way of vital reforms demanded by the majority opinion in a nation of a hundred millions of people, and embodied in law by the people's own representatives in the legislative and executive departments. The same attitude is held toward the courts of the States as toward those of the Nation, except that the feeling is more intense in the case of the former than of the latter. That important changes will be made in some of the State judicial systems is apparently inevitable. How far this movement will go and to what extent the federal judiciary may be involved before the end is reached, the future alone can tell. Whether wisely or unwisely, whether promoting or retarding real democracy, whether helpful or hurtful to true liberty, the demand is put forward for a limitation of judicial power. The courts are being made an issue in contentious politics.

The Courts and Contentious Politics. — This in itself is an interesting and significant fact. The courts are supposed to be independent, impartial, non-partisan tribunals which lie outside the realm of partisan, controversial politics. It is a rule of the courts to have nothing to do with political questions and to confine themselves to the strictly judicial function of interpreting and applying the law to the legal controversies that come before them. This rule is followed with marked consistency. Yet the decisions of the courts again and again are important factors in the struggles between the political parties, both in and out of Congress. This is due to the fact that they exercise their power, when in their judgment there is need, to hold void legislative acts which involve partisan issues. In doing this the courts are performing their strict duty as courts of law, yet their actions are profoundly political or controversial in their consequences. When the Supreme Court, by declaring an act of Congress unconstitutional, makes it impossible for a great national policy, which is strongly desired by a majority of the people, to be carried out, it is inevitable that the Court's action will be made the subject of partisan debate and strife, no matter how coldly judicial the court may be, how sincerely it may strive to avoid all political entanglements, and how strictly it confines itself to questions of law. Upon political questions, as such, the Court will refuse to pass, but legal questions, properly presented to it, cannot be avoided, however serious the political consequences may be. For instance, in a great case involving the validity of State laws providing for the initiative and referendum, — the point at issue being whether or not such laws contravene the principle of republicanism, — the Supreme Court evaded a definite decision on the ground that the question of what constitutes a republican form of government, which is guaranteed to each of the States by the Constitution, is a political question which it is the function of Congress and not of the Supreme Court to determine. Here was a case in which there was a keen public interest and which involved the interpretation of a constitutional clause, yet the Court refused to give an opinion because it considered the issue political. But in another great case involving the validity of an act of Congress establishing an income tax, — a law which was of the very essence of political controversy, — the Court did not hesitate to declare the act void. In this instance the issue was a question of law and the Court decided it, with complete indifference to the political effects of the decision. The result was bitter public criticism and an attack upon the Court in the national platform of the Democratic party. This income tax case of 1895, decided by a five-to-four vote, is a striking example of how a great national policy demanded by public opinion may be defeated through the judicial power. And it is also an excellent illustration of the fact that it is impossible for the Supreme Court, deciding as it must sometimes cases involving partisan issues, to keep free from contentious politics. It rivals in these respects, indeed, the famous Dred Scott decision of 1857, which Abraham Lincoln did not hesitate to criticize and condemn.

In another way, also, and through the use of another power, the federal courts have at times been forced into the foreground of public, partisan discussion. This is through the power to grant injunctions and the great freedom with which the power has been employed, particularly in connection with labor disputes. Most of these troubles involve citizens of different States, and so application to the federal courts for relief is always possible. Injunctions at times of labor disturbances have most frequently been sought by employers against the methods and purposes of organized labor. Many of these have been granted by the courts, so many, indeed, that workingmen pretty generally feel that the courts have been on the side of the employers and justice to the workers has been denied. In view of the great strength of organized labor in the United States, the injunction in labor troubles was certain to be made a political issue, sooner or later. The leading parties have been compelled to place injunction planks in their platforms looking toward a restriction of the judicial power. Not only, therefore, has the issuance of injunctions made the judiciary the center of political discussions, but it also has caused large numbers of people, workingmen and their friends, to distrust the courts and to feel that they are too much under the influence of the big business interests of the country; to believe that the rights of property are held unduly sacred by the judges, and the rights of man, the rights of the worker, are ignored and abused. That this belief, whether with cause or not, is widespread and deep-rooted is one of the profoundly significant facts of American political life. Its existence makes continued agitation for judicial reform, if not its attainment, so much a certainty that the student who seeks to comprehend the inner, vital things of American politics must give it careful study. The position of the courts in the United States is so central, their power so great, and their service to the Nation in the past so unmistakable, that even a latent distrust of them by any considerable proportion of the people becomes a matter of supreme interest. The developments of American politics from the beginning have been profoundly influenced by the work of the judiciary. Its authority was never greater than at present, and whether that authority shall continue to grow still greater or shall be diminished is one of the problems with which the democracy in America must struggle.

REFERENCES

BALDWIN. *The American Judiciary.*
BEARD. *American Government and Politics*, Edition 1914, Chap. XV.
BEARD. *The Supreme Court and the Constitution.*
BRYCE. *The American Commonwealth*, Edition 1910, Vol. I, Chaps. XXII, XXIII, XXIV.
CORWIN. *The Doctrine of Judicial Review.*
The Federalist, Nos. 78 to 83 inclusive.
HAINES. *The American Doctrine of Judicial Supremacy.*
MCCLAIN. *Constitutional Law in the United States*, Chaps. XXV to XXIX inclusive.
REINSCH. *Readings on American Federal Government*, Chap. XIV.
SMITH. *The Spirit of American Government*, Chap. V.
WILLOUGHBY. *The Constitutional Law of the United States*, Vol. II, Chaps. L, LI, LII.
WILLOUGHBY. *The Supreme Court of the United States.*
WILSON. *Constitutional Government in the United States*, Chap. VI.
WOODBURN. *The American Republic*, Chap. VI.
YOUNG. *The New American Government and its Work*, Chap. XV.

CHAPTER XXII

Constitutional Readjustment by Amendment

In every truly constitutional government the question of constitutional readjustment is one of supreme interest. This is particularly the case where there are written constitutions, which have a tendency to retard needed changes in government and to make the existing political order permanent. In the United States this tendency is especially notable. One of the chief weaknesses of the American Constitution is its rigidity, its fixed form, its unwillingness, so to speak, to change itself, or be changed, in accord with the constantly developing and enlarging political life it controls. It tends to make politics static, to keep things as they are. Yet politics, in large part, is elementally dynamic. It is in continuous motion, and to stop this is to kill the state itself. The development of civilization everywhere means greater complexity in social and economic relationships, and, therefore, greater governmental activity. The functions of government multiply as democracy becomes more real. It is axiomatic that governmental activities must change to meet the needs of changed social, economic, and political conditions. This inevitably means constitutional readjustments, sooner or later. The constitution of a living state is itself a living thing and must accommodate itself to new problems. If it cannot do this, so much the worse for it. If the changes that are needed can be brought about in the formal, prescribed constitutional manner, all well and good; if they cannot be attained in this way, they will be made in some other. The life and work of a state cannot stop at the commands of a written constitution.

Yet the tendency is strong with great numbers of people to oppose changes in the fundamental law. The wisdom of the past is to be exalted and that of the present to be distrusted. The constitution of the fathers becomes a sacred thing, to be preserved inviolate. To lay hands on this constitution for the purpose of changing it is not only profanation, but subversion of the governmental structure. To such persons the most effective argument against any proposed policy is the assertion that it is unconstitutional. This tendency and this attitude of mind have been particularly prevalent in the United States, where the written Constitution has been held up as an object of veneration and as the embodiment of the highest wisdom of which the American people are capable. This has been due to different reasons, — to the inherent tendency of many persons to oppose changes of any kind; to the almost universal disposition to idolize the great leaders who framed the Constitution and set up the national government; and, it must be added, to the assiduous efforts of those who profit financially and politically by the existing order to cultivate among the people a belief in the sanctity of the Constitution and an attitude of reverence for its provisions. The result has been an unwillingness to modify the Constitution which is hard for the outsider to understand; for nowhere else is a written constitution looked upon in quite the same way.

Singularly, however, yet naturally, this was not the attitude toward the Constitution of the men who framed it. To them it was far from sacred, far from ideal. It was probably not satisfactory to a single one of them, and it was submitted for ratification with misgiving. Some of them had little hope of its proving permanently successful. It is true that changes in it were looked forward to with some anxiety, but this was not because they considered the Constitution perfect, but because they feared that it might be made even more imperfect through alteration. Men of the clear vision and deep knowledge of Washington, Hamilton, and Madison could not be misled as to the imperfections of the instrument drafted under such trying circumstances and in the face of such conflicting interests and theories as confronted them and their associates in the constitutional convention. It was never their thought that the Constitution would long continue in force without change. The fact that the process of amendment was made difficult and not easy does not indicate that they looked upon the Constitution as incapable of improvement. As suggested, it indicated rather that they thought it might be made worse, and therefore quick, carelessly considered amendments were made impossible.

But that it should never be altered at all, regardless of defects which experience might reveal, was certainly far from their mind. Their position is fairly stated by Madison: " That useful alterations will be suggested by experience, could not but be foreseen. It was requisite, therefore, that a mode for introducing them should be provided. The mode preferred by the convention seems to be stamped with every mark of propriety. It guards equally against that extreme facility, which would render the Constitution too mutable; and that extreme difficulty, which might perpetuate its discovered faults. It moreover equally enables the General and the State governments, to originate the amendment of errors, as they may be pointed out by the experience on one side or on the other."[1]

The Amendment Process. — The prescribed method of amendment, given in the Constitution, is as follows: " The Congress, whenever two-thirds of both Houses shall deem it necessary, shall propose amendments to this constitution, or, on the application of the legislatures of two-thirds of the several States, shall call a convention for proposing amendments, which, in either case, shall be valid to all intents and purposes as parts of this constitution, when ratified by the legislatures of three-fourths of the several States, or by conventions in three-fourths thereof, as the one or the other mode of ratification may be proposed by the Congress; Provided that no amendment which may be made prior to the year one thousand eight hundred and eight shall in any manner affect the first and fourth clauses in the ninth section of the first article; and that no State, without its consent shall be deprived of its equal suffrage in the Senate."

The first exception under the proviso has long been of no consequence. It was due to the existence of slavery and the influence of the slave States. The first part of it related to the importation of slaves, Congress, by the clause referred to in Article I, being forbidden to prohibit such importation prior to 1808. The second part of this exception related to the imposition by Congress of a capitation or other direct tax, this kind of tax being forbidden unless levied in proportion to the census which was ordered in a previous section of the constitution. Of course after 1808, amendments concerning either of these questions were permissible.

[1] *The Federalist*, No. 43.

The second exception, that no State, without its own consent, shall be deprived of its equal representation in the Senate, is still binding. This means that what is called the "statehood" of a State cannot be destroyed without its own consent, as long as the present Constitution stands. The provision was clearly inserted at the demand of the small States, some of which were very much afraid that their powers and place in the Union would be destroyed through the votes of the larger States. Madison observes somewhat ponderously that this exception "was probably meant as a palladium to the residuary sovereignty of the States, implied and secured by that principle of representation in one branch of the legislature; and was probably insisted on by the States particularly attached to that equality."[1] It is an important exception, though, and might under certain conditions give rise to serious trouble. It clearly gives to some States a decided advantage over others as far as voting in the Senate is concerned. Nevada with a population of 81,875 in 1910 offsets in the Senate the vote of New York with a population more than one hundred and ten times as great. New York with a population equal to one tenth of that of the entire United States has one forty-eighth of the voting power in the Senate.

It will be seen that the Constitution provides for two methods of proposing amendments and two methods of ratifying them. Congress, by a two-thirds vote in each house, may propose amendments, or the States may take the initiative. In the latter case, if the legislatures of two thirds of the States demand it, a convention must be called by Congress for the purpose of proposing amendments. In this, Congress has no option; it must arrange for the convention when the necessary number of States have requested it. A convention of this kind has never been held because application for it has never been made by a sufficient number of States. In connection with the amendment providing for popular election of Senators it seemed likely for a time that the requisite number of States might act, but Congress finally submitted an amendment to the States and a convention was not necessary. So it happens that in every instance in which the Constitution has been amended, the proposal has come from Congress. It is to be noted, in passing, that the

[1] *The Federalist*, No. 43.

two-thirds vote in each house, required by the Constitution, has been held to mean merely two thirds of the members present and not two thirds of the entire membership. A " house " for this purpose is defined to be a " quorum of the membership." A quorum is all that is necessary to constitute a house for the transaction of business and a part of the legitimate business of each house is to propose constitutional amendments.

Of the two methods of ratifying amendments, one is by the legislatures of the States and the other is by conventions within the States called for the purpose. In either case three fourths of the States must give their approval before the amendment is adopted. Congress is given the right to say which method shall be employed. Thus far the convention method has not been used. Each of the amendments adopted has been proposed by Congress and ratified by the State legislatures. Each State, when it gives approval to a proposed amendment, certifies its action to the Secretary of State, in whose office a record is kept. When a sufficient number of States have acted favorably, official proclamation of the fact is made and the amendment becomes a part of the Constitution. If a State has once ratified an amendment, it may not rescind its action. That action is final. But if a State rejects an amendment, it is free to reconsider its action and vote its approval. The amendment is open for favorable action until it has been ratified by three fourths of the States. Then further consideration of it ceases, as it becomes at once a part of the Constitution, binding upon all the States alike.

Growth of the Constitution by Amendment. — The extent to which the Constitution has been altered by formal amendment is slight. In a century and a quarter, only seventeen amendments have been adopted. Of these, the first ten, known as the Bill of Rights, were proposed by the first Congress in 1789, only a few months after the government was set in motion, and may properly be looked upon as parts of the original Constitution. They embody guaranties of certain fundamental rights, such as freedom of speech, of the press, of religion, and of peaceable assemblage; right of trial by jury; protection against unreasonable searches and seizures, and against excessive and cruel punishments; protection against depriving a person of life, liberty, or property without due process of law.

Many other fundamental guaranties are included. Some of the States demanded amendments of this nature before they would give their approval to the Constitution. In fact, it seems clear from the records that ratification by the necessary nine States would never have been obtained if the understanding had not prevailed that amendments would immediately be submitted to the States. On September 25, 1789, therefore, Congress proposed the first ten amendments, which were ratified by the States during the next two years and became parts of the Constitution in 1791.[1]

The eleventh and twelfth amendments may also fairly be looked upon as parts of the original Constitution; they are only a little less directly connected with it than is the Bill of Rights. They, like those that preceded, were made necessary by the difficult task of setting up and starting in motion a new national government. The eleventh amendment was proposed in 1794 and became a part of the fundamental law in 1798. It is the one which makes it impossible for a suit to be brought against a State by the citizens of another State or by citizens or subjects of a foreign state. The circumstances of its adoption have already been given.[2] The twelfth amendment was proposed by Congress in 1803 and was declared ratified the following year. This amendment provided for a change in the method of voting to be observed by the presidential electors. As explained in a previous chapter, the original Constitution provided that the electors should vote for two men, and the one receiving the highest number of votes should be President, and the one having the next highest vote should be Vice President, provided, of course, each had a majority of the whole number of electors.[3] This plan gave no trouble until political parties sprang up and the presidential election became a real party contest. Then, since the winning party wished to control both the presidency and the vice presidency, the full vote of its electors was cast for two men as authorized by the Constitution, with the result that they had the same vote and neither could be declared elected as President. This happened in 1800 in the case of Jefferson and Burr, the Democratic-Republican candidates, and the final choice was thrown into the House of Representa-

[1] Twelve amendments, in fact, were proposed by Congress, but two of them were rejected by the States.   [2] Above, p. 256.   [3] Above, Chap. V.

tives. It was evident at once that the electoral college plan, as originally devised, had broken down and that unless the Constitution were modified, the election of a President would, in each instance, very probably devolve upon the House of Representatives, — an outcome which was violently contrary to the intention of the Constitution. A change was therefore imperative and the twelfth amendment was the result. Under its provisions the electors cast separate ballots for President and Vice-President, so that all possibility of a situation such as occurred in 1800 is eliminated. As suggested, this amendment, like the eleventh, was necessary in order to get the government running smoothly. It involved no fundamental change in the constitutional system, but was concerned only with a detail of procedure on the part of presidential electors.

From 1804 until 1865 no change was made in the Constitution, although many suggestions were offered and many resolutions proposing amendments were introduced into Congress. In the latter year mentioned the thirteenth amendment, abolishing slavery in the United States, was proposed and ratified. This was followed by the fourteenth in 1868, which conferred citizenship upon negroes and provided for other things made necessary by the abolition of slavery and by the events of the Civil War. The fifteenth amendment was adopted two years later, in 1870, providing that the right of citizens of the United States to vote shall not be denied or abridged on account of race, color, or previous condition of servitude. These three amendments were distinctly " war amendments," growing out of the great Civil War struggle and the abolition of slavery. They were the result of thoroughly abnormal conditions. Their ratification, in fact, was forced upon some of the States. Their adoption can in no way be looked upon as a result of the insistent pressure of public opinion such as characterizes free governments. Moreover, like those that preceded, they involved no changes in the structure of the governmental system, although they are of the highest importance and have brought the Nation face to face with problems of the gravest nature, which are yet clamoring for solution.

Following the adoption of the fifteenth amendment, a period of forty-three years elapsed before the Constitution was again formally altered. On February 25, 1913, after a long period of agitation, the sixteenth amendment authorizing Congress to levy income taxes became operative. This change was the outgrowth of the decision of the Supreme Court in 1895, declaring unconstitutional the income tax law of the preceding year. The position of the Court was that the provision of the Constitution forbidding Congress to levy direct taxes except when apportioned among the States according to their populations, applied to incomes from real and personal property. The question of a tax of this kind became an issue in party politics, and public opinion finally forced Congress to submit to the States an amendment making it constitutional. Accordingly, in 1909, a resolution finally passed both houses providing that Congress shall have power " to lay and collect taxes on incomes, from whatever source derived, without apportionment among the several States and without regard to any census or enumeration." After almost four years the amendment was ratified by three fourths of the States and was declared to be in force.

In the year 1913, also, the seventeenth amendment was added. This provides for the so-called popular or direct election of United States Senators, in place of election by the State legislatures. No other proposed change in the Constitution has been the cause of so much discussion or has been under consideration for so long a time as the one embodied in this amendment. More than seventy-five years prior to its adoption, an amendment of this character was called to the attention of Congress. Repeatedly thereafter, particularly in the last thirty or forty years, the suggestion was renewed and resolutions were introduced into Congress. Twenty years before its final adoption an amendment of the kind received the necessary two-thirds vote in the House of Representatives, but was rejected by the Senate. At other times in later years the same thing occurred, the Senate standing in the way of the reform, notwithstanding an overwhelming popular demand for it. Party platforms declared for it; more than two thirds of the State legislatures indorsed it by resolution, many of them asking Congress to call a convention as provided for in the Constitution; and everywhere it was discussed and urged upon Congress. In 1912 at least twenty-nine of the States sought by various kinds of primary election laws to attain popular control over senatorial elections by providing for direct nomination of candidates.[1] Finally, the Senate was forced to yield and in 1911 passed an amendment resolution. The two houses did not agree at first, however, as to the content of the amendment, and it was not until 1912 that final action was taken, and the amendment was submitted to the States. About a year later, May 31, 1913, it was proclaimed to be in force.

Amendments Difficult to Obtain. — From the standpoint of a study of the amendment process, the sixteenth and seventeenth amendments are of peculiar interest. They are the only amendments that have been adopted in really normal conditions, under pressure of public opinion. They were not the result of war, as were the thirteenth, fourteenth, and fifteenth amendments, and they were enacted under conditions altogether different from those which compelled the adoption of the first twelve amendments. Moreover, the seventeenth amendment is the only one adopted that has involved a fundamental structural change in the constitutional system. This is a fact of great significance. It is noteworthy, to say the least, that a new government should be established according to an untried plan, with many novel features, and continue in operation for a century and a quarter before a single change in its fundamental structure was accomplished in the manner prescribed by the Constitution. That fact might indicate several things. It might indicate, for instance, that the Constitution as drafted was a most perfect instrument and that the people have been highly content with its provisions. Or, it might suggest that the process of amendment is so difficult that public opinion has been unable to force changes even where experience has shown them to be wise. Again, it might suggest that needed alterations, difficult or impossible to obtain through the formal amendment procedure, have been brought about by circumvention in ways and through agencies that lie outside of the Constitution. The truth is, however, that all of these things, rather than only one, are indicated. The Constitution, though far from perfect, has proven itself a wonderfully efficient instrument, and in the main the people have shown themselves pretty well satisfied. That the work and organization of the govern-

---

[1] Beard, "American Government and Politics," New and Revised Edition, p. 243.

ment have been profoundly influenced by extra-constitutional devices is one of the most obvious facts in connection with American politics. Merely to mention the party system is all the evidence necessary. And that the amendment process is exceedingly difficult is a fact easy to demonstrate. Experience has abundantly proven it. The fact that only seventeen amendments have been adopted out of some twenty-two hundred that have been suggested is itself indicative of the truth.

With respect to the last point, the difficulty of amending the Constitution, the struggle for the popular election of Senators may be cited again. The history of the seventeenth amendment shows how comparatively easy it is to delay indefinitely, if not prevent, the adoption of an amendment, and how overwhelming and insistent the demand must be at times to force Congress to act. The fact is that the majorities required for the proposal and ratification of amendments are so large that formal constitutional readjustments become pretty nearly impossible. It will not do to assert that they cannot be made; the sixteenth and seventeenth amendments disprove that. Yet it is within the truth to say that under ordinary conditions the large majorities required,—two thirds in each house of Congress, or two thirds of the State legislatures necessary for the proposal, and three fourths of the States, either through their legislatures or conventions, necessary for ratification,— make amendments practically impossible, except when there is tremendous public pressure. The full significance of this is coming to be understood by the masses of the people, and a strong demand has developed for an easier method of amendment. The Progressive party in its platform in 1912 inserted a plank pledging itself " to provide a more easy and expeditious method of amending the federal constitution." The conviction that the amendment process should be changed is not confined to members of one party, however. The question is not a party issue. Various suggestions have been made as to what the process should be. One of the most interesting was embodied in a resolution introduced into the Senate in 1912, which provided that the amendment procedure be changed so as to permit amendments to be proposed either by a simple majority in each house of Congress, or by the action of the legislatures or by direct vote of the people in ten states, and ratified by a

… majority of the voters in a majority of the States.[1] This would not only make amendment easier by reducing the majorities now required by the Constitution, but also would democratize the amendment process and bring it into accord with the spirit of the age.[2]

Amendment Process Undemocratic. — That the method of amendment worked out by the framers of the Constitution is highly undemocratic cannot be denied even by those who most ardently defend it. Yet the United States, in spite of constitutional checks, has become a democratic Nation, and the people demand governmental institutions that are thoroughly responsive to their will. The fact is that the Constitution was not designed to be democratic and the amendment process was not intended to make it easy for the people to institute changes in the fundamental law. It was the deliberate intention, rather, to make such changes difficult. Trust in the wisdom of the people and belief in their capacity to run their own government unchecked, in no way characterized the men who were responsible for the Constitution. One of the great objects they had in mind, and of which they spoke again and again, was stability; but stability with a democratic government they believed to be impossible. Popular control they did not want and were determined not to have if drastic checks upon popular action could prevent it. Making amendments to the Constitution difficult was one way to help accomplish their purpose.

The significance of the amendment provision as a check upon democracy was clearly seen by leaders who were in sympathy with popular government. A notable expression of what it meant was made by Patrick Henry in an argument against the ratification of the Constitution before the Virginia convention. It is worth while to quote somewhat freely from this statement.[3] " To encourage us to adopt it, they tell us that there is a plain easy way of getting amendments. When I come to contemplate this part, I suppose that I am mad, or that my countrymen are so. The way to amendment is, in my opinion, shut. Let us consider this plain, easy way." After quoting the amendment

---

[1] Introduced by Senator La Follette of Wisconsin.   [2] Below, p. 643.
[3] Elliot's Debates, Vol. III, pp. 48–50. Quoted in Smith's "The Spirit of American Government," pp. 44–46. Professor Smith's chapter on the Amendment of the Constitution is keenly interesting and suggestive.

provision of the Constitution, he goes on: "Hence it appears that three-fourths of the States must ultimately agree to any amendments that may be necessary. Let us consider the consequence of this. However uncharitable it may appear, yet I must tell my opinion — that the most unworthy characters may get into power, and prevent the introduction of amendments. Let us suppose — for the case is supposable, possible, and probable — that you happen to deal those powers to unworthy hands; will they relinquish powers already in their possession, or agree to amendments? Two-thirds of the Congress, or of the State legislatures, are necessary even to propose amendments. If one-third of these be unworthy men, they may prevent the application for amendments; but what is destructive and mischievous, is, that three-fourths of the State legislatures, or of the State conventions, must concur in the amendments when proposed! In such numerous bodies, there must necessarily be some designing, bad men. To suppose that so large a number as three-fourths of the States will concur, is to suppose that they will possess genius, intelligence, and integrity, approaching to miraculous. It would indeed be miraculous that they should concur in the same amendments, or even in such as would bear some likeness to one another; for four of the smallest States, that do not collectively contain one-tenth part of the population of the United States, may obstruct the most salutary and necessary amendments. Nay, in these four States, six-tenths of the people may reject these amendments; and suppose that amendments shall be opposed to amendments, which is highly probable, — is it possible that three-fourths can ever agree to the same amendments? A bare majority in these four small States may hinder the adoption of amendments; so that we may fairly and justly conclude that one-twentieth part of the American people may prevent the removal of the most grievous inconveniences and oppression, by refusing to accede to amendments. A trifling majority may reject the most salutary amendments. Is this an easy mode of securing the public liberty? It is, sir, a most fearful situation, when the most contemptible minority can prevent the alteration of the most oppressive government; for it may, in many respects, prove to be such. Is this the spirit of republicanism?"

That experience has shown that the difficulty in inducing Congress or the States to propose amendments has been greater than that of obtaining ratification of the few that have been proposed, does not detract from the force of Patrick Henry's argument even when applied to present conditions. The point he made, indeed, is even more telling now than it was when he gave it expression. As far as amending the Constitution is concerned, the claim of majority rule in the United States is simply farcical. An exceedingly small minority can block the way to constitutional changes. It has been computed that according to the census of 1900, " one forty-fourth of the population distributed so as to constitute a majority in the twelve smallest States could defeat any proposed amendment."[1] At the present time, due to the marvelous increase in the population of some of the larger States, it is doubtless true that even a smaller minority properly distributed, could defeat proposed amendments, although their rejection by thirteen States is now necessary to that end. The conclusion is unavoidable that the amendment feature of the Constitution is extraordinarily undemocratic and that if genuine popular government is to prevail in the United States an easier method of amendment must be provided.

The rigidity of the United States Constitution is one of its most marked characteristics. Yet rigid constitutions, hard to modify, are incompatible with the spirit of truly free government, unless they are supplemented by statutory provisions which eliminate the need for constitutional changes — and this cannot always be done — or are circumvented by extra-constitutional processes which practically nullify constitutional limitations. " All democratic constitutions are flexible and easy to amend. This follows from the fact that in a government which the people really control, a constitution is merely the means of securing the supremacy of public opinion and not an instrument for thwarting it. Such a constitution cannot be regarded as a check upon the people themselves. It is a device for securing to them that necessary control over their agents and representatives, without which popular government exists only in name. A government is democratic just in proportion as it responds to the will of the people; and since one way of

[1] Smith, " The Spirit of American Government," p. 46.

defeating the will of the people is to make it difficult to alter the form of government, it necessarily follows that any constitution which is democratic in spirit must yield readily to changes in public opinion."[1] If the formal Constitution of the United States is to be in keeping with the democratic spirit of the people, its amendment section must be radically revised. That this will be done in time can hardly be doubted; but exactly what the change shall be is one of the real problems of American politics.

REFERENCES

BEARD. *American Government and Politics*, Edition 1914, Chap. IV, pp. 60–71.
BRYCE. *The American Commonwealth*, Edition 1910, Vol. I, Chap. XXXII.
SMITH. *The Spirit of American Government*, Chap. IV.

[1] Smith, "The Spirit of American Government," p. 40.

CHAPTER XXIII

CONSTITUTIONAL READJUSTMENT THROUGH LAW, CUSTOM, AND
JUDICIAL CONSTRUCTION

WHAT has been said thus far concerning constitutional readjustment has had to do exclusively with the formal Constitution and the formal method of changing it. But the formal Constitution is by no means the real, the working Constitution. The latter is made up of the former plus a good many other things. Moreover, the formal amendment process is by no means the only way of modifying fundamentally the formal Constitution. It may be, and, indeed, has been profoundly influenced, supplemented, rounded out, in other ways. And it is this larger Constitution that is vital. To understand it is to understand the real processes of government and the many ways in which they act and react upon one another; and to be content with less than this is to be content with an incomplete, distorted, false view of what the United States has done, and is doing, to solve the problems of free government. In addition, therefore, to the formal procedure of amendment, are to be noted certain other ways in which the written Constitution has been supplemented and modified. There are three of these, — statutory provisions, judicial interpretations, and custom.

Growth through Legislation. — Supplemental legislation by Congress, providing for many really fundamental parts of the governmental structure, was made necessary by the written Constitution. The machinery of government specifically established by the Constitution, in fact, was incomplete, and without additional features authorized by law could never have met the demands put upon it. For instance, the constitutional provision authorizing the federal court system was wholly inadequate. Without action by Congress, there could be no federal courts, not even a Supreme Court. The statutes, therefore, by which the courts have been created and organized may properly be looked upon as "constitutional," that is, as part of the broad, working Constitution of the United States. And so, also, with laws affecting fundamentally the other departments of government. It is by the Constitution that the powers and instrumentalities of the government are distributed and harmonized. Any statute, then, like the Judiciary Act of 1789, or its successor, the Judicial Code of 1911, or like those establishing the executive departments or regulating the election of members of Congress, must be considered parts of the true Constitution. The extent of such legislation is very great. Speaking of what he calls "statutory elaboration of the constitution," Professor Beard says: "... If we regard as constitutional all that body of law relative to the fundamental organization of the three branches of the federal government, — legislative, executive, and judicial, — then by far the greater portion of our constitutional law is to be found in the statutes. At all events, whoever would trace, even in grand outlines, the evolution of our constitutional system must take them into account."[1] To illustrate the kind of statutes in question, this writer observes that the twelfth amendment is hardly more important than the law of 1887, "which elaborates it in great detail by providing the modes of counting the electoral votes and determining controversies." No particular additional comment is needed to emphasize the significance of these laws. It should be added, however, that though they are as much law as the written Constitution itself, yet their status with respect to modifications is not the same as that of formal constitutional provisions. They are ordinary law and may be changed by the ordinary legislative procedure.

Judicial Construction. — A second method by which the Constitution has been expanded is that of judicial construction. To the courts, and in the end to the Supreme Court, alone, belongs the function of interpreting the Constitution. This means that, in the last analysis, the formal Constitution, the part which may be subjected to construction by the judicial power, is simply what the Supreme Court says it is. It is for the Court to determine what the Constitution provides. Whether or not the judgment of the Court accords with the opinions of the legislative and executive departments, or with the desires

[1] Beard, "American Government and Politics," New and Revised Edition, p. 72.

of the people, is a matter of no moment. The Court's decision is conclusive as long as the Court permits it to stand. To get at the meaning of the Constitution, then, the written document must be read in the light of all the interpretations of it made by the Supreme Court in the cases that have come before it for adjudication. Necessarily there have been many calls upon the Court to construe various constitutional provisions. This was inevitable in view of the extreme brevity of the Constitution and the very general terms in which it is written. With respect to some things the Constitution is minute in its provisions, but to a large extent it deals with general principles in general terms. To apply these principles to the specific questions that have arisen has been a most difficult task and has made the function of constitutional construction one of supreme importance. From the generality of the phraseology of the Constitution, the courts, when called upon to construe it, have been in a position to influence profoundly the industrial and political life of the Nation. A tremendous power was thus placed in the hands of the judges. And this power has become of more and more importance with the passing years because of the marvelous development of the United States and the rise of new problems, necessarily unforeseen by the makers of the Constitution. In thus adapting the Constitution to unanticipated conditions, there have been unavoidably both expansion and modification. The Constitution to-day is a much more inclusive document than it was when it was accepted by the States in 1789. Undoubtedly the powers of the national government are much greater now than they were intended or expected to be by those who framed and ratified the Constitution.

Perhaps the most notable instance of constitutional expansion through judicial construction is found in the power of the courts to declare legislative acts unconstitutional. As brought out in the discussion of the relation of the courts to legislation, this power was not given to them by express grant of the Constitution. It is exceedingly doubtful whether it was the intention that the judicial power should extend so far. Yet the courts do declare legislative acts void and have done so since 1803, when the power so to do was asserted in the case of Marbury *v.* Madison.[1] The reasoning upon which the court based

[1] 1 Cranch 137.

its right has already been given. Whether it is sound or not, is not pertinent here. The prime fact is that the courts exercise the power and the power is derived by judicial construction.

The Doctrine of Implied Powers. — Other examples of the importance of judicial construction are found in powers recognized as belonging to the Nation, but which come to it by implication and not by direct grant. From the beginning the rule has been to construe liberally all grants of power made by the Constitution. The Supreme Court, from the very first, has recognized the right of the national government to exercise all those powers which are necessary and proper for the effective use of the powers specifically conferred. This is the essence of the doctrine of implied powers; though the doctrine complete covers, in addition to those suggested, the powers which may be implied from the general nature and purpose of the Constitution. The full, conclusive statement of the principle was made by the Supreme Court in the famous case of McCulloch v. Maryland, decided in 1819.[1] An implied power is just as definitely a " grant " of power as is one specifically enumerated, and is to be construed with the same liberality.

Through the use of this principle of implied powers the authority of the nation has been greatly extended. A number of highly important matters have become the subjects of congressional legislation which the words of the Constitution in no way suggest and which the framers of the Constitution could not possibly have had in mind. Two or three examples will be sufficient to show the great importance of the principle and the way in which it has worked to the extension of national power. In the case of McCulloch v. Maryland one point at issue was whether the Congress had the right to incorporate the Bank of the United States, which had been created by law in 1816, inasmuch as the Constitution did not in express terms confer this authority upon Congress. The court held that Congress acted within its powers, notwithstanding the absence of a specific grant. The power was one to be implied fairly from provisions which are specific. " Although, among the enumerated powers of government, we do not find the word ' bank ' or ' incorporation,' we find the great powers to lay and collect taxes; to borrow money; to regulate commerce; to declare

[1] 4 Wheaton 316.

CONSTITUTIONAL READJUSTMENT THROUGH LAW

and conduct war; and to raise and support armies and navies." If to carry out any or all of these powers a United States bank was deemed necessary or proper by the Congress, its right to establish the bank could not be questioned. To Congress alone is given the right to determine what means it shall employ to carry out a purpose authorized by the Constitution. In this instance, Congress was given specific control over the Nation's fiscal affairs, and, therefore, could establish and make use of a bank or any other agency which might commend itself. On the same basis, there have been created by Congress a national currency and a vast system of national banks, minutely regulated by law. The law of 1914 reorganizing the banking system and establishing a number of reserve banks was enacted under this implied authority.

Another illustration of the expansion of national authority is afforded by the protective tariff system maintained for so many years. By this means the economic opportunities and industrial activities of individuals, States, and sections may be effectively controlled by national regulations. Yet the Constitution does not expressly give Congress power to levy customs duties for the purpose of protecting industries. It does give Congress power, however, to lay and collect taxes and imposts, and regulate commerce with foreign nations. The purpose and the method of this regulation are for Congress to determine. The result is that during nearly the whole of its life, the United States has levied tariff taxes which have not been merely for the sake of revenue. The influence of this policy, both industrially and politically, has been far reaching, and the question of the degree of " protection " to be afforded is still, as it has been from the beginning, one of the large questions in the field of controversial politics.

Again, there may be cited the power exercised by Congress over interstate commerce. The constitutional provision is merely that Congress shall have power to regulate commerce among the several States. In the early days of the Republic this was a power of slight importance as compared with what it has been for many years. The growth of great railway systems, traversing many States, and the development of multitudes of corporations, large and small, doing an interstate business, have made this power one of the most vitally important powers which Congress possesses. There is, in fact, no more difficult problem confronting the American people than that involved in the control of corporations, trusts, and monopolies, and it is through its power to regulate interstate commerce that Congress may deal with it. One of the greatest departments of the government, the Interstate Commerce Commission, with its large power of control over interstate carriers, was established under this power. All the antitrust legislation, beginning with the Sherman law of 1890, has been enacted under the same authority. The tendency has been to appeal more and more to the national power for the control of industry. But the purpose is not always industrial. Sometimes it is distinctly moral and social. A splendid example of this is the so-called Mann white slave act which calls into use the power of Congress over interstate transportation to forbid the carrying of persons from one State to another for immoral purposes. This act was vigorously attacked in the Courts, but its constitutionality was upheld. Another evidence of this is the proposed national child labor law by which it is sought to forbid the interstate shipment of all goods in the manufacture of which the labor of children under a specified age shall have been used. This kind of legislation has until recently been looked upon as coming exclusively within the power of the States. The fact that an insistent and increasing demand has developed for national action clearly indicates the great expansion that the power of Congress over interstate commerce has undergone.

Still other illustrations of the development of national authority through the principle of implied powers could easily be cited, but these are sufficient to show how the principle works. The enumerated powers are comparatively few, but these give rise to many implied powers. The exercise of one calls for the exercise of another, and these call still others into being. In the apt words of Bryce: " Each has produced a progeny of subsidiary powers, some of which have in their turn been surrounded by an unexpected offspring." [1]

The great point to be remembered in this connection is that all these various implied powers come to the national government by judicial construction. Had the Supreme Court chosen,

[1] Bryce, "The American Commonwealth," New and Revised Edition, Vol. I, p. 382.

as it might, to accept the arguments of the strict constructionists — and there have always been strict construction adherents in the United States; had it chosen to apply the strict letter of the Constitution and not the spirit, the powers of the Nation and its relation to the States would be vastly different from what they are. American history would not read as it does. With such an ideal of national union as the strict construction theory called for, and with such national impotency as it would have made inevitable, the strain of the Civil War could never have been withstood. The debt of the Nation to the Supreme Court is great.

Supreme Court and Constitutional Expansion. — By a good many persons the Supreme Court has been sharply criticized for the part it has had in the adaptation of the Constitution to new conditions, and the consequent enlargement of national power. Thomas Jefferson spoke for a host of followers when he said that the Court in assuming the right to declare legislative acts unconstitutional has usurped a supreme power which did not belong to it, and that the Constitution, if the Court alone can explain it and determine its meaning, " is a mere thing of wax in the hands of the judiciary which they may twist and shape into any form they please." He was equally the mouthpiece of a multitude when he asserted that the federal judiciary is the " subtle corps of sappers and miners constantly working under ground to undermine the foundations of our confederated fabric. They are construing our Constitution from a coördination of a general and special government to a general and supreme one alone." Though the Supreme Court's critics have not always been as severe in their comments as was Jefferson, it has never been free from hostile criticism. It has often been charged as guilty of " judicial legislation." By this is meant that it has, through its power to construe both Constitution and statutes, read into them things that were never intended by the framers of the Constitution or by Congress; and by so doing, the assertion is, it has stepped beyond the proper limits of judicial power. The truth of the general criticism will be denied by few. The powers of the Nation have been amplified, and those of the States have been restricted by judicial construction. Statutes, as, for example, the Sherman antitrust law, have been given meanings not intended by

Congress. The results of this have been profoundly political. But that the Supreme Court has purposely transformed itself from a judicial into a political body, and has maliciously, or even intentionally invaded the province of either the legislative or the executive department, there are few to assert. It has never sought to cripple the other departments. On the contrary, it has striven to respect and protect their powers, and in an admirable manner has adhered faithfully to the judicial function of interpretation and construction. The critics of the Supreme Court have too frequently been misled by the consequences of its work. Those consequences oftentimes have a deep political significance; but that by no means indicates that the court was actuated by political motives. It has with splendid consistency confined itself to the adjudication of the legal and constitutional rights involved in the controversies before it. Its record is not perfect, of course, — the judges are men; but to the impartial observer its record challenges admiration, nevertheless.

With respect to the part which the Supreme Court takes in the modification of the formal Constitution, it is to be borne in mind that its function is one of vital necessity. The Constitution must be adapted to the needs of the Nation and keep pace with its growth. In part this readjustment is brought about by formal amendments and by processes which lie outside the field of constitutional authorization; but in large part it must continue to be brought about, as it has in the past, by judicial construction. The Constitution is a living thing and, therefore, a changing thing. It must continue to live, and continue to grow and change, unless it is to become a stumbling-block in the way of the Nation's progress. To the Supreme Court, in large part, falls the duty of elaborating it by interpretation so that it will respond adequately to the demands made upon it from generation to generation. The powers given to the national government by the express grants of the Constitution are the same now as they were in the beginning; but the express powers are wholly inadequate, and, as new conditions arise, with their attendant problems, new and hitherto unanticipated implied powers must be brought to light. To the Supreme Court, therefore, the Nation must look for continuous elaboration and adaptation of its fundamental law. The

CONSTITUTIONAL READJUSTMENT THROUGH LAW

necessity of this is apparent; also, its danger and difficulty. No other function of government calls for broader vision, higher wisdom, and clearer understanding of the spirit, ideals, and principles of free institutions.[1]

Development through Custom. — There remains to consider the third way in which constitutional readjustment is accomplished, other than by formal amendment, namely, custom or usage. Strictly speaking, of course, political customs, no matter how long standing, cannot be said to be a part of the constitutional law of the United States. In case of a clash between a venerated custom and the written Constitution, it is the latter which would be given force by the courts. Nevertheless, the formal Constitution has been materially influenced in its working by certain customs and traditions. Indeed, custom plays an unusually large part in the actual operation of the United States government. To the American, as well as to the foreigner unfamiliar with the facts, it comes with somewhat of a shock to discover how profoundly the organization and the processes of government have been affected in this manner. As has been pointed out in previous discussions, the constitutional system set up in the United States, though based upon vital experience, was almost wholly the result of deliberate choice, of conscious analysis. From the very first, however, changes began to occur by common consent. The general result is that customs or understandings play quite as large a part in the control of governmental operations in the United States as they do in European countries. Even in England the customs of the constitution are hardly more important than are those of the United States. Some leading examples will be given to illustrate their force.

The most consequential development that has come about through custom, — one which revolutionized the spirit of the constitutional system, — is the development of the political parties with their vast and complicated systems of organization. It will be recalled that the framers of the Constitution were opposed to parties and tried and hoped to prevent their rise. Yet parties have, almost from the beginning, dominated the government in all of its activities. The President, contrary

---

[1] Wilson, "Constitutional Government in the United States," p. 158. For contrast as shown by Australian methods see below, Chap. XLV.

to all desire and expectation, is a party man, and not only that, but the leader of his party. Appointments to office have been largely partisan appointments, and are so still, except in so far as they are now controlled by civil service regulations. Each house of Congress is organized and dominated by the majority party. Even the courts come within the range of party influence. Yet all this is without constitutional authorization or even recognition. The party system in the Nation has nothing but custom, long-standing habit, to rest upon. Though this system is not a part of the formal Constitution, yet it is clearly a vital part of the real, working constitutional system. It is sheer nonsense to look upon it in any other way. No understanding of constitutional government in the United States can be had without a study of the political parties and their methods.

Growing out of the existence of parties, other customs of the Constitution have developed. One of the most notable is that by which the constitutional method of choosing the President has been set aside, and there has been substituted for it what is called a popular election. As we have seen, this is not a strictly popular election, but a choice by States through popular elections. It is, however, a strictly party election. The presidential electors are party agents, committed in advance, not legally but morally, to vote for their respective party candidates for President and Vice President. The whole electoral college scheme has been transformed. Yet the selection of the President by a popular party vote is absolutely opposed to the Constitution as it was in the beginning. Of course this is not a legal modification of the formal Constitution. The electors unquestionably still have a perfect legal and constitutional right to vote for others than their party candidates. But the great fact is that they do not vote for others and have not done so since parties came into being. The change that has occurred is vital and fundamental.

Again, the position, power, and influence which the Speaker of the House of Representatives has come to hold is in no way due to provisions of the written Constitution. The Constitution neither gives him powers nor assigns him duties. It merely declares that the House " shall choose their own Speaker," — a declaration which tells absolutely nothing about him and his work. And even this simple statement has been rendered meaningless by custom, for, although the technical, legal election of the Speaker is by the House of Representatives, the real choice is made by the caucus of the majority party. Furthermore, the vast influence of the speakership is due to custom observed by the House, with the tacit approval of the people, and to rules of the House's own making. The Constitution points to a speakership that is a purely parliamentary office, but it is, as a matter of fact, a party institution.

The committee system maintained by the Congress affords another excellent example of how inner, vital processes of government are controlled by agencies which lie outside the Constitution. Each house of Congress legislates by means of standing committees. No legislation, except under the most extraordinary conditions, is enacted without reference to committees. The committee system is absolutely central in the organization of each house, yet it is unknown to the Constitution. It rests only on rules of the houses and could be completely destroyed at any moment.

The party caucus is another important extra-constitutional body. Each party in each house of Congress has its caucus. The caucus of the dominant party in each house determines its organization. And, as has been pointed out, and need not be elaborated again, the very content and form of important legislative measures may be finally determined in the caucuses of the majority party, so that the action of the houses becomes a mere formality. On custom alone these institutions are based.

The President's cabinet is an unofficial body, based on custom, and lying wholly outside the Constitution. The Constitution recognizes the existence of heads of departments, but there is nothing in it to suggest a cabinet. Both the term " cabinet " and the idea it suggests were almost unknown at the time the Constitution was adopted. The cabinet, a collective body of advisers to the President, is the outgrowth of custom.

Still other customary practices affecting constitutional relations may be mentioned without special comment. The Senate controls presidential appointments in a way not contemplated by the Constitution. The appointment of cabinet officers, however, is not interfered with by the Senate. The President uses the veto power for reasons not originally intended. The two-consecutive-term tradition has become pretty firmly established although under the Constitution a president may be reëlected indefinitely. Heads of departments are not permitted to participate in the discussions of Congress, though there is nothing in the Constitution to prevent their doing so. For more than a century the Presidents observed the tradition of sending written messages to Congress and not delivering them orally. This tradition, however, was broken by President Wilson, who restored the practice of Washington and Adams. Originating revenue legislation is only nominally an exclusive power of the House of Representatives.

From the illustrations given, it is evident that custom is a significant factor in the operation of the United States government. It has given rise to institutions and practices which have affected profoundly the Nation's development and brought into existence some of the Nation's greatest problems. The fact is also apparent from what has been said in preceding portions of this chapter, that custom is only one of several methods of constitutional readjustment and development. By amendments, by supplemental legislation, by judicial construction, and by custom, the constitutional system has been elaborated and modified until it is little short of amazingly different from what its creators designed it to be. By these different processes the skeleton outline of government given in the written Constitution has been filled in and rounded out until it is a complete, workable, efficient, though imperfect, system. By the same processes, other modifications and enlargements, unforeseen at present, will be made in the years to come. Constitutional development must go on as long as the Nation lives.

REFERENCES

BEARD. *American Government and Politics*, Edition 1914, Chap. IV, pp. 72-77.
BRYCE. *The American Commonwealth*, Edition 1910, Vol. I, Chaps. XXXIII, XXXIV, XXXV.
TIEDEMAN. *The Unwritten Constitution of the United States.*

CHAPTER XXIV

The States — Constitutional Position and Powers

The bed-rock principle of the constitutional system in the United States is that of federalism. Indeed, the United States is the most conspicuous example of federation known to history, and her great success in developing a unified, efficient national government without destroying the independence of the States of the Union, or even seriously impairing their autonomy, constitutes one of her most notable contributions to the science of politics. The United States is not merely a large and powerful state with a hundred million people, governed by a President, a Congress, and a judiciary, but is a Union of forty-eight commonwealths which are independent of one another and largely independent of the national government, each with a complete governmental organization of its own. Understanding of the nature of the American Union and the functions of the commonwealths which form it is absolutely essential, therefore, for a clear comprehension of the United States government, and any description which fails to include an account of the States is obviously incomplete, if not fallacious. It is necessary, consequently, to give at least brief consideration to the States and their governments.

The elementary though vital fact is to be kept in mind that the national government is one with conferred or limited powers, and that the States possess the original or inherent powers of government. Except with respect to those powers delegated exclusively to the Nation and those other powers definitely prohibited to the States, the latter possess all the residual powers of government and may use them as they please as long as the requirements of the federal Constitution are properly observed. As stated in the first chapter of this book, it must be shown positively that a power has been prohibited to the States before its exercise can be denied them, whereas in the case of the national government it must be shown affirmatively that a power has been conferred by the Constitution before its exercise can be considered valid. To a person accustomed to a unitary government and unacquainted with the conditions surrounding the formation of the American Union, this is likely to appear a reversal of the proper order; to such the logical, natural arrangement is to have the national government one of reserved powers and the commonwealths possess only delegated authority.[1] But under the circumstances which prevailed at the time the Constitution was adopted, the American arrangement was not only logical, but inevitable. The States already existed. Each one had a fully developed governmental organization and, in a theoretic sense, at least, possessed supreme or sovereign power. If a national government were to be created with authority to control even only a few matters of national concern, it could be done only on condition that the powers in question should be taken from the States and transferred to the Nation. The States had all the powers that were possible before the Constitution was adopted; by its adoption their powers were curtailed and some of those which they formerly possessed were delegated to the new central or national authority. Because of the jealousies, rivalries, and antagonisms, which characterized the original States in their dealings with one another prior to the establishment of the Constitution, and because of the devotion of the people to their respective State governments, a full surrender of the latter's inherent powers was an impossible action. The utmost that could be reasonably hoped for was the delegation to the Nation of sufficient power to enable it to control in matters that were national or interstate in character; all local or intrastate questions must lie within the control of the States themselves. Thus the constitutional position of the States in their relation to the Nation was dictated by the conditions which gave rise to the need for a new and efficient central government.

The Equality of the States. — As a natural consequence of the conditions which governed in the formation of the Union, the States have a position of perfect equality under the Constitution. Consent to the establishment of the new government

[1] See discussion of Canada and Australia, Chap. XLV.

could be obtained on no other basis. Moreover, this equality in law belongs to the States admitted to the Union since the adoption of the Constitution as well as to the original States. A restriction which rests upon one, rests upon all alike; a power possessed by one belongs to the others in equal degree. In theory it must be held that the powers of the national government come from the States admitted to the Union by national authority to the same extent as from the States that were in fact responsible for the setting up of the Constitution. To the admitted States as well as to the original States belong the inherent powers of government. No distinction is or can be made. In the words of the Supreme Court, a State upon its admission to the Union " becomes entitled to and possesses all the rights of dominion and sovereignty which belong to the original States." [1]

It is true that in admitting a number of States Congress has sought to impose restrictions and exact promises which were to be considered binding upon the States thus pledged until they were freed from their obligation by some prescribed process. It was required of Ohio and a number of other States, for instance, that they should agree not to tax for a period of years all public lands sold by the United States. Missouri was forced to declare that its legislature under authority of the State constitution should never be permitted to enact a law denying to the citizens of other States any of the privileges and immunities conferred on them by the federal Constitution. It was demanded of Nevada that her constitution should be in accord with the Declaration of Independence and that persons should not be denied the right to vote on account of their color. Of Nebraska it was required that the voting privilege should not be denied because of race or color, Indians excepted. Utah was required to provide for religious toleration, public schools free from sectarian control, and the abolition of polygamy.

The restraints which Congress has sought to impose upon States at the time of admission are of two kinds, " those that attempt to place the State under political restrictions not imposed upon all the States of the Union by the federal Constitution, and those which seek the future regulation of private, pro-

[1] *Bolln* v. *Nebraska*, 176 U. S. 83 (1900).

prietary interests."[1] These are vitally different from the point of view of enforceability. The political restrictions are not enforceable. The Supreme Court has so ruled upon repeated occasions. When a State is once admitted to the Union it cannot be subject to political restraints which are not obligatory upon all the States alike. The powers of the States are identical. A Territory seeking statehood may be forced to accept conditions imposed by Congress that involve political restrictions, but when it becomes a State it may disregard those conditions if it chooses. A recent illustration is found in the case of Arizona which was forced to modify its proposed constitution, particularly with respect to the recall of judges, before Congress would give its approval. The authority of Arizona, however, as of any other State, to provide for the recall of judges is beyond question. Restrictions of this kind are simply of no force. If they were of force, the equality of the States under the Constitution would be destroyed. The second kind, however, those relating to the regulation of private, proprietary interests, are enforceable and the Supreme Court has so declared. Such restrictions amount merely to agreements between a State and the Nation, constituting valid contracts which are binding, but which in no way impair the political equality of the States.[2]

Decline in State Prestige. — It is essential to note that though there is constitutional equality among the States, yet relatively the States are not now so important as the original States were in 1789. With the growth of the Nation's power and influence, the States have declined in prestige. They are still vital, imperatively necessary elements in the constitutional

[1] Willoughby, " Constitutional Law of the United States," Vol. I, p. 240. The above statement concerning the attitude of Congress is based on Professor Willoughby's discussion.

[2] Professor Willoughby, upon this point, cites as "most illuminating" the comparatively recent case of *Stearns* v. *Minnesota*, 179 U. S. 223 (1900). "That case involved the construction and application of an agreement made by the State with the United States at the time of its admission to the Union, with reference to public lands, within its boundaries, owned by the United States. The court in its opinion says: 'That these provisions of the Enabling Act and the Constitution, in form at least, made a compact between the United States and the State, is evident. In an inquiry as to the validity of such a compact this distinction must at the outset be noticed. There may be agreements or compacts attempted to be entered into between two States, or between the State and the Nation, in reference to political rights and obligations, and there may be those solely in reference to property belonging to one or to the other. That different considerations may underlie the question as to the validity of these two kinds of compacts or agreements is obvious.

system, since without them the national government could not exist, but they do not hold the central place in the affections of the people which they once did. At the time of the adoption of the Constitution practically the whole of the people's loyalty was given to their respective States. In the beginning the Nation received little or no devotion from the masses and had no real place in their political consciousness. The States towered above the Nation, the latter being looked upon generally as merely the agent of the former for the control of certain questions which were of common concern and which the States acting separately could not settle satisfactorily. Service of the States was quite commonly looked upon as of higher dignity and honor than service of the new central government. Not infrequently men resigned from high places in the national government to accept offices in the States. The governorship of a State was everywhere looked upon as superior to membership in the United States Senate. This attitude of the people was natural under the circumstances, and nothing else could reasonably be expected. But a striking and fundamental change has taken place, and now the Nation is most distinctly first in the regard of the people. This has long been true, and particularly so since the great Civil War, which put an end to the extreme States' rights doctrine, gave a tremendous impetus to nationalism, and settled for all time the question of whether the Union is of the confederate or federal type. The spirit of nationalism has developed steadily from the beginning. With its growth, the relative importance of the States, and, to a considerable degree, their actual political power, have declined.

It has often been said that a State admitted into the Union enters therein in full equality with all the others, and such equality may forbid any agreement or compact limiting or qualifying political rights and obligations; whereas, on the other hand, a mere agreement in reference to property involves no question of equality of status, but only of the power of a State to deal with the Nation or with any other State in reference to such property. The case before us is one involving simply an agreement as to property between a State and the Nation. That a State and the Nation are competent to enter into an agreement of such a nature with one another has been affirmed in past decisions of this Court, and that they have been frequently made in the admission of new States, as well as subsequently thereto, is a matter of history. . . . We are of the opinion that there was a valid contract made with these companies in respect to the taxation of these lands, — a contract which it was beyond the power of the State to impair; that this subsequent legislation does impair that contract and cannot, therefore, be sustained.'" — "Constitutional Law of the United States," Vol. I, pp. 242-243.

Two significant facts may be suggested as partial explanation of this decline. The first is the rapid, revolutionizing industrial development of the United States, with its attendant problems, dangers, and evils. This has involved fundamental, far-reaching changes in the life of the people and in the relations of the States to the Nation, the true significance of which is by no means fully comprehended even now. It must be remembered that the industrial life of America in 1789, and for many years thereafter, was very simple and easily regulated as compared with that of to-day. The people were for the most part agriculturists, and manufacturing industries were both small in size and few in number. Industry and trade were essentially local or intrastate in character and accordingly could be effectively controlled by the States. Interstate and foreign commerce, it is true, were becoming of increasing value and complexity, and, consequently, the source of difficulties which were hard for the States to settle; but, nevertheless, the transfer from the States to the Nation of the control over both interstate and foreign commerce, important as they were, did not at the time tend to undermine seriously the States' authority or divert popular interest and loyalty from them to the newly established national government. But with the development of the vast railway systems, reaching into every corner of the land, and the growth of multitudes of industrial corporations, large and small, engaged in interstate and foreign trade, a new industrial order has come into being. The effect of this upon the political life of the States and of the Nation has already been profound; and the ultimate consequences are still to be revealed. Readjustments and more or less of redistribution of political powers were inevitable, regardless of the letter of the Constitution or the intention of its makers. By the very force of circumstances and the nature of their needs the people have been compelled to look more and more to the national authority for relief and protection from corporate abuses and monopolistic greed and oppression. The result has been a weakening of the States and a strengthening of the Nation. Power has been transferred from the one to the other, with a consequent loss of prestige by the States. In the field of national politics now lies the largest opportunity for statesmanship and leadership, as far as industrial affairs are concerned. However, it should be noted, signs are not lacking that the pendulum may swing somewhat in the other direction. In very recent years there has been a sort of rejuvenation of the States through the agitation for a more democratic governmental organization and a larger exercise of their police powers in the promotion of social welfare policies. The opportunity thus afforded is proving attractive to men of vision and high abilities, and may cause the States to regain some of their lost glory and influence.

The second fact which beyond question has had a good deal to do with the relative decline of the States is the artificiality of many State boundaries, with the consequent arbitrary division politically of communities and regions which properly belong together. The States as a rule are not natural economic and social units. The influence of this fact upon the political activities of the States is obvious. It tends not only to eliminate dissimilar features in the State governments and promote uniformity, but also to make the people willing to have the common central government act in the place of their respective States. If a problem is common to all or many of the States, and since a uniform solution is desirable, what is more natural than to look to the national government for that solution, even though the problem, under the letter of the Constitution, lies within the province of the States and not of the Nation? It is easy to overemphasize the potency of an influence like that under discussion, and the suggestion must not be carried too far; but that the artificiality of State boundaries and the lack of social and economic distinctions among the States tend to make the American people somewhat complacent in the face of a transfer of political power from the States to the Nation can hardly be disputed.

Besides, the people are accustomed to the same artificiality and to a high degree of central control in their local government units, particularly the counties and townships. The normal township is a block of territory six miles square and its boundaries are wherever the surveyors' lines happened to run, regardless of economic, social or geographical considerations. The county is a large district, with equally artificial boundaries, composed of, say, sixteen townships. These local units are mere divisions and subdivisions of the State and in their political activities are controlled by State laws. The natural influence of these local adjustments is to tend to make the people satisfied to have the States, which are, after all, only divisions of the Nation, more or less under the control of the national authority.

Relation of the States to One Another. — Frequent reference has been made to the fact that the States are independent of one another. This is a fact of significance and is entirely true with respect to the operation of their own local laws. The authority of each State ceases absolutely at its boundaries, however artificial they may be. The States are not, however, in the position of true foreign states, because their relations with one another, so far as they may have such relations, are controlled by the federal Constitution. Four important constitutional provisions in this connection are to be noted. The first requires each State to give full faith and credit to the public acts, records, and judicial proceedings of every other State; the second provides that the citizens of each State are entitled to all the privileges and immunities of citizens in the several States; the third requires that a person who is charged in any State with a crime and who flees from justice and is found in another State, shall upon the demand of the executive authority of the State from which he has fled, be returned to the State having jurisdiction of the crime; and the fourth provides that no State shall, without the consent of Congress, enter into any agreement or compact with another State, or with a foreign power. It is also to be noted that the States are prohibited absolutely from entering into any treaty, alliance, or confederation.

These constitutional restrictions and requirements make plain the fact that the States cannot do as they please in their dealings with one another. It should be clear that the full faith and credit clause applies only to civil judgments. The penal laws of a State are without force in the other States and no State is under obligation to help enforce the criminal laws of another. Concerning this point the Supreme Court says: " The rules that the courts of no country execute the penal laws of another applies not only to prosecutions and sentences for crimes and misdemeanors, but to all suits in favor of the State for the recovery of pecuniary penalties for any violation of statutes for the protection of its revenue, or other municipal laws, and to all judgments for such penalties. If this were not so, all that would be necessary to give ubiquitous effect to a penal law would be to put the claim for a penalty into the shape of a judgment."[1] The fact that each State's authority comes to an end at its own boundaries and that its laws are without force in another State becomes particularly important in connection with violations of its criminal laws. "A crime is to be punished if committed against the laws of a State only within the limits of that State, and the courts of another State cannot take cognizance of such a crime for purposes of punishment; nor has any State the authority to send its officers into another State for the purpose of arresting and bringing back a fugitive from justice, save as provided by the federal constitution."[2] Under the constitutional regulation it is the duty of the executive of a State to which a criminal has fled to deliver him, upon proper request, to the executive of the State in which the crime was committed. It is a noteworthy fact, however, that there is no way to compel the performance of this duty. It is for the Governor of a State, and, under the accepted rule, for him alone, to say whether a fugitive from justice shall be delivered up. If extradition is refused, the State requesting it has no redress. Congress has by law regulated the extradition of criminals, but no remedy is provided in case of a refusal to surrender the accused person. Neither by State nor national judicial process can a governor be compelled to act. If he takes action, however, this may be reviewed by the courts.

That the commonwealths of the Union do not have toward one another the status of sovereign foreign states is made clear by the absolute denial by the Constitution of their right to enter into any treaty, alliance, or confederation, and by the requirement that no State shall, without the consent of Congress, form any agreement or compact with another State or with a foreign power. As far as treaties with foreign powers are concerned, and participation by the States in the control of international relations, these constitutional provisions are wholly unnecessary, because the management of the nation's foreign relations rests exclusively with the national government. The absolute prohibition of alliances or confederations among the

[1] *Wisconsin* v. *Pelican Insurance Company*, 127 U. S. 265 (1888).
[2] McClain, "Constitutional Law in the United States," Second Edition, p. 269.

States, and the introduction of the qualifying clause, "without the consent of Congress," with respect to compacts or agreements, are points which deserve some emphasis. The effect of the two provisions is to make it possible for the States, if they have the approval of Congress, to enter into compacts with one another, providing such compacts do not constitute alliances or confederations, as those terms are used in political language.[1] The political significance of the compact is what brings it under the restriction, for the Supreme Court has held that there are some things which may be the subjects of agreements which may be entered into without the consent of Congress. As illustrating these, the court suggests that it would be the height of absurdity to hold, for instance, that States threatened by the spread of deadly diseases could not unite to provide means to prevent disaster without first obtaining the consent of Congress, which might not at the time be in session. It goes on to say that "it is evident that the prohibition is directed to the formation of any combination tending to the increase of political power in the States, which may encroach upon or interfere with the just supremacy of the United States."[2] The object of the restriction is, thus, to prevent the States, through agreements among themselves, from undermining national authority. The power of the Nation must be maintained intact. Its supremacy in the sphere set for it by the Constitution is neither to be questioned nor interfered with.

Relation between States and Nation. — In this connection it is proper to call attention to the obligation which the States are under to accord full respect to the agencies and organs of the federal government. The functions of the latter are performed through its own officers, who are not to be interfered with in any way by action of a State. It is to be remembered that though the powers of the federal government are limited in number, yet in the case of each one of these powers its authority is absolute. This means that the States may not hinder the national government in the utilization of its powers or federal officers in the discharge of their official duties. The agencies created by the federal government for the performance of its work under the Constitution cannot be subject to the control

---

[1] Willoughby, "Constitutional Law of the United States," Vol. I, p. 235.
[2] *Virginia* v. *Tennessee*, 148 U. S. 503 (1893).

of any State or group of States. If such control could be exercised, efficiency in national administration would be impossible. For illustration, the States may not tax the instrumentalities of the federal government. This was settled by the Supreme Court in the well-known case of McCulloch v Maryland, in which the principle of non-interference with federal agencies was definitely asserted. In the words of the court: "If the States may tax one instrument employed by the government in the execution of its powers, they may tax any and every instrument. They may tax the mail; they may tax the mint; they may tax patent rights; they may tax the papers of the custom-house; they may tax judicial processes; they may tax all the means employed by the government to an excess which would defeat all the ends of government. This was not intended by the American people. They did not design to make their government dependent on the American States." The general principle of non-interference with federal agencies by the States is given emphatic expression in the statement of the court's conviction that " the States have no power, by taxation or otherwise, to retard, impede, burden, or in any manner control the operations of the constitutional laws enacted by Congress to carry into execution the powers vested in the general government."[1]

On the other hand, the federal government may not interfere with the officers or agencies of the States in the performance of duties which come within the constitutional powers of the States. The same reasoning which leads to the conclusion that the States may not interfere with the Nation in its work, leads to the conclusion that the Nation may not hinder the States. The efficiency of the States in the discharge of their constitutional functions is dependent upon their freedom of action. For the Nation to tax or otherwise burden the agencies of the States would be to undermine, if not destroy, the States themselves; yet the existence of the States is essential to the existence of the Nation, and in impairing them, the Nation would be doing injury to itself. The argument may be stated again in the words of the Supreme Court: " If the means and instrumentalities employed by that [the general] government to carry into operation the powers granted to it are, necessarily, and, for the

[1] 4 Wheaton 316 (1819).

sake of self-preservation, exempt from taxation by the States, why are not those of the States depending upon their reserved powers, for like reasons, equally exempt from federal taxation? Their unimpaired existence in the one case is as essential as in the other. It is admitted that there is no express provision in the Constitution that prohibits the general government from taxing the means and instrumentalities of the States, nor is there any prohibiting the States from taxing the means and instrumentalities of that government. In both cases the exemption rests upon necessary implication, and is upheld by the great law of self-preservation, — as any government, whose means employed in conducting its operations, if subject to the control of another and distinct government, can only exist at the mercy of that government. Of what avail are these means if another power may tax them at discretion?"[1]

The constitutional position of the States thus involves a large sphere of independent action and freedom from national interference in the performance of their legitimate functions. But this independence is not without restriction. The States are under the same obligation to respect the authority of the Nation as the latter is to respect their authority. Without the States, the Nation would perish; without the Nation, the States, though they might continue to live, would be weak and inefficient.

REFERENCES

BEARD. *American Government and Politics*, Edition 1914, Chap. XXII.
BRYCE. *The American Commonwealth*, Edition 1910, Vol. I, Chaps. XXXVI, XXXVII, XXXVIII.
COOLEY. *Constitutional Law*, Chaps. X, XI.
McCLAIN. *Constitutional Law in the United States*, Chap. XXXIII.

[1] *Collector* v. *Day*, 11 Wallace 113 (1871).

CHAPTER XXV

THE STATES — SUFFRAGE AND CITIZENSHIP

THE point has been made that the federal government carries on its work through its own officers, and is not dependent on the States for the performance of its functions. This is quite true, yet it could not live without the States, and in certain respects is wholly dependent upon them. The voting privilege, for instance, is under the control of the States, yet members of both houses of Congress are chosen by popular vote. The right of suffrage is not held under national authority; the Nation has nothing to say as to who shall vote and who shall not. The only regulations in the federal Constitution relating to suffrage are those found in the fourteenth and fifteenth amendments, which were enacted as a result of the abolition of slavery. In the first of these it is provided that if the right to vote for presidential electors, members of Congress, State executives and legislative officers, is denied in any State " to any of the male inhabitants of such State, being twenty-one years of age, and citizens of the United States, or in any way abridged, except for participation in rebellion, or other crime," the basis of representation in the Congress shall be reduced " in the proportion which the number of such male citizens shall bear to the whole number of male citizens twenty-one years of age in such State." In the second it is provided that the right of citizens of the United States to vote shall not be denied or abridged, either by the United States or by any State on account of race, color, or previous condition of servitude. These amendments were adopted soon after the Civil War and were clearly designed to protect the Negroes in the enjoyment of their newly acquired rights. They in no sense deprive the States of control over suffrage. It is for the States to say, subject to the restrictions noted, who shall vote and what franchise tests shall be established. They may provide property qualifications for voting if they wish, although requirements of this nature have been almost entirely done away with. They may confer suffrage upon women, as a number of them have done, or upon alien residents who have not yet become naturalized citizens under federal law.[1]

Suffrage and National Elections. — The point of interest to take note of here, from the standpoint of the Nation, is that the right to vote at State elections, resting wholly upon State law, carries with it the right to vote at all elections of national officers. In the case of members of the House of Representatives, the only national officers made elective by the original Constitution, it was provided that the electors participating in their election should have " the qualifications requisite for electors of the most numerous branch of the State legislature." Uniformity in the franchise qualifications in the several States is manifestly not required. Each State may do as it pleases, subject only to the requirements of the fifteenth amendment. Women may vote in one State, for instance, and be debarred from voting in another. If they are permitted to vote for members of the " most numerous branch " of the State legislature, they may vote for members of Congress. The right of women to vote for presidential electors, however, does not follow the right of suffrage for members of the State legislature. Under the Constitution the method of selecting presidential electors is left wholly to the legislatures of the States. Their selection by popular vote is not required. Consequently it is entirely permissible for the legislatures to admit women to the suffrage for local and State officers and deny them participation in the choice of presidential electors.

It is obvious that the Nation does not possess an entirely complete government of its own; that in vital respects it is dependent upon the States. Two of its great departments, in fact, the executive and the judicial, would fall to the ground at once if the States failed to perform the functions expected of them. If the State legislatures were to make no provision for the selection of presidential electors, there would be no constitutional method of choosing a President; and the federal

---

[1] In some States suffrage has been conferred upon aliens who have declared their intention to become citizens but have not yet taken out their final papers, and, therefore, are not yet naturalized citizens.

judiciary is dependent upon executive appointment of the judges. It is difficult to see what remedy would lie with the federal government. Practically, of course, such a situation would never develop, but the constitutional possibility of it shows the peculiarly close and vital connection between the States and the Nation.

Before passing from the subject of suffrage, two additional facts need to be brought out. The first is that the possession of the voting privilege in one State does not mean necessarily its possession in another State. This naturally follows from the fact, previously discussed, that the laws of a State are without force beyond its own boundaries. Each State protects the electoral franchise by residence and registration requirements, and otherwise, as it sees fit. No State is under obligation to admit a person to the suffrage because he has enjoyed that privilege in some other State. The second fact, to be noted, as the foregoing discussion intimates, is that the participation in the election of public officers is not recognized as a natural right, nor is it looked upon as a necessary element in citizenship. According to ordinary usage, this is commonly spoken of as a right, but like the so-called right to hold office, it is merely a privilege conferred upon individuals by authority of the commonwealth.[1] The electoral franchise is conferred upon no one by the federal Constitution. Of course, this privilege conferred upon a person by State law becomes his legal

[1] *Minor v. Happersett*, 21 Wallace 162 (1875). In this case, in addition to the question of citizenship, the point was raised that a State, in which women of proper age are debarred from voting, does not maintain a republican form of government as is required by the Constitution. This contention the Court denies. "The guaranty is of a republican form of government. No particular government is designated as republican, neither is the exact form to be guaranteed, in any manner especially designated. Here, as in other parts of the instrument, we are compelled to resort elsewhere to ascertain what was intended. The guaranty necessarily implies a duty on the part of the States themselves to provide such a government. All the States had governments when the Constitution was adopted. In all, the people participated to some extent, through their representatives elected in the manner specially provided. These governments the Constitution did not change. They were accepted precisely as they were, and it is, therefore, to be presumed that they were such as it was the duty of the States to provide. Thus we have unmistakable evidence of what was republican in form, within the meaning of that term as employed in the Constitution." The Court then goes on to show that in these States the suffrage was not conferred upon women, and not even upon all men, and concludes: "Under these circumstances it is certainly now too late to contend that a government is not republican, within the meaning of this guaranty in the Constitution, because women are not made voters."

Y

right, as long as the law stands and he meets the law's requirements. In such circumstances his right to exercise the privilege conferred on him by the law cannot be questioned. The law, though, may be changed whenever and however the State pleases, except only as restrictions are imposed by the fifteenth amendment.

Citizenship. — The question of citizenship in the United States is one of peculiar interest. Both the States and the Nation are involved in it. There is a citizenship of the State and a citizenship of the Nation. The two are not identical. One may be a citizen of the United States without being a citizen of a particular State. The rule of the Constitution is contained in one of the provisions of the fourteenth amendment, as follows: "All persons born or naturalized in the United States, and subject to the jurisdiction thereof, are citizens of the United States and of the State wherein they reside." This makes it impossible for a State to deny State citizenship to any citizen of the United States who acquires a permanent residence within it. The acquiring of this residence is necessary, however, although there is no particular term of residence prescribed. "A State may require residence for a specified period as a condition for enjoyment of the elective franchise; but the moment that residence in a State by one who is a citizen of the United States commences, or the moment one who resides in a State acquires citizenship in the United States, that moment such person becomes a citizen of the State. By residence is meant, not merely a temporary abiding within the State, but residence in a legal sense, that is, a permanent residence. The term in this connection is synonymous with domicile and involves residence in fact, with intent that it shall continue until subsequent removal with the intent of abandoning such residence and acquiring another."[1]

Until the enactment of the fourteenth amendment the Constitution was silent as to the meaning of the term "citizenship," whether of a State or of the United States. The word "citizen" was used, but it was not defined. An eminent writer asserts that before the adoption of the fourteenth amendment, the Supreme Court was inclining to the view of the leaders of the States' rights party who held that citizenship of the United

[1] McClain, "Constitutional Law in the United States," Second Edition, p. 276.

States was merely a consequence of citizenship in some State, as was indicated by the decision in the famous Dred Scott case in which the position was taken that a Negro could not be a citizen either of a State or of the United States. He says that this amendment reversed the previously established rule. "According to it, citizenship is primarily of the United States; and secondarily and consequently, of the locality in which the citizen of the United States may reside. Citizenship, both of the United States and of the commonwealths, is thus conferred by the constitution of the United States and the laws of Congress made in accordance therewith. The commonwealths can neither confer nor withhold citizenship of the United States. A citizen of the United States is now, *ipso jure*, a citizen of the commonwealth in which he fixes his residence; and if any commonwealth should undertake to defeat the spirit of this provision by the enactment of hostile laws in regard to the gaining of residence within its limits, any individual suffering injury from the same may invoke the interpretation of the term residence by the United States judiciary, and the aid of the general government in the protection of his liberty under this interpretation."[1]

Citizenship by Birth. — Under the constitutional provision, citizenship is acquired either by birth or by naturalization. Though the language of the provision is simple, many difficulties have been encountered in applying it to different classes of cases, particularly those involving citizenship by birth. The fact is that cases may arise which are not within the constitutional provision. A detailed discussion of these cannot here be given, but two or three illustrations may be cited. For instance, the citizenship status of children born abroad of parents who are citizens of the United States is not determined by the Constitution. They are not subject to the jurisdiction of the United States. By act of Congress, however, passed in 1855, before the fourteenth amendment was added to the Constitution, — a law which is still in force, — such children are declared to be citizens by birth if their fathers are citizens of the United States. Likewise, the status of alien women married to citizens of the United States is not covered by the provision, although by law citizenship is conferred upon them if they are

[1] Burgess, "Political Science and Constitutional Law," Vol. I, p. 219.

capable of naturalization. Cases have been determined by the courts involving the citizenship rights of children born in the United States of parents who are not citizens. The general rule is that if the parents are subject to the jurisdiction of the United States, the children are citizens by birth. For instance, it has been decided, that although the subjects of China cannot, under the laws in force, become citizens, the children of Chinese parents who have a permanent residence in the United States are citizens by birth.[1] An exception to this rule seems to be made with respect to children born in the United States of foreign parents who are residing in that country only temporarily, notwithstanding the fact that such parents, except in the case of representatives of foreign nations to whom the international rule of extra-territoriality applies, are within the jurisdiction of the United States. With a child of such parents an option or right of choice is recognized. If he remains in the United States until of sufficient age to exercise an intelligent choice, he may claim citizenship by birth. If, however, he is taken by his parents to the country of which they are subjects, and his choice is to remain there, he becomes an alien to the United States, notwithstanding the fact that he was born in that country.[2] Other cases have arisen from time to time, and been passed upon by the courts, in which difficulties not mentioned here have been involved; but the ones suggested are sufficient to show that the constitutional provision is not all inclusive.

Citizenship by Naturalization. — The other method of acquiring citizenship, that of naturalization, lies wholly within the control of the national government. By the Constitution Congress is given power to " establish an uniform rule of naturalization." The States are not specifically denied the power to set up naturalization rules of their own, but, of course, by implication, the authority of Congress is necessarily exclusive, else it could not establish a uniform rule throughout the Nation. By act of Congress a general naturalization law has been provided which prescribes the procedure which an alien must observe in order to become a citizen of the United States, and, therefore, of the State in which he resides. It is to be noted

[1] *United States* v. *Wong Kim Ark*, 169 U. S. 649 (1898).
[2] McClain, " Constitutional Law in the United States," Second Edition, p. 278.

that the authorization of Congress to impose a uniform rule does not mean that the same rule must apply to all classes of aliens. The uniformity feature of the constitutional provision applies only to the operation of the law in the several States of the Union. It is fully within the power of Congress to restrict the privilege of naturalization to whatever races and nationalities it may think best, and to enact special laws for special classes of aliens, if it so wishes. Under the general law, as it stands, only white persons and members of the African race can be naturalized. The Chinese, Japanese, and all colored persons except Negroes, are excluded. The exclusion of the Chinese has, in addition, been made the subject of special legislation. It must be kept in mind, though, that with respect to all persons excluded by law, whether general or special, the restriction applies only to naturalization and does not prevent the acquiring of citizenship by birth. As previously pointed out, the children of parents who permanently reside within the jurisdiction of the United States, are citizens by birth, even though the parents themselves cannot become citizens. Also, it should be repeated, the enjoyment of political privileges, such as voting, holding office, and serving on juries, is not involved in the question of naturalization or citizenship. The latter lies within the province of the Nation, while the former is to be determined by each State for itself. Furthermore, the fact should be mentioned that the regulation of the naturalization of aliens is not confined to statutes enacted by Congress; this may be accomplished by treaties, as well, whether the purpose be exclusion from or admission to the privilege of naturalization. Treaties, by express provision of the Constitution, are a part of the supreme law of the land and are binding upon all of the States, as well as upon the Nation. Obviously the question of expatriation, both of aliens desiring to become citizens of the United States and of citizens of the United States who wish to become citizens of other countries, is a proper subject for treaty negotiations.

What Citizenship Means. — The meaning of citizenship of the United States, with respect to the privileges conferred by it, is still to be touched upon. Though citizenship does not carry with it political privileges, yet it involves rights and privileges, both at home and abroad, which are of fundamental importance. A citizen traveling or temporarily residing abroad is entitled to the protection of the United States in the enjoyment of his rights under international rules and treaty provisions which may have been established. Of course, such citizen is subject to the laws of the foreign state, for the time being, and must accord them proper respect and obedience; but it is the business of the United States to see that he is not subjected to discrimination and unfair treatment. In regard to the privileges of citizenship at home, the Constitution of the United States gives certain fundamental guaranties. The provisions of the so-called Bill of Rights, or first ten amendments to the Constitution, are here involved, as well as that clause of Article IV which guarantees to the citizens of each State " all the privileges and immunities in the several States " and that part of the fourteenth amendment which says that no State " shall make or enforce any law which shall abridge the privileges or immunities of citizens of the United States." The prohibitions of the first ten amendments apply to the national authority, while the others mentioned apply to the States. Precisely what privileges and immunities are guaranteed against State interference cannot be stated. Some things, however, are clearly included and have been passed upon by the Supreme Court, although the attempt has not been made to define the phrase specifically. Some brief excerpts from the Court's decisions may be used to show what is involved. In a leading case, calling into question the force of the provision that the citizens of each State are entitled to all the privileges and immunities of citizens in the several States, these words are used: " It was undoubtedly the object of the clause in question to place the citizens of each State upon the same footing with citizens of other States, so far as the advantages resulting from citizenship in those States are concerned. It relieves them from disabilities of alienage in other States; it inhibits discriminating legislation against them by other States; it gives them the right of free ingress into other States, and egress from them; it insures to them in other States the same freedom possessed by the citizens of those States in the acquisition and enjoyment of property and in the pursuit of happiness; and it secures to them in other States the equal protection of their laws." [1]

[1] *Paul* v. *Virginia*, 8 Wallace 168 (1868).

THE STATES — SUFFRAGE AND CITIZENSHIP

In another case involving the same clause of the Constitution the court declared itself as follows: "Attempt will not be made to define the words 'privileges and immunities,' or to specify the rights which they are intended to secure and protect, beyond what may be necessary to the decision of the case before the court. Beyond doubt, those words are words of very comprehensive meaning, but it will be sufficient to say that the clause plainly and unmistakably secures and protects the right of a citizen of one State to pass into any other State of the Union, for the purpose of engaging in lawful commerce, trade, or business, without molestation, to acquire personal property, to take and hold real estate, to maintain actions in the courts of the States, and to be exempt from any higher taxes or excises than are imposed by the State upon its own citizens."[1] And in the famous Slaughter House Cases,[2] decided in 1873, the Supreme Court discussed the meaning of the "privileges and immunities" clause of the fourteenth amendment. It does not try to state the exact meaning of the clause, but merely calls attention to some of the rights included. Among these are the rights of the citizen to visit the seat of government for the purpose of transacting business with it or seeking its protection; to have free access to the Nation's seaports and to the courts of justice; to demand the care and protection of the federal government over his life, liberty, and property when on the high seas or within the jurisdiction of a foreign government; peaceably to assemble and petition for redress of grievances; to use the navigable waters of the United States; to become a citizen of any State of the Union, upon acquiring a legal residence, with the same privileges as the other citizens of that State. Other rights are enumerated, but need not be given here; those already mentioned are sufficient to show that the privileges and immunities enjoyed by citizens of the United States are of fundamental importance, even though political privileges are not included. They also show clearly that the fourteenth amendment, which definitely placed the whole question of citizenship under national control, has imposed far-reaching restrictions upon the States. It is unnecessary in this place to discuss all of the provisions of this amendment and their effect upon the powers of the States, but it may be said that the restrictions involved in

[1] *Ward* v. *Maryland*, 12 Wallace 418 (1871).   [2] 16 Wallace 36.

the privileges and immunities clause, great as they are, are by no means all that are imposed. Indeed, as affecting State powers, the clauses which immediately follow, providing that no State shall deprive any person of life, liberty, or property, without due process of law, nor deny to any person within its jurisdiction the equal protection of the laws, are probably of still more vital significance. Though these provisions were apparently designed to protect the Negroes in the enjoyment of constitutional rights acquired by the overthrow of slavery, it is behind them that corporations, in their capacity of legal persons, have sought and found shelter against much restrictive legislation by the States. Multitudes of cases have arisen involving the rights of corporations under the fourteenth amendment and many attempts of the States to regulate corporate activities and management have been thwarted by action of the federal courts. Corporations are not entitled to the privileges and immunities of citizenship, but they, together with natural persons, come in for full protection under the " due process " and " equal protection of the laws " provisions. As has been the case in other matters, the development in connection with citizenship, particularly that growing out of the fourteenth amendment, has resulted in an expansion of national power and a restriction upon that of the States.

REFERENCES

BURGESS. *Political Science and Constitutional Law*, Vol. I, pp. 218-232.
COOLEY. *Constitutional Law*, Chap. XIV.
COOLEY. *A Treatise on Constitutional Limitations*, Chap. XVII.
McCLAIN. *Constitutional Law in the United States*, Chaps. XXXIV, XXXV.
RICHMAN. "Citizenship of United States," *Political Science Quarterly*, Vol. V, p. 104.
VAN DYNE. *Citizenship of the United States*.

CHAPTER XXVI

THE STATES — POLICE POWER AND CONTROL OVER LOCAL GOVERNMENTS

THE various references that have been made to the restrictions upon the States and to the relative decline of their powers are not to be interpreted as suggesting that the States are unimportant political organizations, with insignificant functions. Nothing could be farther from the intention of this discussion, or more at variance with the truth. The States are not only essential to the existence of the Union, but they exercise powers of the highest rank and perform functions that are absolutely necessary for the orderly on-going of society. And these powers they have, not by sufferance from the national government, but of their own right. Moreover, they are to be used as each State sees fit, subject only to the restrictions of the federal Constitution. It is necessary merely to mention that those great powers of government called police powers, and that the entire control of all local governments and their functions, rest with the States, to indicate how vital the States are in the government of the American people. Brief comment upon the police power and the relation of the States to the local governments is desirable.

Significance of Police Power. — It is not necessary to try to define specifically what is meant by the police power of the States; indeed, no precise, authoritative definition of the term has been developed. All that is needed here is to indicate roughly its nature and scope, and thus make clear one of the supremely important functions of the States. The broad, fundamental significance of this power is suggested in these words by the Supreme Court: " But what are the police powers of a State? They are nothing more or less than the powers of government inherent in every sovereignty to the extent of its dominions. And whether a State passes a quarantine law, or a law to punish offenses, or to establish courts of justice, or requiring certain instruments to be recorded, or to regulate commerce within its own limits, in every case it exercises the same power; that is to say, the power of sovereignty, the power to govern men and things within the limits of its dominion. It is by virtue of this power that it legislates. . . ."[1] Considered in this broad sense, the police power is utilized in the prevention and punishment of crimes, the control of private conduct, the regulation of the ownership, use, and management of property, the promotion and maintenance of public education, the prevention of vice and immorality, the promotion and protection of health, the regulation of domestic relations, the control of the relations between employer and employee, the protection of individuals against fraud, oppression, and injustice; in short, through the exercise of this power, the " whole of the ordinary field of law " comes within the control of the States. It is through it that the States possess " all the ordinary legal choices that shape a people's life."[2]

But a narrower and perhaps more accurate interpretation of the police power is frequently made, namely, that it is the power used by the States for the promotion of the public welfare through the establishment of restraints and regulations upon the use of liberty and property. " The police power restrains and regulates, for the promotion of the public welfare, the natural or common liberty of the citizen in the use of his personal faculties and of his property."[3] Much of the protection of liberty and of property, and many of the limitations upon each of these, the purpose of which is the advancement of the public welfare, are found in the common law which prevails in the States. " But no community confines its care of the public welfare to the enforcement of the principles of the common law. The State places its corporate and proprietary resources at the disposal of the public by the establishment of improvements and services of different kinds; and it exercises its compulsory powers for the prevention and anticipation of wrong by narrowing common law rights through conventional restraints and positive regulations which are not confined to the prohibition of wrongful acts. It is this latter kind of state control which

---

[1] License Cases, 5 Howard 504 (1846).   [2] Above, p. 7.
[3] Freund, " The Police Power," p. 17.

constitutes the essence of the police power. The maxim of this power is that every individual must submit to such restraints in the exercise of his liberty or of his rights of property as may be required to remove or reduce the danger of the abuse of these rights on the part of those who are unskillful, careless or unscrupulous." [1]

A word more should be added concerning the police power in relation to the courts and judicial control over property. The significance of this relationship is brought out in a stimulating way by Professor Ely, who argues that " the essence of police power is social control over property," [2] and whose statement concerning the nature of the police power, according to the modern acceptation, is here reproduced. In this, emphasis is placed upon its judicial character. Says Professor Ely: " The police power is regarded as primarily a legislative power, and it is true that legislative bodies provide in their enactments materials for the work of the courts. But the legislative power has no inherent limitations, and as in all lands, so in the United States, it goes without saying that legislatures are presumed to seek the public good only. What is peculiar in the United States is that controlling influence of courts given them by American Constitutions; this peculiarity has given rise to the modern use of the term ' police power.' As a peculiar institution, the police power is essentially judicial, and it is as a judicial power that it requires discussion in the present connection; and from this point of view we may define it as follows: The police power is the power of the courts to interpret the concept property, and above all private property; and to establish its metes and bounds. The judges, in their decisions upon the accordance of legislative acts with written Constitutions, tell us what we may do with property or what acts bearing on property are allowable. The police power shapes the development of the social side of property. It tells us what burdens the owner of property must bear without compensation. . . . Many efforts have been made to define police power, but . . . from the economic point of view, so far as property is concerned, it is essentially the power to interpret

[1] Freund, " The Police Power," p. 6.
[2] Ely, " Property and Contract in their Relations to the Distribution of Wealth," Vol. I, p. 225.

property and especially private property and to give the concept a content at each particular period in our development which fits it to serve the general welfare. The police power means the general welfare theory of property. It signifies the 'principle of public policy' with respect to property. This idea above all others gives unity to the concept of police power."[1]

An important fact to be borne in mind is that the police power is not negative merely in its effect, but is also definitely positive; it not only says what shall not be done with property, in the interest of the general welfare, but also declares what shall be done. In this connection Professor Ely quotes the words of Mr. Justice Holmes of the United States Supreme Court: "The police power extends to all the great public needs. It may be put forth in aid of what is sanctioned by usage, or held by the prevailing morality or the strong and preponderant opinion to be greatly and immediately necessary to the public welfare."[2] Although the police power is not confined to the regulation of property, real difficulty is not encountered in its exercise except where property and economic relations are concerned. "No one objects to general benevolence — to doing good without cost — so when we consider police power, its essence is the interpretation of property, and when we consider the real essence of the police power as found in the leading American decisions, we find that it is consistent with this concept. It is that power of the courts committed to them by American Constitutions whereby they must shape property and contract to existing social conditions by settling the question of how far social regulations may, without compensation, impose burdens on property. It seeks to preserve the satisfactory development of the individual and social sides of private property and thus to maintain a satisfactory equilibrium between them."[3]

Further comment is hardly necessary to show that the governmental institution that exercises this great power and discharges this elemental function of organized society, is one of prime importance. It is in the field covered by this power

---

[1] Ely, "Property and Contract in their Relations to the Distribution of Wealth," Vol. I, pp. 206–207. [2] *Noble State Bank* v. *Haskell*, 219 U. S. 110 (1911).
[3] Ely, "Property and Contract in their Relations to the Distribution of Wealth," Vol. I, p. 220.

that the great bulk of governmental activity is found. It is therefore through action of the States that the American citizen comes into most immediate and most frequent contact with governmental authority. This must continue to be true as long as the present constitutional system is maintained. The functions of the States, therefore, their powers and machinery of government, are subjects of fundamental significance, and he who seeks to understand the American system of government in all of its essential relationships must give a large place in his thoughts to the States and their work.

The States and Local Government. — In the matter of local government, the States are supreme. No authority whatsoever is lodged in the national government over local affairs or organizations. These may not be touched or in any way affected by national authority, unless they in some manner act contrary to the provisions of the federal Constitution; in which case, their acts would be set aside by judicial process, if appeal were made to the courts. Any restraints which may rest upon a State with respect to its control over the organization, powers, and duties of the local governments within its limits are self-imposed restraints. The people of a State through the State constitution may provide for any kind of local government they may wish. They may set up local governments which are independent of the legislative and executive authorities in the State government, or they may give to one or the other of these authorities direct supervision over all local activities. It is for the people of a State to say, if they wish, through the State constitution, what the entire system of government, both State and local, shall be, subject only to the requirement of the federal Constitution that the State government itself shall be republican in form. The relationship between the State government and the various local governments, therefore, may be determined specifically by the State constitution, enacted by the people of the State according to the prescribed method of procedure. If this relationship is not thus fixed, however, it will be determined by the State legislature in whatever way the latter may prefer, subject, of course, to any prohibitions and restrictions that may be imposed by the State constitution. The reserved powers of a State are vested in its legislature, except as the State constitution may forbid.

The right of a legislature, free from constitutional restraints, to create new local governments or alter or abolish old ones, is therefore beyond all question. In such circumstances it has a free hand.

The local governments, whether counties, townships, towns, cities, or incorporated towns, possess no inherent governmental authority, but exercise only delegated powers. These powers are derived either directly from the constitution of the State or from the acts of its legislature. The local governments, therefore, can do only what they are permitted to do; they are not free to do as they wish, unless forbidden by State authority. In this respect their position is radically different from that of cities in continental Europe, which in general resemble the American States in that they have all powers not taken from them. They are created by the States for specific purposes and are given the powers that are considered necessary or advisable. If these prove inadequate, relief can come only through a further grant of powers from the State. The nature of the powers possessed by the local governments and the constitutional principle which controls, are clearly shown in the following statement by an eminent writer: "It is a general and undisputed proposition of law that a municipal corporation possesses and can exercise the following powers and no others: First, those granted in express words; second, those necessarily or fairly implied in, or incident to the powers granted; third, those essential to the declared objects and purposes of the corporation — not simply convenient, but indispensable. Any fair, reasonable doubt concerning the existence of power is resolved by the courts against the corporation, and the power is denied. Of every municipal corporation, the charter or statute by which it is created is its organic act. Neither the corporation nor its officers can do any act, or make any contract, or incur any liability, not authorized thereby, or by some legislative act applicable thereto. All acts beyond the scope of the powers granted are void."[1]

The fact that the local authorities have only delegated powers is one of great practical importance, both from the standpoint of legislative efficiency in the State and administrative efficiency in the local governments. As a consequence of the development

[1] Dillon, "Municipal Corporations," Fourth Edition, p. 145.

of multitudinous, conflicting local interests, and particularly of the rapid growth of cities, both in number and in size, the legislatures of the States are constantly under pressure to enact new legislation for the benefit of the local governments and to confer upon them additional powers. The result is that a relatively large part of the time and thought of each legislature is given to the consideration of problems of local government which is needed in the determination of important questions of State policy. State interests naturally suffer to a greater or less degree. On the other hand, because of the general constitutional rule against special legislation and the requirement of State constitutions that laws must be of general application, the conflicting interests and needs of the localities are inadequately provided for, to the serious impairment of the efficiency of the local units. The natural outcome is a steadily increasing demand for a larger independence, — home rule, — on the part of the local governments. This demand is particularly marked in the case of cities, but it is also more or less prevalent with respect to counties. There is increasing objection to State supervision and control in purely local affairs. In all of the States, but, of course, in some far more than in others, the tendency is to give to the local governments larger powers and independence in the settlement of their own problems. It may be expected that future years will witness fundamental readjustments in the relations between State and local governments, for the question of what these relations shall be is one of the pressing practical problems of American politics.

Nature of the State's Control. — Emphasis is to be placed on the fact that the control which the States exercise over the cities and other local governments is primarily legislative in character and not administrative. The careful administrative supervision, so common in Europe, is largely lacking, although in recent years there has been a marked tendency to increase the State's administrative control. The usual plan has been to confer upon the local governments the powers considered necessary and then allow them to use these powers pretty much as they please, without being held accountable to established State authority. The results of this policy have been far from satisfactory, however, and a more centralized administrative direction is being established in many States. Recognition is growing of the idea that the vital question is not so much that of what powers the local governments shall have, but of how they utilize their powers. The need is for efficient supervision of their administrative work, — a need which the States are coming to see and to meet. The development that is taking place is similar to that which has occurred in England; the legislative control is giving way, in part, and is being supplemented by administrative control. The result is likely to be a system which in character stands mid-way between the extreme legislative system, so familiar to America, and the extreme administrative system, so common in European countries. It is to be observed, however, that the supervision is centralized, State supervision, whether it be of one type or the other. The local governments have powers or do not have powers, they are free or not free, just as the States prescribe through their constitutions or the acts of their legislatures.

The local governments, created thus by State action and exercising only delegated authority, have a dual function to discharge. They are instruments for the control of local affairs, as far as their limited powers go, and they are at the same time agents of the State, charged with the duty of assisting in the enforcement of State laws and in administering State affairs. What the exact powers of any particular local government are, depends upon the class to which it belongs. The towns and townships do not have the same powers as the counties; and the powers of the counties are not identical with those of the cities. Moreover, the cities of a State are frequently divided into classes, according to population, each class having powers that differ more or less from those of the other classes. As a rule, the grant of powers is uniform to all local governments of the same kind or class. In the case of cities, the movement for a larger independence of State control has made much progress in recent years, and a number of States have, by amendments to their constitutions, conferred upon municipalities the right to frame their own charters, subject only to constitutional requirements and the general police regulations of State law. The same object is being sought, also, through statutory provisions. Where this home rule principle is applied, the local government, though it continues to exercise delegated power, is freed from supervision and interference on the part of the legislature. In this way each community can adapt its institutions to its own requirements, and carry out policies designed to meet its own peculiar needs.

Local Governments Agents of the State. — As agents of the States, the local governments have important duties to perform. For example, their law enforcement officers are charged with the enforcement of State laws. The States, as a rule, have no regular police of their own and are dependent upon local officers, largely, for the prevention of crimes and the punishment of offenders. The conspicuous fact should be remembered, in this connection, that local enforcement of State police regulations is often far from what it ought to be. Locally elected officers are much inclined to govern their official conduct by the sentiment of the communities they serve. The enforcement of State laws against gambling or the illegal sale of liquor, for instance, in a community where such offenses are winked at, or to a degree openly approved by local opinion, is very likely to be lax and of little result. This has become a very serious problem, in fact, in all of the States and a growing sentiment is discernible in favor of more stringent State supervision over the work of law enforcement, if not the actual establishment of a State police. In some States, the chief executive may remove local officers for failure in this respect and in others the Department of Justice may, through court proceedings, oust them for cause.

But the functions of the local governments as agents of the States are not confined to enforcing police regulations. They are also important administrative districts of the State. Three distinct purposes for which they are used may be cited. The first is the administration of the revenue laws. The local units are taxation districts, not merely for obtaining local revenues, but also for obtaining State revenues. The State revenue systems differ, of course, in many ways, and some have sources of income which others do not have. Also the process of levying and collecting taxes is by no means identical in all the States, but the traditional practice of the States, with respect to the general property tax, which has been the chief source of State and local revenues, has been to intrust to the officers of the local governments the duty of assessing the property and collecting the taxes according to the levies made by the State and local authorities. The funds belonging to the State, collected by the local collection officer — the county treasurer usually — are turned over, under provisions of law, to the State treasurer and become available for the purposes to which they have been appropriated by the State legislature. Thus this vital function of administering the State's tax laws is to a large extent in the hands of locally elected officers in the local government districts, the county, township, town, and city. Needless to say, abundant fault may be found with the manner in which this system works. Probably no other of the States' activities has given cause for more complaint and greater dissatisfaction. The extreme decentralization of revenue administration has been the chief weakness. This has come to be so widely understood that in recent years more than half the States have provided for centralized supervision through State tax commissions.

The local government units are also election districts for the State. The county, particularly, is important in this connection. In fact, the county in most States is the real election district. Some of its officers, in general, are responsible for the administration of the election laws. Ballots are printed under their direction. The returns from the townships, wards, or other election precincts are sent to the proper county officers to be canvassed officially. This applies not merely to the election of county officers, but to the election of all State officers, United States Senators, and presidential electors. Election expenses are provided for out of county funds. The county is the usual unit of representation in the State legislature, and it is by a grouping of counties, except in the large cities, that the larger election districts, such as congressional districts, are formed. Elections are under the strict control of the States, except as Congress has prescribed regulations which must be observed in the election of national officers, and are conducted according to a procedure required by State law. The counties and the smaller election precincts, as far as State elections are concerned, are merely State administrative agents.

Likewise, the local governments are districts for the administration of justice. And here, again, the county is the district of most consequence. In all the States there are courts of general civil and criminal jurisdiction in the counties, which hold regular sessions as required by State law. These courts are parts of the State judicial system, but their administrative officers are county officials receiving compensation from the county funds. The sheriff of the county, and the county attorney, or, as he is frequently called, the district attorney, are officers of these courts, though they are usually chosen by the voters at the polls, and are the county's chief agents in the enforcement of the laws. The grand juries which bring indictments before these county or district courts are county bodies, with authority to consider only offenses which are committed within the limits of the county. In short, these courts, though they may not be known as such, are really county courts, and the records of their work are kept at the county seat, and the expenses incurred by them are paid out of county funds. The minor justice of the peace courts and various municipal courts in the larger cities are also agencies of the State in enforcing the laws and administering justice. The State depends in large measure upon its administrative divisions and subdivisions for the maintenance of law and order.

Further discussion is not necessary to show the relationship of dependence which exists between the State and the local governments. The latter exist only at the will of the former; their powers and duties are what the States prescribe. And the States have chosen to depend upon the local governments for the discharge of functions which are vital to their own existence.

REFERENCES

BEARD. *American Government and Politics*, Edition 1914, Chaps. XXVII, pp. 579–584, XXIX.
BRYCE. *The American Commonwealth*, Edition 1910, Vol. I, Chaps. XLVIII, XLIX, LII.
COOLEY. *A Treatise on Constitutional Limitations*, Chap. XVI
ELY. *Property and Contract in their Relations to the Distribution of Wealth*, Vol. I, Chap. VII.
FAIRLIE. *Local Government in Counties, Towns, and Villages.*
FREUND. *The Police Power.*
GOODNOW. *City Government in the United States*, Chaps. II, IV, V.
GOODNOW. *The Principles of the Administrative Law of the United States*, Book III, Chaps. I, II, III, IV.
MUNRO. *The Government of American Cities*, Chaps. III, IV.
YOUNG. *The New American Government and its Work*, Chap. XXIV.

CHAPTER XXVII

STATE LEGISLATION

THE governments of the States are very much alike in their general outlines, but are dissimilar in many details of organization and procedure. This fact makes the task of describing them in general terms, within the limits of a few pages, one of some difficulty. To present an outline of the governmental system of any one State would be a simple task, but to let such outline stand as representative of the governments of the other forty-seven States, would be to ignore essential differences among them, particularly in administrative organization, and to imply a degree of uniformity which does not exist. It is desirable, therefore, briefly to discuss the State governments in terms which, in general, will apply to all alike. The purpose here is not to give a detailed treatment of the State organizations, but merely to describe their essential characteristics, suggest some of the important developments that have taken place, and indicate the manner in which the States are discharging their functions as members of the American Republic.

Uniformity Among State Institutions. — The tendency of the States to copy the laws and institutions of one another has already been briefly commented upon. This is both a significant and a natural tendency. As new regions were settled and developed by the pioneers who pushed on to the westward from the older States, it was inevitable that the political institutions, which in time were established, should be patterned after the institutions which had existed in the States from which the settlers came. This is the case with the local governments as well as those of the States; perhaps it is even more the case with them, since the first governments set up in the frontier regions were purely local in character. When the time came to seek membership in the Union and organize as a State, the logical thing in the drafting of the new constitution was to provide for a framework of government substantially identical with those of the older States. Moreover, it is to be remembered that the original States, when they became independent commonwealths and established the Union, retained practically the same organizations they had when they were colonies under British rule. These, in their main outlines, were essentially the same in all the States, the chief differences that prevailed being found in connection with the local governments. Consequently there was a long experience with a fairly uniform scheme of State government, which had given general satisfaction, to be drawn upon by the founders of new States and the framers of new constitutions. The general success of the familiar State institutions which this experience revealed assured their acceptance in the newer commonwealths, and discouraged attempts at innovation and experimentation with untried agencies of government.

Furthermore, the influence of the national government, which grew in strength and effectiveness as the Nation developed, tended strongly in the same direction. As we have seen, the national government was modeled chiefly upon the governments of the Colonies and the States, and so gave additional evidence, upon a magnified scale and in a conspicuous manner, of the inherent worth of the institutions and the organization of government to which American conditions and experience had given rise. The marked influence of the States upon one another and upon the Nation, and of the Nation upon the States, is one of the notable aspects of American politics. Under all the circumstances, therefore, it is not to be wondered at that there is a high degree of uniformity in the fundamental features of the State constitutions. Anything else, considering the similarity of the problems which the States must meet and the fact that their powers and functions are identical, could not reasonably be expected. Yet there are important differences, whose significance should not be overlooked; and, as previously pointed out, one of the distinct advantages of the American federation plan is that the States have the opportunity to originate and apply new theories and methods. Though they have utilized this opportunity in the past only to a slight extent, yet a tendency to make freer use of it is indicated by the events of recent years. A few of the States, in order to make their governments more truly democratic and solve pressing problems which have grown out of changed and changing industrial conditions, have made radical departures in the enactment of new legislation and the establishment of new administrative agencies. Wisconsin, with her state insurance, income tax, and multitude of administrative commissions, is a good example.

Development of State Constitutions. — Looking at the development of the States from the time they gained their independence to the present, it is seen that not only have their institutions of government been similar, but also that their experience with those institutions and the attitude of the people toward them, have been strikingly similar. This may be shown by reference to the development which has occurred in connection with the State constitutions, and the altered positions of the legislative and executive branches of the State governments. This development is profoundly significant and is directly related to some of the greatest questions now before the people of the States.

The early constitutions were short documents which dealt in general terms with the fundamental structure of the State governments. They created the instrumentalities of government, distributed powers among them, and harmonized the use of those powers. They were essentially grants of powers to the departments of government which they established; they were not codes of restrictions upon the departments. In other words, they merely created the framework of the State governments. Indeed, some of them were called "frames," a term suggestive of their nature and of the intention of those who were responsible for them.[1] These instruments were not designed to regulate the conduct of private individuals, through a multitude of provisions, but to create the machinery of government and determine the relations among its parts. Under them the department of government which was of highest importance was the legislature. As compared with it, the executive department was distinctly inferior. The executive, in fact, was largely the agent of the legislature. To the latter was given the function of controlling the State. The inherent powers of the State, unlimited powers of legislation, in fact, were in the hands of the legislature, except as it was limited by the State constitution, and — after the

[1] Jones, "Statute Law Making in the United States," p. 4.

national government was formed — by the federal Constitution. This is the theory which was accepted at that time and which is still accepted. When the independence of the States was declared, their legislatures fell heir to the plenary powers of the English Parliament, whose authority in America came to an end. As this constitutional adjustment implies, the people had large confidence in their State legislatures and only slight confidence in their executives. Because of their experience with British authorities, particularly the colonial governors, they were distrustful of executive power. There was constant fear of executive encroachments. Consequently, as stated, the executive held a relatively subordinate place in the State government and the legislature was exalted as the champion and protector of the newly acquired and dearly bought liberties of the people.

The People and the Legislatures. — This expresses the general attitude which prevailed at the time the national government was established, and which continued to prevail for a number of years. But at length a change began to take place. The State legislatures began to lose some of their prestige. Gradually the confidence of the people in them began to wane. The great respect shown to the legislatures in the earlier times changed to a widespread, freely expressed disrespect. Distrust of them sprang up, — distrust of their motives, their integrity, and their capacity. The consequence was numerous readjustments of the State governments and frequent revisions of State constitutions.

The outstanding feature of these revisions was the marked restriction placed upon legislative power. At first the restrictions were comparatively slight, but as time passed and the popular distrust increased, they became more numerous and more sweeping in their effect. Upon many questions the hands of the legislatures were tied. Powers, which formerly were exercised without restraint, were specifically forbidden. The sphere in which the legislature was free to work its will, untrammeled by constitutional restrictions, was cut down until the legislature's position was strikingly different from what it had been when the Union was formed. But the development did not stop with merely placing constitutional restrictions upon the legislature. In time the practice grew up of incorporating in the constitutions veritable codes of laws regulating in detail all kinds of questions which formerly had been left to the legislature's discretion. The purpose was not merely to restrain the legislature, but absolutely to prevent action by it upon the questions covered by the Constitution. In this way the character of the State constitutions came to be changed. Originally they were intended to express only the fundamental principles underlying the State governments. The laws of the States, in the ordinary sense, the details of legal regulations, were left to the legislatures to prescribe. But under the influence of the movement which has been described, the constitutions have come to be filled with a multitude of details which really have no place in them, the effect and purpose of which are to deprive the legislatures of powers which properly belong to them. " Our later constitutions have included an ever increasing body of concrete rules drawn with some local or temporary abuse in view. By putting the rule in the constitution it was thought to protect it against the possibility of easy repeal should the people subsequently, through their legislature, decide that it should be modified. When legislators wrongly used their power, resort was had to taking the power permanently away from them instead of taking the legislator out of power at the succeeding election. As a result of this process our constitutions are padded with restrictions, which make the legislator no longer a free agent in the proper field of legislation and encourage resort to subterfuge by which that may be accomplished indirectly, the doing of which is forbidden." [1]

To illustrate this phase of constitutional development, writers frequently call attention to the great length of the present State constitutions as compared with those in the earlier times. A few examples will be sufficient to show this tendency toward expansion. Louisiana in 1812 had a constitution of twelve pages; the present constitution has ninety-five pages, containing forty-five thousand words. Virginia in 1776 was content with a constitution of four pages; that of 1902 numbers fifty-eight pages. The South Carolina constitution in 1778 had nine pages; that adopted in 1895 has thirty-eight. Alabama adopted a constitution in 1819 with eighteen pages; in 1901 a new constitution went into effect with fifty-two pages. And thus it is in all the States where constitutional revisions have occurred. The newer States, those admitted in recent years, all have long

[1] Jones, " Statute Law Making in the United States," p. 5.

constitutions. Oklahoma in 1907 accepted a constitution with seventy-three pages, containing more than thirty-three thousand words, while New Mexico in 1911 adopted one with forty-seven pages. This tendency to expand the constitutions is found in all the States, though it is less in evidence in the New England commonwealths than elsewhere, and, as pointed out, is largely due to the desire of the people to legislate directly upon many important questions and, by placing this legislation in the constitutions, protect it absolutely against changes made by their legislatures. That the general effect of this is far from good seems obvious. The detailed "law provisions" of the constitutions soon become out of harmony with the conditions they are designed to meet, and demand alteration. This means that constitutional readjustments are constantly being urged, — a condition which is hardly wholesome and conducive to efficient administration of government. And if changes are not made, many provisions of the constitution become unsatisfactory and ineffective, and attempts at evasion are constantly made.[1]

Development of the Executive. — In connection with this constitutional development and the change in the attitude of the people toward their legislatures, there should be noted another equally significant fact, and that is the changing attitude of the people toward their State executives. Whereas in the beginning the executive branch of the State governments was distrusted and held an inferior place, with greatly restricted powers, it has come to hold relatively a high place in the public esteem, and has acquired, through new constitutional grants, greatly augmented powers and responsibilities. In a rough way it may be said that as the legislatures declined, the executives grew in popular favor; as the powers of the legislatures diminished, those of the executives increased. Reliance upon the executive has come to characterize more and more the public attitude. More and more the natural leadership of the executive has come to be recognized, as has the high importance of administrative functions and problems. This expansion of executive power and growth in executive influence are evidenced by many changes in the State constitutions. Not all of the in-

---

[1] For further discussion of the growth of State constitutions and the consequences which result, see Jones, "Statute Law Making in the United States," pp. 4–8, and Bryce, "The American Commonwealth," New and Revised Edition, Vol. I, p. 455.

crease in the length of the constitutions, to which reference has been made, is due to additional restrictions upon the legislature; some of it is due to new provisions imposing new duties upon the executive, and conferring and regulating executive powers. The shift in public sentiment which this implies, and the enlarged sphere of executive action which has resulted from it, constitute one of the most deeply significant developments in American politics. And, it is well to note, this executive expansion has not been confined to the States. A similar change has occurred in the Nation. The President is vastly more powerful now than in the beginning. Indeed, it may be said, that not a little of the change that has taken place in the relative positions of the legislative and executive departments of the States, is due to the development of the President's leadership in the Nation, and the growing confidence and satisfaction of the people in that leadership. As executive leadership proved itself in the Nation, the demand for it sprang up and grew in the States; and this demand has never been more insistent than at the present time. All the signs point to a still larger development of administrative functions.

The general plan of the State governments is the same as that of the Nation. There are the three departments, resting upon a constitutional foundation, each with its own powers, its own duties, and its own sphere of action. In the States as in the Nation, the principle of the separation of powers is fundamental. Consciously, and because of a firm belief in the soundness of this principle, the people of the States have set up the three departments and hedged them about by restrictions in order to protect them in the enjoyment of their respective powers and prevent encroachments upon one another. The departments must touch one another at certain points, of course, in order to make the machinery of government run with reasonable smoothness, but, nevertheless, each has its own work to do and must be free to do it without unauthorized interference by the others. In general, the same complex system of checks and balances, both legal and extra-legal, is to be found in the States as in the Nation. The chief executive has his part in legislation, similar to that of the President. The legislature possesses the power of impeachment over both executive and judicial officers, and in other ways may influence them, much as the Congress may do with national officers. The judiciary may pass upon the constitutionality of the acts of the legislature, and set aside executive actions which lie outside the executive sphere, just as the federal courts may do in the national field. By this system, suggested here in only general words, the departments are kept to the paths marked out for them by the State constitutions. The relation of the departments to one another will be brought out more in detail in the description of them given in this and succeeding chapters. The first to be considered is the legislature.

The State Legislative Departments. — The legislatures of the States are all of the same character, although they differ more or less in their internal organization. Each is composed of two houses, whose members are chosen by popular vote from districts into which the States are divided. One house is called the Senate, and the other, in most instances, is known as the House of Representatives, though in a few cases it is called " The Assembly " and in others " The House of Delegates." The Senate is the smaller body and is frequently spoken of as the " upper " house, while the larger body is referred to as the " lower " house. Though the two houses are equal, coördinate branches of the legislature, the Senate is usually more influential than the House of Representatives, and membership in it, because of its smaller size and the fact that its members represent larger constituencies, is everywhere considered more desirable than membership in the lower house. The legislative powers of the two bodies are essentially the same. Following the national plan, the power of impeachment belongs to the House of Representatives, while the duty of trying impeachment cases is imposed on the Senate. To the latter, also, as is the case with the national Senate, is given the power to confirm many executive appointments. The general nature of the legislative powers of the two houses has already been discussed somewhat at length in preceding chapters and need not be considered here. It is to be remembered that all the original powers of government are vested in the legislature, except as prohibitions are placed upon it by the national and State constitutions. The powers which the legislatures of the several States may actually exercise depend upon the State constitutions. The national Constitution, of course, applies to all alike, but the restrictions of the State constitutions vary a great deal.

There is much variation, also, in the size of the legislatures. In the case of the Senate, the number of members varies from seventeen, in Delaware, to sixty-three, in Minnesota. Two States, New York and Illinois, have Senates with fifty-one members. In four States the number is fifty; in one, forty-seven; in two, forty-five; in two, forty-four; in three, forty-two; in four, forty; in two, thirty-eight; in four, thirty-five; in twelve, from thirty to thirty-five; in ten, besides Delaware, less than thirty. The average membership is about thirty-seven. In the case of the House of Representatives, the variation is even greater, and the average membership much larger. The number of members runs from thirty-five to three hundred and ninety. In five States the House numbers more than two hundred. In thirty States the number is one hundred or more, sixteen of these having a House membership of from one hundred to one hundred and twenty. In twelve States the number is below seventy-five.

The qualifications of members of the legislature are fixed by the State constitutions. These differ a good deal. There is usually an age requirement for eligibility, that of a Senator being higher ordinarily than that of a Representative; say, thirty and twenty-five years. In some States the age is fixed at twenty-five and twenty-one years. Residence within the district represented is the regular rule. This may be required either by the constitution or by law. The residence rule, it should be said, is practically always observed in the United States, with respect to all elective offices. Other eligibility restrictions also may be imposed on State legislators, as, for instance, the exclusion of certain classes of persons. Public officers receiving salaries are regularly excluded.

In a majority of the States the term of office of Senators is longer than that of Representatives. In nineteen States, however, the term is the same. In a few more than half of the States the senatorial term is four years. In most of the others it is two years, only two having a one-year term. One, New Jersey, has a three-year term for Senators. In almost all of the States the Representatives serve for two years. The exceptions are four States where the term is one year, and three where it is four years. With the exception of two of the States having a four-year term, Representatives are elected for only one regular session of the legislature. In Louisiana and Mississippi both Representatives and Senators serve during two regular sessions. The ordinary rule, in those States where the term of Senators is twice that of Representatives, is that only half the Senators are elected at one time, thus making the Senate a permanent body, similar, in this respect, to the United States Senate.

With respect to compensation of legislators the practices of the States also differ. In thirty-one States the compensation is a fixed sum per day, ranging from three to ten dollars. In almost all of these the legislative session is limited to a stated number of days. In only one, Vermont, where a per diem salary of three dollars is provided, is there no limit to the number of days the legislature may remain in session. In two States, Rhode Island and Texas, there is no limit to the legislative session, but the compensation is limited to five dollars per day for a period not exceeding sixty days. In nine States there is a regular per annum salary, ranging from one hundred and fifty to fifteen hundred dollars. Five States pay a fixed salary for each regular session, the amount varying from four hundred to one thousand dollars.

In most of the States the legislatures hold biennial sessions. In only six is there an annual session. One, Alabama, has a quadrennial meeting of its legislature. In the great majority of the States the sessions begin sometime in January, the exact day being prescribed by law. As previously suggested, the sessions are frequently limited to a certain number of days. Seventeen States fix no limit. In the others the sessions vary from forty to ninety days.

Legislative Organization and Procedure. — Each house, when the legislature convenes, organizes for work by the election of a staff of officers, the appointment of committees, and the adoption of rules of procedure. The Lieutenant-Governor of the State is usually the presiding officer in the Senate and bears the title, President of the Senate. Frequently he appoints the Senate's committees. Where this is not the rule, the committees are elected by the Senate, as is done in the Congress of the United States. The power to appoint the committees gives to the Lieutenant-Governor great influence upon the work of the Senate, although he is not elected as a legislative officer. Not infrequently important committees are made up in a way to prevent legislation to which the Lieutenant-Governor and his friends are opposed. In the House of Representatives, the presiding officer is elected by the House and is known as the Speaker. He appoints the standing committees. In addition to the presiding officers, there is in each house a large number of officers and employees, including a chief clerk, reading clerk, sergeant-at-arms, doorkeeper, and their assistants, and many committee clerks, secretaries, and messengers. These are all technically elected by the houses. In reality, however, the selection of all the important officers is made by the party caucuses, just as is done in the Congress. The majority party in each house fills all the chief places and most of the inferior places with its own adherents, leaving to the minority party only a few offices of minor consequence. The committees are made up so as to give the majority party control of each by a safe margin. Each house, it thus is seen, is always organized on strict party lines, although the amount of strict party voting in the legislatures is very slight. In the process of organization, the election of the Speaker of the lower house is usually the event of most interest and concern. As in the national House of Representatives, the actual selection of the Speaker is made by the caucus of the dominant party, the election by the House being only a formal ratification of the caucus action.

By the State constitutions each house is authorized to prescribe its own rules of procedure. Some important regulations, though, are set up by the constitutions themselves which, of course, the houses cannot change, such as the requirements that bills shall be read three times, that every act shall embrace but one subject and this subject shall be clearly expressed in the title, that a majority of each house shall constitute a quorum, and that the yeas and nays shall be called upon the request of the designated number of members. Except where constitutional restrictions interfere, however, the houses may adopt whatever procedural regulations they may prefer. These cover the preparation and introduction of bills and resolutions, their reference to committees, their debate and amendment in the houses, and all the other steps which must be observed in the enactment of laws. The number, size, and jurisdiction of the committees also are regulated by the rules, as are the order of business and the duties of officers.

Without going into the details of a typical procedural system, attention may be called to the great importance of the legislature's rules. The efficiency of the legislature is determined to a large extent by them. However good may be the intentions of the legislators, the value of their service is affected materially by the procedure which they must observe. That the State legislatures have failed, in most instances, to provide rules which promote efficiency in the processes of legislation is one of the outstanding facts revealed by a study of their methods and the character of their work. It should be mentioned, however, that much of the fault which attaches to the State legislatures is not due to the failure to adopt rules of procedure, which, if observed, would prove fairly satisfactory; it is due in part to the non-observance of the rules which are adopted. It is a familiar though significant fact that the formal procedure which the rules prescribe is by no means always the one which is observed. Not infrequently the rules are practically set aside and bills are rushed through without regard to the normal requirements. If the leaders of the majority and minority groups are agreed — and such agreement is common — great laxness in the observance of the rules is likely to prevail. This lax procedure, as Professor Reinsch remarks, "has been encouraged through the general apathy of the people towards the State legislatures." The people as a rule give little thought to legislative procedure about which they are generally ignorant. "So it has come about that in States where the majority party has a strong organization or machine, the various forms of procedure have been treated as fictions, and the legislative body has automatically registered, in the last days of the session, and with a downright disregard of rules, those pieces of legislation which the party managers had agreed upon. Thus it is very common that the full readings of bills required by the constitution are entirely dispensed with, that the committee action on certain bills is treated as a pure formality, that objections and demands for roll-calls are ignored, and even that votes, which in fact were insufficient, are recorded as satisfying the legal requirements."[1] It is plain, therefore, that a mere study of the formal organization and procedure of the State legislatures will give both an inadequate and a false view of these important governmental

[1] Reinsch, "American Legislatures and Legislative Methods," p. 160.

bodies. With them, as with all the agencies of government, the vital thing is the manner in which they actually work, and not the way in which they were intended to work. It cannot be denied that the procedure prescribed by the rules commonly adopted by the State legislatures is far from perfect; but it is equally indisputable that much better results could and would be attained if the requirements of the rules were accorded the respect that is their due.

Character of the Legislatures' Work. — As the foregoing discussion indicates, the work of the State legislatures is far from satisfactory. Many reasons for this exist. Much of the work is done with indifferent spirit and in careless manner. The laws enacted are often very faulty in character, with respect to both form and content. Responsibility for what is done is often difficult, if not impossible, to determine. The committee system is usually cumbersome and preventive of harmonious action, — the committees being too many in number and too large in size. Publicity as to committee procedure is usually lacking. Objectionable lobbying and improper influence upon legislators are frequently brought to light. Narrow party spirit is too often displayed. Members of legislatures are too frequently unfitted for legislative service, through lack of ability, training, serious purpose, or appreciation of the responsibilities of their positions. Because of a rather distrustful, suspicious attitude on the part of the general public, coupled with the necessity of making a vigorous campaign to obtain an election, many men of character and ability are disinclined to seek legislative service. Moreover, the salaries of members are usually so small that they do not compensate for the sacrifices demanded by the political campaigns and the time which must be devoted to legislative duties. Furthermore, the increasing number of constitutional restrictions upon legislative powers has made service in the legislatures unattractive to many men of talent and capacity for leadership in public affairs. For these, and other reasons, the State legislatures have failed to measure up to a very high standard. The natural consequence has been that, as the people have become aroused to the need of more responsive and efficient government, a demand has sprung up for fundamental changes in legislative organization and methods. Three of the leading reform movements may be noted, those to provide for scientific legislation, to bring about thorough reorganization of the State legislatures, and to promote direct legislation. Only brief comment upon these is here necessary.

The movement for higher standards of legislation is of recent origin and thus far has involved two important proposals. One is the establishment of legislative reference libraries or bureaus for the purpose of collecting information needed by the legislature in the formulation of policies and of assisting legislators in preparing for their duties. The other is the establishment of drafting bureaus where bills may be put in proper form by experts in the art of drafting laws. It is an indisputable fact that the great majority of State legislators have neither the knowledge nor the ability necessary for the proper framing of laws dealing with many of the difficult, complex questions to which modern industrial conditions have given rise. The need for accurate information, so that the laws enacted will adequately fit the conditions which they are designed to meet, and the need for expert, scientific drafting of laws, so that they will fit perfectly into the existing body of law and meet all the constitutional requirements, thus being able to stand the severe test of judicial scrutiny, are among the genuinely vital needs of the American legislatures. Recognition of this fact has been growing rapidly in recent years and a number of States, following the lead of Wisconsin, have established reference libraries which are rendering service of the very highest value. Some of the States, also, have provided for official draftsmen. The growing consciousness of the value of well-framed laws and the great confusion and loss from faultily drawn measures, with the consequent burdens they impose upon the courts, give cause to think that in time all of the States will make adequate provision for assisting legislators along both of these lines.

The movement for reorganization of the State legislatures looks to fundamental structural changes. A number of different plans have been suggested, all seeking the same end, — greater legislative efficiency, more responsiveness to public opinion, more direct responsibility, simplification of the legislative process, a higher type of legislator, and more capable leadership. All of the suggestions contemplate a marked reduction in the membership of the legislatures, particularly that of the lower and most numerous branch. The most radical and most interesting proposal is to abolish the bicameral legislature and substitute a single chamber, with a relatively small membership, in which the chief executive officers should have seats. This plan, which involves the payment of adequate salaries and calls for the entire time of the legislators, has met with a good deal of public favor, and there is fair prospect that, sooner or later, it will be adopted by one or more of the States. It is to be borne in mind, however, that the bicameral legislature is deeply rooted in American experience, and the overthrow of so old an institution is a work of difficulty. In all the history of the American States, only three have experimented with a single chamber legislature, and even in these an executive council was provided as a check upon the legislature. Not since 1836, when Vermont abolished the council and divided the legislature into two houses, has the unicameral plan been used. With the merits of these reform projects, it is not the purpose here to deal. Attention should be called, however, to the growth of the sentiment in favor of a closer relation between the legislative and executive departments. A waning of the popular faith in the rather extreme separation of these departments, so characteristic of American government, is clearly discernible. The belief is undoubtedly growing that the presence in the legislative assembly of the heads of the chief executive departments would be in the interest of better legislation, as well as more efficient administration. That this belief is well founded, there is abundant evidence to show.

The third legislative reform mentioned, and the one which has made greatest progress, is the movement for direct legislation through the popular initiative and referendum. Representative government, both in State and in Nation, controlled largely by the exigencies of party politics and confronted by the great industrial problems and forces which have developed, has proven far from perfect. In fact, in the minds of many persons, apparently increasing in number, it has proven inadequate, if it has not actually broken down. The State legislatures, particularly, under the influence and sometimes the domination of political bosses and big business interests, have been, as has been pointed out, indifferent in their work and unresponsive to public opinion and the desires of a developing democracy. The result has been a demand for direct participation by the voters in the work of legislation. In a number of States amendments to the constitution have been put through which give to qualified electors the right, upon petition, to initiate legislation and decide at the polls whether it shall become law, as well as the right to demand a referendum upon bills passed by the legislature. That the movement for direct legislation is gaining in force cannot be questioned. In more and more States the demand is growing for constitutional amendments providing for the initiative and referendum. The experience of the States that have adopted the plan of direct legislation is being observed and studied by the others, as a basis upon which to determine their own actions. The extent to which this movement will develop is a matter for conjecture only, as is the ultimate effect of it upon the legislative assemblies. In the minds of some, a general acceptance of the initiative and referendum will cause a still further weakening of the State legislatures and a still further loss in prestige and efficiency. In the minds of others, the opposite effect will result, and the true representative principle will be strengthened and the legislatures improved in character and influence. Time must tell which opinion, if either, is correct.[1]

It is to be noted that the legislative reforms mentioned are not antagonistic to one another. They are, in fact, supplementary to one another. Whatever the effect of direct legislation may be upon the legislative assemblies, it is nowhere contemplated that the legislatures shall be abolished. Whether composed of two houses or one house, the legislature is certain to be an important organ of government, and the same need will exist for closer affiliation with the executive leaders, and for expert assistance and accurate information in the drafting of laws, as now exists. With all of its weaknesses and faults, with all of the changes that are likely to occur, the State legislature will continue to hold a vital place in the American system, and if some of the reforms contemplated are carried out, and work as they are anticipated to work, it will acquire a position and influence such as it has not had since the early days of the Republic, for these reforms look to the strengthening of the legislature and not to its injury.

The States as Political Experiment Stations. — In connection with this discussion of the legislatures and their work, and as

[1] For discussion of direct legislation in Switzerland, see Chap. LIII.

illustrating the part which they will undoubtedly continue to play in American politics, attention may be called to the profoundly significant part which the States have in solving the problems of free government. The possession of the inherent or original powers of government and their independence with respect to the control of their own affairs give to the States a strategic position; and it is to be remembered that, except as the State constitutions forbid, these inherent powers are exercisable by the legislatures. The States, acting through their legislatures as well as by direct legislation, may be, if they wish, great experiment stations for the development and testing of new institutions of government, for trying new policies, and evolving new methods of administration. They are frequently spoken of as political laboratories; and such they are, to a greater or less degree, to the enrichment of the political life of the whole Nation. The States are so related to one another and to the national government, that each can experiment in the solution of problems that are common to many or all of them. The possible advantages of this are so obvious that comment upon them is unnecessary. A number of States with a common problem, under similar conditions, may be seeking its solution along radically different lines. Some may fail and some may succeed. By a comparative study of their experiences and the results attained, the policy best suited for all of the States interested may be discovered. By this procedure much time and a great waste of energy and of money may often be avoided.

It must be said, however, that the States have not utilized to the extent possible, the opportunity that is always before them to carry forward political experiments which may prove mutually helpful. In fact, though in recent years a number of States have boldly tried new policies and new devices in their attempts to achieve a more genuinely popular government, the general tendency in the past has been to adhere to a markedly uniform scheme of government and to oppose innovations. The result has been less advance than might reasonably have been expected. This situation is undoubtedly changing, however, and under the influence of the great democratic movement which has been developing for a number of years and is now rapidly gaining headway, the States are becoming more active and more inclined to venture upon untrodden paths and to test by actual experience new principles and new theories. The reference here, of course, is to principles and theories hitherto untried by the American States, not necessarily new to the experience of foreign countries. It is in the States, indeed, that the growing democratic spirit and the demand for the democratization of government in all of its agencies, have first revealed themselves and have been most insistent. Naturally the influence of this movement for a more thoroughgoing democracy in the States has extended to the Nation and now no branch of government, national, State, or local, is free from it.

To illustrate the service of the States in this connection, reference may be made to some of the great reforms in government achieved by them in recent years. One of the most notable of these is the legalization of the political parties and their functions and the thorough overhauling of the procedure for the nomination of candidates for public office through the enactment of popular or direct primary laws. The old voluntary convention system, evolved by the political parties, unrestrained by law, is rapidly being supplanted by direct primaries. In practically all the States the primary, in one form or another, is in operation. In a majority of them, a statewide primary prevails, applying to United States Senators, members of the House of Representatives, Governors, and other State officers, as well as to members of the State legislatures and to local officials. And, as pointed out in the discussion of the party system, a strong demand has developed for the nomination of presidential candidates by a similar method.[1] The whole purpose of these laws is to popularize the State governments by making the party organizations legal institutions and giving the members of each party the right to choose the party candidates. Discussion of whether the ultimate results of the primary plan will be what has been hoped for does not lie within the scope of this book; opinions differ radically upon this, and a much longer experience with the system is needed before final judgment may be made. It may be assumed with some assurance, however, that popular nominations, by one plan or another, have come to stay and that the direct primary will in time be extended to all the States.

Many other new governmental devices and policies are being tested by some of the States, which are being scrutinized care-

[1] Above, p. 203.

fully and to a greater or less extent copied by the others. Among these, in addition to the initiative and referendum previously discussed, may be mentioned the recall of public officers, including judges of the State courts, by popular vote, — a reform which is new and which only a few States have adopted; control of public utilities, local as well as State, by State commissions; public ownership of municipal utilities; taxation reforms and centralized tax administration; legislation for the construction of permanent highways; coöperative enterprises of various kinds; the short ballot; stringent corrupt practices acts and control of election expenditures; State insurance; and social justice or social welfare legislation, such as minimum wage, child labor, and workingmen's compensation laws, and mothers' pensions. As stated previously, the States have become very active in recent years in the enactment of social welfare legislation, and the keenest interest is shown in the legislative experiments of the more advanced States. A plan which proves successful in one State is certain to be adopted, in whole or in part, by some of the others. Some experimentation is always in progress, and through a comparative study of the results all of the States are enlightened and helped. The benefit which comes from this mutual exchange of ideas and experiences is too manifest to be seriously questioned. Whatever may be thought of specific measures that may be enacted, it must be admitted that one of the distinct advantages that comes from the federal system of government lies in the reaction of the States upon one another in their attempts to solve difficult problems which are of common interest.

Uniform Legislation. — Complete diversity of laws, each State going its own way, no matter how similar the conditions may be, is plainly not desirable. On the other hand, absolute uniformity is hardly to be desired. Such a condition would tend to check progress in meeting adequately the problems that arise. It is of supreme value to the American democracy to have the individual States free to handle their own peculiar problems in their own way. There are some questions, however, upon which uniform laws would be of great benefit, though these questions, under the constitutional arrangement that exists, are exclusively within the jurisdiction of each State. Marriage and divorce may be cited as examples. If the laws of one State upon these questions are very stringent and those of an adjoining State are very lax, it is evident that the purpose of the former can easily be defeated by the latter. The advantage of having the same law, or substantially the same law, prevail in both States is clear. Some of the States have had at times rather unsavory reputations because of the resort to them by people from other States for the purpose of taking advantage of their lax divorce requirements. There is little reason to doubt that a satisfactory uniform law on this subject would be in the interest of morality and public welfare.

It is perhaps in connection with the control of industry and business, however, that the need for uniformity is most noticeable. Restrictive legislation designed to remedy abuses or prevent evils in business is difficult of enforcement in a State, if other, perhaps adjoining States, do not have laws of a similar character. Control of this kind, though it may be proper control and clearly in the interest of the general public welfare, may in fact impose burdens upon business enterprises which they cannot successfully carry in competition with similar businesses in other States that are free from such control. Difficulties of this nature have frequently prevented in some States the enactment of laws greatly needed for the protection of helpless classes of people. For instance, the passage of child labor laws has been much retarded, and in some instances prevented, by the fact that industries to which the laws applied would be compelled to compete with those of other States in which similar laws did not exist. Yet adequate protection of child workers is necessary. Similar situations arise in connection with minimum wage laws, workingmen's compensation laws and other restrictive social welfare legislation. The difficulty is a very real one and the progress of movements for the protection of workers and the improvement of industrial conditions has been delayed materially by it. If all of the States, or those of them interested in a particular problem, could be induced to act uniformly, it is undeniable that the solution could be found for many questions which are as yet unsolved. But experience has shown that it is extremely difficult to obtain this uniform action, notwithstanding the marked inclination of the States to copy from one another. Unquestionably, however, there is a growing sentiment in favor of concerted action in some matters, and it may reasonably be expected that in time uniform laws will be more common.

REFERENCES

BEARD. *American Government and Politics*, Edition 1914, Chaps. XXIII, pp. 461–471, XXV.

BRYCE. *The American Commonwealth*, Edition 1910, Vol. I, Chaps. XXXIX, XL.

DEALEY. *Growth of American State Constitutions*, Chaps. I to VIII, inclusive, XV, XVI, XVII.

JONES. *Statute Law Making in the United States*, Chaps. I, II, III.

MCCARTHY. *The Wisconsin Idea*, Chaps. VIII, IX.

Proceedings, American Political Science Association, 1907, Vol. IV, pp. 69–137; 1913, Vol. X, pp. 191–233.

RAY. *An Introduction to Political Parties and Practical Politics*, Chaps. XVIII, XIX, XX.

REINSCH. *American Legislatures and Legislative Methods*, Chaps. IV to X, inclusive.

REINSCH. *Readings on American State Government*, Chap. II.

CHAPTER XXVIII

State Administration

DECENTRALIZATION characterizes the executive organizations in the States. In this respect the State governments differ materially from the government of the Nation. Executive power in the States is not centered in one chief executive, as the executive power of the Nation is centered in the President; on the contrary, it is divided among a number of State officers and commissions, some of whom are entirely independent of control by the nominal chief executive, the Governor. The State administrative system is not a unit; its parts do not constitute a hierarchy of administrative agencies, each carefully adjusted to the others with a view to obtaining the highest efficiency. Thus far the fact which stands out with most striking clearness in connection with the governments of the States is this decentralization in administration, this diffusion of executive power, with its consequent diffusion of responsibility. The extent to which this policy has been carried and the results which flow from it, will be indicated in the discussion that follows. It is suggested here, merely, that decentralization, though it is natural for the States, considering the circumstances which prevailed at the time the Union was formed and the traditions of the American people, has proven very ineffective under modern conditions, and constitutes one of the grave, urgent problems of the present day.

The fact is to be emphasized that the administrative organization which prevails in the States was developed under conditions that were very different from those that now exist. When the Union was formed the functions of the State governments were few in number and simple in character. The general social and industrial life was far from complex. The States were not organized to engage in large operations such as they are now called upon to undertake, and consequently the administrative machinery is not adapted for the work they must do. Governmental institutions and processes, if they are to prove adequate, must change with changing conditions and problems. In the case of the States this necessary development has not occurred, with the result that they are falling far short of what they should achieve and what, in some manner, they must be made to achieve. The conclusion is inescapable that the State governments must undergo important changes before they will be able successfully to do the work which, under the American system, they alone can do. That this is becoming apparent to the people of the States is one of the significant developments of recent years.

The Governor. — In describing the State administration, it is natural to begin with the Governor, who is looked upon as the chief executive and the head of the State government. Each State has its Governor and except in one instance, Mississippi, he is everywhere elected by popular vote.[1] He is practically always a party man, nominated for his position at a party primary or convention, and elected as a partisan. Quite generally he is looked upon as the head of his party in the State, for the time being, though sometimes he is overshadowed in this respect by a United States Senator or by an unofficial party boss. The position he holds is so high, however, notwithstanding the limitations upon him, and the opportunity for aggressive leadership which he has is so great, that the Governor who is made of the right stuff, can, regardless of the party conditions which surrounded his election, make himself a conspicuous power in the affairs of the State, and not infrequently acquire national fame and influence. He is the natural State leader and the general public, completely reversing the popular attitude in the early years of the Republic, has come to look to him for guidance in State affairs in much the same way as it looks to the

[1] In Mississippi an unusual system of indirect election prevails for the selection of all State officers. Elections are held in the several counties and legislative districts of the State at which the voters express their preferences among the candidates for the various offices. The person receiving the highest number of votes cast in any county or district, for any office, "shall be holden to have received as many votes as such county or district is entitled to members in the house of representatives, which last named votes are hereby designated 'electoral votes.'" The candidate who receives a majority of all the electoral votes of the State, and also a majority of the popular vote, is declared elected. — Mississippi Constitution, Section 140.

President in national affairs. The office of Governor is undoubtedly growing in importance, and, taking the States as a whole, its occupants are measuring up to higher standards of independence and leadership. It is an office that is potentially great and that calls for men of statesmanlike qualities and abilities. As in the case of the presidency, its actual influence at any particular time depends largely upon the character and powers of the man who holds it.

The term of office for which the Governor is elected is fixed by the State constitution. As in the case of members of the State legislatures, no uniform rule is observed. In twenty-three States the term is two years, and in twenty-three, it is four years. One State, New Jersey, has a three-year term, and one, Massachusetts, elects its Governor annually. A tendency has been apparent, in recent years, to substitute the four-year for the two-year term. The opinion is growing that it is in the interest of popular government, as well as of more efficient administration, for the Governor to have at least four years of service, free from the excitements and distractions of a campaign for reëlection, and in a number of States agitation is under way looking to the adoption of the longer term. It requires time for a Governor to become proficient in his work and the two-year term is not long enough to enable him to do this and utilize this newly acquired proficiency to the best advantage. That the tendency is clearly in the direction of the longer term is indicated by the fact that two of the three States last admitted to the Union, Oklahoma and New Mexico, provided for the election of their Governors every four years.

The compensation of the Governors varies greatly. In some States the amount is definitely fixed in the constitution, and in others it is left to the discretion of the legislatures. The salaries range from $2500 to $12,000. Six States pay their governors $10,000 or more, and thirty-two pay $5000 or more. In two States the sum is $2500 and in four, $3000.

The qualifications of Governors are determined by the State constitutions. An age limit is everywhere prescribed, the usual requirement being that the Governor must be at least thirty years of age. He must be a citizen and have been a resident in the State for a prescribed number of years. It is quite the regular rule to forbid the Governor to hold any federal office during the time he is serving as Governor. In some States he is made ineligible to succeed himself, but in others no limitation is prescribed as to the number of terms he may serve. The two-term custom, however, is quite generally observed. In a few States it is prescribed that the Governor shall not be elected to the United States Senate during his term of office.

The Governor as an Executive. — The powers of the Governors of the several States are similar in character, though, as a matter of course, they differ more or less in detail. The Governor is generally charged by the State constitution with the exercise of the executive power of the State and is made responsible for the faithful enforcement of the laws. He thus becomes the State's " chief executive." It is to be noted, however, that this vesting of the executive power in the Governor does not give him a place in the State government like that which the President has in the Nation as a result of a similar grant in the national Constitution. The President is in fact the Nation's chief executive and is responsible for the national administration. The executive departments are under his direct supervision and control, and their heads are appointed by him and may be removed by him at will. But in none of the States is the Governor given such a position of dominance in the State administration. There are in each State executive officers, chosen by popular election, who are in charge of important departments of administration, and who are independent of the Governor. Their responsibility is to the electors just as is the Governor's. Consequently the declaration of a constitution that the " supreme executive power " of a State shall be vested in the Governor is not to be understood as conferring the authority to direct all of the State's administrative activities. As remarked previously, the State's administrative organization is decentralized, while that of the Nation is highly centralized. The Governor is thus only one of a number of executive officers in the State; and over his associates he has very little, if any, control. Certainly as long as these officers, to whom definite duties have been assigned by the constitution or by law, observe the requirements set for them, the Governor can have nothing to say concerning the manner in which they conduct their offices. However, if they should violate the laws or fail to enforce those for which they are responsible, it would be the duty of the Governor, under the constitutional requirement, to take whatever action is permitted him to see that the laws are enforced and that those guilty of their violation are punished. This means, usually, that he may start legal proceedings against the offending officer. In some instances the power to suspend an officer temporarily is conferred on the Governor, but this is by no means common. As a usual thing, he is dependent upon court processes. It is clear, therefore, that the Governor, as the " chief executive " of the State, holds a peculiar position and that his relation to the general State administration is very different from that of the President to the administration of national affairs.

In the enforcement of laws violated by private individuals, the Governor, when he takes the initiative, acts by ordering a prosecution in the courts by the law officers of the State. In cases of this kind resort is almost always had to court proceedings. It sometimes happens, however, when riots occur or extreme disorder prevails, that martial law is declared by the Governor, and the military forces of the State, the militia, are called out to enforce obedience. This drastic action is by no means a frequent occurrence, but occasionally it has been necessary. Usually, when it has been taken, the necessity for it has arisen in connection with the violence and disorders attendant upon bitter, long-continued controversies between striking laborers and their employers. If the disorder is so widespread and of such a character that the Governor feels that he is unable to cope with it, he may call upon the President for the assistance of federal troops. Of course the President is under no obligation to grant the request, if he thinks that the Governor has failed to use all the power at his command, and he will assent to it only when he is convinced that there is real need for federal interference. In this connection it is to be noted, as these statements imply, that the Governor is the head of the State militia except when it is in the service of the United States, when, of course, it becomes a part of the United States army and is under the command of the President.

Another significant power, possessed by the Governor, is that of granting pardons, reprieves, and commutations. This power is related to his executive functions, but is really quasi-judicial in character. The practices of the States in this, as in the exercise of so many other powers, are by no means uniform. In some States the Governor alone exercises the pardoning power, and in others he shares it with the legislature or with a board of pardons. In some instances a board of parole exists with power to parole prisoners and make recommendations to the Governor concerning applications for pardon. Sometimes the Governor is bound by such recommendations and sometimes he is not. The pardoning power may not be used in impeachment cases. The granting of pardons, reprieves, and commutations is a very important function of government and has been greatly abused in many of the commonwealths. It affects vitally the administration of the criminal laws, a work in which the American States are notably weak, and is central in the great problem of prison administration and reform which presses for solution in all of the States.

Appointment and Removal of Officers. — A part of the Governor's work as an executive officer is the making of appointments to office. With respect to this the practices of the States differ greatly. In some States the Governor's power of appointment is large because, either by constitutional provision or by requirement of law, he is charged with the appointment of many important officers. In other States this power is relatively small because the elective principle is applied to all or practically all important positions. The present tendency, as shown by the developments of recent years, is clearly in the direction of a larger use of the appointive principle and a reduction in the number of elective offices. If this movement achieves substantial results, the Governor's position will undoubtedly become one of far greater power, influence, and responsibility than it is now or ever has been. It is usually the practice, where the Governor is given authority to make appointments, to require their confirmation by the upper house of the legislature. In this the influence of the national practice is clearly discernible. As with the President, some of the Governor's appointing power comes from the constitution, and some from authorization by the legislature. In the latter case, the legislature is usually free to require confirmation or not, just as it pleases. In some States, indeed, the legislature itself is empowered to make important appointments. In a few, the State Treasurer, who is commonly looked upon as one of the most important State officers and one whom the electors should choose directly, is appointed by the legislature. The regular rule, however, is to give the appointing power to the Governor, in the case of heads of departments, members of State boards and commissions, and judges of the courts, if the appointive method is employed. The appointment of deputies and other subordinate officials in the departments is usually left to the department heads. To some extent, in some States, civil service laws are in force, which limit the appointing power of the Governor and other State officers. There is no uniformity in this regard, however, and, in general, the civil service requirements of the States are meager and not of a high order. In this field lies one of the great opportunities of the States for notable reform and progress.

Consideration of the appointing power suggests the power of removal. Here, again, the position of the Governor is very different from that of the President. In the case of the Governor, there seems to be no general or inherent power of removal, such as is recognized as belonging to the President. Whatever authority he has of this nature comes to him from specific authorization by the State constitution or by legislative enactments. As would naturally be expected, this authority varies greatly from State to State. Not only this, but a number of radically different methods of removal are employed by the States. Professor Beard calls attention to six of these, three or more of which will be found in almost any commonwealth, and remarks: "Not only do we discover a great variety of practices among the several commonwealths, but in each State we find different methods of removal applied to officers of equal rank as well as officers of different grades."[1]

The first of these methods, common to all of the States, is that of impeachment. As a rule, the procedure observed is about the same in the various States and is similar to that which is followed by the houses of Congress as prescribed by the federal Constitution. The indictment or impeachment charge is brought by the lower house of the legislature and the case is tried by the Senate. In some instances judges of the highest State court sit with the Senate. This is the case in New York,

[1] Beard, "American Government and Politics," New and Revised Edition, p. 508.

where all of the judges of the Court of Appeals participate in impeachment trials. One State, Nebraska, imposes the duty of hearing impeachment cases exclusively upon the judges of the Supreme Court, the impeachment being made by the two houses of the legislature in joint session. No uniform rule exists among the States as to what officers are subject to impeachment. In some, all civil officers may be impeached, while in others the impeachment process is limited in its application. The offenses which may cause impeachment are, with one exception, stated in the constitutions. South Carolina gives to the legislature full authority to determine the offenses which call for impeachment. Among the causes of impeachment, in addition to treason, bribery, crime, and misdemeanor, may be mentioned the following: "drunkenness, malfeasance, gross immorality, extortion, neglect of duty, incompetency, and misconduct."[1] Conviction on an impeachment charge usually involves removal from office and disqualification from holding any office of profit or trust in the State, but as under the national Constitution, it does not free the offending officer from arrest, conviction, and punishment under the criminal laws of the State.

The other methods of removal are by the legislature, by the Governor and the Senate acting together, by the Governor alone, by the courts, and by recall by the electors. These methods are not employed by all of the States, of course. Removal by the Governor and Senate is quite common. Removal by the Governor alone, however, is not a common practice, although in a number of States the Governor is given authority to remove officers whom he appoints. The popular recall is a new device, first applied to State officers in 1908 when it was made a part of the Oregon constitution. It involves the holding of an election, upon the petition of a designated percentage of the voters, to determine whether or not the officer under charge shall continue in office or be removed. A number of States in recent years have adopted the recall and given it state-wide application. In the cities governed by commissions it is quite generally provided for.

The Governor and Legislation. — The Governor, in addition to the executive and quasi-judicial functions which have been

[1] Beard, "American Government and Politics," New and Revised Edition, p. 509.

noted, has a vital relation to State legislation. In general, this relation is very similar to that which the President has to national legislation. While the principle of the separation of powers is fundamental in all of the State constitutions, the Governor is everywhere permitted to share in the legislative function. Some of his power, as with the President, is constitutional in its origin and character and some of it extra-constitutional. The Governor, like the President, is more than an executive officer under the constitution and the nominal head of the government of which he is a part; he is also the head of his party and, as such, has an important work to do in the formulation of State policies.

Following the practice in the Nation, the State constitutions give to the Governor the right to recommend to the legislature the enactment of laws and the adoption of policies which he deems wise. He does this through messages, either sent in written form to be read to the two houses by their own officers, or delivered in person by the Governor. At the beginning of each legislative session, he addresses the legislature in one or the other of these ways and calls attention to the new laws, or the modification of existing laws, which he thinks the legislature should take under consideration. During the session, also, special messages may be addressed to the legislature for the same purpose. It is understood, of course, that the legislature is not bound to act upon the Governor's recommendations. It is free to do as it pleases, just as Congress may do whatever it wants to with the suggestions of the President. But the Governor, like the President, may appeal directly to the people through speeches or printed articles in an attempt to arouse public sentiment in favor of the policies he stands for and thus bring public pressure to bear upon the legislature. Moreover, the Governor is given authority to call the legislature in extraordinary session, and if it fails to act as he desires at the regular session, he may thus force it to approve or reject the measures he has recommended to it. In attempting to influence the legislature, the Governor has the same weapons to employ that belong to the President in his dealing with Congress, though, of course, their effectiveness is less in the hands of the former than in the hands of the latter. Patronage sometimes plays its part; personal persuasion is often effective; the influence of party leaders and workers is sometimes brought to bear. But the great weapon of the Governor is the privilege he enjoys of appealing directly to the people, to whom he is alone responsible, and of explaining his position and soliciting their approval. Public opinion, when it is clear and unmistakable, is the great, irresistible force in politics.

In addition to his right to recommend laws, the Governor has the power to veto acts of the legislature which he disapproves. Only one State, North Carolina, withholds the veto from the Governor. The constitutional authorization of the veto is a part of the general provision requiring that all bills must be submitted to the Governor for his signature. The general practice is similar to that prescribed in the federal Constitution. The Governor is given a definite period in which to consider a measure submitted to him by the legislature, the time varying in the different States from three to ten days. If he signs it, the legislative process is completed, and the law goes into effect at the time prescribed by the constitution or by the law itself. If he wishes to veto the measure, he returns it to the branch of the legislature in which it originated, together with a statement of his objections. It is then the privilege of the legislature to pass the bill over the Governor's veto. The usual vote required for this is two thirds in each house, although three States provide a majority of three fifths, and a few require only a majority vote. In some of the States the Governor is permitted to veto single items of bills, a privilege which the President does not have. More than half of the States give this authority to the Governor in connection with appropriation bills. Ordinarily, as is the case with the President, the veto is an effective weapon in the hands of the Governor.

Mention has been made of the fact that an important part of the Governor's influence upon legislation does not rest upon formal constitutional provision, but is due to his position as a party leader. This is an aspect of the matter which should not be overlooked, but which cannot be given here a detailed discussion. The Governor's recommendations to the legislature carry weight by reason of his party leadership. For the same reason his veto is difficult to overcome, if the bill in question deals with matters that are the subjects of partisan controversy. In general, it may be said upon this point, that the Governor's party position in the State is relatively the same as the President's position in the Nation, although the actual influence of the Governor by no means measures up to that of the President. Each has power in his own field because of his relation to his party. What this power really amounts to depends, in the case of the Governor, as in the case of the President, upon himself, — upon his character, will, capacity for leadership, and conception of the functions of the office he holds. He can be a leader in legislation, or not, just as he chooses.

The Lieutenant Governor. — Closely related to the office of Governor, is that of Lieutenant Governor, although the latter is not an administrative office. The Lieutenant Governor, usually elected by popular vote, holds in the State relatively the same position as the Vice President in the Nation. By provision of the State constitution he succeeds the Governor in case of the latter's death or disability or removal from office by impeachment. As a usual thing, the Lieutenant Governor is the presiding officer in the State Senate and, under constitutional authority, casts the deciding ballot in case of a tie. As previously noted, the Lieutenant Governor is given power in some of the States to appoint the Senate committees. Where this is done he is an important factor in legislation, differing in this respect from the Vice President. A majority of the States have a Lieutenant Governor.

Independent Executive Officers. — Passing from a consideration of the State's "chief executive," the Governor, and his legal successor, it is necessary to give attention to other administrative officers. In all the States there are several executive officers who are independent of one another and, for the most part, of the Governor also. Each has his own work to do by authorization of the constitution or the statutes, and is responsible to the people of the States. These officers are heads of departments, and as a rule are chosen by popular vote for definite terms of office. Their terms usually coincide with that of the Governor. They are almost always chosen as party men and as a rule receive compensation as fixed by the legislature. At least five of these officers may be given special mention.

In all of the States there is a Treasurer who is charged with the safe-keeping of all moneys which come into the State treasury from taxes, fees, rentals, and other sources of income. He is placed under a heavy bond for the faithful discharge of his duties. Money may be paid out of the treasury only upon authorization by the legislature and upon proper warrants issued as provided by law.

All the States have an officer called Secretary of State who performs important ministerial duties. He is the custodian of the State archives and keeper of the State seal; publishes and distributes the laws enacted by the legislature; distributes public documents of all kinds; issues election notices and certificates of election; compiles and publishes election returns; usually serves as *ex officio* member of various State boards; makes annual reports of the work of his department; receives reports and fees from various officers, and performs many other miscellaneous duties imposed by law. Frequently he is required to issue certificates of incorporation to companies organizing under the laws of the State, collect the incorporation fees, receive the annual reports of corporations, and have general supervision over the enforcement of the corporation laws. Naturally the duties of the Secretary of State vary greatly, in detail, from State to State.

Another official found in all of the States is the Attorney-General, who is the chief law officer. In general, his duties are of two kinds. He prosecutes cases for the violation of State laws and defends the State in actions brought against it; and he acts as legal adviser to State officers and departments when they are in need of his services. Clearly the work of the Attorney-General is of high importance. Upon him in no small degree rests the responsibility for the faithful enforcement of the laws. His powers differ a good deal in the several States. In some he has close relation with the law enforcement officers of the local governments and may interfere on behalf of the State if they fail or are lax in the enforcement of State laws. It may be said that the function of the Attorney-General is coming to be looked upon by the people with increasing concern and general improvement in the work of his office may confidently be expected.

In most of the States there is an officer called Auditor or Comptroller, the former being the more common name. As the name suggests, it is the function of the Auditor to audit accounts against the State and draw warrants on the treasury for the payment of money authorized by law. It is only upon the proper warrant from the Auditor that the Treasurer may pay out money in his possession. The Auditor is an important factor in the management of the fiscal affairs of the State. In some States special duties are imposed upon him with respect to the supervision of insurance companies, banks and loan and trust companies. He is everywhere in close relation with county officials, and, like other State officers, is frequently *ex officio* a member of boards and commissions.

The fifth officer to be mentioned especially is the Superintendent of Public Instruction, in some States called the Commissioner of Education. This officer is found in most of the States. It is his duty to administer the laws of the State relating to education, as far as the general public school system is concerned, and promote the educational interests of the State. A phase of his work which is particularly vital is that in connection with the development and management of the rural schools, one of the big and fundamentally important problems in America. In many States, the Superintendent of Public Instruction is elected by popular vote, while in others he is appointed, usually by the Governor.

Besides the officers mentioned there are many other independent executives, with widely varying duties, to be found in the States. The work of the State governments has increased enormously with the growth of population and the rapid development of industry and commerce. It is to be borne in mind that America practically has ceased to be a country with a vast unclaimed public domain, with fertile agricultural lands to be had at very low prices, and has entered upon the industrial phase of her development. The result is a complexity in social, business, and political relationships which was entirely lacking not many years ago. This development is clearly reflected in the great increase in governmental functions both in States and Nation. Public offices have multiplied rapidly in recent years. The States have not developed along identical lines, and naturally there is great diversity as to the character and purposes of the offices which have been established. Furthermore, there has been comparatively little thought taken in any State to insure a systematic, harmonious administrative system.

"These new state offices have been created one after the other as new demands have been made upon the legislature; and as the federal policy of classifying and subdividing into departmental hierarchies has not been adopted by our commonwealths, the result has been the creation of a system which is the very apotheosis of chaos and irresponsibility."[1]

State Boards and Commissions. — One aspect of this development is deserving of particular emphasis, for it represents a noteworthy tendency in American politics and is the occasion of a good deal of uneasiness and criticism on the part of many persons who cling tenaciously to the traditional ways of administering public functions. This is the marked and rapid increase in the number of boards and commissions which have been charged with the management of important, difficult administrative problems. To these commissions have been given great executive powers. The number of members on the commissions varies a good deal; sometimes there are three, sometimes five, and frequently only a single commissioner is provided for. The questions placed under commission control cover a wide range. Among them may be mentioned the regulation of railways and other public utility companies, both State and local; tax administration; civil service; public health; highways; minimum wage laws; workingmen's compensation laws; agriculture; management of the State's charitable, penal, and reformatory institutions; control of the State institutions for higher learning; food and dairy laws. Some States have gone much farther in this direction, of course, than others, but in all the States the movement for " government by commission," as its critics have called it, has gained great headway. That this is having a marked influence upon the State governments cannot be questioned, but the ultimate effect must be left for time to reveal.

In explanation of the commission movement, three points may be suggested. First, legislating in minute detail upon complex social and industrial questions is a difficult thing, and State legislators, often unwilling to assume the full burden of legislation, take the easier course of creating a commission and authorizing it to work out a system of control. Though

[1] Beard, "American Government and Politics," New and Revised Edition, p. 501.

the work of the commission is really executive in nature, this is really delegating to the commission a task which, according to the traditional American practice, the legislature itself should perform. Second, it is often impossible for the legislature to provide in precise terms for all phases of the work which must be done. A commission is created, therefore, and given certain discretionary powers which will enable it to fit the general legislative requirements to the needs of the time. Third, there are unquestionably developing in America a demand for expert administration and a belief that many of the great problems of the day cannot be solved by the direct act of the legislature. It is held that the legislature adequately discharges its function when, in general terms, it expresses its will and sets up reasonable requirements, leaving to administrative officers the task of ascertaining in detail what the legislative will is. The practical application of this will is not legislative, but executive in character, and in the hands of trained officers assures effective execution of public policies. There is clearly a disposition on the part of many Americans to attempt to graft on the typical Anglo-Saxon practice of governing through detailed legislation some of the administrative features of governmental organization in the Roman Law countries where legislation is in general terms and executive authority is large. The administrative achievements of Germany, in particular, have had a very positive influence upon some of the American States. Wisconsin may be cited as an example. In that State, administration through commissions exercising large discretionary powers, has reached perhaps its highest development in America.

As stated, the commission idea has been subjected to a good deal of hostile criticism; but with the merit of this criticism the discussion here is not concerned. It is sufficient to call attention to the development that has occurred and to indicate its significance in relation to traditional American methods of administration. One fact, in addition to what has been said, however, should be noted; that the method of administrative control through commissions has become firmly established in national affairs. Its use is not confined to the States. As evidence of this, it is only necessary to mention the Interstate Commerce Commission, with its vast power over the management, service, and charges of railways, the Federal Trade

Commission, and the Civil Service Commission. In Nation, as well as in States, the idea of expert administration is gaining recognition.

Movements for Administrative Reorganization. — From the review of the executive organization in the States which has been given, it is plain that administrative functions are performed under conditions of chaos and irresponsibility which make real efficiency impossible. This fact has come to have general recognition. As a natural consequence, a strong demand has developed in a number of States for thoroughgoing administrative reorganization, in the interest of economy, efficiency, and genuine democracy. This has led to the consideration, both official and unofficial, of a number of proposed schemes of reform. Space is lacking for a detailed discussion of these. One feature, however, which is fundamental in all of them, is the centralization of executive power and the definite fixing of responsibility for its exercise. This involves, of course, systematic regrouping and coördination of executive departments and offices. The purpose, in general, is to substitute an executive organization similar to that of the national government, in which the President is directly, definitely responsible for the conduct of the administrative departments, for the loose, decentralized, irresponsible system which prevails in the States. Readjustment according to a uniform plan is hardly to be expected, but the tendency as revealed in the reorganization plans proposed is clearly toward some arrangement modeled upon the national executive. The belief is coming to be widely held that there should be a marked reduction in the number of elective State offices and a corresponding extension of the Governor's appointing power. Heretofore, diffusion of power has characterized the State governments, the opinion prevailing that only with a decentralized system, in which the offices were elective, could popular control be made effective. But this opinion is yielding and the people of the States are coming to see that a multiplicity of elective offices is not essential to democracy, and that a centralization of executive power is not opposed to the spirit of free government.

Special emphasis is to be placed upon this need for administrative reform. In all nations the great bulk of the work of government is administrative in character; yet in the United

States administration has been notably, and at times notoriously, weak. This is particularly true of the State and local governments; but the national government as well has, at times, been conspicuous for its administrative failures. These failures, in State and Nation, have been exceedingly costly, not only in a financial sense, but also from the standpoint of popular government. The people of America are becoming increasingly insistent that government in all of its aspects shall be thoroughly democratized, but as yet, generally speaking, they have failed to comprehend the supreme importance of administration and its vital relation to democracy. If democracy, if true free government, is to succeed, efficiency in all of the processes of government must be attained. In the United States public attention has usually been centered upon the legislative function, the determination of public policies, and comparatively little thought has been given to the administrative function, the machinery and methods by which the policies determined upon are actually carried into effect. Yet public policies, however wise in character, will prove disappointing, to say the least, if they are carelessly, inefficiently administered.

It is of fundamental importance that the people of the United States awaken to a realization of this fact, and set to work to develop an administrative system that will insure the effective execution of the public will. This must be done, indeed, if the government is to be genuinely popular and the experience of the United States in solving the problems of free government is to count for what it should in the promotion of world democracy.

In the case of the States, what the ultimate outcome will be of the movement for the reorganization of their governments cannot be foretold. It seems certain that important changes will be made. But, whatever plan may be adopted, it may be expected that there will be some centralization of executive power and a more rational coördination of administrative departments. Necessity compels readjustment of this character.

REFERENCES

BEARD. *American Government and Politics*, Edition 1914, Chap. XXIV.
BRYCE. *The American Commonwealth*, Edition 1910, Vol. I, Chaps. XLI, XLIII, XLIV, XLV.
DEALEY. *Growth of American State Constitutions*, Chaps. XIII, XXII.

FINLEY and SANDERSON. *The American Executive and Executive Methods*, Chaps. I to XIV inclusive.
GOODNOW. *The Principles of the Administrative Law of the United States*, pp. 94–109.
MCCARTHY. *The Wisconsin Idea.*
REINSCH. *Readings on American State Government*, Chaps. I, V.
YOUNG. *The New American Government and its Work*, Chaps. XVII to XXII, inclusive.

CHAPTER XXIX

The State Judiciary

The judicial power of the States, like the legislative and the executive, is an original or inherent power of government. It does not belong to the States by reason of any constitutional provision, and is not limited to specific questions or to controversies involving particular classes of persons. Because of this the State courts differ fundamentally from the federal courts with respect to jurisdiction. The latter exercise delegated authority; their powers are limited to certain kinds of cases enumerated in the federal Constitution. But the courts of the States are courts of general jurisdiction. They may hear any kind of case, except as limitations are imposed upon them by authority of the Constitution. Thus their field of action is very large. It is in connection with them that the citizen most frequently comes in contact with judicial processes, and through their decisions that his private rights and obligations most often receive judicial recognition and enforcement. This makes the State judiciary an institution which is of high concern to every person within the State's control.

It is to be borne in mind, in thinking of the work of the State courts, that the ordinary field of private law for the most part lies within the powers of the States. The rights of person, property rights, domestic relations, business relations of all kinds, the definition and punishment of crimes, are all within the State's control, and may be regulated as the State legislature sees fit, except as restrictions are imposed on the legislative authority by the State constitution. The volume of law which is administered by the State courts is naturally very large. This has increased enormously in recent years, under the pressure of a rapidly changing, developing social and industrial life. The larger the number and the greater the complexity of the laws, the greater is the work of the courts and the more vital is the judicial function in the promotion of the public welfare and the advancement of social progress. This is the case in all political societies, but especially so in America where the courts exercise the right to nullify legislative acts on constitutional grounds. Because of this power the courts have direct, positive influence upon public policies. Therefore the problem of court organization and methods and the attainment of judicial efficiency become matters of supreme consequence. If the States are to perform well the parts they must play in the evolution of the American democracy, the administration of justice by the courts must be well performed. For good or for ill, the American system gives to the judiciary a central place in the governmental organization. This is no less true of the States than of the Nation. It is therefore a necessity on the part of the States to develop a judicial establishment that will meet the peculiar needs of a politically virile, active, democratic people who, by the nature of the government which has been developed, are dependent upon the courts to a degree unknown in other countries. That the State judiciary, on the average, has satisfactorily met this requirement, few will assert. It is a fact not to be disputed by any one conversant with American politics that there is urgent need for radical changes in the organization and methods of the judiciary in most of the States. It may be said that this is one of the problems of fundamental importance now pressing for solution. Indeed, it may be doubted whether there is any other question before the people of America which is so supremely important as this. To its solution thoughtful, discerning minds are turning with increasing interest and growing appreciation of its elemental character.

The State Judicial Systems. — The judicial systems of the several States are difficult to describe in general terms because of the many variations in organization and powers, as well as in the nomenclature applied to the courts. With the courts, as with all their other institutions, the States have been free to do as they pleased, and although a certain degree of uniformity exists, the differences are so numerous and in some instances so striking that a large amount of detail is necessary for a comprehensive treatment. This, however, is impossible in this place and only certain general features of the State judiciary may be commented upon.

There are at least three parts to the judicial organization in all the States. These are the small local courts, with limited jurisdiction; the highest court of appeal, the head of the judicial system; and certain intermediate courts with general original jurisdiction and appellate powers over cases which are appealable from the local courts. The main outline of this system is always provided for in the State constitution.

In most of the States the highest court is called the Supreme Court, although in some instances other names are used such as Court of Appeals, and Court of Errors and Appeals. Its work is appellate and its decisions, of course, are binding upon the lower courts. For the most part it passes upon questions of law and not of fact. It is composed of a number of judges, say seven or nine, the number varying in different States. The size of the court, as also the question of compensation, is usually left to the discretion of the legislature. The State Supreme Court has in the State system relatively the same position as that held by the Supreme Court of the United States in the federal system. One of its important powers is to pass upon the constitutionality of State laws.

The court at the bottom of the State system is the Justice of the Peace court, which has jurisdiction over petty offenses and civil cases which involve only small sums. Its powers and procedure are fixed by statute. In some instances, in the larger cities there are two sets of these courts, one for hearing criminal cases and the other civil cases. These Justice courts are notably faulty and inefficient in their work. As a usual thing special knowledge of the law is not required of the justices in charge.

The intermediate courts vary a good deal in organization and powers. Two kinds of courts in this group are to be noted. One is the County Court which is to be found in many of the States. Its jurisdiction is limited, though much larger than that of the Justice courts. It may hear a good many civil cases involving fairly large sums, though the limit varies greatly in different States, and also has jurisdiction in most criminal cases which arise in the county. Ordinarily it passes upon appeals from the Justices of the Peace. In some of the States, furthermore, certain administrative duties are imposed on it by law. In two States, West Virginia and Missouri, the County

Court is really not a court at all, having only administrative functions to discharge. In a few States this court has probate jurisdiction and certain administrative functions, but no jurisdiction in civil and criminal cases.[1] These courts are sometimes known as District Courts or Courts of Common Pleas.

In a good many of the States there are courts above the County Courts, but inferior to the Supreme Court. These bear different names, such as District, Superior, or Circuit Courts. Their powers are larger than those of the County Courts, involving original jurisdiction in both civil and criminal cases. It is customary to allow these courts to pass final judgment in cases in which the sum involved is not in excess of a fixed amount, the latter varying from State to State. When appeals are permitted, they are taken to the Supreme Court.

In some States the distinct County Courts do not exist and the District or Circuit Court is the only one intermediate between the Supreme Court and the Justices of the Peace. A number of counties are grouped together to form the district or circuit. The judges, of whom there may be several, go from county to county within their district and hold court at stated times. Though the judges are from a district larger than a county, this court in effect is a real county court. The cases tried in any particular county, except when there has been a change of venue, are those which arise only in that county. The records of the cases are kept at the county seat. The clerks, sheriffs, and prosecuting officers are county officials. The jurors, both grand and petit, are residents of the county. Thus essentially the court is a county court, though bearing another name.

There are in some States, in addition to those of the regular hierarchy, a number of special courts whose duty it is to look after particular kinds of questions and cases. Such are the probate or surrogates'. courts for the settlement of estates; juvenile courts to pass upon the delinquencies of children; courts of claims; chancery or equity courts; and special municipal courts in the larger cities. Except as provided in the State constitution, the judicial organization is subject to change or extension at the discretion of the legislature. New courts are established when there is need.

[1] Fairlie, "Local Government in Counties, Towns, and Villages," p. 98.

Selection and Compensation of Judges. — In the selection of the judges various methods are employed in the different States. The most common is that of election by popular vote, usually for short terms of service. This applies to Supreme Court judges as well as to judges of the lower courts, although the members of the high court usually serve longer terms than do the lower judges. Where popular election has prevailed, it has been customary for the political parties to put up candidates for judicial positions just as for other public offices. Sentiment is tending away from partisan judicial elections, however, and in some States attempts have been made by law to insure non-partisan elections. Many serious objections are made to popular election of judges, particularly to partisan popular election, combined with short terms. Bryce's expression upon this is to the point, and represents the view of many Americans. "Popular elections throw the choice into the hands of political parties, that is to say, of knots of wirepullers inclined to use every office as a means of rewarding political services, and garrisoning with grateful partisans posts which may conceivably become of political importance. In some few States, judges have from time to time become accomplices in election frauds, tools in the hands of unscrupulous bosses. Injunctions granted by them were moves in the party game. Now, short terms, though they afford useful opportunities of getting rid of a man who has proved a failure, yet has done no act justifying an address for his removal, sap the conscience of the judge, for they oblige him to remember and keep on good terms with those who have made him what he is, and in whose hands his fortunes lie. They induce timidity, they discourage independence."[1]

Another method of selection is appointment by the legislature. This is used in four States, two in New England, — Vermont and Rhode Island, — and two in the South — Virginia and South Carolina. Election by the legislature does not meet with much approval; in fact, it is generally condemned. The legislatures are made up of party men and election by them is likely to be quite as partisan as popular election. The standard of political morality in the State legislatures is not always very high and the log-rolling methods so commonly employed are particularly objectionable in the appointment of judges.

[1] Bryce, "The American Commonwealth," New and Revised Edition, Vol. I, p. 512.

The third method of selecting judges is that of appointment by the Governor, subject to confirmation by the Governor's Council[1] or by one or both of the houses of the legislature. Seven States, including Massachusetts whose judiciary has always ranked high, employ this method. In two of these, Massachusetts and New Hampshire, the appointment is for life. This is true, also, of Rhode Island, in which the judges are appointed by the legislature. In all of the other States the election or appointment is for a definite term, the length of which varies from two years in Vermont to twenty-one years in Pennsylvania for members of the Supreme Court. A six-year term is provided in some States, and in others one of twelve years.

With regard to the manner of selecting judges and the length of their terms, it is difficult, indeed impossible, to forecast what the years will develop. Dissatisfaction with popular election is unmistakable and is undoubtedly growing; but this practice is deeply rooted, and a vast amount of prejudice exists against entrusting the appointment of judges to the Governor, even though his action must be approved by the legislature or by one of its houses. The power of the courts to nullify legislative acts is looked upon as a political power of the utmost importance, and the opinion prevails that the judges who exercise it should be directly responsible to the people. There is some indication, however, that sentiment is slowly developing in favor of the appointive plan, particularly in connection with the higher judgeships. The general success of the federal courts, whose judges are appointed under life tenure, has had its effect upon popular opinion. What is safe and satisfactory for the Nation should be equally so for the States. The right to elect the local judges is everywhere jealously guarded and there is little to suggest any marked departure from the method in use.

The compensation of judges is low, much lower than that given judges in England and other European countries. The highest salary paid to any of the State judges is $17,500, the compensation received by Supreme Court justices in certain districts in the State of New York. The chief justice of the New York Court of Appeals, the highest court in that State,

[1] The Governor's Council, common in the early life of the States, is retained by only three of the Commonwealths — Massachusetts, Maine, and North Carolina.

however, receives only $14,200 a year, and the associate judges $13,700. In Vermont members of the Supreme Court receive only $2500. This is the lowest salary paid in any State to judges of the highest court. Salaries of from $5000 to $6000 are found in many States and are about the average. Of course judges of the lower courts receive, as a rule, a proportionately lower compensation. The general effect of the low salaries is obvious. The strongest, most capable lawyers are not drawn to service on the bench. An attorney with an income from five to ten times as large as the salaries of the judges before whom he practices ordinarily is not inclined to seek judicial honors. Yet the courts should command the highest talent if their work is to be of a high order.

Jurisdiction of State Courts. — As observed in the opening paragraph of this chapter the State courts have a general jurisdiction; they are not confined by constitutional provision to a limited field of litigation. The significance of this is clear, but it becomes all the greater when it is recalled that the judgments of the State courts are final in all matters that lie within the control of the States. Their decisions are not subject to review by the federal courts, unless rights are claimed under federal law or the federal Constitution. In that case, of course, if the alleged rights are denied, the federal courts themselves must determine whether the question at issue comes within the authority of the States or that of the Nation. The Nation's supremacy in its own sphere must be maintained by its own agents, if its authority is challenged.

The bulk of the work falling upon the State courts arises out of litigation involving the State's own laws. In the application of these the court of last resort in the State gives the final, authoritative interpretation, if there is no conflict with federal authority. But the State courts are not confined to the application of State laws; frequently they are called upon to administer federal laws. The federal Constitution, statutes, and treaties are, by the terms of the Constitution itself, the supreme law of the land, and are as much binding upon the State courts as upon the federal judiciary. It is the duty of the State courts to apply these federal laws, therefore, if it is necessary to do so to settle cases before them. It is only in case the rights asserted under federal laws are denied that the national authority concerns itself in the matter. The Nation cannot permit its laws to be nullified by the States.

Under authority of an act of Congress a suit may be removed from a State court to a federal court if it is of such character that it might have been brought in the federal court in the first place. If the State court should refuse to grant the transfer when asked, and satisfactory showing is made, the federal court of proper jurisdiction may itself order the removal, if the application has been made according to the method prescribed by law. As stated in the discussion of the federal courts, their jurisdiction in the cases recognized by the Constitution as lying within their field is not exclusive unless Congress makes it so by law. That is, if Congress permits, the State courts may exercise a concurrent jurisdiction. This has been authorized in a good many instances, but, as observed, removal of such cases from the control of the State courts is provided for if this seems necessary to protect the federal authority. Discussion of the technical procedure by which this is done is aside from the present purpose; all that is necessary here is to make plain the possibility of removal.

Character of State Law. — As remarked above, the chief part of the State judiciary's work is administering the State's own laws. These are exceedingly numerous and give occasion for a huge volume of litigation. A word concerning their general character is desirable.

Two kinds or bodies of law prevail in the States. These are the Common Law and the statutory law. Statutes, of course, are now the chief source of law. The Common Law was transplanted to America from England by the early colonists and made the basis of American jurisprudence. Its influence upon American development, as upon that of England, has been profound. All of the States except one have the Common Law in force to a greater or less extent. Louisiana, the exception, has the Roman Law system, based on the Code Napoleon [1]; but even that State has, by statute, adopted the Common Law of crimes. In the Nation the Common Law does not prevail, the federal courts administering it, when occasion demands, only as a part of State law. The Common Law in America is not now identical with that of England, of course, because of the

[1] Below, Chap. XLIX.

adaptation which has been made by the rulings of the American courts to New World conditions. For the same reason the Common Law system of one State may vary materially from that of another. The fact is to be borne in mind that the courts of a State are independent in their judgments; they are not bound by the decisions of the courts in other States. They may be influenced by these decisions; they may, indeed, choose to follow them, but they are at liberty to apply the law in their own way. The result is that the principles of law accepted and enforced in one State may differ a good deal from those in another. Of course a decision of a State's high court is binding upon all of the lower courts.

Of statutory law, little need be said. Its volume is rapidly increasing in every State. Hundreds of statutes are likely to be added at each session of a State legislature. Many of these are sadly at fault both in content and form. The consequence is new causes of litigation and a steadily increasing burden upon the courts, — a burden which would be lightened to a considerable extent, if the statutes were properly drafted. The general effect is to make the courts objects of criticisms which really should be directed to the legislatures. It is a conspicuous fact, indeed, that the courts are frequently held blameworthy for setting aside legislative enactments and interpreting statutes contrary to the legislative intent, when the fault was with the legislatures themselves which should have seen that the laws were drafted so as to stand the severest judicial scrutiny.

It should be noted in this connection that a large proportion of the statutes enacted by the legislatures deal with governmental organization and functions, with administrative methods and problems, and therefore do not affect the general body of private law. This does not mean that private law is not subjected to legislative control and modification, for it is thus controlled in many important respects. It does mean, however, that to a large degree the development of private law is left to the courts. The tendency is clearly toward an invasion of the Common Law field by statutory regulations. As illustrating the activity of the legislatures in this respect, attention may be called to the statutory penal codes which have been substituted in many States for the Common Law of crimes, and to the enactment of laws regulating in detail both criminal and civil procedure. In some States, New York especially, codification of the Common Law upon particular subjects has been carried out and the Common Law provisions have been transformed into statutes. In a few States the attempt has been made to codify the entire civil law. This has not been particularly successful, however, and it may be doubted whether the States generally will go to this extreme. The belief is widespread that extended codification tends to make the law too inflexible.

In connection with the Common Law, it is important to note that the English system of Equity was also transported to America and was adopted by most of the States essentially as it was administered by the English courts. It will be recalled that Equity jurisdiction is conferred on the federal courts by the Constitution of the United States. Equity rules are still enforced in the States. In some there are distinct Equity courts, but in others, as is also true of the federal judiciary, the same courts administer both Law and Equity. In still other States the distinction between legal and equitable remedies has been abolished by statute. This does not mean, however, that the Equity principles are abolished; the change affects merely the remedies afforded by the Equity system, which, under the change, are applied according to the same procedure as those of the Common Law. It is a significant fact that in States where the Law and Equity systems are maintained distinct, whether administered by the same courts or not, there is apparently an increasing disposition to resort to the Equity jurisdiction, which is administered by the judges without the aid of juries, in preference to that of the Law. This is due to the imperfect working of the jury system. Attorneys, where the choice of remedies exists, frequently prefer Equity actions before judges to Law actions before juries. Moreover, litigants of their own choice frequently have the same preference. Though the jury system is a highly cherished institution, it is generally conceded that under the rules usually governing American courts its working is far from ideal.

A word may be added concerning the juries, which are important parts of the judicial machinery. Both the grand jury and petit or trial jury are generally used. The function of the former is the returning of indictments upon criminal charges.

In the federal courts, by constitutional provision, no person may be tried for a criminal offense except upon a grand jury indictment. In many of the States a similar provision is contained in the State constitution. In some States, however, a grand jury charge is not necessary; prosecution may be begun upon the filing of an information by the prosecuting officer. The trial jury is everywhere used, but the rules governing it vary from State to State. The usual thing is for the jury to pass only upon questions of fact, leaving to the judge the determination of the law. The size of the jury varies somewhat, even in the same State, depending upon the nature of the suit at trial. It is not possible to discuss here in detail the rules applying to juries or to enumerate the various criticisms made concerning their work. One point only will be mentioned, — the usual requirement of a unanimous verdict. This makes it possible for one juror to " hang the jury " and prevent a verdict. This is a common occurrence, in fact, and many mistrials have resulted from the obstinacy or corrupt action of a single juror. In some States the requirement of a unanimous verdict has been done away with.

Criticism of the State Judiciary. — Criticism of the courts is widely prevalent in America. There is, indeed, very great dissatisfaction with judicial administration. Justice has by no means always been done. Equality before the law oftentimes has been a fiction rather than a fact. The legal rights of the rich not infrequently are much more certain of protection than are the rights of the poor. Particularly has the administration of the criminal law been faulty. In every State glaring examples may be found of breakdowns in the administration of punitive justice. The conditions are far worse in some States than in others, as a matter of course, but, taking all the States together, criminal law administration is notably, inexcusably weak. A common opinion is expressed in the frequently quoted statement of President Taft: " No one can examine the statistics of crime in this country and consider the relatively small number of prosecutions which have been successful, without realizing that the administration of the criminal law is a disgrace to our civilization." [1] The reasons for this lamentable condition are numerous. As suggested above, the working of the jury

[1] Reinsch, " Readings on American State Government," p. 177.

system is in part responsible. The machinery of the courts is cumbersome and slow moving. Judges fail to retain proper control over the trial of cases or are prevented from doing so by rules of procedure imposed by the legislature. The right of appeal is carried to unreasonable lengths. Technicalities of procedure are often exalted in the estimation of judges to a place which is beyond all reason. In many instances guilty persons go free of punishment because of minor procedural errors which in no way affect the question of their guilt. The seeking of justice is made wearisome by needless delays and by unnecessary expense. Flagrant failures to carry out the constitutional provision, found in all of the States, which guarantees "speedy" trials to persons charged with crime, are notoriously common. In short, inefficiency characterizes to a high degree the criminal law administration in the American States. But this inefficiency is not confined, however, to the enforcement of criminal laws; it frequently characterizes civil procedure as well. It is not to be understood, of course, that the courts of all the States are equally open to the criticisms which have been suggested, and to others which might be added. But in every State the problem of judicial administration is of prime importance, and in every State modification of judicial procedure is urgent.

As would naturally be expected, the unsatisfactory conditions which have been mentioned have led to a demand in many States for radical reforms in connection with the judicial system. There is no unanimity, however, as to what should be done. It is urged by some that there should be a popular recall of judges. It is urged by others that there should be a thorough revision of the rules of procedure and that the judges should be given greater power in the conduct of cases. By still others it is argued that a complete reorganization of the judicial system is necessary. Important changes in the relations of the bar to the courts are suggested, as are, also, changes in the jury system. These and many other proposed reforms with respect to particular matters have been brought forward, but future developments must determine what fundamental changes shall be made. In some States substantial progress has been made in the simplification of court procedure and in expediting judicial business. The results of these attempts at reform have been wholesome and give promise that ultimately in all of the States the administration of justice will be upon a high plane of efficiency.

It needs no particular emphasis to make it clear that the whole problem of judicial administration is one of fundamental concern to the American people. The courts have a peculiar function to perform in the evolution of the American democracy. Their position is such in the constitutional system that upon them may depend political as well as legal developments of far-reaching influence.

REFERENCES

BALDWIN. *The American Judiciary.*
BEARD. *American Government and Politics,* Edition 1914, Chap. XXVI.
BRYCE. *The American Commonwealth,* Edition 1910, Vol. I, Chap. XLII.
REINSCH. *Readings on American State Government,* Chaps. III, IV.

PART II

ENGLAND, FRANCE, GERMANY, AND SWITZERLAND

ENGLAND

CHAPTER XXX

The Cabinet System

The Cabinet system involves a division of the executive into partisan and non-partisan elements. It places the non-partisan functions in the hands of a monarch or, as in the case of France, a president, while the partisan functions pass into the hands of the chief ministers of state. The body of chief ministers constitutes the Cabinet. They are usually members of the legislature and as party leaders, whether members of it or not, they control the legislature. Separately each member of the Cabinet, with an occasional exception, administers a department of the executive, but they are jointly responsible for the conduct of the government. At the head of the Cabinet is the Prime Minister who presides at its meetings and is its chief spokesman in the legislature and before the country. The system thus requires two official heads. The King or President is the nominal head, or ruler of the entire people, and his duties are non-partisan. The Prime Minister speaks with authority on all matters of disputed party politics.

"Parliamentary government" is a term often used as a synonym for Cabinet government. The system has arisen out of conflict between monarchs and representative assemblies. In an absolute monarchy the monarch rules through officers whom he appoints. Monarchy becomes limited, or constitutional, when a representative assembly is added, although the chief officers in the executive may still be subject to appointment and removal by the monarch. A constitutional monarchy becomes a Parliamentary or Cabinet government when the representatives of the people assume the power of dismissing the King's ministers. Political power then passes from the monarch to the legislature. There is a sense in which it may be said that the Cabinet controls the legislature, because it must command the continuous support of a majority of the legislature. The legislature also in a sense controls the Cabinet, because at any time the majority may be changed to a minority, thus forcing the Cabinet to resign. The term "Cabinet government" is suggestive of the control of the Cabinet over both administrative and legislative business. The term "Parliamentary government" emphasizes the authority of the legislature. Another synonym is equally significant. Cabinet government is denominated "Responsible government." The term calls attention to the united, concentrated responsibility for both executive and legislative business which rests upon the Cabinet. The Cabinet is directly responsible to the representatives of the people for its policies. This relation to the legislature is the essential feature of "Responsible government."

These few characteristic qualities are found in every form of Cabinet government. A brief comparison of the English and American systems will serve to bring out more clearly these distinguishing features. In the Cabinet system the legislature and the working executive are united. Those persons who are responsible for the administration of the laws are not merely, as usual, members of the legislature; for the time being they also control legislation. The members of the Cabinet hold office because they have the support of a majority in the legislature. When they cease to have this support they give place to ministers who do lead or control or, at least, have the support of the legislature. Bagehot calls the Cabinet a hyphen, or a buckle, by which the two departments of government are united.[1]

The American system involves a separation of the executive and the legislature. The two departments are assumed to be equal and coördinate, but the lawmakers are not responsible for administration. Executive officers are not members of the legislature. They recommend legislation and may appear before committees of the legislature in support of their measures; but they are not members of either house of the legislature, and it is a rare exception for an executive officer to be permitted to take part in legislative procedure. The theory of the Constitution requires complete separation of departments. Both the Chief Executive and the members of the legislature are chosen by the people and are equally, coördinately, and independently

[1] Bagehot, "The English Constitution," p. 82 (Edition of 1877).

responsible to the people for the performance of governmental functions looked upon as separate and distinct.

Personal *vs*. Corporate Responsibility. — Executive responsibility in the American system is personal. The President of the United States as Chief Executive is individually responsible for the entire field of federal executive business. The heads of the departments of administration are appointed by him, are removable at his will, and are held responsible to him. The chief advisers of the President are, as a body, called a Cabinet, but they are not a Cabinet in the English sense of the term. They advise the President on matters of general executive policy, but he may entirely disregard their advice. Each member of the President's Cabinet is responsible to his chief for the administration of a separate department as, for example, the war, navy, or post-office department; but there is no such thing as joint cabinet responsibility.

The English Cabinet is itself a sort of corporate personality. As a body it is held responsible both to the legislature and to the people. The Cabinet and not a chief person rules and governs. It is true that most members of the Cabinet are the heads of separate departments of the executive; but this fact is obscured by the emphasis given to the joint responsibility of the body as a whole, for both legislative and executive policies. The American executive is personal; not a body of men, but a *man* governs in the case of the general government, or a half dozen men independently elected, in the case of the state executives, but in either case the rule is personal and not corporate.

King or President in Cabinet Government. — The English Cabinet, however, does not include the whole of the executive. The system requires a person, King or President, who is nominal head of the state, and who is, in a sense, above both Cabinet and legislature. This chief person performs important functions in the making up of cabinets and the harmonizing of cabinet and legislature. He is usually described as irresponsible. He is not responsible to the legislature, because his duties in certain emergencies may require him to traverse the will of the legislature. He is not responsible to the Cabinet, for the same reason, and because, nominally, the cabinet members are his ministers and act in his name. In an important sense, however, the chief person is responsible to the people. It is his solemn duty to seek to give effect to the will and choice of the nation. In no case is he permitted to enforce his own will against the will of the nation. Fully developed Cabinet government is a democracy. In so far as the nominal head of the state exercises personal power against the will of the people, the government is not that of a cabinet, but that of a despot.

In England the nominal head of the executive attains and maintains his position by birth and education. In France the two houses of the legislature in joint session elect a President once in seven years, not to govern, but to harmonize the functions of those who do govern.

The Judiciary in the Two Systems. — The contrasts between Cabinet and Presidential systems of government are by no means exhausted in the relations of the executive to the legislature and the personnel of the two executives. The judiciary of the two systems presents differences equally notable. Cabinet government is an agency for expressing the will of a ruling voting constituency. The Cabinet represents and personates contentious politics. For the time, it is the agent of the dominant party as represented in the legislature. As the agent of the legislature the Cabinet acts without legal restrictions. In a Cabinet government there can be no legal restrictions. The legislature, including as it does the executive, represents supreme power, and the system does not admit of legal checks. Are the courts, then, at all times subject to the will of Parliament? Assuredly they are. To one trained under the English system it is unthinkable that a court should presume to set aside an Act of Parliament. Parliament ordains and establishes the courts and defines their functions. Judges are removable by act of the two houses. If the judges interpret a law in a manner not satisfactory to the government of the day, the law may be changed. The judiciary is non-political, or outside of contentious politics. Judges are trained to respect the will and intention of the lawmakers in their interpretation of statutes and to consider public opinion in their interpretation of Common Law. Hence the Judiciary is, in fact, largely independent of party politics.

The American system is strikingly different. In it the powers are divided and set one against the other, so that no officer or combination of officers is in a position to express without restraint the will of the state. The legislature acts subject to limited executive veto; and when a law has been approved, the judiciary may nullify the act, basing the decision on some clause or some principle embodied in the written Constitution. In theory the people may change the Constitution, but in the case of the federal Constitution the method is so complicated as to render a change extremely difficult. The result is that the judiciary is continuously brought into political partisan controversy.[1]

The Natural *vs*. the Artificial in Government. — Again, the two systems of government are contrasted in respect to origin and nature. One is derived from a process of evolution; the other is a product of logical analysis and artificial construction. Bagehot is surely correct in saying that a Cabinet government could never have been the result of deliberate plan and intention. It could have originated only through a long process of adjustment of forces to solve temporary difficulties. The system as known to-day is of recent origin.

The distinctive features of the presidential system are the result of conscious logical analysis. The system could never have come into existence except as the result of a deliberate plan. Each of the systems stands for certain well-known and enduring qualities found in all governments, the artificial and the natural. The English were continuously seeking to create specific agencies for the safe-guarding of liberty and the promotion of efficiency, but these, for the most part, failed.[2] The Cabinet developed unconsciously as a by-product of continuous striving for limitations on the Crown.

When experienced Europeans were transplanted to America, there ensued a great contribution to conscious, artificial state-building unhampered by custom or tradition. Where old names were used and old customs were apparently followed in the new environment, they became essentially new. Men knew when and how each governmental institution was created in the wilderness. Boundary lines were artificially drawn, crooked

[1] Above, pp. 277–280.
[2] Conspicuous examples of such efforts are the appointment of twenty-five barons for the enforcement of Magna Charta, the Provisions of Oxford, Temple's scheme for the organization of the executive.

lines became straight, townships, counties, and States became rectangular and were bounded by meridians and parallels. Everything was given an artificial cast. Statesmen of the American Revolution distrusted direct popular rule, so they ordained by a constitution which the people could not easily amend, that executive power should rest in the hands of a President indirectly chosen, and that abuse of power should be prevented by separating the legislature, executive, and judiciary, and making each a check upon the others. It was a device to give effect to a theory. Thus the two Governments of England and America show diversity in origin; in one the unconscious element is dominant, in the other the conscious, yet in practice this difference grows less distinct, each form of government tending to assume the qualities of the other; for government is by nature partly artificial and partly natural.

The Relation of the Cabinet to Party. — The English Cabinet is identified with a political party; it is itself the one organ for giving final expression to party opinion and party policy. By the very acts of assuming and exercising responsible government the Cabinet fulfills party pledges and formulates party platforms. Cabinet government of the English type is a real government. The Cabinet holds office because at a partisan election their party has obtained a majority in the House of Commons. The life of the Cabinet is dependent on the continued approval of a majority of the House. When a Cabinet fails to command a majority it ceases to govern, though it still maintains its integrity as a body of party leaders. The system assumes that there shall be two ruling parties which shall alternately assume control of the government. The defeated Cabinet still holds its position in Parliament as the leader of the party. It is variously described as the King's Opposition or the "Shadow Cabinet." The rival groups of leaders continually face each other in Parliament, the one in office and the other a candidate for office. The Opposition serves the country as expert critics of the Government. The policy of the Cabinet is continually modified by the criticism of leaders of the opposing party.

Only the English type of Cabinet government identifies government with a party. On the Continent of Europe cabinets are composed of combinations of leaders of various parties.

The cabinet is not itself the organ of a party; it usually represents a number of party groups. No single party commands a majority in the legislature. Temporary majorities are made by coalitions of parties. The Cabinets are, indeed, made up of party leaders, but leaders of different parties. The parties influence government, but they do not govern. No Shadow Cabinet confronts the government ready to take office as soon as the ruling Cabinet is defeated. After a cabinet crisis often a number of the same party leaders will reappear in the newly organized Cabinet.

The President and the Monarch. — The Presidential system of government was organized with the distinct intention of excluding monarchy. In this connection it is a matter of interest to note that in its practical working the American system has tended to give increased prominence to personal rule and personal leadership. This is true in respect to legislation, as well as in executive policy. So great have been the difficulties in attaining efficiency and responsibility in legislative bodies with restricted powers, that the people have been led to look for these qualities in the mayors of cities, the governors of states, and in the President of the United States. Some would say that the discarded monarchy is being restored by a process of evolution. On the other hand, in countries where the monarchy is retained, personal rule is being eliminated from government. The nominal chief magistrate personates power and symbolizes unity, while a corporate body of men actually exercise power. It can no longer be maintained that monarchy and democracy are exclusive terms.

It is now well understood that hereditary monarchy is not at all necessary to the maintenance of the Cabinet system. The experience of France proves that an elected President may readily take the place of the monarch in that system. The American government could be transformed into a cabinet government by fusing together the executive and the legislature, and still remain a republic. In that case the President would cease to be the responsible executive, but would remain the dignified and apparent head of the state, and would become the coördinator and adjuster of the governmental powers. In other words, the President would become practically a king in a democratic state, but if the American President should become a hereditary monarch, still retaining all his powers, the state would be essentially despotic. The Cabinet is the one clearly recognized agency for preserving democratic monarchy.

REFERENCES

BAGEHOT. *The English Constitution*, Edition Second, Chaps. I and II.
DICEY. *The Law of the Constitution*, Edition Eighth, Chap. I.
LOWELL. *The Government of England*, Edition 1908, Chaps. I and II.
OGG. *The Governments of Europe*, Edition 1914, Chaps. I to III.
WILSON. *The State*, Revised Edition, Chaps. X and XI.

CHAPTER XXXI

THE NATURE OF THE ENGLISH CONSTITUTION

THE state in England is personified in its King. In his name all the processes of government are carried on. By his Ministers the laws are executed; as his agents the two houses of Parliament make and amend laws and vote supplies; in his name the courts of the realm dispense justice. Every official act is nominally that of the sovereign. Nevertheless "the King reigns but does not govern." He may influence administrative and legislative policies, but the real power rests with a representative assembly under the guidance of groups of party leaders whose leadership is entirely unknown to the law. The government is of two parts, the one formal and legal, the other not recognized by law but active and efficient.

All this is as different as possible from the form of government in the United States. For the most part, the formal Constitution of the United States and the actual working constitution are identical; at least they are not directly contradictory. A fundamental law coming from the people as the source of power created the office of President and in part defined its powers. This law also called into existence and empowered the two houses of the legislature. It laid upon Congress the duty of organizing a judiciary whose powers it in part defined. The work was done consciously with the purpose of creating "a republican government."

The Kingship and the House of Lords. — In the English Constitution, no conscious effort toward democracy is evident. The present form of government is a growth, not a creation. The origins and early character of the Kingship, the central fact of the legal Constitution, is shrouded in the mysteries of the past. It is known that in the fifth century conquering chiefs from the Continent displaced Roman authority in the British Isles. Numerous petty kingdoms arose, and in the course of time became united under the West Saxon rulers. The conquests of Danes and Normans in the eleventh century brought modifications in the kingship. Thus, by a series of accidents and favorable conditions, the Crown came into existence. At no time was the office definitely established. By habit, by custom, by legal fiction, the monarch came to be accepted as the source of all law, all authority, and these legal fictions remain in the processes of government to-day.

The House of Lords is equally venerable and uncertain in origin. Freeman, the historian, considers the Upper House of Parliament at least as old as the monarchy itself. Before there were hereditary monarchs, tribal or national assemblies existed whose members chose leaders of the host in time of war, and who were active in changing the temporary leader into a permanent ruler. The early kings were elective. The Council selected a member of the ruling family. As the kingship grew in importance the Council remained as the chief agency through which the king maintained working relations with his people. Its early Saxon name was Witan or Witenagamote. After the Norman Conquest it was known under various names as *Curia*, *Commune Concillium*, Council, or Assembly of Notables. Later, after elected members had been added and these had separated to form a House of Commons, the old assembly continued under the designation of House of Lords.

The House of Commons and the Judiciary. — The House of Commons is not so old as the institution now called the House of Lords, but its origin is scarcely less mysterious and uncertain. A definite date, 1295, can be assigned, however, as an important period in the history of the Lower House of Parliament. In that year Edward I called to the meeting of his Great Council representatives from counties, boroughs, and cities. To this assembly the name " Model Parliament " has been given. Earl Simon had called a similar assembly as early as 1265 and on many occasions counties and boroughs had been invited to send representatives to confer with the King in Council. The House of Commons did not originate in the Model Parliament of Edward I. It came into existence, no one knows how, during the long reign of Edward III (1327–1377), when the members chosen from counties and boroughs became separated from the Council and formed a distinct House.

The word Parliament came into use with the Normans from France. It was early applied to meetings of the King in Council when engaged in judicial business. Later the term was used to designate the ordinary meetings of the Council. When representatives were added, and two houses were formed, Parliament remained the convenient designation of the body composed of the King and the two Houses.

In the early days the King in Council exercised all the high powers of government, legislative, executive, and judicial. The Council with the King was then the highest court of the realm. As early as the reign of Henry I (1100–1138), members of the King's Council visited the counties and administered justice in the King's name. During the reign of Henry II (1154–1189), a body of men under the name of *Curia Regis*, became differentiated from the Council, as a Judicial Committee administering justice in the counties. A hundred years later committees of the *Curia Regis* took the form of permanent courts of law separated from the Council. The King, however, still retained supreme judicial power. The Council was still the highest court of appeal. As a heritage from these, its early powers, the House of Lords to-day is the highest court of appeal for nearly all cases in the United Kingdom, and a committee of the Privy Council is the highest court of appeal for India and the Colonies. Thus the courts of England, like the two Houses of Parliament and the Crown, have been gradually evolved out of the habits, customs, and incidents of English history. The English form of government has come into existence through a long process of adaptation and adjustment.

Written *vs.* Unwritten Constitutions. — In outward form resemblances exist between the English and American governments. The President and his Cabinet suggest the King and his Ministers; the upper and lower houses of Congress, the two houses of Parliament. In both countries a distinct and separate judiciary exists. These are the most striking likenesses. All the American organs of government have been created by the enactment of a written Constitution which is their warrant for existence, and their relations are in a measure defined by this document. The courts recognize it as supreme law. Any law enacted by the President and Congress must be in harmony with the Constitution or the judges will refuse it judicial sanction if its validity is questioned. The position of the Judiciary in England is radically different. Anything which the King in Parliament does or enacts is legal. All power rests with the King in Parliament or the King in Council. Parliament itself determines the rules that shall govern the conduct of Crown, Commons, and House of Lords in their relations to one another. For the most part these rules are mere understandings that have grown up in the past. Disagreements arising among the three constituent parts of Parliament must be settled by argument, compromise, or force. There is no superior law or constitution to compel harmony. Parliament cannot do an unlawful thing because it is supreme in all matters of law.

The English Judiciary, then, is distinctly subordinate to Parliament. It is not, as is the judiciary in the United States, an equal and coördinate branch of the government. Nearly all the courts were created by act of Parliament or by act of the King in Council, and their continued existence is dependent upon Parliament. No court in England could rule that any act of Parliament is illegal. There are a few acts of Parliament providing for the establishment of the high courts and the regulation of their procedure, and a few acts limiting the power of the Crown. These may be called a part of the Constitution, but most of the rules that regulate the high powers of government in their relations to one another have been made by custom without any formal enactment. The Constitution is largely unwritten.

Common Law as an Analogy. — How such an unwritten Constitution could be evolved and used may be made more comprehensible by reference to a similar development in English law. The Common Law which prevails in England and America to-day has grown out of the rulings of the courts. The judges have given legal force to the common sense of justice among the people. Rules of conduct that were approved by the courts and enforced in the King's name became law.

As society was ever changing and new rights arose, the law was adapted to meet the new conditions, or [1] the king was called upon to render justice despite the rules of common law, or Parliament was called upon to enact new laws in amendment to or

[1] Discussion of the courts of equity is omitted from this brief description, introduced here merely for analogy.

modification of or repeal of the common law. Thus two sorts of laws grew up in England, viz., those that originated in the rulings of the courts and the statute laws. These two kinds of law are alike in that their authority comes ultimately from the same source, the King in Parliament. In formulating Common Law the judges have acted under the authority of the sovereign. The Constitution is analogous to Common Law in that it has grown out of mere habit and custom and has undergone constant change to meet new conditions.

There is, however, a striking contrast between the common law and the rules of conduct regulating the relations one to another of the high offices of state. Common Law is law because its rules are enforced by the courts. The fact of enforcement makes it law. The customary rules observed by the monarch in his relation to the two houses of Parliament and the rules observed by them in their relations to each other and to the Crown cannot be enforced by the Judiciary; the Judiciary is itself subject to the sovereign will of Parliament. Any line of action agreed upon by the three branches of Parliament is legal, not because it can be enforced by the courts, but because it proceeds from and is an expression of the will of the sovereign.

The Rise of Democracy. — The relations of the three branches of Parliament to one another have been subject to constant change and readjustment. The Crown has at times dominated the two Houses. At one time they, acting without the monarch, declared the throne vacant and proceeded to fill it by electing an alien prince. The House of Lords has clearly overshadowed the House of Commons during certain periods of English history. The general tendency, however, has been to transfer power from the Crown to the two Houses, from the Upper House to the Lower House of Parliament, and, finally, from the Lower House to a newly created voting constituency. This revolution has been produced by a gradual process; by calling into existence agencies of government which the laws of England do not recognize and by transferring to these new agencies the high powers of government. Consequently it has been possible to retain the old institutions, the ancient legal forms and phrases in all lines of governmental procedure, the legal forms which apparently center all power in the Crown, and at the same time to maintain an actual government which centers supreme power in a voting constituency. The real Constitution which is now in force in England is not only not written; it is not legally recognized as existing. Nowhere do the laws or legal forms recognize political parties, yet England is governed by two competing party organizations appealing for support to the voting constituency. The laws do not recognize the Cabinet, yet in each of the two ruling parties there is a group of twenty or more statesmen ready to take office and govern the British Empire whenever the voting constituencies give them the majority in the House of Commons. One of the groups is always in office and is known as the Cabinet, or the King's Government; the chief leaders of the other group face the Government in the House of Commons and are known as the leaders of the Opposition or the "Shadow Cabinet." These party leaders with the support of the House of Commons exercise nearly all the high powers of state formerly exercised by the King in Council or by the King in Parliament. But the Cabinet, while ruling in the name of the king, tends actually to express the authority of the enfranchised Democracy.

Meanings of the Term "Constitution."—The term "English Constitution" has been used with a variety of meanings. It denotes, for instance, the actual government of a king and a representative assembly which has endured for more than a thousand years. England stands as the most conspicuous example of a constitutional monarchy. It has always been constitutional; no king has ruled without a council which conditioned his action. It is natural, therefore, that the Constitution should become an object of veneration and worship, a sentimental bond of union for the English citizenship, a word to conjure with in political controversy. Burke calls upon his fellow-citizens to understand the Constitution according to their measure; and to venerate when they are not able to comprehend.[1] As thus used the term appeals to the sentiment of patriotism; it summarizes all that has made England great. To analyze and define such a Constitution would destroy its usefulness. As Bagehot said of a similar attitude toward royalty, "If you begin to poke about it you cannot reverence it."[2] Not until the creation of other national constitutions which

[1] Burke, "Works," III, p. 114. Quoted by Dicey, "The Law of the Constitution," p. 1.
[2] Bagehot, "The English Constitution," p. 127.

forced comparison did the term denote in England anything more definite than that form of government which has given to England a favored position in European history.

The comparison of the Constitution of England with that of the United States has led to a real analysis and a more definite understanding of the former. Following the American analogy, we may say that a part of the Constitution is written. Magna Charta, the Petition of Right, the Habeas Corpus Act, and the Bill of Rights are laws to guard the liberties of the citizens, such as appear in the fundamental laws of American States and also in the federal Constitution. In England these Acts have not usually been considered a part of the Constitution. They stand simply as landmarks in the long series of conflicts between kings and the people's representatives. The Constitution as generally understood cannot be reduced to writing and enacted as positive law. Its great merit consists in the fact that it is not rigid; that it is not definite and explicit; that it admits of an infinite variety of delicate adaptations to changing conditions. Analysis also reveals the fact that the English Constitution is constantly the subject of controversy. The Crown and each of the two Houses are wont to appeal to ancient and time-honored custom as warrant for their authority. There has always been controversy as to the limits of their powers. Each of the parties to the dispute has been wont to assume that there is an ancient and unchanging Constitution which is essential to the well-being of the state, and that the line of action insisted upon by their opponents is a violation of that authority. As soon, however, as a particular controversy is settled by a new law or an agreed line of conduct it ceases to be of any constitutional interest. In the terms of contentious politics in England, the two ruling parties have for centuries been engaged in nothing else than violating and destroying the Constitution. Yet all parties agree that during all this time the Constitution has been enriched and amplified and better adapted to meet the needs of the people.

In a more restricted and specialized sense the English Constitution is the guaranty for that part of the governmental system that exists to-day in apparent contradiction to the legally recognized government. The Cabinet and the political parties are constitutional agents of government, but they are not legal agents. Every official act of the King, of Parliament, of the House of Lords, the House of Commons, or the Privy Council, is legal. These authorities are all legally recognized, and what they do has the force of law. No act of the Cabinet or of the party organizations is legal. When the Cabinet wishes to give legal effect to a policy it must do it through the Privy Council, through the administrative departments, or through the Crown and the two Houses of Parliament. The Cabinet looks to the Constitution of England as the warrant for its authority. In this new sense of the term, the Constitution becomes a sort of higher law since it requires the setting aside of some of the rules of the earlier Constitution. As long as the King in Parliament was recognized as exercising sovereign power there could be no contradiction between the Constitution and legal form. The contradiction has arisen from recognizing the Democracy as the political sovereign while permitting ancient forms and institutions to remain.

Yet the new democratic Constitution is firmly anchored to the past. Its supporters are not a whit behind others in laying claim to all that is useful for them in past history. The representative feature was always present in the English government. Many believe that the popular element was much more efficient in the earlier day than in the middle period under alien kings. It was always in order for King and Council to hearken to the appeals, the petitions, and the complaints of their subjects. It involves no real break in the continuity of the monarchy to increase its deference to the manifest wishes of its subjects, to consent that government be influenced by the advice of those in close touch with the people. The present advisers of the King, that is, the Cabinet, are chosen in a sense by the people and act with their authority. Since whatever the king, with the Lords and the Commons, does is legal, they may legally consent to be governed by the voting constituency. No break with the past has come from making the House of Commons the dominant factor in the English government. That house has become the leader when the King and the Lords have yielded their power to it. For this there is legal sanction. King, Lords, and Commons may also, without a break with the past, recognize that the voting constituency possesses political sovereignty and may execute their sovereign will. But this involves a transfer of sovereign power. It is a revolution. It sets up a new political sovereignty while permitting a legal sovereignty to remain in other hands. Under the new Constitution the King, Lords, and Commons, although remaining nominally supreme in government, become actually subject to a new authority. So long as this condition remains the new Constitution must be accounted as extra-legal or super-legal, a higher law supplanting a portion of the formal law.

REFERENCES

(See References to Chap. XXX.)

ANSON. *Law and Custom of the Constitution*, Vol. I, Chaps. I to III.
BRYCE. *The American Commonwealth*, Fifth Edition, Chaps. III, IV, and XXXIII.
COURTNEY. *The Working of the Constitution of the United Kingdom*, 1901, Chap. I.
HEARN. *The Government of England*, 1886, Chap. I.
MACY. *The English Constitution*, 1897, Chaps. I to III.
MEDLEY. *English Constitutional History*, Second Edition, Introduction and Chap. VI.

CHAPTER XXXII

Sources of the English Constitution found in Local Government

Counties, townships, hundreds, parishes, towns, and cities, transplanted from Europe to North America in the seventeenth century, became the foundation for a great federated republic. The same institutions are giving to England a unified democracy. The constitutions of the two countries have a common origin in the devotion of the people to their local liberties. In the United States devotion to local freedom resulted in federation; while in England through the party system power became centralized in the Cabinet and the House of Commons. Yet in England as in America the Constitution is accounted for by tracing the relation of the high offices of state to counties, parishes, boroughs, and cities. These are older than the kingship, older than Parliament and the high courts. The original English county, or shire, is a survival of a petty kingdom, and the United Kingdom was in the beginning an enlarged county.[1] The county is the one institution which goes farthest in explaining the relation of King, Parliament, and courts of law to the people. To account for the formal legal Constitution which makes the King in Parliament sovereign, the Crown would be given the central place in history; but to account for the democratic Constitution requires attention to the development of the counties and their local subdivisions.

History. — The history of local government may, for our present purpose, be considered in five periods. *First*, the Formative Period extending from the Saxon Conquest in the fifth century to the Norman Conquest in 1066. In these centuries county and hundreds courts became popular representative assemblies. *Second*, the Period of Royal Control over local government, extending to the Model Parliament of 1295.

[1] Stubbs, "The Constitutional History of England," Vol. I, pp. 109-118.

Norman and Plantagenet Kings sent their representatives to county courts and only gradually substituted for this system the calling of county, borough, and city representatives to attend Parliament. *Third*, the Period of Factional Wars extending to the establishment of the Tudor Monarchy in 1485. While the nobles and the kings fought for control of the central government, order was maintained in the country by the squirarchy of the counties and the merchants of the towns; local institutions survived under royal neglect. The *Fourth* Period, from 1485 to 1832, covers the centuries during which Parliament became more and more the recognized bulwark of the people and local organs of government were left unchanged. *Fifth*, from 1832, with the repeatedly enlarged franchise, attention has again been drawn to local institutions, and new local areas have been created by the central government to meet new needs.[1]

Formative Period. — The Saxon invaders of Britain brought with them some sort of tribal organization under chieftains and wise men. Out of their little known primary institutions they gradually evolved numerous petty kingdoms which, during the eighth and ninth centuries, became absorbed by that of the West Saxons. But the smaller kingdoms instead of being destroyed were preserved as convenient local units. The smallest survived as shires, and he who had been king became Ealderman or earl, the presiding officer in the shire-council or county court. These counties, therefore, are simply survivals of kingdoms in which the King in Council has become the earl. Larger kingdoms were subdivided into two or more counties, but the existing model of organization was naturally followed. The whole kingdom was thus divided into shires, or counties, each of which had its county court. The shire was subdivided into hundreds, boroughs, or cities. The hundreds were again divided into townships, or parishes. Boroughs and cities existed as specialized local governments for dense populations. The hundreds court received suitors and representatives from townships and parishes within its area. The county court was a popular assembly attended by large numbers of suitors and representatives from hundreds, boroughs, and cities.[2] In the

---

[1] Lowell, "The Government of England," Chap. XXXVIII; Ogg, "The Governments of Europe," p. 176 *et seq.*

[2] Green, "History of the English People," Vol. I, p. 353.

beginning, also, the King in Council represented what was actually an overgrown and amplified shire court for the entire country. The county, or shire, both in its origin and throughout most of its history, has been the chief coördinating agency between the local and the central government.

The foundations for democratic government had been laid before the Normans came to England. An orderly system of local government had been evolved. The people had become thoroughly grounded in the belief that the chief duty of the King and his advisers was the protection of the people in the enjoyment of their local liberties. The government was their friend. Law and liberty had become identified. King Alfred and other Saxon rulers personated liberty in their efforts to defend the people against alien conquerors. They did not succeed in shutting out the conquerors, but, far better than that, they did succeed in forming a system of government strong enough to withstand foreign encroachment and ultimately to compel all rulers to obey English law.[1]

Royal Control. — William the Conqueror introduced many important changes into the organization of the county court, but he found in the institution itself an effective means of control over the people. The king's sheriff as his special representative became the presiding officer in the county court and linked the shire more closely to the throne. The introduction of feudalism tended to restrict ancient English liberty and produced changes in the townships and hundreds. Many freemen in the townships became slaves or serfs. The area itself often became a manor, and the manorial courts of the feudal lords absorbed a considerable part of the business formerly transacted in the hundred court.[2] But the Norman and Plantagenet kings maintained control over the county courts, and through them protected the English from encroachments on the part of the Norman barons. To this end they transferred much of the business which had been transacted in the popular hundred court to the county court. Thus they exalted the shire as the one reliable means of limiting the power of the feudal chiefs. The result was that, in the course of centuries, all the functions of the hundred court disappeared.[3]

[1] Green, "History of the English People," Vol. I, p. 94.
[2] Stubbs, "The Constitutional History of England," Vol. I, p. 273.
[3] Lowell, "The Government of England," Vol. II, p. 130.

Norman and Plantagenet kings were probably not greatly interested in the preservation of the ancient liberties of the English people, yet they saw in the people's devotion to their time-honored customs a means of upholding royal power against the attacks of their armed feudal chiefs. The growth of feudal power was arrested by the king's sheriffs and the king's justices in county courts. Cases under dispute were decided in favor of the English and the decrees of the monarch were enforced with a high hand.

On the death of William I (1087) the people supported the younger son, William, against Duke Robert of Normandy, who relied upon the barons. And again, when William II died, the English, for the better protection of their local liberties, rallied to the third son, who became Henry I (1100–1135). Henry I strove in many ways to keep the support of the English people. His general charter of liberties was made the basis, a hundred years later, of Magna Charta. Boroughs and cities had been strongholds of opposition to the new Norman nobility. Henry increased their independence by giving numerous charters that insured the perpetuation of English liberties. He also punished many Norman nobles and with their confiscated lands created a new English nobility. Through a small council composed of the new English nobles, the King maintained very close relations with the county courts. He sent members of this council to visit each county and there to administer justice in the King's name.[1]

Henry II (1154–1189), the first of the Plantagenets, continued and developed the policy of Henry I. Through the members of his council, through sheriffs, through police and military officers, whom he appointed, he kept in touch with his supporters in the counties. The county court, in the meantime, had lost much of its earlier popular character, but Henry, through the organization of the Jury system, maintained a part of its representative connection with the hundreds and boroughs. Effective control over the judiciary, over the police and the militia, and over a wider range of financial resources, was giving to the crown the means for completely destroying the independent power of the nobility. Under conditions then existing, kings would have tended to become absolute and

[1] Stubbs, "The Constitutional History of England," Vol. I, p. 527.

tyrannical and themselves the destroyers instead of the preservers of ancient freedom had they not been prevented by their powerful nobles.

Origin of the Charter. — The feudal lords were themselves learning important lessons from the policy of the king. It was possible for them also to curry favor with the people by assisting them to preserve their local privileges against royal encroachment. The outrageous tyranny of King John (1199–1216) gave to the barons their great opportunity. It should be remembered that at the accession of King John there had been a full hundred years since Henry I created a distinctly English nobility and drilled them to habits of government according to ancient English custom. Many barons of Norman families also had become English in knowledge and sympathy. When, therefore, John through evil practices had turned all classes of his subjects against him, the barons were prepared to take an active part in the formulation of Magna Charta and in compelling John to sign it.

The Great Charter of Liberties was several years in preparation. The bishops and the barons were in possession of Henry's charter of 1100. This charter was issued at a time when men still lived who were personally acquainted with the government under the last Saxon monarch. Magna Charta is a sort of written constitution for the restoration of former rights and liberties and for the removal of all present grievances. Many conferences were held for its preparation. Representatives from counties, cities, and boroughs consulted with the nobility and clergy. Thus in the process of its construction it was prophetic of the future method of regaining liberty, while in its contents it was a faithful catalogue of existing ideals of free government.

John had no intention of submitting, but he died before his plans for resistance were completed. Henry III (1216–1272) promised to observe the charter, but he fell under the influence of the foreign party and drifted into a war with the supporters of the charter. During this conflict both parties attempted to strengthen their influence with the people by calling representatives from counties and boroughs to take council with them. In 1265, when the King was a prisoner, Earl Simon, the leader of the barons, called a representative assembly similar in character to the later Model Parliament of Edward I in 1295. In this way a new method of approach is established between the king's government and the people and a new chapter is opened in the history of local government.

Factional Wars. — Before counties and boroughs were represented in the central government, the King, through his sheriffs and through members of his council, visited the counties and administered justice and secured in county court a vote of supplies. A close and intimate relation was thus maintained between the central and the local governments. But, when the movement is reversed and boroughs and counties go to the King, that intimate relation is at an end. No longer is the stress of conflict for the control of counties and cities, but rather for the control of Parliament. Local government is neglected.

County courts themselves were in process of reorganization. The king's justices, who formerly presided over the county court,[1] had become in a sense separated from the older institution. They held courts of their own and the counties became simply geographical areas defining their jurisdictions. The older court, which in the earlier time was composed of numerous representatives from hundreds, cities, and boroughs, gradually fell into the hands of local magistrates, justices of the peace, appointed by the central government. These, with the grand and petit jurors, were in time united into a Court of Quarter Sessions. As thus constituted the court lost its popular character. The magistrates were appointed for life and the eldest son usually succeeded the father. It was a government by a local aristocracy. The Court of Quarter Sessions attended to a wide range of business, judicial, legislative, and administrative. It was in fact a comprehensive local government for all purposes. In boroughs and cities also, government, for the most part, drifted into the hands of a few of the wealthier class. In both borough and county the franchise was much restricted; yet the wealthy middle-class folk, with little help from king or parliament, for centuries maintained an orderly local government. Those who had the franchise made their peace with the people, preserving order, administering justice, and fulfilling local needs.

[1] After Henry II (1154–1189) members of the King's court displaced the sheriffs as presiding officers in the county courts.

Anarchy and confusion ruled in the central government. Much of the time there was a disputed succession to the throne and actual or threatened civil war. Yet the squirarchy in the counties maintained the ancient traditions of law and order for the masses of the people. In speaking of the Wars of the Roses at the close of this period, J. R. Green says: " The ruin and the bloodshed were limited in fact to the great lords and their feudal retainers. Once or twice, as at Townton, the towns threw themselves into the struggle on the Yorkist side, but for the most part the trading and the industrial classes stood wholly apart from and unaffected by it. Commerce went on unchecked. The general tranquillity of the country at large, while feudalism was dashing itself to pieces in battle after battle, was shown by the remarkable fact that justice remained wholly undisturbed. The law courts sat quietly at Westminster; the judges rode as of old in circuit." [1]

Political Interest Shifts from Local to Central Government. — No important changes are made in the forms of government in county and city during the fourth period under discussion, 1485 to 1832; but there are significant changes in the relation of the local organizations to the central government. Hitherto the great service of county and city had been to preserve order while feudal chiefs were at war. When Tudor monarchs completely subdued the unruly classes, this function was at an end. The Tudors were careful not to offend greatly the orderly classes in town and county though they maintained a high degree of royal power. The Stuarts who succeeded them did offend the people represented in the House of Commons, and after a century of conflict they were driven from the throne. This is not the place to describe the conflict between the Stuart rulers and the House of Commons, but rather to note some of its effects upon the local organization of the people.

Origin of Parties. — Religion was an important factor in the conflict. First the English people were divided into Catholics and Protestants and later into Dissenters, or Nonconformists, and supporters of the Established Church. These differences in belief had the effect of greatly extending the scope of local religious organization. Dissenters maintained separate religious

[1] Green, "Short History of the English People," p. 301. Cf. "History of the English People," Vol. II, p. 18.

bodies, and Church people gave added attention to their local parish organizations. Few people, as noted above, had any direct share in county and town government. Many participated in church organization and practically all were intensely interested.

Moreover, the religious groups coincided in large measure with the ancient divisions in the membership of the House of Commons. The House was composed of representatives of boroughs and cities and representatives from counties; that is, of burghers and country gentlemen. Dissenting bodies were mainly formed in towns and cities, while the Church was largely identified with the Squirarchy in the counties. Religious controversy thus gave added emphasis to this ancient division.

The same cleavage among the people is seen in the organization of political parties, which appear at the end of the Stuart century. The Tory party has always found its chief support in the rural classes and the clergy, while the opposing party has won the adherence of Nonconformists and industrial classes in towns. It is true that throughout this period there were few voters and local party organization was very meager. Yet, whenever there was a contested election, agents for the rival candidates appeared and lined up the supporters of their parties. As will appear in a later chapter, the mob as well as the legal voters took an active part in contested elections. The masses sympathized with and gave moral support to one or the other of the rival parties.

All of these disturbing contests; the prolonged conflict with Stuart monarchs, the division of the people into rival church organizations, the advent of political parties with their appeal for local favor, tended to concentrate attention on the House of Commons as the one authoritative representative institution. The English people apparently lost all sense of their dependence for their liberties upon their ancient local institutions. When the time came for extending the franchise, the primary aim was not the recovery of local freedom but a more complete popular control of the central government.

In striking contrast with the loss by the English people of a sense of dependence on local institutions is the experience of the colonists in North America. At the beginning of the conflict with the Stuart monarchy, English counties, towns, and parishes were organized in the New World. So great has been the attachment of the people to these institutions and so profound has been the sense of dependence upon them for the maintenance of liberty that it has been difficult to secure an efficient central government. Americans escaped the centralizing tendencies which in their ancestral home finally localized power in the hands of a party Cabinet and a House of Commons.

Democratic Municipalities. — The period since the enfranchisement of 1832 will be more adequately treated in future chapters on local government and on local party organization. By the acts of 1834 and 1835, provision is made for reorganizing city governments with the use of an enlarged voting constituency and also for relieving the parishes and the Court of Quarter Sessions from the care of the poor and committing that business to a popularly elected board. With this modification the county government remained without further change until the Act of 1888, creating popularly elected county councils. For more than five hundred years local magistrates holding office by life-tenure had governed the counties. They governed by appointment, yet with acquiescence and common consent. At no time was there a sustained general demand for a surrender of their power. The change came by a voluntary yielding of power to the new democracy. The agricultural laborers had just been enfranchised and the Tory party, the party of the squirarchy, handed over to them the privilege of electing their local rulers.

REFERENCES

FREEMAN. *History of the Norman Conquest*, Vol. 2, Chap. III.
GREEN. *History of the English People*, Vol. I, Book II, Chap. III.
KEMBLE. *Saxons in England*, Vol. II, Chaps. I to VI.
LOWELL. *The Government of England*, 1908, Vol. II, Chap. XXXVIII.
OGG. *The Governments of Europe*, 1914, Chap. VIII.
STUBBS. *Constitutional History of England*, Vol. I, Chaps. III–VI, XII.

CHAPTER XXXIII

THE RISE OF THE CABINET

IN describing the growth of the kingship in a former chapter, little notice was taken of the immediate advisers of the monarch. The Cabinet was mentioned as nominally fulfilling the advisory function to-day, while actually performing a service in apparent contradiction to its nominal position. Like every vital part of the English Constitution, the Cabinet did not originate at any one time or place; it simply grew out of English history. The Crown always commanded the services of a body of advisers and councilors. The Witenagamote, or great council, met at intervals and was together for a brief period. The smaller council was always with the monarch giving advice and administering the laws. There was always a tendency for the smaller body to acquire distinct institutional recognition. The *curia regis*[1] of Henry II for a time filled the place of the smaller council. When the members of the *curia regis* became occupied in the holding of the Common Law courts, other officers took their place in the King's Continual Council. As a board of regents, the smaller council actually governed England for a dozen years during the minority of Henry III (1216-1272). These were the men who had formulated Magna Charta and they ruled in harmony with its provisions. When Henry assumed control, he discarded the former councilors and selected as advisers men of the foreign party who were opposed to the provisions of the charter.

There was never any clear line of demarkation between the powers, functions, and duties of the two councils. The King in Council exercised all powers, legislative, executive, and judicial,

[1] *Curia regis* was a name given to a body of high officers of state associated with the King in the administration of the laws. For its relation to the Exchequer, or financial administration, and to the larger common Council see Stubbs, "The Constitutional History of England," Vol. I, pp. 376, 387-390; also Anson, "The Law and Custom of the Constitution," Vol. II, pp. 10-13, 87.

whether the council was large or small. Magna Charta specified very explicitly that certain taxes should be levied in full council. There was always a tradition that acts of the full council, or Parliament, carried with them greater authority than the acts of the minor council; yet in practice this rule of action has never been applied in such a way as to deprive the minor council of a large measure of power independent of, and coördinate with, the acts of Parliament. An order in council to-day carries with it equal authority with acts of Parliament. Orders in council led the United States to declare war on England in 1812. This is in apparent contradiction to the modern theory of the complete sovereignty of Parliament. Yet, as lawyers say, whatever Parliament permits, it sanctions.

Since the days of Magna Charta there have existed the two rival methods of giving expression to the sovereign will. The full council, or Parliament, has always enjoyed the greater weight and authority, while the smaller council has had the advantage of being in actual possession of the powers of government.

The Relation of the Crown to its Ministers. — Before giving further details in the conflicts between these rival institutions which have resulted in the modern Cabinet, it is well to define the English Crown and the meaning of the phrase, "the King can do no wrong." As noted above, the English monarchy has always been a constitutional state. No English king could ever dream of saying, "I am the state." The kingship always included, as a part of itself, a body of Ministers who were themselves members of the national representative assembly. The smaller council was always included in the full council. The sovereignty was thus directly or indirectly linked to the national assembly and the Crown is a composite of two elements, the person and his ministers, or advisers. The person of the monarch is sacred. He is held inviolate. He is the mystical fountain of justice, the source of law. "The King can do no wrong." If the King's government goes wrong, the blame rests with the King's ministers. It early became an established principle of the Constitution that the Crown acts only upon advice of ministers and that for its acts the ministers are responsible. The King cannot be punished; ministers may be punished.

Another phrase much in use in later political controversy throws light upon the earlier conflicts. "The prerogatives of the Crown " denotes all the powers which may be exercised by the King in Council without consulting the Houses of Parliament. The prerogatives of the Crown became pretty clearly defined and understood during and after the revolutions of the seventeenth century. But before that time the monarch had two distinct agencies, Parliament and the Privy Council, through which he could exercise his powers of government, and there was no agreement as to their respective limitations.[1]

King John was forced to appoint twenty-five barons whose duty it was to compel the King to observe the charter.[2] This is a striking exemplification of the difficulty of harmonizing government by a representative assembly with government by a King in Council. The barons forced upon Henry III, 1258, the adoption of a new mode of government, the Provisions of Oxford, whereby administration should be placed in a committee of their own number. This is another futile attempt to harmonize the King in Parliament with the King in Council. Again, twelve "Ordainers" were forced upon Edward II to act as his council of state. The king, through the agency of Parliament, displaced the ordainers; but a little later the opposing party deposed the monarch. There was continuous effort on the part of those opposed to the policy of the government to exert a controlling influence over the Ministers. The process of impeachment was instituted during the closing years of the reign of Edward III (1327–1377). Richard II (1377–1399) was induced for a few years to accept a council from his Parliament. When he reverted to a policy of personal rule he was deposed and the Duke of Lancaster (Henry IV, 1399–1413) ruled by parliamentary title. During the Wars of the Roses, which resulted in the exclusion of the Lancastrians from the throne, the two Houses of Parliament were used as a weapon of warfare. Alternate factions assembled parliaments to complete the destruction of their enemies by bills of attainder. Many noble families were thus wiped out of existence and their estates confiscated.

Rule by Privy Council. — Early in the Lancastrian period (1399–1461), the name " Privy Council " came into general

---

[1] Dicey, "The Law of the Constitution," pp. 392–395; Anson, "The Law and Custom of the Constitution," Vol. II, p. 2, *seq.*
[2] Section 61, Magna Charta.

use in place of the older term, "Continual Council."[1] From the accession of Henry VII (1485) to the meeting of the Long Parliament (1640) the prerogatives of the Crown were, except for brief periods, clearly in the ascendant over the two Houses of Parliament. England was governed by the King in Council. The Privy Council resembled in many respects the modern Cabinet. The number of members was usually about the same, eighteen or twenty. Privy Councilors filled the high offices of state.[2] They were members of one or the other of the two Houses. Through his Council the monarch was kept in close touch with parliament. The King in Council could create peers *ad libitum* and could thus control the House of Lords. He could create and destroy city and borough corporations and thus maintain voting constituencies loyal to the Crown. Through the power of patronage and other forms of bribery, the Crown controlled votes both in the constituencies and in the two Houses of Parliament. Through these and other agencies Henry VIII (1509–1547) made himself complete master of Parliament.

This, however, is but the indirect and weaker side of royal prerogative. The King in Council could exercise practically all the powers claimed by the two Houses. There was, indeed, a traditional restraint in the matter of direct taxation, but the prerogatives of the Crown furnished various means of supplying the royal treasury. For eleven years preceding the Long Parliament, Charles I (1625–1649) ruled without Parliament. Under the name of "Ship Money" he levied and collected a general tax and for this policy secured the approval of a majority in his high court.

The Judiciary and Royal Prerogative. — It was, however, through the control of the judiciary that royal prerogative reached its highest development. The King in Council has been from the beginning the court of last appeal. From this fact we have the explanation of the coexistence of two supreme courts to-day. One is the King in the House of Lords, the original Council, the other is the King in the Privy Council. The other high courts are the creation of the King in Council. With a few exceptions the courts have been loyal and sub-

---

[1] Stubbs, "The Constitutional History of England," Vol. II, p. 260; Vol. III, p. 245.   [2] There were occasional exceptions to this rule.

THE RISE OF THE CABINET

servient to their creator. Edward I brought his obstreperous bishops to submission by simply giving notice that he would withhold the protection of his courts.[1] Sir Edward Coke, the Chief Justice of England, pronounced some of the acts of James I illegal, and for this temerity was deposed and imprisoned. Not only did the Crown maintain control over the ordinary courts through the power of appointment and removal, but, until the act of the Long Parliament denying the right, the monarch had a clear field for bringing into existence new and arbitrary courts with practically unlimited powers. Henry VII, by means of his Star Chamber, made the higher nobility subservient to his will. By fines and confiscations and arbitrary exactions he left a full treasury to his successor. Henry VIII failed to obtain a suitable decision from existing courts in a matter of divorce and he forthwith created a special court to legalize his predetermined exchange of wives. By arbitrary courts created out of hand by the Crown, royal power was made complete over Ireland and over large sections of England. Even after the acts of Parliament abolishing the Star Chamber and other arbitrary courts and denying to the Crown the power to set up such courts; after the execution of Charles I and after the restoration of the monarchy with new promises and guaranties for respecting the rights of Parliament, the judiciary still remained an effective tool of injustice and royal tyranny. James II (1685–1688) experienced little difficulty in securing juries and judges in the ordinary courts to execute his brutal and despotic orders. The Act of Settlement (1700) by depriving the Crown of the right to remove judges from office finally laid the foundation for a judiciary free from royal dictation.

Thus it appears that from the beginning until the Revolution of 1688, the King with the smaller council of his advisers was more than a match for the full Council, or Parliament. Only in revolutionary times could Parliament force its will upon the Crown. It was Parliament's fatal weakness that the monarch was conceded the chief place in the administration of law. Until the conflict with the Stuarts in the seventeenth century, the monarch was also accounted the source of law. Even when the two Houses had established their position as the final authority in lawmaking, they could not govern England. Cromwell kept

[1] Green, "Short History of the English People," p. 224.

order for eleven years, but he did it as an "uncrowned king." He could not live with a parliament. Much less could he submit his policy to the dictation of a parliament. To avert anarchy or irresponsible despotism, Charles II (1660-1685) was called to the throne. It was, however, still possible for the monarch to thwart the will of Parliament, to suspend by royal decree the operation of its acts, to pack a House of Commons with royal supporters by creating new voting constituencies in the boroughs. The two Houses could assert a theory, but they could not govern. Even after they had gone to the limit of declaring the throne vacant, filling it by an imported ruler from Holland and enacting a Bill of Rights which specifies a full list of royal abuses and declares them all illegal, the problem of government was still unsolved. The Crown was still left in full possession of many high prerogatives and the formal Constitution was not essentially changed. Kings had never been accustomed to pay much attention to legal requirements forced upon them in times of revolution. Despite the Bill of Rights and the circumstances of its enactment, government might have continued along the old lines. But there were accompanying changes in the unwritten Constitution which mark the beginning of a real revolution. Important among these changes was one mentioned in a previous paragraph, by which the Crown lost its control over the judiciary. James II was the last king to make a tyrannical use of courts and juries. By common consent this ancient abuse was done away.

King Dependent on Parliament. — Deprived of the aid of the courts, the Crown became dependent on Parliament for necessary funds. James and Charles secured money from Louis XIV of France, but no succeeding monarch had other than parliamentary sources of supply. The Crown was thus continuously tied to the two Houses. Annual parliaments became a necessity.[1] These two changes made it impossible for monarchs to continue to govern by the use of a council acting independently of and in competition with the two houses of Parliament.

[1] Since the Revolution of 1688 the policy of voting supplies for the year has been maintained, thus creating parliamentary control over taxation. Parliament established continuous authority over the army by means of the Mutiny Act which authorizes the pay of officers and the disciplinary powers of the army for only a single year. Each of these policies necessitates annual Parliaments. See Green, "History of the English People," Vol. IV, pp. 44, 45.

THE RISE OF THE CABINET

The king and his council thus became firmly anchored to the legislature. By various acts of royal prerogative they might influence or control the action of the houses, but they could not ignore them or override them in the old way.

Before the Revolution of 1688 the monarch and his ministers were usually one in sentiment and purpose, since the king chose ministers to execute his own policies. The Council, apart from the monarch, had no policy, no will of its own. The modern Cabinets, according to legal forms and fictions, are still identified with the Crown, though they act upon their own sense of responsibility to the public. It is a violation of the Constitution for the monarch to intervene to thwart their will. The Cabinet has gained the initiative and has become an active part of the Crown. The sovereign yields to the advice of the Ministers. It was a long time after the exclusion of the Stuarts before this principle was fully recognized.

In its origin the modern Cabinet carried with it no suggestion of a radical change in the exercise of the powers of the Crown. It was always true that the monarch had a small number of advisers upon whom he relied for special guidance. The name "cabinet" as applied to such a group appears as early as the time of Charles I. Charles II had a few ministers who became conspicuous as his chief ministers. The "Cabal," as these men were called, is especially noteworthy as a group of five ministers who for a time held high office and filled the place of king's council. There were at the time fifty or sixty men who held the rank of Privy Councilor, too numerous a body for use as confidential advisers. So long as kings could rule through a council independently of Parliament they might use a body of considerable size and thus add weight to their government. But such a body is impractical when the chief business in hand is the securing of Parliamentary support. The Privy Council which had been the chief governing body for more than two hundred years was falling into disuse. There was an effort to revitalize the Council by forming out of it a committee of thirty, half of whom should be members of Parliament; the other half an executive council outside of Parliament. Charles gave his assent to the law and then continued to govern by secret advisers, giving no heed to the statute.[1]

[1] Green, "History of the English People," Vol. III, p. 426.

In the same way and for similar reasons, William III (1699–1702) ruled with the use of a small council or cabinet. At first he selected members from the three parties, Tories, Trimmers, and Whigs; but finding that the Whigs were in the majority in the House of Commons, he chose Whig ministers. His object was to control Parliament with the least expenditure of money or official influence. Later, when the Tories had secured a majority in the Commons, the King chose Tory ministers. During the reign of Queen Anne (1702–1714) the ministerial and party movements were similar. A Tory ministry was followed by a Whig ministry and that again by a Tory ministry, all with reference to securing the continuous support of Parliament. The House of Lords at one time failed to support the Tory ministry and the Queen secured a majority by creating twelve new peerages.[1]

The Beginning of Conflict between Law and Constitution. — In all this there is little indication of a radical change in the principles of government. The monarch was apparently still in control of the powers of the Crown. The Ministers were the servants of the Crown. They met in the royal presence and rendered their humble advice. At the death of Queen Anne nothing had occurred to raise any question of conflict between the Constitution and the forms of law. It is true that many acts of Parliament were being overlooked or disregarded; but it had always been so. Not yet was there any understanding or rule of the Constitution which would make a legal act unconstitutional. A provision in the Act of Settlement of 1700 marks the beginning of a distinct separation of law and constitution. The statute was contingent upon the advent of another foreign ruler from the Continent upon the death of Queen Anne. In that case it was ordained that all matters "properly cognizable in the Privy Council by the laws and customs of this realm, shall be transacted there, and all resolutions taken thereupon shall be signed by such of the Privy Council as shall advise and consent to the same."[2] Another clause forbade office-holders and pensioners of the crown from holding seats in the House of Commons. The object of these provisions was to put an end to the new custom of substituting

[1] Anson, "The Law and Customs of the Constitution," Vol. I, pp. 192 and 331.
[2] Adams and Stephens, "Select Documents," p. 478.

a small secret cabinet in place of the Privy Council and also to the method of controlling the votes in the Commons by means of offices and pensions. But the new custom survived despite the law.

The Prime Minister. — This, however, of itself does not make a discrepancy between constitution and law. So long as the monarch is the recognized head of the Cabinet or smaller council, the procedure is both legal and constitutional even though in direct conflict with a statute. The discrepancy arose later when a Prime Minister displaced the monarch as the head of the Cabinet, when the Prime Minister and his associates held meetings apart from the King, when the policies to be followed were agreed upon in secret Cabinet meeting and the Prime Minister afterwards secured the approval and coöperation of the monarch. All this took place under the leadership of Robert Walpole during the reign of George I (1714–1728) and the first part of the rule of George II (1728–1760). Walpole created the office of Prime Minister, and by means of that office he for twenty-one years maintained harmonious relations between the Crown and Parliament. The Prime Minister and his associates held continuous control over the House of Commons, using for this purpose persuasion, the bribery of office, money, and influence or bribery among the voting constituencies. There was a loyal and subservient House of Lords. At no time did Walpole permit his party or faction to be defeated in the House of Commons. Bills which he found it convenient to support in the House of Commons in order to gain favor with the voters, though he was unwilling to enact them into law, he would arrange to have defeated in the upper House. The head of the Cabinet had succeeded in gathering into his own hands the effective powers of the Crown and by means of these controlled the two Houses.

During the twenty-one years of the continuous rule of the first Prime Minister there is no evidence that the monarchs were conscious of being deprived of any of their royal prerogatives. George I lived and died under the impression, some would say under the delusion, that he was himself exercising royal power.

Circumstances and conditions favored this marked change as to the exercise of kingly authority. The first George was a foreigner who did not understand the English language and for this reason absented himself from Cabinet meetings. Both George I and George II were dull and easily imposed upon. The security of their crown was dependent upon the support of the Whig party. During the whole of the Walpole régime there was a possibility, and some of the time a probability, of a restoration of the Stuarts. The situation gave opportunity for the rise of the new order of government. But opposition to Walpole finally became serious. Pitt and Chesterfield led an opposing faction of Whigs in the House of Commons, and at last, in 1742, the majority for the Ministry was reduced to one vote and Walpole resigned.

There was at the time no Cabinet, in the modern sense of the term, with its joint corporate responsibility. Much less was there a Shadow Cabinet ready to take office. The Prime Minister had lost his majority and he alone ceased to be a minister of the Crown. Pitt and Chesterfield had gained a controlling position in the Commons by criticizing the Government. The King naturally accepted their criticism as personal and refused to accept the obnoxious statesmen as his Ministers. At the same time the House of Commons refused to support a Ministry unless Pitt and Chesterfield were given office. Finally the entire body of the chief ministers refused to remain in office unless Pitt and Chesterfield were added to their number. There was at the time a formidable rebellion which threatened to restore the Stuarts to power. The monarch was thus forced to accept as members of the Cabinet his personal and political enemies. After this event there was no doubt of the fact that a new institution had come into existence which, without changing the legal, formal relations of King and Council, does in reality under given conditions reverse those relations. The new custom, which later becomes recognized as constitutional, requires that the monarch shall yield to those who in legal form are his servants.

Tory Reaction. — When George III (1760–1820) came to the throne, the government had been almost continuously in the hands of Whigs since the revolution of 1688. The Cabinet, which had taken the place of the Privy Council and had gathered to itself a large share of royal power, was viewed as a Whig institution. George III had had a Tory training. He accounted it his high mission to regain the lost power of the Crown. There was no longer any thought of a Stuart restoration,[1] and the king had a free hand to institute new policies. During the first decade there were frequent ministerial changes and the King was all the while seeking to break up the cabinet system and to rule through ministers under his personal direction. Finally, in 1770, he found in Lord North a man after his own heart and with Lord North as chief adviser he ruled for eleven years. There was no Cabinet or Council, only ministers separately directed and controlled by the king. The American colonies were driven into rebellion, and England was involved in war with a large part of continental Europe. The personal rule of the monarch came to an end with the loss of the American colonies and the threatened ruin of the country through disastrous foreign war. George was forced to appoint a Whig ministry and a little later he was compelled to accept a detested coalition ministry. Finally the younger Pitt was induced to form a ministry with the distinct understanding that the Cabinet system of government should again be restored.

Pitt had been a Whig, but through a division and realignment of parties he became known as a Tory leader. Under his leadership the Tory party became thoroughly identified with the Cabinet system. The theory of the government was now clearly defined. The Cabinet was recognized as including the king's responsible advisers, from whom alone was he to seek advice. He was at no time to seek to thwart the policies agreed upon with the Cabinet, but to give effect to all such measures.

Neither George III nor George IV (1820-1830) ever really observed the constitutional requirements of the Cabinet system. They were continuously exerting an influence at variance with some part of the Cabinet program. In some cases the king refused to carry out a policy previously agreed upon. It became increasingly evident to leading statesmen of both parties that with an Upper House subject to the direct control of the Crown and a Lower House subject to indirect influence and control from the same source, continuous Cabinet government would be impossible. Either the Cabinet or the monarch would control

[1] May, "Constitutional History of England," Vol. I, pp. 35 ff.

Parliament by royal prerogative. In the one case the government would become an oligarchy, in the other it would be an irresponsible monarchy. As between the two forms, personal rule would prevail. A method of escape from irresponsible personal rule was found in the reform act of 1832. By this act a large voting constituency was created which was subject to the control of neither oligarchy nor king. Through a House of Commons, elected by these voters, royal prerogative, however exercised, became subject to the will of the nation.[1]

The Cabinet and the House of Commons. — Enfranchisement carried with it as a natural consequence the subordination of both the Crown and the House of Lords to the national will as expressed in the House of Commons. Only in the Lower House could the people make known their will. The leaders of the Upper House perceived this result and resisted with desperation the act of enfranchisement. Their submission was secured by a threat emanating from the King to create enough new peers to pass the bill. Thus, among the three parts of the ancient government of the King in Parliament the House of Commons is advanced to the place of final authority. In the meantime, out of the ancient body of the king's ministers, there has been developed a separate and distinct institution which is above the House of Lords and, in a sense, is above the House of Commons, since that House has no way of doing anything except as it yields itself to the guidance of the Cabinet. It is true the House may drive the Cabinet out of office by refusing to support its policy. It is likewise true that the Cabinet may dissolve the House and appeal to the voters to elect a new one. The electors mediate between the Commons and the Cabinet. Members are nominated and elected with a distinct understanding that they will support the leader of one of the great parties in the formation of a Cabinet, in the administration of the laws, and in the making of new laws. The Cabinet thus becomes the direct voice and expression of the democracy and the members of Parliament are chosen to give effect to the promises of party leaders.

The Shadow Cabinet. — The final stage in the development of the system is reached in the appearance of the institution known as the King's Opposition or the "Shadow Cabinet."

[1] Walpole, "History of England," 6 Vols., Vol. III, pp. 206-244.

As noted above, the Whigs ruled almost continuously from 1688 to 1760. From 1760 to 1830 the Tories were in office nearly all the time. Since 1832 party leaders have changed places in Parliament, on an average, every six years. There are thus two definite bodies of trained statesmen actively engaged in determining the policy of the government. One of these groups holds the chief offices of the executive and is responsible both for lawmaking and law administration. The other group is in Parliament, its members acting as expert critics of the government both as to its administrative and legislative policies. The system thus constantly conserves the experience of the leading statesmen of both parties. The Cabinet and the Shadow Cabinet are constantly engaged in discovering and revealing to the democracy improved policies in government. There are thus five instead of three institutions involved in the exercise of sovereign authority in England. The King and the two Houses are still nominally sovereign, while real sovereignty has passed to the people through the instrumentality of two party institutions not recognized by the laws.

To summarize the stages in the evolution of the Cabinet: 1. There was the inner circle of the Privy Council and of the earlier Continual Council on whom the king relied for advice in government. The name Cabinet was applied to this group as early as the reign of Charles I. 2. Charles II began to substitute the inner circle in place of the Privy Council. 3. William III and Anne identified the Cabinet with party leaders. 4. George I absented himself from Cabinet meetings. 5. Robert Walpole created the office of Prime Minister which served as an entering wedge in the transfer of the exercise of royal prerogative from the King to the Cabinet. 6. The Cabinet supported by the House of Commons forced George II to give Cabinet places to Pitt and Chesterfield. 7. After George III had for twenty-five years tried to discredit and destroy the Cabinet its authority was restored under the leadership of the younger Pitt as head of the Tory party, thus committing both parties to the system. 8. Finally, beginning with the act of 1832, the nation is becoming enfranchised, the people are recognized as the source of final authority, there are frequent changes in party rule, and the people express their will by alternate choice between two competing Cabinets. The mechanism is such that the people retain the continuous services of both groups, one as actually governing, the other as pointing out methods of improvement.

REFERENCES

ADAMS and STEPHENS. *Select Documents of the English Constitutional History*, 1901, *Act of Settlement*, p. 475.

ANSON. *Law and Custom of the Constitution*, Vol. I, Chap. II, Vol. II, Chaps. I and III.

DICEY. *Law of the Constitution*, Edition 1915, Chap. XII.

MAY. *Constitutional History of England*, Vol. I, Chaps. I and II, Vol. II, Chap. VIII.

MEDLEY. *English Constitutional History*, Second Edition, Revised, Chaps. II and VI.

OGG. *The Governments of Europe*, Chap. II.

WALPOLE. *History of England Since 1815*, Vol. III, Chap. XI.

CHAPTER XXXIV

THE RELATION OF THE CABINET TO THE EXECUTIVE AND TO THE JUDICIARY

THE Cabinet as a whole arose from an adaptation of an ancient institution to meet changing needs and consequently a number of the offices included in it are survivals of ancient offices. Significant among these posts is that of the Lord President of the Privy Council, always a member of the Cabinet, nearly always a peer and, since the functions of the Council have been absorbed by the Cabinet, an officer left practically without duties. All Cabinet members are made Privy Councilors so that the Cabinet becomes the active Council.[1] The Board of Trade and Board of Education originated as committees of the Privy Council, and the President of each of these boards is included in the Cabinet. The "Boards" are mere fiction; the Presidents are the boards and fill the places of Ministers of Trade and Education respectively. As stated in another chapter, a Committee of the Council serves as the Supreme Court for the Colonies and for the Established Church. The Lord High Chancellor is a member of this court. He is also the presiding officer of the House of Lords. The Chancellor was for centuries the most confidential adviser of the Crown, "the keeper of the king's conscience." The duties of the Chancellor, both as presiding officer in the Upper House and as a member of the high courts, are non-partisan in character, though he is a member of a partisan Cabinet. This office exemplifies the early union of all powers in the King in Council.

[1] The Privy Council numbers more than 200 members, and now consists of all the members of the Cabinet; all who have been Cabinet officers; most of the chief administrative officers in the departments of the government; and a large number of eminent persons upon whom the rank of Privy Councilor is conferred as a complimentary distinction. It rarely acts as a whole, but performs its duties — now mainly executive rather than advisory — through numerous committees. See Anson's "Law and Custom of the Constitution," Vol. II, pp. 106-107, 141-143; Macy, "The English Constitution," p. 86.

A fifth member of the modern Cabinet represents an office, whose duties have vanished, the Lord Privy Seal. When it was proposed to abolish the office, Mr. Gladstone alleged as a reason for continuing it the desirability of furnishing the Cabinet an additional councilor who might not have the strength to administer a department.[1]

Until the death of Queen Anne in 1714 the Lord High Treasurer had control of finance. Since that date the duties of the office had been assumed by the Chancellor of the Exchequer. The ancient title has been dropped and in its place there remains the First Lord of the Treasury, who is also an officer without duties. The Prime Minister is usually appointed First Lord of the Treasury[2] and thus is secured to him time and energy for other arduous duties. Occasionally, however, the Prime Minister prefers another office. Lord Salisbury was Foreign Secretary and Prime Minister.

In addition to the six officers named above, the Cabinet includes the five Secretaries of State; viz., those for the Home Department, for Foreign Affairs, for the Colonies, for War, and for India. The Navy is represented by the First Lord of the Admiralty. Ireland is represented either by the Chief Secretary or by the Lord Lieutenant of Ireland. A number of other officers, such as the Secretary for Scotland, the Postmaster General, the Presidents of the Board of Agriculture and of the Local Government Board, the First Commissioner of Works, and the Chancellor of the Duchy of Lancaster, may be included. Since the year 1900 cabinets have numbered twenty members. During the nineteenth century the number varied from ten to twenty. The enlargement of the field of government has involved an increase in the size of the Cabinet.

Change of Cabinets. — When in case of a general election it becomes evident that the ruling party is defeated, the Prime Minister resigns office and the King sends for the leader of the victorious party and requests him to form a government. He consults with his immediate party associates and they distribute among themselves the offices to be represented in the

[1] Ogg, "The Governments of Europe," p. 65, note 1.
[2] Anson, "The Law and Custom of the Constitution," Vol. II, p. 174; Lowell, "The Government of England," Vol. I, p. 127.

Cabinet, and a list of the appointments to be made is handed to the king. The press at once announces the names of the new Cabinet members and the office held by each. As stated in a former chapter, an actual Cabinet and a potential Cabinet are always on duty in Parliament. These change places when the acting Cabinet is defeated at an election. In respect to many of the offices it is understood in advance who will fill them, and the work of the Prime Minister is thus simplified. The questions in doubt as to how many and what officers shall be included and who shall be appointed to particular places are decided by the Prime Minister alone or in consultation with his friends. It is the aim of the leader to make the party strong in Parliament, strong with the electors, and as harmonious and efficient as the conditions will permit. The King has a legal right to select whom he pleases as his ministers of state; yet the well-established rule of the Constitution requires him to appoint the leader of the triumphant party to the office of First Lord of the Treasury, or to whatever office he may prefer, and leave to him the distribution of all the other positions in the Ministry. Besides the Lord Chancellor, whose duties are mainly judicial, and three or four sinecures, the Cabinet is composed of about sixteen Ministers who are heads of the chief departments of the executive.

The Duties of the Cabinet. — The amount of executive business in the British government is enormous. Comparison with that of the American government helps to make this clear. The United States is so situated as to be comparatively exempt from the anxiety of a dangerous encounter with any foreign power. Military requirements are correspondingly slight. The situation of England is such that its continued existence has been felt to be dependent upon the maintenance of an efficient standing army and a navy superior to that of any two rival states. As to colonies, America owns islands with less than ten millions of inhabitants, while England is responsible for the government of more than one seventh of the human race. In respect to domestic matters, the contrast is equally striking. The Government at Washington has nothing to do with local government, except as it concerns the District of Columbia, which includes the national capital. Local government with the enlarged franchise is new in England and the Local

Government Board in the Ministry is a hard-working department. It does for cities and counties what is done in America by the forty-eight separate States. The English habit of depending upon the central authority for minute, detailed supervision of local interests still persists and places heavy burdens upon the central office. Again, the entire police system of the country is under the supervision of the Home Secretary.[1] A few years ago, that important official gave directions in person for the arrest of desperadoes in East London. Scandal has assailed a whole Cabinet and imperiled its very existence on account of the mistake of a policeman in arresting a respectable woman — a local event which would hardly make acceptable copy for an American newspaper.

The separate American States assume the burden of public education. The federal government does, indeed, coöperate and assist in a variety of ways; but the general responsibility and most of the financial support is borne by the States. In the English Cabinet the President of the Board of Education is a very important minister, and the Government interests itself in educational details in ways unknown in America. The union of Church and State, carefully repudiated by the founders of the American Commonwealth, gives rise in England to two rival systems of schools, both recognized and regulated by law, and involving very difficult problems to be dealt with by the Minister of Education.

The onerous burdens of the English Cabinet are made heavier by the fact that those who execute the laws are at the same time responsible for their existence. The blame for a law which works badly cannot, as in America, be shifted to the shoulders of an independent legislature or, as in some instances, a court. The Government of the day is held responsible for retaining any laws which are a source of injustice, as well as for the formulation of new and needed projects of legislation. Executive duties are thus complicated. The Government inaugurates a new policy in the face of partisan rivals for office. The Cabinet incurs all the odium arising from temporary maladjustments due to change of policy.

[1] London police are subject to direct control; other police are subject to the supervision of the central government. — Lowell, "Government of England," Vol. I, p. 106.

The Cabinet has been called a committee of the Privy Council, because it was evolved out of and takes the place of the Council. It has been called a committee of Parliament because it depends for its continued existence on the support of the House of Commons. The Cabinet is in fact a self-appointed national party committee and as a ruling party committee, it formulates party policies, both legislative and administrative, and maintains its position by securing party support in Parliament and among the constituencies.

Ministerial Responsibility. — Each minister is individually responsible for his own department. If matters go wrong with the police, the Home Secretary may be criticized; if diplomatic delinquencies are charged, the Foreign Secretary may be blamed. But the Cabinet as a whole stands or falls together. Personal defects may lead to a change within a Cabinet, but this is exceptional. The body as a whole is responsible. It is compared to a chain which is no stronger than the weakest link. A vote of censure directed against the war department would cause a Cabinet crisis. Joint responsibility promotes a spirit of watchfulness over all departments to avoid hostile criticism.

Besides the members of the Cabinet, there is in the two Houses of Parliament a larger number who are members of the Ministry. Each of the departments has a Parliamentary Secretary. The war and navy departments each have three parliamentary members in the Ministry, two of whom are not in the Cabinet. In the Ministry and not in the Cabinet are four party Whips, a number of officers of the King's household, and a few heads of minor departments. The ministry numbers more than fifty in all. These all resign their offices with the Cabinet changes; all are members of the party. Each minister is bound to vote with his party, to apologize for and defend the policies adopted, to seek in every legitimate way to strengthen the party. Ministers not in the Cabinet have no direct share in determining the policies of the government. They are not consulted, do not share Cabinet secrets. They are salaried or paid adherents of the government. If they cannot yield loyal support to it, their duty is to resign. The parliamentary secretary is directly responsible to the head of the department. When the Cabinet member is a peer the Secretary is always in the House of Commons and upon him may rest the chief burden of defending the policy of the department, though he speaks for and on behalf of his chief and not as a Cabinet minister. Some of the departments always and a number of them usually have a spokesman in each House, but all officers of the Treasury sit in the Commons.[1]

The members of the ministry receive salaries ranging from £1000 to £20,000, but these are practically all of the salaried partisan positions. The public service outside of Parliament is permanent and strictly non-partisan. Membership in Parliament marks the distinction between salaried party supporters and the officers who serve both parties with equal loyalty. Without this sharp line of distinction, a democratic Cabinet would be difficult or impossible. Previous to the popular enfranchisement Parliament was controlled through pensions and the bribery of office. With the enfranchisement came the general recognition of the principle that partisan appointments should be restricted to the membership of the two Houses.[2]

Permanent Under Secretary. — The English executive thus possesses some of the qualities of a bureaucracy. In each department next to the Parliamentary Secretary is the Permanent Under Secretary of the Department. This officer is like a bureaucratic chief in that he holds his place on account of his ability as an administrator. He lives with the department, is familiar with its details, and is acquainted with both the theory and the practice of administration. Yet the Permanent Secretary is subject to the orders of a parliamentary Minister. Some of the departments are involved in heated partisan controversy, and the secretary is subject, with a change of parties, to orders from a chief who, as a party leader, is bitterly opposed to a law just enacted by the defeated party. The Liberals came into office in 1905, in large part because of intense opposition to an Educational Act of the Conservative party. Because of obstruction in the Upper House, they were unable to amend the law and it thus became the duty of the party to administer an

[1] Lowell, "The Government of England," Vol. I, p. 78.
[2] There remains, however, a limited amount of patronage which may be used for partisan purposes, such as the bestowal of lesser titles and temporary offices of a personal character. *Ibid.*, Vol. I, p. 449.

obnoxious law which the country had condemned. This, however, was done in such a way as to avoid serious criticism. It is customary for both parties to administer statutes which as partisans they have condemned. The skilled under secretary and the permanent service facilitate uniformity of administration in the face of frequent changes in the heads of departments. In some cases it is an administrative policy which becomes an issue at a general election. Then the victorious party may be pledged to make specific reforms or a radical change in policy. In the heat of partisan debate, promises may have been made which are difficult or impossible of fulfillment. The permanent secretary then has the delicate task of saving the service while giving it the appearance of fulfilling a party pledge made without an appreciation of the difficulties involved. He needs to be a skillful politician without being a partisan.

Non-partisan Civil Service. — It is a violation of one of the delicate rules of the Constitution to refer to or to quote an officer of the permanent service in parliamentary debate. Gladstone reproved one of his associates for failure to observe this rule.[1] The parliamentary chiefs are alone responsible. They alone are to be criticized. It is expected that the permanent service will remain absolutely impartial. These officials are not expected to discuss in public the affairs of their departments or to give information to others than their superiors to be used in public debate. A clerk in one of the departments was laboring day and night to furnish information to a party leader to be used in an important debate. Upon being asked if his department would be equally alert in gathering information for the opposition, his reply was, that a request coming from the leader of the opposition would be treated with almost the same respect as the one from the party in power, yet they would be greatly surprised to receive a request for statistics from such a source to be used in a partisan way. This would tend to confusion. The opposition understand this and are willing to wait until they themselves are officially in command. The leaders on both sides are bound to respect and to protect the independence and the impartiality of the civil service. Those in the civil service, on the other hand, are equally loyal to both parties. They may vote at elections, but they take no

[1] Lowell, "The Government of England," Vol. I, p. 191.

other part in politics. It is not good form for them to attend political meetings. At least they take no active part in a campaign.

The Prime Minister and other Leaders. — There are three distinct classes in the public service. First is the inner circle of the ministry, the Cabinet. Second, the non-cabinet Ministers in Parliament. These are all identified with a ruling party. Third, the public officers not in Parliament. These, as officers, belong to both parties. The Cabinet itself is composed of two parts, a leader and his followers. The office of Prime Minister is to be thought of as an institution quite apart from the Cabinet as a corporate body. The Prime Minister has many duties which are distinct from those of other members of the body. The office preceded the Cabinet in the order of development. Around the chief Minister the Cabinet has been formed. He is the president of its meetings, the spokesman for Cabinet policies. He is the party disciplinarian. He gives the final word in party disputes. He is the chief intermediary between the Monarch and the Cabinet. Before Parliament and before the country his word, for the time, carries the force of supreme authority. The Prime Minister is kept from being a despot because he has no authority except that which is derived from a large, intelligent voting body. By excelling others in discerning and giving expression to the will of the nation he comes to the place of supreme power, and he gives place to a competitor when he ceases to excel in leadership. The party chief and the inner circle of his associates secure and hold their positions by actually leading the party or some section of it. In this sense they are self-appointed, yet conditions may arise which cause doubt as to who shall be the leader. Within the ranks, as already stated, doubts are solved by the party chief. When the leader himself vacates his office there may be a question between two or three associates as to who shall fill the place. Salisbury succeeded Beaconsfield without question as leader of the Conservative party, and Balfour succeeded Salisbury; but when Balfour resigned a successor was not easily found. In such cases the leader is selected by informal conferences among party leaders, or there may be a caucus including all the party supporters in the two Houses of Parliament. If at the time of Cabinet crisis there is doubt as to leadership, the King may act upon his own judgment in selecting the leader most likely to harmonize the party.

The organization is normal when one man is the accepted party chief and is Prime Minister when his party is in office, and leader of the opposition when it is out of office. The official party leader is the leader of debate in the House of which he is a member. In the other House some party member is an officially recognized leader of debate. There are thus two leaders in each party. When the chief leader is a peer the leader in the Commons holds a position of almost equal importance. The Prime Minister, however, remains the official spokesman and the disciplinarian of the party. Normally, the official leaders are the actual leaders of the Cabinet; yet not infrequently other Cabinet officers overshadow the official leaders in commanding public attention.[1] With increased numbers in the Cabinet there is a tendency to subdivide that body into smaller groups, four or five of whom form an inner cabinet.[2]

Rank in the party has no necessary association with any particular office in the executive. Even the Prime Minister may select an office other than the traditional one of First Lord of the Treasury. The Chancellor of the Exchequer must be a financier of marked ability. The office of Lord High Chancellor goes to a jurist of eminence. But the fifty or more places in the Ministry are subject to frequent and indiscriminate changes. They are filled by ambitious men. Even when the same party is long continued in office there are frequent shifts in the distribution of office, while a change of party involves a clean sweep of the entire Ministry.

Party Rule and Administrative Efficiency. — A standing criticism against the cabinet system is that it places the control of the executive business in the hands of politicians who are ignorant of the details of administration in the departments for which they are responsible.[3] The bureaucratic character of the permanent service described above is in part an answer to this criticism. A further answer is found in the fact that the parliamentary side of the executive is likewise, in a sense, permanent. It is true that the tenure is usually brief as related to

---

[1] Joseph Chamberlain, in the Tory Cabinet, and Lloyd George, in the Liberal, furnish illustrations.

[2] Lowell, "The Government of England," Vol. I, p. 59.   [3] *Ibid.*, Chap. VIII.

any one office, yet the holder of the office has either had long training in governmental business or possesses a genius for public affairs. For every place in the Cabinet there are probably ten men in Parliament who have seriously contemplated the possibility of attaining Cabinet rank. Membership in Parliament is a career, a life work. A young man entering the service naturally expects to come to the front. To remain in the House of Commons he must satisfy a single constituency of his continued usefulness, or he must so commend himself to the leaders of his party that they will secure for him a new constituency in case of need. Each of the parties has numerous districts which may be relied upon to elect any one whom the leaders nominate. The fact that there is no residence requirement makes it possible to secure unbroken service for the superior man. He demonstrates his superiority by his ability to throw light on public affairs. Outside of the fifty who hold office, there are others who are demanding recognition. Already they have made themselves familiar with the business of administration. Their training begins before the "maiden speech" in Parliament and, subject to the law of survival of the fittest, it goes forward until a position in the inner circle is reached. The heads of Departments have either had experience in subordinate positions in the ministry or have manifested conspicuous ability.

Yet after all that may be said by way of mitigation, the criticism still holds. To parcel out, in a more or less haphazard way, twenty of the high offices of state does not fulfill the requirements of an ideal scientific administration. It does involve waste and misfits in the association of men with office. The system, however, is capable of yielding a high degree of practical efficiency and it insures the executive against serious and long-continued scandals.

The English and American Systems Compared. — It is in order here to refer briefly to the distinguishing feature between the Presidential and the Cabinet types of government. The American States and the General government of the United States were organized upon the theory of a separation of the three departments. The Legislature, the Executive, and the Judiciary are made as far as possible independent of one another. Each is supreme in its own sphere. No officer is permitted to serve at the same time in any two of the departments. In actual fact, complete harmony between theory and practice has not been secured. The tendency has been for the governors of States and the President of the United States to become leaders in legislation as well as executive chiefs. The American governor or president as a party leader may gain a controlling influence over the legislature without becoming responsible to it. The Executive is elected by the people and is responsible to the people. The Cabinet is in a sense chosen by a popular election, but it is chosen for the double purpose of making laws and administering laws. It is directly responsible to the House of Commons whose vote may at any time drive it out of office. The Americans intended by their constitutions to exalt the legislature and give it an independent position. Present tendencies are in the direction of subordinating the legislature to an independent executive leader.

The President, like the Prime Minister, selects his own associates in the Cabinet, but in this respect he has a much freer hand. Occasionally a party leader is so related to the newly elected President as to command a place in the Cabinet, but this is exceptional. In general, the President may appoint any one he pleases. He cannot, however, choose a member of Congress. The Prime Minister must select members of Parliament and must fulfill as far as possible the reasonable expectations of every member of his Cabinet. There are no surprises in the ordinary make-up of the English Cabinet.

The President's Cabinet is not a cabinet at all in the English sense of the term. The relation of cabinet members to the President almost exactly fulfills the ideal of George III, who set himself to destroy the English Cabinet. The heads of departments are independent of one another. Each is directly responsible to the President. There is no joint or corporate responsibility. American Cabinet authority is personal. The Chief Executive is alone responsible. He may appoint or remove members at will. He may entirely disregard their advice. He may seek and follow the advice of whomsoever he pleases. The President *is* the Executive. If matters go wrong in the foreign service, blame may attach to the Secretary, but the responsibility is with the President. Members of his Cabinet as such have no share in legislation.

Contrast also the positions of the judiciary in the two countries. It was the intention of the Americans to make the courts not only independent, but far removed from partisan controversy. Judges in most of the States as well as in the federal government were at first appointed for life. As the courts have assumed and exercised the power to nullify acts of the legislature, they have come into political and partisan controversy. States have very generally adopted the policy of nominating and electing judges by the same process as other political officers. In England the courts were an effective tool of royal tyranny until the revolution of 1688, but coincident with the development of Cabinet government, the judiciary became entirely non-partisan. At the same time the Lord High Chancellor, a member of a partisan Cabinet, presides over the House of Lords as a supreme court, is a member of the judicial committee of the Privy Council and of other high courts, appoints the judges in lower courts, and is active in all matters of judicial procedure and reform, while the judiciary remains as completely out of politics as does the permanent service in the administrative departments.

The English Constitution began with all powers, legislative, executive, and judicial, united under the control of the Crown and an assembly. In its relation to the monarch and to Parliament the Cabinet still exemplifies the union, but by common consent one department, the judiciary, has come to be treated as independent, leaving legislation and administration fused together and united under partisan control. The description of the relation of the Ministry to Parliament will follow an account of the organization of the two Houses.

REFERENCES

ANSON. *Law and Custom of the Constitution*, Vol. II, Chap. IV.
BAGEHOT. *The English Constitution*, Chap. II.
COURTNEY. *The Working of the Constitution of the United Kingdom*, Chap. XII.
DICEY. *The Law of the Constitution*, 1815, Chap. II.
LOWELL. *The Government of England*, Edition 1908, Vol. I, Chaps. II–X and Chaps. XVII and XVIII.

CHAPTER XXXV

THE HOUSE OF COMMONS

THE House of Commons has been the chief coördinating agency in the British Government. Beginning as a feeble institution intended to enable the king to increase his revenues, it gradually gained a share in all acts of legislation. Henry VIII used the lower House as a means of control over the House of Lords. The House of Commons was always the one branch of the government having a direct connection with a voting constituency. In the name of the people Parliament was exalted above the Crown. In the name of the people the House of Lords has been subordinated to the House of Commons. The right to vote for members of the House measures the progress towards democracy. By successive acts of Parliament the elective franchise has been extended to five sixths of the male population twenty-one years of age, and further extension is under consideration. From every point of view the House of Commons holds the place of primary interest in the present and future government of the British Empire.

To the student of politics the very center of the British Empire is the small, oblong room in the Palace of Westminster known as the House of Commons. It is not an imposing legislative hall, for when it was rebuilt in 1834 the proportions of the old room were retained so that no inducement should be given to " loud-voiced oratory." Consequently the benches can accommodate only about half of the present membership of the House (670), and even with the seats reserved for members in the side galleries they are not sufficient. From the entrance lobby a broad aisle leads up the center of the House to the Speaker's chair before which stands the table for the clerks. At the end of this table lies the mace, — upon the table when the House is sitting, on a bracket below when in committee. The Chairman of Committees occupies a seat in front of the Speaker's chair when he presides during sessions of the Committee of the Whole House or of the Committee of Ways and Means. On either side rise tiers of green leather-covered benches, divided halfway down the side of the hall by a narrow cross aisle, called the gangway. At the lower end is another aisle beyond which is a shallow tier of cross benches for members and a few visitors. Under the high stained-glass windows runs a gallery, reserved on the sides for members, at the lower end for strangers, and back of the Speaker's chair for the press. Above the Press Gallery and behind a heavy grating is the Ladies' Gallery, which is technically outside the House.

Composition of the House. — The front bench at the Speaker's right is occupied by those Members of the Ministry who sit in the Commons, and is called the Treasury Bench. On the front Opposition Bench at the Speaker's left sits the "Shadow Cabinet" composed of the members of the party out of power who have held or are expecting again to hold ministerial office. Thus, facing one another across the table sit the two party leaders with their lieutenants at their sides and their immediate supporters just behind. Below the gangway sit members less closely bound to the leaders. Irish Nationalists habitually occupy seats below the gangway on the left even when their Liberal allies are in power. Except in this general way no seat belongs to a particular person, but before "prayers" a member may reserve his seat for the day's session by marking it with his card or his hat. At question time and when a very important debate is in progress the House is well filled, but most of the time a comparatively small number of members is in actual attendance. They are, however, not far distant, and the sound of the division bell or the report that a leader is speaking brings them flocking to the House from the committee rooms, the library, the refreshment rooms, and other parts of the building.

Of the 670 members who make up the House of Commons 465 represent England, 30 sit for Wales, 72 for Scotland, and 103 for Ireland. These are elected to represent counties, municipal and provincial boroughs, and the universities. Most of the Constituencies now elect only one member; but twenty-three boroughs, the " City " of London,[1] and three universities, — twenty-seven constituencies in all, — elect two members each.

Constituencies vary greatly in size. The last distribution of seats, that of 1885, did not pretend to make them equal, and the subsequent shifting of population has increased the discrepancies. In 1912, the largest constituency was the Romford division of the county of Essex with 55,951 electors; the smallest, the borough of Kilkenny in Ireland with 1690. Twenty-five boroughs in Great Britain and four in Ireland, each have less then five thousand electors. One two-member constituency and the three universities, returning two members each, have less than ten thousand electors. Five county constituencies in Great Britain and sixteen in Ireland also have less than five thousand electors. In general, Ireland is over-represented, as her population has been decreasing for several decades, while that of Great Britain is increasing.[2]

Great confusion in respect to the suffrage has been the result of the policy, extending over many centuries, of dealing with the subject by special acts, many of them of local application. The qualifications were different for boroughs and counties, different for the parliamentary franchise, and for local governments. The great democratic enfranchisement began with the Reform Act of 1832 and was extended by the Acts of 1867 and 1885, but the confusion remained. A considerable number of the adult male citizens are still debarred from the privilege of voting. On the other hand, the abuse of plural voting persisted, since unrepealed ancient laws gave the franchise to property owners in each district in which they held property.

The nomination and election of members is more fully described in the chapters on political parties. A dissolution of the House of Commons is followed at once by the election of a new House. According to the old law several weeks are required before a newly elected House may be organized. The voting extends over a period of two or three weeks. This arises from

---

[1] The City of London has less than 30,000 inhabitants. It is about a mile square and contains the chief business houses; it is still governed by the ancient merchant guilds.

[2] Lowell, "The Government of England," Vol. I, pp. 197–201; King and Raffety, "Our Electoral System," Chap. IV.

the fact that the Returning Officer in each district "has a choice of dates for giving notice of the election, a choice, again, in fixing the date of nomination, and a further choice in fixing the date for the poll, a minimum and maximum number of days in each case alone being prescribed."[1] The proposed act designates a single day for the election of all members.

No change is proposed in the matter of residence requirements for members of the House; members are not required, either by law or custom, to reside in the districts which they represent. Scotsmen or men of Scottish descent usually represent Scotch districts, but they are not required to live in Scotland. The same is true as to Wales and Ireland. There is the greatest freedom in the selection of representatives from all the constituencies. This fact has a great influence on the character of the House. It is possible for a statesman of ability to choose a parliamentary career and remain continuously in the House of Commons. Each of the parties has a number of districts at its disposal, which may be relied upon to elect any candidate whom the leaders may nominate. The laws provide for an official nomination by petition after due notice. If only one candidate is nominated, the nomination itself is an election; no poll is ordered. Each of the parties controls a number of such districts. The system makes it possible for members of cabinet or ministerial rank to continue in Parliament. Party leaders usually represent districts which are contested, and their relations to the district are such that even when their party is defeated they carry their own districts. But if an accident should occur and the leader be defeated, he is kept in office by the use of a constituency which the party controls. This system is essential to the maintenance of the English type of Cabinet Government.

Permanence and continuity in the legislative career tend to secure a high grade of ability in the House of Commons. The fact that a number of seats are to be disposed of by mere party nomination has in the past tended to keep in the House mere appointees of influential families who are sometimes men of inferior intelligence. Party rivalry tends to diminish this evil, for capable leaders seek the support of followers of real ability.

[1] King and Raffety, "Our Electoral System," p. 86.

Members are elected for a term of five years or until a dissolution is ordered. Since 1911, each member receives a salary of £400 a year, except when he is in receipt of a salary as an officer of the House, as a Minister, or as an officer of His Majesty's Household. Although members are elected for five years, they seldom, if ever,[1] are allowed to fill out their term to the close. A dissolution, involving a general election, may occur at any time and will occur whenever, in a political crisis, the Cabinet prefers an appeal to the country to resignation. When the end of a term approaches, the Government endeavors to secure a dissolution at the time most favorable for their own reëlection.

For a long time Parliament met in annual session early in February and was usually prorogued in August; but in recent years the limit has often been extended in either direction. At the opening of the session the Commons are summoned to the bar of the House of Lords to hear the King's Speech. The Speech from the Throne outlines the Government policy for the session as laid down by the Ministry. The House then prepares an Address in reply, the discussion of which may occupy two or three weeks. Amendments to the Address are often moved expressing regret that certain matters were not mentioned by His Majesty, etc. An actually hostile amendment carried is equivalent to a vote of no confidence and involves the immediate resignation of the Ministry.

The Speaker. — The Speaker is elected by the House and confirmed by the King for the life of one Parliament, but in practice he is always reëlected as long as he will serve, and on his retirement he is given a peerage. He is chosen from the ranks of the party at the moment in power; but as soon as he is elected he is expected to lose all partisan bias and to become the impartial presiding officer of the House. Since 1835 the reëlection of a Speaker has never been opposed and his seat is not usually contested at a general election. In 1895 Mr. Gully was chosen Speaker under conditions which offended the Conservatives. An opposing candidate contested his election to Parliament, yet the Conservatives in the House reëlected him as Speaker.[2]

---

[1] Since 1837 the longest term closed July, 1865, and was six years, seven months, and six days. The legal limit was seven years.
[2] Lowell, "The Government of England," Vol. I, p. 259.

Especially since the introduction of new rules governing closure and other matters of parliamentary procedure the powers of the Speaker are very great. His decisions are treated with the utmost respect and from them there is no appeal. His disciplinary powers include " naming " a member and even his suspension from attendance in the House. The right to suspend a sitting in case of grave disorder has occasionally been exercised since it was granted to the Speaker in 1902.[1] The impartial and respected position which the Speaker holds is well shown by the agreement to leave with him the delicate decision as to what is a money bill, and so the power of declaring what bills shall come within the scope of the Parliament Act of 1911.[2] Only in the case of a tie does he cast a vote, and then he bases his decision, not upon his own opinion of the measure, " but upon the probable intention of the House as shown by its previous action, or upon some general constitutional principle." [3] His whole position is the exact opposite of that of the Speaker in the American House of Representatives, who is himself a party leader, participates in the organization of the house, and directs debate with the interests of his own party in mind, although since the change in the house rules in 1910 his powers are diminished.

Committees. — The presiding officer, when the House is in Committee of the Whole, is regularly the Chairman of the Committee on Ways and Means, called Chairman of Committees. He is nominated at the beginning of a Parliament by the Ministry from among their prominent supporters and serves until they resign. Like the Speaker, he is expected to preside in a strictly non-partisan manner, and he speaks and votes in the House only on questions that have no political significance. In the absence of the Speaker, he also presides over regular sessions of the House. Since 1902, a deputy Chairman has been chosen in addition, to preside in the absence of the Speaker and the Chairman of Committees, so that no interruption may come to the business of the House.

For the dispatch of business, the House resolves itself into three great committees or one committee of the Whole House

---

[1] A recent instance is that in the autumn of 1912, when feeling was running high over the Home Rule Bill.   [2] Ogg, "Governments of Europe," p. 112.
[3] Lowell, "The Government of England," Vol. I, p. 262.

acting under three names. The Committee of Ways and Means considers all matters of revenue. The Committee of Supply deals in detail with all estimates laid before the House by the various government departments; and revenue accounts of India are reviewed by the Committee for India. The Committee of the Whole House discusses the clauses of Government and Private Members' Bills that are not referred to Standing or Select Committees. In Committee greater freedom of debate is possible than in a regular session and members may speak on the same question as often as they please. The Chairman of Committees presides when any one of these committees is in session. When the House is in Committee, the mace is not on the table, — showing that the body does not then exercise full legislative powers. At the opening of the session, Select Committees [1] are appointed on Privileges, Standing Orders, Selection, Public Accounts, Railway and Canal Bills, Public Petitions, Police and Sanitary Affairs, the Kitchen and Refreshment Rooms. Their chief duties are indicated by the names they bear. Fifteen is the usual number of members, but it may be smaller and, by special leave of the House, may be made larger.

The Committee of Selection [2] is a nominating committee of eleven members, chosen by the House at the beginning of the session. Its membership is really determined by the leaders of the two parties. It is an important body made up of six members of the Government and five of the Opposition. It acts in a non-partisan manner and almost never divides along party lines. This Committee appoints most of the members of the other Select Committees, also the four great Standing Committees, described below, and the Chairman's panel.

Nothing better illustrates the impartial character of these Parliamentary committees than the Chairman's panel. This panel of from six to eight men is chosen by the Committee of Selection at the opening of the session. The panel then appoints from among its own number Chairmen for the four Standing Committees, sometimes called Grand Committees. The object is to secure experience and continuity of policy in the presiding officers. The conduct of business in committee is

---

[1] Ogg, "The Governments of Europe," p. 124.
[2] Lowell, "The Government of England," Vol. I, p. 266.

very largely in the hands of the Chairman, and upon his skill and impartiality the success of the system mainly depends.

The four Standing Committees of from sixty to eighty members are appointed at the beginning of the session. Every bill that is read a second time and is not sent to a Committee of the Whole House is referred to one of these Committees. The Scottish Standing Committee is one of the four and is composed of all the members representing Scottish constituencies and not more than fifteen other members nominated for the consideration of any bill, by the Committee of Selection. All public bills relating to Scotland are referred to this Committee. A Standing Committee conducts its business like a Committee of the Whole House and is, indeed, a substitute for such a committee. In its organization and personnel, it reflects the various points of view of the larger body and carries on discussions in the same way. It reports to the House the bills referred to it, with or without amendments.

Other Select Committees than those nominated at the beginning of the session are appointed by the House to inquire into special questions or measures as they arise. Sometimes they are Joint Committees acting with an equal number of members of the House of Lords. The Committee of Selection names Private and Provisional Order Bills Committees of four members to deal with individual bills. Public Bills affecting private interests are referred to hybrid committees appointed partly by the House and partly by the Committee of Selection.

Parliamentary Bills. — Bills that come before the House are divided into four classes, — Government, Private Members', Private, and Provisional Orders Bills. First in importance stand Government Bills, introduced by the Ministry in fulfillment of promises made in the Speech from the Throne, in Parliament or on the platform. Such measures follow a special procedure and have peculiar facilities for being passed. But any member may introduce a bill dealing with public questions, and these are classed as Private Members' Bills. They have to take their chances in a ballot for places on the calendar, and little time is permitted for their consideration. No Private Members' Bill that is opposed by a determined minority has a chance of being passed, unless it is adopted by the Government. The third class is that of Private Bills by which private persons, companies, or local governments in particular places are affected. They often deal with matters of local police, sanitation, the granting of powers to municipal corporations or private companies for supplying public conveniences, such as gas, water, electric light, or tramways. Their passage through Parliament is facilitated by committees. The objects of Private Bills must be advertised before the bills are presented to Parliament, in order that all persons affected by their proposals may be informed. In Parliament they must comply with a large number of Standing Orders. The real discussion of a Private Bill takes place in a Private Bill Committee of four members who hear the evidence presented by all persons affected by the Bill and report their decision to the House. In most instances the report of such a committee is accepted as final. In order to secure greater uniformity in legislation on railways and canals, all bills dealing with those subjects are referred to one large committee which appoints from its own members the Chairmen of separate committees of four to deal with each bill. A similar method is followed in reference to police and local sanitation.[1]

Provisional Order Confirmation Bills are dealt with in the same way as Private Bills, by special committees.[2] These are brought in by representatives of government departments which have issued, under statutory powers, the provisional orders requiring sanction. They are not, however, treated in any sense as Government bills. Private and Provisional Orders Bills relating to Scotland are dealt with by a special process.

Passage through Parliament. — The steps through which a Bill must pass before becoming law have been numerous and tedious, but the tendency of Parliamentary procedure as the volume of business increases is to eliminate, or at least to make purely formal, many of the historical processes. Discussion is limited at the very most to five stages.

---

[1] Private bills pertain to some local, corporate, or private interest. They are subject to a special procedure in Parliament. Private Members' bills deal with general legislation and are like Government bills, except that they are introduced by members not in the Cabinet. Private members may introduce Private Bills, but such bills do not thereby become Private members' Bills. The distinction is in the subject matter.

[2] Lowell, "The Government of England," Vol. I, p. 384 *et seq.*

Important Government Bills are still introduced by asking permission, and they occasionally are discussed at this stage. The first reading offers no chance for debate. On second reading, the first real debate, — a discussion of the general principles of the bill, — takes place, and then if it is not shelved, the bill goes either directly to the Committee of the Whole or to a Standing Committee, or is referred first to a select Committee, and then to one of the two former. In Committee the bill is considered in detail and may be amended clause by clause. When a bill has been reported, with amendments, from a Committee of the Whole, and when it has been reported, with or without amendments, from a Standing Committee, it is discussed in detail by the House on the report stage. Not only the amendments made in committee, but new ones, may then be proposed and discussed. The third reading allows only verbal amendments and discussions of the bill as a whole. If a bill passed in one House is amended in the other, it is sent back for consideration of the amendments. When agreement is reached between the two Houses, it is ready for the Royal Assent.[1]

Private bills must be preceded by petitions and public notices stating their objects. If the preliminary regulations have all been complied with, the bill then goes through all the stages of a public bill, but in addition, if there is opposition, it must go through a judicial process in a private Bill Committee. This Committee hears the arguments of those who support and those who oppose the bill, amends it when it thinks best, and reports to the House, which may emend, recommit, or pass the bill to its third reading.

Although private members are permitted to bring in public bills, their chances of getting them through are very small, for the Government appropriates to its own uses every sitting except the evening sittings on Tuesdays and Wednesdays, and the sittings on Fridays. But the Tuesday evening sitting is given to the Government by Standing Order after Easter, and the Wednesday one after Whitsuntide, and all but the third and fourth Fridays after Whit Sunday. The Government also often seizes even more time by moving to take the whole time

[1] Money Bills and Accounts follow a special process and will be discussed later. See p. 476.

of the House, before the specified holidays. In 1911, Government business, including the time for election of Speaker, swearing in of members, King's Speech, Supply, etc., occupied a hundred and sixty-three of the hundred and seventy-two days in the session, leaving nine full days for some six hundred and thirty-five members to bring in their bills and resolutions.

Limiting Debate. — As the length of debates increased, and especially since the systematic obstruction by Irish Nationalists began in 1880, some means of limiting debates has been found necessary. Closure of debate, introduced in 1882, has been extended until now, after a question has been proposed, any Member may move " That the question be now put," and unless the Chair considers the motion an abuse of the rules of the House or an infringement of the rights of the minority, it is put without amendment or debate; the only requirement being that it must have the support of at least 100 votes.

The same rule has been applied to Standing Committees, where twenty members may force a closure. Since 1887, a system of " closure by compartment " has gradually developed, by which a certain amount of time is allotted for the discussion on various portions of a bill. This method of concluding debate is often called " The Guillotine," because of the inexorable close which it brings to discussion. The system has been further developed by allocating time to the various sections of a Bill before discussion begins and so avoiding the evil of allowing full debate on the first clauses and none on the later clauses of a Bill. In 1911, a variation of this system of closure was introduced and nicknamed " The Kangaroo Closure." It gives the Chair power to choose out of a selected group of amendments those he holds it most profitable for the House to discuss, " and the alertness and celerity of its movements account for its name." [1]

Process of Voting. — Voting is carried on in the following manner. The Chairman puts the question to an oral vote and announces its result by saying, " I think the Ayes (or Noes) have it." If any member of the minority challenges his decision, a division is called. The clerks turn a two-minute sand glass, bells are rung, and " Division " shouted by the police in all parts of the building. All members who enter within six minutes have a right to vote on the question. The outer doors

[1] " Liberal Yearbook," 1913, p. 8.

of the House are then locked, the vote is repeated, and if again challenged, two tellers are named from each side by the presiding officer. They station themselves in the division lobbies at either side of the House and the Members record their votes by passing through these lobbies where clerks record their names. The "Ayes" go to the right of the Speaker's chair and leave the House by a door behind it; the "Noes" go to the left and leave by the other end of the room, and return in reverse order. When the lobbies are clear, the four tellers report the vote to the Chairman. "A Member may vote in a division, though he did not hear the question put, but he is not in any case obliged to do so, and can remain in the Chamber while the division is in progress without recording his opinion."[1] If the Chair thinks a division frivolously called for, he may command a rising vote instead.

When the Government considers a question vital to itself, Government whips are appointed as tellers and its supporters are expected to vote with the Government. The Opposition similarly indicates whether it considers the vote a party matter. If private members are appointed as tellers, any member may vote as he pleases without being reproached.

REFERENCES

ANSON. *Law and Custom of the Constitution*, 1901, Vol. I.
BAGEHOT. *The English Constitution*, Edition 1904, Chaps. V and VI.
COURTNEY. *The Working Constitution of the United Kingdom.*
DICKENSON. *The Development of Parliament during the Nineteenth Century.*
Liberal Yearbook, 1904, and annually since.
LOWELL. *The Government of England*, 1908, Vol. I, Chaps. IX–XXII.
OGG. *The Governments of Europe*, Chaps. IV–VI.
PIKE. *Constitutional History of the House of Lords*, 1894.
REDLICH. *The Procedure of the House of Commons*, three Vols., 1910.
TEMPLE. *Life in Parliament.*
TODD. *On Parliamentary Government in England*, Edition 1889.

[1] "Liberal Yearbook," 1913, p. 7.

CHAPTER XXXVI

The House of Lords

More venerable than the House of Commons, as old as the Crown itself, the House of Lords stands as a monument to English conservatism. The name came into use when the representatives from counties and boroughs separated themselves from the Great Council and formed the House of Commons; while the old Council continued under the new name. First among western European nations the English achieved a monarchy with a dominant position, but it was a monarchy which could never become absolute because there was ever at hand a council of dignitaries from whom the monarch received his crown. Better than any other institution the House of Lords expresses the unbroken continuity of the government.

The Meeting Place. — The Chamber of the Lords is much more imposing than that of the Commons, although the general arrangement of the two rooms is the same. Instead of the somber hues that prevail in the Commons, the Hall is rich with gold and crimson. The Throne at the upper end of the room dominates all. Before it, in the broad aisle, is placed the Woolsack, a not too comfortable seat for the Lord Chancellor to occupy. A few cross benches stand in the broad aisle for peers who have not allied themselves with either party and beyond them is the table for the clerks of the House. At the lower end of the room beyond the Bar, a few seats and standing room for the public are provided. Peeresses may sit in the gallery which runs round three sides of the room. The general arrangement of seats and of parties corresponds to that in the Commons. The room is larger and the attendance much smaller than that of the popular Chamber, so that the red-leather cushions are usually revealed in all their glory. As in the House, the leaders of debate for the two parties sit facing one another on the front benches at the right and left of the Lord

Chancellor. Only a very small proportion of the Ministry, especially in the Liberal party, sits in the House of Lords.

Composition of the House of Lords. — The Lords Spiritual and Temporal, 641[1] in number, compose the Upper Chamber.

The Lords Spiritual are all Bishops of the Church of England and number twenty-six. The Archbishops of Canterbury and York, the Bishops of London, Durham, and Winchester sit by virtue of their offices, and the twenty-one senior Bishops also have seats. They are members of the House only because they are Bishops, and cease to be members when they leave their offices. Of the Lords temporal, the most important and numerous are the hereditary peers of the United Kingdom from princes of the blood royal down to barons. The Scottish peers are represented by sixteen elected peers, chosen from among their own number (31) for the duration of one Parliament by all the peers of Scotland. Ireland is represented by twenty-eight peers who are elected for life from among the Irish peerage as vacancies occur. In 1915 there were 19 Scotch peers without seats in the House of Lords and 59 Irish peers.[2] Scotch peers who are not elected to the House of Lords have no right to be elected to the House of Commons, but Irish peers may be elected for any constituency outside of Ireland. In order to supply more legal talent for the important judicial functions of the House of Lords, Sir James Parke was created a life peer in 1856; but the right of the Crown to create life peers was denied by the House. In this case the difficulty was solved by giving Sir James an hereditary peerage as Baron Wensleydale. In 1876, however, two life peers, Lords of Appeal in Ordinary, were created, and the number has since been increased to four. They hold their position and receive their salaries like other judges and also have a right to sit in the House after they have ceased to serve as judges.

The House of Lords is popularly thought of as representing mainly the ancient landed aristocracy of the United Kingdom, and in its sympathies it does so, yet only about one fourth of its members sit there by virtue of peerages dating before 1800. In 1830 there were 400 members of the House of Lords, but the number has rapidly increased. From 1830 to 1911 the liberal ministers added to the membership of the House 286 new peer-

---

[1] Correct for 1914.   [2] "The Statesman's Yearbook" for 1915, p. 5.

ages, and the Conservative ministers 181, sixty-four of these being created by the Liberal Ministry between 1905 and 1911. This constant stream of additions tends to change the political color of the House, but it is counteracted by the conservative traditions of the Lords. About four fifths of the members of the House belong to the Conservative party.

As there is much less business to be transacted by the Lords than by the Commons, their sittings are not so long. The House usually meets at a quarter past four o'clock on the first four days of the week, and does not usually sit on Friday or Saturday. The sittings do not ordinarily extend into the evening. Attendance, except upon rare occasions, is very meager; the average is less than fifty. The small number of three is necessary as a quorum, but no vote by division can be taken unless at least thirty lords are present.

Discipline and Procedure. — The Lord Chancellor, who is usually but not necessarily a peer, presides in debate, as Speaker, but without the authority of the Speaker of the House of Commons as guardian of order. He does not even decide which of two speakers shall have the floor and he has no casting vote in case of a tie. The House itself decides who shall speak, and also maintains order.[1] A motion to cast the duty of deciding on points of order upon the Lord Chancellor and the Lord Chairman was rejected in 1908. A Lord Chairman of Committees is elected for the life of a Parliament and is given full power to decide points of order in Committee. He also has great influence over private bill legislation.

In general, procedure in the House of Lords resembles that in the Commons. A bill must pass through the same stages as in the Lower House, but it is usually not discussed until the second reading when it may be passed with the understanding that important amendments are to be made in Committee. A bill after passing the second reading or after passing through committee of the Whole House, may be referred to a Standing Committee. It is not usual to oppose a bill on its third reading unless the majority at previous stages has been so small as to leave the real opinion of the House uncertain, in which case a bill may receive real opposition on the last reading and may even be defeated.

[1] Lowell, "The Government of England," Vol. I, p. 402.

Since the Lords need to spend very little time on finance legislation and are not eager to be heard in debate for the sake of their constituents, they are not so much pressed for time as are the Commons and they do not need any rule for closure of debate. Their share in the work of legislation is, however, still far from negligible. In the committee stage they often whip into shape a bill that has been much mutilated and distorted in a contested passage through the Commons. Amendments made in either House to a bill sent in from the other may be accepted, rejected, or modified by that other. Provision is made for conference in case of serious disagreement, but such a method of settlement has long been wholly formal and since 1911 the will of the Commons can be made ultimately to prevail. Opposed private bills are referred to committees of five members, nominated by the Committee of Selection, over which the Chairman of Committees presides. No peer is compelled to serve on such a committee, but if he consents to serve, he must attend during the hearing of the whole case.

The Lord Chairman of Committees exercises more influence than any other person over all private bill legislation, for he examines all private bills, even before they are read by the Speaker's Counsel in the House of Commons, and endeavors to protect public interests and to remove objectionable clauses before the bills come to the Committees. This he does, not through the Committees, but through conferences with the promoters who are practically obliged to comply with his wishes, as the Lord Chairman always moves the third reading of a private bill in the House of Lords and he would refuse to act if the bill were not altered to meet his advice.

Because the House of Lords is less pressed for time, the Government sometimes introduces a few of its less important measures in that House, but this can only be done with success by a Conservative ministry, since the Lords would always amend a Liberal Government bill that displeased them, and no time would be gained. Private Members' Bills fare even worse, since even if such a bill has been passed by the Lords, it stands but little chance of getting through the Commons in the crowded days toward the end of the session. The result is that of the few private Members' Bills enacted each session only about one sixth originate with the peers. Private Bills, however, fare better in the Lords than in the Commons, and the Private Bills Committees of the Upper House are regarded with more favor than those of the Lower, because of their greater experience. The more leisurely House thus is really of great importance to the country in respect to non-political measures which are really vital to the local and general welfare of the nation.

The House of Lords is the remnant of that Great Council of the King which in former days exercised nearly all the functions of government. Traces of all its varied powers remain, although its importance has steadily waned as the power of the Commons has increased. It is still, however, the highest court of appeal for the United Kingdom, except in ecclesiastical cases. Any lord has the right to attend when the House sits as the Court of Appeal, but actually only the Law lords and others who have the necessary legal talent and experience do take part in the Court.

The Relation of the Peers to the Commons. — As a coördinate branch of the legislature, the House of Lords must give its assent to every act of Parliament before it becomes law. Until the passing of the Parliament Act in 1911, the real division of power between the two Houses had not been definitely stated, and repeated struggles over the passage of bills occurred. As early as 1671, the Commons asserted "That, in all aids given to the King, by the Commons, the Rate or Tax ought not to be altered by the Lords." The right of the Lords to amend financial bills was thus early disputed and came gradually to be discarded, although the right of absolutely rejecting a money bill continued to be asserted. The dispute over the paper duties Bill in 1860 led to the inclusion of all taxes in one great measure of Supply, which, it was assumed, the Lords could not reject. The device of "tacking" or adding measures not of a financial nature to privileged financial legislation has at times been attempted by the Commons, but it has been dropped of late years, and various devices for allowing the Lords to express their will in altering money bills have been developed.

In 1909, however, the House of Lords definitely rejected the annual Budget and created a deadlock in legislation which threatened to wreck the very parliamentary system itself. The general election of January, 1910, was fought out very largely on the issue of the Lords' vote, and after the accession of George V (1910–   ) the second general election of 1910 was practically a referendum on the Government and Opposition schemes for reform of the Upper House so as to limit its power. The Government was sustained, and accordingly the Parliament Bill of 1911 passed the House and was submitted to the Lords who passed it, rather than have enough new peers created to carry the Bill through. This act, which had been passed in identical terms by the Commons in 1910 and 1911, recognizes that ultimately a reform in the composition of the Upper Chamber must be effected, but provides for at once removing the absolute veto of the House of Lords. If a Money Bill which has passed the House of Commons and has been sent up to the House of Lords at least one month before the end of the session is not passed by the House of Lords within one month, it may be presented to His Majesty for the Royal Assent and may become an Act of Parliament without the assent of the Lords. The Speaker of the House of Commons is empowered to decide whether a Bill is a Money Bill and whether proposed amendments change its character as a Money Bill.

"If any Public Bill other than a Money Bill . . . is passed by the House of Commons in three successive sessions (whether of the same Parliament or not), and, having been sent up to the House of Lords at least one month before the end of the session, is rejected by the House of Lords in each of those sessions, that bill shall, on its rejection for the third time by the House of Lords, unless the House of Commons direct to the contrary, be presented to his Majesty and become an Act of Parliament on the Royal Assent being signified thereto, notwithstanding that the House of Lords have not consented to the Bill: provided that this provision shall not take effect unless two years have elapsed between the date of the second reading in the first of those sessions of the Bill in the House of Commons and the date on which it passes the House of Commons in the third of those sessions."[1]

The Act also substitutes five for seven years as the maximum duration of a Parliament.

[1] The Parliament Act, 1911, 2. George V.

Relieved of the incubus of a permanently Conservative Upper House with unlimited powers of obstruction, the Liberal Government can now pass its Budget at once and can put through other legislation in from two to four years.

REFERENCES

(See References to Chap. **XXXV**.)

CHAPTER XXXVII

THE MINISTRY IN PARLIAMENT

In the olden time an English king was accustomed to call together the national Assembly, or Parliament, and to deliver before it an address submitting for its approval the policies decided upon and asking for supplies to support the government. Upon their side the members of the Assembly were permitted to present petitions for redress of grievances. Many of the old forms are still followed, but the King's Speech with its presentation of governmental policy has become the program of a political party. The chief items in this program have been for many months, and often for many years, subjects of debate between the parties; some of them have been party issues in the previous election, and the victorious party comes to the Parliament with a mandate from the people to do certain things. Months before the meeting of Parliament in February, the party leaders meet to agree upon measures which they will submit for the action of Parliament, and before the session opens the details of the various bills to be presented have been formulated. The King's Speech is written by the party leaders and the program outlined is presented on behalf of the people.

Relation to People and Parliament. — Each of the ruling parties constantly lays claim to superior wisdom and efficiency in discovering and carrying out the will of the people in respect to all sorts of governmental business. When the people by their votes have given to one party a majority in the House of Commons, the leaders then have an opportunity to make good their claim. At a parliamentary election the voters have in mind the choice of a party leader and his associates, who will form a Government. The people thus virtually elect the Prime Minister and his Cabinet by voting for members of the House. The party is the important factor in the election, the individual member voted for being of minor consequence unless he chance to be a party leader or one of the inner circle who will form the Government.

A responsible Ministry, in the English sense of the term, is a body of men who have come into office under certain pledges, promises, and expectations. They are responsible to the House of Commons. With the support of Parliament they exercise full political power and are also responsible to the people, as an account of their stewardship must be given at a general election within the five years following. Ministers may at any time ask for a new mandate from the people, but as long as they hold office their responsibility is complete because their power is supreme.

Agreement between Parties on Essentials. — The working of the party government is greatly facilitated by the practical coöperation and agreement of the two parties upon the great body of executive and legislative policies. Only in respect to a few questions is there at a given time a serious conflict of opinion. The exigencies of partisan debate, however, tend to exaggerate the differences, while there is nevertheless a real unity and coöperation arising from a common, intelligent interest in the general welfare and a common appreciation of the cabinet system as a unique contribution to the cause of free government. Both parties believe in the system and are willing to make sacrifices for its support. It was noted in the chapter on the executive duties of the Ministry that each party is accustomed to accept in good faith the deliberate acts of Parliament and faithfully to administer laws whose enactment they may have strenuously opposed. Much of the formal controversy in the House of Commons has an air of unreality. The Opposition Party consents to assume the rôle of " devil's advocate " and to say everything that can be said against a Government measure before it goes into effect. The leaders of the parties frankly coöperate in the formation of the Committees of the House and in assigning to them the non-partisan legislation. The larger number of Government Bills pass into law without serious opposition from any quarter. There remain, however, a few questions involving matters of peculiar interest to the constituencies or certain sections of them on which the parties radically differ.

The Prime Minister. — Nearly every member of the House is known as an habitual supporter of the Government or as a supporter of the Opposition, and on each side of the House there is one man who speaks with the authority of his party. On the side of the Government he is the Prime Minister, unless that leader chances to be a peer. With the changed relations of the two Houses following the Act of 1911, it is likely that the Prime Minister will always be in the Lower House, or at least that the leader of the Government in that House will be chief leader of his party. The relation of the Prime Minister to the other members of the Cabinet depends upon the personality of the man and upon the political issues dominant at the time. Other leaders may be equally conspicuous and influential with the official head of the Government, but it is the Prime Minister alone who is in a position to speak for his party with supreme authority. In like manner, the recognized leader of the Opposition is the unquestioned spokesman of his party.

The Cabinet is a thinking machine for the state. The House of Commons has been described as an assembly having more sense than any one of its members. The Cabinet, as a whole, ought to be wiser than any leader, yet actual thinking is an individual operation, and in each Cabinet one man, or a very few men do the chief part of the guiding and directing. All may give counsel; few lead. All must sacrifice individual preference, but some much more than others. If twenty men must present one mind to the public, it is economy of effort to find an individual mind that will meet the requirements. More than half the Ministers are outside the Cabinet though they are equally bound to give loyal support to the Government. They must defend its policy when called upon in Parliament and when they address the public they must take pains to say nothing which will cause it embarrassment. The responsible party leaders think with the public and for the public. They reflect the various shades of opinion in the party and they are open to suggestions from outside. Whether the coördinating and harmonizing of opinion within the Cabinet is the work of one or of many, the result is the same.

Political Problems and Party Issues. — The questions recognized as party issues are those in respect to which opposing parties have already reached contradictory conclusions. A few party issues become so fixed that cabinets are powerless to change them. A Conservative Cabinet must, for example, defend the Established Church and the existing social order. There are, on the other hand, several problems of common public interest which make an identical appeal to the rival parties. For example, the fight against disease is non-partisan. A third class of questions of great public interest remains which are, or may be, highly contentious in their nature, but which have not yet become party issues. These furnish to party leaders the real problem of corporate thinking. Every Cabinet must make up its mind whether to espouse one side or the other of the controversy and thus create a new party issue. Home Rule for Ireland was for a few years a non-partisan matter; then it became partisan by the act of a Liberal Cabinet. In that instance, Gladstone, the Prime Minister, did the thinking for the Government.

The policy of free trade *versus* a policy of protection and especially the proposition to tax food, has long been a subject for sharp conflict in opinion. It was treated as non-partisan until Mr. Chamberlain, as Colonial Secretary in a Tory Cabinet in 1903, outlined a policy of imperial federation which involved a tax on wheat. But Mr. Chamberlain was not the authorized leader of the Government. His utterance, therefore, meant either that the party was already committed to a policy involving a tax on food, or that there was a divided Cabinet. The Prime Minister, Mr. Balfour, assumed a tolerant attitude towards Mr. Chamberlain's program, while yet not wholly committing his party to its adoption. For a time the Cabinet appeared before the country as having two heads, or rather no head at all. The anomalous situation was relieved by the resignation of Mr. Chamberlain. The party, however, was rapidly becoming committed to the policy of protection. After the Liberals had returned to office in 1906, Mr. Bonar Law, a noted protectionist, was made the leader of the opposition. In a public address he definitely pledged his party to a tax on wheat, in case the colonies should wish such a tax. There was an immediate agitation among his supporters in the House of Commons; the members were hearing from their constituents. A paper was signed by nearly every private member in the House, defining the party position on the policy of protection in such a way as to exclude, for the time at least, a tax on food. These facts exhibit with unusual distinctness the English methods for attaining party harmony upon a new and divisive issue. The Liberals had a similar experience in dealing with the question of women's suffrage. Cabinet officers were known to hold opposing views on the subject. Promises were made to the suffragists which could not be fulfilled. To conciliate those who were offended the Cabinet promised to give the right of way to a private bill granting the vote to women.

It is apparent that the real balance of the Constitution comes more and more to rest with the two ruling parties in their attitude towards the conflicting and divisive interests of the public. The parties are the two eyes which enable the state to see the two sides of important questions; the two hands which may work together to fulfill accepted common needs; the two feet enabling the body politic to advance step by step. There is a constant shifting of support from one party to the other in the outside public, and this tendency is reflected in the House of Commons.

The Relation of Leaders to their Supporters. — Within the House leaders and followers act and react upon one another, while the opposing parties maintain a continuous duel. On the Government side three distinct elements appear, the Cabinet, the Ministers not in the Cabinet, and the private members. The Cabinet alone determines the policy, the other ministers being only official and salaried supporters. The entire Ministry, however, acts as a unit; its members stand or fall together. The private members of Parliament who usually support the Government are the ones to determine whether the Ministry shall stand or fall. If the Government has a majority of a hundred, fifty members may cause a cabinet crisis by voting with the Opposition. Yet the fifty who thus act cannot govern. They either make themselves subject to the leaders of the other party or they secure a new election which may, perchance, change the policy of their own party. On all party questions, the Ministry usually has against it the entire opposition party, and on some of the party issues it may incur the opposition of some of its habitual supporters. The determinate action of the House is thus in the hands of a few government supporters. Private members may criticize the Government respecting a distinctively cabinet policy, but this is not permitted to a member of the Ministry. The power of the House as contrasted with that of the Cabinet rests with the conduct of private members. In a sense, the Cabinet guides, directs, and controls the House of Commons. The House also guides, directs, and controls the Cabinet; but the House can only act in a rough, crude, and destructive way. It cannot really govern without at the same time submitting to ministerial control.

The Opposition in the House is also subject to constant stress and to tendencies toward readjustment between the leaders and their followers. Some are in danger of being won over by attractive government policies, or they may give support to some specific plan which the "Shadow Cabinet" opposes. It is, however, much easier for the Opposition than for the party in power to keep its followers together. They can more easily conceal their discordant views. They are not subject to a daily questioning and a constant fire of criticism on matters for which they are held responsible. Yet even in opposition, a party has need of a positive program. Elections are not usually carried on mere criticism and negation. The case just cited of the Tory party's attitude towards a tax on food is an illustration in point. The Opposition experienced a party crisis, and the same sort of sharp line of distinction was drawn between leaders and followers as subsists, on the Government side, between ministers and private members. Twenty-seven of the members of the Opposition were not asked to sign the petition to the party leaders, because it was deemed not good form for one member of the opposition Bench to petition another.

Two Ruling Parties and Minor Groups. — In theory the English system provides for two parties and only two. It is assumed that the voters and the country at large will find their way in matters of government by the use of two competing organizations. But no government ever works in practice in strict harmony with a definite theory. There is always a tendency to form more than two parties. In all countries outside of the British Empire where cabinet government prevails, there are numerous parties and cabinets supported by a number of parties which have agreed to stand together for the carrying out of a prescribed program. In England this tendency to form numerous party groups has for the most part been kept within the lines of the two governing parties.

The most formidable attack thus far made upon the system came from the Irish Nationalists under the leadership of Mr. Parnell. Eighty-seven members who resolutely stand together in opposition to both parties are able to destroy or paralyze the system. This condition arose in 1885. Neither party could gain a majority large enough to overcome the Irish opposition. The Liberals effected an affiliation with the Nationalists by yielding to their demand for Home Rule for Ireland. This led to a division in the party, and a separate Liberal-Unionist Party was organized, which acted with the Conservatives in their resistance to Home Rule. The balance was thus restored to the ruling parties, but each was now composed of two distinct sections. By a long process of party adjustment, the Unionists and Conservatives have become fused in a single organization having a variety of names, as Unionist, Conservative, Tory,[1] Constitutionalist. A similar process has been in progress in the other party, but the fusion is less perfect. The Nationalists organized for a single purpose and with the attainment of that end the reason for its existence ceases.

The case is different with the Labor Party. It arose to give support to permanent policies of government which affect the interests of the wage-earning class. The "Laborites" profess to be equally ready to coöperate with either of the old parties. They have no intention of aspiring to become a ruling party, but only maintain an independent position for a group of members in order to make their demands more effective. During the Asquith ministry (1910–) the members supported the Liberal Government, while the Conservatives were bidding for their favor. If parties of this type should become numerous, they would tend to change the English into the Continental type of cabinet government.

The King's Speech and Vote of Censure. — As already explained in the chapter on the House of Commons, much of the non-partisan legislation in Parliament is remanded to the various committees, and nearly all the time of the House is devoted to a duel between the two parties over the contentious policies of

[1] The word "Tory" as the name of an English party carries with it no stigma such as the term acquired in America at the time of the Revolution. It is an ancient and

government. The party program as outlined in the King's Speech is attacked by the Opposition and two weeks or more devoted to criticism of the various measures proposed.[1] Attractive substitute measures may be brought forward and the Government is forced to carry a majority of the House against them or to resign office or dissolve Parliament.

In February, 1885, Mr. Jesse Collins introduced a resolution expressing regret that the Government had not included in their program a measure to provide allotments of land for agricultural laborers. The resolution was carried: Parliament was immediately dissolved and there was an appeal to the country over the question described in party parlance as "three acres and a cow" for farm laborers. The address in reply to the King's Speech cannot be amended by an opposition vote. Such a vote is a notice to the Government to surrender to the Opposition. Any member of the House may produce a cabinet crisis by carrying a vote to amend the reply to the King's Speech.

There is another form of the vote of censure which, if carried, is fatal to the continuance of the Government. In this case the Leader of the Opposition moves a vote of want of confidence in the ministry. The Government must defeat such a motion or immediately resign or dissolve Parliament.

Cabinet on the Defensive. — With the improved discipline of the supporters of the Government and the increased efficiency in the organization of the parties these direct attacks are less formidable. In fact, they make it easy for the Government to muster its full strength in an impressive manner. What really tries the life of a Cabinet is the effect of the divisions on doubtful questions; the defects in their bills revealed in debate; the amendments which they are induced or forced to accept; the perpetual criticism from a trained and alert Opposition. The Government may incur defeat on a minor issue without serious injury, but in all such cases the Opposition will call for a resignation. Through a partisan press, the public is notified that the Government is on its last legs. Repeated defeat does rapidly weaken the position of the Government; hence it behooves it always to have at hand a majority on all divisions however

honorable name of a great party and in recent years its use has been revived in the phrase Tory Democracy.

[1] Lowell, "The Government of England," Vol. I, p. 308.

trivial. Occasionally the Opposition takes the Government by surprise. A time is chosen when few members are present and enough voters are spirited in through concealed entrances to the House to defeat the Cabinet. An amendment to the Home Rule Bill was thus carried in 1912. The Government was then hard pressed for time to complete its program and the Prime Minister gave notice that he would simply rescind the action of the "snap" majority and proceed with the Bill. To do this, involved a radical change in a long-standing custom of the House, the removal of one more check upon "hasty legislation." In the instance mentioned the Opposition prevented this action by means of riot and disorder. The Government was forced or induced to follow the old custom of framing a new amendment which virtually destroyed the effect of the one carried by the snap vote; but this consumed a week of precious time.

It is economy on the part of the Government never to lose its hold on its majority, never to be taken off guard. It is likewise good politics for the Opposition to keep its supporters well in hand; but with the Government this is a necessity if pledges are to be fulfilled.

Party Whips. — The Party Whips and their assistants are the chief agencies for marshaling the forces of the contending armies. Four salaried officers in the Ministry serve as whips, while the corresponding officers for the Opposition act without salary or are paid out of party funds. The Whips are in the Ministry, but not in the Cabinet; they take no part in debate. The Chief Whip may be promoted to a place in the Cabinet or rewarded with a peerage. With his numerous aids and assistants, the Chief Whip fills a place scarcely less essential to the working of the system than that of the Prime Minister himself. He serves as eyes and ears for his leader, who must be kept informed as to the various movements among his followers in Parliament. He needs also to be informed as to tendencies among the voters. On such questions, the Whip speaks with authority. He is a trained politician of the first order. He not only knows how to report public opinion, but, in a successful party, he is master of the various devices for the direction of public attention to partisan ends. He knows who among the leaders of his party make a favorable impression on the public, and for these he may furnish occasions for frequent public appearances.

There may be a public ceremonial function which apparently has no connection with politics, yet an alert Whip may seek to have the right man in his party selected to preside. Prizes are to be distributed to young people who will soon be voters and the Whip sees an advantage in having the embryo voter receive the prize at the hands of a prominent party leader or a member of his family. The Whips are not themselves leaders; they do not formulate or create public opinion; but they see to it that available sources of opinion or influence are directed to the strengthening of their party.

The relation of the parliamentary Whips to local party agents is described in the chapter on party organization. At present we are concerned with their principal work, which pertains to the House of Commons. By means of these officers the leaders keep their hands on their supporters. On all party divisions the Whips act as tellers. The leaders have an artificial way of indicating to their followers how to vote. If the leaders do not request the Chairman to appoint their Whips as tellers, he will select tellers from private members. This is an indication that members are to vote as they please.

The word "Whip" has two distinct meanings. The term is derived from the "Whipper-in" at the fox hunt, and is applied, by analogy, to the men who round up the party supporters on Government divisions. The message by which this is effected is also called a "whip." All the members receive these notices to be present at a given time. If there is a question of doubt as to the party standing of a member, the "whip" itself solves the doubt. All are members who receive the notice. The Irish and Labor parties have their separate Whips who send "whips" to their members. Nearly all members of the House are thus officially recognized as belonging to one of the parties, and are classified as supporters or opponents of the Government. A simple notice means that it is highly desirable that the member should be present. A "whip" underscored means increased urgency; underscored with four black lines it is a notice to be present on penalty of being accounted a traitor to the party. The Whips are gifted with powers of persuasion. They make personal appeals to refractory members. They dispense party patronage and administer party funds. Loyal voting constituencies may be called upon to "whip" in a member who is in danger of going astray. Among the members of the Ministry, the Prime Minister is the chief party disciplinarian; among private members this duty devolves upon the Chief Whip.

The Relation of the Ministry to Finance. — The fusion of the legislative and executive departments is well exemplified in the management of the finances. This business has always been largely, and is now completely, monopolized by the House of Commons. Under rules adopted early in the eighteenth century all matters pertaining to the spending of money and the raising of revenues are considered in Committee of the Whole. Thus the House vindicates its right to be informed as to the details of financial policies, but the business itself is retained in ministerial hands. In Committee of the Whole on Supply all the information comes from the heads of departments in the Ministry; there is no way for a private member to be heard in favor of any appropriation not included in the ministerial reports. Likewise, when the House is in Committee of Ways and Means, every item in the measures for raising revenue comes from the Crown. By long-standing rule private members are forbidden to introduce any petition or bill involving an increased charge upon the revenues. A private member may, however, propose a reduction of taxation along lines not included in the Government program.

Finance, then, is emphatically a cabinet business. The House may ask questions; it may criticize; it may refuse assent; but it may not initiate any important change in the ministerial policy. While the House is in Committee of Supply it is quite in order for the Leaders of the Opposition or any private member to expose any weak point in the administration of the particular department under consideration. Thus the departments, one by one, are brought under public notice and an opportunity is offered for the exposure of delinquencies.

The Chancellor of the Exchequer is the efficient head of the Treasury. He receives from all the departments the estimates of expenditures for the fiscal year ending March 31. These are considered and compared, and from them a careful estimate is made of the aggregate expenditure. The Treasury officers likewise make an estimate of the revenues of the state. Upon the basis of the estimated needs for the fiscal year and the income from permanent revenues the Chancellor of the Exchequer formulates such modifications in the taxing system as seem best. The appropriations for the various departments and the changes in the system of taxation are all embodied in one project of legislation. This is known as the Annual Budget. In it is often embodied the most important legislation for the year.

The contrast with the government at Washington is evident. There large expenditures are made upon the irresponsible initiative of private members who may wish to supply a friend with a pension or a town in their district with a public building. Supplies are awarded to the departments through a half dozen or more unrelated committees. Taxes are levied with only incidental reference to the annual expenditures. The separation of the Executive from the legislature makes fiscal control more complex and more difficult.

REFERENCES

ANSON. *Law and Custom of the Constitution*, Vol. I, Chaps. VIII, IX.
DUPRIEZ. *Les Ministres dans les principaux pays d'Europe et d'Amerique*, Edition 1893.
HEARN. *The Government of England*, Chaps. VI, VII, IX.
LOWELL. *The Government of England*, Vol. I, Chaps. XVII, XVIII.
MEDLEY. *The English Constitution*, Edition 1898, Chap. VI.
OGG. *The Governments of Europe*, Chap. III.

CHAPTER XXXVIII

THE CROWN

THE parties govern with little reference to the Crown; nevertheless there is a king in England. No institution seems more firmly established than the monarchy. Coincident with the advent of democracy the Crown has grown more popular. How could England be England without a royal family? That democracy excludes monarchy is a crude notion arising from a false analysis of government. Democracy is not a mere form of government, it is a principle inhering in every form; it may assume many forms. The term "monarchy" does stand for a particular form of government; but the form admits of infinite adaptations to every grade of popular control.

Monarchies Classified. — Between the absolute monarchy, in which all power is conceded to the person of the monarch, and the complete democracy, in which all power is conceded to the voting constituency, there are unlimited varieties in governmental mechanism. It may be helpful to an understanding of the subject to reduce all monarchies to four classes: viz., Absolute, Limited or Constitutional Monarchy, Parliamentary, and Democratic Monarchy.[1] Of the first, autocracy or absolute monarchy, Russia has been the standing exemplification, but with the establishment of the Duma there ensued a transition to the second class, viz., Limited Monarchy. England was from the first a limited monarchy. There was always an assembly which participated in government. England became a Parliamentary Monarchy in the Revolution of 1688. The person of the monarch then ceased to be the chief source of authority. The Crown became subject to the Assembly. Ministers of state became responsible to Parliament. In a limited, or constitutional monarchy, the assembly exerts an influence, it may be at times a controlling influence, over the monarch. In a parlia-

[1] Seignobos, "A Political History of Contemporary Europe," Vol. I, p. 117.

mentary monarchy the monarch exerts an influence over parliament; at times he may even exert a controlling influence, yet the governmental center of gravity remains with the assembly. In the democratic Monarchy all this is changed; both the Crown and the Parliament become subject to the will of the enfranchised nation. Since 1832 England has gradually changed from parliamentary to democratic monarchy. Those who had been rulers became servants of the public. Autocracy does exclude democracy; monarchy does not. Norway is an intelligent, fully enfranchised democracy, yet Norway deliberately adopted monarchy without abating one whit of its democracy.

Royal Aid to Free Government. — English devotion to monarchy is not based upon blind, unreasoning sentiment, but rather upon an intelligent comprehension of the facts of history. The story is already told in the chapter on local government. Saxon kings wrought with the people in securing to them the enjoyment of local liberties. Normans and Plantagenets defended them against feudal tyrants. High-monarchy Tudors rid the country of civil war and subjected lords and bishops to parliamentary rule. The reaction against the innovating Stuarts led to the subjection of the Crown also to parliamentary rule. In 1832, when the time had come for the first great act of enfranchisement, the House of Lords stood like a stone wall athwart the path of progress. In this emergency it was the king who made it possible to take the step without a bloody revolution. William IV gave to the Prime Minister the written statement that, in case the peers again refused to pass the bill for extending the franchise, he would create enough new peers to pass it. Again, in 1911, the obstruction of the hereditary House was removed by the simple announcement of the Prime Minister that, in case of further refusal to pass the pending bill, the king would be advised to create new peers. Four monarchs in succession, their reigns covering the entire period of the enfranchisement, have learned to coöperate with and assist the servants of the people. It is, therefore, a mark of intelligence as well as of right sentiment for the democracy to approve of the monarchy.

Relation of Crown to Cabinet. — The Cabinet system requires that there shall be an executive head above the party leaders who shall mediate between the parties. If there is not a king, then there must be a president or some other officer. The Prime

Minister represents a party, not the entire state. There must be an executive head who represents the state.

The mere formal act of receiving the resignation of a defeated Prime Minister and sending for the leader of the victorious party and asking him to form a new ministry is a necessary and an important service. But there are times when no party has a clear majority; times when, within the party, there is confusion in leadership. At such times it may become the duty of the king to act upon his own judgment, to take a personal share in bringing order out of confusion. Lowell gives four instances in which Queen Victoria determined by her personal choice who should be Prime Minister.[1] A fifth instance, in 1890, illustrates another phase of royal service. The Queen first sent for Lord Hartington, who was nominal head of the party; but Gladstone, who had retired a few years before, had resumed actual leadership. Hence it became the duty of the Queen to give effect to the changed condition by making Gladstone Prime Minister.[2] All these services are indispensable. Within the parties and between the parties conditions are constantly arising which may call into play the personal exercise of royal prerogative. So long as the cabinet system works according to the theory of the modern super-legal Constitution, executive power rests with the inner circle of the Ministry. The monarch himself is a distinctly subordinate minister to the Cabinet. He does what he is told to do. But if the machinery is out of order, if there is an actual or a threatened deadlock in government, there at once ensues a tendency to revert to the earlier Constitution, and the monarch, from his vantage ground of an experienced, non-partisan observer, may call the ministers to his aid to restore the government to its normal condition.

Changed Relations to the Democratic Cabinet. — Bagehot, writing in the late sixties of the last century, has much to say of the rights of the monarch to be informed as to contemplated ministerial policies and the possibility of his securing a modification or a change of policy by his advice and council.[3] The government was then parliamentary but not democratic. Under the more recent democratic Constitution, it is no longer desirable

---

[1] "The Government of England," Vol. I, p. 34.
[2] Morley, "Life of Gladstone," Vol. II, Chap. VII.
[3] Bagehot, "The English Constitution," Chap. III.

that the monarch shall be informed in advance as to the cabinet policies in order that he may advise or warn or in any way seek to change the policy. It is enough that the Cabinet meet the demands of their new masters, the people. Only harm and confusion and waste of energy are likely to result from any sort of royal interference with the partisan cabinet policies. Queen Victoria was in many ways an ideal parliamentary monarch, but there is evidence that much royal energy was worse than wasted because she did not understand the changes involved in the transition to a democratic monarchy.

The usefulness of the monarch in his relation to the democratic Cabinet consists in his remaining entirely aloof from everything partisan. The Cabinet should formulate its policy without advice or influence from the Crown, and royal approval should follow as a matter of course. Disraeli was at one time rightly reproved for presenting to the Crown a choice of policies. It is unfair thus to bring the monarch into contentious politics. So long as the parties work normally, the Crown has nothing to do but to let them work. It is, however, desirable that the monarch be informed as to the difficulties and the exigencies of party politics, so that in case royal interference is needed, it may be given intelligently. In some respects the position of the king resembles that of the permanent under secretary whose duties require him to serve with equal faithfulness the party chiefs of each party. The secretary assists in overcoming party difficulties in respect to the minor details of administration. If the king takes no share in any partisan policy, unless a threatening emergency has arisen, then he may act with authority in such a way as to command general acquiescence. It was a serious question in 1910 whether the Crown was justified in forcing the peers to pass the measure depriving them of the power of veto. The chief object of the general election had been to test the will of the electors on that question. The monarch then expressed a willingness to act upon the advice of his ministers in the matter of the creation of new peers. The House of Lords yielded, and the controversy was at an end.

The fact that the monarch has no share in ordinary party government by no means detracts from his field of usefulness. We have seen that, at any given time, only a few questions are the subjects of party controversy. In this narrow field, party leaders have a monopoly. The wide field of national life is still open to the royal family. The warfare against disease has never been partisan. King Edward VII took an active and intelligent interest in the fight against cancer. The encouragement of agriculture and other lines of industrial improvement are fit subjects for royal activity. Members of the royal family are especially in demand at public functions, such as the opening of a school or a library, the dedication of a monument. They are active in works of charity. Outside of the narrow field of party politics, the opportunities for service are unlimited.

Foreign Affairs. — The relation of the Crown to foreign affairs has been especially close and intimate. The two houses of Parliament have no share in the making of treaties. Legally the business is in the hands of the King in Council. Constitutionally it belongs to the responsible Government of the day. But in the middle of the last century the monarch was still active in foreign affairs. For instance, the Queen and the Prince Consort modified the dispatches sent to America at the beginning of the Civil War in such a way as to avoid war. Such business now would rest entirely with the Cabinet; the monarch would not be personally involved. By being entirely separated from the controversial side of foreign relations, the monarch may now be even more useful in facilitating right international conduct. It is understood that King Edward was signally efficient in removing friction and promoting a good understanding in the relation of England to France and to the other states of Europe. The feeling of Europe towards England does not involve personal censure of the Crown as the corresponding sentiment towards Germany involves censure of the Emperor. The latter is the object of censure because of specific personal acts, such as the dispatch to Kruger at the time of the Jameson Raid in the Transvaal. The King of England can be under no such censure, although, knowing the mind and temper of his Ministers, he has unrivaled opportunities for securing for them favorable hearing in other states.

Democratic Monarchy is of very recent origin. England is still in the midst of the transition; the work of political enfranchisement is not yet completed, a considerable number of the male adults being still debarred from the privilege of voting, while the voting privileges of women are much restricted.

Property enjoys an excess of privilege which gives to a few landholders enough votes to change the result of a close election. The House of Lords has been deprived of much of its former power, but it is yet to be reconstructed so as to harmonize with the accepted Democracy. The House of Commons is overworked and relief is sought by a proposed devolution of power upon provincial legislatures. These are all questions which have to do with the mere mechanism of government involved in the transition to democracy. To describe a democratic monarchy, then, involves the description of an institution which is in the process of making. No state thus far exhibits a perfected example.

The Crown as a Disguise. — Bagehot, writing more than forty years ago, gave as a chief function of the monarchy to serve as a disguise, a source of deception to the masses of the people, causing them to think that they were cared for by a beneficent royal family, while in fact they were governed by party leaders. Bagehot wrote under the impression that monarchy was likely to decline with the rise of democracy, and he feared that with the decline of monarchy, free government was in danger of losing the Cabinet system which he regarded as vastly superior to the Presidential system. He argued that, even if monarchy should fail, it was still possible to continue the Cabinet with an elected President. Monarchy, however, since that time has continuously grown more popular and the people, whose advent to power Bagehot looked upon with fear and dread, are in no need of a dignified institution to humbug them into a belief that they are governed by processes which they do not understand. It has now become evident that it was Bagehot himself that was under a delusion as to the services of the Crown as a disguise. The common people have apparently been quite correct in their opinions as to how they were governed.

As a Symbol of Unity. — Much more fortunate is Bagehot's designation of the Crown as the symbol of unity, the object of patriotic sentiment. The King personates the state. Loyalty to a person worthily fulfilling such a mission is different in the sentiment involved from loyalty to a flag or to a temporary President; but monarchy is not at all essential to a strong and persistent sentiment of loyalty. Probably no state has ever existed which has more sentimental patriotism than has Switzerland to-day. The sentiment may exist and abound without a person or a personating head. Yet, if the state has a personal office of this sort associated with a thousand years of fortunate history, it is an asset of considerable advantage. Americans cultivate a sentiment of loyalty towards the stars and stripes, but it is a sentiment created by effort, by association; it does not arise naturally as does the sentiment towards a royal family. Americans give the personal touch to their patriotism by making of George Washington a patron saint and a symbol of unity in the early day, and of Abraham Lincoln a savior and a deliverer in the critical middle period of our history. Patriotism is assisted by a personation of the state. This is one great function of the English Crown and it seems as helpful to this end under the democracy as under the high-monarchy Tudors.

The royal family has been and continues to be an important factor in binding together the different parts of the empire. Scotland and England, after centuries of war, became united through a branch of the royal family. Edward I (1272-1307) conquered Wales and conciliated the people by presenting to them the new-born heir to the throne as "Prince of Wales." This ceremony continues to be repeated and the Crown has no more loyal subjects than the Welsh. It is a thousand pities that there was not early found a "Prince of Ireland" also. The royal family has neglected Ireland to the lasting detriment of the country. It is significant that during recent democratic days, royal neglect of Ireland has been recognized and efforts made to repair the injury.

The service of the Crown is not less apparent in its relation to the outlying possessions and dominions. Victoria was made Empress of India to promote loyalty and strengthen the hands of the Empire. Members of the royal family visit this great possession for the same purpose. This is a reasonable adaptation of means to an end, though the results may not be easily measured. There is, however, no uncertainty about the relation of the Crown to the Dominion of Canada. The Canadians are intensely loyal, after both the sentimental and the rational manner. The sentiment is based upon the realization of what they believe to be a superior form of democratic government. Instead of the king they have in Canada a member of the royal family or some other statesman who serves as a non-partisan executive head. He fulfills for Canada the functions of the king in England, and the political parties govern as they do in England. Canadian loyalty has grown out of a conviction that the English Cabinet system fulfills the needs of the Dominion better than any other government. A similar condition prevails both in Australia and New Zealand, dominions thoroughly democratic and self-governing in all domestic affairs, yet bound to the British Crown by hoops of steel. In South Africa there are Dutchmen (Boers) who a few years ago hated the English as implacable conquerors and enemies. But the chief of the Boers, as Prime Minister of the Union of South Africa, became a loyal subject of the British Crown. This is not a blind, unreasoning sentiment, but a reasonable recognition of favors received. It is as the head of a group of self-governing democracies that the monarchy of England is attaining its greatest glory.

All, therefore, which Bagehot said of the service of the Crown as an object of patriotic sentiment remains in force when applied to the democratic monarchy. The same is true of the services of the royal family as exemplars of morality and religion. The publicity demanded by democracy tends to realize in the royal family a fulfillment of ideal domestic virtues. The self-conscious and enduring democracy will see to it that those who are born to the office of the head of the state shall be trained to the right fulfillment of the duties of the office. Abundant opportunity is offered in the non-partisan public service to make it easy and convenient to combine theory and practice in the training of the members of the royal family.

A standing argument against Democracy is the apparent absurdity of depending upon a chance majority of an ignorant and untrained mob to decide intricate questions of statesmanship. American State and Federal Constitutions are considered mere mechanisms to enable the few to rule, despite the temporary preferences of a majority of the people. The English Cabinet system, however, has had the effect of committing the Tory party, the party of reaction and conservatism, to the advocacy of immediate direct and unchecked democracy; to the policy of deciding the intricate questions at issue between the parties by a direct vote of the people.[1] The Radical party in

[1] Cf. "The Problem of Democracy and the Swiss Solution," in the *Edinburgh Review*, Vol. 218, pp. 257-277, January, 1913.

England can scarcely afford to be less democratic than their opponents. For the first time in human history, a great empire is pledged to a policy of immediate, direct, and unchecked popular rule. This position has been reached not through actual belief in the principles of democracy, but by a process of exclusion by a forced choice between policies regarded as evils.

Government by Unanimous Consent. — The Monarchy gives institutional expression to a complete refutation of the chief argument against democracy. It is an observed fact that loyalty to the Crown is practically unanimous. We have here a demonstration that a democracy may be unanimous on one important subject. The English Crown has always stood for an indefinite range of powers. The Cabinet is coming to be associated with a narrow range of the few policies which are under dispute. Here, then, are two institutions exemplifying two lines of governmental business — the field of unanimous consent and the field of controversy. It is the common concern of all patriots to enlarge the field of general agreement and to narrow that of controversy. So long as the principle of democracy was under dispute the Crown, on account of past associations, was reduced to its lowest terms. To establish democracy, the Cabinet, at least in theory, had to make good its claim to plenary powers. But with democracy conceded, there is nothing in the way of extending the services of the monarchy in the growing field of non-partisan conduct. This is a unique service of the Crown in a new and untried form of government — that of giving institutional expression to the unity of the state.

Education as a Means of Securing Public Servants. — Closely allied to this is another lesson which the democracy needs to learn; namely, that there are other ways of securing reliable public servants besides the method of nomination and election. The royal family are born, educated, and trained to the service of the state. This principle admits of indefinite extension. Democracy in the past has been militant. It has been forced to fight for existence, forced to elect full-grown fighting men, men often abounding in obvious defects and imperfections. But with the end of warfare, a new spirit will ensue. Education and training will hold a larger place in the determining of position in the service of the state. It is said that in some of the Swiss communes where democratic forms are comparatively old, some families choose and follow official life much as others follow watchmaking or agriculture.[1] The experienced democracy will avail itself of heredity, natural aptitude, education and training in public life as well as in private industry.

Members of the royal family in England have been trained to service in the army and navy. This arises from the close hereditary association between the Crown and public defense and from the fact that in the crude beginnings of democracy, militarism strikes the fancy of the public. In the experienced democracy, this will be changed. The education of the future king will be in the line of his actual services to the state. These pertain primarily to the solution of problems which arise in party government. As a non-partisan arbiter between parties, he needs to be well informed in the details of the party system. Much more to the purpose would it be to place the heir apparent and the heir presumptive under the tutelage of a board of under secretaries than under the orders of a military captain. It is no part of the duties of a democratic king either to obey orders or to give orders. His high mission is to assist in discovering and giving adequate expression to the will of the people. A properly educated monarch would know when and where to proffer his services and many a wasteful party crisis would be forestalled. The Crown, as has been pointed out, naturally gives emphasis to the agreements between the parties. The trained monarch would coöperate intelligently with the leaders of both parties in securing efficiency. The very process of educating the future king would tend to improve the civil service. Training for the office concentrates attention of all parties on agreed methods of improving the service. The trained monarch would unite with party leaders in directing the education of the future permanent officials. The natural result of this would be to secure to the cabinet system the economies of a bureaucracy without sacrificing the advantages of suggestion and criticism from rival party leaders who are alternately heads of the departments. The system itself would tend to define and restrict the limits of partisan controversy to the few questions in respect to which there is real, widespread difference of opinion. Even in respect to the few questions of doubtful policy the important advantage

[1] Lowell, " Governments and Parties in Continental Europe," Vol. II, pp. 225 and 226.

to the state rests not upon the assumption that the majority is necessarily correct in its decisions, but upon the assured educational advantages derived from the attempt to settle doubtful policies by securing a majority. Undoubtedly, a majority may prove to be mistaken, but so long as the state rests for its stability on unanimous agreement in most things, a majority of but one comes by so much nearer the ideal. No better way has ever been discovered or suggested for obtaining a working basis for action on the few questions which are in themselves doubtful. The method of obtaining majorities ought to be such as tends to secure unanimous agreement. Getting majorities by free and fair debate has such a tendency. The democratic monarchy has an advantage over other forms of free government in that it tends to draw a distinct line between the agreed and the controverted policies of government.

Different Systems Compared. — Comparison between the French and the English forms of cabinet government is more fully discussed in a later chapter. It may be in order to state here that if an elected president takes the place of the hereditary monarch, there are both gains and losses incident to the change. The president, it may be assumed, is a man of experience, a leading statesman chosen to dedicate several years of his mature manhood to the public service. The system ought to yield a uniformly high standard of ability in the office. The occupant has also had experience in dealing with men on equal terms. On the other hand it is much more difficult for the president to be non-partisan or to be regarded as non-partisan. If the Prime Minister, a party leader, is made President by party votes in the legislature, partisan association inevitably goes with him into the higher office. Whatever advantage there is in the royal family as an object of patriotism and as both a sentimental and a practical bond of union in the state is largely sacrificed in the case of the temporarily elected chief. The American Executive furnishes no ready means of distinguishing between partisan and non-partisan policies. The President is party leader, Prime Minister, and King all in one person.

The Relation of the King to Parliament. — The time-honored phrase "The King in Parliament" has become an empty form of words in the evolution of the democratic monarchy. The King has practically nothing to do with Parliament, though ancient forms are still scrupulously observed. The crowning of the monarch is a parliamentary ceremony; Parliament prescribes the coronation oath. The ceremony of calling, proroguing, and dissolving Parliament by royal order remains unchanged. The monarch enters the throne prepared for him in the House of Lords and reads the " King's Speech " to the two Houses at the opening of Parliament. All these are survivals of ceremonies which once marked the close relation of the King to the Legislature. There is no law nor is there an established rule of the Constitution which debars the monarch from suggesting changes in a cabinet program, yet the " king's speech " is written by the Cabinet, and the ministers alone are responsible for every item. The monarch, in common with every subject, has the right to request a modification of the laws. It is understood that the coronation oath was modified at the request of George V. But supreme lawmaking power now rests with the Cabinet in Parliament and the Constitution consigns the monarch to a subordinate position.

Queen Anne (1702-1714) was the last ruler who refused to sign a bill passed by the two Houses. There has been no change in legal form, yet executive veto has entirely disappeared. The Cabinet takes the place formerly held by the King. Executive assent is assumed in every measure introduced by the Government. The Ministry controls legislation. It may effectively arrest or veto any measure it chooses during the process of enactment. But when a bill has passed the final stage in Parliament, royal assent follows as a mere clerical act.

It has already been made evident that the monarch has no connection with the Judiciary. The police and the courts of law, formerly agents of royal power, are now far removed from any sort of influence from the Crown. Through the Home Secretary, the Cabinet exercises the pardoning power and directs the conduct of the police. Through the Lord Chancellor, judicial appointments are made and judicial procedure modified.

The Supreme Service of the Crown. — With all its limitations, the Crown fills a useful and important place in the cabinet system. It is false and misleading to call the monarch a mere figurehead. He is the real Head of the nation. At any moment it may become his transcendent duty to exercise supreme power in the name of and with the authority of the democracy. With all the people united in loyalty to the Crown, political parties may with comparative safety indulge in a great variety of disruptive conflicts. Party leaders enter the lists conscious of a visible special Providence whose services may be invoked to prevent irretrievable disaster. It is almost treason to suggest such a thing, yet it is a fact that the old prerevolutionary Constitution of the Stuart monarchs still survives. Every form has been religiously preserved. If the occasion required it, these forms would admit of being vitalized and the earlier Constitution might by reversion become again the actual Constitution. Such a thing could never be thought of unless a condition has been reached which would call for a dictator. But this background of history is fitted to give courage both to the royal family and to the radical democratic leaders in the work of perfecting a system of government which will meet all the demands of a government of the people, by the people, and for the people.

REFERENCES

ANSON. *Law and Custom of the Constitution*, Vol. II, I–III.
BAGEHOT. *The English Constitution*, Edition 1904, Chaps. III, IV.
HEARN. *The Government of England*.
LEE. *Queen Victoria*, A Biography.
LOWELL. *The Government of England*, Vol. I, Chaps. I, II.
OGG. *The Governments of Europe*, Chaps. I–III.
Queen Victoria's Letters (Editors, Benson & Esher, three Vols., 1909).

CHAPTER XXXIX

Origin of Political Parties

Political parties are found in all free states. Even in a despotism there are rival factions contending for power. States pass from the rule of a despot to the rule of the people through the medium of voluntary organizations which appeal for support to the people. The party may be defined as an organ of public opinion directed to political ends. Parties then are a necessary agency in all states in which public opinion is recognized as a factor in government.

Various Uses of the Term. — States may be divided into two main classes with reference to their relation to party: first, those in which permanent party organizations assume control of the government, and, second, those in which parties do not govern, but simply influence the government. England and the United States illustrate party government with two ruling parties as an integral part of the government. In the United States the party organizations are legally recognized and, in the States, regulated by statutes. In England, parties are constitutionally recognized in such a way as to place party rules above the law. America and England exemplify two radically different types of responsible party government.

Outside of the Anglo-Saxon world, it is difficult to find any state in which permanent "institutional" party government prevails. In France, Italy, and other states, where some features of the cabinet system are found, legislative majorities are maintained by temporary party coalitions. The permanent parties influence but do not control government. In Switzerland, where democracy has arisen directly out of local communes and cantons, a so-called political party maintains a majority in the national legislature, but it does not presume to govern in the English or the American sense of the term.

Like everything vital in the English Constitution, the party has its roots deep in past history. After 1066, two peoples,

English and French, lived in the Island, representing two diverse systems of government. For three hundred years two languages were spoken, and it was much more than three hundred years before the ideals of local liberty prevailed against innovating foreign rule. All that has been said in previous chapters on local government, the origin of the Crown, the House of Lords, the House of Commons, and the courts of law, is contributory to an understanding of the origin of parties. Every line of that history is an integral part of the history of the rise of responsible party government.

The charter of liberties of Henry I (1110–1135) marks a great triumph of the English faction over the French. The *curia regis* of Henry I (1154–1189) and his compact system of local government appeared for the time a death blow to the French feudal party. When feudal lords drew their swords on behalf of English liberty and compelled King John to sign Magna Charta, 1215, they won another great triumph of the English over the French faction. For two hundred and sixty years after Magna Charta continuous actual or threatened civil war prevailed. Dukes and earls were pitted against one another and contended for the control of the government. This was not party government; it was not primarily government by appeal to public opinion; but it was analogous to party government in that for a long time it did involve a fairly equal balance between two contending factions; it did compel continuous attention to political questions on the part of a large body of the citizens. Moreover, the class which, united, would have been most dangerous to liberty was divided and weakened; and one other effect of the centuries of conflict and war was to call into existence an experienced middle class in the counties and cities, who were capable of withstanding the later encroachments of royal despotism.

As noted in former chapters, the Tudor rulers, relying upon the support of the middle and lower classes of the people, made an end of civil war and brought the unruly factions under the dominion of the courts. Then the middle-class folk in county and city, with the House of Commons as a chief agency, supplemented for a few years by an army under Cromwell, made the Crown subject to Parliament. But just at the time that the Crown was becoming subordinate Parliament itself was passing under the control of permanent party organizations.

Relation of Party to Religious Controversy. — But to understand the material out of which parties are evolved it is needful to take account of the religious history of England. The English are by nature a religious people and their religion has tended directly to the strengthening of the spirit of brotherhood, which is the very essence of democracy. The early religious teaching added greatly to the popular ability to resist tyranny in the parishes, hundreds, and counties. The pastors and priests who lived with the people often cast in their lot with them, while the higher clergy were giving aid to their oppressors.

Each of the great national religious revivals in the twelfth, thirteenth, and fourteenth centuries, added strength to the popular aspirations for liberty. The third of these, led by John Wyclif, threatened a complete revolution in Church and State. The higher clergy were exposed as tyrants and the masses of the poor were led to feel the injustice of their position. Under the preaching of the Lollards they arose in rebellion, occupied London, slew the Archbishop, and so frightened all sections of the ruling classes that they combined under the Lancastrian monarch to make an end of the open profession of Lollardy. Wyclif's teachings, however, were secretly kept alive among the common people and became an important factor in making England the leading Protestant nation of Europe two hundred years later.

The Christian religion strengthened democracy in many ways. Lollardy was suppressed because it openly espoused the cause of the wage earner. All combinations of laborers to improve their conditions were forbidden, but the poor, nevertheless, gained permission to unite in the support of a sacred altar or for the rendering of a religious drama, and their rulers discovered after a time that under the guise of religion these societies were attempting to raise wages. Local religious organization was always a means of training for democracy, and when the great schism came in the English Church large masses of the people were found to be already qualified to take an intelligent part in the national controversy.

The political party system, which became the organ for the modern triumph of democracy, grew out of religious controversy. Queen Elizabeth found England equally divided between Romanist and Protestant and she left it nearly all Protestant. In the meantime Protestants had become divided into reactionaries and reformers, or Puritans. The House of Commons opposed the Stuart monarchs on many questions other than religious, but it was religion especially that nerved the people to actual war against Charles I.

Origin of Party Names. — Roundheads and Cavaliers were the immediate precursors of Whigs and Tories. Roundheads stood for Parliament and for a reformed Protestant religion. Cavaliers upheld the Crown and the established order. Had they fought out their disputes in Parliament and before voting constituencies, instead of on a bloody field of battle, they would have been political parties. Incident to the war, the execution of the king and the setting up of a Commonwealth, there arose a distinct spirit of democracy. Free government had already taken root in America and this reacted upon the party of reform in the mother country. A faction arose favoring direct rule by the people in church and state alike and at no time since has democracy been without advocates.

The monarchy was restored under a wave of reaction against Puritan rule. Drastic measures were taken to crush out dissent in the church and as a result nearly half of England became permanent Dissenters, separated from the established Church. Since the restoration, one party has usually had the adherence of the established Church and the other party has received support from dissenting churches.

The names Whig and Tory came into use as party designations in 1680. Shaftsbury as leader of the parliamentary party was securing petitions for the calling of Parliament with the intention of excluding James II from the throne and making the Duke of Monmouth the successor of Charles II. Counter petitions were circulated by the other party. Shaftsbury's supporters were called "petitioners" and their opponents were dubbed "abhorrers." The more odious term "Whig" was fastened upon the petitioners by their enemies, thus associating them with alleged treasonable covenanters in Scotland. The Whigs retaliated with the term "Tory," carrying with it an association with Irish bandits. Names thus given in contempt remained to designate honorable ruling parties.

Petitioners and abhorrers it would seem were not all of them voters. Few citizens at that time had a right to vote, but for centuries the great mass of the unenfranchised had been trained to take an active interest in politics. Especially had this been the case for more than a hundred years when religious opinion and church discipline had been the chief divisive issues in party politics. The parties appealed to the mob as well as to the voters for the support of their policies.

Factions become Parties. — With the advent of Whigs and Tories there comes a reversion to that evenly balanced conflict between contending factions which had come to an end at the close of the Wars of the Roses in 1485. Again dukes and earls in rival camps contend for the control of the state. The earlier method of warfare was by the use of actual arms. Parliament was used as a tool of victorious generals to complete the destruction of their enemies by impeachments and bills of attainder. Whigs and Tories now found Parliament in continuous possession of the powers of government. In order to govern, it was necessary to control Parliament, but not by a victorious army, for no civil war worthy of the name has arisen under the party system. Parliament has been controlled by means of elections, by persuasion, by bribery, and by appeals to the mob threatening civil war. At every stage in their history party conflicts in England exhibit their ancient background of war. The language is military, the spirit is military, and much of the actual conduct has been violent. Wilkes as a leader of mobs, 1780, vindicated the right of a constituency to decide who should be its representative in the House of Commons. The unenfranchised classes took part in elections and in the conflicts between Pitt and Fox as rival leaders; the election of a member often degenerated into street fights continuing many days. Militancy has not even yet wholly disappeared; witness the conflict over the Home Rule Bill for Ireland. American parties have not the ancient background of war and party conflicts are less violent

Prior to the enfranchisement of 1832, the Whig party was composed of leading families of the nobility supported by voting constituencies in the towns and cities. The Tory nobility on the other hand looked for their following to the squire and parson in the counties. The two parties thus reflected ancient and fundamental divisions in local government. The Whigs were sponsors for the trading and industrial classes chiefly located in cities or boroughs; while the Tories had the larger support from the counties. This division is quite in harmony with the relation of the parties to the churches, described in a previous paragraph. The dissenters or non-conformists who supported the Whigs lived for the most part in towns, while the Established Church predominated in the country. These divisions were at no time complete; Whigs always had some support from the counties and from the Established Church, and the Tories had some city members.

The democracy is gradually removing the separate party alignments of town and country. Disraeli, as Tory Prime Minister, made a direct bid for the city vote by the enfranchisement act of 1867. This is usually characterized in party slang as "dishing the Whigs." The Liberals responded in 1884 by a corresponding act enfranchising agricultural laborers. The Conservatives replied by a comprehensive bill providing for direct democratic rule in all the counties and in London. A dispute over the property rights of the Church and over the relation of the Church to education has tended to prolong the ancient party alignments based upon religion. With the settlement of these disputes, church policy in England would cease to be a party question as it has ceased to be in Switzerland, the United States, and Norway.

From Queen Anne (1702–1714) to George III (1760) the House of Lords was Whig; since that date it has been Tory. There was a party realignment when Pitt became a Tory leader in 1784. A more drastic realignment followed when Tory reformers supported a Whig ministry in the passage of the Reform Act of 1832. Party names were changed at this time. Liberal was substituted for Whig, and in course of time the term Whig entirely disappeared as the name of a party. Conservative was likewise substituted for Tory, but both names still survive. On account of the rise of Liberal-Unionists, previously described, a third name has been added. So that the same party is called at different periods Tory, Conservative, or Unionist.

REFERENCES

CHURCHILL. *Life of Lord Randolph Churchill.*
Constitutional Yearbook.
COOKE. *The History of Party from the Whig and Tory Factions in the Reign of Charles II to the Reform Act, 1832*, three Vols., 1837.

DICKINSON. *The Development of Parliament during the Nineteenth Century.*
HARRIS. *History of the Radical Party in Parliament.*
KEBBEL. *History of Toryism.*
LECKEY. *History of England in the Eighteenth Century,* seven Vols., 1903.
Liberal Year Book.
LOWELL. *The Government of England,* 1908, Chaps. XXIX-XXX.

CHAPTER XL

THE PARTIES IN PARLIAMENT

The President of the United States and members of Congress come into office pledged to carry out a party platform adopted at a National Party Convention. In England the Parliament itself takes the place of the National Convention. The King's Speech is the platform for the session and the Cabinet is the authoritative party committee. Surrounded by their supporters in the House of Commons, the party committee proceeds to fulfill its promises to the voting constituencies under the criticism of the party committee of the defeated party. It is as if the National Nominating Conventions of the ruling parties in America were to meet together in one room, and the party of the majority were in actual possession of the government and obliged to formulate and to carry out both legislative and executive policies in the presence of the minority party. The House of Commons is the meeting place of the ruling parties. The proceedings are peculiarly interesting because the makers of the party platform are at the same time carrying it into effect. The interest is increased because the rival party is present in force, and at every stage is striving to convince a majority of the assembled supporters of the two parties that they are themselves in possession of a better policy. Publicity is thus secured. Under the fire of expert criticism, the Government modifies its policy and, as finally executed, the program embodies the wisdom of both parties. At the opening of the daily sessions, an hour is consumed by the Ministers in giving account of their conduct in answer to questions of which previous notice has been given. This is an important part of the machinery for keeping the House and the country informed on matters of public interest.

Relation of the Cabinet to the Two Houses. — Party, or cabinet, government is complicated by the existence of two houses in the legislature. The rise of the Cabinet, as has been shown, belongs to the period in which the House of Commons held the leading place in Parliament. It is preëminently a House of Commons institution and its responsibility is to that House, though a considerable number of both cabinet and non-cabinet ministers have always been members of the Upper House. Much of the time the Prime Minister has been a peer. The system requires a recognized official party leader of each party in each House. One of these is the leader who becomes Premier when his party wins the majority in the Commons. The other is the leader of debate in the other House. If the Premier is a peer, the leader of debate in the Commons holds a position of great responsibility. He is on the field of battle and must respond to the changing moods of the conflict. Yet only the Prime Minister is in a position to give utterance to the final conclusions of the party on disputed issues. Greater unity and efficiency are secured by combining the office of party leader with leadership in the lower House. With both of the parties thus organized the varying positions assumed in the exigencies of the conflict carry the weight of final authority. Only in the House of Commons are there party whips. Here the two parties must keep their supporters well in hand. The battle is on all the time and pickets are set to watch the soldiers of the enemy. The whips and their assistants are always on the alert to discover a party advantage.

The members of the Ministry in the House of Lords have fewer political and legislative burdens. The sittings are brief, the business not exacting, and Ministers are more free to attend to the administrative duties of their office. One argument in defense of the Upper House has been that it furnishes numerous ministers who were not overburdened with other than ministerial duties. When the head of one of the departments is a peer, the parliamentary Secretary of that department must be a commoner. Some one in the Commons must answer for the conduct of each department. When the chief is a commoner, the Secretary is likely to be a peer. It is not, however, essential that all the departments be represented in the Upper House. The Treasury is never thus represented.

Until 1832, the theory of equality between the two houses had prevailed. Except as to matters of taxation, the Lords equally with the Commons participated in legislation. The act of Queen Anne in changing a Whig into a Tory House by the creation of twelve new peers was viewed as unconstitutional. When, however, after long debate and an appeal to the constituencies, William IV gave notice that in case the peers again refused to pass the reform bill, it would be passed by the creation of new peers, a distinct change was effected in the Constitution. Henceforth, the political constitution made it the duty of the peers to pass all government bills which in their opinion had the support of the country. They still had a right to amend bills or to reject those of doubtful support.

It is one of the marvels of English history that the House of Lords should have maintained its position without further change for nearly eighty years, controlled during all this time by one party. When the Conservatives were in power, every act of Parliament was in the hands of its friends in both houses. No government bill would be rejected and if amended, it would be in a friendly spirit. There could be no conflict between the two houses. Tory ministers in both houses could coöperate with the full assurance that they were in command of the entire legislature. For one of the parties Parliament became practically a single chamber. When the other party was in power, there were two chambers and one of them was politically hostile to the other. Numerous bills passed by a Liberal government have been rejected by the House of Lords. The principle had been clearly enunciated that it was the duty of the peers to follow the lead of the Commons, not to obstruct legislation which the people's representatives approved; but the rule of action was indefinite. Just when should the lords yield? How should they know what bills had the support of the country?[1] Some expositors answered by saying that the peers had a right to reject all bills, but if the same measure should be sent up a second time, it should be passed. Especially should the peers yield, if, upon the rejection of a bill, Parliament should be dissolved and the same government should be returned to power. In practice, however, the peers had a free hand in rejecting a large proportion of the bills passed by a Liberal Government. Not only so, but by amendment they changed the character of much of the Liberal legislation which they consented to pass.

[1] Dicey, "The Law of the Constitution," p. 384 (1885).

That such a condition should continue so long is proof of the conservative character of the radical party.

The change came in 1911, after the House of Lords had refused to vote for the Government Finance Bill of 1909. For many years there had been growing hostility toward the Upper House. Numerous plans for its reform had been proposed. The rejection of the Budget precipitated action.[1] The peers have still the power of delaying a cabinet measure for a period of two or more years. It has, however, become possible for a strong Government ultimately to pass a bill despite the resistance of the peers.

The Act of 1911 satisfies neither party. The Liberals secured its enactment as a makeshift pending a more thorough reform. They object to it, because it still comes short of securing equality between the parties. The Upper House is more hostile than before and there is still opportunity for obstruction and delay. The Conservatives view the measure as an act of destruction, depriving or threatening to deprive the time-honored Second Chamber of all its powers and committing the government of the country to a single-chambered legislature. The reform yet to be wrought will seek to place the two parties on an equality in their relation to support from the Second Chamber.

The cabinet system tends to concentrate political power in one house. The Cabinet is a unit; it cannot be equally responsible to two houses. In some way they must be made one. The American system admits of two houses of the legislature, each elected in the same way, each having equal power. But organize a cabinet in such a legislature and place in its hands the responsibility for both lawmaking and law administration, and there would be trouble. A cabinet cannot both make laws and govern, unless it has a continuous party majority. The Australians are trying the experiment of a cabinet system with two houses each elected by popular vote. Provision is made, however, for a joint assembly of the two houses in case of emergency. Canada maintains the cabinet system by making the second chamber distinctly subordinate and filling it with appointees who consent to eschew party politics. It is theoretically possible to construct a second chamber which would do useful non-partisan revisory work for both parties in matters

[1] See above, p. 463.

of legislation and at the same time furnish to each of them experienced administrators. The English House of Lords may be developed in this direction and cease to be a tool of one party. As nearly as may be its membership will then be divided between the parties. Such a House might readily make itself useful in the growing field of coöperative legislation between the parties. It might be serviceable also as a revisory chamber for all government bills. To this end, the Second Chamber should be freed from suspicion of partisan bias. The relation to the Democracy should be similar to that of the Crown, both becoming efficient and active agents in matters of common agreement. Thus differentiated, the House of Commons would become the one chief agency for the discovery and the formulation of the will of the state on the few questions in respect to which there is serious diversity of opinion. The ideal of cabinet government requires that the two parties shall have equal opportunity to make their wills go. Thus far England has had no such government.

Merits and Demerits of the Cabinet System. — Dual party government of the cabinet type is one among many forms for democratic government. It is the most interesting, the most spectacular, and withal the simplest. No other form has had so wide and far-reaching an influence. In the interest of the great future of free government it is desirable that it should not be abandoned until its reasonable possibilities have been thoroughly tested. Along with the party conflict involving radical changes in the House of Lords have come propositions which suggest modifications of the cabinet system. The Tory party proposes a direct vote of all the electors as a substitute for the parliamentary vote on the more important of the controverted measures. Thus far the system has derived its chief interest from the fact that the rival parties are the sole agencies for formulating and adopting projects of legislation in the field of contentious politics. Forty or fifty men divide themselves into two rival camps. They "line up" and "whip in" their supporters in Parliament. They seek to extend their organization so as to include every vote in the United Kingdom. They thus become two rival schools for the education and training of all the people. The school is always in session. Its lessons are interesting, because they profoundly affect the well-being of the people.

The teachers are the men who both say and do at the same time. It is the one business of the rival party leaders to keep the entire nation informed as to what they have done and what they propose to do, and their position is such as to secure the maximum of responsibility for every promise made to the public. Statesmen formulate policies with the intention of winning and maintaining a majority in the legislature, and if they succeed, then they must make good their claims, or give place to others.[1]

The system has also its limitations. It leaves to members of the legislature little room for independent action. Members of the Cabinet cannot be independent because they must all speak and act as one man. Ministers not in the Cabinet are bound to uphold, vote for, and defend every Government measure. There may be independence among private members, but the tendency of the system is to make every member an unquestioning supporter of his party leaders. Treason against the party is likely to be followed by political death. As shown in the next chapter, party leaders control nominations and the independent candidate finds little place. The voters are independent, but they are limited in their choice to the two rival groups of party leaders in whose selection they have no direct share. As to the securing of desired legislation or the prevention of a detested act, the people must persuade or frighten the party leaders. This is done by agitation, petition, and public demonstration.

If the referendum should be adopted, it would furnish an alternate method of preventing the passage of an act which the voters did not approve. The House of Lords has served as a check on one of the parties, often vetoing bills or compelling an appeal to the country over a party issue, — a sort of indirect referendum. With the removal of the Lords' veto, the proposition for a direct referendum appears. This democratic measure would probably be followed by the popular initiative. In any event, the cabinet system would be so far set aside or modified. The Cabinet could no longer carry the full measure of responsibility. There would be at least a divided responsibility and there would be a division in popular interest. Rival parties could no longer monopolize political attention. There might

[1] By means of a coalition Cabinet the system readily adapts itself to a realignment of parties or to a great emergency which overshadows contentious politics.

in the end be worked out a more satisfactory democratic government, but it would not be in the full sense a cabinet government.

Another proposition which comes quite naturally with the referendum is to deprive the Cabinet of the power to dissolve Parliament, to have a fixed term, say four years, for the House of Commons; this in the interest of independence on the part of the members. But with a fixed term for Parliament and direct participation of the people in legislation, party government would be in a measure set aside.

REFERENCES

(See References, Chap. **XXXIX**.)

CHAPTER XLI

LOCAL PARTY ORGANIZATION

ENGLISH and Americans have ever been preëminent in organization. English liberties were first defended and maintained through the coöperation of the people in counties, cities, and townships, or parishes, with one or another of the opposing factions in the king's government. When political parties were organized in England they focused popular attention upon the central government. In a sense, the party may be said to have taken the place of local government. In the meantime Americans were laying the foundations for a great federated republic by the use of counties, cities, and townships transplanted to the New World. When America became independent, national parties arose and assumed control of the government. Permanent parties were formed there out of the local party caucuses in the voting precincts. The organization of the party followed the order of the organization of the nation: first the town and city, then the county, the State, and, finally, the federation of States. The national parties have looked to the local caucus as the ultimate source of their authority. The series of conventions culminating in the great National Convention, in theory, speak and act with the authority of the local caucus, or primary. Every voter is assumed to belong to one of the parties and to be a member of the local primary of the party whose candidates he usually supports. The organization is voluntary and separate from the government. Party conventions speak with the authority of the people, who nominate candidates, and, by means of the party platform, dictate the policy of the government. Candidates are nominated and elected as pledged to carry out policies formulated by the people's representatives in party convention.

This is quite unlike the place and work of the party in England, where the Cabinet has always held the supreme party authority and was in the beginning the sole party organization. There followed a lining up of party supporters in the Ministry and in the two houses of Parliament; but it was a long time before the organization extended further. While in America the political party is an agent of the masses of the people for the purpose of choosing the officials and controlling the government, in England the party is the government. Cabinet government is literally a party in full possession of political power. It can brook no superior. Outside organizations may strengthen and support, they cannot control it.

Preliminary Training. — Not until the extension of the franchise in 1832 did the organized parties include those outside of the two Houses of Parliament; but the people in general had not lacked training in ways of working together for definite ends. For centuries they had been developing habits of local organization for religious, social, industrial, and political purposes. Long before Whigs and Tories began to contend together in Parliament, Churchmen and Non-conformists had parted England into rival religious bodies, and at no time have these organizations lacked political significance. Both Henry VII (1485–1509) and Henry VIII (1509–1547) were upon occasion compelled or induced to forego the collection of taxes voted by Parliament, on account of the organized opposition of the taxpayer. Such early training in united resistance to governmental measures prepared the people for more direct and effective political action. The American colonists were practicing a very ancient custom of their ancestors when they organized resistance to the collection of a tax of two pence a pound on tea in Boston harbor.

Equally significant were certain combined movements among the English for securing positive reforms. Catholics and Nonconformists each maintained an active, organized propaganda for the removal of legal restrictions upon their religious beliefs; and for sixty years before the passage of the first Reform Act many organizations for the securing of a variety of reforms and for the promotion of diverse philanthropies were receiving the attention of large numbers of the people. It is sufficient to mention the sustained, organized, and successful efforts of the associations for securing the abolition of the slave trade, the prohibition of slavery in the British Empire, and the abolition of the Corn Laws, — all with a more or less definite political aspect. Other societies sprang up among the people having as one object among others the gaining of more direct influence upon the government.

The Birmingham Plan. — Candidates for Parliament have long been accustomed to employ agents to look after their elections. With the extension of the franchise the labors of these functionaries were greatly increased. Rival agents representing opposing candidates busied themselves in efforts to secure full registration of the voters and to prevent the opposite party from gaining the benefit of false registration. During the period from 1832 to 1867 incipient party organization was incident to the process of registration and getting out a full vote at the election. After the passage of the Act of 1867, organization in both parties was extended and improved in an effort to secure and retain the support of the newly enfranchised laborers. In the city of Birmingham a local caucus was adopted which very much affected the organization of the Liberal party. The new law gave to Birmingham the right to elect three members of the House of Commons on a general ticket, each voter being limited to two votes. Those two votes might both be given to one candidate or one to each of two candidates. The intention was to elect one member from the minority party. But the Liberal party managers found it possible so to distribute the votes of their supporters in the nineteen different wards as to elect all three of their candidates. To accomplish this the voters were enrolled under pledge to act as directed by the Central Council of the party. By this method the Liberals elected the three members of Parliament and also nearly all the members of the City Council.

The National Liberal Federation. — The Birmingham Liberal Association was simplified and perfected in 1873 under the astute leadership of a young manufacturer, Mr. Joseph Chamberlain. It was Mr. Chamberlain's ambition to extend the Birmingham plan of local party organization throughout the kingdom and to unite all local organizations in a National Liberal Federation. That organization was effected in 1877 with Mr. Chamberlain as its first president. To this position he was annually reëlected until he became a member of the Gladstone Cabinet in 1881. He had previously entered Parliament as an already recognized national party leader. As a cabinet officer he soon became a promising candidate for the first place in the Government.

The Chamberlain plan involved the enrollment of all the supporters of the Liberal party in local associations united by a series of committees and councils into one representative body capable of giving authoritative expression to the party sentiment. The Federation was expected to assist in finding candidates for office and in carrying election, but its primary object was to serve as a school of national politics, to propagate liberal principles, to discover the subjects demanding the immediate action of Parliament and thus to guide the conduct of parliamentary leaders. It was, in effect, designed as a sort of second parliament to enable the democracy to formulate and express its views. Mr. Chamberlain was accused of an attempt to Americanize the English party, to build up a machine nominally based upon local democratic caucuses but really playing into the hands of the party manipulator.

Chamberlain Deposed. — The test of the machine came in 1886, when Gladstone espoused the cause of Home Rule for Ireland and Chamberlain refused to follow his party leader. A special meeting of the Council of the National Liberal Federation was called to give utterance to the sentiment of the party on that question. In the vote taken at a full and representative meeting the Chamberlain faction was overwhelmingly defeated and the Gladstone ministry was sustained. Hitherto the Federation had been closely associated with one man and one city. Organized at Birmingham, the central office had remained in that city, and Mr. Chamberlain had been its chief sponsor. Immediately upon his defeat he withdrew from the Federation and proceeded to organize a National Liberal-Unionist party on the same general model, with the central offices in London. The new organization was rapidly extended. As the recently enfranchised agricultural laborers had furnished a large and fruitful field for Liberal organization, it now appeared as one of the ironies of political life that the Liberal party should find its chief weapon of defense in the system devised and perfected by its most influential opponent and former leader.

For many years the National Liberal Federation was inspired by, and is still influenced by the Chamberlain idea of a separate and independent organ to formulate and express party opinion. Its annual meetings became occasions for adopting resolutions on a great variety of subjects after the manner of American national party conventions. All the good doctrines previously accepted were reaffirmed and others were added. Finally, at a meeting held at Newcastle in 1891, a definite "platform" of great length was adopted and Gladstone's Annual Address expounded its various "planks." All this could take place without apparent injury to the party, so long as the Liberals were out of office. But within a few months a cabinet crisis placed them again in power and their responsible statesmen were confronted with the obligation of giving answer to demands for the fulfillment of the "Newcastle Program." The thing was clearly impossible; and the fact that an apparently responsible party organization had adopted such a platform became a source of embarrassment and weakness to the Government.

It must be remembered that the British Cabinet cannot receive dictation from an outside party organization. The Cabinet forms its own platform in the actual tug of war with its opponents in the House of Commons.

A problem was thus presented to the Liberal leaders: how to preserve all that was helpful in the National Liberal Federation and at the same time to prevent embarrassing interference. This has been accomplished by modifications of the rules and changes in the central offices. The constitution of the Federation under the new order consists of an Executive Committee, a General Committee, and a Council. The Executive Committee is composed of the officers of the Federation and not more than twenty other members. This small body of leaders manages the business of the Federation. The General Committee appoints from its own number the Executive Committee and is itself composed of numerous representatives from local associations and all the Liberal members of Parliament. It has few duties as a committee, but serves as a connecting link between the Executive Committee and the local organizations. The Council includes all the members of the two Committees with additional delegates from local associations. It is the all-inclusive Central organization.[1] The new rules exclude from the representative General Council discussion or voting upon

[1] "Liberal Year Book," 1912.

any matters not presented by the General Committee. This committee, consisting of more than a thousand members, is entirely too large for deliberative purposes. It has been found useful in extending the local organizations to all parts of the country in the work of publishing and distributing party literature and in gathering information on the trend of public sentiment on all public questions. In its meetings there is much greater freedom than in those of the more popular Council. But the real sifting out of the subjects to be presented to the Council is left to an Executive Committee, consisting of the five officers of the Federation and twenty members elected each year by the General Committee. This small committee of twenty-five is the important factor in harmonizing the caucus and the Cabinet. The committee arranges that the caucus representatives in council shall act only on such matters as shall encourage and strengthen the party in Parliament. The annual meeting of the Council is called to ratify and approve, but not to oppose the program of the leaders. The entire machinery, however, is fitted to furnish useful guidance to the leaders in the preparation of their program. Still a show of independence is maintained. A rule forbids the election of a member of Parliament to the Executive Committee of the Federation, and it is good liberal politics to assert that the parliamentary whips never seek to influence the committee. This actual subservience of the Liberal party to its parliamentary leaders is contrasted with the place of the Executive Committee in the national Conservative organization which is presided over by the Chief parliamentary Whip. In practice, however, the same result is attained.

Superior Organization of the Conservative Party. — The Tory party has always been more homogeneous and better organized than its opponent. The local magistrates who ruled the counties were its supporters. The squire and the parson were relied upon to send Tory members to Parliament. When the right of suffrage was limited to few, members were often chosen by nomination without the form of an election. In case of a contested election the candidates employed agents to conduct their campaign.

The Agents who served members of the House of Commons by looking after their interests in elections and seeking to keep their chiefs in touch with their supporters furnished the nucleus for the first form of party organization outside of Parliament. The employment of such agents was at first temporary — for the conduct of a single campaign; but as the number of voters increased the service became permanent. The agents became a class of professional politicians devoting their lives to the service of their party. They receive small return for their useful labors — salaries ranging from a few hundreds of dollars to two thousand — and are wholly devoid of personal ambition for governmental office. Professing no political opinions of their own, they become highly skilled observers of the opinions and sentiments of others. They receive without question the doctrines of the party leaders; they distribute party literature and arrange meetings for party lectures or campaign speeches; they keep an open eye for all means of conciliating voters or strengthening the party in their district and they organize and direct the work of the voluntary, unpaid local party workers. When the time comes for enrolling all party supporters in local caucuses or associations, the said agents in the Conservative party simply add this duty to their regular work.

The Conservative National Union. — When in 1867 the franchise was extended to laborers in industrial centers, the Conservative party was already prepared to enroll the new voters in local associations. Delegates from fifty-five constituencies met and promptly organized the Conservative National Union ten years before Mr. Chamberlain effected that of the National Liberal Federation at Birmingham. So, when the Radicals were only beginning to organize the local caucus, the Tories were already perfecting a national party union of local associations, growing out of and in close affiliation with the older central organization of the party in Parliament.

Organization in Parliament. — Before the organization of national unions or federations parties were organized in Parliament. Whips had been employed to secure the continued adherence of the other party members in Parliament. A Central Office was early established in each party to facilitate the coöperation of the leaders and the Whips. The working of this central office in its relation to Parliament has been described, but its relation to the public is equally important. It is the high mission of the Chief Whip to gain for his party continuous public support. He is the custodian and distributer of party funds, and his advice goes far in the bestowal of honors or office. The central office is a meeting place for candidates seeking constituencies and for constituencies seeking candidates. It gives direction to local agents in matters of registration and the canvass of the voters, and the agents employed by the members of the House of Commons are thus brought into close relation to the office. Local agents who have distinguished themselves in organizing campaigns and in carrying elections in one district are employed to assist in other districts. Finally, a Chief Agent was selected to act with the Chief Whip in the Central Office. It thus becomes possible to include in one central organization all the supporters of the party. Paid local agents were accustomed to extend as far as possible the spirit and practice of voluntary coöperation, and under their guidance local associations grew up which furnished the basis for national organization. The Conservative National Union arose from an effort of the Central office to enroll the new voters as party members. The delegates composing the Union assembled, not to express opinions, which might embarrass the party leaders, but to educate and train the adherents of the party and to devise more effective agencies for extending its influence. As one of the founders expressed it, " The Union had been organized rather as what he might call a handmaid to the party, than to usurp the functions of party leadership." [1] With one exception, to be described later, the Conservative National Union has been kept in strict subordination to the Central Office of parliamentary leaders. The permanent secretary of the Union has usually been at the same time the Chief Agent of the party. The agents are subject to the Whips and the Whips are the servants of the leaders. Neither the Whips nor the agents have a right to promote their own private opinions. It is their duty to give effect to cabinet policies as expressed by the Prime Minister or the official leaders.

Contrast between Caucus and Central Office. — The Birmingham Caucus embodied a radically different idea. It was organized with the intention of promoting free and independent discussion of party policies and of giving, in the National Council of Delegates, an authoritative expression of party opinions.

[1] Lowell, "The Government of England," Vol. I, p. 537.

LOCAL PARTY ORGANIZATION

The Liberal party already had a Central Office similar to that of the Tory party. The Caucus was therefore in a sense a rival to the older organization. Through the office of the Chief Whip, assisted by the agents of the party, the leaders were already kept in constant touch with the constituencies. It was the duty of the local agents to inform the leaders of the trend of public opinion. From such a source the leaders could receive guidance free from the implication of dictation. But the caucus proposed to dictate policies and thus became not only a rival, but a discordant organization. By long process of adjustment, the discord has been removed in the National Liberal Federation, and, like the Conservative National Union, it has become a mere handmaid to the Central Office of parliamentary leaders. In both parties the Chief Whip remains the head of the party organization in Parliament and in the voting precincts.

An episode in the history of the Tory party throws added light on the relation of the central parliamentary organization to the National Union. In 1883 the National Liberal Federation with its popular local caucuses was apparently giving strength and efficiency to the Liberal party. By means of the organization Mr. Chamberlain was being rapidly advanced to the first place in the leadership of his party. There was discontent in the Tory party because their National Union was kept under the control of the Central Office of leaders, Whips, and paid agents. This condition furnished the opportunity for the promotion of Lord Randolph Churchill to a leading place in the Tory Cabinet. He gained partial control of the Conservative National Union and proceeded to infuse into it the spirit and purpose of the Birmingham Caucus. This led to an acute conflict with the leaders of his own party over the question of the relation of the Union to the older parliamentary organization. Lord Randolph was defeated in his attempt to transfer party control to the National Union, but, like Mr. Chamberlain, he gained a personal triumph by securing a place in the Cabinet.

This incident furnishes additional proof in support of the proposition that the Cabinet itself is the sole authoritative party organization. The Whips are the servants of the Cabinet. The Chief Whip in each party organizes and directs the paid agents of the party. Through the use of the whips and the agents the leaders may extend the organization so as to include as members of local clubs or associations all party supporters. The local associations may be induced to send delegates to the National Union or the Council to receive instruction from the party leaders, to ratify the policies adopted, to furnish inspiration and party enthusiasm; but thus far the experience in both parties seems to prove that the national organization cannot dictate party policy. As long as the Cabinet is the Government it cannot be subject to an external organization. Except during the two years of Lord Randolph Churchill's ascendancy, the Conservative party organization has been under the control of the Central Office of which the Chief Whip is *ex officio* chairman. The Liberal party became locally organized on a contradictory principle, and has attained harmony and efficiency by eliminating the idea of caucus dictation to party leaders.

The local organizations in so far as they work in harmony with the agents and the Chief Whip are a source of great strength to the leaders. While they may not dictate a policy, they do greatly aid in furnishing information and in extending the field of parliamentary debate. Millions of party members acquire the habit of following the debates in Parliament. They become educated in respect to public questions, and competent to furnish useful guidance to the party leaders.

English and American Party Methods. — A few words by way of comparison of campaign methods in England and the United States may well be added. The Americans know in advance the date of the campaign, which comes at the end of a four-year period. An entire year is devoted to special preparation for the event. The intervening three years are designated as " off years " in politics. Political interest is made intermittent by fixed rule. The people become accustomed to alternate periods of relaxation and stress. The English have no such periods of rest from party anxiety. The campaign may be delayed for five years, and it may occur on any day. Immediately following the organization of a newly elected House of Commons the defeated party begins the preparations for another appeal to the people. Party platforms are all the time in process of evolution in the House of Commons. By-elections are of frequent occurrence and party leaders make much of these as indicating the trend of public opinion. The English live in an atmosphere of political agitation.

Another contrast in campaign methods arises from the fact that in the one government political power is centralized, while in the other it is diffused. From the nature of their government the English have the shortest possible ballot. The voter exhausts his possibilities for the election of his rulers by casting a vote for one member of the House of Commons. No other officers are chosen at a Parliamentary Election. The electors choose the members of the House in separate districts and the House governs the country. Interest in the campaign is thus concentrated upon the party candidates in the various districts. In America party interests are diffused among numerous state and national candidates to be voted for at a single election. Americans extend the active campaign over four or five months. In England it is limited to a few weeks, though party machinery is always kept in order and the campaign may be said to be continuous. When the dissolution of Parliament actually occurs, the closely contested districts which are relied upon to determine the politics of the House of Commons are subjected to a few days of most active and intense campaigning.

REFERENCES

OGG. *The Governments of Europe*, Chap. VII.

OSTROGORSKI. *Democracy and the Organization of Political Parties*, Vol. I, Parts II–III.

Report of the Annual Conference of the Labor Party.

ROSEBERY. *Life of Lord Randolph Churchill.*

TREVELYAN. *England in the Age of Walpole.*

WALPOLE. *History of England from 1815.*

WATSON. *The National Liberal Federation from its Commencement to the General Election of 1906.*

CHAPTER XLII

RELIGION AND THE CHURCH

IN the foregoing discussion frequent references have been made to religion and to church organizations. Religious controversy was a cardinal factor in the origin of parties, and it remains a subject of great importance in present-day party conflicts. It is not possible to understand the government of England without a knowledge of the part of the Church in its historical development. The few facts here recorded are intended to throw light on the present relation of the Church to the government.

Before the state was centrally organized, England possessed a centrally organized Church, with the Archbishop of Canterbury at its head.[1] In a way it furnished the model and was itself a chief agency in effecting a union of the petty kingdoms into one united state. Many of the early statesmen were bishops and other church dignitaries who coöperated with the West Saxon rulers to promote that union. Church and state became and remained fused together as one government until after the Norman Conquest in 1066. The higher clergy were by right or by custom members of the King's Council. The bishop sat with the earl as presiding officer in the County Court. In the lower courts of the hundred and the *vil*, or township, church affairs were administered along with other local business.

Relations of Church and State. — A radical change was therefore effected when William the Conqueror separated the church courts from the secular courts, eliminated the bishops from county courts, relegated matters of religion formerly adjudicated in county and hundred courts to the hands of the bishops and lower clergy. One apparent object of the king in separating church courts from secular courts was that he might

---

[1] Wakeman, "History of the Church of England," Chaps. I–III.

gain more complete control over both, that he might use both as a weapon against the nobility. Later changes, as has been pointed out, completely effaced the functions of the hundred. The township remained as an important local institution; though, because of the fact that much of the secular business passed into the hands of local magistrates and the county court, the term "Parish," which had been used to denote the religious functions of the township, gradually displaced the older term. But in the parish there has never been a complete separation of religious from secular affairs.

England was at the time a part of western Christendom of which the Pope of Rome was the recognized head. The popes habitually asserted a larger measure of authority over the subjects of kings and emperors than these were willing to concede. Separate church courts in England might readily have been made a tool in the hands of the popes for encroaching upon the king's authority. This was guarded against in many ways. The kings for the most part maintained the chief control over church appointments. They carefully examined all communications between the Pope and the national Church. William I (1066–1087) and Henry II (1154–1189) asserted supreme rights over all questions of appeal from the bishops' court in England to the See of Rome. Carried to its logical conclusion, this system would have given the King in Council full power over the English clergy. To avoid this result Becket, the Archbishop of Canterbury, resisted Henry II to the death. The duel between King and Archbishop was a drawn battle. The church courts retained a modicum of independent power and the popes a limited right of interference in English affairs, but by far the greater authority over the Church remained with the King in Council.

No detailed account can be given here of the part which the Church has played in the conflicts which have led to the modern Constitution. During the earlier part of the four hundred years of strife between king and armed nobility, the Church at times held the balance of power. Throughout the disputed reign of Stephen and Matilda (1135–1154) the Church was a dominating factor in the government. The strife which led to the exacting of Magna Charta from King John began with a dispute among the King, the Pope, and the English clergy over the election of the Archbishop of Canterbury. Finally, when King and Pope united their forces, the English clergy, coöperating with the armed nobility, controlled the situation. Again, when Henry III (1216-1272) fell under the influence of the Pope and the foreign faction of nobles, the English clergy united with the home faction of the barons and exacted from the King the Provisions of Oxford, in 1258.

But the ordinary relation between bishops and barons was that of rivalry, jealousy, and hostility. The king usually commanded the support of the higher clergy against the great lords. After the reign of Edward I (1272-1307) a distinct decline in the independent power of the bishops followed. Such power as they had was usually at the disposal of the king. The Church was becoming rich, timid, and corrupt. The great Wyclif revival during the last half of the fourteenth century had the effect to weaken still further the clerical power. The religion of the masses became pitted against the ecclesiastical organization. Henry VII (1485-1509) found the Church a convenient tool to employ in accomplishing the complete subjugation of the feudal nobility. Henry VIII (1509-1549) took advantage of the great Protestant uprising to advance the Crown to the position of chief authority in the Church. Arbitrary courts were created to displace papal dominance. Religious houses were destroyed and their property confiscated.

The transition from Roman Catholicism to Protestantism was thus accompanied by a transfer of the enormous property endowment of the Church to the Crown, but no step was taken towards disestablishment. In fact, Church and state in the higher organization of the Government became more closely fused together. In law, as well as in fact, the powers previously claimed by the Pope now belonged to the King, and the monarch became the head of the Church. The King in Parliament was made the supreme lawmaking power in all matters of religious belief and church discipline, while the King's Privy Council became and remained the highest court of appeal in the administration of church affairs. The great revival of religion which accompanied the advent of Protestantism tended greatly to magnify the importance of the Church. The support of bishops and clergy counted for much in the government. Had it been possible to attain a united and harmonious church with all powers centering in the Crown, its position would have been invulnerable. But just when Henry VIII had secured for the Crown a maximum of power the country became permanently divided on questions of religion. The chapter on the rise of political parties shows that at first Catholics and Protestants contended for supremacy. No sooner had Protestants gained ascendancy than a Puritan party arose within their own body to dispute with the monarch the control of the Church. So fierce was this struggle of the Puritan Revolution that in its course both a king and an archbishop were executed by act of a Puritan Parliament. When monarchy was again restored, in 1660, it was with a permanently divided Church. Half the people were dissenters, or non-conformists. An effort on the part of James II to revive Catholicism led to a temporary coöperation between dissenters and churchmen whereby the Catholic dynasty was rejected and two Protestant monarchs were introduced from the Continent.

The effect of the coöperation between dissenters and bishops first in the exclusion of James II and the calling of William and Mary to the throne and later in the passing of the crown to George I, was greatly to diminish the violence of religious controversy. The division remained, but never again did either party presume to destroy the other by force.

Church Organization and Disestablishment. — The organization of the Church to-day and its relation to the government can be understood only by reference to the remote facts in its history. There are two archbishops. One is the Archbishop of Canterbury who has the title of " Primate of all England "; the other is the Archbishop of York who is " Primate of England." This arises from the fact that pagan England was converted by two groups of missionaries, one from Ireland, working in the north, and the other group sent directly from Rome and beginning work at Canterbury. In the final adjustment between these competing authorities two archbishops were recognized with two convocations, or synods, which remain to the present day. The synod of York is but a feeble transcript of the chief convocation of the South. As to the time and the manner of organization of the Convocation of Canterbury historians are not informed. It was an institution of importance as early as the time of Edward I (1272–1307).

The Convocation consists of two houses, an upper house of bishops and a lower house made up of the deans and canons of the cathedrals, archdeacons, and proctors. The two houses transact part of their business in joint session. Convocation is the chief legislative assembly of the Church, although at the present day it has no really independent powers. It meets at the call of the Crown; takes action upon such subjects as the Crown suggests, and its acts become valid as a part of the law of the land only by the approval of Parliament. The Prayer Book of 1549 was formulated by a Church Commission and was then adopted by Parliament. In like manner were enacted the Thirty-Nine Articles of 1571 and the revised Prayer Book of 1661. Parliament is the real lawmaking body for the Church as for the nation. The clergy are without independent power either in matters of belief or of discipline. Should the Church be disestablished, the bishops would leave the House of Lords and the Church synods would come into complete control of church government. For this reason some of the clergy favor disestablishment.

Another change also would come with disestablishment which would be very generally approved by the clergy. The church courts to-day have little effective power or influence. They are subject to the secular courts and all appeals of important matters go to the Privy Council whose members may be non-Churchmen. After disestablishment all questions would be decided according to rules adopted by the Church and officers of its own choosing.

The important offices of the Church are now filled upon the recommendation of persons who are or may be non-Churchmen. Bishops and deans are appointed by the Crown upon the recommendation of the Prime Minister. Many of the canons are also thus chosen. The rectors, vicars, and perpetual curates are in large part appointed by the Lord High Chancellor, and others by private persons who have by law the right to recommend for church office. These advowsons, or rights to present to church livings, are in law private property and may pass by inheritance or by contract as other property. " They may pass into the hands of Dissenters, Jews, Turks, infidels and heretics, who can nevertheless present to the living." [1] Such a system

[1] Lowell, "The Government of England," Vol. II, p. 366.

would never be tolerated except for the fact that it is an inheritance from the middle ages. Disestablishment would surely give to the church the right to select its own religious leaders. Why, then, does the great body of Churchmen resist disestablishment? The prestige of the name, "state Church," is a factor of importance. Crown and Church are linked together in the glorious past. The state Church still maintains the fiction that all the inhabitants of a parish who have escaped formal excommunication are ever and always members of the Church with a right to its ministrations. To sever the Church from the state would destroy this fiction. The Church in England, like the Episcopal Church in the United States and Canada, would become one among numerous religious sects. Perhaps a more important reason for continuing the old system is the question of title to church property. Much property has already been taken from the Church. Until a recent date Dissenters were compelled with others to pay taxes for the support of the Church. It still owns much land from which it receives the entire rental. From other lands it receives tithes. Then there are the great cathedrals in which the nation as a whole, regardless of special church affiliation, lays claim to a common proprietary interest. These conflicting claims to property tend to unite the people in the maintenance of the peculiar and illogical relations of the Church to the state which are inherited from the past.

In Scotland, Ireland, and Wales quite a different and peculiar history pertains to the Church. While the English Roman Catholic Church was becoming the Protestant Episcopal Church, Scotland was becoming Protestant and Presbyterian and stoutly resisted the imposition of the English Establishment. In the war between King and Parliament in England the Scots sided with the Puritans and were an important factor in the outcome. When Parliament finally triumphed over the Stuart monarchs in 1688 the state Church as by law established in Scotland was the Presbyterian organization, and one division of Presbyterianism is to-day the state Church.

The advent of Protestantism in England coincided with a bitter conflict between English and Irish. The attempt to force upon the Irish the use of the new English Prayer Book tended to make the masses of the Irish people belligerently

Catholic. Even the English colonists in the north united with their Celtic neighbors in resistance to the alien form of religion and were drawn into the Irish Catholic Church. Later importations of Presbyterians from Scotland and from England served to renew the old conflict. Religious fanaticism was thus added to the old race hatreds. Crimes of massacre and rapine were committed in the name of religion. Stuart monarchs, hard pressed by their English and Scotch subjects, looked for aid to Ireland. James II driven from his English throne sought aid of the French and the Irish to bolster up his power in Ireland. The Ulster Protestants resisted his army and a decisive battle, fought July 12, 1690, established English authority over the whole of the island. But much of the old bitterness has survived. The anniversary of the battle of the Boyne is still observed by an order of Protestant Irish "Orangemen," to commemorate the triumph of the supporters of William of Orange over James II. The English Episcopal Church was forced upon Ireland, as it was upon Scotland.

While the Scots were able to rid themselves of the burden of a church establishment not in harmony with the national sentiment, the less fortunate Irish remained restive and refractory under the incubus until relieved by Act of Parliament in 1868. Since that date there has been no state Church in Ireland.

The Welsh became loyal subjects of the British crown long before the rise of Protestantism and accepted the change along with the English. Although in the later subdivision within the Church the Welsh almost wholly adhered to the Dissenters, the Episcopal Establishment was maintained in the province until the year 1914.

REFERENCES

GREEN. *Short History of the English People*, Chaps. VII, VIII.
GREEN. *The Making of England*, Chap. VII.
HUNT. *History of the English Church.*
LOWELL. *The Government of England*, XLI, XLII, XLIII.
TREVELYAN. *England Under the Stuarts.*
TREVELYAN. *England in the Time of Wycliffe.*
WAKEMAN. *The Church of England*, 1908, Chaps. I–III.

CHAPTER XLIII

THE COURTS AND LOCAL GOVERNMENT

NEARLY all the facts here presented appear in former chapters. They are repeated for purposes of review and especially to show their relations to the differentiation of the three departments of government, — legislative, executive, and judicial.

At first there was no differentiation. King's Council and county and hundred courts attended to all sorts of governmental business. The separate church courts of William the Conqueror stand as an important landmark in the separation of judicial from other functions. A hundred years later further progress was shown in the system of Henry II (1154–1187), who made use of two councils, the full assembly of all the notables, both spiritual and secular, and a smaller body, the *curia regis*, through whose agency he administers his government. The larger assembly is especially associated with important legislation and the smaller with administrative and judicial functions. The king's quarrel with the archbishop, Thomas à Becket, over the right of appeal to the Pope of Rome suggests the importance of a separate judiciary. Still no sharp line of differentiation of functions had yet been established. The monarch through the smaller council, or *curia regis*, could issue orders which had the force of law. The members of the council in county courts decided cases of law, administered the law of the land, and granted petitions for changes in local by-laws.

During the next century, a really distinct judiciary was evolved. Committees of the *curia regis* became continuously occupied in discovering and applying the rules of law. One committee attended especially to finance and taxation; another to cases of conflicting rights between citizens; a third to offenses against the crown and those affecting the rights of the crown. In the system of Edward I (1272–1307), the old *curia regis* is eliminated and in its place are the three courts of common law, corresponding to the three committees just mentioned, the court of the Exchequer, the court of Common Pleas, and the Court of the King's Bench. These are entirely occupied with judicial business and have become separated from the king's council.

Origin of an Independent Judiciary. — When the *curia regis* thus became transmuted into the common law courts, its place was taken by another body, which later became known as the Privy Council. The king in this smaller council, as well as the king in the greater council, later called Parliament, embodied all the high powers of government. Each council remained a supreme court of appeal from the common law courts, while the lower courts gave legal effect to the customary rules of conduct found among the people. In cases of injustice the high court of the King in Parliament or that of the King in Council amended the law or ordered a different ruling or interpretation. With a rapidly changing society the rigid rules of the common law courts caused continuous friction and injustice. So constant became the appeals to the king to give relief against the common law rules, that it led to the establishment of a new court of equity with more summary and less rigid rules of procedure. Yet the King in Council still remained the highest court of appeal. There seemed to be no limit to the power of the king to call into existence new courts to serve his purposes. Henry VII (1487–1509) by the use of an arbitrary court called the Star Chamber humiliated the great lords and enriched his treasury. Henry VIII (1509–1547) by means of a newly created court rid himself of an obnoxious wife and made himself the head of the Church. Charles I (1625–1649) revived the Star Chamber and called into existence various other high courts that gave him despotic powers in the north of England, in Ireland, and over church matters for the United Kingdom. One of the early acts of the Long Parliament was to compel Charles I to sign a bill abolishing the Star Chamber and all the arbitrary courts and denying to the monarch the right to create such courts. A few years later Charles himself was tried, condemned, and executed by order of a special court which the House of Commons had set up. There was no such thing as a permanent independent judiciary until after the Crown became subjected to the rule of Parliament. James II (1685–1689) found in the common law courts his last and most effective tool for royal tyranny. When these failed him he fled for his life.

The Act of Settlement, of 1701, deprived the monarch of the power to remove judges from office except upon the petition of the two houses of Parliament. England has since enjoyed an independent judiciary removed, for the most part, from partisan strife. No governmental act is more significant in the transformation of a limited monarchy into a parliamentary monarchy than is this Act of Settlement, which divested the crown of the privilege of removing judges. This power, passing from the sovereign to the two houses, carries with it the subjection of the Executive to the law of the land. It is no longer possible for the monarch to call judges and jurors to his aid in order to pervert the law or prevent its execution. By means of this Act the judiciary becomes really independent. The judges are no longer subject to the arbitrary dictation of either the monarch or the houses of parliament. Parliament, indeed, may at any time change the law and the courts will enforce the new legislation. The judges are themselves subject to the law. It is their duty to apply the law as they find it, assuming no responsibility for its appearance on the statute books. The independence of the English judiciary means that the magistrates are entirely subject to the lawmaking power. In theory, and as far as possible in fact, the separation is complete. The courts have no right to change the law.

The ancient fusion of powers is still reflected, however, in the forms of organization. The complete union of all the governmental forces is personified in the Lord High Chancellor. He is a member of the various high courts of the realm, and an active participant in their decisions. At the same time he presides over the upper house of the legislature and is a member of a party cabinet. Yet when the chancellor acts as a judicial officer he rids himself of all partisan bias; he ceases to think as an executive or as a lawmaker and, with other judges, seeks simply to discover and apply the existing law.

In like manner, when the House of Lords acts as the highest court of appeal for cases arising in the united kingdom of Great Britain and Ireland, it is not really the lawmaking body which constitutes the court. The judicial function of the House of Lords is discharged by the life peers and other members who hold or have held high judicial office. A similar condition prevails in the Privy Council. Cases arising in the Church courts and all cases from the Empire outside of Great Britain and Ireland go to the Council as the court of last appeal. But for such a purpose the Council is made up of a judicial committee consisting of the Lord High Chancellor and other members of high rank in the judiciary. These are now, however, courts of law, as really independent as if they had been newly created and filled by jurists who have no connection with the other departments of government.

Union of Legislature and Executive. — While the judiciary has become separated from the other departments of government, the latter have, on the contrary, been more thoroughly fused together. The Cabinet unites lawmaking and administration. Parliament makes and amends the laws and at the same time looks after the details of administration. So complete has this union of powers become in the central government that the same policy is carried into the local governments of county and city. The city council passes ordinances and, through its committees, also administers them. The English are familiar with a fusion of the two functions. In local as in general government the executive is incorporated with the legislative functions.

Much light is thrown upon the relation of the three departments of government to one another by a comparison of the English and American experiences. The Colonies were founded during the century of conflict between the Crown and the Parliament for the control of the government, and the current debate gave marked emphasis to theoretic distinctions between the three departments, legislative, executive, and judicial. Sir Edward Coke, chief justice of England, made an early plea for the independence of the judiciary. Parliament at the beginning of the controversy conceded to the Crown executive responsibility, but claimed for itself a monopoly of the lawmaking power. The executive and legislative remained united because there was discovered no practical means of separation.

Separation in the United States. — Statesmen of the Commonwealth (1649–1660) formulated a definite theory of government as consisting of three distinct and independent fields of authority. Conditions in America at the time favored the development of this theory. The colonists were especially devoted to their own provincial legislatures. These colonial assemblies were the only institutions which were all their own. In most cases their chief executive and the judiciary came from England. When governors and judges administered in good faith the acts of the colonial legislatures there was peace and harmony; when they did not there was friction and warfare. In any event the three departments of government were separated and contrasted. When the Colonies became States, an elected governor filled the office previously occupied by an appointee from England. Later, an elected President was charged with duties corresponding to the executive functions of king and cabinet in England. Both in the States and in the General government the Americans placed executive and legislative business in separate hands, thus carrying into actual practice the theory of government which prevailed in England during the century of colonization.

The result has been that in the United States the executive has come to be associated with a chief person, President, Governor, or Mayor, who is individually responsible for administering the laws. In England the attempt to separate the powers failed; a corporate body, the Cabinet, became the responsible executive and at the same time the controller of legislation. Likewise in the English city, the council governs, — the Mayor is a figurehead.

Local Courts and Local Governments. — The lowest court in the present English system is that of the Justice of the Peace in petty sessions. This court is held by one or more justices; it initiates processes to be adjudicated in the higher courts and it has jurisdiction over minor offenses. The justices of the peace in quarter sessions [1] have jurisdiction over more serious offenses against the law. Before the creation of the county courts of 1846 the justices of the peace in petty and in quarter sessions had civil jurisdiction also.

The courts held by these local magistrates, appointed by the Crown, have had a continuous history for more than five hundred years. During the thirteenth and fourteenth centuries, while

---

[1] As the name implies, this court meets four times a year. It is attended not only by justices of the peace, but also by grand and petty jurors. It hears appeals from the justices in petty sessions and tries cases of serious crime. It may not try a case involving the death penalty.

the common law courts were being developed out of the king's smaller Council, while the Great Council was being transformed into the two houses of Parliament, the business of the local courts in the counties and in the hundreds was passing into the hands of local peace officers. In petty and in quarter sessions the justices of the peace attended to local affairs of all sorts, judicial, administrative, and legislative. They constituted the local government in matters financial and secular. Church matters had been eliminated from the county court, but in the townships, or parishes, secular and church functions were still united. Instead of the old town meeting there remained the parish vestry, participating in the support of the parish church, the care of the poor, assessments and taxation, and many other matters which would now be classified as secular.

Local Government Reorganized. — These are the local institutions that for many years maintained law and order among the people while kings and lords and bishops were engaged in acts of strife and threatened revolution. The Squirarchy consisted not alone of country gentlemen in the courts of petty and quarter sessions, but it included also the priests in the parishes.[1] As stated in the chapter on the history of local government the court of the magistrates maintained possession of the full round of its powers until the Act of 1888 established a popularly elected county council which relieved the court of quarter sessions of nearly all of its legislative and administrative powers. Its judicial functions still remain.

The parish experienced its first radical change in the Act of 1834 creating a new board for the care of the poor. Parishes had become entirely inadequate to this important function. The act created larger districts, called Unions, which have little regard to county lines or other local areas. The administration of the poor laws was placed in the hands of a board of nine members in each union. Later acts encroached upon the spiritual functions of the parish. Dissenters were relieved from the requirement to pay taxes for the support of the Church. Finally, in 1894, an act was passed providing for the election of parish councils whose work is supplemental to that of the county councils. The counties are thus provided with a complete democratic government separated both from the judiciary and from the Church.

[1] (The Parson and the Squire composed the Squirarchy.)

Popular government was extended to towns and cities much earlier than to the counties. The first municipal councils act was passed in 1835. By various amendments to this act the government of cities has been kept in harmony with the growing democracy. In some of the towns and cities judicial service is supplied by the ordinary county courts; in others by modifications of quarter sessions or by a substitute recorder's court. The varieties are so numerous and complex as not to admit of a general description. The Recorders, who in some cities perform the duties of quarter sessions, are salaried judicial officers chosen like other judges from the profession of barristers.

The effect of these various measures has been to create a separate and independent local judiciary and to place other local, secular business in the hands of popularly elected boards or councils. The local councils are little parliaments, or cabinets; all are subject to the great Parliament at London and they are all supervised in their policy by the Cabinet acting through the President of the Local Government Board. Great cities have already attained a large measure of legislative and administrative independence. It is to be expected that with prolonged experience like freedom will come to counties and parishes. But legally all power rests with the central government; local boards are subject to its minute supervision and direction.

The development of modern industry made it impossible for local magistrates to attend adequately to both civil and criminal litigation. As stated above, civil cases were assigned to a county court created by act of Parliament in 1846. These courts are several hundred in number. They are held by permanent judges appointed from the barristers. The districts are formed without reference to county lines. Their courts relieve the old county court of a large share of its business, but are themselves county courts only in name. They are rather small debts courts, whose jurisdiction in ordinary cases is limited to £100, and in equity cases to £500.

There are thus four sets of judicial officers derived from the ancient county governments:

1. The Justices of the Peace in petty sessions.
2. The Justices of the Peace in quarter sessions.
3. The Recorders in towns and cities, and
4. The County Courts of 1846.

The High Courts. — By various acts of reform, beginning in 1873, the courts intervening between the local courts and the two courts of final appeal have been reorganized and the procedure simplified. The three common law courts and the court of equity have been merged into one Supreme Court of Judicature. This court may adopt rules of procedure, but for the trial of cases it is divided into a Court of Appeals and a High Court of Justice. The latter is itself divided into a Court of Chancery, a Court of the King's Bench, and a Court of Admiralty, Probate, and Divorce. The High Court of Justice, acting through its three divisions, is a court of general original jurisdiction, and it also hears appeals from the lower courts. Appeals from the three divisions of the High Court go to the Court of Appeals and from this Court the appeal is to the House of Lords. The House of Lords also hears appeals from the courts of Scotland and Ireland. As stated above, the Privy Council hears appeals from the Church courts in England and from the courts of the Empire outside of Great Britain and Ireland. London has a system of courts peculiar to itself and in other cities the modifications are numerous.

All the members of the House of Lords have a legal right to participate in the hearing of appeals, but by custom the business is confined to the Lord High Chancellor, who presides, the life peers [1] appointed for the purpose, and any other peers who hold or have held high judicial office. The Court, by recent statute, is empowered to transact business when the House of Lords is not in session. Since appeals come to the House of Lords from Ireland and Scotland, care is taken to secure representatives in the Court from those countries. Procedure of the Court is analogous to the ordinary procedure of the House; the issues are debated and voted upon, and a majority decides.

The other Court of final appeal, the Judicial Committee of the Privy Council, is composed for the most part of the Judges who decide cases of appeal in the House of Lords. But, since the Privy Council hears cases appealed from Church courts in England, and a great variety of cases from the colonies and from

---

[1] A part of the measures for reform consisted in adding to the House of Lords four Lords of Appeal in Ordinary. These are made peers for life. The object was to strengthen the House as a Court for final appeal. — Lowell, "The Government of England," Vol. II, p. 464.

India, the Court is strengthened by representatives from the Church, from India, and from the colonies. The two supreme courts are thus composed of a body of English Jurists with a few members added to meet the special needs of the separate courts.

The Act of 1873 provided for a Supreme Court of Judicature to which was to be transferred the judicial functions of the House of Lords and the Privy Council. It was designed to be the Court of final appeal in place of the House of Lords and the Privy Council; but before the Act went into effect it was amended so as to restore the judicial functions to the older bodies. The Supreme Court of Judicature, however, remains as a body of judges having some control over matters of procedure, but no duties as a court for the trial of cases. The Supreme Court is divided into two branches — a Court of Appeal and a High Court of Justice. The High Court of Justice has three divisions known as the Chancery, the King's Bench, and the division of Probate, Divorce, and Admiralty.

The Court of Appeals is composed of the Master of the Rolls, the Presidents of the three divisions of the High Court, and five Lord Justices appointed for the purpose. Ex-Chancellors may sit upon the invitation of the Chancellor. All sessions are held in London, and the court works in sections, three Justices usually sitting together. The appeals are from the three divisions of the High Court and in some instances from the lower courts. Until 1907 no appeals were allowed in criminal cases, but a statute of that year provides for a Court of Criminal Appeal composed of judges from the Court of the King's Bench.

The Chancery Division of the High Court of Justice is made up of the Chancellor as President and six other Judges. The King's Bench Division consists of its President, the Chief Justice of England, and fourteen other Judges. The Probate, Divorce, and Admiralty Division is made up of a President and one additional judge. These are all divisions of one court, and the Judges in the various sections may be freely transferred from one division to another. The object of the system is to simplify procedure and economize labor. When a single judge from any one of the divisions holds a court, it is a session of the High Court. Judges from the King's Bench Division are commissioned to hold courts in the various Counties. On circuit a single judge acts for the Court. In civil cases doubtful questions may be referred to the London Session, where two judges hold the court. The High Court of Justice is, therefore, simply the name of a body of Judges who, either singly or in pairs, exercise general jurisdiction over all matters of litigation, as indicated by the three parts into which the court is divided.

The following is a list of the Courts:

1. The House of Lords.
2. The Judicial Committee of the Privy Council.
3. The Supreme Court of Judicature.
4. The Court of Appeals.
5. The High Court of Justice, composed of
    (*a*) The Chancery Division.
    (*b*) The King's Bench Division.
    (*c*) The Division of Probate, Divorce, and Admiralty.
6. The County Court.
7. The Court of Quarter Sessions.
8. The Justices of the Peace in Petty Sessions.

REFERENCES

ANSON. *Law and Custom of the Constitution*, Vol. II, Chap. X.
CARTER. *History of the English Legal Institutions*, Fourth Edition, 1910.
HOLDSWORTH. *History of English Law*.
LOWELL. *Government of England*, Vol. II, 1908, Chaps. LIX–LXIII.
MAITLAND. *Justice and Police*, 1885.
MARRIOTT. *English Political Institutions*.
MEDLEY. *English Constitutional History*, 1894, Chaps. VII–VIII.
OGG. *The Governments of Europe*, 1914, Chap. VIII.
POOLE. *The Exchequer in the Twelfth Century*.

CHAPTER XLIV

WALES, SCOTLAND, AND IRELAND

THE government thus far described is that of England proper, both in its history and in the forms of its organization; yet in a broader sense the terms used apply to three additional peoples in whom there is a strong sense of separate nationality. The four peoples, English, Welsh, Scotch, and Irish, are all of mixed ancestry. Celtic, Saxon, Danish, Norman, and many other racial strains mingle in these nations. Common to all the four races is the fact that they have grown out of conflicts between natives of the Islands, usually classified as Celtic, with conquerors from the Continent. The Angles, or English, were one of the conquering tribes, and the original inhabitants who remained under the direct dominion of the early conquerors all became English in sentiment as well as in name.

Wales and Scotland. — The Welsh are distinguished from their brethren who became English, in that they held out longer against their conquerors. Having kings and princes of their own, they developed an intense patriotism which expressed itself in music and song and a high order of literature. Yet they were finally subdued or were induced to submit to English rule. They were permitted, however, to retain their own language and to cultivate their own literature and, to a large extent, to follow their own local customs. Since 1307 the heir to the English throne has been called the Prince of Wales. The loyalty of the Welsh was won by fair and considerate treatment. This was so thorough and came so early in the national history that on the political side the fusion was complete. Nearly all laws apply indifferently to the two countries. Yet the fact remains that in no other part of the United Kingdom is native race, language, and literature so well preserved, and local patriotism so intense.

Scotland has a different history. The English conquerors extended their dominion also to the north. For a long time they ruled the country as far as the Firth of Forth. Strenuous efforts were made to bring the whole of Scotland under English rule, but lowlands and highlands finally united and established and maintained an independent kingdom. The union with England was nominally achieved in 1603 when James VI of Scotland became James I of England. A hundred years later the union was perfected, when the Scottish Parliament was disbanded and the people accepted representation in the English Parliament. The Scots retained their own local governments, their own laws, and system of jurisprudence, which is entirely different from that of England. They repudiated the English Church, and they maintained their own system of education.

Representation in Parliament. — Legally, when the Scottish Parliament became extinct, the people were subject to a government of whose membership their own representatives are a small minority. To serve in the House of Lords the peerage of Scotland elects sixteen of their number at each election of the House of Commons, — a small fraction of the entire membership. The Allotments Act of 1885 gave to Scotland 72 members in the House of Commons, to Ireland 103, and to England and Wales 495. Scotland, thus, has 72 out of a total of 670. For a long time after the union the administration of laws in Scotland was carried on through the office of the English Home Secretary, but in 1885 the office of Chief Secretary for Scotland was created and Scottish administration passed into his hands. The Chief Secretary is a member of Parliament and of the ministry, and is usually a member of the Cabinet. In judicial matters the union of the two countries carried with it the right of appeal from the high court of Scotland to the House of Lords. Scottish jurists are represented among the law Lords.

Scottish Influence in the Government. — In outward appearance a small country thus became subject to a great and powerful state; but the actual facts are far otherwise. It is nearer the truth to say that the small country has dominated the larger state. Scotland gave to England the Stuart monarchs, and from the same source came the determining power in saving England from their despotic rule. The Scots did not consent to abandon their own Parliament until it became evident that the Parliament at London was gaining the mastery over the Crown. In the British Parliament the Scotch representatives have, to a large extent, maintained control of legislation for Scotland; they have constituted a sort of parliament within the larger assembly for the government of their own country. While effectively resenting the interference of the English in dictating legislation for Scotland, they have been active and efficient in making laws for England and for the Empire. In like manner, in matters of administration they have maintained effective control over Scotland. Even while they were nominally subject to the English Home Secretary, Scottish affairs were really managed by the Lord High Advocate for Scotland, unless, perchance, the Home Secretary was himself a Scotsman and preferred to look after the details of the administration of his own country. The English have been shut out from local administration in Scotland while the Scots have secured for themselves a large proportion of the offices for the government of England. Wherever the British flag goes Scottish officers go. In politics and officeholding the Scots are English and lay claim to a share in all the glories of the Empire. But in local matters they remain a distinct people and are possessed of a large measure of local national patriotism.[1]

The Conquest of Ireland. — The conflicts which led to the subjugation of Wales and to the independence of Scotland were already well advanced before the English conquest of Ireland began. Henry II (1154–1189) inaugurated the policy of overrunning parts of that island, confiscating the lands and establishing English colonies upon them. There was then no central government, the country being held by rival chiefs contending for the supremacy. The English invaders of Ireland either maintained against the natives a brutal and exterminating war or they became themselves Irishmen. It was comparatively easy for English armies to overrun the country, but for centuries it was impossible to govern it. English colonists residing there often united with the native chiefs to resist the later incursions of the English. They not infrequently became the most inveterate enemies of England. Irish patriotism and the feeling of nationality was thus not so much a matter of race, language, or religion as it was a sense of common danger inspired by a powerful enemy. Besides the English, the Danes, Normans, and others from the Continent made incursions. These mingling

[1] Lowell, "The Government of England," Vol. I, pp. 272, 273.

races were gradually amalgamated by a common resistance to English rule. After numerous conquests and many attempts to govern the country, English authority had become generally recognized at the beginning of the reign of James I in 1603. To assist in holding the country Puritan and Presbyterian colonists were settled upon confiscated lands. The bitterness of religious controversy was added to the old conflict of opposing nationalities. English common law was being gradually extended over a people hostile in sentiment and whose local customs were not adapted to the system. In the name of law the people were deprived of their lands. Irish estates passed into the hands of English landlords, many of whom remained in England, and the country was ruled by a foreign army. Nearly the whole of Ireland except the newly imported Presbyterians, who were the direct beneficiaries of the English rule, became or remained Roman Catholic. The conflicts between Puritan and Crown in England extended to Ireland. There were brutal massacres by both parties. The Irish took the side of James II in his efforts to regain the throne of England. Ulster Protestants fought on the side of William of Orange in the decisive battle of the Boyne, July 12, 1690. Since that date English rule over Ireland has not been seriously threatened.

The Character of the English Rule in Ireland. — The Irish have submitted as unto a foreign ruler. The law, the police, the church, the schools, were all in the hands of the conquerors. England won the loyalty of Wales and Scotland by respecting the preferences of the people. The enmity of Ireland has been fostered by disregarding the preferences of the people. Until the rise of democracy in England the masses of the Irish people were deprived of all political rights. The wave of democracy which carried the extension of the franchise in 1832 removed many of the political disabilities of the Irish Catholics. The further extension of the franchise in 1867 was followed by the disestablishment and disendowment of a church which for centuries had been forced upon the Irish. Later, as the democracy in England has become more self-conscious and more securely dominant, many abuses of long standing have been removed.

In the meantime the spirit of nationality in Ireland has not one whit abated. The Irish have never had a king of their own race. Their executive and judiciary have always been viewed as alien impositions. The one institution which could be looked upon as national in its character has been a legislative assembly which has existed in the island at various times. Irish patriotism has therefore expressed itself in a demand for the restoration of an Irish legislature.

At the time the last legislature was abolished, 1801, the Irish peers were permitted to select twenty-eight of their own number to sit in the House of Lords. The privilege is still continued. But unlike the Scottish members the Irish peers held the office for life and are not reëlected for each parliament. To the Irish was also granted proportionate representation in the House of Commons. The present number, 103, gives to Ireland some thirty members more than their just proportion. This arises in part, however, from a decrease in Irish population.

The Irish executive has been developed out of an army of occupation. The Lord Lieutenant of Ireland was in the beginning the commander of an alien military force. The police are only slightly modified English soldiers. The government is thoroughly military in its form of organization. The laws passed by the British Parliament have made it easy at any moment to transform the Irish executive into actual military rule. The Lord Lieutenant is a member of the English Ministry. Sometimes he is a member of the Cabinet. His salary of £20,000 he is expected to expend in the maintenance of a palace in Dublin. In recent years the Chief Secretary to the Lord Lieutenant, who is always a member of the House of Commons, has assumed the chief duties of the office. This has led to the Chief Secretary's taking the place in the Cabinet formerly held by the Lord Lieutenant. Note again the contrast with the Scottish executive, a government from which all English interference is excluded.

The judicial system is simply the English system imposed upon the people by the use of the army. From the highest court in Ireland the appeal lies to the House of Lords.

During the seventeenth century by the use of the army, by the use of the courts, by the use of Protestant Irish legislatures, Irish lands amounting, it is estimated, to one third of the agricultural lands of the island were transferred, without compensation, from Catholic to Protestant owners.[1] This and other acts

[1] Gardiner, "Students' History of England," Vol. II, p. 595.

of like import have given rise to a land question of peculiar piquancy.

The Governments of Ireland and India Compared. — For many decades the English have maintained a government over a large proportion of the human race in Asia. They are wont to regard this government as distinguished for its efficiency and for its success in winning the loyalty of its subjects. During a like period the government of Ireland has, from the standpoint of the English rulers, been honest and efficient. To the English governing classes it has been a matter of surprise that the Irish do not, like the people of India, show fitting gratitude for such a government. But there are points in the comparison which have been entirely overlooked. The English have never tried to force upon the people of India an alien religion, a foreign land system involving a transfer of title from Mohammedans or Buddhists to Christians. Another point of difference is that the Irish are not Asiatics. They are in race and lineage not far removed from the English themselves. The reiterated assertion that Irish peculiarities demand a peculiar treatment is not well founded. On the contrary, the Irish are like their neighbors on the larger island, they have persistently refused to submit peaceably to a government which they did not approve. They are, however, peculiar in this, that in the maintenance of a resistance which has given distinction to the Anglo-Saxon race the Irish have fought a longer and a harder battle. For thus persevering to the end they deserve and will receive the lasting gratitude of militant democracy in all lands. When Gladstone said that Ireland must be governed in harmony with Irish opinion, he gave utterance to a primary axiom in the modern view of government.

Training for Imperial Rule. — The four ill-defined local nationalities which make up the United Kingdom have been an important factor in the training of British statesmen for imperial rule. They make politics interesting. How often a question arising in a parliamentary debate receives illumination from each of the four parts of the kingdom. Local English politics become varied, saved from the dead level of commonplace stupidity. When the English county council's bill of 1888 was under discussion, the Irish members took an active part, furnishing enlightening details as to Irish local government which prepared the way for the later extension of a similar measure to Ireland. Such experience in comparative government growing out of the coexistence of four nationalities has had no small share in training the British for successful imperial rule.

The movement for home rule in Ireland has become associated with a plan for the federation of the United Kingdom. The four nationalities would naturally furnish the basis for such a federation. Wales and Scotland might each be granted a legislature, and England one or more provincial assemblies. The government of England would thus be harmonized with those of the largest of the self-governing dominions, Canada, Australia, and South Africa, — all federated states. By means of such a system the imperial Parliament might be relieved from the care of local legislation, and the central government from the details of local administration. The democratization of local government tends to increase rather than to diminish the demands upon the central government and such labors might well be passed over to the governments in the several provinces.

REFERENCES

BROWN. *History of Scotland*, Three Vols.
Cambridge Modern History, Vol. XII, Chap. IV.
MORLEY. *Life of Gladstone*, Vol. II, Book IX, Chap. V, and Book X, Chaps. I–V.
TOUT. *Political History of England*, Chap. XXXVI.
LOWELL. *Government of England*, Vol. I, pp. 137–144.

CHAPTER XLV

THE SELF-GOVERNING DOMINIONS

ENGLAND's contribution to free government does not rest chiefly upon what has taken place within the United Kingdom of Great Britain and Ireland, but rather upon the extension of democracy through the process of colonization. Not only have the independent republics of the New World arisen from English colonization and influence, but there remain three self-governing dominions, each with a territory almost equal to that of the United States, still loyal to the British Crown. English colonies have created the federated form of government now being rapidly extended upon all the continents.

The Dominion of Canada. — After the United States had become independent it was only a question of time when Canada should either become incorporated into that Republic or should attain for itself a free government. Civil war broke out between French Catholics and English Protestants in 1837. Some English statesmen then encouraged the policy of union with the United States; but the Canadians opposed it. The alternate policy was, first, federation between the two disturbed Provinces of Upper and Lower Canada in 1841, followed in 1867 by a plan of federation for the whole of British America. Statesmen from the four Provinces of New Brunswick, Novia Scotia, Upper and Lower Canada, the two latter under the new names of Ontario and Quebec, first formulated the plan of union and secured its adoption by the English Parliament under the name of the *British North American Act*. New provinces have since joined the Union, and the Dominion government now exercises authority over the entire country.

In framing their government the Canadians took the United States as their model. They accepted the principle of division of powers between the Provinces and the Dominion government; but instead of making the separate States the possessors of the residuary powers they assigned them to the general government. The Constitution assigns certain powers to the Provincial legislatures, all others being reserved to the government of the Dominion. Sixteen clauses define the powers of the provinces: twenty-nine clauses describe those to be exercised by the Parliament of Canada; but the reservation is made that this is not to be so construed as to restrict the general power " to make laws for the Peace, Order, and good Government of Canada in relation to all matters not assigned exclusively to the Provinces." As compared with the United States, the general government has a much wider range of powers, and, as just said, it is assumed that the Dominion may exercise any power which has not been exclusively appropriated to the Provinces.

The Canadian Constitution is, in form, an Act of the British Parliament. It is English in its phraseology. All executive power is vested in the King, and is exercised through a Governor-General appointed by him. All official acts are in the name of the King. The Governor rules with the advice of a Privy Council whose members he appoints. No mention is made of a Prime Minister or a Cabinet; but in Canada the Privy Council is the Cabinet and the head of the Council is the Prime Minister. The Privy Councilors, being members of a ruling Cabinet, secure and hold office as leaders of the party having a majority in the Lower House of the legislature. Both in the Dominion government and in that of the Provinces the English cabinet system prevails. A Lieutenant-Governor for each Province, appointed by the Governor-General, is the nominal executive head. With him is associated a Council, which serves as provincial Cabinet and is the efficient and responsible government for the Province. Parties in Canada follow the English model, using the same names, Liberal and Conservative; and, although party issues are different, there is a natural sympathy between the parties of the same name in the two countries.

The Canadian Parliament is made up of two houses, a Senate and a House of Commons. The Senate is composed of members appointed for life by the Governor-General (that is, by the government of the day), and are distributed among the Provinces in three equal parts, Quebec and Ontario each having the same number. Qualifications for Senators as to age and residence are the same as in the United States. There is a substantial property qualification. Though tenure is for life, the office may be vacated in various ways, — by resignation, by failure to attend two consecutive sessions, by becoming bankrupt, or failing to maintain the required property qualification. The number of Senators is less than a hundred.

The House of Commons is composed of more than two hundred members distributed among the Provinces according to population. They are elected by ballot for a term of five years. The House is subject to dissolution by the Governor-General.

The Lower House is the controlling branch of the legislature. Not only do money bills originate there, but nearly all important measures also. It is the forum for political controversy. The party leaders are in control, as in the English House of Commons. The Leader of the Opposition receives several thousand dollars *per annum* in addition to the regular salary of twenty-five hundred dollars.

The Senate is a mere revisory body. Its political affiliation changes as one party or the other controls the government for a term of years; but it has been constituted and maintained with the understanding that it should not obstruct the measures agreed upon by the popular assembly. The Dominion is therefore governed by a Cabinet responsible to and identified with the House of Commons. Three of the Provinces have but a single chamber each.

Canadian legislatures, containing as they do under the Cabinet system the efficient executive, hold a distinctly dominant position, the judiciary being remanded to a distinctly subordinate place. Yet the federal system necessitates the coexistence of distinct grades of legislative authority. The Constitution, or the British North American Act, is in the place of supreme authority. Next in order stands the Dominion Parliament, and then the Provincial legislatures. What is done in case legislatures in Canada enact laws in violation of the Constitution? To meet such a contingency the Governor-General, or the Dominion Government, is given veto power over Provincial legislatures, and thus unlawful acts are forestalled. The Governor may also veto or reserve for the consideration of the Crown acts of the Dominion Parliament, if he deems them to encroach upon the rights of the British government. But with two authorities as closely interrelated as are the Provincial and the

Dominion legislatures, numerous statutes are enacted whose administration raises the question of infringement upon or overlapping of authorities. Such matters come into the courts in process of litigation, and the Judges may be of the opinion that an act of a legislature is *ultra vires*, or not warranted by the Constitution. The Court having final authority to nullify a legislative act is the English Privy Council. Here is seen a resemblance to the powers exercised by American Courts in nullifying acts of the legislature on grounds of unconstitutionality; but the similarity is apparent rather than real. In the American governments the Courts are given equal authority with the legislature. That is, a court, as an equal and coördinate branch of the same government, may nullify an act of the legislature. This in effect places the court above the legislature. But in Canada the court of a superior and more comprehensive government sets aside an act of an acknowledged inferior government. It is as if a State court should rule that an ordinance of a subordinate municipality was *ultra vires* and void.

At one time the Supreme Court of Canada became affected with the idea of equality as a coördinate branch of the government. The Dominion Parliament passed an act compelling the Justices of the Supreme Court to answer questions put to them by the Governor-General in respect to the constitutionality of a proposed measure of legislation. The Court held that this law was an interference with their independence and was, hence, unconstitutional. The Privy Council sustained the act and made it very clear that the court was a creature of the legislature and subject to its laws. The Privy Council has uniformly maintained the English position of the supremacy of the legislature. Statutes are nullified only when they create confusion between interrelated authorities or are clearly forbidden by the Constitution. Laws are not declared void because in the opinion of the Judges they are unjust or confiscatory. The responsibility for bad laws rests with the legislatures, not with the courts. It is the duty of the Judges to administer statutes as they find them, asking no questions as to their wisdom. Judges are not permitted to enter the field of lawmaking under the guise of protecting the rights of citizens. Constitutional law in Canada is public law. Its field is the harmonizing of authorities, leaving to the legislature the disposal of private rights.

Canada's judicial system is highly centralized. With the exception of local magistrates all Judges are appointed for life by the Governor-General and are subject to removal by petition from the Dominion Parliament. A uniform system is established for all the States. Criminal law and procedure are controlled by the Dominion government. The separate Provinces legislate upon civil matters, and incidentally penal provisions are attached to aid in enforcement. Hence a distinction arises between criminal law and penal law. The same courts administer both Dominion and Provincial statutes. The Dominion government may command the services of Provincial officers; and in some cases Provincial legislatures rely upon Dominion officers for the enforcement of their laws. Notwithstanding the close relation of the two governments, a vigorous and active local and Provincial life is maintained.

With the government thus constituted British America becomes in all matters of local concern a great free and self-governing republic; only in matters of diplomacy and in foreign relations are Canadians subject to British authority. Even in the making of treaties and the adoption of foreign policies, when Canadian interests are involved Canadian opinion is consulted. There is intense loyalty to the British Crown because of the freedom and independence which are secured to the people. Canadians know that if they should wish to join the United States or to set up a completely independent republic, the British government would offer no forcible resistance. The relation between them is entirely voluntary.

New Zealand and Australia. — Before the Canadian Constitution had been adopted English colonies had been planted in Australasia and South Africa, and the policy of encouraging local self-government was everywhere adopted. New Zealand gained legal recognition as a colony as early as 1840. In 1907 the term Dominion was substituted for Colony, the change of name being intended to denote more clearly the independent position of the state in its relation to the home government. For several decades New Zealand has been conducting experiments in government which are of great interest to all free states. Its present form of government is of the English Cabinet type, with a legislature of two Chambers, one appointive and the other chosen by universal suffrage. The people early grappled with the problem of the use and disposal of the public domain and have adopted a policy which aims to forestall monopoly and secure to large masses of the people the use of land. A system of taxation was adopted which gave to the public a considerable part of the unearned increment of land values. Significant has been the policy of arbitration and conciliation in disputes between wage-earners and employers. Government officers interfere by legal right to prevent strikes and other forms of industrial warfare. New Zealand also introduced the extension to women of the elective franchise on equal terms with men, a plan finally adopted in all the Australian States. It is an excellent example of the small state, favorably located, working out experiments in democracy which are of universal interest. Australian States have been especially influenced and benefited by the study of New Zealand's progressive experimentation.

On the first day of the twentieth century the Commonwealth of Australia was proclaimed. Six States formed the Union and a seventh was added the following year. Some of these communities had already a history of more than a hundred years. All were democracies of the New Zealand type. More than a decade had been consumed in efforts to form a constitution acceptable to all the States. Not only had the Australians the guidance of American and Canadian experience, but in the meantime Switzerland had become a conspicuous teacher of federated democracy. The Canadian Constitution of 1867 was drawn up by statesmen from four Provinces and presented to the British Parliament without popular sanction. The Australian Constitution came direct from the hands of the people. All its provisions had been carefully discussed. Various tentative forms of union had been abandoned on account of popular disapproval. As finally adopted the formal, popular approval preceded enactment by the British Parliament. Unlike the British North American Act the Australian Constitution prescribes a method for its own amendment. A majority of the two Houses of the Legislature may propose an amendment which becomes valid when approved by a majority of the voters so distributed as to include a majority of the States. This is an exact copy of one of the formulas for amending the Swiss Constitution. The people make and amend their own constitution. The formal enactment by Parliament gives final legal sanction.

The Constitution of Australia confers certain specified powers upon the legislature of the Commonwealth and reserves all other powers to the separate States. This is a reversion to the plan prescribed in the United States Constitution. The government is less centralized than is that of Canada, though the list of conferred powers is more ample than that found in the American Constitution.

The method adopted for maintaining the Cabinet system in the Commonwealth and in the States through the offices of a Governor-General, and Lieutenant-Governors for the States, is practically identical with that of the Canadian Constitution. The Australians adopted the American names for the separate Chambers of their legislature, Senate and House of Representatives, and for the two Houses the British name, Parliament. Both Senators and Representatives are elected by universal suffrage. Senators are chosen for terms of six years, six from each State, and the terms are so arranged that half of them are elected every three years. The term of office for Representatives is three years and they are distributed to the States according to population, the whole number to be as nearly as practicable twice that of the Senate. Control of financial legislation is vested in the House of Representatives; but to the Senate is given coördinate power over all other matters. How can the cabinet system be made effective with a legislature having two chambers of equal power? In the case of Australia it was evidently intended that the life of the Cabinet should depend chiefly upon the lower House; but it was conceded that a popularly elected Senate would have unusual power of obstruction. To overcome a deadlock the Constitution provides that in case the Senate twice refuses to give assent to a measure passed by the Representatives, with three months intervening between the times of refusal, then both Houses may be dissolved and all the members newly elected. If the newly elected House of Representatives still persists in the passage of the bill under dispute, and if the Senate still refuses assent, then the bill may come before a joint session of the two Houses. This is a new device for securing harmony between a Cabinet and a bicameral legislature.

The Constitution as originally framed provided for a complete and independent judicial system, the Supreme Court of the

Commonwealth being the final Court of appeal instead of the English Privy Council. This feature was modified, however, so as to permit in exceptional cases an appeal to the Privy Council. The Australian judiciary remains substantially independent of the English judiciary, with some new and interesting developments resulting in the relation of the judiciary to the legislature. The Supreme Court of Australia is of the same grade of authority as the Parliament of Australia. It becomes the duty of the court to rule on questions of the constitutionality of acts of the Commonwealth Legislature. Acts of the legislature have been held void as *ultra vires*. For rendering such decisions the court has been attacked, as being partial or prejudiced. The mere fact of a transfer of power from the Privy Council to a local court is having unforeseen effects. The Judiciary is becoming involved in local partisan politics in a way which would be impossible had the final interpretation of the Constitution remained with English jurists who were accustomed to look to legislatures rather than to courts for the righting of political wrongs. If present tendencies continue in Australia, it will no longer be in order for publicists to say that the United States is the only country in the world in which a court of the same grade of authority with the legislature has the power to nullify its acts. It will be impossible, however, for this policy to be developed in Australia as it has been in America, because of the facility for amending the Constitution. As soon as a serious issue arises between legislature and judiciary there at once follows a movement for amending the Constitution, and the court is thus shielded from prolonged and bitter attack.[1]

Union of South Africa. — The Constitution for the Union of South Africa was framed in 1908 by a delegate Convention from the four colonies of Cape Colony, Natal, Transvaal, and Orange River Colony. In 1909 it was adopted by popular vote in each colony and was enacted by the British Parliament September 20, 1909. During the following year the Constitution was carried into effect Before the Union there had been a century of rival colonization by Dutch and English, and a war had occurred, resulting in the Conquest of two Dutch colonies, 1899 to 1902.

[1] See "The First Decade of the Australian Commonwealth" H. G. Turner, Melbourne, 1911, p. 188.

The South African Union marks the last and in many respects the greatest of the triumphs of the British policy of federation. The submission of the Dutch colonies was immediately followed by the coöperation of the English authorities in securing to the Boers complete self-government in their separate colonies. Hostility disappeared as by magic. The Dutch took a leading part in the agitation for a more perfect union between English and Dutch colonies, and General Botha, the Dutch hero of the Boer War, became the first Prime Minister of the United state.

Conditions in South Africa call for a strong central government. There is a large native population, a shifting body of miners, and members of various races are found in all the Colonies. To secure a government capable of dealing with the numerous perplexing questions arising, the four Colonies were led to surrender their independent powers and become local provinces in a unified state. Instead of a Lieutenant-Governor and a Legislature under the cabinet form of government, as in the case of the Canadian Provinces, there is an Administrator in each province appointed by the Governor-General of the Union, who governs with the assistance of an Executive Council and an elected Legislative Council of not less than twenty-five members. A number of powers and duties are assigned by the Constitution to the Provinces, and these may be indefinitely extended at the discretion of the Central Government. The government is, therefore, on the borderland between a federated union and a state divided into provinces with a large measure of local autonomy.

The Union government is of the thorough English cabinet type. There is a Senate partly elective and partly appointive, with a provision that it may be entirely elective after ten years. Members of the Lower House, called the House of Assembly, are elected for a term of five years. To secure unity of action between Cabinet and legislature the two Houses of Parliament may be called into joint session, or they may be both dissolved at the same time, or either House may be dissolved separately.

The provisions for a judiciary resemble those in Australia, except that in the case of the South African Union the Privy Council in England, instead of the local Supreme Court, decides whether a case may be appealed to the Privy Council.

The four Dominions thus described, together with the United Kingdom of Great Britain and Ireland, constitute a state with a peculiar type of government possessing federal qualities. In their relations to the outside world all are united as one state; all are subject to the British Government. In respect to matters local and domestic, the four Dominions are practically independent. England does not tax them, she does not command their services in case of war. Whatever aid the Dominions furnish for the common defense of the Empire is voluntary. The union is one of good will and mutual loyalty to common interests. The Governor-General is not sent to the Dominions to govern, he is sent to enable the Dominions to govern themselves by means of the English cabinet system.

The spirit which finds expression in the self-governing Dominions is being diffused throughout the government of the British possessions in general. Democracy in England inevitably seeks to provide for the training of the people of India and the Crown colonies for local autonomy and for ultimate self-government.

REFERENCES

An Analysis of the System of Government Throughout the British Empire, Macmillan & Co., 1912, Part II.
EGERTON and GRANT. *Canadian Constitutional Development.*
EGERTON and GRANT. *Federation and Unions within the British Empire.*
KEITH. *Responsible Government in the Dominions,* Three Vols., 1912.
MOORE. *The New Australian Commonwealth.*
TODD. *Parliamentary Government in the British Colonies.*
TURNER, H. G. *The First Decade of the Australian Commonwealth.*

FRANCE

CHAPTER XLVI

Origin and Nature of the French Constitution

THE study of comparative free government begins naturally with England and the United States, since, historically considered, they have led the world in the development of democracy and from them have come the two types of organization most widely adopted. Above all other states they possess the literature of democracy, and their reaction upon other states is most significant and most easily observed. These two governments have, therefore, been described in considerable detail.

The state next to be examined in the enlargement of the field of comparison is indicated with equal certainty by the facts of history. It is France that has been from very early times most intimately associated with the development of the English state and, later, with that of the United States, and it is not improbable that, in the distant future, France may be seen to have played an equally influential part in determining the ultimate forms of the free governments of the world.[1]

The Anglo-Saxons have wrought out their political destiny under exceptional conditions, and it was to be expected that the result would be the evolution of qualities not adapted to incorporation into the governmental forms of states developed under the quite diverse conditions prevailing upon the European Continent. Especially is this true of the experience of the United States with its three hundred years of practically unhindered and independent growth upon a virgin continent, exempt from the perplexing problems afflicting the peoples of the Old World. England's insular position, though furnishing an isolation less

[1] Munro, "Government of European Cities," p. 7.

complete, has also proved favorable to the fostering of an independent development in consonance with the inborn temper and instincts of her people, while her nearness to the European Continent has also proved advantageous in that the enforced association with other and different peoples has contributed to the quickening of ideas and the enrichment of thought. France has worked out her history, her race development, her political ideas, her power of keen and logical thought, through close connection with the turbulent, ever changing life of the great continental states about her, and she is uniquely fitted to make most important contributions to the final forms of world democracy.

Comparison of France and England. — A superficial view reveals marked similarity in the histories of France and England. Both were originally occupied by Celtic peoples; both were subject for centuries to Roman rule; both were later conquered by German tribes and were exposed to incursions and occupation by the Danes; and to each the name of a German tribe became affixed. But Britain adopted the language of the invading Teutonic tribes, while the people of Gaul first accepted that of their Roman rulers and then taught it to the conquering German Franks. French is therefore a modified Latin tongue, and French civilization has been profoundly affected by its intimate relation to an earlier and powerful political development. It has most perfectly embodied the dominant tendencies of Western Europe. Under the Cæsars Gallia had become as Roman as Italy itself and Roman law became and remains the basis of the French legal system. In France the conquering Teutons attained their most brilliant successes. There only did the feudal system reach perfection, and when the time came for monarchy to triumph over feudalism, its most perfect work was displayed in France. When, finally, the day of democratic revolution dawned, in France alone did its unbridled spirit fully work its will.

Contrast all this with corresponding movements in England. There conquest by the Roman was only partial, as was that of the Angles and Saxons who followed. The Norman triumph did not destroy the earlier institutions, which the new rulers were, indeed, careful to preserve. The feudal system never entirely prevailed in the Islands, for neither feudal lords nor kings ever completely gained dominion over the people and the ancient institutions to which they clung. Different ideals in government and society lived on side by side, each modifying the others and no one becoming permanently dominant. Democracy came through a long series of slight adjustments and adaptations, all in harmony with the steadfast, determined, cautious English character.

Reciprocal Influence of France, England, and the United States upon One Another. — The constant influence of France upon England has been a potent factor in the development of democracy. Norman and Plantagenet kings had large possessions in France. By defending English local liberties they avoided in their island kingdom the weakness of the early feudal monarchs of France. Factions in England arose through conflict between French foreigners and native English. It was Philip Augustus of France as well as the English barons whose pressure obliged King John to sign Magna Charta. The liberated peasants of England gained a new sense of importance from their triumphs over the feudal armies of France, and their persistence hastened the downfall of feudalism in both countries. French monarchs encouraged and assisted Stuart Kings in their warfare against Parliament. Fear and distrust of France was one of the causes leading to the triumph of the Whig party in the Revolution of 1688, and for two generations British Toryism was discredited on account of suspicions of French influence. English religious history was also often modified by the experiences of her neighbor across the Channel. The Massacre of St. Bartholomew in 1572 helped to make England Protestant.

No less significant has been the relation of France to America. Rival settlements, begun at the same time in North America by both France and England, led to prolonged territorial conflicts. Fear of France caused England to adopt a liberal policy toward her American colonies. Wars between France and England involving intercolonial contests gave the settlers a trained soldiery. When French authority had been finally excluded from North America, France aided the English Colonies in a war for independence.

England and America have in turn exerted an influence upon France. The victims of Bourbon tyranny were encouraged to thoughts of resistance by the example of the freer peoples. Montesquieu, Rousseau, Voltaire, and other French writers gave precise and logical expression to the theories of freedom engendered by the conflicts between England and her Colonies. The thoroughness of the autocratic rule under which the French lived tended to promote thoroughness in their theory of democracy. The time and effort required to indoctrinate a great nation with the new teaching gave rise to a profound conviction of its truthfulness and importance. When the doctrines of the French philosophers at last found expression in a Declaration of Independence and in the birth of a free nation in America, the reaction upon France was tremendous. The Revolution came like a deluge. Its excesses caused a conservative reaction in England: in France it produced Napoleon. As France helped America to get rid of George III, so England helped France to get rid of the first Napoleon. Both England and the United States were active in moderating the pretensions of the restored Bourbons after 1815. The House of Orleans, in 1830, distinctly recognized the English parliamentary system. After a succession of revolutions France, having been overrun by German armies, was left without a government. The Third Republic was extemporized to meet the emergency. While some of its features were borrowed from the American Republic, it is English in its characteristic method of harmonizing the Executive and the Legislature. England and America are thus contributors to the shaping of the present French government.

Successive French Constitutions. — The present French Constitution is the eleventh which has been enacted since the beginning of the Revolution of 1789.[1] The state has more than fulfilled Thomas Jefferson's ideal of a new constitution every twenty years. Some of these documents have been reactionary in certain of their provisions, but all are based upon the constitution and government of the great Revolution. Before that event, the masses of the people were subject to the arbitrary personal rule of kings, nobility, and clergy. After that, and especially after the completion of the civil code of 1804, the people were protected by laws administered by a fairly just and independent judiciary. Subsequent constitutions specifically guaranteed to the people the continued enjoyment of their own

[1] Ogg, "Governments of Europe," Chap. XV, p. 289.

local courts of arbitration.[1] No reactionary government has presumed to return to the brutalities of personal rule. Another change, equally significant and permanent, appeared. Before the Revolution the land, which was in the hands of nobility and clergy, had become an agency of tyranny and oppression. The Revolution transferred the land to the proprietorship of the peasant occupants and no later government has called in question the validity of the title.

Other provisions of the original constitution could not be rendered effective in so short a time. A trained voting constituency cannot be extemporized. Provisions for the exercise of the right of suffrage were much more liberal than those which prevailed at the time in England and in the United States; but experience was lacking. No one who understands the difficulties involved will deny that during the past century France has made phenomenal progress in the development of an intelligent popular use of the franchise. The statesmen of the Revolution believed that a state founded upon universal suffrage required universal free education, but the realization of this ideal in France has involved a conflict with the established church. Although delays have been numerous the third Republic is now in process of realizing universal education and the separation of church and state.

Centuries of tyranny had effaced from the minds of the people nearly all memory of local government. To meet the popular needs for local administration and legislation an elaborate system of local geographical areas was created. Napoleon utilized these local areas as administrative districts for the central government and the Napoleonic system of local government still survives. France is now apparently engaged in the more important task of proving that a great state may have a centralized government and yet become thoroughly democratic. Already there are signs of the rise of local autonomy, especially in the communes and cities. With assured democracy in the central government it is to be expected that the development of local home rule will be rapid.

---

[1] The lowest French court is presided over by a Justice of the Peace (*juge de paix*) whose first duty is not to hear law suits, but to prevent them by acting as arbiter in a *preliminary conciliation*. Many judicial cases are arbitrated by him and thus settled without coming to trial.

Respecting the more fundamental part of the constitution, which pertains to the distribution of the high powers of state and the attainment of their harmonious working, France has been subjected to many changes scarcely less notable than those that have taken place in England and America during the corresponding period. At the time of the French Eevolution the ideas that prevailed in England respecting the relations of the King to his ministers, of the ministers to one another, of the ministers jointly and severally to Parliament, of the two Houses to each other and to King and Cabinet, differed greatly from those of to-day. Theories as to these relationships have undergone radical changes in the course of the century. The American States were especially fitted by their past training as colonies to reduce to practice Montesquieu's theory of the division of government into three departments, each composed of separate officials and all serving as checks one upon another. Having done this, they naturally applied the same principle to the frame of the general government. The theory of a separate executive with independent powers determines the Presidential type of government. At no time, indeed, has the government been in entire harmony with the theory of the founders, and the discrepancy increases as the business of governing becomes more exacting and complex.

Unlike the States of the American Union, France had no past experience suited to encourage a trial of the system advocated by French philosophers. It was easy to provide for an assembly having supreme legislative powers, but it was not easy to harmonize the working of such a legislature with an independent executive. King, committees, directory, consuls succeed one another in rapid succession. Somewhat of fixity was reached when Napoleon, the First Consul, became Emperor of the French, in 1804. But in the meantime the legislature had been so organized that it could not transact business, and both executive and legislative power were left in the hands of the Emperor and a Council of State of his own choosing. When the Bourbons were restored, in 1815, it was with the distinct provision that the legislature should be resuscitated, and the principle recognized that ministers should be responsible to the legislature. This was made more emphatic under Orleanist rule, from 1830 to 1848.

Carried along by the great European wave toward free government, the French proclaimed the Second Republic in 1848. The new Constitution provided for a single-chambered legislature elected by universal suffrage and for a President, elected in the same way. This was distinctly an experiment in the American Presidential type of government. Louis Napoleon, the first President, soon made himself master of the state. In the Constitution which he issued in 1852 the independence of the Executive is clearly stated. Neither Emperor nor minister was made responsible to the legislature. But a few years before his abdication Napoleon III was forced to proclaim anew the principle of the responsibility of ministers.

Organization of the Third Republic. — The century of experimenting and constitution-making has been highly educative, and the Third Republic came into existence under conditions favorable to the final union of the people in the support of a free republic having the English, rather than the American, form of organization. A single-chambered Assembly was chosen in 1871, primarily to make a treaty of peace with Germany. Although there was an insistent popular demand for a restoration of the Republic, the peculiar conditions existing at the time of the election gave to the Assembly a large majority of monarchists who refused to declare a republic. They did, however, elect a President as chief executive with power to appoint and dismiss his ministers. President Thiers himself favored a republic; but, not having the support of the Assembly, he resigned after two years. The Assembly elected Marshal MacMahon, a pronounced monarchist, as his successor. Because of a division among the monarchists no royal candidate could command an immediate majority.

Finally, in 1875, the Assembly, which had been elected to meet a temporary emergency, proceeded to set up a more permanent form of government, and adopted a constitution which is still in force. By this document legislative power is committed to two houses, a Senate and a Chamber of Deputies. The Senate at first consisted of three hundred members, three fourths of them chosen by a process of indirect election in the various Departments, the other fourth being selected by the Senate itself. This law was afterwards altered so that all Senators are elected by an indirect process in the Departments. The body which chooses the Senators is composed of: members of the Lower House representing the Departments; the departmental Council General; the Councils of the *Arrondissements* into which the Department is divided; and Delegates elected by the Communes.[1] All of these various classes are chosen by universal suffrage. The legislative power of the Senate is concurrent with that of the Lower House, except as to the introduction of money bills. Only with the consent of the Senate may the President dissolve the chamber of Deputies.

The Deputies number 602, all elected at one time by universal suffrage. Their term of office is four years. If a dissolution should occur, the newly elected assembly would still be entitled to the full four-year term, barring another dissolution. Two methods of electing deputies have been made the subject of much dispute in French politics. The Assembly that provided for the organization of the Chamber of Deputies in 1875 was itself elected by the voters in the various Departments who cast their ballots for all the members to which the Department was entitled. This is called *scrutin de liste*. It is as if the members of the Lower House of the American Congress from each State were elected on a general ticket. The Constitution of 1875 left the method of electing Deputies to be determined by law, and the method adopted has been election by single districts — called *scrutin d'Arrondissement* — except between the years 1884 and 1889, when the other method was followed. The age requirement for members of the Chamber is 25 years; for the Senate, 40 years. There is no residence requirement. Provision is made for the payment of members, and since 1906 the salary in each house has been 15,000 francs.

In the acts for the reorganization of the government (1875) President MacMahon was left in full possession of his office, and provision was made for the election of future Presidents by an absolute majority of votes of all the members of the Senate and the Chamber of Deputies united in National Assembly. The term of office was fixed at seven years, and the incumbent was made eligible to reëlection.

The President has the initiative in legislation concurrently with the two Houses. He is without veto power, except that

[1] Lowell, "Governments and Parties of Europe," Vol. I, p. 20. For local government areas see below, pp. 567–569.

he may require the two Houses to reconsider a bill. He promulgates the laws, superintends their execution, grants pardons, disposes of the armed forces, and is the ceremonial head of the nation. Still, for every official act the name of a minister is required. The Constitution expressly states that: " The ministers are jointly and severally responsible to the Chambers for the general policy of the Government and individually for their personal acts. The President of the Republic is responsible in case of high treason only;"[1] the President may be tried before the Senate for high treason and the ministers may be arraigned for lighter offenses. The obvious intention of these provisions is to set up a responsible cabinet government in which the President instead of a king is the formal head.

It should be remembered that a majority of the framers of the Constitution of 1875 were monarchists, as was their President also. All that was needed to fulfill their desires was for the President to give place to the Count of Paris as an Orleanist King.

The first elections under the new Constitution gave to the republicans a large majority in the Chamber of Deputies, while in the Senate monarchists and republicans were nearly balanced. A conflict ensued between the republican Chamber and the monarchist President, the latter, contrary to law, taking an active part in party politics. In 1877 the Chamber was dissolved with the consent of the Senate, and the election following returned a still more determined and radical republican majority. The Senate having become republican also, President MacMahon resigned in 1879, and M. Grévy, a radical republican, succeeded to the office. All branches of the government have since remained in the hands of the republican party.

The Constitution of 1875 was the result of a compromise between monarchists and republicans. Each party expected to carry the election and thus to control the future government. The monarchists, while incidentally recognizing the existing republic, hoped by slight changes to adapt its Constitution to a monarchy. In either case the government would be in the hands of a Cabinet of ministers responsible to the legislature. Of all the French constitutions that of 1875 is the briefest. Everything is omitted except the bare framework of the executive and legislative departments of government. No refer-

[1] Law on the Organization of the Public Powers, Feb. 25, 1875, Art. 6.

ence is made to the judiciary. Details are left to be filled in by the legislature or by the executive. The method of choosing Senators was, however, described with considerable particularity; yet, by an amendment of 1884, it was declared that this part of the act should cease to have constitutional force, thus leaving the legislature in full control of the matter. Amendments have been added to insure the permanence of the Republic. All members of the families that have reigned in France are excluded from office, and the Constitution, as changed, makes it illegal to propose an amendment to restore the monarchy.[1]

The method of amending provided for in the Constitution of 1875 requires each House, by majority of all its members, to vote that a change in the constitution is desirable. Then the two Houses must meet in joint session as a National Assembly and act upon the proposed changes. Amendments to the Constitution are thus secured by a modified process of legislative action. No popular ratification is required. Only twice has the National Assembly been called to consider changes in the Constitution. Except the acts referred to above, the changes are of minor consequence. Although the Constitution is written, although it is solemnly enacted law, there is no means of enforcement other than an appeal to public opinion or to the agencies relied upon for enforcing the ordinary statutes. President Poincaré expresses the conviction that if a National Assembly should pass an act restoring the monarchy, it would be the duty of the President to refuse to promulgate it; yet he qualifies the statement by the observation that the strength of the Republic rests with public opinion rather than in constitutional prohibition.[2]

French, English, and American Constitutions. — A few words on the nature of the French Constitution as compared with those of England and of America are in order here. It is contrary to the genius of the French people to permit any custom, or understanding, or usage, either to obscure the law or to usurp the place of law. French courts are not permitted to interpret or apply the law according to a previous decision of the same or of another court. Each court, at the time of action, is required

[1] Lowell, "Governments and Parties in Continental Europe," Vol. I, p. 12.
[2] Poincaré, "How France is Governed," p. 163.

to apply the law as then understood. If there are uncertainties or confused and contradictory decisions, the remedy is sought either through new statutes or new administrative rules, or through a bench of jurists intrusted with the especial duty of promulgating general rules for the guidance of judges. In any event, the assumption prevails that the law is definite and positive, equally well understood by all subjects; that law is not a mysterious rule of action discoverable only by the high priests of an occult science.

It is unthinkable that such a people, keen, positive, and logical in their mental habits, should endure a constitution based upon mere sentiment, or composed of customs, or understandings, or rules of conduct, which are not themselves laws, but which traverse the law and are treated as if they were above law. In France the rule making the ministers responsible to the legislature is a written law. In England the rule is a mere understanding, while the old forms of law subjecting the ministers to the Crown remain unchanged. Custom and understandings have been permitted to nullify the law. The French as well as the English have customs; they have certain ways of doing things; but when a conflict between custom and law is raised, either custom is condemned or the law is changed. The greater part of the English Constitution is a subjective experience, a state of mind associated with a thousand years of national history. There was no distinctly recognized constitution in France until a state of mind induced by a long period of tyranny expressed itself in the destruction of despotism and the substitution of government founded upon the will of the people. Their Constitution was not merely a written declaration of principles, but an embodiment of these principles in an actual frame of government. The French method requires that when the government changes, corresponding alterations shall take place in the written Constitution. The eleven constitutions have each and all embodied the fundamental principles of the original one; they are so many attempts to harmonize the letter of the law and the actual government. How many constitutions would have been issued in England during the same period if the French method had been followed? It is the glory of the English Constitution that its marvelous adaptation to the ever changing demands of public opinion " cometh not with observation." After ten trials the French have apparently created a constitutional government with all the flexibility of the English, while at the same time subject to definitely enacted law.

The contrast with the Constitution of the United States is scarcely less striking. Both countries have written constitutions which are definitely enacted law. In America the real constitution is not found in the words of the document, but in the rulings of the courts interpreting it, a vast body of constitutional law resting upon judicial decisions. The French Constitution consists of a few brief enactments providing for a Cabinet form of government. Executive and Legislature are left with a free hand to do what seems best for the state, not influenced or hampered by appeals to custom or usage as in England, and in no way controlled by judicial decisions as in the United States. The only appeal to past experience is by way of reminder that there are yet unfulfilled ideals in the principles proclaimed in the Revolution of 1789.

REFERENCES

DODD. *Modern Constitutions*, Edition 1909, Vol. I, pp. 283 ff.
LOWELL. *Governments and Parties in Continental Europe*. Vol. I, Chaps. I, II.
OGG. *The Governments of Europe*, Chaps. XV–XVIII.
POINCARÉ. *How France is Governed*, London, 1913, Chaps. I–VI.
SEIGNOBOS. *A Political History of Contemporary Europe*, London, 1901, Vol. I, Chaps. V–VII.

CHAPTER XLVII

The Executive in France

THE President of the French Republic serves for a term of seven years. He is eligible for reëlection, has a salary of 600,000 francs ($120,000), and an equal allowance for household expenses. The pomp and circumstance of the office are like those of a king or emperor. The office is open to all citizens except the members of families which have reigned in France. One would think that an office with such attractions would make a disturbing appeal to the ambition of politicians. As a matter of fact the election of the President commands little public attention or general interest. A month before the end of the presidential term the two Houses of the Legislature meet in National Assembly at Versailles and choose the next President. He is usually one of their own number, is sure to be a statesman of experience, and is naturally associated with the party groups which at the time command a majority in the Legislature.

Various attempts have been made in France to separate legislative and executive powers, but in each case either anarchy or the subordination of the legislature has ensued. Monsieur Thiers (1871), the first President of the Third Republic, was chosen by the Assembly and was, in a sense, responsible to it, though he personally exercised the power of appointing and dismissing his ministers. The President, being at the same time, in effect, Prime Minister also, was subject to the continuous criticism of the Assembly. When he found that his policies were not supported he resigned (1873). MacMahon, the second President, was in a like position until the adoption of the Constitution of 1875. Then the President was no longer responsible to the Assembly. He was removed from personal contact with the Parliament and in his place was established a responsible Cabinet of Ministers. France was thus transferred to the cabinet type of government with an elected President holding the place of the monarch in England.

The President thus chosen cannot be the object of patriotic sentiment and the symbol of unity in the state as is the King of England. When the citizens of the Republic do honor to a public officer, sentiment attaches not to individual or family, but to the state. The symbol of unity is the tricolor.[1] If the President is not criticized, it is because his acts are not deemed worthy of criticism, rather than because of any sentiment associated with the office. Since 1875 three Presidents have been induced to resign on account of adverse criticism. MacMahon resigned on account of his failure to restore the monarchy. Grévy resigned (1877) because of revelations of corruption in his family, and Cassimir-Périer, called to the office upon the assassination of Carnot in 1894, resigned after a few months, because of difficulties in maintaining a ministry. Only three Presidents have served the full term of seven years. In the normal working of the system the President is not the object of criticism, because his duties are usually not of a partisan character. The Prime Minister and the Cabinet bear the brunt of partisan attacks. It is a great advantage of the Presidency as compared with the Monarchy that the chief executive is always a man of mature age, an experienced statesman and politician. Perchance, he has himself been Prime Minister or President of one of the Chambers of the Legislature, and is thus thoroughly acquainted with the working of the government. On the other hand, it has been shown in the chapter on the English Crown, that monarchy has likewise certain advantages which can never attach to a temporary chief executive, and the balance of merit may be fairly even. It is hence of interest to the free governments of the world that both systems should continue to exist. France is, at least, rendering valuable service to all peoples living under a monarchy by making a demonstration of an easily available substitute for an unsatisfactory royal family.

President, Cabinet, and Councils. — The powers and duties which the French President may exercise upon his own responsibility are not numerous. Of these by far the most important

[1] The refusal of the Bourbon candidate to recognize the flag of the Revolution caused his defeat in 1877.

is the formation of a ministry. The President must select a body of men who are responsible to the legislature and to the country for the conduct of the government. This duty in France is far more onerous than the corresponding service in England. The King has practically no choice in the matter, if English parties are in their normal condition. But the normal condition in France lays upon the Chief Executive the often difficult task of discovering a statesman willing and able to form a workable ministry. The Prime Minister in France is a legally recognized officer, his official designation being President of the Council. The outgoing Prime Minister countersigns the decree appointing his successor, but it is the President of the Republic who really makes the selection.

With the Prime Minister in office cabinet responsibility begins, other appointments being upon the recommendation of the chief minister. Cabinet crises in France follow each other in rapid succession. Rarely does a ministry endure for two years. On an average, there is a new ministry every year. An adverse vote in the Chamber of Deputies produces a cabinet crisis; the members resign in a body and the President must find a new President of the Council. It is quite in order for members of the former Cabinet to accept office under the new Prime Minister. In fact, a complete change in the membership of the Cabinet is unusual.

The President of the Republic remains in much closer touch with the Cabinet than does the King of England. He not only attends, but he presides over the meetings of the Council of Ministers. These occur usually twice each week. Once a week or oftener the Ministers also hold a session of their own at which the Prime Minister presides. This is called a Cabinet Council. Of these meetings President Poincaré says, " The Council of Ministers deals with the more important business, the Cabinet Council with current questions of internal politics."[1] Both councils are composed of the same ministers. The meetings are secret; no minutes of the proceedings are kept. Through this direct connection with the ministers the President may exert much influence, but for all official acts the ministers are responsible. The Constitution gives to the President the power to negotiate and ratify treaties, but permits him to exer-

[1] "How France is Governed," p. 197.

cise this power only by and through a responsible minister and with cabinet approval. A list of subjects for treaties which require legislative approval before they are valid is given in the laws. There are, however, important treaties which are entirely in the hands of the Executive, and their terms may be state secrets. The alliance with Russia is the result of such a treaty.

The President undoubtedly has a free hand in the appointments to office in his household, although appointments in general are ministerial rather than presidential. Pardons, the general administration of the laws, the disposing of military forces, are all in the hands of the Council of Ministers, subject to such influence as the President may exert.

Besides the Cabinet Council and the Council of Ministers, there is a third body called the Council of State, composed of more than fifty members, selected, in recent years, by the Council of Ministers. The Council of State originated in the system of the First Napoleon. It exercises legislative and judicial as well as executive functions. With the rise of the Cabinet many of the legislative and administrative duties of the older body passed to the Council of Ministers, while in recent years its judicial functions have been greatly amplified. Historically, the Council of State fills an important place in the evolution of the Cabinet. Napoleon governed by means of this Council, whose membership he controlled. With the increase of power in the legislative assemblies the powers of the Council of State diminished. With the advent of the Cabinet the older Council became an assistant to the Council of Ministers. Through its committees it aids the ministers in various lines of administration, and it may also be called upon to formulate a system of by-laws for the Executive.

French Method of Legislation. — No proper comparison can be made of the relation of the executive and legislative departments in France and England without taking account of a radical difference in the partition of business between the two departments. In England and in the United States, it is the aim of the Legislature to furnish in the statutes minute, detailed directions to the Executive. The laws are so drawn as to leave to the administrative officers little or no discretion. The ideal set before the legislators is to foresee and provide in the wording of the bills for all possible contingencies. In France, and in all other countries apart from the Anglo-Saxon world, the work of the Legislature is comparatively simple and easy. There is no effort to foresee and provide for doubtful contingencies. The statutes are drawn in general terms giving clearly the requirements of the state, but leaving to the Executive the addition of all needed details. Administrative officers thus assume and fulfill the more difficult functions of English and American Legislatures.

To supply needed rules supplementary to the statutes, the President of the French Republic issues general orders and decrees; the Council of Ministers formulates by-laws; each Minister gives general orders and directions in his own department; or, the ministers may call upon the Council of States to prepare a system of by-laws on assigned subjects. Moreover, in each Department there is a Prefect and in each Commune a Mayor, who has the power of issuing by-laws. In these various ways the executive department amplifies, explains, and applies the acts of the legislature. In theory, at least, no by-law is permitted to change or violate the statutes; all are intended to meet their requirements. Even in matters of finance there is a limited field for executive discretion. Revenues may be increased and credits extended to meet unforeseen needs. Under such a system the work of the Cabinet in the Legislature cannot be as exacting and as important as in England; and the administrative *rôle* is correspondingly more important.

Responsibility of Ministers. — The French Constitution states that Ministers shall be jointly and severally responsible to the Legislature, but gives no intimation as to the number of Ministers or as to who shall organize the administrative departments. The Executive itself has, therefore, assumed the function of organization. The Legislature, by implication, expresses approval of the act by voting supplies to each new department. There are not, as in England, non-cabinet Ministers. Neither are there sinecures, as in the English ministry, nor officers corresponding to parliamentary and under secretaries. Twelve men, each of whom is the head of an important administrative department, assume the entire burden of a responsible Ministry. The following are the names of the departments: Justice; Foreign Affairs; Interior, or Home

Affairs; Finance; War; Marine; Public Instruction; Public Works; Commerce; Agriculture; Colonies; Labor.[1]

The Prime Minister chooses any one of the departments. If he is not the Minister of Justice, the holder of that office is *ex officio* Vice President of the Council of Ministers. Ministers are nearly always, though not necessarily, members of one of the two Houses of the Legislature. All the members of the Cabinet, whether members of the Legislature or not, have free access both to the Senate and to the Chamber of Deputies. In each of the Houses the ministers are privileged speakers on all matters pertaining to the business of their several departments. Because of this privilege, the officers of government monopolize a large proportion of the time of the legislature, especially of the Chamber of Deputies.

The letter of the Constitution makes the Cabinet responsible to the two Houses; but various features of the law tend to restrict this responsibility to the Lower House. The Senate is a permanent body. Its members serve for a long period — nine years. They are elected by an indirect process, one third of the number every three years. Naturally the Senate, with its high age requirement, responds more slowly to changes in public opinion. It is evidently fitted to be a conservative, regulative Second Chamber. There is no provision for dissolving the Senate, and its consent is required for a dissolution of the Chamber. In practice, therefore, ministerial responsibility is to the Chamber, which receives a direct mandate from the voters once in four years, or oftener in case of dissolution. An adverse vote in the Senate does not cause a cabinet crisis. The few instances where the attitude of the Senate has appeared effective in driving a Ministry from office are explained as exceptions or as mere excuses for resignation on the part of a weak Cabinet lacking adequate support in the Chamber of Deputies.[2] The real political battles which count in the Government of the country are waged in the popular Chamber.

The administration of the central government extends to the minutest details of local government. The country is divided into 86 Departments, 362 Arrondissements, nearly 3000 Cantons, and more than 36,000 Communes. In its chief outlines

[1] The War Cabinet of August 26, 1914, had 14 members.
[2] Lowell, " Governments and Parties in Continental Europe," Vol. I, p. 22.

the system is a product of the Revolution. It is artificial in the extreme, the boundaries being fixed without reference to former community life. The statesmen of the Revolution intended to create, out of hand, a complete system of local government. They did create the geographical boundaries for local government, but they could not create the habits and experience required for successful local autonomy. The First Napoleon organized a centralized system of administration, using the local areas as a framework and, with some important modifications, it still survives.

For purposes of convenient local autonomy there are too many subdivisions; a citizen cannot maintain a lively corporate interest in four distinct areas. Both the Arrondissement and the Canton are mere districts, with no corporate qualities. They own no property and do not of themselves levy and collect taxes. The Arrondissement, as a subdivision of the Department, serves as a district for departmental administration. It has a Subprefect, who is subject to the orders of the Prefect, and an elected Council with only advisory powers. It is also the legislative district for choosing members of the Chamber of Deputies. Cantons serve as districts for the Justices of the Peace and for choosing members of the Council General of the Department.

The Department and the Commune are corporate bodies. Potentially they are centers for the development of local government; they are, however, under the control of the Central Government.

The Prefect of the Department is the officer through whose agency France is governed. One may gain an idea of the significance of this office by eliminating the American State officers and placing in the hands of a single appointee of the President the business of the state legislatures, the state executives, and, to a large extent, of the counties, cities, and school districts. The Prefect governs the Department subject to the orders of the Minister of the Interior. This was the character of the office as established by Napoleon I. Under the Third Republic modifications have been introduced which are fitted to develop into a limitation on the power of the central government.

Local Government. — Each of the Cantons within the Department elects, by universal male suffrage, one member of a

Council General for the Department. Members of this Council hold offices for a term of six years, one half retiring every three years. The Council holds two short sessions each year, and no important powers are conceded to it. Subject to the veto of the Central Government, it may adopt resolutions on purely local matters and apportion direct taxes to the Arrondissements. All the acts of the Council are under the guidance of the Prefect of the Department. He prepares the budget to be voted. Even the measures enacted by the Council General are in his hands to be enforced or not at his will. The Council has no means of enforcement. There is, however, a representative committee, or commission, appointed by it, whose duties are purely advisory. In fact, the Council General has no independent authority. The Prefect or the Minister of the Interior may issue orders which are enforced as law; but the acts of this representative assembly are treated as recommendations, not as laws. Its very existence is precarious, since it may be dissolved by the Central Government. The importance of the Council General consists not in what it has done, but in what it may yet become. President Poincaré, after describing the Council in action, says: " If you have attentively followed the proceedings of the council you will doubtless receive the impression that there are unemployed forces here, and that the citizens ought to strive to make the departmental organism more active and energetic." [1] This, it may be seen, is the expression of a hope for the future of French democracy rather than an attainment. Primary interest is still absorbed in the one problem of gaining a more effective popular control over the general government. Democracy in France has not yet reached the decentralizing stage.

The communes, like the other local institutions, received the stamp of artificiality. They were made practically identical in their forms. A rural commune consisting of less than a hundred people has a frame of government similar to that of Bordeaux with nearly half a million. Paris and Lyons are, however, favored with special local organizations. In each commune there is a Council elected by universal suffrage every four years. The number composing it varies, according to

[1] Poincaré, "How France is Governed," p. 70; Lowell, "Governments and Parties in Continental Europe," Vol. I, p. 38; Ogg, "The Governments of Europe," p. 346.

population, from ten to thirty-six. All members are elected at the same time and by *scrutin de liste*, or general ticket. The Mayor, with one or more Assistants, is elected by secret ballot in the Council from its own number.

While in its present form of organization the commune is recent and artificial, it is associated historically with the remote past. Towns and cities played an important part in the destruction of feudal despotism. The larger cities maintained also traditions of resistance to centralized autocracy. The commune, therefore, is the one modern local institution which calls forth strong personal sentiment. It also has a modicum of independent governmental power. Unlike the department, it is provided with a locally elected executive. The mayor and his assistants perform the double function of administering general and local orders. As agents of the General Government they act under the direction of the Prefect of the Department. As local officers they carry into effect policies adopted by the Communal Council. On a few matters purely local the Council and mayor may act without consulting the higher authorities, though the exercise of independent powers is guarded in many ways. The Mayor may be suspended for a month by order of the Prefect; for three months by the Minister of the Interior; and he may be removed from office by the President of the Republic. Only a limited number of the resolutions of the Council are of themselves valid; others require the approval of the Prefect; still others more important, the approval of the central government; others more important still must be submitted to the Senate and the Chamber of Deputies. A few of the great cities have a larger measure of local autonomy than the smaller communes.

From this brief description it is evident that the President of the Republic and the twelve members of the Cabinet are responsible for the administration of the entire government, local as well as general. Not only do executive officers administer the laws; to a large extent they also make the laws, since they issue acts supplementing the brief statutes emanating from the legislature. In local matters administrative officers rather than municipal assemblies exercise the lawmaking function. Powers are thus centralized in the Executive. The one means of popular control is through the two houses of the

Legislature. The system involves cabinet responsibility to the Chamber of Deputies.

The relation of the Executive to the Judiciary is discussed in later chapters. In the French use of the term an independent judiciary means a judiciary which in no way interferes with administrative officers: *i.e.*, Judges do not hear complaints on account of official wrongdoing. If citizens suffer from illegal acts, they may appeal for redress to higher officers in the executive or they may call the Cabinet to account in the Chamber of Deputies. A third method of protection against administrative abuse is provided for in administrative tribunals in which cases of alleged violation of law may be investigated and decisions rendered. Associated with the Prefect in each department there is a Council which acts as a tribunal in matters of administrative disputes. The Council of State also serves as a tribunal to hear appeals from the departmental councils and complaints against the higher officers of state.[1]

REFERENCES

(See Chap. **XLVI** for general references.)

MUNRO. *The Government of European Cities*, Chap. I.
POINCARE. *How France is Governed*, Edition 1913, Chaps. VII, VIII.
SHAW. *Municipal Government in Continental Europe*.
WILSON. *The State*, Edition of 1898, pp. 224–244.

[1] For further elaboration of the topic see below, p. 589.

CHAPTER XLVIII

THE LEGISLATURE AND POLITICAL PARTIES

LEGISLATIVE halls on the Continent of Europe have the seats arranged in a semicircle, facing the presiding officer. In all of these assemblies there is the same traditional arrangement for the location of the party members. Extreme conservatives and reactionaries occupy the seats to the right of the President; extreme radicals occupy the seats to his left; the moderates sit in the center. Parties are named from their respective positions in the hall, as, — the Party of the Right and of the Right Center, the Party of the Left and of the Left Center. There may be a fifth designation, — the Party of the Center. The actual party organizations are usually more numerous and their relations to one another more complex and confusing than is this division into four or five leading groups; but in its chief outlines this order holds true for party divisions in Continental legislatures.

In some of its features the English Cabinet system is quite unworkable in a legislature so organized. The multiplicity of party groups calls for a different plan. The French Chamber of Deputies is a good example of the Continental type of cabinet government. Like the English, the French system fuses Legislature and Executive; it makes the Cabinet responsive to and dependent upon the votes of the Assembly. It is a true cabinet government having corporate responsibility, but its relation to the political parties is radically different. The French Cabinet is not itself a party organization, as is the English. Parties in France are organized to influence government; not to govern. The English Cabinet is confronted at every point in Parliament and before the country by a "shadow cabinet" of equal numbers, equally organized and seeking to win a majority. The system requires two governing parties, whose joint constituencies include practically all the voters of the nation. The French plan will admit of nothing of the sort. Its legislature, on the contrary, exhibits an ordinary minimum of at least four permanent major party groups.

The Political Parties.[1] — First, there are citizens who have lost some privilege in government which they have greatly cherished. Something is passing or has passed which they deem of primary importance. To defend what is threatened and to recover the lost is their mission. These are the reactionaries, or the extreme conservatives, — the party of the Right. Second, there are those who set a high value upon the dearly bought experiences of the past; they would not lightly sacrifice anything of value, though they recognize the facts of progress, and are actuated by a desire to harmonize the new with the old. These are the moderate conservatives, — the Right Center. In the third class are the idealists who seek to gain for the state blessings never yet attained, reformers who would adventure into new fields of statesmanship. They would not wantonly destroy the present order, neither would they permit the present order to block the way to the attainment of greater good. These form the Left Center. The Fourth class are idealists who find in the present order of society an obstruction to the new order which they would substitute in its place. These are the Radicals, Socialists, and Anarchists of the Left. The history of the Third Republic shows the shifting of power from one to another of these main groups. The Party of the Right — Clericals and Royalists — held a dominant place until 1877. The Right Center, — Moderate Republicans and Progressists, — with the help of radicals, was then in control until 1898. Since 1902 the Radicals, assisted by Socialists, have been in the ascendant. The movement has been from Right to Right Center and on to Left Center. Some theorists would give a permanent place to a fifth party group, a party of the Center, whose special function should be the coördination of the prevailing tendencies in the State in times of emergency. Of such a party Waldeck Rousseau was leader during the period of transition from Right to Left, from 1898 to 1902.

---

[1] The description of parties in France given here follows freely the work of M. Léon Jacques, " Les Partis Politiques sous la IIIe République," Paris, 1913. For a full discussion of party groups and their component parts the student is referred to this admirable work.

The actual condition of parties in France is by no means so simple as this description would indicate.[1] In each of the four sections there are subdivisions with distinguishing names and organizations. Numerous intermediary organizations tend to obscure the lines of division between the major parties. In the legislative hall sit men who were elected under one party designation and who act and vote under another. Some members are allied with more than one party group.

It should be remembered that in each of the ruling parties in England there appears a tendency to form minor organizations for the promotion of special interests. In each party are extremists and moderates. Numerous combinations appear, looking to political ends. Yet in the House of Commons practically every member is a supporter of one of the two party leaders. The English system forces all organizations into at least a temporary alliance with one of the parties. Within the separate parties and between the parties there is continuous readjustment. In the French Chamber, however, this kaleidoscopic rearrangement take places within the Assembly. In an important sense the English Cabinet is master of the Assembly, but French Ministers hold no such masterful position.

The Organization of the Chamber. — The Chamber of Deputies organizes itself according to rules which prevailed long before any Cabinet had appeared. It appoints a bureau of sixteen of its own members to have general charge of its business and to act on behalf of the Chamber during recesses. The head of this Bureau is the President of the Chamber. He is not an impartial presiding officer, as is the Speaker of the House of Commons. Nor does he control the House as a party leader, after the manner of the Speaker in the American House of Representatives. The President of the Chamber of Deputies is an experienced political leader; he takes an active part in the debates of the Assembly; he may or he may not agree with the Cabinet; but his advice is sought by the President of the Republic in the selection of a leader to form a new ministry at the time of a cabinet crisis. The presiding officer thus exercises

[1] Lowell, describing the party divisions in 1876, says, "In the Chamber of Deputies were the Left Center, the Republican Left, the Republican Union, the Radical Left, and the Extreme Left; and each of these, like the fractions into which the Right was split, was organized with president, secretary, and executive committee of its own." — "Governments and Parties in Continental Europe," Vol. I, p. 78.

large responsibilities in preserving order and in assisting the Chamber to fulfill its mission. Other members of the bureau of sixteen fill the offices of vice presidents, secretaries, and auditors for the Chamber.

To organize for the transaction of business the six hundred Deputies, following an ancient custom, divide themselves by lot into eleven sections, or bureaus, as nearly equal in number as possible. This division takes place every month. These eleven sections assist the Assembly in determining the validity of the elections of its members; they discuss briefly the bills presented to the Chamber, and determine the attitude of the members upon these bills before they are referred to a committee. But by far the most important service of the Bureaus is the appointment of committees to consider and report upon the bills brought before the House. The separate sections first give enough attention to a bill to determine who are in favor of and who are opposed to it; and then each bureau names one of its members to serve on the committee to examine the bill, suggest amendments, and report to the House. The plan, as will be seen, provides for a special committee of eleven to consider each bill. Measures of peculiar importance may have a committee of two from each Bureau, or even three. The Budget and the auditing of accounts go into the hands of committees of thirty-three each, appointed for a year. Committees on the Army, on Labor, and on a few other topics calling for much legislation, are made practically continuous in service, and all bills pertaining to those subjects are referred to them.

There are thus two sorts of bureaus: the permanent Bureau of sixteen made up of the President and other officers of the Chamber, and the eleven temporary bureaus into which the members of the Chamber divide themselves by lot each month. There are, likewise, two varieties of committees to consider and report upon bills. Measures pertaining to Finance, Army and Labor, and a few other subjects of primary importance are referred to permanent committees, all other bills are referred to special committees appointed by the eleven bureaus, each bureau naming one or more of its members to serve on the committee.[1]

At the opening of each legislative session the Prime Minister presents a brief outline of the policy of the Cabinet and the pro-

[1] Lowell, "Governments and Parties in Continental Europe,' Vol. I, p. 111.

posed legislation, and ministerial bills are prepared and introduced.

The Cabinet has been injected into an Assembly already organized to perform its duties without executive guidance. How can such an organ secure support from such an Assembly? This is accomplished through definite modifications in the working of the system. The leaders of the stronger party groups agree in advance upon the composition of certain committees of special political importance. The fact that the ministers are privileged speakers in both Houses of the Legislature enables the Cabinet to monopolize the time and dominate their action. There is, indeed, constant friction between the Cabinet and the Committees, and it is evident that the later system is not yet fully harmonized with the earlier one.

The Cabinet members have seats in a central position in front of the Presiding Officer. No opposition of trained critics confronts the Government, as in the House of Commons in England. Ministers address the Chamber from the Tribune, which is a raised platform lower than the seat occupied by the President and placed immediately in front of him. From the same place come speeches for and against Cabinet measures; and from various parts of the chamber spring sallies of attack upon or defense of government proposals.

French Ministers are accustomed to be called to account for their policy by two quite distinct processes. First, there is the ordinary Question, directed to the Premier or to any one of the ministers. The Question requires notice and previous consent of the minister who gives the answer; and only the member who asks the question has a right to reply to the minister. Second is the Interpellation, which may proceed from any member of the House and may pertain to any part of the ministerial policy. The Interpellation is a formal challenge, and the Ministry is compelled to make answer within thirty days, a day being fixed for the reply. The Ministry adopt a form of words explaining their attitude on the policy called in question by the Interpellation and then move to proceed with the regular order of business. Upon this motion there ensues a general debate attacking and defending the policy of the Cabinet. At the end of the debate, if the ministerial motion receives a majority vote, the government is sustained.

A negative vote does not necessarily cause a cabinet crisis, since the interpellation may pertain to a trivial matter which the government decides to ignore; yet such a vote always weakens the Cabinet and usually is followed by resignation. About half the French cabinet crises are produced by an adverse vote following an interpellation.

The Senate. — The organization and working of the Senate is similar to that of the Chamber. It elects a President and a body of officers to manage the business of the House. It divides into nine, instead of eleven, bureaus; the committees, therefore, number nine or a multiple of nine; that on the Budget consists of eighteen members. The salary of the members is the same as that of the Deputies. While the election[1] is by an indirect process, still, all the persons of the various classes qualified to vote for Senators in the Departments are themselves chosen by the voters who elect members of the Chamber of Deputies. Politics enters into the choice of Senators.

All the great parties have members in the Senate, but some of the minor ones are not represented. Party changes are less rapid than in the Chamber, yet the permanent tendencies are reflected in the Senate as in the Lower House. The fact that all the Ministers are privileged speakers in each of the two Houses tends to secure harmony of action and to avoid prolonged conflicts. There are frequent disputes over the power of the Senate to amend or change bills for raising revenue, but thus far serious conflict has been avoided. Government bills strongly supported in the Chamber can usually be got through the Senate.

The French Senate is vastly more influential and important than is the House of Lords in England;[2] on the other hand it is correspondingly inferior in power to the Senate of the United States. The French Senate has one peculiar judicial function. Like the United States Senate, it serves as a court for the trial of impeachments, and in addition to this it may be transformed into a high court for the trial and punishment of any one who is accounted dangerous to the Republic. In 1889 Boulanger, who had for several years been a disturbing element in politics,

[1] See above, p. 556 et seq.
[2] Lowell, "Governments and Parties in Continental Europe," Vol. I, pp. 21–26; Bodley, "France," Vol. I, pp. 26 ff., London, 1898.

was summoned to appear before the Senate for trial. Instead of appearing he chose to become an exile.

Party Organization. — To understand the relation of the French Cabinet to the voting constituencies involves a knowledge of the party organizations. In the States of the American Union the fact that one usually votes a certain party ticket entitles him to legal rights as a member of that party and to a voice in the selection of its candidates. On the Continent of Europe the fundamental assumption as to what constitutes membership in a party is different. The habitual voting of a party ticket does not make one a member of a party, nor does it entitle him to any share in the nomination of candidates. The parties are composed of those who have formally joined the organizations and who pay the required fees. The fees are paid annually, monthly, or weekly, and may be high or low. Each party has its own system, but all party membership is conditioned upon paying at least an annual fee. In some parties there are two, three, or even four grades of membership, according to the amounts paid and the corresponding privileges in respect to control of the organization. Parties of the Right in the Chamber of Deputies exact large annual fees; those of the Left small ones. The highest rank in one of the royalist parties requires an annual payment of at least $100, while a socialist may attain a full voting privilege in his party for a few cents per month. High fees with various ranks are characteristic of the Right; fewer ranks and lower fees are characteristic of the Center; and the extreme Left has but one rank and a low uniform system of contribution.[1]

The organization of parties is of recent date in France. Not until after the Boulanger disturbances, which terminated in 1889, were there any systematic national organizations with central offices in Paris. Since that date the leading parties have all attained central organizations with subdivisions in the Departments, establishing a regular means of communication with the local clubs and associations in the communes. The central office in Paris is a clearing house for gathering from and distributing party information to all parts of the country. Party bulletins are regularly issued by the stronger organizations and

[1] Statements respecting local organization of parties are based upon information derived from party officials in 1913.

the party newspapers fill a place of influence which is without parallel either in England or America. Through these numerous organizations and the complicated system of finance which each involves, large numbers of French citizens are rapidly acquiring needed experience in the ability to initiate and to execute a positive program.

The Revolution of 1789 found the people void of organizing ability. They could combine to destroy, but the masses were helpless to create a new order. Socialists began at once to combine to proclaim new gospel, but it required almost a hundred years for them to create an effective organization. Poverty of organizing ability among the revolutionists has inured greatly to the advantage of the ecclesiastical orders with their superb system. Poverty of organizing ability has also undoubtedly been an influential factor in inducing the Freemasons of France, as a society, to enter politics as a counterpoise to the Roman Church. To the same cause may be attributed the failure of labor unions in France. Unable to form and execute positive programs of amelioration, the wage earners become victims of policies of destruction, "sabotage," "syndicalism," or revolution. Socialists, on account of their superior organization, are winning the laboring classes to the support of more moderate and conservative policies. They go farther than any other party in extending their membership to include all who habitually vote for their candidates.

All the parties seek to increase their membership. To this end there is a tendency toward reduced fees, some of the organizations even permitting local clubs to join the party by simply paying a single membership fee. The ideal will be fulfilled when all who habitually vote for the candidates become paying members of the party. American voters enjoy full party membership without financial sacrifice. The French who become members of a party are trained to expect an assured demand upon their incomes to promote the objects of their party.

Improved organization is naturally followed by more insistent demands upon public officers. Beginning about the year 1910, the better organized parties required that members of the legislature whom they elect shall hold together and vote as a body. The new rules establish closer relations between the members and the party councils. This latest development corresponds to the rise of the Caucus in England, when, under the leadership of Chamberlain and Churchill, the party councils undertook to dictate policies to the Cabinet.[1] It was then seen that since the English Cabinet, from its essential nature, was itself the supreme party council, it could not submit to dictation from an outside organization.

In France the case is different; the Cabinet is not a party organ. Greater simplicity and efficiency are likely to result from a closer association between public officers and the party councils. The parties and the public press with which they are identified are become the great organs of public opinion. They enable the lawmakers to feel their way. The French Cabinet cannot, as does the English, keep in touch with the voters through Whips and paid agents. Nothing of the sort exists in France. There is need, therefore, of some reliable source of guidance; and the stronger parties are assuming this *rôle*. Recent developments are likely to diminish the number of party names by drawing into a few great organizations the allied groups. Nothing, however, has thus far occurred to lead to the expectation that parties on the Continent will finally be reduced to two and thus make way for the English cabinet system. Belgium has been quoted as a Continental state exemplifying the English system. But one of the so-called Belgian parties is the Roman Catholic Church, and the other is composed of numerous groups opposed to the Church. This has no real resemblance to the English system, but means a prolonged duel between the Church and its opponents.[2]

The French cabinet system is in the formative stage. It has not yet had a fair trial. Its very existence is still seriously threatened. Royalists and Bonapartists would restore a monarchy with independent executive powers. The Church still maintains a propaganda against the Revolution. These are all discordant elements. What form the government will assume when all classes shall have accepted the existing Constitution is for the future to determine. The probabilities are in favor of a continued parliamentary system, but one with a Cabinet which is decidedly un-English in its relation to party

[1] See above, Chap. XL.
[2] Seignobos, "A Political History of Contemporary Europe," Vol. I, pp. 246–250.

organizations. England is as likely to adopt the multiple party system of the Continent as continental states are to adopt two-party government of the English type.

REFERENCES

(See references for Chaps. XLVI and XLVII.)
BODLEY. *France* (1900), Vol. II.
JACQUES. *Les Partis Politiques Sous la IIIe République*, Livres I, II.
MARRIOTT, J. A. R. *Second Chambers*, Oxford, 1910, Chap. X.
PONDIA and PIERRE. *Traité pratique de droit parliamentaire*, Eight vols.

CHAPTER XLIX

The Roman Legal System and Modern Government

The preceding chapters have discussed the State of France as having a typical Continental Government differing in many ways from the Anglo-Saxon democracies. This radical distinction in the forms of government and in the types of law which separates Anglo-Saxon countries from all others can in a measure be accounted for by a consideration of the way Roman law and government have affected England. The present chapter is devoted to a sketch of legal development in England and the United States and on the Continent of Europe. Necessarily brief, it merely suggests some of the fundamental influences which account for radical differences in the distribution of the powers in the governments.

The Romans have given to the world a system of law fitted to become universal. The English system of Common Law is best understood as a recent and peculiar modification of the Roman system. The men who first organized government in England were versed in the Roman system. It was only late in the thirteenth century after separate high courts had been set up that the peculiar English differentiation arose. Common Law has a history of less than seven hundred years. Roman Law has a continuous history of some three thousand years. The Roman system prevails in nearly all civilized countries outside of the British Empire. The peculiar Common Law modification is for the most part confined to England and countries colonized by Englishmen. English law has been extended to Wales and Ireland, while Scotland retains the Roman system, as do Quebec, South Africa, and the State of Louisiana. What will be the ultimate system in India and other British possessions is for the future to determine. The Common Law system is, then, a special Anglo-Saxon institution, though it embodies certain principles of liberty which entitle it to recognition in all free states.

Early Roman Law. — Roman Law, like English law, originated in a struggle for liberty. Before the Laws of the Twelve Tables were enacted centuries of progress had been leading towards an enlarged citizenship. The Plebeians had already obtained many civil rights. The Patricians held the chief offices when the Plebeians, having superior force, made an effective demand that the laws should be codified and published, so that all might be equally informed as to their rights. The result was that after the first great Roman Code of 451 B.C., all distinctions between Patricians and Plebeians gradually disappeared. Roman citizenship was afterwards extended to the poorer unorganized classes. Strangers living in Rome secured at the hands of Roman magistrates the administration of the laws which they had been accustomed to enjoy in their own countries. As the Romans annexed new territory the local territorial laws were still administered. Magistrates thus became expert in the administration of a great variety of laws and in the selection and extension of those rules of conduct which were found to be most beneficial. Selected Roman Law became the common law for a great variety of tribes and peoples in a growing empire. The extension of the Empire carried with it the benefits of an improved legal system. At first no distinction was made between private and public law. " Private law furnishes the foundation upon which public law rests."[1] Plebeians and the proletariat contended for political as well as for property rights. During the later centuries the Roman rulers became obsessed with the idea of world conquest and great changes ensued in the organization of the government. " The young Empire which arose over the ruins of Carthage bore the seeds of its own destruction within it." The masses became subject to the rich. " While Rome's serfs were growing into freemen, her power was steadily in the ascendant; when the masses of her small freemen lapsed into serfdom, her power was doomed. Christianity came to proclaim the gospel to the masses, but it arrived too late to effect any decisive reform in the existing economic conditions."[2]

Early Roman statutes were enacted by large assemblies of citizens in which was no opportunity for discussion or debate. The Roman Senate was quite as much an executive as a legisla-

---

[1] Sohm's "Institutes of Roman Law," p. 36, Third Edition. Tr. by Ledlie, Oxford, 1907.   [2] Sohm's "Institutes of Roman Law," pp. 44–45. Tr. by Ledlie.

tive body. The Twelve Tables were prepared by a commission appointed for the purpose and were enacted by vote of the *comitia centuriata*. Roman law was largely developed from discoveries made by administrative officers. When a prætor was set to rule over a district he administered the laws and customs which he found among the people. He issued general orders of instruction to the judges and these orders when sanctioned by the general government became laws. His doubts were solved by seeking instruction from higher officers. This policy produced a class of experienced students of law. The Commentaries of the Jurists and expert students were often enacted into law. Through various agencies private law was perfected by the elimination of differences and by a selection of such rules of conduct as, based upon experience, were found most helpful in securing domestic harmony. Numerous codes were prepared for the guidance of public officials and for the instruction of the people. For more than a thousand years the legal codes were, in theory, based upon the laws of the Twelve Tables. When the Emperor Justinian (527–565 A.D.), with the help of eminent jurists, made a complete codification of the entire system of ancient Roman law, the Justinian legislation furnished a new starting point for the development of the Roman system.

Later, or Private, Roman Law.—It is to be observed that the later Roman Codes embody only a part of the law developed by the early Republic. They contain no bill of rights, no recognition of the right of subjects to a share in the government. Only such laws are found as may be administered by a corrupt and tyrannical government. Caracalla (212–217 A.D.), who made all free subjects of the Empire Roman citizens, was noted for corruption and tyranny. Citizenship had long ceased to imply any important political rights.

When Rome became a conquering empire, military chiefs found it to their advantage to extend and perfect only that part of the law of the Republic which pertained to private and personal rights. Hence, during the centuries of conquest the laws governing the ownership and transfer of property, family relations, and the punishment of crime, became dissociated from any idea of a share in the government. In the realm of private law, Roman conquest carried with it the great boon of justice and equity to the subject peoples. By the separation of private from public law corruption and tyranny in the government were enabled to coexist with progress in the development of a system of private justice. It is a remarkable fact that Roman private law was perfected during a period of degeneracy in the government. Bryce designates the four hundred and fifty years from the end of the First Punic War (241 B.C.) as the time occupied in the completion of the Roman system.[1] The result is thus described by Sohm: "Towards the commencement of the third century (in the reign of Caracalla), the Roman franchise was extended to the great bulk of the subjects of the Empire. . . . To be a citizen of Rome was now to be a citizen of a world-wide Empire. The Roman Civil law — at one time a narrow kind of private law, circumscribed and limited by national idiosyncrasies — expanded into a private law for the citizen of the *orbis terrarum*, a law for the private person as such, a law, in other words, in which the essential and indestructible elements of the private personality found expression. And at the same time the rules regulating the ordinary dealings between man and man widened into a system in which the essential character of such dealings was brought out, a system not restricted to the dealings of any particular age, but applicable in all ages alike. Herein lay the secret of the imperishable strength of Roman private law."[2]

A corrupt and decaying government thus perfected a system of justice received from an earlier free and progressive Republic. The government perished, but the system of law did not perish. Barbarian conquerors were induced to accept this gift from the past and transmit it to modern free states.

English, or Common, Law. — The early development of English law was not unlike that of Roman law. In each case the people were contending for their rights, personal and political. Neither in Magna Charta nor in the Twelve Tables of Roman law is there any suggestion of a separation of private from public law. In England the contest continued along the original lines of a struggle for both private and public rights. While Roman emperors had restricted the magistrates to the administration of private law, English kings followed a different course, creating new courts by means of which they restrained the power

---

[1] Bryce, "Studies in History and Jurisprudence," p. 114. Essay II, § VIII.
[2] "Institutes of Roman Law," p. 46.

of feudal lords. The people were taught to look to the king's courts for the defense of political as well as private rights. Public officers were held amenable to the ordinary courts and nobility and clergy were made subject to the law. In course of time kings also were deprived of arbitrary power and were rendered submissive to Parliament.

By a gradual and imperceptible process the Roman people had lost all share in their government, while at the same time Roman rulers were perfecting a system of private law. Gradually, also, in course of centuries, the English people have gained recognition as themselves the source of all political power and authority. The English kings did not intend to build up a democracy. They labored to increase and perpetuate their own power, as did the Roman emperors. But the barbarian conquests and the resulting feudal system had created a break in the continuity of Roman administration. Private and public law were again fused together, and local conditions favored the development of political rights.

Space does not permit of detailed description of the sharply contrasted systems of English and Roman law. Only a brief notice of three characteristics which explain the peculiar English distribution of the high powers of state will be given.

In the first place, as already noted, English courts administer both public and private law, and the judiciary is thus enlarged at the expense of the executive. Administrative officers are held accountable before the ordinary courts for any alleged illegal acts.

A second, more radical, difference is found in the fact that a considerable part of English law is derived from the judiciary.[1] As the king's justices passed from shire to shire securing to the people their local rights and customs, the rulings of the courts transmuted custom into law. This was undoubtedly a potent agency in strengthening the position of the Crown, which also gained in prestige as the High Court of Appeal. The rulings of the courts became important sources of both public and private law.

The spirit of the Roman Law is radically different. It is the business of the Roman Law court to apply the rules of law to cases of disputed right, not to determine what the rules

[1] Above, p. 406.

are. If there are uncertainties as to the rules, light is sought from administrative officers or from the legislature. It is the aim of Roman Law to inform litigants in advance as to what are the rules of law; to make the statement of the rules so clear and distinct that to understand them calls for no unusual technical knowledge. Chance decisions of cases in litigation are not permitted to obscure the rules of law, and judges are warned against the evil tendency to follow precedent in their decisions. They are admonished to do justice in each case regardless of former decisions. If new light is required, it is not sought among the utterances of magistrates in deciding previous cases. The Roman system thus restricts the ordinary judiciary, first, by confining it to the field of private law, and, second, by preventing the courts from becoming a source of law.

The third difference lies in the exaltation of the legislature as a lawmaking body. The process of lawmaking in England at first did not greatly differ in form from the Roman method. Magna Charta, like the Twelve Tables, was a brief summary of private and political rights. The Petition of Right exacted from Charles I (1625-1649) was also a brief summary of rights. Neither Charles nor John had any intention of obeying the laws which were exacted from them by force. It was the difficulty of securing royal obedience which led Parliament to introduce into the statutes minute details and then to secure their administration through a Cabinet controlled by the legislature. The king, as chief executive, was thus restricted in his power to interpret and apply the acts of Parliament. This enlargement of the functions of the distinctive legislative assemblies is, therefore, a very recent innovation in the Roman system, and is strictly limited to Anglo-Saxon countries. In other modern free states the Roman method of general lawmaking prevails.

Each of the three English modifications of the Roman system deprived the administrative department of a portion of its power. First, by administering without discrimination both public and private law, the courts rendered executive officers accountable to the judiciary. Second, English judges performed functions that in Rome had fallen to administrative officers. They both expounded and applied the law, and enlarged and adapted it to changing conditions. Third, Parliament was led by fear and distrust of the king to introduce minute details into its statutes, thus depriving the executive of the right to expound and apply the laws.

Constitutions and Law in the United States. — A more radical departure from the ancient system is found in the United States. Roman public law was in the beginning evolved from preëxisting customary or private law. In the United States the process is reversed, public law is made fundamental. There is no law, there are no legal rights, either private or political, except such as are authorized by the Constitutions. The American system is the exact opposite of the Roman system. It begins with public law; private rights are made dependent on public law. Romans made sure of private rights, leaving public law in the hands of tyrants. Neither system will be complete without the other. Many centuries were required to perfect the Roman scheme. Americans have entered upon the more difficult task of perfecting and harmonizing both public and private law. Thus far time for only a crude and imperfect beginning has elapsed.

Bagehot has called attention to the fact that, at a certain stage in the evolution of the race, quantity of government is of greater importance than quality. It seems America's high mission to fulfill vicariously this quantitative service for the world in its transition from despotism to democracy. In the earlier history of the American States there was little real demand for government of any sort, but as a rule each State was supplied with two separate legislative chambers supplemented in some cases by an executive council. The English practice of minute statutory legislation was adopted. States and Nation were each supplied with distinct sets of independent governmental machinery. Not only so, but towns and cities were likewise, for a time, provided with governments after the same model. Comparatively small cities were organized with city legislatures having two houses, and with independent executives and judiciaries. This governmental machinery was again duplicated by local, state, and national party organizations, through whose agency popular election was substituted for the constitutional method of choosing the President of the Republic. In many ways the parties assumed and exercised governmental functions. Numerous corporations have also been called into existence which appropriated governmental powers. The

American system, moreover, forces the judiciary into the thick of the fight in partisan or contentious politics. Thus the entire government in its manifold forms has been engaged in the gathering of experience for the future democracy. From the standpoint of mere quantity nothing more could be desired. The one purpose of finally making sure of popular control of the government as a means of securing all rights, has constantly become more determined and more clearly defined.

The Americans adopted the three English innovations upon the Roman system and added thereto a notable innovation of their own. Not only did they make the executive amenable to the ordinary courts, but they gave to the courts the power to nullify acts of the legislature. The judges are the final interpreters of the Constitutions. If in their judgment a legislative act violates the Constitution, they declare the act void in case its constitutionality is questioned. This feature has led to the development of an extensive body of Constitutional law derived from judicial decisions. In no other country are the political powers so adjusted as to render possible the development of such a body of public law.

The French Legal System. — The United States is not alone in the attempt to create a legal system designed to enable the people to govern themselves. France also entered upon the task the very year that the American Constitution went into effect. A brief comparison of the two results is given in a previous chapter. A few points are recalled here because of their relation to the contrasted method of English and Roman government.

France is becoming democratic with a minimum of departure from the Roman system. In the southern provinces the influence of Roman law survived throughout the feudal period and gained new life as feudal power diminished. One of the first demands of the Revolution was the restoration of Roman Law and the response is found in the Civil Code and four minor codes issued by Napoleon during the years from 1804 to 1810. This Napoleonic legislation is a modern summary of Roman Law comparable to the Justinian legislation of the sixth century. At the same time a series of courts was organized to administer these codes. The organization is thoroughly Roman in form.

An Act of 1790 forbade the judges to entertain any charge against a public officer. The French place confidence in their administrative officers and protect them from any interference on the part of the judges. Under the Third Republic special administrative tribunals have been established to hear complaints against public officers and to assist in the administration of public law. Referring to these tribunals, President Poincaré says: " Administration and justice are two separate domains. The better to ensure their reciprocal independence, the disputes arising out of the execution of the commands of the administrative authorities are not submitted to the judicial authorities. A Minister or a prefect issues an order. If this order is illegal the Government may be interpellated in the Chambers, but the civil courts will not have the right to annul the order. It is not their place to judge the executive power nor its officials. This is a principle which was solemnly proclaimed by the Revolution."[1] The French system is a continuation of the Roman system in that it exempts the executive from judicial interference, but the Romans did not provide for an " interpellation in the legislature," nor did they set up tribunals whose special business it was to hear complaints against the executive. The French plan implies practically two sets of courts, one to administer the ordinary law and the other to decide questions arising out of the rapidly accumulating administrative law. It becomes impossible always sharply to distinguish between private and public law, and a Tribunal of Conflicts has hence been established composed of judges from the high court and from the highest administrative tribunal. It is the duty of this court to harmonize the administration of private and public law and to decide doubtful cases involving both jurisdictions.

In the making of laws the French likewise follow the Roman system. Statutes are couched in general terms, and the executive is required to amplify them, to issue ordinances explaining their meaning, and to modify them to meet the various exigencies of administration. This is all distinctly Roman. But the two houses of the legislature are English rather than Roman. As French democracy becomes more self-conscious and insistent the importance of debate in the houses becomes more apparent. It should be borne in mind that both the English and the French legislative innovations upon the Roman method are of comparatively recent origin. In England the changes arose from an

[1] Poincaré, "How France is Governed," p. 270.

unconscious striving after a more tolerable government; in France from the first crude attempts at a revolution whose purpose was only partially attained.

The French revolutionists proclaimed the doctrine of popular sovereignty, but their method of realization has been the adaptation of the Roman system to the needs of the democracy. The United States substitutes a radically different plan. Private law, as such, is abolished. In its place State and federal constitutions are made a guaranty for all legal rights. Public officers of every sort are engaged in the elaboration of a political scheme which will in the end secure to the people their private rights. But many of these private rights are made dependent upon the previous satisfactory adjustment of the relation of the States to the Union, and of the various departments of government to one another and to the people.

The future of free government is the more secure because the two great republics of the world illustrate distinct and diverse methods of approach. They are at one in the declaration of the principles of popular sovereignty, but the United States repudiates ancient forms and lays anew the foundations of the state in a popularly enacted fundamental law, while France adapts the ancient forms to modern needs.

The constitutions enacted in all countries since 1789 have been greatly influenced by that of the United States, many of its features having passed into other constitutions. French codes of law have also influenced subsequent legislation in all parts of the world. Latin republics in the New World have copied with modifications the Constitution of the United States while adopting the French civil code. As is shown in later chapters, a marked tendency appears among them to follow French models in the final organization of their governments.

REFERENCES

An Analysis of the System of Government Throughout the British Empire, pp. 43–53. Macmillan.
BRYCE. *Studies in History and Jurisprudence*, Essays II, XV.
BRYCE. *The Holy Roman Empire*.
SOHM. *Institutes of Roman Law*, Tr. by Ledlie, Edition 1907, Introduction by Grueber, and Chaps. I, II; Part II, Chaps. I–III.
WILSON. *The State*, Chap. XIII.

GERMANY

CHAPTER L

The Origin of the German Empire

CHARLEMAGNE (768-814) founded a great empire including the greater part of Italy, the whole of France, and much of the present dominions of Germany and Austria. In the year 800 Charlemagne received at the hands of the Pope the crown of the Cæsars and thereby became the head of the Holy Roman Empire. The old Roman Empire had become Christian in 325 A.D. As the secular power of the Cæsars decreased the spiritual power of the Popes increased. The Church bore no small share in binding the empire together under its spiritual rule. It took over a considerable part of the government. Roman law was already a perfected system. The Church appropriated Roman law and adapted it to its own needs. Canon law, or the law of the Church, became an important part of modern Roman law. The conquering barbarians were rapidly converted to Christianity. In the transition from heathenism to the religion of Rome the idea of a world empire with just laws divinely sanctioned took definite form. Of this Empire the Pope of Rome was the spiritual head, and the dynasty of the Cæsars the temporal head. It was to be a holy and righteous empire which was to give peace and order to the entire world.

Origin of the Holy Roman Empire. — The temporal office was transferred to Constantinople, but the spiritual office remained in Rome. The fiction of a world dominion was still maintained even after the entire west was subjected to Teutonic conquerors. The popes continued to acknowledge the Byzantine emperors as the secular heads of the Holy Empire. After Justinian (527-565) the Eastern Empire rapidly declined. When Charlemagne entered the city of Rome with a conquering army, in 800 A.D., there was a vacancy in the office at Con-

THE ORIGIN OF THE GERMAN EMPIRE

stantinople, and the symbol of the secular unity of Christendom was transferred from Constantinople to Paris.

The idea was grand and inspiring. A just system of private law was already an accomplished fact. If, under the sanctions of religion, order could be established among the rulers of all nations, the predicted millennium would have been fulfilled. Many obstacles stood in the way of immediate realization of the ideal. Popes and secular rulers seldom agreed as to the respective limits of their powers; instead of harmony there was perpetual conflict. The Empire of Charlemagne terminated at the death of his son in 843 by a division into three parts. France and Germany became permanently separated. The Empire was at no time coextensive with the Roman Church. After the division independent states were formed in France and Italy and the Holy Roman Empire became in practice a local German Empire, though it retained some of the mythical symbolism of the unity of Christendom.

The office of Kaiser, or Emperor, was at no time clearly defined. It passed partly by inheritance, partly by the choice of the imperial diet, sometimes by papal influence to one or another of the rulers of German States. In 1438 the office became permanently associated with the house of Hapsburg, the rulers of Austria. It was contrary to the theory of the office that the Emperors should confine their authority to a single State or part of Christendom, but, except among German States, they had little influence. In Germany the Emperors could not form a strong centralized government; they had, however, influence enough to prevent the formation of strong rival governments. The imperial office furnished a nucleus for a loose confederation of petty kings and princes.

In the German States local tribal law or special state statutes took the place of the ancient law. Frederick Barbarossa (1152–1190) and other imperial officers favored the introduction of Roman law. Roman jurisprudence was taught in the universities. Roman law was continuously administered in northern Italy from the downfall of the old empire, and in 1495 it was introduced from Italy into Germany. The local laws were not entirely displaced and the two systems were administered concurrently. The educated classes became indoctrinated with the principles of Roman justice.

During the century following the introduction of Roman law Germany was disrupted by the religious Reformation. Part of the States became Protestant while the others remained Roman Catholic. Germany bore the brunt of the religious wars of the seventeenth century and at the end of the Thirty Years' War (1648) much of the country had become depopulated. By the Treaty of Westphalia (1648) the leading nations of Europe recognized both Protestant and Catholic states and small states were guaranteed independence. The idea of international right based upon agreement between numerous sovereign states displaced the older idea of imperial unity. The Holy Roman Empire thus ceased to be even a symbol of the unity of Christendom.

Out of the ruin wrought by the religious wars Prussia arose to a position of eminence in the north and became a counterpoise to Austria in the south. Prussia and Austria included a mixed population of Slavs and other alien races, while the smaller western States were more distinctly German. Germany thus became divided; the two great rival States having mixed populations composing one part, the group of smaller States the other.

These few facts furnish a basis for the explanation of modern Germany. It was undoubtedly conducive to national pride that for so many centuries the German Kaisers as successors to the Roman Cæsars typified the unity of Christendom. In harmony with the same ideal was the study of Roman law and its introduction as a part of the law of the land in 1495. The comparative independence of numerous states led to the organization of a number of active and vigorous universities. Within the dominions of the Holy Roman Empire the spirit of religious reform became rife almost as early as in England. Germany became the heart and soul of the Great Protestant Reformation. Along with the Reformation came the best system of general education in any part of Europe. Foundations were thus laid for a unified language and a great literature. These and many other forces tended to the formation of a great state. National aspirations, however, found no adequate means of political expression.

Influence of the French. — Educated Germans were profoundly affected by the European movement which found expression in the French Revolution. Many Germans became republicans, States adjoining France being especially infected with liberal sentiments. The Napoleonic codes of Roman Law were adopted by many German States, superseding the older Roman Law which had been the common law of the States, but was for the most part discontinued with the advent of Protestantism. The older law had become associated with Roman tyranny, while the new French law implied greater freedom and equality.

In 1804 Napoleon assumed the title of Emperor of the French. He had already made himself master of a considerable part of Europe. Two years later Francis II of Austria resigned his imperial office and retained simply his hereditary dominions under the title of Emperor of Austria.[1] This terminated the Holy Roman Empire and Austria became simply one of the German States. For Napoleon the ancient Roman title carried with it the idea, not only of conquest, but of a reorganized and an improved government. His system of laws was temporarily imposed upon Germany. Three hundred petty dominions in northern Germany were reduced to less than forty. Napoleonic pressure also induced the King of Prussia and other German rulers to inaugurate great and far-reaching reforms, but the great mass of the peasantry were still serfs, bound to the soil.

While France was creating a new system of land tenure upon the ruins of the old, educated reformers, of whom Baron Stein was chief, were making a profound study of the needs of Germany. A comprehensive plan of reform was perfected, involving not only the liberation of the serfs and changes in land tenure, but also improvements in local government in town and country. Frederick William III, the autocratic King of Prussia, stood like a stone wall against the proposed reforms, but when, finally, in 1807, Napoleon was threatening the complete destruction of Prussia, the opposition of the King gave way and Baron Stein became chief minister of state. From Prussia the reforms extended to other States and in 1813 she became an effective leader in the war of liberation from Napoleonic rule.

A More Perfect Union. — Germany's great need was for some adequate means of giving expression to German public opinion. The consciousness of common interests among the States had been growing for centuries. The wars of liberation from Na-

[1] Bryce, "The Holy Roman Empire," p. 366.

poleonic rule greatly intensified the national spirit. To render effective the pending reforms called for a central government. At the end of the Napoleonic wars (1815) conditions favored a united Germany under a liberal government. A new federation was formed. Many of the smaller States adopted constitutions providing for parliamentary governments. But the two most powerful States, Austria on the south and Prussia on the north, clung to the old absolute monarchy and through their influence free government in the other States was suppressed. The fact that Austria and Prussia contained a mixed population of alien races increased the difficulty of union. The States of the west made various attempts to form an exclusively German state with a liberal government. All such efforts were brought to naught by the overpowering despotic States. Both Austria and Prussia gave effective support to the reactionary monarchial party in each State. The princes were restored to full power. The Diet, the only organ of the Confederacy, was controlled by the absolute monarchies. Free government in the small States was treated as revolutionary. A strict censorship was established over the teaching in schools and universities, and over the public press.[1] Public meetings were forbidden except under police control. The enemies of democracy everywhere gained control of the actual agencies of government; no opportunity was given for the people to acquire practical political experience. Agitation, however, was continued, and as a result of the popular uprisings of 1848 both Austria and Prussia were induced to accept constitutions which recognized popular rights. But the Austrian concessions were at once repudiated and the Prussian Constitution was so modified and so interpreted as to retain supreme power in royal hands.

The revolutions of 1848 greatly weakened the confederation, which included both Austria and Prussia. An insistent demand had arisen on the part of the Liberals that a federated state should be formed to take the place of the existing loose confederation. Delegates from all the German States met at Frankfort in 1848 to provide for a more perfect union, and a liberal Constitution was formulated. The majority of the convention was unwilling to admit Austria to the union with all her non-German provinces, and Austria was unwilling to divide her em-

[1] Seignobos, "A Political History of Contemporary Europe," Vol. I, p. 385.

pire for the sake of membership in the union. A decision was finally reached to exclude Austria and to offer to the King of Prussia, with the title of Emperor of the Germans, the chief place in the new federated state. Frederick William IV had masterful views concerning the divine right of rulers. He believed that the people had no right to usurp divine authority in the choosing of kings and emperors, and he therefore refused to accept the office at the hands of a representative assembly. All efforts to obtain a national representative government failed, and the old, discredited confederation was continued with Austria in control.

The King of Prussia was induced through fear of violence to issue a constitution in January, 1850, which is still in force. It emanates directly from the monarch and involves no form of ratification or acceptance on the part of the people. Many of its articles are taken from a liberal constitution which a representative assembly had approved; but they are so selected and are so interpreted as to leave the royal will supreme. The Upper House of the Prussian legislature is composed of appointees of the king. The members of the Lower House are elected in separate districts by universal manhood suffrage; the method of electing, however, gives the actual choice of members to the rich. The election is indirect. Three sets of electors, equal in number, are chosen at a primary election. The wealthy voters, who pay one third of the taxes, choose one third of the electors. The poor, who are a large majority of the voters, elect a third of the electors. The moderately wealthy elect the remaining third. By this process one tenth of the voters may secure a two-thirds majority in the electoral college which names the members of the Lower House in the legislature. Moreover, the numerous officers in the public service are admonished by an imperial rescript interpreting the Constitution that they are to support the government at elections.[1] With one house directly subject to the dictation of the king and the other thus hedged about and restricted it would seem impossible for the people to gain control of any official agency. Yet such was the popular reprobation of the arbitrary rule following the promulgation of the Constitution that the party of opposition to the Crown did gain control of the Lower House in 1861.

[1] Below, p. 600.

The King, Frederick William IV, became permanently insane in 1858 and his brother William ruled as regent until the death of the King (1861). William I had for many years been exceedingly unpopular on account of his opposition to reform. For a time he was expatriated. His insistence upon a greatly amplified and reorganized military system had aroused great opposition during the regency (1858-1861). On assuming the crown William I gave explicit expression to the traditional doctrine of the Dynasty, declaring that the crown was a direct gift from God to the royal house and that the monarch had no right to submit to dictation from the representatives of the people. The Lower House refused to vote approval of the military budget and after repeated dissolutions became practically unanimous in opposition to the King. There seemed no reason to doubt that the legislature expressed the sentiment of the people, and rather than submit to the popular will as expressed in the Assembly William I determined to resign his office. He was, however, induced to reconsider that decision and to call upon Prince von Bismarck, a notorious opponent of parliamentary government, to organize a fighting ministry in support of the Crown.

The Policy of Blood and Iron. — On assuming the office of Chancellor, Bismarck gave expression to a matured policy for securing German unity. "The unity of Germany," said he, "is to be brought about, not by speeches nor by votes of majorities, but by *blood and iron*." [1] The Prussian army, not Prussian liberalism, was to unite Germany. For several years the government was conducted in utter disregard of the hostile assembly. A war against Denmark was waged in 1864 for the conquest of Schleswig-Holstein. In 1866 was waged a brilliantly successful war against Austria. This made an end of the Confederacy of 1815.

With Austria severed from the rest of Germany it became possible to organize a federated German state under the leadership of Prussia. To this end, a constitution was formulated and accepted by a majority of the States in 1867. With the army triumphant, a Prussian Legislature was elected which voted approval of past acts and sustained current policies of the government. Four important States held aloof from the federa-

[1] Seignobos, "A Political History of Contemporary Europe," Vol. II, p. 461.

tion. They were, however, induced to unite in the war against France in 1870 and after the triumph over Napoleon III, all the States joined the Union. At Versailles, January 1, 1871, William I, King of Prussia, was crowned President of the Empire with the title, *German Emperor*. The Constitution of 1867 was transformed into a frame of government for the Empire. Thus Bismarck's promise was literally fulfilled; Germany was united by a policy of " blood and iron."

Royal Interpretation of the Constitution.—The Constitution of Prussia and the Constitution of the Empire have been formed by those who were actively opposed to parliamentary government. Every attempt on the part of the people to achieve liberty of action has been brought to naught. Serfs have received emancipation as the gracious gift of absolute rulers and from the same source has come the right to vote. When Bismarck, in 1866, expressed a willingness to have one house of the proposed Legislature composed of delegates elected by universal suffrage from all parts of the Confederation, the proposition seemed to be in flat contradiction to all his previous policies. It was, in fact, the Chancellor's highest bid for a united, Prussianized Germany. He needed popular support to compel the other German monarchs to submit to the rule of the King of Prussia. By means of this provision in the Constitution of the Confederation liberal sentiment was conciliated.

But it was still far from Bismarck's intention that the people's representatives should govern the Empire. Germany was to be ruled by Prussia, and Prussia was effectively controlled by the army and the bureaucracy. By means of the army, opposition in the Prussian legislature had been overcome. Bismarck's intention is made clear by an order issued in 1882 explaining Article 44 of the Prussian Constitution, which reads: " The King's Ministers are responsible. All government acts (documentary) of the King require for their validity the approval of a minister, who thereby assumes responsibility for them." [1] The liberals maintained that this article was a guarantee for parliamentary government. A rescript was issued by William I signed by Bismarck to correct this interpretation. It emphatically denies that ministerial responsibility deprives the monarch of complete independence of action. The significant clause

[1] Larned, "History for Ready Reference," Vol. I, p. 598.

reads: "It (the liberal interpretation) is therefore not admissible, and leads to obscuration of the constitutional rights of the King, when their exercise is so spoken of as if they emanated from the Ministers for the time being responsible for them, and not from the King himself. The Constitution of Prussia is the expression of the monarchial tradition of this country, whose development is based on the living and actual relations of its Kings to the people. These relations, moreover, do not admit of being transferred to the Ministers appointed by the King, for they attach to the person of the King. Their preservation, too, is a political necessity for Prussia. It is, therefore, my will that both in Prussia and in the Legislative Bodies of the realm there may be no doubt left as to my own constitutional right and that of my successors to personally conduct the policy of my Government.... It is the duty of my Ministers to support my constitutional rights by protecting them from doubt or obscuration and I expect the same from all State servants who have taken to me the official oath."[1] The rescript further states that all officers shall refrain from all agitation against the Government and vote for those who support government policies or be removed from office. It is to be noted, also, that the principle here announced is applied not only to Prussia, but to all officers and official bodies in the Empire. The royal interpretation is thus placed in apparent contradiction to the words of the Constitution, and the principles of democracy are distinctly repudiated.

In a book on "Imperial Germany" written a hundred years after the war of liberation Prince von Bülow says: "In the German Empire, Prussia is the leading State. The Social Democratic movement is the antithesis of the Prussian State.... The peculiarity of the Prussian State, which is the backbone of our political life, makes a solution of the Social Democratic problem particularly difficult for us. The practical *modus vivendi* with the Social Democrats, that has been attempted here and there in Southern Germany does not seem possible in Prussia. Prussia attained her greatness as a country of soldiers and officials, and as such she was able to accomplish the work of German union; to this day she is still in all essentials a State of soldiers and officials."[2]

---

[1] Larned, "History for Ready Reference," Vol. I, p. 601.
[2] von Bülow, "Imperial Germany," p. 226.

This utterance of Prince von Bülow summarizes the points of chief interest in the relations of the Empire to free government. First, it points out that the Prussian government is opposed by the Prussian people. Second, it contrasts Prussia with the more liberal German States. Third, it emphasizes the military as opposed to civil authority. Germany exhibits on a grand scale the age-long conflict between autocracy and democracy.

REFERENCES

BISMARCK. *The Man and the Statesman; Reflections, etc. by Himself.*
BRYCE. *The Holy Roman Empire*, Edition 1887, Chap. XIX, and Supplementary Chap.
BÜLOW. *Imperial Germany.*
HOWARD. *The German Empire*, Chaps. I–VII.
OGG. *The Governments of Europe*, Chap. IX.
SEIGNOBOS. *A Political History of Contemporary Europe*, Vol. II, Chaps. XIV, XV.
SOHM. *Institutes of Roman Law*, by Ledlie, Edition 1907, Part II.
WILSON. *The State*, pp. 191 ff., 1896.

CHAPTER LI

THE PRESENT CONSTITUTION AND GOVERNMENT

To complete the union of the German States it was necessary in the first place to determine the relation of the State of Prussia to the proposed government. This was done by giving to the Prussian King the office of President of the Federation. William I wished to be crowned Emperor of Germany, but the other rulers, jealous of their own rank, refused to accede to his desire. A compromise was effected which gave to the President the title of *Deutscher Kaiser* — German Emperor. The German union is not itself a monarchy, but a federation of monarchs and free cities under a President having the title of Kaiser, and the King of Prussia is *ex officio* Emperor.

The Frame of Government. — The second object to be attained was a united governing body for the twenty-two monarchies and the three Free Cities. Through the creation of the Bundesrath, a Federal Council of fifty-eight members, this was accomplished. In the council Prussia has seventeen members with seventeen votes;[1] Bavaria has six; Saxony and Würtemburg four each; Baden and Hesse three each; two other States have two each, and all the rest one each.

The Bundesrath is not what is usually called a deliberative body, but rather an assembly of delegates appointed by the princes of the States and the Senates of the Cities, who act under instructions from the rulers who appoint them. If a State is entitled to more than one vote, all the votes are cast by the head of the delegation. For instance, the six votes of Bavaria are cast by the King of Bavaria. The "unit rule" in voting prevails. On nearly all questions a simple majority is required to bind all the States. The assembly of delegates is designed to enable the monarchs to control all departments of

[1] Three additional votes are controlled by Prussia. — Lowell, "Governments and Parties in Continental Europe," Vol. I, p. 260.

the government, legislative, administrative, and judicial. Though the Constitution concedes to the popular House the right to initiate legislation, in practice all important measures, including taxation, originate in the Bundesrath. Bills prepared there are submitted to vote in the Reichstag, and the members of the Upper House are expected to enter the Lower House freely, seeking to persuade its members to adopt the measures proposed.

The growing sense of nationality among the people was recognized in a representative Assembly — the Reichstag — elected by secret ballot, all male citizens twenty-five years of age having a right to vote. The Constitution assigns one member for every 100,000 inhabitants.[1] The election is by single districts and each district must lie wholly within a single State. When the Constitution was adopted there were 382 districts entitled to one member each in the Assemblies; in 1873 15 were added for Alsace-Lorraine. In the distribution Prussia receives 236, while a number of the States have but one each. No redistribution of seats has taken place since 1871. The number remains 397 and great inequality prevails. Growing centers of population, such as Berlin, for example, have only a small proportion of the representation to which they are entitled. The term of office in the Reichstag is five years, though the House may be dissolved by the Emperor with the consent of the Bundesrath.

These institutions form the framework of the Imperial Government. To Prussia as the leading kingdom is conceded the office of Emperor. The Bundesrath is the agent of the ruling powers of the various States, and the Reichstag is a concession to the people of a voice in the government. From many points of view the Constitution is unique and most interesting. Only those features of the government can be discussed here which appear to throw light upon the conflict between autocracy and democracy.

The Chancellorship under Bismarck. — As shown in the preceding chapter, the office of Chancellor of the State of Prussia came into prominence as an agency for resisting the threatened development of parliamentary power. Through the astute Bismarck as Chancellor, the Prussian State became subservient

[1] Howard, "The German Empire," p. 85.

to the Crown. The Imperial Constitution of 1871 was so drawn as to imply that the Imperial Chancellor should be the same person as the Chancellor of Prussia and should fill a corresponding place in the general government. The office was created by Bismarck to be filled by himself, that he might be at the same time the head of the Prussian ministry and the sole responsible administrator of the Empire.

To the Imperial Chancellor is assigned the duty of presiding over the meetings of the Bundesrath. It was Bismarck and not the Kaiser who actually controlled the one assembly of highest authority. His duties and powers as chairman of that body are numerous. He arranges the order of business, receives petitions, and may appoint a Vice Chancellor to preside in his place.

While the Constitution does not declare in express terms that the Chancellor and Vice Chancellor shall always be members of the Prussian delegation to the Bundesrath, yet such is the implication and such has been the practice. With the full power of the great State of Prussia, the Chancellor wields a tremendous influence over legislation. He is chief sponsor for government bills; as a member of the Bundesrath he has free access to the Reichstag, and in some way he secures majorities in the popular assembly for the measures of the government.

Orders and decrees issued by the Kaiser are countersigned by the Chancellor, who thereby becomes responsible for their execution. All administrative business is in his hands. The heads of departments, though in form appointed by the Kaiser, are in fact chosen by the Chancellor and are subject to his commands. All officers in the administrative service are likewise subject to his orders. The prerogatives of the Kaiser are, indeed, exercised by the Chancellor.

Relation of the States to the Central Government. — The separate States do, however, in practice, limit the power and responsibility of the Chancellor, since a large proportion of the laws passed by the Imperial Legislature are left to them for execution. All civil, criminal, and commercial codes adopted for the Empire are executed by the individual States. At the same time it is the duty of the Kaiser to supervise the action of state officers in executing federal laws. But this too is done through the Chancellor. So long as state officers satisfactorily administer Imperial laws they are independent of the Chancellor. But if a State fails in that respect, it is the Chancellor's duty to bring the matter before the Bundesrath, and that body may order an execution. In such a case the Chancellor has the Imperial army at his command for coercing the State into compliance with the laws.

To understand the obvious contrast between the German and American types of federation one must recognize the fundamental difference between the Roman and the Anglo-Saxon legal systems previously described. The German Imperial Codes deal mainly with private rights. Many of the States had been long accustomed to administer the *Code Napoleon*, and the codes which were substituted in the Empire were similar in both form and substance. It is natural that the Roman Law Codes should continue to be administered by state officers. But the decentralized administration is by no means restricted to the defense of private rights. Laws pertaining to Imperial taxation, banks, insurance, labor organizations, etc., which are enacted by the general legislature are executed by the separate States. Bavaria and Würtemburg secured especial concessions in respect to postal and telegraph service. These constitutional provisions testify to the jealousy of the States in guarding their administrative independence. Although the Empire is highly centralized in legislation, the States have retained a wide range of administrative power.

It is clear, however, that the limitations upon the authority of the Chancellor arising from the decentralized administration are more apparent than real. In the first place it must be remembered that nearly two thirds of the people of the Empire live in Prussia, and that Prussian and Imperial legislation are in the same hands. So far as Prussia is concerned, separate state power is favorable to the autocracy because of the restricted Prussian franchise. In the other States also Imperial control is maintained by the reservation of important administrative business immediately in the hands of Imperial officers. Such are the entire foreign service and the management of naval affairs. The Prussian army system is extended into every State and, with slight concessions to state authorities in the matter of appointments, the Emperor controls the military forces. Postal and telegraph officers subject to the will of the Kaiser carry Imperial influence into every part of the country. Add to all this the power of the Imperial Chancellor to interfere in all matters affecting the interests of the Empire, and it is plain that the spirit and methods of the Prussian bureaucracy effectively prevail in every State. The whole country has been essentially Prussianized.

King, Chancellor, and People. — The Imperial Constitution grew directly out of the contest between King and people in the State of Prussia, and by making Prussia the controlling member in a union of German States it has become possible thus far to eliminate thoroughly the people from any effective share in the government. There can be no doubt of the intention of the framers of the Constitution to continue to maintain and extend this autocratic dominion. By the rescript quoted above,[1] which was issued eleven years after the adoption of the Constitution of 1871, the principle of autocracy is specifically reaffirmed and every vestige of parliamentary government repudiated. Prince von Bülow declares: " He [Bismarck] held the reins of Government with such an iron grip that he never ran any risk of letting the least scrap of power slip into the hands of Parliament."[2] The German Constitution is a constitution by the autocrat and for the autocrat. King, Chancellor, Kaiser were three in one, and, so long as the Old Emperor and Bismarck belonged to the trio, that one was the Chancellor. It was Bismarck who had restored to the Prussian King his crown when he had determined to surrender it. He it was who had welded the German States into a mighty Empire and had created the new title of Kaiser. Until the death of William I, in 1888, King and Chancellor ruled as one man.

Necessarily the Constitution, in form, places the authority in the Kaiser's hands. None of it whatever pertains of right to the Chancellor. He is the Emperor's chief ministerial officer, appointed by him, removable at his will, and responsible to him alone. Yet in the eyes of the public Bismarck held a position not inferior to that of the Kaiser himself as the recognized custodian of Imperial authority. The Emperor Frederick is understood to have been favorable to parliamentary government; but to inaugurate a policy based upon that principle would have

[1] P. 600. [2] von Bülow, "Imperial Germany," New York, 1914, p. 175.

involved a break with Bismarck. The Emperor's illness and untimely death forestalled a change in policy.

William II came to the throne imbued with high notions concerning the divine right of the Hohenzollern Dynasty, but Bismarck had discouraged any flaunting of dynastic pride. As defined by the Constitution the Kaiser's office is simply that of President of the Empire. The third incumbent has magnified his office. He has effaced the distinction between King of Prussia and the German Kaiser, and has compelled other monarchs of the Empire to submit to a dominion which they repudiated in the beginning when they accepted the Constitution. Bismarck was dismissed from office in 1890, and a foreign policy which had been consistently condemned by the old Chancellor was inaugurated. William II rules in his own name; he has never permitted a minister to overshadow him or seriously to detract from his royal prestige. The possible permutations in the relations between Kaiser and Chancellor are by no means exhausted. The first Chancellor humiliated a legislature and exalted a King. It is not impossible that a future Chancellor may humiliate a Kaiser and exalt a popular assembly.

The Constitution of 1871 is still the law of the land and implies, without explicitly so stating, that the Imperial Chancellor as a Prussian minister is a member of the Prussian delegation in the Bundesrath. As the head of that delegation he controls, under the King's direction, one third of the votes of that assembly. Other rulers of States are likewise accustomed to send their chief ministers as delegates. It follows, therefore, that those who participate in the enactment of Imperial statutes are, as State officers, active in their execution.

Administrative and Judicial Functions of the Bundesrath. — The Bundesrath itself likewise has important administrative functions. Its consent is necessary for a dissolution of the Reichstag. It shares with the Kaiser the treaty-making power. Except in case of invasion, the Kaiser must have its consent to a declaration of war, and it shares in the making of appointments. Twelve committees of the Bundesrath are appointed each year to coöperate with the Kaiser in Imperial administration. Those upon the Army and Navy are named by the Kaiser. Of all the committees except the one on Foreign Relations the chairmanships belong to Prussia and are filled by the King of that State.

The committees correspond in general to the various administrative departments, and it is their duty to furnish information for the guidance of the executive.

In the description of the French government it was shown that an Executive Council and various other administrative officers perform the duty of amplifying the statutes, explaining their meaning and issuing ordinances for their more effective administration. In Germany this work is divided between the Emperor and the Bundesrath. In the first instance the power to issue ordinances rests with the Bundesrath, but by statute the Emperor is empowered to put forth ordinances in specified lines of administration. Hence, the same authority that initiates projects of legislation requiring the approval of the Reichstag for their validity also issues supplementary orders which are valid without further sanction.

Germany is in form a federal state in which twenty-five States composing the Empire share with the general government the power of legislation on the same or allied subjects; in which the statutes and ordinances of the general government are executed and adjudicated by officers of the separate States; in which Imperial officials bound to obey the Kaiser deal with the same subjects as do the local officers subject to the orders of local chiefs. Inevitably, numerous occasions must arise for clashing between authorities. In contests involving private rights disputes are usually settled in the ordinary courts of the State. Yet, if serious delinquency is alleged so that justice is denied, the cause may be carried to the Bundesrath. It is the Bundesrath that issues the order for the coercion of a State. Disputes between States may also be settled or adjudicated in that body. And in case of any sort of disagreement which finds no other means for adjustment recourse is had to the one institution which represents all the sovereigns united in the Empire.

Thus far the Bundesrath has been controlled by Prussia in the interest of autocracy; but should democracy gain a predominant influence in the States, a new type of delegate would be sent to it. Without essential change in the letter of the Constitution, the present ruling body might become so organized as to serve the democracy in matters judicial and administrative, while in respect to legislation it would be transformed into an innocuous or compliant " Upper House."

The Popular Assembly.

The Reichstag is at present the one check upon an autocratic government. Its members are elected by secret ballot in 397 districts, each district choosing one member. The Constitution says that the members of the Reichstag shall be representatives of the entire people; they are not subject to local instruction as delegates from individual States. The institution is thoroughly national. It has power to organize itself, to adopt its own rules of procedure, and to discipline its own members. Votes and utterances in the Reichstag are not to be called in question elsewhere. The meetings are public and "truthful reports" of proceedings are permitted. Members have immunity from arrest or legal interference during sessions. To dissolve the House before the end of the five years for which members are elected requires the consent of both Kaiser and Bundesrath, and a new House must be elected and assembled within ninety days. During the session the Emperor may adjourn the meetings for a single period of thirty days. The Constitution gives to the Reichstag the right to originate legislation, as well as to approve or reject measures presented by the Bundesrath. Oddly enough, members of the Reichstag are permitted to accept office and still remain members of the House if reëlected by their constituents. This rule is identical with that followed by the British House of Commons in respect to cabinet appointments.

As compared with the popular assemblies of other countries one notable weakness appears in the Reichstag. It has not the exclusive right to originate money bills. Article 35 of the Constitution specifies a long list of sources of Imperial revenue, such as customs, the taxation of salt, tobacco, etc. The income from these sources not even the Bundesrath has power to withhold from the treasury. A proposition to diminish such taxes may be vetoed by the presiding officer of that Chamber, that is, by the Chancellor, as instructed by the King of Prussia. For additional support to the treasury an annual grant is required, but the Constitution is not clear as to the rights of the Lower House in voting supplies. All expositors agree, however, that a levy of new taxes or a proposition to increase the rates is not valid without the approval of that House. But when supplies have once been legally granted and are deemed continuously necessary for the carrying out of approved policies, the government has acted upon the theory that the annual approval of the Reichstag is not required.

As a forum for public utterance the Reichstag has accomplished all that could be expected. It has let in the daylight upon all departments of public affairs. It has become a training school for the discovery and expression of public opinion. The House is itself a guaranty of larger freedom for the schools, the churches, and the public press. Drastic and effective suppression of liberty of speech, such as prevailed early in the last century, becomes impossible. This was demonstrated in the case of the duel between the government and the Socialists from 1878 to 1890. Laws were enacted for the complete destruction of the socialist organization. But the soldier and the policeman could not follow the Socialist in the Reichstag, and the party flourished under persecution. The effort at suppression served only to demonstrate the helplessness of the government, and after twelve years of failure the destructive policy was abandoned.

Political Parties. — The century of agitation that preceded the creation of the popular House gave to large classes of the citizens experience in organization. At times publicly organized political parties appeared. When the parties were suppressed the propaganda for free speech was often maintained in secret. Under the Prussian Constitution of 1850 a party arose in the legislature in opposition to the government. So important were the issues and so fierce was the conflict that the two parties absorbed almost the whole membership; the Conservatives upheld the army and the " divine right " pretensions of the King, while the Progressives urged the superior rights of the Parliament.

When the Reichstag was organized the Prussian parties were naturally carried over into the new national assembly; but in the transition important subdivisions and modifications took place. Free Conservatives separated themselves from the original party and took their place as Moderate Conservatives. The Progressives likewise divided permanently into Liberals and Radicals, Prussian Liberals uniting with those from other States to form the National Liberal party. These four parties which appeared in the first meetings of the Reichstag have ever since held leading places in the Assembly. They conform in general to the orthodox model furnished by the French Chamber of Deputies — two parties of the Right and two of the Left. For six years Bismarck secured his majorities by uniting the two moderate sections of the Right and the Left. At the beginning of the fight with the Socialists, in 1878, he was led to rely upon a fifth permanent party of great strength. This is the Catholic party, which in the Reichstag is called the party of the Center. Of all the five permanent parties throughout the entire history of the Reichstag the Catholic party has been the largest, the best organized, and the most uniform in its membership. The Social Democrats elected two members to the first Reichstag in 1871, and since that date the number has been increased at almost every election. In 1914 they numbered 110 and formed the largest of the party groups. There are in addition a half dozen small groups representing local or special interests.

These few facts suffice to show that the Reichstag has all along been performing the elemental political function of training a citizenship for the assumption of the duties of self-government. To furnish such preparation to Swiss and Anglo-Saxons required many centuries of constant endeavor. The French have labored continuously at the problem for more than a century. In spite of certain appearances to the contrary, the Germans in a single half century have made distinct progress toward democracy.

As soon as the Great Chancellor had ceased to lead the government forces, his successors were compelled to come to terms with the party groups. The principal issue dividing them was the question of the rate of taxation on imports. The Agrarians favored a high rate on competing importations, the Industrials a low rate. The extreme demands of the farmers were resisted by means of the formation of a party coalition, or *bloc*, made up of the Catholic Center supported by various conservative groups. The rule of the *bloc* lasted for more than a decade.

In the meantime opposition to the military policy of the government under the leadership of the Social Democrats became a chief party question, and after the election of 1903 the government had great difficulty in maintaining a majority. A prolonged contest was now inaugurated to establish the principle of parliamentary government. The Reichstag was dissolved in 1906. By means of official manipulation the number of Social Democrats in the Chamber was reduced from seventy-nine to forty-three at the election of 1907, while at the same time the Socialist popular vote was increased by almost a quarter of a million. Then came a direct attack upon the Prussian policy of governmental interference with elections. A national demand arose for the amendment of the Prussian Constitution, in order to admit the masses of the people to equal suffrage, and in 1912 the reform of the Prussian election laws became one of the issues of the Imperial election. At that election the Social Democrats made a gain of a million votes and their membership in the Reichstag grew from forty-three to one hundred and ten. The fact that a vast majority of the people were opposed to the policy of the government was fully demonstrated at that time. Multitudes who are not Socialists voted the Social-Democratic ticket in order to support the strongest party in opposition to the government. Partly as a result of this election measures of reform were introduced into the Prussian legislature. Thus, after forty years of public discussion the Reichstag had practically won a great victory for free government. It had become the one constitutional agency for giving expression to the will of the German people. The issue was already joined against the one effective barrier to German liberty — that is, the Prussian " divine right " autocracy. This was the condition of things at the breaking out of the War in 1914.

The German movement towards liberty has been, in its main features, thoroughly orthodox. The undisguised absolute monarchy ruled down to the Revolution of 1848, which forced the concession of a Prussian Constitution. Following that success, a contest was at once begun to transform the Constitutional Government into a parliamentary one; and in 1862 the Prussian Parliament was apparently triumphant. But the monarchy gained a new lease of life and power when the union of the German States was secured by means of foreign wars. The Union having been effected, the Reichstag became the one reliable agency for advancing the cause of free government. Political parties immediately appeared and began to exert pressure upon the government. Forty years of continuous experience placed the people of the Empire in a position to give forceful assistance to the people of the State of Prussia seeking to get control of their state government. But again progress was arrested by the Great War.

Parliamentary government successfully established in Prussia will inevitably be followed by free government in all the States. Ministers chosen by the people will sit in the Bundesrath in place of personal representatives of the monarchs, and that Chamber will freely concede to the Reichstag the place of supreme authority.. The Upper House may then serve the democracy as efficiently as it has hitherto served the autocracy. The office of Chancellor may be readily transformed into that of Prime Minister. If orthodox lines are followed, the Chancellor will cease to be the special agent of a single State and will become the Chief Minister of the Imperial Democracy. As such he will be transferred to the ruling branch of the legislature, where he will surround himself with a cabinet of responsible associates.

REFERENCES

(See Chap. L.)

DODD. *Modern Constitutions*, Edition 1909, Vol. I, pp. 321 ff.
LOWELL. *Governments and Parties in Continental Europe*, Chaps. VI, VII.
OGG. *The Governments of Europe*, Chaps. X–XIV.
SEIGNOBOS. *A Political History of Contemporary Europe*, Vol. II, Chap. XVI.
WILSON. *The State*, Index Titles, Chap. XII.

SWITZERLAND

CHAPTER LII

Origin of the Swiss Government

Although the Swiss Government is neither Presidential, after the American type, nor Cabinet, after the English or the French type, Switzerland is among the freest and most democratic of states. In this little land perched on the roof of Western Europe rise the head waters or tributaries of four great rivers, the Rhine, the Rhone, the Danube, and the Po, flowing to four seas. Swiss glaciers have ground from the mighty Alps the soil which these streams have carried to form adjacent countries. Up these same river valleys have pushed or have been driven German, French, and Italian settlers. The Swiss people is therefore made up of three races, Teutons, French, and Italians who speak four [1] native tongues, three of which are recognized as official. Sharp religious controversies have ended in toleration and harmony between Catholic and Protestant citizens. Notwithstanding this diversity in race, language, and religion, the Swiss have become one people loyal and devoted to the Swiss Republic.

Early Swiss Confederation. — From the Germanic tribes that overran Switzerland in the fifth and sixth centuries primitive local institutions have survived in the communes and in the isolated mountain valleys; these have preserved much of their ancient democratic character. Poverty and inaccessibility protected these communities from oppression and greed and they were enabled to retain a large degree of autonomy. A town-meeting of male citizens governed the commune, enacted by-laws, and appointed executive officers. Cantons developed from the union of neighboring communes and at first were governed in the same way. Six of the smaller cantons still

---

[1] In the Grisons a corrupt form of Latin, called Romansch, is still spoken.

hold an annual mass meeting, or *Landsgemeinde*, of the primitive sort, composed of all the citizens. In this assembly laws were enacted and executive officers appointed. For centuries the early cantons conducted themselves like sovereign states, making treaties with one another and with foreign powers and providing for their own defense. In other cantons representative assemblies of delegates elected by the communes constituted the governing body. Permanent confederation between cantons began to be effected more than six hundred years ago, in 1291, when the three forest cantons of Uri, Schwytz, and Unterwalden formed a "perpetual league" against the Hapsburgs. About this nucleus other cantons gathered and, through various governmental vicissitudes, by the end of the Napoleonic wars (1815), Switzerland with its present boundaries and twenty-two cantons [1] had worked out for itself a constitution called the Federal Pact, which was formally approved by all the cantons.

Under the Federal Pact no real union was effected; the cantons reverted nearly to the independence of their earlier history and the Diet had no power to enforce its nominal authority. At the same time individual, political, and religious liberty declined and democratic institutions were at a low ebb, save in the smaller and weaker cantons.

The revived revolutionary spirit in Europe in 1830 was in Switzerland accompanied by a reassertion of democracy. Many of the cantonal constitutions were revised.[2] In 1848 a new general Constitution was adopted embodying various needed reforms and expressing a decided trend toward centralization and radical democratic institutions. A later Constitution, that of 1874, a revision of the previous one, embodied many amendments, improved the federal organization, and gave to Switzerland the satisfactory democratic government of the present day. The popular uprisings of 1848 found the country already prepared to yield local privilege and to become a democratic nation, and since that date centralization and democracy have gone hand in hand.

[1] Three of these are divided into half cantons, so that for purposes of local government the number of units is twenty-five.

[2] The period between 1830 and 1848 was marked by no fewer than thirty revisions of cantonal constitutions, all in the direction of a broader democracy. Ogg, "The Governments of Europe," p. 409.

Each of the twenty-five political units which now compose the Swiss nation possesses a large measure of political independence. As in England and the United States, the democracy of the general government of Switzerland has been the result of a contest for local privilege. In local affairs the Swiss have from the earliest days maintained democratic forms, and when the French Revolution gave to them the theory of democracy they appeared, as it were, to the manner born. Still, it was through many and diverse experiments, involving times of reaction and failure, when many citizens were deprived of their political rights, when religious tolerance and individual liberty were no longer enjoyed, and even through revolt and bloodshed, that they strove on towards that ideal which they seem now to have securely attained.

Unlike the other states of Continental Europe Switzerland possessed a background of experience that made for liberty. It is apparent that in each country, there have been local peculiarities and conditions which determine or modify the special forms that free government assumes. In America an experienced, liberty-loving people on a vacant continent worked out a federated republic based upon local autonomy. An age-long conflict between political factions endangering the local liberties of the people finally gave to England a peculiar party government in which power became centralized in two competing groups of party leaders. In France local autonomy was early destroyed by long-enduring tyranny, but it became the high mission of France to give theoretic expression to the principle of human freedom and finally to organize a centralized democratic state. In Germany the local feudal states have survived until a recent date, and federation has been effected through the ancient method of war under the leadership of the strongest states. Still, democracy in the smaller German States has forced the hand of the more despotic one and secured a representative assembly based upon a form of universal suffrage. No two states are alike though all exemplify different phases of the universal movement towards free government.

The distinctive features of the Swiss state are largely due to the physical nature and situation of the country. Thrift, courage, daring, and independence grew from the soil. It may be assumed that the most venturesome and liberty-loving of the several peoples moved farthest up the valleys, where they made the final stand for freedom. The country was too poor to be worth conquering or, being conquered, it was not worth governing. Surplus wealth was not adequate to the support of a despotic government long enough to change local customs. Federation appeared as the obvious means of making liberty more secure against ambitious and warring neighboring states. Independent Switzerland came to be early recognized as a safeguard, a protection to adjacent states. The friendship of the Swiss as the best fighters in Europe became worth cultivating.[1] Neighboring states found it good policy even to contribute new Cantons to the Confederacy. The Congress of Vienna in 1815 was only carrying on a time-honored policy when it added the last three Cantons to the Confederacy and made the whole neutral territory.

The growth of the Swiss Republic resembles in some respects that of the United States. In each case the Union was formed out of preëxisting governments. The thirteen States of the American Union had had a prolonged history as colonies, and were united for a brief period of confederation before they adopted the Constitution. The Swiss cantons had a much longer history, with centuries of confederation preceding the adoption of the Constitution of 1848.

Under the earlier confederation, policies adopted by Diet or representative Assembly and accepted by the Cantons were executed by the separate Cantons. This feature persists in the latest constitution. The national legislature has power to make laws binding upon the cantons without their consent, yet the execution of the statutes is still left to the cantons. Foreign relations, the collections of customs, postal and telegraph service, and a few other lines of business, are administered by federal officers, but the larger body of federal legislation is administered by local officials. If that administration is not satisfactory to the federal authorities, local authorities are admonished; and if they persist in refusal to execute the laws, money due the canton is withheld. As a last resort soldiers are sent into the canton. These " do not pillage, burn, or kill, but are peaceably quartered there at the expense of the canton, and literally eat it into submission." [2]

[1] Moses, "The Federal Government of Switzerland," pp. 19–22.
[2] Lowell, "Governments and Parties in Continental Europe," Vol. II, p. 197.

As in the case of the States of the American Union, the cantons remain in possession of "all the rights which are not delegated to the federal government and are not forbidden to the states."[1] Still, in the practical working out of this principle there is a marked difference between the two countries. The fact that the Cantons execute federal laws tends to obscure the partition of powers between the local and central governments. Cantons readily submit to an expansion of federal legislative rights, while they retain to themselves the function of administration. And, since it is the duty of the Federal Executive to see that cantons do their duty, the habit of looking to the central government for guidance and admonition ensues. Very few powers are exercised exclusively by either government, while the concurrent powers are numerous. To the federal government pertain matters of education, labor, monopolies, insurance, highways, civil rights, criminal law, and many others, which in the United States are dealt with by the States, and the tendency to expand the field of federal legislation grows. In 1912 a complete civil code for the entire country which had been fourteen years in preparation was enacted. A criminal code of like scope is being prepared by experts. These civil and criminal codes, although enacted by the national legislature, will nevertheless be administered by the cantons.

Before the adoption of the Constitution of 1874 a prolonged debate was held between the advocates and the opponents of centralized government. The Constitution of 1848 and the revised Constitution involved a compromise; yet the marked tendency in Switzerland is towards greater centralization. The Constitution gives to the national legislature supervision over the cantons in the matter of amending their constitutions, and no amendment is valid without national approval. Every change in the constitution of a canton must also be submitted for approval to the voters of the canton. Federal authorities may enter the cantons on behalf of the civil rights of the citizens, and they may appear, without invitation, to preserve order therein.

At no time has there been developed any clearly defined theory as to the relative positions of the two governments: practical considerations determine those relations. The Swiss

[1] Chap. I, Art. 3, Const.

know nothing about "implied powers" of the Constitution. The one hundred and twenty-three articles in the document furnish adequate guidance to all public officers. There is no demand for a learned expositor of their meaning. However, a Federal Tribunal exists, a part of whose duties is the decision of cases of conflict between authorities. By this Court acts of cantonal legislatures which violate the constitution either of the canton or of the Federal government may be held invalid.[1] But an entirely different rule holds in the case of acts of the national legislature. The Constitution requires the court to give effect to any legislative act. The Federal Assembly is itself the final judge as to the constitutionality of its own acts. The national legislature is the authorized custodian of the entire process of constitution-making, and supervises the making of the frame of government for the cantons. If the two Houses are agreed, constitutional changes for the Confederacy are enacted by the same process as are statutes. But constitutional amendments do not become valid unless they are sanctioned by a majority of the people, the majorities being so distributed as to include a majority of the Cantons. If the legislature fails to provide an amendment to the constitution which the people require, a petition signed by 50,000 voters may initiate a process to secure the change. By various methods of comparatively easy amendment, the letter of the Constitution is kept in harmony with the policies of government, and political energy is not wasted on account of defects in governmental machinery. The people really make their own constitutions in both canton and Federation; and by peculiar Swiss processes they keep legislative assemblies in such close touch with themselves that those bodies are truly representative. Rasping conflicts between the people and their public agents are thus reduced to a minimum. No other government works with such smoothness and efficiency as does that of the Swiss Republic.

REFERENCES

General References for Switzerland.
DODD. *Modern Constitutions*, Vol. II, pp. 253 ff.

[1] In that case the law is not nullified but it becomes the duty of the national executive to induce the canton to change the statutes. See below, p. 630.

LOWELL. *Governments and Parties in Continental Europe*, Vol. II, Chaps. XI–XIII.
MCCRACKEN. *The Rise of the Swiss Republic*, Book V, Chap. X.
MOSES. *The Federal Government of Switzerland.*
OGG. *The Governments of Europe*, Chaps. XXII–XXIII.
SEIGNOBOS. *A Political History of Contemporary Europe*, Vol. I, Chap. IX.
VINCENT. *Government in Switzerland.*
WILSON. *The State*, Chap. VIII.
WINCHESTER. *The Swiss Republic*, Edition 1891, Chaps. II–IX.

CHAPTER LIII

THE FRAME OF GOVERNMENT

AT no time has serious or prolonged dispute arisen as to the relation of the Swiss people to their Executive or as to the relations of the three departments of government to one another; the Executive is as popular and as fully trusted as any other part of the government and it is the great harmonizer and unifier of the system. The little Federation, with its twenty-two cantons, some with aristocratic history and traditions, others profoundly democratic in both; its more than three thousand communes, of endless variety and puzzling complexity in their local requirements; its population widely diverse in origin, in temperament, tradition, ideals, and aspirations, is nevertheless governed, and well governed, by the same general laws. And these laws deal with such intricate, such divisive matters as a State Church, Popular Education, Capital and Labor, Government Monopoly of the Alcoholic Liquor Traffic, and Government Control of General Utilities. To understand how this is achieved a study of the whole frame of government is necessary.

The common English names for the five national institutions of Switzerland often cause confusion because the words themselves denote nothing distinctive. The attention of the reader is therefore called to the following definitions: Federal Council (*Conseil fédéral, Bundesrath*), the national executive board of seven members, one of whom is annually chosen President of the Swiss Republic. Federal Assembly (*Assemblée fédérale, Bundesversammlung*), the national legislature in joint session of the two houses. As a united body it has a few distinctive duties. Council of States (*Conseil des Etats, Ständerath*), the upper house of the legislature, or the Senate of forty-four members. National Council (*Conseil national, Nationalrath*), the lower house of the legislature of 167 members, elected directly in proportion to the population. Federal Tribunal (*Tribunal fédéral, Bundesgericht*), the Supreme Court.

The Executive. — The laws of Switzerland are executed by a hierarchy of Executive Councils or committees. In the communes the town meeting, — in some instances the voters by ballot, — elects a communal council, consisting usually of from five to nine members. This council is responsible for communal administration. In the cantons councils numbering from five to thirteen members are elected, in more than half the Cantons by popular vote, in the others by the legislature. The term of office in cantonal and communal councils varies from one to five years.

Each grade in the series of executive councils may share in the administration of most of the laws. Only a few subjects of federal legislation are reserved for the exclusive control of the Federal Council, and the administration of certain acts of the cantonal legislatures pertains entirely to the cantonal Executive. It is always in order also for the higher authorities to assist, encourage, or administer, in respect to any matter deemed to be of general interest; and it is the duty of the higher authorities actively to interfere in case of violation of the laws of the canton or of the Confederacy, or in case of delinquency in the execution of the laws.

The Communes adopt numerous by-laws covering a wide range of topics, which are executed by the communal councils or other local officials. Upon the communes rests also a large share of responsibility for the execution of the general statutes of Canton and Federation. In the administration of local affairs the executive council acts as a body, with the mayor as presiding officer; but in the execution of the more general laws the mayor is held individually responsible. This is the one instance in the Swiss system of important individual executive responsibility. The mayor and council have official charge of the town meeting, although the members of the meeting have a nominal right to introduce measures. The regular order is to refer all resolutions to the council. The meeting simply approves or rejects the program presented by the council. In the larger communes the communal council is virtually a legislative committee preparing by-laws to be voted upon by the people.

The Cantons have their own constitutions, guaranteed by the Confederation, and they exercise extensive powers in forming and carrying out their own governments. Each has a single-chambered legislative council in some of which the executive councilors are included as voting members. To all of them the executive officers have free access. They work with the cantonal legislators in all matters of legislation and finance. The chairman, or president, of the executive council holds a position of dignity and honor in the canton, although as an officer he is merely a member of a governing board, the council as a body being responsible for the government. In certain cantons curious survivals of ancient forms of independent, democratic government are found. Such is the *Landsgemeinde*, a primitive mass meeting of all citizens. [1]

The Federal Council of seven members is elected at the first session of each new Federal Assembly to serve for three years. Its members are chosen rather as men of business ability than as leaders of a party, and are not expected to control governmental policy. A restricted area in federal legislation is reserved to the Federal Council, but its legislative duties are chiefly advisory or such as pertain to the conducting of the administration. It mediates between diverse political views, interests, and opinions. No one of its members is authorized to propose any legislation in the Assembly save by vote of his colleagues. Each Councilor, including the Chairman of the Federal Council, who is also the President of the Swiss Confederation, presides over one of the seven departments of administration, and, at the same time, shares in the joint responsibility for the acts of the Council.

The business of the Federal Council is divided into seven departments, one department being assigned to each member. They are: Foreign Affairs; Interior; Justice and Police; Military Affairs; Imports and Finance; Posts and Railways; and Commerce, Industry, and Agriculture. Since, as we have seen, the members have practically a life tenure, the heads of the separate departments are correspondingly permanent. They naturally acquire much skill and specialized experience, yet the Constitution fixes full responsibility for every act upon the entire council. In practice this means that every official act shall have the support of a majority of the Councilors. There is nothing to force an artificial unanimity, such as prevails in a cabinet government. The Federal Council presents a bill to the

[1] Freeman, " The Growth of the English Constitution," Fourth Edition 1884, Chap. I; McCracken, " Teutonic Switzerland," Chap. XI.

Legislature for its approval, yet in the legislative Houses individual members of the Council may appear as opponents of the same measure. The debate begun in the Council is thus continued in the Legislature. Even a member of the Council who has voted in favor of presenting a certain measure to the National Assembly for action may appear in the two Houses as opposed to its passage. This means that he believes the Houses ought to have a chance to act upon the bill, while in his own judgment it would be better not to adopt it. Again, it may occur that the Federal Council, being entirely united in the advocacy of a bill, may use all possible influence in favor of its passage, and approval may still be withheld by one House or by both. This would imply no censure or lack of confidence. It would involve no cabinet crisis. No one would think of resigning and the same Legislature would continue to reëlect the Council whose pet measure it had rejected. The Executive has no need of the support of the Legislature in the performance of its distinctive duties and the Legislature is expected to exercise entire freedom in acting upon executive recommendations. Mutual independence prevents friction.

One of the seven heads of the executive departments is designated each year by the Federal Assembly to serve as President of the Republic, and another is chosen as Vice President of the Council. It has become the established custom to promote the Vice President to the Presidency each successive year. As neither of these officers is permitted to succeed himself these honors become distributed to all the members.

The President of the Republic, being head of a department and supervisor of the work of the other departments, is the ceremonial head of the state and, as such, has a few special duties, — the receiving of representatives of foreign governments, for example; but he does not possess any more power in the administration than do the other Councilors. Switzerland has never had a King nor even a President of the Republic whose position corresponded to that of the President of the United States. The Swiss Cantons have had no governors nor chief magistrates. All executive power rests in the hands of the councils or committees chosen directly or indirectly by universal suffrage. The one apparent exception to this rule is that of the mayor of a commune, previously mentioned, and this arises from the double function of the commune as a local government area and as administrator of cantonal and federal law.

Special reasons may be pointed out as contributing to the remarkable harmonizing, unifying results, noted in the working of the Swiss form of government. Its legal system is based upon Roman Law, which maintains a sharp distinction between private and public law. The courts of the cantons administer private law, but have no jurisdiction over official misconduct. No special tribunals have been set up to administer public law, as has been done in France, a large part of such service being rendered by the series of executive councils. Appeals are made to the cantonal councils to correct abuses in local areas. From the cantons cases are carried to the Federal Council. The jurisdiction of the Federal Tribunal has been extended to include a part of the field of public law, although a considerable portion of such business yet remains with the executive councils. In either case the highest court of appeal is the National Assembly, a joint session of the two houses of the Federal Legislature. That body may set aside a decision of the Supreme Court or of the Federal Council, in judging a case of official misconduct.

Swiss statutes are enacted in the form of brief indications of the will of the state, leaving the executive to furnish supplementary details. In France the Council of Ministers issues general orders explaining the acts of Legislature. The Swiss Council publishes few general orders, but it exercises very wide executive discretion in adapting general measures to local conditions. Many acts of the cantons and the communes are of the nature of supplemental legislation or by-laws relating to the enforcement of federal statutes.

The unifying influence of the Executive is further seen in its relation to the Legislature. In both communes and cantons the mingling of the two functions is constant. Executive officers enter freely into the legislative debates, although they may have no votes. A similar close relation subsists between the Federal Council and the houses of the National Assembly. The Councilors take part in the proceedings of the legislature, though they are not members of it. They prepare bills to be acted upon by the Houses, they are consulted in the preparation of measures, and bills are referred to the Council for suggestions and advice. The Swiss Executive, in fact, performs important services to the state in each of the three departments of government — the Executive, the legislative, and the judicial.

The Legislature. — The Swiss Executive is always, in a sense, subordinate to the Legislature. Executive councils are, one and all, mere committees of the Legislature, whether or not they are appointed by it. When they assist in making laws they act as an aid to the Legislature; when they issue general orders they do it to supplement and enforce a statute, not to override or change the law. When the Executive Council sits as a court to decide issues of public law, its decisions are subject to reversal by the Legislature. No executive body serves as a check upon the Legislature or is endowed with independent powers by which it may thwart the will of the Legislature. This is the fundamental distinction between the Swiss government and that of the United States.

The legislature of the commune is an assembly of all the male citizens over twenty years of age. Two of the cantons and four half cantons also still maintain the ancient *Landsgemeinde*, or mass meeting of all the voters, as the supreme legislative body. In these cantons the legislative councils hold a distinctly subordinate place. In more than half of the others all acts of the legislative councils go to the voters for approval. The rest, with possibly one or two exceptions, provide for a popular veto on legislative acts. Legislation in the cantons is therefore an act of the entire citizenship. The legislature is supreme because the people rule. But the legislative assemblies, and the executive councils, and the judiciary are, in a sense, equal and coördinate, all being subject to orders from the body politic.

It is one of the curiosities of constitution making that Swiss cantons continue to repeat the form of words taken from the constitutions of American States distributing the powers of government to the traditional three departments. Not unnaturally these words appeared in the early constitutions, since in 1848 uncertainty still existed as to the final distribution of governmental powers. There was much copying from the United States, and it was natural that statesmen should expect political development along American lines. Representative assemblies had been little influenced by the referendum; the popular initiative had been adopted in only one canton.[1] Even in the United States

[1] Vaud adopted it in 1845. Lloyd, "A Sovereign People," p. 66.

the theory of independent coördinate powers has been since the middle of the century progressively discredited. In Switzerland, especially in the cantons, the theory has no apparent influence on actual policies, though the form of words is repeated as a harmless anachronism.

When the Constitution of 1848 was adopted there was nowhere in Switzerland a bicameral legislative assembly. Cantons had always used the single chamber, and the early union also possessed an Assembly of one House, in which all the cantons, large and small, had equal voice. One reason for adopting the double chamber for the new Federal Legislature was the facility which it offered for effecting a compromise between large and small cantons. The condition was almost identical with that which prevailed when the thirteen American States attempted to form "a more perfect Union." The Swiss, following the American example, conceded equal representation of the cantons in one house and representation according to population in the other.

The Swiss upper House, usually called the Council of States, is made up of 44 members, two from each of the twenty-two cantons. Three of the twenty-two cantons are divided, making, for all local purposes, each half an independent state. Practically the cantons number twenty-five, though six of them count as only half cantons in national representation. Each of the cantons elects its members of the Council of States as it pleases, pays them as it chooses, and determines their term of office. Naturally the conditions of membership vary. There is a growing tendency to elect by popular vote and to make the term three years to coincide with the term of membership in the National Council.

The National Council is composed of representatives from the cantons apportioned according to population, — one member for each 20,000 inhabitants, and an additional member for fractions of that number above 10,000. They are elected by universal manhood suffrage. All citizens except clergymen are eligible. The election is from districts determined by the Federal Legislature; but a district may not include parts of two cantons. No general rule has been adopted as to the population of districts. Some districts elect one member, others five. A census is taken every ten years for the apportionment of members. That of 1910 gave to the House a total of 167 members. Their term of office is three years, and their salaries are paid from Federal appropriations. In respect to general powers and duties the two Houses of the Assembly hold positions of exact equality. Measures of legislation and of finance may originate in either house. In earlier times the smaller House presented superior attractions; but with the advent of democracy preponderating influence passed to the larger assembly. Members of the Federal Council are more likely to be chosen from the National Council than from the Council of States.

The Judiciary. — The Federal Tribunal consists of a single court of fourteen members, appointed for terms of six years by the Federal Assembly. This court has a limited original jurisdiction both civil and criminal. Civil jurisdiction extends to cases between cantons, between cantons and individuals or corporations, and between cantons or individuals and the Federal government. Criminal jurisdiction covers cases of treason, violations of international law, and crimes which threaten serious disturbance of public order. The Federal Tribunal is not a high court of appeal for the cantons, although a limited class of cases may be thus appealed. The jurisdiction of the Court is dependent upon federal legislation and has been extended to cases of public law involving conflicts between authorities and official abuses of the rights of citizens. There is final appeal in matters of administrative jurisdiction to the Federal Assembly.

Each canton has its own distinct judicial system, at the base of which stands the ever present Justice of the Peace. Arbitration fills a large place in the duties of the local justice. His chief business is to forestall and prevent litigation. Some of the cantons even require that arbitration shall be a prerequisite in every trial of disputed rights.

Between the Justice of the Peace and the Supreme Court of the canton there are usually intermediate district courts. Separate courts are provided for civil and criminal causes. Several Justices are usually engaged in a trial. Appeals may be taken to the Supreme Court of the canton, whose Justices are in most cases appointed by the legislature; the others are elected by popular vote. These courts administer Federal as well as cantonal laws and in most instances there is no appeal to the Federal Tribunal.

The Swiss Judiciary resembles that of France in that the Roman system of distinguishing between private and public law is maintained; yet there are marked contrasts in the methods of development. Roman law had little influence over the peoples in the fastnesses of the Alps, while southern France became thoroughly Romanized. The decline of feudal rule in the eleventh century was accompanied in France by a revival of Roman law, and with the advent of the great Revolution the laws were codified and adapted to modern needs. All this is foreign to the Swiss experience. With legislature and executive in complete accord in the communes and cantons there was little need of a distinct judiciary. As courts were established they followed the French, or Roman order of limiting the legal sphere to the maintenance of private rights. The French system was a creation of the Revolution and the Napoleonic era. It emanated from the Central Government and large provision was made for appeals to the higher courts.

In Switzerland an independent judiciary arose in each of the Cantons. So devoted were the people to their own local systems that when a Federal Tribunal was called into existence in 1848, the judiciaries of the cantons were left intact, and the jurisdiction of the new tribunal was restricted to intercantonal rights. Even Federal laws were adjudicated by the cantonal courts with no appeal to the federal court unless some intercantonal right was involved. One of the serious problems of the centralizing Swiss democracy was how to secure harmony among the numerous independent judicial systems. In recent years, the solution has been sought by extending both the original and appellate jurisdiction of the Federal Tribunal and by the enactment of carefully prepared civil, criminal, and commercial codes, adapted to the needs of the entire Republic.

Thus far the Swiss exhibit no tendency to follow the lead of the French in creating administrative tribunals to administer public law. The settlement of controversies involving public officers is mainly retained in the hands of the executive councils and the legislature. Yet the Federal Tribunal has been empowered to make investigation and to decide questions of right in that domain. This is an apparent exception to the rule in Roman Law countries that ordinary courts shall not administer public law. It is, rather, an instance of the use of the same judges in the two separate capacities. As an administrative court they follow a separate procedure.

The federated system with written constitutions creates a condition in which we might expect to find a hierarchy of laws, as in the United States, and progressive gradation of authority does indeed exist. Communes are subject to cantons and cantons to the Confederation. But nowhere are the courts empowered to nullify a statute either of the canton or of the Federal Legislature. Swiss Constitutions have no higher authority than statutes. If Cantons enact laws which traverse federal authority, the issue is joined between the Federal Council and the cantonal legislature, not between the cantonal statute and the Federal Constitution in a court of law. It is the duty of the Federal Council to induce the cantonal legislature to change its conduct. If the case is referred to the Federal Tribunal that court proceeds, not with the cantonal statute to determine whether it is good law, but to investigate the question at issue between the federal executive and the cantonal legislature and to assist the executive in discovering rules for harmonizing authorities. The real decision still rests with the federal executive or, finally, with the federal legislature. There is therefore no gradation of laws, as such, but a gradation of administrative and legislative authorities. The rule of the Federal Constitution requiring the courts to administer the statutes, even though they are in apparent conflict with that constitution, is applied to cantonal statutes as well as others. If the statutes are wrong, they are to be altered, not to be interpreted out of existence by the judiciary.

Switzerland and the United States represent extreme developments of the two systems of law. In the Anglo-Saxon world the judiciary has been used both as a bulwark for liberty and as an agency for repression. For centuries the high courts were the most reliable tool for the support of despotic power. The judiciary has always held the central position between contending forces of liberty and reaction, or conservatism. Both sides lay claim to judicial support; both have contributed to the exaltation of the courts. In England, this led to the subordination of the Executive to the courts; in America the courts retain all of their accumulated powers over the Executive and, by means of a hierarchy of laws, they have, to a large extent, subordinated the legislatures as well. In France the Roman law with the magistrates to enforce it has been an aid to liberty. The triumph of liberty has tended to emphasize the importance of the judiciary. In Switzerland there has been no sustained despotism as in France, no prolonged conflict between classes as in England, no gradation of laws as in the United States; so there has been little use for a judiciary. Nevertheless more recent democracy is conceding to the courts of law a modest and dignified, but subordinate position in the government.

REFERENCES

(See Chap. LII.)

CHAPTER LIV

The Working of the System

Switzerland has passed beyond the stage of belligerent democracy into that of assured popular rule. The transition is marked in the Constitution of 1874. The advent of assured democracy is indicated by the disappearance of checks and balances. The belligerent democrat naturally looks upon the referendum as a check upon the representative assembly; but this idea is being eliminated. The object of the Assembly is to discover and express the wishes of the body politic. The referendum aids the representatives in the discovery of the general will and enables them to act with greater assurance. Once accept the principle that the legislative assembly is the servant and not the ruler of the people, and the so-called popular veto becomes not a limitation upon, but a guide to its course. It is the business of the Assembly to discover in advance the will of the state. Yet in case of doubt the legislature has a free hand, because if a mistake is made, it may be immediately corrected. In the cantons, where the popular initiative prevails, legislative assemblies have an additional guiding agency. By means of the initiative the body politic may secure the right to vote on a statute which the legislature has failed to enact. It is noteworthy that with the continuous growth of democratic consciousness the popular initiative has not been extended to federal legislation. The people may, by petition of 50,000 voters, secure action upon the amendment of the Federal Constitution, but they may not thus initiate a statutory change. This is explained by reference to the fact that the Federal Council is adequately responsive to popular wishes. As representative democracy approaches perfection there will be less demand for either the initiative or the referendum.

Coöperation Replacing Checks and Balances. — The two houses of the Federal Assembly with their exact equality of function naturally suggest a check of the one upon the other, a safeguard against hasty legislation. Such was the original intention. The principle of artificial checks was recognized and approved in 1848, but the spirit of coöperation has always characterized the relations of the Houses. A presiding officer is chosen by each house from among its members. A Chancellor is elected by the joint session of the two Houses, who serves as a custodian of state records, and, with an assistant, keeps the minutes of the two Houses. He is also Clerk of the Federal Council, though not a member of it. The Presidents of the two Houses with the Chancellor and the Federal Council act as a steering Committee for both Houses. It is the duty of these officers to have business prepared for the opening of each session. Through the Chancellor they are informed as to the exact condition of the unfinished business of the previous session.

The Federal Council is in continuous session. It prepares bills on measures referred to it by the legislature; it receives petitions from all sources for new legislation, and prepares bills of its own to supplement defects revealed by its experience as Chief Executive for the Republic. The Chancellor, as clerk both of the Federal Council and of the legislature, keeps a record of all these measures. The Presidents of the two houses meet and agree upon the measures to be first acted upon by each house. Instead of serving as checks and hindrances, the houses coöperate to a common end under the guidance of a single committee. Thus directed two sessions of about four weeks each suffice for transacting the annual business.

The Swiss system actually attains among the representatives of the three departments of government a condition of equality not found in countries where checks and balances prevail. The Legislature is, in a sense, supreme because of the nature of its business. But with the laws emanating directly from the body politic, legislative assemblies take their place beside the executive and the judiciary as coördinate guardians of the commonweal. The three distinct functions of government are clearly recognized. Each line of business is in the hands of separate officers, and in the performance of their peculiar duties they act independently : one department does not dictate to the other. Authority is derived from the same source and there is a marked uniformity in the machinery provided for its exercise.

The judiciary is made up of groups of justices, each one elected for a brief term of office. In courts of higher rank than the justice court no single judge is permitted to decide a case at law; a bench of justices renders the decision. In matters of private law the decision of a single court is in most cases final. Neither the executive nor the legislative assembly interferes with ordinary courts, nor do the courts interfere with the coördinate branches of government.

Besides the distinctive duties exercised independently by the departments, there are many duties not distinctive, which are exercised coöperatively. It is not necessary to describe farther the continuous coöperation between Legislature and Executive. They work together, although they remain free and independent in action. The judiciary also has its coöperative duties. The work of the judges in promoting arbitration and preventing litigation is not essentially different from that of administrative officers who strive in much the same way to secure compliance with the laws. The courts also assist in legislation. In some cantons they are required to report to the legislature, specifying needed changes in the laws, and this service is everywhere permissible. Moreover, in the matter of administering public law and deciding cases involving conflicts of authority all the three departments share. Various executive councils continually strive to solve all such difficulties. A limited number of problems, whose solution transcends the wisdom of the executive councils, may be brought before the National Tribunal for solution; but a joint session of the two houses of the Legislature is the final court of appeal in questions of public law.

Salaries. — The highest salary paid to any public officer is that of the President of the Republic, 13,000 francs ($2600). His associates in the Federal Council receive 12,000 francs, and the members of the Federal Tribunal receive the same. Members of the National Council have a small daily compensation while in attendance at legislative sessions. Much of the service in communes and cantons is gratuitous. Officeholding is honorable, but nowhere remunerative. The spoils system is forestalled by taking care that there be no spoils. Notwithstanding meager compensation and short terms of office, the state in all its departments secures the continuous services of citizens best fitted for office. The Federal Council may be

THE WORKING OF THE SYSTEM

used to illustrate the general custom as to permanency in the service. Its members are elected in a body, once in three years, by the Federal Assembly, and they are continuously reëlected as long as they live or are willing to serve. The average period is more than ten years; the maximum period, more than thirty years. In some of the communes and cantons a sort of aristocracy of public service is discernible; a promising son of a faithful official is often chosen to succeed his father. The public officer makes sacrifices for the good of the community. For this he is held in high esteem and receives a vote of confidence at each election. Frequent elections promote stability and permanence in office by keeping alive the conscious appreciation of service rendered. Such conditions make exciting contests for office impossible. The personal element is eliminated from elections. Political interest is centered in the issues involved, not in parties or party leaders.

Political Parties. — Switzerland, like all free states, has its distinct party system. Since there are no spoils of office and no positions which admit of personal leadership, parties are kept in close relation to political issues. The relation of the cantons to the central government is the one issue that goes farther than any other in accounting for the formation of parties.

Prior to 1848 there was prolonged debate over the question of a stronger union. The Constitution was a compromise; yet it marked the triumph of the radical party which favored centralization. A period of party confusion followed on account of the injection of new issues. Private or public ownership of railways was for many years a divisive question. Threatened war with France over the seizing of Savoy called forth a new alignment. Race jealousy between Germans, French, and Italians was for a brief period a disturbing element. The division between Catholics and Protestants over questions of education and the support of the church was a factor of importance. The general state of party disarrangement terminated in a ten years' agitation for a new constitution. The Constitution of 1874 provides for a still more centralized government and gives to the people direct control over constitutional amendments and a negative veto on legislation. Under the new order political parties assume a permanent position and for forty years have incurred little change.

After the year 1867 the Catholics became consolidated into a party of the Right, resisting farther centralization of the state. The Radical party, or the party of the Left, favors centralization and the use of federal authority to support secular education. The Liberal party, the party of the Center, is mainly composed of bankers and manufacturers. They are Protestant, favoring secular education, and they turned the scale for the Radicals in the adoption of the new constitution. They are, however, less disposed to extend the field of state control over industries than are the Radicals.

The Swiss are a people with great organizing experience, though they do not apply that ability to their political parties. The Catholics have the best organization, but even they do not work together as a united party. Among Radicals and Liberals are numerous subdivisions. At the extreme left are a few pronounced Socialists. Next to these are Social Democrats, who make up the more active section of the Radical party. The parties have no duties which call for close organization. In office they do not govern. Legislative party members do not pretend to vote as a unit. If a caucus is held, its object is enlightenment, not the securing of united action. Among the constituencies the absence of contest for office leaves little for parties to do by way of nomination and election of representatives. The parties appear as convenient permanent divisions of the citizenship to promote discussion for the instruction of voters. Much of the political life is limited to the cantons and cities. Local parties confined to a single canton abound.

Socialism and Other Reforms. — Besides the parties there are numerous organizations to promote special reforms. Such associations appeal to all parties or to the whole citizenship regardless of party. The relation of reform associations to the party system is illustrated by the position of the Swiss Socialists.

The socialistic propaganda began early in the last century. For many decades it was but one among numerous reform organizations. When socialism became an active political factor in surrounding states the question was raised whether the Swiss Socialists should not go into politics as a party. The prevailing sentiment has been in favor of remaining aloof from party and seeking quietly to permeate the citizenship with their doctrines.

Many of the Social Democrats, however, are Socialists. In some localities the socialist organization has been drawn into political contests, and in Zurich, at one time, they made up nearly half of the Executive Council. Their leaders were even fearful lest at the next election they should have a majority in the Council. Because of the fact that the Socialists are more thoroughly organized than any other party, an actual majority would raise the embarrassing question of party responsibility, — a thing which is alien to the Swiss mind. In Germany, France, Italy, in all countries where parties either rule or try to rule, socialist organizations become political parties. Swiss Socialists seek to maintain the same thoroughness of organization, but they strive to keep it out of politics. Except for a few brief periods, the Radical party has maintained an actual majority in the Swiss Legislature since 1848. Had the party been organized as are the Socialists, and had it, as a party, advocated precise and definite policies, this could not have been. The parties survive with little change because they do not seek to govern, though they do supply needed light to the governing bodies.

Closely related to this function of enlightenment is the rise of Proportional Representation. The advocates of the system aim not only to give to the existing parties representation in legislative and executive councils in proportion to their numbers, but to secure representation to smaller bodies of citizens. As nearly as may be the Legislature is intended to reflect the views of all sections of the body politic. If in such a system one political party happens to have a clear majority over all others, it is because that party is most loosely organized and reflects in itself the widest range of diverse opinion. Only the party least fitted to rule can have a majority.

During the agitation for the new Constitution of 1874 the Radicals had for a brief period less than a majority and the Liberals held the balance of power. Liberals gained a majority in the Federal Council. A few years later the Radicals had regained a majority in the Legislature, but the Federal Council continued to be Liberal, though the party of that name was not one fifth of the Assembly. The executive officers are continued in office without regard to party affiliation. Not one instance has occurred since the triumph of direct democracy in 1874, of failure to reëlect a Federal Councilor who was willing to continue in office. When vacancies do occur places are filled for the good of the service, not for party advantage. There is a growing conscious effort to have all parties represented in the Council. The Clericals, always a small minority and the most reactionary of the parties, have found a place in the Council. Socialists also have been conceded representation.

REFERENCES

See Chap. LII.

CHAPTER LV

SWITZERLAND COMPARED WITH THE UNITED STATES AND ENGLAND

THE fundamental distinction between the two leading types of free government is, that the cabinet system unites the executive with the legislature, while the presidential system separates them. Upon this basis the Swiss government belongs to the presidential, or American type, rather than to the cabinet class. Even in the cantons where the executive councilors are made voting members of the legislative councils, the legislative and executive functions remain distinct. The executive council is not responsible to the legislative council for its policy of administration. In communes and cantons, where the legislature is the entire electorate, the executive council is, in a sense, responsible to the legislature though as a subordinate committee or representative body. If the legislature is the body politic, then the executive is subject to it, as are all other officers. Nevertheless, the Swiss government is not of the presidential type. It is a government approaching direct democracy.

Personal *vs.* Joint Responsibility. — Comparing the three systems with reference to the personnel of the executive, it is to be noted that both the English and the American executives have a chief person at the head. The king is by law the chief executive. According to the Constitution, the Prime Minister with a body of associates whom he has chosen make up the responsible Government. Executive power is either personal or is personated by the party leader.

Personal rule is even more obvious in the United States. The President is the responsible Executive. The members of his Cabinet are assistants and advisers, but responsibility rests with the President. The governor is the chief executive in each of the States, and, for the most part, the mayor is chief magistrate in the cities. The rule is personal and responsibility rests with an individual officeholder.

It is difficult to imagine a greater contrast than Switzerland presents to the American system. Nowhere, either in the executive, the legislature, or the judiciary, are important responsibilities lodged with a single officer. The President of the Republic is not the chief executive. He has a minimum of ceremonial duties, he is permitted to serve only one year, and for all of his important official duties six other members of a governing board share in the responsibility. The President is the chairman of the Council, but he presides over a Cabinet of equals of which he is simply a member. The President of the United States is not a member of his Cabinet. Like the Swiss Executive Council, the Cabinet is made up of the heads of departments, but each member is individually responsible to the President for the conduct of his department. Joint responsibility is no part of the American plan. The cabinet members give advice to the President, which he is not required to follow. A fair degree of unity and harmony is maintained in the American Cabinet, because the President would not tolerate a member who refused to support or acquiesce in his policies. The Swiss heads of departments hold office by legislative appointment for three-year terms: all are chosen at the same time, but the custom of reëlection makes it practically a life service. Cabinet positions in America are held at the will of the President; it is exceptional for a member to remain in a Cabinet after the expiration of the official term of the President who appointed him.

Joint responsibility is a term used in describing both the English Cabinet and the Swiss Federal Council, though it denotes something radically different in the two countries. Joint cabinet responsibility in England grows out of the fact that the Cabinet is the chief agency for responsible party government. Positions in it are held at the will of the House of Commons and all its members stand or fall together. Not only are the members jointly responsible for the acts of the Cabinet, the system requires also that they hold, or at least profess, identical opinions on the leading issues of the day. It is an artificial unity growing out of the exigencies of party government. But the Swiss repudiate party governmental control, seeking instead to attain representative government in the executive as well as in the National Assembly. As far as possible they would have all parties and all shades of opinion represented. The heads of departments belong to different parties, and are expected to be representative, not necessarily unanimous, on seriously controverted matters. Neither in their relations to the legislature nor to the community at large is there any demand for unanimity. Joint responsibility means that all measures adopted shall have the approval of at least four of the seven members, and, if there is serious delinquency or wrongdoing on the part of one, all are subject to criticism.

The Swiss have never experienced the need of limiting the power of a tyrannical executive by means of legislative restraints. They have found no occasion for elaborate detail in the formulation of statutes. The Roman method of giving clear expression in brief general terms to the will of the state, leaving to the executive the filling out of needed details, is followed. This explains the fact that a mass meeting can in a single day enact all the statutes that the canton needs for a year. Legislation is simple, easy, and satisfactory. Between legislature and executive no jealousy or rivalry exists.

Scope and Functions of the Legislatures. — The American model was undoubtedly influential in determining the form of the Swiss Federal Assembly. The Council of States corresponds to the Senate of the United States with equal representation from the cantons, and the National Council is like the House of Representatives, having at least one member from each canton and additional members for every 20,000 inhabitants. There are, however, differences in the apportionment of their functions and in their practical working. The houses of the Congress of the United States meet in joint session once in four years to canvass the votes for President and Vice President. If no one has been elected to the Presidency, the Lower House proceeds to elect a President; and, in case of failure of a majority for Vice President, the Senate elects. The Swiss Federal Assembly each year elects the President of the Republic and a Vice President of the Federal Council; once in three years it elects the seven members of the Federal Council and a Chancellor who keeps the records of both executive and legislature. Once in six years it elects the fourteen members of the Federal Tribunal, or supreme court, and it elects the generals of the army. Besides these electoral duties the joint session exercises the pardoning power and serves as a final court of appeal in cases of public law or of conflicts between authorities. The joint legislative session is, then, in Switzerland, an important institution, while in America its labors are confined to the one act of determining the result of an election.

A two-thirds vote of the Senate alone is required to validate a treaty of the American government. A majority vote of the two houses of the Swiss Legislature, sitting separately, is required to validate a treaty already agreed upon by the Federal Council. Appointments not otherwise provided for by law are made by the President of the United States with the advice and consent of the Senate. In Switzerland this power is lodged with the Federal Council, and no legislative approval is required. It should be noted, however, that, owing to the fact that federal laws are administered by the cantons, federal appointments are few. The American Lower House exercises the power of impeachment while the Senate sits as a court for the trial of such cases. The Swiss make no provision for impeachments.

Bills for raising revenue must originate in the Lower House of Congress. In the Swiss National Assembly they may originate in either house. The election of Senators is regulated by the Constitution and by the federal statutes. The election of members of the Council of States is left entirely to the separate cantons. The salaries of the members of Congress are fixed by federal law and are paid out of the federal treasury. The members of the Council of States receive compensation from the cantons which they represent. The members of the lower house in the National Assembly are paid out of federal appropriations. No age requirement is fixed for membership in either Swiss house. Any voter who is not a clergyman may be elected to the Lower House. The same rule holds in the other House unless, perchance, some canton may have adopted a different rule. All the members of the more numerous body are elected at one time and serve three years. Some of the cantons elect their members of the Upper House yearly, but the greater number elect for terms of three years.

The fundamental principle to be observed in the comparison of the two legislatures is that in America there exists a considerable differentiation of functions between the two houses, while the Swiss houses maintain a complete identity of function. In joint session one house is outvoted by the other nearly four to one. If the Houses were in controversy over matters for joint action, the more numerous council would rule. But controversies are unusual. It is observed, however, that executive Councilors are more likely to be chosen from the larger chamber and that chamber attracts greater political interest. Neither house has any dignity or prestige to defend; cordial coöperation under executive guidance is the rule. No bills are introduced for political effect; no speeches are made for distribution in election campaigns. During the brief sessions of four or five weeks each, the members of the houses attend strictly to business. Inevitably some measures fail of enactment for lack of assent from the smaller House, yet no general criticism arises on that account. One house is as democratic as the other. There has been an agitation for the extension of the Popular Initiative to federal legislation. This has failed because the legislature is so constituted that it can be relied upon to pass any measure which the people want. If anything in the form of obstruction or minority rule should appear, the initiative would surely be adopted.

Making and Amending the Constitution. — The relation of the two houses of the Federal Legislature to making and amending the Constitution illustrates the high degree of confidence placed in them. The constitutions of all the cantons are subject to approval by each of the two Houses acting separately. Every amendment to the constitutions of the cantons takes place under federal supervision. If the two houses of the National Assembly agree upon an amendment to the Federal Constitution, they adopt it by majority vote just as they would a statute. The proposed amendment then passes to the people for approval, and to become valid it must receive not only a majority of all votes cast upon the question, but the majority must be so distributed as to include a majority of the cantons. If one house desires a change in the Constitution and the other does not consent to it, the appeal is made to the voters. Finally, if the people wish a change in the Constitution, 50,000 petitioners may secure a vote on a specifically formulated amendment. All that the Legislature does in that case is to present the proposed act to the voters for approval. The same number of petitioners may require the Legislature to submit the question of a general revision to the voters. If a majority of the voters favor revision, this has the effect of dissolving the existing Legislature, and a newly elected National Assembly is chosen which proceeds to prepare the desired revision of the Constitution to be submitted for approval. The Legislature, therefore, is the guardian of the entire process of constitution making both in the States and in the Confederacy. With the single exception of a specific amendment demanded by petition, the Legislature formulates all changes in the Constitution. The same body in joint session of the two Houses is the final interpreter of the Constitution.

The legislative experience of Switzerland and that of England so widely differ that it is difficult to make a helpful comparison in brief, general terms. England was first to develop the bicameral form for legislative assemblies. Switzerland for many centuries held to the single chamber and when finally two houses were set up for the federal legislature they were used in such a way as to retain many of the features of a single chamber.

The British Parliament has been made up of discordant and opposing elements, — the Crown, the Lords Spiritual, the Lords Temporal, and the Commons. Nothing of the sort has appeared in the Swiss legislatures: King and Lords are omitted. In the United States, in England, and in Switzerland alike, democracy has arisen out of the devotion of the people to their local privileges. The prolonged duel between the English Crown and Parliament resulted in centralizing democracy in a representative assembly. Modern towns, counties, and parishes receive their popular privileges at the hands of Parliament. France exhibits this same order of development in a more extreme form, but a precisely contrary order has controlled the democratic evolution in Switzerland. There the communes and the cantons held their dominant positions until the rise of the spirit of national democracy. The radicals are now securing an efficient centralized government despite the resistance of the conservative reactionaries who defend some form of local privilege.

The contrasts between the judicial systems of the different countries are equally significant. England was the first and Switzerland the last to develop a distinctively national judicial system. It is unnecessary to repeat here the story of the rise of the early English judiciary out of the habit of the people to look to the King's Justices for the defense of local liberties, and to show how this led to a complete fusion of private and public law. Swiss local liberty is older than Magna Charta, yet no higher authority has ever arisen in the name of law to strengthen the hold of the people upon their local privileges. When disputes have arisen they have been settled by committees or by boards of arbitration. Laws have been executed by representative boards, and interpreted and applied by similar institutions. Arbitration still holds a fundamental place in the Swiss judicial system.

REFERENCES

See Chap. LII.

PART III
DEMOCRACY IN OTHER STATES

CHAPTER LVI

THE SMALL STATES OF EUROPE

SMALL states have been great teachers. Palestine teaches the world religion and morality. The little Greek states surpass all others as teachers of art, literature, philosophy, politics. It was when Rome was a small state that the principles of Roman law were developed. The law was extended through the comparative study of other small states, or communities. That which is of permanent good to the race came from the winnowing of experiences gathered from innumerable small communities. Imperial Rome was corrupt, degenerate, in many ways a curse to mankind. Morality and the manly virtues emanate from local community life, while the great conquering states have often transformed brave men into cowards. The Swiss, who have never been subjected to the emasculating influence of imperialism, have been distinguished for bravery. Not until the advent of self-conscious, belligerent democracy and the federal principle in government has it been possible to protect the people of a great state from wholesale degeneracy. The battle for liberty in the great states may do much, but the lesser states on the Continent of Europe are in a position to render a unique service to humanity.

Three Groups of States. — Europe is divided into three distinct governmental groups. The five leading continental countries of France, Germany, Austria, Russia, and Italy, with England, make up the Concert of Europe, and their policies are determined by imperialistic ideas. The eight minor states of Switzerland, Denmark, Sweden, Norway, Holland, Belgium, Portugal, and Spain stand second. The Balkan states, formed out of the Turkish empire, complete the list.

These minor states share in the world's commerce and colonial possessions to an extent out of all proportion to their population. The little state of Norway maintains a merchant marine greater than that of any state on the Continent except Germany, and the merchant marine of the three Scandinavian states is nearly equal to that of Germany. Holland does a carrying trade more than one fourth that of Germany, and during the ten years ending 1914 the rate of increase in the Dutch merchant marine was twice that of the German. Seven small states of the Continent maintain a merchant marine in proportion to their population six times that of the five military and naval states. In respect to colonies and foreign possessions the facts are equally striking. Each of the three states of Holland, Belgium, and Portugal rules over a greater colonial population than does Germany; and together their colonial subjects are nearly twice those of France. Although they have no huge armies and navies, they have yet been comparatively secure in their possessions, and their experience is a lesson of great value to the law-abiding in all lands.[1]

Each one of the minor states is an independent school of domestic politics. Switzerland has been described. Spain has passed through the various experiences of a people subjugated, liberated, risen to imperial dominion and then incurring the degeneration incident to such rule; while, in recent years, the state is being rejuvenated by the development of a citizenship devoted to popular education and self-government. Absolute monarchy has given place to constitutional monarchy and this in turn is being transformed into a parliamentary monarchy or into a republic. Portugal, whose history has been closely linked to that of Spain, has assumed the republican form of government.

Belgium and Holland have won the lasting gratitude of all lovers of liberty for their persistent refusal to submit to tyrannical rule. In defending their own local liberties they have protected other peoples from oppression. Germans and English have been beneficiaries of their valor. A Dutch army assisted the English in ridding themselves of a tyrannical king, and for several generations the people of the Low Country took a leading part in imposing restraints upon the disorderly and imperialistic rulers of Spain and France. Belgium and Holland early established constitutional governments and the Bel-

[1] This paragraph describes the condition at the beginning of the War of 1914.

gian constitution served as a model for the framers of the constitutions of the more liberal German states.

Equally important are the contributions of the Scandinavian states to the cause of freedom. More than thirty years before the Swiss discarded the rule of the aristocratic oligarchy in their Confederation the Norwegians had become thoroughly democratized. In 1814 the nobility was abolished and a liberal frame of government adopted. By outside pressure Norway was forced into a union with Sweden and for nearly a hundred years continual friction existed between the two states, until, in 1905, by mutual agreement Norway became independent. At the time of the separation from Sweden the people were divided in their preference as to the form of government. Some favored a republic after the model of the United States; others preferred a cabinet government after the English form, but all were equally democratic. The subject was thoroughly discussed, and the difficulty of reaching agreement on a form of republican organization led, finally, to the acceptance of the monarchy. The people, however, remain in complete control of their government. The King, who was chosen by the people, accepts the condition that he is in no way to interfere with the people's representatives in the management of public affairs. The ministers are made responsible to a legislature of a single chamber elected by universal suffrage,[1] and all matters pertaining to the Royal Household are subject to regulation by law.

Sweden, like England, has been developing a parliamentary kingdom out of earlier monarchical forms, but the movement toward democratic government has not yet gone so far nor exactly along the same paths as in England. The Constitution of 1809, under which the country is now governed, took the form of an agreement between the newly chosen King and the Four Estates acting for the people, in which each party made certain promises and certain concessions. Although the King described himself as "Sovereign by the Grace of God and by the right of birth," the Estates asserted their right to give to the country a new constitution and to abolish all the fundamental laws in force. They had deposed one King and now, in the name of the people, invited Charles XIII to occupy the throne. Of the three Scandinavian States, Sweden concedes the most

[1] Suffrage now practically universal.

of royal authority to parliamentary monarchy. The Swedish King retains much executive power as commander of the army and navy, and as having a general initiative in political affairs. He is granted general oversight and control of many details of legislation and administration, and is invested with an authority almost unlimited in the matter of external politics. At the same time, he is obliged to choose a Council of State whose members are his advisers, and every royal decree, except military orders, must be countersigned by the Minister at the head of the department most concerned, and this Minister is responsible for the advice acted upon. The Swedish Riksdag consists of two Chambers theoretically of equal powers. The Upper Chamber, of one hundred and fifty members, is elected by indirect proportional vote through the provincial and municipal councils. A candidate must be thirty-five years of age and must have held for at least three years previous, land valued at 50,000 kroner ($13,500) or have paid taxes on an annual income of 3000 kroner ($800). The term of office, since 1909, is six years, one sixth of the members being elected annually. The Lower Chamber, of two hundred and thirty members, is elected once in three years by universal manhood suffrage of those twenty-four years of age.

From 1665 to 1849 the little Kingdom of Denmark was under an absolute monarchy. The first half of the nineteenth century saw agitation for a constitution and the grant of slight concessions to popular interest in the government. In 1849 the King and the national assembly adopted a constitution which recognized a parliament of two representative Chambers and made possible a comparatively free government. The difficulties over Schleswig-Holstein and the resulting war with Germany in 1864 led to its abandonment and the substitution of various short-lived constitutions. But after the Duchies of Schleswig-Holstein had been lost, the people demanded the restoration of the Constitution of 1849, and in 1866 the instrument was reissued in a revised form.

Within the century the Scandinavian states have exhibited all the varieties of kingly government from absolute monarchy to extreme democracy. Autocracy has given place to constitutional monarchy and constitutional monarchy to Parliamentary monarchy, and in the case of Norway the final form is reached.

The history of Europe is thus rehearsed in these three small states. Of late years Sweden and Denmark have been rapidly following the example of Norway. The various unions and attempts at union between the Scandinavian powers have thrown important light on the general problem of federation.

Less fortunate has been the history of the Balkan States under the deadly shadow of imperialism. Subject as they had been for many centuries to the corrupt Roman Empire, followed by a thousand years of the debasing rule of Byzantian imperialism, they became in the fifteenth century a part of the tyrannous Ottoman Empire. No chance has come to them to share in the expanding thought, the fermenting life of Western Europe. Crushed by the peculiar type of persistent governmental despotism for which the Turks have shown an actual genius, all possibility of any sort of union among the various peoples of Southeastern Europe has been forestalled and prevented. Jealousy and discord between the diverse races have been systematically fomented according to Turkish policy. Distinctions of race, language, religion, and sentiment have been carefully preserved. Suspicion and hatred have not been allowed to yield to natural neighborly kindness and human brotherliness even in the smallest villages and towns, where the different peoples have gathered by themselves in hostile sections and dwelt side by side in distrust and fear of one another. Industrious and frugal, they have been kept poor by oppressive Turkish tribute and submissive by frequent massacres.

When at last this age-long subservience of the oppressed nationalities began to break under the stirrings of a new life; when western ideas began to penetrate the darkened minds, and one state after another emerged and achieved autonomy or independence, then a new danger assailed the unhappy Balkan peoples. They became the victims of plots and counter-plots among the European powers greedy for dominant influence in the crumbling Turkish Empire. It became the common practice of the powerful states of Europe to parcel out the territories of Western Turkey among themselves with scant reference to the interests of their inhabitants. Rising against intolerable wrongs, the Balkan peoples in 1912 waged a successful war of independence; but they were not allowed to enjoy the full fruits of their victory. Ancient race hatred and jealousy survived, and a second conflict followed between Bulgarians and Greeks and Servians, and it was the Balkan incident which was made the occasion for beginning the War of 1914.

The modern states of Southeastern Europe have had a brief history. Greece, the oldest, dates from 1830. Bulgaria became autonomous after the war between Russia and Turkey in 1877. Considering the limited time and opportunity for development which they have enjoyed, they have made commendable progress. Their present condition makes a profound appeal to all lovers of liberty on account of their prolonged endurance of imperial despotism. No people should yield to despair, if Greeks can yet be Greeks again after two thousand years of crushing tyranny.

Small States and International Law. — The smaller states have an important place in respect to the development of international law. Law among nations is analogous to law among the classes within a single state. The common people are the first to become law-abiding. In theory every just rule of law implies equality, since it is equally binding upon the rich and the poor, the great and the humble. In actual practice it is indeed long before real equality before the law is achieved. In all states it is as yet an unattained ideal. The humble obey the law, appreciating more keenly its advantages, and they ultimately generate a force which will compel or induce the great and the strong to become law-abiding.

Equality between states is a fundamental principle of international law. Regardless of size or strength or previous condition, all the states which the high contracting powers recognize as sovereign or independent are accounted equal. All are alike bound to observe international rules. All share alike the benefits which they secure. A primary object on the part of the great states of Europe that first began to formulate the rules of international law, was to make an end of wars of conquest, to assign to each state its metes and bounds, and to agree upon rules for its protection; to substitute justice and fair dealing in place of the brutalities of war. Numerous weak states were acknowledged as independent, and as having equal rights with all other states. The small states have uniformly observed the rules of international law. They understand its advantages; they admire its principles of justice and equality. The powerful states, on the other hand, have not been law-abiding. Among nations, as between citizens within each nation, there is one law for the humble and the weak and another law for the great and the powerful. The small, law-abiding states, therefore, furnish a sure reliance for developing a force which will compel or persuade the great to become law-abiding.

The problem is the same within the states and between the states. It is the problem of democracy. There can be no prevailing democracy in any state whose government is disposed to encroach upon the rights of other states. It is therefore the especial duty of the democracy in every state, great or small, to rally to the defense of the weak states threatened by unruly neighbors. If the weak can be made secure in their rights, that will go far toward insuring international justice.

REFERENCES

Cambridge Modern History, Vol. XI.
DODD. *Modern Constitutions*.
HALL. *International Law*, 1904, pp. 47–51.
OGG. *The Governments of Europe*, Chaps. XXVIII–XXXIV.
OPPENHEIM. *International Law*, Two Vols., Vol. I, pp. 15–20, 170–177.
SEIGNOBOS. *A Political History of Contemporary Europe*, Vol. I, Chaps. VIII, X; Vol. II, Chaps. XVIII–XXI.

CHAPTER LVII

South America and Free Government

To the student of politics South America is both an interesting and a fruitful field. Numerous and striking contrasts are to be found between her institutional life and that of the United States or that of any of the free states of Europe. Forms and principles of government are being tested under widely varying conditions. New illustrations of the difficulties to be overcome in the attainment of free government are revealed on every hand. Particularly is it made plain that governmental forms and processes, if they are to be effective, must be adapted to the needs and conditions they must meet. Abundant evidence is furnished of the familiar fact that a governmental organization which may be entirely successful in one state may be wholly unsuited for another. In the experience of South America the problems inherent in artificial state building are revealed in all their perplexing aspects. Lessons which the nations of the world at large need to learn are to be drawn from both her failures and successes. Her institutional life is rich in suggestion and throws light upon many political problems. It is for this reason that careful study of South America is so much worth while for those who are genuinely concerned about the future of democracy.

It is well to be reminded that the world has had much experience with what may be called paper democracy; with institutions that are democratic in theory, but essentially oligarchic in operation. Constitutions embodying principles of free government have been set up in many states which have been powerless to control political practices. If history teaches anything, it teaches the futility of mere constitutional forms. Written constitutions have their virtues and are aids in the attainment of democracy if they are supported by intelligent, alert, liberty-loving people. But it requires more than a written constitution, however democratic in character it may be, to make a government free. It is trite, of course, to give expression to so obvious a fact; yet indisputably its significance is not comprehended by multitudes of people who are content with mere constitutional formalism and who, in the face of long experience, confuse the shadow of liberty with the substance. One of the great lessons which believers in free government need to learn is that democracy is not a form or method; no more so than is religion a ritual or ceremony.

Perhaps nowhere are the effects of political formalism more strikingly manifested than in the states of South America. Though they have constitutions which have been carefully drafted and which are adequate in themselves for the needs of free states, yet free government, in the only sense in which that term is properly used, namely, real popular government, does not exist. The leaven of liberty is working, but to discuss the democracy of South America is, generally speaking, to enter the realm of prophecy and discuss what is yet to be. Nevertheless progress is being made and it is evident that in the future development of the world-wide movement for freedom, South America is destined to hold a prominent place. Her states will be the scenes of intense struggles between the friends and foes of free institutions. The cause of liberty and justice will win in the end, just as it has won and is winning in other lands. The final achievement of popular government may long be delayed, for the obstacles to be overcome are both many and great, but its ultimate triumph is certain. In this struggle for liberty the free states of the world, large and small alike, are deeply concerned. The possibilities that lie before the South American states are too vast, their potential influence upon world politics too great, for other nations to ignore what they do or be indifferent to what they become.

It cannot be denied that political progress in South America has been slow; so slow, indeed, as to cause much questioning concerning future developments. It is to be remembered, however, that real democracy is everywhere a thing of slow growth; it is an evolution, and its development can only to a degree be forced by hot-house methods. The failures of the South American states, whatever they may be, are not essentially different from those which long characterized the political life of France, Italy, and other states which now rank high among the nations of the world.

To comprehend at all clearly the working of political institutions in South America, it is necessary to consider some of the reasons for her backwardness. The operation of government is everywhere influenced, if not determined, by the economic and social conditions that prevail. In the case of South America this influence may perhaps be more in evidence than in other countries, but in none is it absent. In considering the shortcomings of the South American states, therefore, several important social and economic facts should be kept in mind. Failure to do this is likely to result in either a false understanding of the manner in which the governments work, or great injustice to the progressive leaders and thinkers of South America who are laboring diligently to overcome the conditions which retard her development. The fact is to be emphasized that it is unfair to judge the states of South America by the standards that are applied to the United States or England.

Reasons for South America's Backwardness. — An unbiased analysis of South American politics can be made only by keeping clearly in mind the background of Spanish despotism from which the South American states slowly emerged. Though a century has passed since the Spanish yoke was thrown off, the spirit which characterized the exploitative, despotic Spanish control still widely persists. The whole Spanish régime in the South American colonies was opposed to freedom and gave no opportunity to their people to develop the qualities of mind and character which are essential for citizenship in a free state. It is a fact of supreme significance that the great majority of the people of South America have no sufficient background of local self-government, no adequate traditions of free government upon which to build a democratic society. They are without experience in the processes of democracy, and have little understanding of its spirit or ideals. They lack the long training that is necessary for the successful operation of free institutions. In this respect they are notably different from the people of North America, who have behind them centuries of experience with local self-government and long-standing traditions of popular rights and control. In the circumstances it is hardly to be wondered at that progress toward political liberty has not been more rapid in South America.

Another fact to be noted, but which needs little comment, is that the great majority of the people of South America are without education. Popular education has been sadly neglected, even in the most progressive states, with the result that, considering South America as a whole, fully seventy per cent of the inhabitants are illiterate. They therefore not only lack the inspiration that comes from attempts in the past to acquire and maintain popular government and equitable industrial conditions, but are without understanding of their present problems and needs. Because of the prevailing ignorance there is no extensive interest in democracy; no general desire for free government. In a truly democratic society public opinion is the great controlling element; but public opinion, as that term is used in North America and in Europe, does not exist in South America. The ignorance of the people and the general indifference to political and social questions make an effective public opinion impossible, and constitute a dead weight upon progress which is superlatively difficult to overcome. As an eminent American sociologist suggestively remarks, there is no " people " in the sense in which that term is commonly used in the United States.[1] There must, indeed, be a " people " in order to have a public opinion. As would naturally be expected, conditions are worst in tropical South America; but even in the temperate regions, where foreign influences are most noticeable, interest in popular education and popular government is far below the standard necessary for successful democracy. Even in Argentina, which, on the whole, is the most progressive of the South American states, government cannot be said to rest upon the will of the people.

The absence of a real public opinion is not entirely due, however, to the fact that the people are without education. The lack of racial unity is a factor in the problem which is of prime importance. The sharp racial distinctions lead to antagonisms, prejudices, and social differences which make the formation of general public sentiment and the attainment of united action exceedingly difficult. Professor Ross asserts that " the distribution of the population into whites, mestizos,

[1] Ross, " South of Panama," p. 337.

and Indians makes well-nigh impossible the emergence of a general will and of a government truly reflecting the general will."[1] This statement, however, is not to be taken as intimating that, because of lack of racial unity, government controlled by public opinion cannot be obtained. The governments of Switzerland, Canada, and the United States furnish abundant proof to the contrary. Differences of race, language, religion, and customs, divisive as they are in their influence, are not insurmountable barriers to unity of thought and purpose. In the states of South America little effort has been made to bring the races into harmonious relations and to develop in all the people an interest in the common welfare and the ability to give expression to the common will. That this work of harmonization and education must be done, before efficient self-government can prevail, cannot be questioned, and in it are involved some of the most vital problems confronting the progressive leaders of South America.

Still another unfortunate condition is found in the existence of caste and the greatest economic inequality. A wide and, as yet, impassable gulf separates those who rule from those who are governed; those who have great wealth and live in luxury from those who have little or nothing and live accordingly. The caste spirit is strong and reveals itself in many forms of activity, — social, industrial, political. In general, the land is held in great estates and is worked for the benefit of the landowning classes by those who are little better than serfs. Economic opportunity is for the few. There exist the extremes of wealth and luxury on the one side and the extremes of poverty and degradation on the other. A virile, liberty-loving middle class such as has played so big a part in the achievement of free government in other lands is lacking. Comparatively little free agricultural labor is found. This is especially the case in the West Coast countries, where "the agricultural population is in a state of dependence and stagnation, and there is no such class of intelligent, independent small farmers as have constituted the backbone of democracy" in the United States.[1] The general industrial system has been exploitative in character, little consideration being given, as a rule, to the interests and development of the workers. The influence of this upon state

[1] Ross, "South of Panama," p. 332.

activities is obvious. The powers of government have been utilized for the protection and promotion of the interests of the governing classes, — the wealthy landowners or the designing military leaders who command followers of sufficient strength to place them in power. It is plain that the establishment of democratic government in South America will involve fundamental social and economic changes.

Fault not with the Constitutions. — Other reasons for the backwardness of South America from the standpoint of democracy might be given, but those mentioned are sufficient to indicate the relatively slight advance that has been made and to suggest both the fundamental character and the complexity of the problems which must be solved before popular government can be attained. The fact is clear and should be emphasized again that the fault of the political delinquency of South America does not attach to the constitutions or to the mechanism of government outlined in them. The constitutional forms, in the main modeled upon those of the United States, are adequate for peoples who know how to use them, but the governments in operation, for the reasons suggested, fall far below the standards which the constitutions prescribe. It cannot be denied that the people, generally speaking, are not prepared for citizenship in self-governing commonwealths. Indeed, it may be said that the great leaders responsible for the liberation of the South American colonies from Spanish rule had no real comprehension of the nature and processes of free government. They were profoundly impressed by the spirit and achievements of the French Revolution and admired greatly the Constitution of the United States, which they accepted as a model for the constitutions of their own states; but they failed to see how fundamentally different the conditions in South America were from those which prevailed in the United States. Although the purpose was high and the spirit fine, it was in a very real sense a case of the blind leading the blind. It would be a mistake, however, to conclude that the South American constitutions are without value. They embody, in large degree, the ideals of self-government and, notwithstanding the imperfections of the governments that exist, they point the way to the goal of liberty and are a constant challenge to the champions of democracy to press on in the fight for its ultimate realization. The substantial advance that is being made in the more progressive states gives assurance of the final triumph of the forces of freedom throughout the whole continent. This advance has come slowly, but it is real and is steadily gaining in momentum. The great task of all of the South American states is to develop a citizenship which is trained for its duties and conscious of the responsibilities which free government involves. This will require many years undoubtedly, but that it will be done ultimately can hardly be questioned. In time South America will be free.

REFERENCES

(For References, see Chap. LIX.)

CHAPTER LVIII

Cabinet and Unitary Government in Chile

A STUDY of the formal constitutions and the actual operation of the governments of South America reveals the fact that certain underlying principles of free government, as exemplified by the free states of Europe and North America, are at work and are competing for supremacy. The form of government best suited, in the long run, for the people of South America is not yet determined, but the development thus far is sufficient to disclose tendencies which point to the probable outcome. It is desirable, therefore, to take brief notice of some of the outstanding facts in connection with governmental organization.

Both types of free government, cabinet and presidential, receive recognition. The latter, due to the influence of the United States at the time the South American colonies broke away from Spanish control, is in form the prevailing type. It may be questioned, however, whether either system has been applied under conditions which afford fair opportunity for judging its merits as a form of government suitable for South America. In fact, a really fair test cannot be made of either form until a citizenship capable of self-government is developed. In illustration of the manner in which these main types of free government have been utilized, reference may be made to the so-called "A B C" nations — Argentina, Brazil, and Chile. Following the example of Europe, Chile has attempted to apply the cabinet principle, while Argentina and Brazil have endeavored to develop presidential governments.

In some respects, it should be noted, cabinet government in Chile resembles the French system, although there are important differences. It is very unlike the government of England, however. This dissimilarity is to be expected, considering the fact that Chile and England are so far apart with respect to the power of the people over the government. England, in spite of legal forms to the contrary, is democratic. Chile, in spite of constitutional forms to the contrary, is not democratic. It is commonly said that from one hundred to one hundred and fifty leading families control the Chilean government. Public opinion is not the dominant force in the state. It is plain, therefore, that cabinet government in Chile is more a name than a reality, for true cabinet government necessitates real popular control through a popularly elected legislature. A brief statement concerning the executive organization in Chile, and the relation of the executive to the legislature, may be made to good purpose.

The President and his Powers. — By the terms of the Constitution, the executive authority is vested in the President and the Ministers of State. The President is elected for a term of five years and is ineligible for the next succeeding term. He is chosen by an indirect process, similar to that which, in form, prevails in the United States. Electors are chosen by direct popular vote by the departments into which the several provinces are divided for purposes of administration. These electors meet at a stated time and cast their ballots for President. Records of the votes taken are sent to the Senate and, at the time specified in the Constitution, are opened and counted at a public joint session of the Senate and House of Deputies. If no person receives a majority of all the votes, the duty of selecting the President devolves upon Congress, the procedure of the election being prescribed in the Constitution. The President must be a native of Chile, at least thirty years of age, and possess the qualifications necessary for membership in the House of Deputies.

To the President, by constitutional provision, is confided the administration and government of the state. His authority extends to " everything which has for its object the preservation of internal public order and of the external security of the Republic, observing and causing others to observe the constitution and the laws." [1] Many special powers are enumerated as belonging to him. Among these are the powers to take part in the enactment of laws and to approve and promulgate them; to watch over the official conduct of judges and other

[1] Article 72 of the Chilean Constitution. Dodd, "Modern Constitutions," Vol. I, p. 245.

judicial officers; to appoint and remove ministers of state and departmental officers, councilors of state of his own choosing, diplomatic ministers and other foreign agents, and intendants of provinces; to command the military and naval forces; to declare war with the previous approval of Congress; to supervise the collection and expenditure of public funds; to maintain political relations with foreign powers, receive their ministers, and negotiate treaties.[1] Other powers are named which need not be mentioned here. Those given are sufficient to show that, as far as the formal Constitution is concerned, the President is a person of great authority and heavy responsibilities.

Ministers and Council of State. — In connection with the President must be considered the Ministers of State, or cabinet. The number of these is not fixed by the Constitution, but by law. Under the prevailing arrangement there are six ministers who are heads of the following executive departments: Interior; Foreign Affairs; Worship and Colonization; Justice and Public Instruction; War and Marine; and Finance, Industry, and Public Works. All orders of the President must be signed by the minister of the proper department, and without such signature are invalid. Ministers are " personally responsible for all acts which they sign, and collectively responsible for all acts subscribed to or agreed upon by them with the other ministers."[2] They may be members of the Senate or House of Deputies. If they are not members of Congress, they may attend the sessions of either house and take part in the debates, but may not vote. They may be removed by the President or impeached by Congress.

Another body to be noted in considering the executive organization is the Council of State. This consists of twelve members, including the President, who is the Council's presiding officer. Six of the members are chosen by Congress, three by each house. The remaining five are appointed by the President. He is not entirely free, however, in making the appointments, but must choose from among certain officers named in the Constitution. Cabinet ministers are ineligible for membership. The function of the Council of State is advisory in char-

[1] Article 73.
[2] Article 78 of the Constitution. Dodd, "Modern Constitutions," Vol. I, p. 248.

acter, except in those cases in which the President is required to act upon its advice. The President must consult with it upon some matters and may do so upon all. It has the right to propose the dismissal of ministers of state, intendants, governors of departments, and other public officers, whom it considers incapable or negligent. By provision of the Constitution the President shall submit to the Council, for its advice, all bills which he desires to call to the attention of Congress; measures passed by Congress and sent to him for his approval; questions concerning which the Constitution requires that the Council shall be heard; the annual estimates of expenses to be submitted to Congress; and any other matters upon which he may wish to have the Council's opinion. For the opinions given by them, the councilors of state are responsible and they may be impeached if their advice is contrary to the laws. They do not surrender office when a cabinet crisis occurs.

The Working of the Cabinet System. — It is clear at a glance that the President, though nominally possessing large powers, by no means has a free hand in the performance of executive duties. He is restrained by both the ministers and councilors of state. Moreover, the principle of parliamentary responsibility is carried to extreme. Congress is the controlling element in the government. The President, with the aid of the cabinet and the advice of the Council of State, initiates legislation and participates in the legislative process, but Congress determines the fate of presidential measures. Every rejection of one of these, important or not, by Congress involves the resignation of the cabinet and the formation of a new ministry. The right of appeal to the voters to settle the dispute between the executive and Congress does not exist. Because of the determination of Congress to rule, regardless of the fate of Presidents and ministers, cabinets come and go with almost startling rapidity. The instability of cabinets in Chile is far greater than ever was the case in France. Changes occur so frequently, in fact, that they are not generally looked upon as serious or even important. The effect of this upon the work of administration is obviously harmful.[1] It would require a permanent

---

[1] "The defect in the present Chilean system which makes itself felt most disagreeably consists in the frequent changes of ministries. Excessive instability is thus introduced not only into parliamentary and party life, but into the very ad-

civil service of high excellence, far superior to that which prevails in Chile, to withstand successfully the demoralizing effects of such lightning-like shifts among the heads of executive departments.

It is to be observed that these frequent cabinet crises have no relation to a general public opinion opposed to the policies urged upon Congress by the President and the ministers. They are due to the unwillingness of a majority of Congress to accept executive leadership. The consequence is a domination by Congress such as is hardly to be found in any other state. But this domination is not the result of a popular demand, nor of a clash between great political parties upon important questions of public policy. The congressional leaders are distrustful of executive power. Although the President and the ministers exercise a good deal of authority, they are clearly the agents of Congress and are held accountable by it for what they do. Whatever may be the theory of the Constitution concerning the relation of legislative to executive powers, in practice there is no balance or equilibrium between them. Congress governs in Chile. Executive leadership of the character called for by true cabinet government does not exist.

It is manifest that the cabinet principle has been applied only imperfectly in Chile and the results have been far from

ministration of the republic. We have already seen that ministries change on the average every four months. The record figure of ministerial change in any country is certainly that of eighteen ministers of finance during one administrative period of five years. On account of the confusion in Chilean party life a ministerial crisis happens far more frequently than a real crisis of majorities in parliament. It has been stated that only one out of every three or four crises really is the result of a displacement of majorities in the house. The others depend on the temporary shifting of groups and cliques, in which no principle whatever is involved. Such changes rest entirely upon personal reasons, upon a desire of small groups of representatives to acquire influence with the government, very often for the purpose of gaining a merely local or personal advantage. The effect of this instability upon the administration of public affairs may be imagined. . . . The ministers of state lack continuity of experience. They are in many cases young men who have not as yet acquired representative character, who are put in governmental positions because men of wider experience refuse to submit to the chances of political change. The cabinets, indeed, do always contain men of real ability but they by no means offer a field of activity in which great public characters may be developed through continuity of experience and through a constant sense of responsibility for definite policies and political principles. The tenure of the ministers does not depend upon their excellent conduct of affairs, but upon the shifting constellations of parliamentary cliques and groups." — Paul S. Reinsch, "Parliamentary Government in Chile," *The American Political Science Review*, Vol. III, p. 527.

satisfactory. Naturally, a demand, though of uncertain strength, has arisen for a change in the relations between the executive and legislative authorities. For many years the belief has prevailed among some progressive leaders that a much larger degree of independence should be accorded the executive. This was the issue, raised by President Balmaceda, which was involved in the revolution of 1891. The Congressional faction was successful and Balmaceda's efforts came to naught. Sentiment in favor of more effective executive leadership, however, appears to be growing. The most radical reformers demand the overthrow of the parliamentary system, carried on as it has been to an extreme which is considered ridiculous, and the substitution of a presidential system similar to that of the United States. It is held that this is necessary in order that great national policies may be formulated and successfully carried out. Little or much may come, in the long run, from the agitation for this reform; its strength is merely a matter for conjecture. But its continuance indicates that real dissatisfaction with the parliamentary system exists, and points to an ultimate reorganization of the government.

Chile's Government Highly Centralized. — Not only are the two great types of free government given theoretical recognition in South America, but also both the unitary and federal principles are utilized. Chile, again showing the influence of Europe, particularly of France, has a unitary government of the extreme type and may be cited to illustrate the use of the unitary form in South America. Argentina and Brazil, on the other hand, again followed the example of the United States and established governments of the federal type. The former made use of federation to unite provinces which, following independence, were inclined to maintain separate governments; the latter, after the overthrow of the monarchy, deliberately abandoned a unified government and established commonwealths in order to make federation possible. This was a very unusual action on the part of Brazil. Federation was perhaps a logical, natural system for Argentina to accept, but hardly may thus be characterized in the case of Brazil.

In no other country of South America has the unitary principle been carried to greater lengths than in Chile. It is frequently said that a highly centralized government is the only kind that can successfully meet the needs of Chile, considering the unusual character of her territory. " The government of Chile is wisely preserved as a centralized republic or ' unitary ' system, in which the system of federation has been avoided. In a country of such vast longitudinal extent, wherein political conditions would perforce have to be made to coördinate with climatic zones, the federal system as enjoyed by Mexico or Brazil could scarcely be conducive to national solidarity." [1] This statement may or may not be sound; opinions will differ as to whether mere climatic variations are seriously inimical to federation. The fact is clear, however, that extreme centralization, of the French type, characterizes the government of Chile. By the Constitution the territory is " divided into provinces, the provinces into departments, the departments into subdelegations, and the subdelegations into districts." [2] There are twenty-three provinces and one territory, which are divided for administrative purposes into seventy-five departments. The subdelegations number 855, and the districts 3068. At the head of each province is an intendant, appointed by the President. In the words of the Constitution: " The superior government of each province in all branches of its administration shall be vested in an intendant, who shall exercise his power in accordance with the laws, and with the orders and instructions of the President of the Republic, whose natural and immediate agent he is." [3] The intendant's term of office is three years, but he may be reappointed indefinitely. Removal is by the President. The government of each department is vested in a governor, who is subordinate to the intendant of the province. Governors are appointed by the President upon the nomination of the respective intendants. They may be removed by the intendants with the approval of the President. At the head of each subdelegation is an officer known as subdelegate, who is appointed by the governor of the department and is responsible to him. The power to remove subdelegates vests in the governor. The districts are governed by inspectors who are appointed by and are under the direction of the subdelegates. In each department, also,

---

[1] Enock, " The Republics of Central and South America," p. 304.
[2] Article 106. Dodd, " Modern Constitutions," Vol. I, p. 254.
[3] Article 107. *Ibid.*

municipalities exist under constitutional authorization. The governor is made the administrative head of all municipalities in his department. Municipal ordinances dealing with questions recognized by the Constitution as coming within the powers of the municipalities, must be presented through the intendant of the province to the President for his approval, with the advice of the Council of State.

From this brief summary of the constitutional provisions relating to Chile's internal administration, it may be seen how highly unified the government is. The central authorities control from the top to the bottom of the governmental system. There is no local self-government comparable with that which is held to be so essential in the United States. The results of centralized control over local affairs in Chile are not always good. As illustrative of this fact Professor Ross makes this interesting statement: "The Government of Chile relieves the cities of the burden of pavement, sewers, water-supply, fire protection, police and hospitals, so that the municipality has nothing to do but care for the streets and parks, light them, and provide band music. Its taxation is limited to three mills in the dollar. No doubt, the department of public works has given some cities better water than otherwise they would have. On the other hand, German-managed towns like La Union and Osorno would have good drinking water if only they might provide it for themselves; but, thanks to their dependence on remote Santiago, their water is bad and typhus is rife."[1] The evidence is abundant that the neglect of the central government with respect to local conditions, suggested in this statement, is not confined to questions of water supply and public health. It has fallen far short of both its opportunity and its duty with respect to problems of education, morals, industry, and the general social welfare.

It is important to note, however, that the failures of the Chilean government are not due necessarily to the fact that it is unitary and not federal in character. The difficulty is found in the fact that Chile is not democratic and those in control of the government are not using the powers of the state to promote the interests and welfare of the mass of the people. A centralized government may be democratic, as

[1] Ross, "South of Panama," pp. 353–354.

England and France have demonstrated, and Chile may in time meet her problems, both national and local, effectively and in the spirit of wholesome democracy, without serious changes in the structure of her governmental system. It is a significant thing, which will be commented upon in the next chapter, that the unitary or centralization principle is noticeably becoming stronger in South America. The trend is away from federalism, not toward it. However, if the unitary form is to prove permanently satisfactory, it must be thoroughly democratized and made to serve all the people and not merely the few who govern.

REFERENCES

(For References, see Chap. LIX.)

CHAPTER LIX

FEDERATION AND PRESIDENTIAL GOVERNMENT IN ARGENTINA

As previously stated, the federal form of government finds recognition in Argentina and Brazil. The United States Constitution was a model for both. In the case of Argentina the circumstances out of which federation developed were not unlike those which led to the establishment of the great federated republic in North America. Jealous, warring Provinces, with unstable governments, had to be united under an adequate central authority in order to bring about peaceful relations, and maintain conditions which would admit of permanent political and industrial progress. As in the United States, a unitary government, in the beginning, was impossible. The hope of a satisfactory adjustment of the troubles confronting the Provinces lay in a union of the federal type, in the control of which all should have a fair voice. From the time independence was gained from Spain until 1860, however, the political life of Argentina was characterized by struggles between the champions of federation and the advocates of a unitary government. Because of the final acceptance of the federal principle, which affords an interesting contrast with Chile and the other states with unitary governments, as well as for the reason that Argentina is the most advanced, most progressive of the South American states, it is worth while to consider her governmental organization in some detail.

The Provinces and the Nation. — As in any federated government, a question of fundamental importance is that which involves the relation of the Provinces to the central government. It is seen that this relation is very similar to that which exists between the States and the Nation in the United States. Argentina consists of fourteen Provinces and ten Territories, the latter being completely under the control of the national power. The Provinces, in theory, are autonomous commonwealths with respect to their own internal affairs. The Constitution declares that they shall have their own local institutions and be governed by them, and that they shall elect their governors, legislators, and other provincial officers without interference from the federal government. Article 5 reads: " Each province shall adopt its own constitution which shall provide for the administration of justice in its own territory, its municipal system, and primary instruction, such constitution to be framed upon the republican representative plan, in harmony with the principles, declarations, and guaranties of the national constitution. Upon these conditions, the federal government shall guarantee to each province the enjoyment and exercise of its institutions." [1] The Provinces, thus, are free to do as they please within their own constitutional sphere, subject to the right of intervention by the national government, to be discussed later; but concerning the questions assigned to the national government, they have nothing to say. By specific constitutional provision, they retain all powers not delegated to the Nation. Thus they possess the inherent or original powers of government and the Nation has only the conferred powers. The latter cover a wide range of questions, however, so that the authority of the Provinces is greatly restricted.

The Constitution places upon the Provinces a number of specific prohibitions. They are forbidden to exercise any power delegated to the Nation; declare or wage war upon one another; enter into treaties or alliances of a political character; pass laws relating to domestic or foreign commerce or navigation; establish provincial custom houses; coin money; enact any civil, commercial, criminal, or mining codes, after Congress has enacted such codes; pass laws on the subjects of citizenship, naturalization, bankruptcy, and counterfeiting of money or forging of government documents; arm war vessels or raise armies, except in case of foreign invasion or of danger so immediate as to admit of no delay; appoint or receive foreign agents, or admit new religious orders.[2]

In their relations to one another, the Provinces in Argentina hold a position quite similar to that of the commonwealths in the United States. The Constitution requires that full

[1] Dodd, " Modern Constitutions," Vol. I, p. 4.   [2] Article 108. *Ibid.*, p. 28.

credit shall be given in each Province to the public acts and judicial proceedings of all the other Provinces, under rules prescribed by Congress. The citizens of each Province enjoy in all the others the rights, privileges, and immunities belonging to the citizens of such other Provinces. The extradition of criminals is obligatory upon the Provinces.[1] Interference with freedom of travel and freedom of commerce among the Provinces is forbidden. To all of the inhabitants of the Nation are guaranteed the rights " to work and engage in any lawful industry; to navigate and engage in commerce; to petition the authorities; to enter, remain in, travel through, or leave the Argentine territory; to publish their ideas through the press without previous censorship; to use and dispose of their property; to associate together for useful purposes; freely to profess their religion; and to teach and to study." [2]

Intervention and State of Siege. — In two ways, particularly, the relation between the Provinces and the central government in Argentina differs from that which holds between the commonwealths and the national government in the United States. In Argentina the national government, under certain circumstances, may intervene in the affairs of the Provinces, and in case of domestic disturbance or foreign attack may proclaim a state of siege in the Province or Territory involved. These are important matters from the standpoint of constitutional law and deserve some consideration, even though the rights involved may seldom be asserted. They signify that the Provinces, even in theory, are by no means independent of the central authority.

By the Constitution the national government may intervene in any Province for any one of four purposes: to guarantee the republican form of government; to repel foreign invasion; to maintain the constituted authorities of the Province in power, when requested by them to do so; and to reëstablish them if they have been deposed by sedition or by invasion from another Province.[3] In the case of the first two, intervention may occur upon the initiative and at the will of the national executive; in the last two, upon the request of the provincial authorities. "What happens in case of an intervention is the following.

[1] Articles 7 and 8. Dodd, "Modern Constitutions," Vol. I, p. 4.
[2] Article 14. *Ibid.*, p. 5.   [3] Article 6. *Ibid.*, p. 4.

The National Government sends to the province an Interventor with his secretary and other personnel requisite, and, according to the circumstances, accompanied or not by national troops of soldiery. On arrival at the province, the Interventor becomes the supreme authority and it is his duty to carry out the objects of his intervention with the least possible delay. He inquires into the circumstances which have made his intervention necessary and then takes steps to re-establish the republican form of government, that is to say, he sees that the authorities provided by the Constitution are legally constituted. Sometimes, in case of what is called a revolution, his duty is limited to replacing the deposed Government in power. If, however, he finds that the revolution is justified by the actions of the local government, he declares the authorities deposed and calls for fresh elections. The power of intervention is a most serious one and, practically, places the provincial governments in a state of dependence on the National Government, as it will be readily seen that, if a provincial governor does not fall in with the views of the National Executive, there is nothing easier than to take advantage of any local *emeute*, which is easily got up, and intervene 'motu proprio' to restore the republican form of government. A sympathetic interventor can be relied upon to do the rest." [1]

The right to proclaim a state of siege belongs to Congress, if it is in session when the occasion arises, and to the President, if Congress is not in session. This procedure is authorized in case of domestic disturbance or foreign attack which endangers the observance of the Constitution and the safety of the authorities created by it. During its continuance, constitutional guaranties are suspended within the Province or Territory in which the disturbance occurs. To show the purpose and significance of the state of siege, the words of the writer last quoted may be used. "Unfortunately this measure has had to be resorted to with much greater frequency than the compilers of the Constitution ever contemplated. The declaration of a State of Siege in Argentina is not, however, a declaration of martial law. It is practically the same thing as is, in Great Britain, a suspension of the Habeas Corpus Act. Its application is strictly limited to the National Government and can-

[1] Pennington, "The Argentine Republic," pp. 64–67.

not be usurped by the provincial authorities. . . . The declaration of a State of Siege does not give any punitive powers to the Executive. The President can neither condemn nor impose punishment. He can arrest any person and convey him to another part of the Republic. In actual practice, when a state of siege is declared, the Press is warned not to do or publish anything which may in any way diminish the effects of the measure. Any journal daring to disobey this order is summarily closed either for a few days until repentant or for the whole period of the suspension of the guaranties. Foreigners, who may be deemed detrimentals, are sent out of the country by the authority of a special law which does not require a state of siege for its application. Argentine citizens are sent away from the district where they have influence. Frequently they are retained on board a man-of-war or, in extreme cases, they may be sent down to the cool regions of Tierra del Fuego or Staten Island. The declaration of a State of Siege in no way puts an end to personal rights, except as immediately affected by the causes which have been the ground of the dictation of the measure. In other respects, the constitutional privileges of every inhabitant of the country suffer no interruption. This fact was very remarkably shown during the state of siege declared in consequence of the assassination of the Buenos Aires Chief of Police. The National Government declared a state of siege over the whole country with the object of dealing with anarchists and anarchy. Several provincial governors took advantage of the measure to put in prison persons whose actions were politically displeasing to them. These governors had their knuckles sharply rapped by the National Executive and were ordered, not only to release the persons whom they had imprisoned, but also to take no steps against anyone without first obtaining the authority of the Minister of the Interior. A State of Siege must therefore not be confounded with martial law, with which extreme step it has practically nothing in common." [1]

The National Congress and its Powers. — In the organization of the national government the principle of the separation of powers is followed, the authority of each department — legislative, executive, and judicial — being specifically stated

[1] Pennington, "The Argentine Republic," pp. 67–68.

in the Constitution and protected against infringement. A brief outline of the departments and their constitutional powers will be given.

The Congress, in which is vested the legislative power of the Nation, is composed of two houses, the Senate and the House of Deputies. The Senate is representative of the Provinces and the national capital, each Province and the capital being entitled to two Senators. Those from the Provinces are elected by a plurality of votes of the respective provincial legislatures, while those from the capital are chosen by an electoral college, such as is employed for the selection of the President. The term of office is nine years, one third of the membership being chosen every three years. Senators are eligible for reëlection indefinitely. The qualifications for election as Senator, as prescribed in the Constitution, are the attainment of the age of thirty; citizenship in the Nation for six years; an annual income of two thousand pesos in coin or an equivalent amount of capital; and nativity in the Province which elects him or residence therein for the two years immediately preceding. Each Senator has one vote. The Vice President of the Nation is the presiding officer in the Senate, but has no vote except in case of a tie.

The House of Deputies is representative of the people of the Provinces and of the capital. Its members are chosen by direct vote, a simple plurality being sufficient to elect. The constitutional unit of representation is one deputy for every thirty-three thousand inhabitants or fraction thereof not less than sixteen thousand five hundred. After each census, which shall not be taken more than once in every ten years, Congress is required to fix the ratio of representation upon the basis of such census; this ratio may be increased beyond the constitutional unit, but not diminished. The manner of election is prescribed by a general law of Congress. Deputies must be twenty-five years of age, citizens of the Nation for four years, natives of the Provinces from which they are chosen or residents thereof for the two preceding years. They serve for four years and are eligible for reëlection, one half of the members being elected every two years.

The regular session of Congress begins on the first day of May of each year and continues until the thirtieth of September.

Extraordinary sessions may be called or the regular sessions may be extended by the President. Each house is judge of the qualifications and elections of its own members and determines its own rules of procedure. Neither house is permitted to transact business without the presence of a majority of all its members. The remuneration of Senators and Deputies is fixed by law and is paid out of the funds of the national treasury. The initiation of laws relating to taxes and to the recruiting of troops belongs exclusively to the House of Deputies, as does the right to vote impeachments. The trial of impeachment cases is by the Senate. Members of religious orders are prohibited from serving in Congress and provincial governors may not represent their Provinces during their terms of office. Members of Congress are forbidden to receive appointments or commissions from the executive without first obtaining the consent of the house to which they belong. The customary freedom from arrest during sessions of Congress and from responsibility for the things said in the discharge of their duties, are accorded members of both houses.

Laws originate in either house by means of bills introduced by the members or by the executive. A bill passed by both houses is sent to the President for his approval. If he approve, the legislative process is completed and the measure is promulgated as law. Ten working days are allowed the President in which to consider a measure submitted to him. If it is not returned within that time, the bill becomes a law without executive approval. The President's veto may apply to a bill wholly or in part. A measure thus rejected must be returned to the house in which it originated, with a statement giving the reasons for executive disapproval. To overcome the veto a two-thirds majority is necessary in each house. The vote upon a bill vetoed by the President must be by yeas and nays, and the names of the members voting, together with the reasons upon which their votes were based, and the objections of the President, must be immediately published in the press.

The constitutional powers of Congress cover a wide range of questions. It is unnecessary to give these in detail, but mention may be made of the power to impose import and export duties, which shall be uniform throughout the Nation; to levy direct taxes when occasion demands; to borrow money on the credit of the Nation; to arrange for the payment of the Nation's debt and provide for its fiscal needs; to grant subsidies to those Provinces whose revenues are insufficient to meet their ordinary expenses; to regulate the free navigation of rivers; to coin money and adopt a uniform system of weights and measures; to enact civil, commercial, penal, and mining codes; to pass general laws on naturalization, citizenship, bankruptcy, counterfeiting of money, and establishment of trial by jury; to regulate commerce among the Provinces and with foreign nations; to establish and regulate post offices and post roads; to govern the national Territories and create new Provinces; to establish national courts inferior to the Supreme Court of Justice; to authorize the executive to declare war or to make peace; to approve or reject treaties with other nations; to provide for the military and naval forces of the Nation and establish regulations for their government; to proclaim a state of siege in one or more places in the Nation in case of internal disorder and to authorize the calling out of the militia of any or all of the Provinces if the need arises; and to make all laws and regulations which shall be necessary for carrying into execution the powers granted to Congress and all other powers vested by the Constitution in the government of the Argentine Nation. It is impossible here to discuss the constitutional law of Argentina from the standpoint of legislative authority, but it is plain that the powers of Congress are exceedingly broad and include all matters that are not distinctly local and provincial in character. As far as the Constitution is concerned, Congress is representative of the people, through the electorate, and the way is open for effective public control in all great questions of national policy. The Congress, in composition, organization, and powers, is adequate as an instrument of democracy; the need in Argentina, as in all of the South American states, is for an intelligent, responsible, efficient citizenship.

The Executive Department. — The executive power of Argentina is vested in the President, who is assisted by eight ministers or secretaries. Provision is made for a Vice President to take the place of the President in case of the latter's illness, absence from the capital, death, resignation, or removal. Both of these officers are chosen by an indirect process, almost identical with that which is prescribed by the Constitution of the United

States for the election of President and Vice President. The capital and each of the Provinces elect, by direct vote, an electoral college which consists of twice as many members as the number of Senators and Deputies constituting their respective representation in Congress. Members of Congress and officials receiving pay from the federal government are disqualified from serving as presidential electors. Four months before the expiration of the presidential term, the electors chosen by the Provinces meet in their respective provincial capitals, and those chosen by the capital in the capital, and proceed to elect by signed ballots the President and Vice President, separate ballots being used. Two lists are made of all the persons named for President and two of those named for Vice President, with the number of votes cast for each. Two of these lists, one of each kind, properly authenticated, are sent to the president of the Senate, and the other two are filed with the president of the provincial legislature, and, in the case of the capital, with the president of the municipality. In the presence of both houses of Congress, the ballots are opened by the president of the Senate and are counted by four members of Congress selected by lot. Those receiving in each case an absolute majority of all the votes are immediately proclaimed President and Vice President. If no one receives the necessary majority, Congress is authorized to elect, by verbal vote, one of the two persons receiving the highest number of votes. If the highest vote is in favor of more than two persons, Congress must make its choice from among all of them. This choice must be made by an absolute majority. In case of a tie, the vote is repeated immediately, and if it again results in a tie, the president of the Senate casts the deciding ballot. The election must be concluded in a single sitting of Congress, the presence of three fourths of all the members being necessary.

The President is made the chief magistrate of the Nation and is given charge of its general administration. He is given power to issue instructions and regulations necessary for the execution of the laws; to assist, in the manner prescribed in the Constitution, in making the laws and to promulgate them; the power to veto, wholly or in part, measures which he disapproves; to grant pardons and commute punishments in cases subject to federal jurisdiction, except impeachments; to appoint and remove, with the advice of the Senate, the Nation's diplomatic representatives, and by himself, without senatorial action, ministers of state, officials of the departments, consular agents, and all other government employees whose appointment is not otherwise provided for by the Constitution; to open the annual sessions of Congress and to recommend legislation which he considers necessary and expedient; to extend the regular session of Congress or summon it in extraordinary session; to supervise the collection and expenditure of public funds as provided by law; to negotiate treaties and receive foreign ministers and consuls; to command the land and naval forces of the Nation; to declare war, with the authority and approval of Congress; and to declare, with the consent of Congress, a state of siege, in case of foreign invasion, and upon his own authority, when Congress is not in session, in case of internal disorders.[1]

The President is assisted by the ministers of state, who, by the constitution, "shall have charge of the affairs of the nation, and shall countersign and attest the acts of the President by means of their signatures."[2] This countersignature is necessary for the validity of the President's acts. Each minister is individually responsible for the acts signed by himself and jointly with the other ministers for all acts agreed upon between him and his colleagues. Individual action, on the part of a minister, is confined to the internal affairs of his own department, the work of which is prescribed by law. Ministers are required to submit detailed reports to Congress at the beginning of each session. They may attend the sessions and take part in the debates, but do not have the right to vote. No minister may serve either in the Senate or the House of Deputies without first resigning his position as minister.[3] The ministers do not constitute a cabinet in the parliamentary sense. Their position is similar to that of the President's cabinet in the United States. Unlike the latter, however, they have definite constitutional status. The departments which the ministers direct are as follows: Interior; Foreign Affairs and Public Worship; Finance; Justice and Public Instruction; War; Marine; Agriculture; Public Works.

The Judiciary. — The judicial power of Argentina is vested in a Supreme Court of Justice and in such inferior courts as

[1] Article 86 of the Constitution. Dodd, "Modern Constitutions," Vol. I, pp. 23–25. [2] Article 87. *Ibid.*, p. 25. [3] Articles 88–93. *Ibid.*, p. 26.

Congress may establish. The President is specifically forbidden to exercise judicial functions. The judges of the Supreme Court and of the inferior courts, appointed by the President with the approval of the Senate, hold their office during good behavior, and are subject to impeachment by the House of Deputies. No person is eligible for membership in the Supreme Court who is not a lawyer with at least eight years' practice in the national courts, and who does not have in addition the qualifications necessary to be a Senator. The Supreme Court makes its own rules of procedure and appoints its subordinate employees. Rules for the inferior federal courts may be prescribed by Congress. The important lower courts, established by Congress, are the Appeal Courts and the Inferior Courts or Courts of First Instance. Each Province, of course, has its own judicial system.

The constitutional jurisdiction of the Argentine national courts is very much like that of the federal courts in the United States. It extends to all cases arising under the Constitution, the laws of Congress, or treaties with foreign nations; to cases concerning ambassadors, public ministers, and foreign consuls; to admiralty and maritime causes; to controversies to which the Nation is a party; and to cases which arise between two or more Provinces, between one Province and citizens of another Province, between citizens of different Provinces, and between a Province or its citizens and a foreign state or its citizens. In all cases concerning foreign ambassadors, ministers, and consuls, and in those to which a Province may be a party, the Supreme Court has original and exclusive jurisdiction. In all other cases, it has appellate jurisdiction under such rules and exceptions as Congress may establish.

The Government in Operation. — It is of especial importance to bear in mind that the government of Argentina, as described in the foregoing paragraphs, is the government as outlined in the formal Constitution. The government in actual operation differs from this very materially. This is true, as has been pointed out, in all of the states of South America; indeed, it is true to a greater or less degree of all nations that have formal, written constitutions. In the case of the South American states, however, the departures from constitutional forms have frequently involved practices that are far less democratic than those which the Constitutions prescribe, whereas in other countries, the United States for instance, extra-constitutional practices have developed as a result of a growing democracy. In Argentina, as in Chile, Brazil, and other countries of South America, representative government has fallen far short of the requirements of the Constitution.[1] The balance among the departments, demanded by the doctrine of the separation of powers, is by no means maintained. The executive dominates the government to a degree not contemplated by the framers of the Constitution. Particularly the President is unduly influential in the selection of his successor. Indeed, not infrequently he is able to dictate his successor through the control which the government party has over presidential elections. Judicial administration is notably weak and often corrupt. This is especially the case with the lower courts, but even the standing of the Supreme Court is far below what it should be. Public opinion does not control the government. Popular interest in the election of public officers is lax. In spite of a system which makes use of a secret ballot and of compulsory voting, large numbers of voters do not participate in the elections. The power of the *caudillo*, or political boss, is great, and party life can hardly be said to exist. The Socialists alone seem to constitute a real party. Corruption and force are frequently resorted to in elections. The government, though more liberal, more democratic than that of Chile and most of the other governments in South America, is nevertheless undemocratic, as yet, in spirit and methods. In the Provinces as well as in the Nation political authority is in the hands of the few, and not in the possession

[1] "However generous any particular constitution may be in allowing for the participation of the people at large in government, the fact remains that, to all intents and purposes, the Latin-American countries are ruled either by a virtual autocrat whose effective support comes from certain classes and not from the great body of the people themselves, or else by a relatively small number of persons identified with the interests of the wealthy and the well educated. Professional men, rather than those concerned primarily in industrial pursuits, are apt to be the dominant factor in politics.

"Possibly the two kinds of actual government in question are the only ones that are feasible under present conditions. To establish a more liberal system, so long as the masses remain uneducated, might be unwise. The Latin-American governments, at all events, do not appear to rest on the people, broadly speaking, but only on the 'political' people, on that portion of the population which is believed to possess the knowledge and intelligence needful to enable its members to assume an active share in public life." — Shepherd, "Latin America," pp. 142–143.

of the common people. Federation has not worked out as planned in the Constitution. The national government has dominated provincial politics to a high degree. The central government has extended its activities so widely, in fact, that it "threatens to throw the federal system out of balance."[1] In practice, therefore, the unitary principle has prevailed to a large extent, and a tendency away from federalism seems clearly discernible.

Argentina Becoming Free. — But when all of the adverse criticisms of Argentina are made, and the fact is demonstrated that the theory and practice of her government are widely divergent, it must still be admitted that she is moving steadily forward to a better political and social order. The spirit of democracy is developing, and a demand for general social improvement is growing. Though the control of the government has, in large measure, been somewhat oligarchic in character, yet the domination of the wealthy landowners has been far less complete than in Chile and other South American states. Many governmental projects, particularly in the promotion of internal improvements, such as railways and irrigation works, have been carried through which were clearly not beneficial to the great landed interests. Although the percentage of illiteracy is high, amounting to fully fifty per cent, yet the standard of education is superior to that of any other South American nation and is slowly being raised. While it is true that the interests of property have commonly been given more consideration than those of humanity, yet much labor and social welfare legislation of an advanced type has been enacted. The development of the Socialist movement is indicative of a growing social unrest and points to a larger democracy both in government and in industry. Argentina, in fact, has made rapid and very substantial progress, particularly from the material point of view, but it seems certain that the future, perhaps the near future, is to witness a development that will greatly transcend her present attainments. She is in the process of becoming a great free state and is attaining a place of influence among the nations of the world.

Argentina Contrasted with Australia. — Professor Ross quotes a suggestive comparative statement made by the eminent sociologist, Ernesto Quesada, on return from a visit to Australia, with

[1] Ross, "South of Panama," p. 348.

the remark that "there is no better appraisal of the Argentine state." The statement follows:

"There as here immense territory and sparse population. There as here stock-raising and agriculture lead while manufacturing is secondary. In the one country as in the other is forming a new race; there homogeneous, here heterogeneous. The economic and social problems are the same in both countries, but their solution is diametrically opposed: here, the individualistic criterion governs, there the socialistic.

"Both are countries of immigration: but there it is retarded by racial, linguistic and social standards, while here the gates are open to all. Both export meat and grain, but there the State fosters production and exportation, while here they are left to individual initiative. Both borrow foreign capital, but there the loans are expended in productive works and the State assumes the administration of undertakings of a monopolistic nature, such as transportation, insurance, refrigeration and like industries, representing a business based on the interest of the community; while here the State divests itself of the conduct of such enterprises even if perchance it has them in its hands, as once it had certain railways, and leaves to private enterprise such important public services as telephones, lighting, and docks. There no danger of trustification of any industry because the State intervenes and assumes its management; here private capital is left free to combine, in form more or less covert, and constitute true monopolies. There the absence of great private companies conducting public industries which employ thousands of persons makes unknown the political influence which these inevitably exercise; here such companies wield a considerable influence, which they may be tempted to use, by means of the vote of their employees or by the natural seduction of favors direct or indirect, to the injury of democracy. There the settlers are aided with loans from the public treasury; here they are abandoned to the banks and the private money lenders. There likewise certain agricultural or stock-raising industries are helped by the credit of the State; here the State does not intervene in what is considered to be a matter of private concern. There despite such financial interventions the Treasury reports regularly show a surplus; here, in spite of withholding public money from such purposes, they generally close with a deficit.

"Finally, — to sum it all up, — there the functions of the State are extended wherever the public welfare requires it, and no individual right is valid as against that of the collectivity; here the radius of government action is limited and the State maintains intact the private right of each which the general interest may not set aside."[1]

Tendency Toward Centralization. — In conclusion, attention should be directed to what, from the standpoint of governmental organization, is the most significant tendency in Argentine political life, — the tendency to develop a unified, centralized government. This, however, is not peculiar to Argentina, for, taking the South American states as a whole, it is unquestionable that centralization is the outstanding feature of government. The fact of special importance in the case of Argentina is that federalism, formally accepted as the basic principle of the constitutional system after years of struggle between the federalists and the unitarians, is giving way before the advance of a developing nationalism. Whether or not this will continue until the final overthrow of federation and the acceptance of a unitary government, no one can say. The tendency, however, is plain. Federation, without doubt, is weaker than it used to be; centralized government is stronger.

The question naturally arises as to the reasons for this development. Several points should be noted: the ignorance of the mass of the people; the lack of interest in public affairs; the general absence of traditions of local self-government; the survival of autocratic ideas and practices developed during the colonial régime; the effect of the prevailing legal system upon governmental organization and methods; the influence of continental Europe; and, particularly, the influence of France in her attempts to erect a free government upon the ruins of an absolutism largely identical with that which so long characterized the rule of Spain both at home and in the South American colonies. It is to be observed, however, that these suggestions are not pertinent in connection with Argentina alone; they apply with equal force to the other South American states. Some of them have already been discussed and need only be mentioned here.

Influence of France and the Roman Law. — Two points, though, deserve special emphasis: the effect of the Roman Law

[1] Ross, "South of Panama," pp. 383-385.

system upon government, and the influence of France. The former is discussed at length in a preceding chapter; all that is necessary here is to suggest the applicability of the ideas there developed to the political life of South America.[1] It was pointed out that political institutions in countries accepting the Roman jurisprudence are different from those of countries in which the English Common Law is basic. In the two systems the emphasis upon public rights and upon private rights differs. Under the former, the executive branch of the government, under the latter, the legislative branch, is the dominant element. In other words, administrative control, in general, characterizes Roman Law nations, while legislative control characterizes Common Law countries. It is to be expected, therefore, that presidential government in Argentina, and cabinet government in Chile, will develop along lines which are materially different from those followed respectively in the United States and England, just as cabinet government in France differs fundamentally from the English system upon which it was modeled. Centralization is natural in South America, and it seems safe to assume that it will permanently characterize the governments of her states. The problem in South America, as has been the problem in France, is to democratize centralized government; to develop democracy from the top downward, — the reverse of the process in England and the United States. In this development the example of France is markedly influential. People of education and culture throughout South America speak the French language and are familiar with French literature and French political experience. They find in the history and development of France inspiration for the settlement of their own respective national problems. Indeed, it seems to be a fact that France, more than any other nation, is marking the path which the South American states are to follow in their efforts to attain free institutions. The signs discernible by a careful study of the political life of South America point to the ultimate achievement of governments of the French type, — of centralized democracies.

[1] Chap. XLIX.

REFERENCES

CLEMENCEAU. *South America To-day.*
DOMVILLE-FIFE. *Great States of South America.*
ENOCK. *The Republics of South and Central America.*
Latin America, Clark University Addresses, 1913. Edited by George H. Blakeslee.
PENNINGTON. *The Argentine Republic.*
PORTER. *The Ten Republics.*
REINSCH. "Parliamentary Government in Chile," *The American Political Science Review,* Vol. III, p. 507.
ROSS. *South of Panama.*
SHEPHERD. *Latin America.*

CHAPTER LX

FEDERATION AND DEMOCRACY

A CONFEDERATION is an association of otherwise independent states for purposes of common defense and the regulation of common interests. Each of the States thus united retains its sovereignty, and the officers of the confederation are dependent upon the States for the execution of the policies agreed upon. This form of association prevailed among the states of ancient Greece and more recently among Swiss Cantons and German States. Such was the form of union among the American States until the adoption of the Constitution of the United States. A federation, or a state having a federated form of government, is one which has a central government exercising supreme authority over matters of common interest, but which reserves to the governments within the local areas the control of local affairs. A federation involves the partition of the powers of the state between central and local governments. The United States became a federation under the Constitution of 1789. Swiss Cantons were united under a federal government by the Constitution of 1848. The fact that the words confederation and federation are often used as synonyms tends to promote confusion between the two plans of union. Germans give accurate expression to the distinction in the terms *Staatenbund*, meaning a league of separate states, and *Bundesstaat*, meaning a true federal union of the states under one general government. Since democracy and the federated form of government have a common origin, there is evidence of a necessary connection. Democracy on a large scale is difficult of realization apart from federation, and that form once attained becomes itself a teacher of democracy.

When fugitives from the oppressions of the Old World formed colonies in North America the experiment began which finally resulted in a federal government. The settlements could not be governed from the mother country; they governed themselves in town, parish, and county, and managed affairs of general interest through the colonial legislatures. The colonists became everywhere devoted to the privilege of self-government. They were ready to fight rather than submit to English domination. Even the Cavaliers of Virginia who had sided with the Stuart monarchy in England would not peaceably submit to Stuart rule in Virginia. They would accept the ritual of the English Established Church, but they would not tolerate an English bishop. They were fully determined to govern themselves both in church and state; and when the time came for independence, the Virginian Cavaliers were not a whit behind the New England Puritans in devotion to their cause or in the efficiency with which they supported it. Liberty was the vital principle in the air of the New World, and liberty meant to all the colonists the permanence of their control over their own local institutions.

Coöperation between the colonies in matters of common interest grew up early. In 1643 four New England colonies formed a league, or confederation, which lasted for forty years. With the encouragement of the British government, attempts were made to draw all the colonies into a union for greater efficiency in warding off attacks of the French from Canada. All the elements were at hand for the creation of a common government of the federal type and all the conditions seemed to favor it. Had there been no separation from England, it is not likely that the colonists would have been induced to yield their control over local affairs and hence the principle of federation would have been injected into the British government. By maintaining the right to conduct their own local affairs in their own way, while conceding to the British government the exercise of only such power over them as met with their approval, the colonists were upholding the federal principle in government. Before a Declaration of Independence had been framed; before the meeting of the Philadelphia Convention of 1787 had been called, the federal form for state organization in America was a foregone conclusion. In no other way could the demands for self-government be realized. Had England yielded to the wishes of the colonists, federation would have taken place under British authority, and such a federation would naturally have included Canada as well as the thirteen colonies. Then the course of history would have been different. No great state would have stood forth as originally founded upon the principle of federation. There would have been no Declaration of Independence; no Washington's Farewell Address; no Monroe Doctrine serving notice upon Europe to refrain from interference with the republics of the New World; no Lincoln's Gettysburg speech. But democracy would nevertheless have found embodiment with equal certainty in states securing to their citizens control of local affairs.

The principle of federation fulfills certain permanent and imperative needs of universal free government. First there is the organized neighborhood which secures peace and harmony among families and individuals and gives expression to community life. Among the ancient Greeks the organized neighborhood comprised the entire state. In the United States and Canada it includes town, city, and county. Among adjacent communities conflicting interests arise and there is need of a more general organization to maintain just relations between counties and cities; and there are other industrial and social needs common to all local communities which the separate counties cannot supply. These are met by the State in the United States and by the Province in Canada. Conflicting interests also arise between adjacent States and Provinces, and there are general governmental needs not met by the state organizations. Hence the government of the United States and of the Dominion of Canada to supplement those of State and Province. In the case of Canada a government of still higher authority is represented by the British Crown. These are facts illustrating a common need. The greatest of the Anglo-Saxon contributions to the free government of the world is found in the diversity of forms presented for federated governments.

The United States, Canada, and Australia all present different types of federation.[1] The United States, a highly elaborated federated state, is the original model. The Canadian Constitution was framed at a time when the States of the American Union were undergoing reconstruction after a disastrous civil war. This is, no doubt, one cause for the highly centralized character of the Dominion government. No Canadian Province can ever

[1] For a description of the federated self-governing Dominions of England and of their relation to the Central Government see Chap. XLV.

claim a constitutional right to dissolve the Union. The Province is allowed only such powers as are assigned to it by the Constitution, all others belong to the central government. The central government exercises a veto power over provincial legislation, and the courts of the Dominion or the Privy Council in England may nullify legislative acts of the Provinces. In many ways the Provinces are restricted in their action, yet they have been given by the constitution enough independent power to insure a vigorous and active state life. They control local government and formulate their own constitutions. The same people control both the Provinces and the Dominion government, and, in general, they retain in the separate Provinces all the powers they want.

The Australian Constitution was formulated under entirely different conditions. Jealousy for State rights long prevented the formation of the Commonwealth. In the organization of the union the people of Australia reserved to their separate States all powers not specifically conferred upon the government of the Commonwealth. The States, in appearance at least, retain a more important and independent position than do the Canadian Provinces. Yet in Australia the central government is endowed with a much wider range of powers than is the general government of the United States. Of the three governments compared Canada is most highly centralized, the United States least centralized, while Australia holds an intermediate position.

An interesting fourth grade in the order of centralization is presented by the recently formed Union of South Africa. Dutch and English had long been at enmity and a war of conquest ended in 1902. There was a mixed population in each of the four colonies. Many considerations favored a strongly centralized government. The colonies, therefore, voluntarily surrendered practically all of their independent powers and consented to be governed locally by executive and legislative councils of their own choosing with few powers assigned to them by the Constitution and such additional powers as might be afterwards granted them by the government of the Union. In legal form the South African Union is not a federated state. It is rather a centralized state having highly developed local autonomous provinces. In practice this may not differ greatly from the Canadian type of federation.

These illustrations exhibit the great adaptability of federal forms to varying conditions. The South African provinces are almost entirely dependent on the general government for the powers they exercise. They are subject to the orders of the government as an American county is subject to the state government. The Union of South Africa, however, in its relation to the central English government is almost independent. Only in a very limited way does England maintain authority over any of the dominion governments. There is, however, enough of authority mutually recognized to suggest the federal type of government. That is, with England as a central government and South Africa, Australia, Canada, and New Zealand as subordinate states, a government of the federal type is suggested, but in this case nearly all the real powers of government are in the hands of the separate states.

The federal form of government has called into being a new order of sentimental union, a new variety of patriotism. The framers of the American Constitution of 1789 assumed that the States would continue to hold the chief positions of honor, the leading place in the affections of the people. National patriotism was yet to be created. National patriotism does not in itself detract from local and state pride and devotion. As one values his local and community life, so ought one to value the State which is guardian and promoter of that life. As one appreciates the blessings of an authoritative state or provincial body politic, so one ought to prize the more general body politic which insures harmony and security among the States. To the citizen trained to the full appreciation of the federal system there is one all-inclusive object of patriotic devotion. Canadians are intensely loyal to the British government on account of the rich and satisfying community, Provincial, and Dominion life which such a relation insures to them. There are numerous stimuli to the one sentiment of devotion. The citizen of the parish is made conscious of a vital share in the life of a great empire. In the United States true federation was not attained until the conflict between the devotion of Americans to their States and to the general government had ceased. In a genuine federation an appreciation of any one part includes an appreciation of all.

The new patriotism which the federal system promotes is found able to make an end of the inveterate hatred and rivalry arising from difference in race, language, and religion. English and French had been traditional enemies for centuries. Between the two peoples there was actual or threatened war when English statesmen induced the Canadians to begin the formation of a federal union and assume the powers of local self-government. Serious conflicts were thus brought to an end; French Canadians became loyal British subjects; English Canadians became the willing followers of French Canadian leaders. Sir Wilfred Laurier, a French Catholic, was for many years Prime Minister of the Dominion, and when a movement arose for a closer compact among the different parts of the British empire, the French Canadian statesman was accepted as the most influential personal exponent of the sentiment of imperial union. Another exemplification of the same principle is found in the relations of Dutch and English in South Africa. A vindictive war was followed immediately by friendly coöperation between Dutch and English to found a great free self-governing union. The Boers are becoming loyal to the British government because for the first time in their history they feel secure in the enjoyment of their local community life and at the same time are made conscious of a share in extending the principles of self-government to the ends of the earth.

The Anglo-Saxons by occupation and by political influence have preëmpted the greater part of the New World and of Australia for the federated form of free government and have founded in South Africa a free Republic destined probably to assume the same form.

Switzerland has become a federal state after many centuries of continuous confederation between Cantons. The commune is a primitive institution of the same order as the Saxon town, or township. Communes became united into Cantons and during the thirteenth century these began to unite for mutual protection. Until the adoption of the Constitution of 1848 Switzerland was a Confederation, but by the adoption of the Constitution it became a federal state. From force of habit it is still called a Confederation. Swiss history illustrates the American order for the formation of union. Devotion to local autonomy was determined and persistent. Even the Catholic Church in some Swiss communes took on a form of government similar to that of the Puritan churches in the New England towns; the Communes elected their own priests. Cantons were formed by the union of communes, as American townships united to form Counties. In Switzerland the Canton was the sovereign state. They confederated, but they did not surrender their sovereignty until a Swiss democracy had been developed which could be relied upon to control the central government. The federal governments thus far described present one general line of development. In each case the people, having control of local affairs and realizing the need of a government of wider range and superior authority, call into existence agencies to meet those needs.

In the German Empire a different order is observed; there the government emanates from the rulers instead of the people. It is a government devised by kings and princes. But the popular element does appear in the German Constitution of 1871. Bismarck, having failed to induce the German princes to accept the King of Prussia as their Emperor, appealed for support to the people of Germany. He gave them an assembly of their own choosing. In this way democracy became an essential part of the federation.

A genuine federation involves the union of equal states; equal in their relations to one another and subject to equal rights in their relations to the central government. The German federation does not conform to this ideal. The constitution, however, furnishes evidence of an attempt to do so. The monarchs who formed the union agreed to accept one of their own number as President of the Empire, but refused to subject themselves to the rule of an hereditary Emperor. They were willing to accept the King of Prussia as their President and were content to associate with the office of President the honorary title of Kaiser, or Emperor. The German experience illustrates the great difficulty of forming an authoritative government over a group of absolute rulers. If they permit another to exercise a part of the authority, they cease to be absolute. The Constitution gave to the separate principalities many powers and provided for the management of imperial affairs by delegates appointed by the princes and subject to their instruction. In appearance the Constitution did provide for a federation of kings and princes on nearly equal terms. Had the actual working Constitution conformed to the fictions of equality injected into the frame of government, the union would have been a rope of sand; it would have failed as had previous efforts to secure a united Germany. The success of the Union arises from the fact that a single State had already conquered and annexed the greater part of the German territory. It was a matter of detail whether the remaining States would join by agreement or by force. The form of federation is a mere incident in the creation of an Empire governed by Prussia. The actual government is in conflict with the federal principle of equality between the States. Absolute or Constitutional monarchies may form alliances or confederations, but the experience of the Germans seems to prove that they may not form an authoritative central government of the federal type. Either there will be no government or the weak States will be subordinated to the strong. Should the people of Prussia gain control of their government and establish a parliamentary monarchy, the way would be opened for a genuine federal government. The people of Prussia would unite with the people of other States to control the central government. Authority would pass to the Reichstag in which all the States are proportionately represented. The democracy would naturally seek to extend to the small and weak States equal rights and privileges. This has been the common experience. Rhode Island is as secure in every local privilege as is New York or Texas.

The phenomenal extension of the federal forms of organization during the past century is a prophecy of greater triumphs for the future. Statesmen and philosophers everywhere are learning to think in terms of federation. Some of the thinking finds definite expression in such institutions as the Hague Conferences, the Hague Tribunals, the Quinquennial meetings of delegates from the republics of the New World, and numerous other similar institutions. The actual institutions looking towards a better understanding or a more perfect union among the different states are outnumbered by the various plans of union proposed for discussion. It is impossible that any considerable proportion of the plans should ever be realized; yet the general and rapidly increasing interest in the subject gives reasonable grounds for the belief that the tried and approved plans of federation now in use will be still farther extended and that new and perchance better methods will be discovered.

The plan first evolved in the United States assumed the pre-existence of a people accustomed to take care of themselves in their own local institutions; a people who stubbornly refused to surrender local control to a central government. This condition is found among comparatively few peoples and to nearly all of these the plan of federation has already been extended. Switzerland alone, apart from the British colonies, fulfills the conditions. To farther extend the Anglo-Saxon plan calls for modifications. Americans are training Filipinos for self-government by creating habits of control over local institutions. Something in the same line is being done in India and in other British possessions. This is an important modification of the original plan. Even with this modification the field for its extension is limited. Rulers who are not themselves accustomed to administer a government in which local autonomy prevails will experience peculiar difficulty by beginning with the local institutions. The French experience is an illustration in point. The Revolutionary statesmen had the idea; they proposed to evolve a free state out of local communes and Cantons, but the plan would not work. More than a hundred years have intervened and the goal is apparently as remote as at the beginning. The ideal still survives, but the method of approach has been completely reversed. Instead of the commune the department or some provincial area yet to be formed holds the place of chief interest. The central government will unload some of its burdens upon the provinces and these in turn will cultivate the local democracy. The order of development is from the higher authority to the lower, rather than from the lower to the higher. It is not likely that a system developed in the reverse order will have the same characteristics as the American and Swiss federations. It may have no characteristics which answer to the accepted definition of a federal state; but by federation or by some other agency the local needs will be met.

Important as is the principle of federation in respect to the domestic relations of the people in the great states, it is even more important in its relations to the needs of a world democracy. It is difficult to imagine any agency for giving expression to the sense of justice common to all civilized peoples which does not involve a common agreement of equal states. The United

States of Europe, the United States of North and South America, or the United States of the World involve no new principles, but merely an extension of principles now in full operation. The consciousness of common European needs first found expression in international law, and the fulfillment of international law leads logically to some form of federation. The consciousness of the common needs of the republics of the New World gave rise, first, to the Monroe Doctrine, to be followed by forms of closer and more effective union.

A distinct world consciousness with a lively sense of common needs is of very recent origin, and its natural fulfillment is "The federation of Man."

REFERENCES

See Chap. **XLV**.
BRYCE. *The American Commonwealth*, 1911, Chaps. **XXVII–XXX**.
DICEY. *The Law of the Constitution*, Chap. **IV**.

BOOK LIST

BOOK LIST

THE UNITED STATES

General Government and Politics

ASHLEY, ROSCOE LEWIS. The American Federal State. Revised Edition, New York, 1911.
BACON, EDWIN M., and WYMAN, MORRILL. Direct Elections and Law-Making by Popular Vote. Boston, 1912.
BALDWIN, SIMEON E. The American Judiciary. (American State Series.) New York, 1905.
BEARD, CHARLES A. American Government and Politics. New and Revised Edition, New York, 1914.
—— —— An Economic Interpretation of the Constitution of the United States. New York, 1913.
—— —— Readings in American Government and Politics. New and Revised Edition, New York, 1914.
—— —— The Supreme Court and the Constitution. New York, 1912.
BISHOP, JOSEPH BUCKLIN. Our Political Drama: Conventions, Campaigns, Candidates. New York, 1904.
BROOKS, ROBERT C. Corruption in American Politics and Life. New York, 1910.
BRYCE, JAMES. The American Commonwealth. Two vols. New and Revised Edition, New York, 1910.
CLEVELAND, FREDERICK A. The Growth of Democracy in the United States. Chicago, 1898.
—— —— Organized Democracy. (American Citizen Series.) New York, 1913.
COMMONS, JOHN R. Proportional Representation. Second Edition, New York, 1907.
The Congressional Directory.
COOKE, FREDERICK H. The Commerce Clause of the Federal Constitution. New York, 1908.
COOLEY, THOMAS M. The General Principles of Constitutional Law in the United States. Third Edition, Revised by A. C. Angell, Boston, 1898.
—— —— A Treatise on Constitutional Limitations. Seventh Edition, Boston, 1903.
CORWIN, EDWARD S. The Doctrine of Judicial Review. Princeton, 1914.
CROLY, HERBERT. Progressive Democracy. New York, 1914.
—— —— The Promise of American Life. New York, 1909.

DALLINGER, FREDERICK W. Nominations for Elective Office in the United States. (Harvard Historical Studies.) Cambridge, 1914.
DAVIS, HORACE A. The Judicial Veto. Boston, 1914.
DOUGHERTY, J. HAMPDEN. The Electoral System of the United States. New York, 1906.
FAIRLIE, JOHN A. The National Administration of the United States of America. New York, 1905.
FARRAND, MAX. The Records of the Federal Convention of 1787. Three vols. New Haven, 1911.
The Federalist.
FINLEY, JOHN H., and SANDERSON, JOHN F. The American Executive and Executive Methods. (American State Series.) New York, 1908.
FISH, CARL RUSSELL. The Civil Service and the Patronage. (Harvard Historical Studies.) New York, 1905.
FISHER, SYDNEY GEORGE. Evolution of the Constitution of the United States. Philadelphia, 1909.
FOLLETT, M. P. The Speaker of the House of Representatives. New York, 1909.
FORD, HENRY JONES. The Cost of Our National Government. New York, 1910.
———— The Rise and Growth of American Politics. New York, 1900.
FREUND, ERNST. The Police Power. Chicago, 1904.
FULLER, HUBERT BRUCE. The Speakers of the House. Boston, 1909.
GOODNOW, FRANK J. Politics and Administration. New York, 1900.
———— The Principles of the Administrative Law of the United States. New York, 1905.
———— Social Reform and the Constitution. (American Social Progress Series.) New York, 1911.
GRIFFITH, ELMER C. The Rise and Development of the Gerrymander. Chicago, 1907.
HAINES, CHARLES GROVE. The American Doctrine of Judicial Supremacy. New York, 1914.
HARRISON, BENJAMIN. This Country of Ours. New York, 1897.
HART, ALBERT BUSHNELL. Actual Government as Applied under American Conditions. (American Citizen Series.) Third Edition, New York, 1908.
———— Practical Essays on American Government. New York, 1904.
HAYNES, GEORGE H. The Election of Senators. New York, 1906.
HINSDALE, MARY L. A History of the President's Cabinet. (Historical Studies, Vol. 1.) Ann Arbor, Mich., 1911.
The House Manual.
JOHNSON, ALLEN. Readings in American Constitutional History. Boston, 1912.
JONES, CHESTER LLOYD. Readings on Parties and Elections in the United States. New York, 1912.
JUDSON, FREDERICK N. The Judiciary and the People. New Haven, 1913.
———— The Law of Interstate Commerce and its Federal Regulation. Second Edition, Chicago, 1912.

―― ―― Treatise on the Power of Taxation, State and Federal, in the United States. St. Louis, 1903.
KALES, ALBERT M. Unpopular Government in the United States. Chicago, 1914.
LEARNED, HENRY BARRETT. The President's Cabinet. New Haven, 1912.
LODGE, HENRY CABOT. The Democracy of the Constitution. New York, 1915.
LOWELL, A. LAWRENCE. Public Opinion and Popular Government. (American Citizen Series.) New York, 1913.
MCCALL, SAMUEL W. The Business of Congress. New York, 1911.
MCCLAIN, EMLIN. Constitutional Law in the United States. (American Citizen Series.) Second Edition, New York, 1910.
MCCONACHIE, LAUROS G. Congressional Committees. (Library of Economics and Politics.) New York, 1898.
MCGEHEE, LUCIUS P. Due Process of Law under the Federal Constitution. New York, 1906.
MCLAUGHLIN, ANDREW C. The Courts, the Constitution, and Parties. Chicago, 1912.
MCLAUGHLIN, ANDREW C., and HART, ALBERT BUSHNELL. Cyclopedia of American Government. Three vols. New York, 1914.
MACY, JESSE. Party Organization and Machinery. (American State Series.) Revised Edition, New York, 1912.
―― ―― Political Parties in the United States, 1846–1861. (Citizen's Library.) New York, 1900.
MASON, EDWARD CAMPBELL. The Veto Power. (Harvard Historical Monographs, No. 1.) Boston, 1890.
MERRIAM, C. EDWARD. A History of American Political Theories. New York, 1913.
MEYER, ERNST CHRISTOPHER. Nominating Systems: Direct Primaries versus Conventions in the United States. Madison, Wis., 1902.
OSTROGORSKI, M. Democracy and the Organization of Political Parties. Two vols. Vol. I devoted to parties in England, and Vol. II to parties in the United States. New York, 1902.
―― ―― Democracy and the Party System in the United States. New York, 1910.
PIERCE, FRANKLIN. Federal Usurpation. New York, 1908.
POMEROY, JOHN NORTON. An Introduction to the Constitutional Law of the United States. Tenth Edition, Boston, 1888.
RAY, P. ORMAN. An Introduction to Political Parties and Practical Politics. New York, 1913.
REINSCH, PAUL S. Readings on American Federal Government. Boston, 1909.
The Senate Manual.
SLOANE, WILLIAM MILLIGAN. Party Government in the United States of America. New York, 1914.
SMITH, J. ALLEN. The Spirit of American Government. (Citizen's Library.) New York, 1907.
STANWOOD, EDWARD. A History of the Presidency from 1788 to 1897. Boston, 1898.

—— —— A History of the Presidency from 1897 to 1909. Boston, 1912.
STIMSON, FREDERIC JESUP. The American Constitution. New York, 1908.
—— —— The Law of the Federal and State Constitutions of the United States. Boston, 1908.
STORY, JOSEPH. Commentaries on the Constitution of the United States. Two vols. Fifth Edition, Edited by M. M. Bigelow, Boston, 1891.
THORPE, FRANCIS NEWTON. Federal and State Constitutions. Seven vols. Washington, 1909.
TIEDEMAN, CHRISTOPHER GUSTAVUS. The Unwritten Constitution of the United States. New York, 1890.
TOCQUEVILLE, ALEXIS DE. Democracy in America. Two vols. Paris, 1835–1840. Translation by Henry Reeve. New York, 1898.
VAN DYNE, FREDERICK. Citizenship of the United States. Rochester, 1903.
—— —— A Treatise on the Law of Naturalization of the United States. Rochester, 1907.
WEYL, WALTER E. The New Democracy. New York, 1914.
WILCOX, DELOS F. Government by all the People: The Initiative, The Referendum and The Recall as Instruments of Democracy. New York, 1912.
WILLOUGHBY, WESTEL WOODBURY. The American Constitutional System. (American State Series.) New York, 1904.
—— —— The Constitutional Law of the United States. Two vols. New York, 1910.
WILSON, WOODROW. Congressional Government : A Study in American Politics. Boston, 1904.
—— —— Constitutional Government in the United States. New York, 1908.
WOODBURN, JAMES ALBERT. The American Republic and its Government. New York, 1908.
—— —— Political Parties and Party Problems in the United States. Second Edition, New York, 1914.
YOUNG, JAMES T. The New American Government and its Work. New York, 1915.

STATE AND LOCAL

Annals of the American Academy of Political and Social Science: July, 1910, Administration of Justice in the United States; September, 1912, The Initiative, Referendum and Recall; May, 1913, County Government; March, 1914, Reform in the Administration of Justice.
BEARD, CHARLES A., and SCHULTZ, BIRL E. Documents on the State-wide Initiative, Referendum and Recall. New York, 1912.
BRADFORD, ERNEST S. Commission Government in American Cities. (Citizen's Library.) New York, 1911.
DEALEY, JAMES QUAYLE. Growth of American State Constitutions. Boston, 1915.
—— —— Our State Constitutions. Philadelphia, Annals Supplement, March, 1907.
DEMING, HORACE E. The Government of American Cities. New York, 1909.

DODD, WALTER FAIRLEIGH. The Revision and Amendment of State Constitutions. (Johns Hopkins University Studies.) Baltimore, 1910.

FAIRLIE, JOHN A. Local Government in Counties, Towns and Villages. (American State Series.) New York, 1906.

GOODNOW, FRANK J. City Government in the United States. (American State Series.) New York, 1904.

HOWE, FREDERIC C. Wisconsin, An Experiment in Democracy. New York, 1912.

JONES, CHESTER LLOYD. Statute Law Making in the United States. Boston, 1912.

Kansas Legislative Reference Department. Bulletin No. 1, Legislative Systems. Topeka, 1914.

MCCARTHY, CHARLES. The Wisconsin Idea. New York, 1912.

Manual or *Legislative Handbook* of Each State.

MERRIAM, C. EDWARD. Primary Elections. Chicago, 1908.

MUNRO, WILLIAM BENNETT. The Government of American Cities. New York, 1912.

—— —— The Initiative, Referendum and Recall. (National Municipal League Series.) New York, 1912.

OBERHOLTZER, ELLIS PAXSON. The Referendum in America. New Edition, New York, 1911.

REINSCH, PAUL S. American Legislatures and Legislative Methods. New York, 1907.

—— —— Readings on American State Government. Boston, 1911.

SHELDON, A. E., and KEEGAN, M. Legislative Procedure in the Forty-Eight States. (Nebraska Legislative Reference Bureau, Bulletin No. 3.) Lincoln, 1914.

WILCOX, DELOS F. Great Cities in America. (Citizen's Library.) New York, 1910.

ENGLAND

GOVERNMENT AND POLITICS

ACLAND, A. H. D., and RANSOME, C. Handbook of the Political History of England to 1913. New Edition, New York, 1913.

ADAMS, G. B., and STEPHENS, H. M. Select Documents of English Constitutional History. New York, London, 1901.

ANSON, SIR WILLIAM R. The Law and Custom of the Constitution. Fourth Edition, Revised, Oxford, 1911.

ATLAY, JAMES BERESFORD. Victorian Chancellors. Two vols. Boston, 1906-1908.

BAGEHOT, WALTER. The English Constitution. Revised Edition, New York, 1904.

BLAUVELT, MARY TAYLOR. The Development of Cabinet Government in England. New York, 1902.

BOUTMY, ÉMILE. The English People: A Study of Their Political Psychology. Translated from the French by E. English. London, 1904.

—— —— Studies in Constitutional Law. Translated from the Second French Edition by E. M. Dicey. London, 1891.
CARTER, A. T. History of English Legal Institutions. Fourth Edition, London, 1910.
CHURCHILL, WINSTON SPENCER. Life of Lord Randolph Churchill. Two vols. New York, 1906.
Constitutional Year Books. London.
COURTNEY, LEONARD HENRY. The Working Constitution of the United Kingdom. New York, 1910.
DICEY, ALBERT VENN. Introduction to the Study of the Law of the Constitution. Eighth Edition, New York, 1915.
—— —— The Privy Council. Arnold Prize Essay, 1860. London, 1887.
DICKINSON, G. LOWES. Development of Parliament During the Nineteenth Century. London, 1895.
FREEMAN, EDWARD A. The Growth of the English Constitution. Fourth Edition, London, 1884.
—— —— History of the Norman Conquest of England. Six vols. New York, 1873.
GARDINER, SAMUEL R. History of England 1603-1642. Ten vols. New York, 1883-84.
—— —— History of the Commonwealth and Protectorate. Four vols. London, 1903.
GNEIST, RUDOLPH. The English Parliament in its Transformations through a Thousand Years. Translated by R. J. Shee. Boston, 1886.
—— —— History of the English Constitution. Translated by P. A. Ashworth. Two vols. New Edition, New York, 1910.
GREEN, JOHN RICHARD. History of the English People. Four vols. New Edition, New York, 1904.
—— —— Short History of the English People. New York, 1902.
HARRIS, W. History of the Radical Party in Parliament. 1885.
HEARN, WILLIAM EDWARD. The Government of England. Second Edition, London, New York, 1886.
HUNT, WILLIAM, and POOLE, L. R., Editors. Political History of England. 12 vols. London. Each volume a different date.
ILBERT, SIR COURTENAY. Legislative Methods and Forms. Oxford, 1901.
—— —— The Mechanics of Law Making. New York, 1914.
—— —— Parliament; Its History, Constitution and Practice. (Home University Library.) New York, 1911.
JENKS, EDWARD. Parliamentary England. The Evolution of the Cabinet System. (Story of the Nations.) New York, 1903.
KEBBEL, THOMAS EDWARD. History of Toryism, 1886.
KEMBLE, JOHN MITCHELL. Saxons in England. Two vols. New York.
KING, JOSEPH, and RAFFETY, F. W. Our Electoral System: The Demand for Reform. London, 1912.
LEE, SIR SIDNEY. Queen Victoria, A Biography. Second Edition, London, 1903.
Liberal Year Books. London.
LOW, SIDNEY. The Governance of England. New Edition, New York, 1914.

LOWELL, A. LAWRENCE. The Government of England. Two vols. New Edition, New York, 1912.

MACDONAGH, MICHAEL. The Book of Parliament. New York, 1897.

McILWAIN, CHARLES HOWARD. The High Court of Parliament and its Supremacy. New Haven, 1910.

MACY, JESSE. The English Constitution. New Edition, New York, 1904.

MARRIOTT, J. A. R. English Political Institutions. Second Edition, Oxford, 1913.

MAY, THOMAS ERSKINE. Constitutional History of England. Two vols. London, 1861–1863. Three vols., Vol. III by Francis Holland. New York, 1912.

—— —— Treatise on the Law, Privileges, Proceedings, and Usage of Parliament. Three vols. New Edition, London, 1912.

MEDLEY, DUDLEY JULIUS. English Constitutional History. Oxford, 1894.

MORAN, THOMAS FRANCIS. Theory and Practice of the English Government. New Edition, New York, 1908.

MORLEY, JOHN. Life of William Ewart Gladstone. Two vols. New Edition, New York, 1911.

OSTROGORSKI, M. Democracy and the Organization of Political Parties. Two vols., Vol. I devoted to parties in England, and Vol. II to parties in the United States. New York, 1902.

PIKE, LUKE OWEN. Constitutional History of the House of Lords. New York, 1894.

POLLOCK, SIR FREDERICK, and MAITLAND, FREDERIC WILLIAM. History of English Law before the Time of Edward I. Two vols. Second Edition, Boston, 1899.

POOLE, REGINALD L. The Exchequer in the Twelfth Century. Oxford, 1912.

PORRITT, EDWARD, and PORRITT, MRS. ANNIE G. The Unreformed House of Commons. Two vols. New York, 1903.

POWELL, ELLIS THOMAS. The Essentials of Self-Government. (England and Wales.) New York, London, 1909.

REDLICH, JOSEF. The Procedure of the House of Commons. Translated by A. E. Steinthal. Three vols. New York, 1910.

ROSEBERY, ARCHIBALD. Life of Lord Randolph Churchill. New York, 1906.

SMITH, G. BARNETT. History of the English Parliament. 1892.

STUBBS, WILLIAM. The Constitutional History of England. Three vols. Second Edition, Oxford, 1875.

TASWELL-LONGMEAD, THOMAS PITT. English Constitutional History. Seventh Edition, Revised, New York, 1912.

TEMPLE, RT. HON. SIR RICHARD. The House of Commons. London, 1899.

—— —— Life in Parliament. London, 1893.

TODD, ALPHEUS. On Parliamentary Government in England. Two vols. Second Edition, London, 1889.

—— —— Practice and Privileges of the Two Houses of Parliament.

TREVELYAN, G. M. England in the Age of Wycliffe. New Edition, New York, London, 1909.

—— —— England under the Stuarts. New York, 1905.
WAKEMAN, HENRY O. History of the Church of England. 1908.
WALPOLE, SIR SPENCER. The Electorate and the Legislature. (English Citizen Series.) London, 1892.
—— —— History of England from the Conclusion of the Great War in 1815. Six vols. London, 1911.
WATSON, R. SPENCE. The National Liberal Federation from its Commencement to the General Election of 1906. London, 1907.
WHITE, WILLIAM. The Inner Life of the House of Commons. Edited by Justin McCarthy. Two vols. London, 1904.

COLONIAL GOVERNMENT AND POLITICS

An Analysis of the System of Government Throughout the British Empire. London, 1912.
BOURINOT, SIR JOHN GEORGE. Manual of the Constitutional History of Canada. Montreal, 1888.
BRADLEY, A. G. Canada. (Home University Library.) New York, 1912.
BRADSHAW, F. Self-Government in Canada and How It Was Achieved. London, 1903.
CLEMENT, W. H. P. The Law of the Canadian Constitution. Second Edition, Toronto, 1904.
DENISON, GEORGE T. The Struggle for Imperial Unity. New York, 1909.
DILKE, SIR CHARLES WENTWORTH. Problems of Greater Britain. Fourth Edition, London, 1890.
DOUGLAS, SIR ARTHUR. Dominion of New Zealand. Boston, 1909.
EGERTON, HUGH EDWARD. Federations and Unions within the British Empire. Oxford, 1911.
EGERTON, HUGH EDWARD, and GRANT, W. L. Canadian Constitutional Development. London, 1908.
JEBB, RICHARD. Studies in Colonial Nationalism. New York, London, 1905.
KEITH, ARTHUR BERRIEDALE. Responsible Government in the Dominions. Three vols. Oxford, 1912.
LEFROY, A. H. F. Canada's Federal System. Toronto, 1913.
LE ROSSIGNOL, JAMES EDWARD, and STEWART, WILLIAM DOWNIE. State Socialism in New Zealand. (Library of Economics and Politics.) New York, 1910.
LLOYD, HENRY DEMAREST. Newest England. Notes of a Democratic Traveller in New Zealand, with some Australian Comparisons. Revised Edition, New York, 1904.
LUCAS, SIR CHARLES PRESTWOOD. Historical Geography of the British Colonies. Six vols. New Edition, Oxford, 1914.
—— —— History of Canada. Oxford, 1909.
LUSK, HUGH HART. Social Welfare in New Zealand. New York, 1913.
MOORE, WILLIAM HARRISON. The New Australian Commonwealth. Philadelphia, 1903.
MUNROE, J. E. C. The Constitution of Canada. New York, 1901.
PARSONS, FRANK. The Story of New Zealand. Philadelphia, 1904.

Payne, E. J. Colonies and Colonial Federation. (English Citizen Series.) London, 1904.

Scholefield, Guy H. New Zealand in Evolution; Industrial, Economic, and Political. New York, London, 1909.

Siegfried, André. Democracy in New Zealand. Translated by E. V. Burns. New York, London, 1914.

Todd, Alpheus. Parliamentary Government in the British Colonies. New York, 1909.

Turner, Henry Gyles. The First Decade of the Australian Commonwealth. New York, Melbourne, 1911.

Wise, B. R. The Commonwealth of Australia. Boston, 1910.

FRANCE

Block, M. L'Administration de la Ville de Paris et du Department de la Seine. Paris, 1898.

Bodley, John E. C. France. New Edition, New York, 1900.

Brissaud, Jean. History of French Public Law. Translated by J. W. Garner. (Continental Legal History Series.) Boston, 1915.

Browne, Arthur S. French Law and Customs for the Anglo-Saxon. Third Edition, London, 1914.

Duguit, Léon. Les Transformations du Droit Public. Paris, 1913.

Garner, James Wilford. The French Cabinet. American Political Science Review. Vol. 8, p. 353. Aug., 1914.

Guérard, Albert Léon. French Civilization in the Nineteenth Century. London, 1914.

Guyot, Yves. The Relations between the French Senate and Chamber of Deputies. Contemporary Review, Vol. 97, p. 142. Feb., 1910.

Hanotaux, Gabriel. Contemporary France. Translated by John Charles Tarver. Four vols. New York, 1903–1909.

Jacques, Léon. Les Partis Politiques sous la IIIe République. Paris, 1913.

Morgaud, Léon. La Loi Municipale. Two vols. Seventh Edition, Paris, 1907.

Pierre, M. Eugène. Organization des Pouvoirs Publics. (Constitutional and organic laws of the French Republic.) Paris, 1902.

Poincaré, Raymond. How France is Governed. Translated by Bernard Miall. New York, 1914.

Pondra, and Pierre. Traité Pratique de Droit Parliamentaire. Eight vols. Versailles, 1878–1880.

GERMANY

Binding, Karl. Die Rechtliche Stellung des Kaisers im Heutigen Deutschen Reiche. 1898.

Bismarck, Otto von. The Man and the Statesman. Translated under the supervision of A. J. Butler. Two vols. New York, 1899.

Bryce, James. The Holy Roman Empire. New Edition, New York, 1904.

VON BÜLOW, BERNHARD. Imperial Germany. Translated by Marie A. Lewenz. New York, 1914.
COMBES DE LESTRADE, GAETAN. Les Monarchies de l'Empire Allemand. Paris, 1904.
DAWSON, WILLIAM HARBUTT. Municipal Life and Government in Germany. New York, 1914.
HEADLAM, JAMES W. Bismarck and the Foundation of the German Empire. New York, 1899.
HOWARD, BURT ESTES. The German Empire. New York, 1906.
JAMES, HERMAN GERLACH. Principles of Prussian Administration. New York, 1913.
LABAND, PAUL. Das Staatsrecht des Deutschen Reiches. Fifth Edition, Tübingen, 1913. French Edition, four vols., Paris, 1900–1904.
MAYER, OTTO. Deutsches Verwaltungsrecht. Two vols. 1914.
MEYER, GEORGE. Das Parlamentarische Wahlrecht. Edited by von Jellinek. Berlin, 1901.
―――― Lehrbuch des Deutschen Verwaltungsrechtes. Fourth Edition, Leipzig, 1914.
SCHIERBRAND, WOLF VON. Germany, The Welding of a World Power. New York, 1904.
SEYDEL, MAX VON. Commentar zum Verfassungsurkunde für das Deutsche Reich. Second Edition, Freiburg, 1897.
STILLICH, OSCAR. Die Politische Parteien in Deutschland. Two vols. Leipzig, 1908–1911.
TOWER, CHARLES. Germany of To-day. (Home University Library.) New York, 1913.
ZORN, PHILLIPP. Das Staatsrecht des Deutschen Reiches. Two vols. Second Edition, Berlin, 1895–1897.

SWITZERLAND

ADAMS, F. O., and CUNNINGHAM, C. D. The Swiss Confederation. London, 1894.
DÄNDLIKER, KARL. A Short History of Switzerland. Translated by E. Salisbury. New York, London, 1899.
DEPLOIGE, SIMON. The Referendum in Switzerland. New York.
LLOYD, HENRY DEMAREST. A Sovereign People: A Study of Swiss Democracy. New York, 1907.
MCCRACKEN, W. D. The Rise of the Swiss Republic. Second Edition, New York, 1901.
―――― Romance; Switzerland. Geneva, Basle, 1895.
―――― Teutonic Switzerland. Geneva, Basle, 1895.
MOSES, BERNARD. The Federal Government of Switzerland. Oakland, 1889.
RICHMAN, IRVING B. Appenzell; Pure Democracy and Pastoral Life in Inner-Rhoden. London, 1895.
VINCENT, JOHN MARTIN. Government in Switzerland. New York, 1900.
WINCHESTER, BOYD. The Swiss Republic. Philadelphia, 1891.

SOUTH AMERICA

AKERS, CHARLES EDMOND. History of South America, 1854–1904. New Edition, New York, 1912.
BINGHAM, HIRAM. Across South America. Boston, 1911.
BRYCE, JAMES. South America; Observations and Impressions. New Edition, New York, 1914.
BUCKMAN, WILLIAMSON. Under the Southern Cross in South America. New York, 1914.
Bulletin of the Pan American Union. Washington, D.C.
CARPENTER, FRANK G. South America. Akron, Ohio, 1900.
CLEMENCEAU, GEORGES. South America To-day. New York, 1911.
CURRIER, CHARLES W. Lands of the Southern Cross. Washington, D.C., 1911.
DALTON, LEONARD V. Venezuela. (South American Series.) London, 1912.
DAWSON, THOMAS C. South American Republics. Two vols. (Story of the Nations.) New York, 1903.
DENIS, PIERRE. Brazil. Translated by Bernard Miall. (South American Series.) London, 1911.
DOMVILLE-FIFE, CHARLES W. Great States of South America. New York, 1910.
—— —— The United States of Brazil. New York, 1911.
ELLIOT, G. F. SCOTT. Chile. London, 1911.
ENOCK, C. REGINALD. The Republics of Central and South America. (South American Series.) New York, London, 1913.
FRASER, JOHN FOSTER. The Amazing Argentine. New York, 1914.
GARCIA-CALDERÓN, F. Latin America. Translated by Bernard Miall. (South American Series.) New York, London, 1913.
GUINNESS, GERALDINE. Peru: Its Story, People and Religion. New York, London, 1909.
HALE, ALBERT. The South Americans. Indianapolis, 1907.
Handbooks of the various countries issued by the Pan-American Union. Washington, D.C.
HIRST, WILLIAM A. Argentina. (South American Series.) London, 1910.
KOEBEL, W. H. Modern Argentina. Boston, 1912.
—— —— South America. (Making of the Nations Series.) New York, London, 1913.
Latin America. George H. Blakeslee, Editor. (Clark University Addresses, 1913.) New York, 1914.
MAITLAND, FRANCIS J. G. Chile: Its Land and People. London, 1914.
MANSFIELD, ROBERT E. Progressive Chile. New York, 1913.
MARTIN, PERCY F. Peru of the Twentieth Century. London, 1911.
MARTÍNEZ, ALBERTO B. The Argentine Republic. Buenos Aires, 1910.
MARTÍNEZ, ALBERTO B., and LEWANDOWSKI, MAURICE. The Argentine in the Twentieth Century. Translated from the French of the Third Revised Edition by Bernard Miall. New York, 1915.
PAXSON, FREDERICK L. The Independence of the South American Republics. Philadelphia, 1903.

PENNINGTON, A. STUART. The Argentine Republic. New York, 1910.
PORTER, ROBERT P. The Ten Republics. Chicago, 1913.
REYES, RAFAEL. The Two Americas. Translated From the Spanish by Leopold Grahame. New York, 1914.
ROSCHER, WILHELM. The Spanish Colonial System. Edited by E. G. Bourne, New York, 1904.
ROSS, EDWARD ALSWORTH. South of Panama. New York, 1915.
SHEPHERD, WILLIAM R. Latin America. (Home University Library.) New York, 1914.
South American Year Book.
SPEER, ROBERT E. South American Problems. New York, 1912.
WINTER, NEVIN O. Argentina and Her People of To-day. Boston, 1911.
———— Brazil and Her People of To-day. Boston, 1910.

COMPARATIVE WORKS

ALSTON, LEONARD. Modern Constitutions in Outline. London, 1905.
AMOS, SHELDON. Science of Politics. New York.
ASHLEY, PERCY. Local and Central Government. A Comparative Study of England, France, Prussia and the United States. New York, 1906.
BLUNTSCHLI, J. K. The Theory of the State. Translated from the German. Third Edition, Oxford, 1901.
BORGEAUD, CHARLES. Adoption and Amendment of Constitutions in Europe and America. Translated by Charles D. Hazen. New York, 1909.
BRYCE, JAMES. Studies in History and Jurisprudence. Two vols. New York, 1901.
BURGESS, JOHN W. Political Science and Comparative Constitutional Law. Two vols. Boston, 1891.
Cambridge Modern History. Edited by A. W. Ward, G. W. Prothero and S. Leathes. Fourteen vols. New York, 1902–1912.
CRANE, WILLIAM W., and MOSES, BERNARD. Politics: An Introduction to the Study of Comparative Constitutional Law. New York, 1898.
DICKINSON, REGINALD. Summary of the Constitutions and Procedure of Foreign Parliaments. Second Edition, 1890.
DODD, WALTER FAIRLEIGH. Modern Constitutions. Two vols. Chicago, 1909.
DUPRIEZ, LÉON. Les Ministres dans les Principaux Pays d'Europe et d'Amerique. Two vols. Second Edition, 1892–1893.
FISHER, H. A. L. The Republican Tradition in Europe. New York, London, 1911.
FLAUDIN, ÉTIEN. Institutions Politique de l'Europe Contemporaire. Four vols. Paris, 1906–1909.
GARNER, JAMES WILFORD. Introduction to Political Science. New York, 1910.
GETTELL, RAYMOND GARFIELD. Introduction to Political Science. Boston, 1910.
GOODNOW, FRANK J. Comparative Administrative Law; An Analysis

of the Administrative System, National and Local, of the United States, England, France and Germany. New York, 1893.

HAMMOND, B. E. Outlines of Comparative Politics. 1903.

HOLT, LUCIUS HUDSON. An Introduction to the Study of Government. New York, 1915.

HOWE, FREDERIC C. European Cities at Work. New York, 1913.

LEACOCK, STEPHEN. Elements of Political Science. Boston, 1906.

LE BON, GUSTAVE. The Psychology of Peoples. New York, 1912.

LEFÈVRE-PONTALIS, ANTONIN. Les Élections en Europe à la Fin du XIXe Siècle. 1902.

LOWELL, A. LAWRENCE. Governments and Parties in Continental Europe. Two vols. Boston, 1896.

MARRIOTT, J. A. R. Second Chambers. New York, 1910.

MUNRO, WILLIAM BENNETT. The Government of European Cities. New York, 1909.

OGG, FREDERIC AUSTIN. The Governments of Europe. New York, 1913.

—— —— Social Progress in Contemporary Europe. New York, 1912.

OSBORN, J. L. Second Chambers at Home and Abroad. 1910.

POLEY, ARTHUR PIERRE. Federal Systems of the United States and the British Empire. Boston, 1913.

Report of Royal Commissioners to Inquire into Electoral Systems. Blue Book, London, 1910.

SEARS, EDMUND HAMILTON. An Outline of Political Growth in the Nineteenth Century. New York, London, 1900.

SEIGNOBOS, CHARLES. A Political History of Contemporary Europe since 1814. Two vols. London, 1901.

SHAW, ALBERT. Municipal Government in Continental Europe. New York, 1901.

SIDGWICK, HENRY. Development of European Polity. New York, 1903.

Statesman's Year Book. London.

WENZEL, JOHN. Comparative View of the Executive and Legislative Departments of the Governments of the United States, France, England and Germany. Boston, 1891.

WILSON, WOODROW. The State. Revised Edition, Boston, 1911.

MISCELLANEOUS

ABBOTT, LYMAN. The Rights of Man. A Study in Twentieth Century Problems. Boston, 1902.

—— —— The Spirit of Democracy. Boston, 1910.

Aristotle's Politics. Translated by Benjamin Jowett. Two vols. Oxford, 1885.

AUSTIN, JOHN. Lectures on Jurisprudence, The Philosophy of Positive Law. Abridged by Robert Campbell. New York, 1875.

BONDY, WILLIAM. Separation of Governmental Powers. (Columbia University Studies in History, Economics, and Public Law, Vol. 5.) New York, 1895.

BRADFORD, GAMALIEL. The Lesson of Popular Government. New York, London, 1899.
BUTLER, NICHOLAS MURRAY. True and False Democracy. New York, London, 1907.
DOLE, CHARLES FLETCHER. The Spirit of Democracy. New York, 1906.
DUNNING, WILLIAM ARCHIBALD. A History of Political Theories, Ancient and Mediæval. New York, London, 1902.
—— —— A History of Political Theories from Luther to Montesquieu. New York, London, 1905.
ELY, RICHARD T. Property and Contract in their Relations to the Distribution of Wealth. New York, 1914.
GIDDINGS, FRANKLIN HENRY. Democracy and Empire; With Studies of Their Psychological, Economic, and Moral Foundations. New York, 1900.
GODKIN, EDWIN LAWRENCE. Unforeseen Tendencies of Democracy. Boston, London, 1898.
GUYOT, YVES. La Démocratie Individualiste. Paris, 1907.
HADLEY, ARTHUR TWINING. The Relations between Freedom and Responsibility in the Evolution of Democratic Government. New York, 1903.
HALL, WILLIAM EDWARD. A Treatise on International Law. Edition Six, edited by J. B. Atlay. Oxford, 1910.
HOBHOUSE, LEONARD T. Democracy and Reaction. New York, 1905.
—— —— Liberalism. (Home University Library.) New York, 1911.
—— —— Social Evolution and Political Theory. (Columbia University Lectures, 1910-1911.) New York, 1911.
HYSLOP, JAMES H. Democracy; A Study of Government. New York, 1899.
JELLINEK, GEORG. The Declaration of the Rights of Man and of Citizens; A Contribution to Modern Constitutional History. Translated by Max Farrand. New York, 1901.
—— —— Recht des Modernen Staates.
JENKS, JEREMIAH W. Governmental Action for Social Welfare. (American Social Progress Series.) New York, 1910.
KELLY, EDMOND. Government; or, Human Evolution. Two vols. New York, 1900.
LECKY, W. E. H. Democracy and Liberty. Two vols. New Edition, New York, 1899.
LEROY, MAXIME. La Loi; Essai sur la Théorie de l'Autorité dans la Démocratie. Paris, 1908.
MCKECHNIE, WILLIAM SHARP. The State and the Individual. Glasgow, 1896.
MAINE, SIR HENRY SUMNER. Popular Government; Four Essays. New York, 1886.
MILL, JOHN STUART. Considerations on Representative Government. New York, 1875.
—— —— On Liberty. New York, 1882.
OPPENHEIM, L. International Law, A Treatise. Two vols. New York, 1905.

ORTH, SAMUEL P. Socialism and Democracy in Europe. New York, 1913.
RITCHIE, DAVID G. Principles of State Interference. Four Essays on the Political Philosophy of Spencer, Mill, and Green. London, 1891.
—— —— Studies in Political and Social Ethics. New York, 1902.
RUBINOW, ISAAC MAX. Social Insurance. New York, 1913.
SOHM, RUDOLPH. Institutes of Roman Law. Translated by James Cranford Ledlie. Third Edition, Oxford, 1901.
SPENCER, HERBERT. Social Statics and Man versus the State. New York, 1901.
STICKNEY, ALBERT. Organized Democracy. Boston, 1906.
STIMSON, FREDERIC JESUP. Popular Law-Making. A Study of the Origin, History and Present Tendencies of Law-Making by Statute. New York, 1911.

CASES IN AMERICAN CONSTITU-
TIONAL LAW

CASES IN AMERICAN CONSTITUTIONAL LAW

Supremacy of Federal Authority

Ableman v. *Booth*	21 Howard 506	1859
Calder v. *Bull*	3 Dallas 386	1798
Chisholm v. *Georgia*	2 Dallas 419	1793
Cohens v. *Virginia*	6 Wheaton 264	1821
Collector v. *Day*	11 Wallace 113	1871
Debs, in re	158 U. S. 564	1895
Ex parte *Siebold*	100 U. S. 371	1880
Knox v. *Lee*	12 Wallace 457	1871
Lane County v. *Oregon*	7 Wallace 71	1869
McCulloch v. *Maryland*	4 Wheaton 316	1819
Martin v. *Hunter's Lessee*	1 Wheaton 304	1816
Neagle, in re	135 U. S. 1	1890
Osborn v. *Bank of the United States*	9 Wheaton 738	1824
South Carolina v. *United States*	199 U. S. 437	1905
Tennessee v. *Davis*	100 U. S. 257	1880
Texas v. *White*	7 Wallace 700	1869
United States v. *Peters*	5 Cranch 115	1809
United States v. *Tarble* (Tarble's Case)	13 Wallace 397	1872
Van Brocklin v. *Tennessee*	117 U. S. 151	1886
Veazie Bank v. *Fenno*	8 Wallace 533	1869

Division of Powers between States and Nation

Barron v. *Baltimore*	7 Peters 243	1833
Chae Chan Ping v. *United States* (Chinese Exclusion Case)	130 U. S. 581	1889
Cohens v. *Virginia*	6 Wheaton 264	1821
De Lima v. *Bidwell*	182 U. S. 1	1901
Fairbank v. *United States*	181 U. S. 283	1901
Fong Yue Ting v. *United States*	149 U. S. 698	1893
Gibbons v. *Ogden*	9 Wheaton 1	1824
Gilman v. *Philadelphia*	3 Wallace 713	1866
Houston v. *Moore*	5 Wheaton 1	1820
Juilliard v. *Greenman* (Legal Tender Case)	110 U. S. 421	1884
Kansas v. *Colorado*	206 U. S. 46	1907
McCulloch v. *Maryland*	4 Wheaton 316	1819

Murray's Lessee v. *The Hoboken Land & Improvement Co.*	18 Howard 272	1856
Sturges v. *Crowninshield*	4 Wheaton 122	1819
United States v. *Fisher*	2 Cranch 358	1804
United States v. *Ju Toy*	198 U. S. 253	1905

RELATION OF STATES TO ONE ANOTHER

Atherton v. *Atherton*	181 U. S. 155	1901
Blake v. *McClung*	172 U. S. 239	1898
Bolln v. *Nebraska*	176 U. S. 83	1900
Escanaba & Lake Michigan Transportation Co. v. *Chicago*	107 U. S. 678	1883
Kentucky v. *Dennison*	24 Howard 66	1861
Lascelles v. *Georgia*	148 U. S. 537	1893
McCready v. *Virginia*	94 U. S. 391	1877
Paul v. *Virginia*	8 Wallace 168	1869
Roberts v. *Reilly*	116 U. S. 80	1885
Virginia v. *Tennessee*	148 U. S. 503	1893
Ward v. *Maryland*	12 Wallace 418	1871
Wisconsin v. *Pelican Insurance Co.*	127 U. S. 265	1888

RELATIONS AMONG DEPARTMENTS OF GOVERNMENT

Georgia v. *Stanton*	6 Wallace 50	1867
Gordon v. *United States*	2 Wallace 561	1865
Kilbourn v. *Thompson*	103 U. S. 168	1881
Marbury v. *Madison*	1 Cranch 137	1803
Michigan Central Railroad Co. v. *Powers*	201 U. S. 245	1906
Mitchell v. *Clark*	110 U. S. 633	1884
Public Clearing House v. *Coyne*	194 U. S. 497	1904
Sinking Fund Cases	99 U. S. 700	1879
United States v. *Ferreira*	13 Howard 40	1851

CIVIL AND POLITICAL RIGHTS

Barron v. *Baltimore*	7 Peters 243	1833
Civil Rights Cases	109 U. S. 3	1883
Dred Scott v. *Sandford*	19 Howard 393	1857
Ex parte *Jackson*	96 U. S. 727	1878
Ex parte *Siebold*	100 U. S. 371	1880
Ex parte *Yarbrough*	110 U. S. 651	1884
Hurtado v. *California*	110 U. S. 516	1884
Logan v. *United States*	144 U. S. 263	1892
Minor v. *Happersett*	21 Wallace 162	1875
Pope v. *Williams*	193 U. S. 621	1904
Public Clearing House v. *Coyne*	194 U. S. 497	1904
Slaughter House Cases	16 Wallace 36	1873
Strauder v. *West Virginia*	100 U. S. 303	1880

CASES IN AMERICAN CONSTITUTIONAL LAW

United States v. *Tarble* (Tarble's Case)	13 Wallace 397	1872
United States v. *Wong Kim Ark*	169 U. S. 649	1898
Ward v. *Maryland*	12 Wallace 418	1871

Constitutionality of Legislative Acts

Calder v. *Bull*	3 Dallas 386	1798
Fletcher v. *Peck*	6 Cranch 87	1810
Marbury v. *Madison*	1 Cranch 137	1803
Norton v. *Shelby County*	118 U. S. 425	1886
United States v. *Peters*	5 Cranch 115	1809

Jurisdiction of the Courts

Ableman v. *Booth*	21 Howard 506	1859
Ames v. *Kansas*	111 U. S. 449	1884
Chisholm v. *Georgia*	2 Dallas 419	1793
Claflin v. *Houseman*	93 U. S. 130	1876
Cohens v. *Virginia*	6 Wheaton 264	1821
Debs, in re	158 U. S. 564	1895
Ex parte *McCardle*	7 Wallace 506	1869
Foster v. *Neilson*	2 Peters 253	1829
Kiernan v. *Portland*	223 U. S. 151	1912
Marbury v. *Madison*	1 Cranch 137	1803
Martin v. *Hunter's Lessee*	1 Wheaton 304	1816
Neagle, in re	135 U. S. 1	1890
Ohio & Mississippi R. R. Co. v. *Wheeler*	1 Black 286	1862
Osborn v. *Bank of the United States*	9 Wheaton 738	1824
South Dakota v. *North Carolina*	192 U. S. 286	1904
Tennessee v. *Davis*	100 U. S. 257	1880
The Moses Taylor	4 Wallace 411	1867
United States v. *Texas*	143 U. S. 621	1892

Taxation

Brown v. *Maryland*	12 Wheaton 419	1827
Collector v. *Day*	11 Wallace 113	1871
Crandall v. *Nevada*	6 Wallace 35	1868
Davidson v. *New Orleans*	96 U. S. 97	1878
Dooley v. *United States*	183 U. S. 151	1901
Hagar v. *Reclamation District*	111 U. S. 701	1884
Hylton v. *United States*	3 Dallas 171	1796
Knowlton v. *Moore*	178 U. S. 41	1900
License Tax Cases	5 Wallace 462	1867
Loan Association v. *Topeka*	20 Wallace 655	1875
McCray v. *United States*	195 U. S. 27	1904
McCulloch v. *Maryland*	4 Wheaton 316	1819
Pollock v. *Farmers' Loan & Trust Co.* (Income Tax Case)	157 U. S. 429 / 158 U. S. 601	1895 / 1895

Springer v. *United States*	102 U. S. 586	1881
State Tonnage Tax Cases	12 Wallace 204	1871
Veazie Bank v. *Fenno*	8 Wallace 533	1869

Financial Powers Other than Taxation

Briscoe v. *Bank of Kentucky*	11 Peters 257	1837
Craig v. *State of Missouri*	4 Peters 410	1830
Hepburn v. *Griswold*	8 Wallace 603	1870
Juilliard v. *Greenman*	110 U. S. 421	1884
Lane County v. *Oregon*	7 Wallace 71	1869
Legal Tender Cases	12 Wallace 457	1871

Interstate and Foreign Commerce

Athanasaw v. *United States*	227 U. S. 326	1913
Austin v. *Tennessee*	179 U. S. 343	1900
Baltimore & Ohio Railway Co. v. *Interstate Commerce Commission*	221 U. S. 612	1911
Bowman v. *Chicago & N. W. Railway Co.*	125 U. S. 465	1888
Brown v. *Maryland*	12 Wheaton 419	1827
Champion v. *Ames* (The Lottery Case)	188 U. S. 321	1903
Cooley v. *Board of Wardens*	12 Howard 299	1851
Debs, in re	158 U. S. 564	1895
Geer v. *Connecticut*	161 U. S. 519	1896
Gibbons v. *Ogden*	9 Wheaton 1	1824
Gompers v. *Buck's Stove & Range Co.*	221 U. S. 418	1911
Gompers v. *United States*	233 U. S. 604	1914
Henderson v. *Mayor of New York*	92 U. S. 259	1876
Hoke v. *United States*	227 U. S. 308	1913
Houston & Tex. Central R.R. Co. v. *Mayes*	201 U. S. 321	1906
Houston, E. & W. Texas Railway Co. v. *United States* (Shreveport Case)	234 U. S. 342	1914
Howard v. *Illinois Central Railway Co.*	207 U. S. 463	1908
Kansas v. *Colorado*	206 U. S. 46	1907
Leisy v. *Hardin*	135 U. S. 100	1890
License Cases	5 Howard 504	1847
Loewe v. *Lawler* (Danbury Hatters' Case)	208 U. S. 274	1908
Minnesota v. *Barber*	136 U. S. 313	1890
Northern Securities Co. v. *United States*	193 U. S. 197	1904
Passenger Cases	7 Howard 283	1849
Paul v. *Virginia*	8 Wallace 168	1869
Pensacola Telegraph Co. v. *Western Union Telegraph Co.*	96 U. S. 1	1878
Plumley v. *Massachusetts*	155 U. S. 461	1894
Postal Telegraph Cable Co. v. *Adams*	155 U. S. 688	1895
Rahrer, in re	140 U. S. 545	1891
Simpson v. *Shepard* (Minnesota Rate Case)	230 U. S. 352	1913
Smyth v. *Ames*	169 U. S. 466	1898

CASES IN AMERICAN CONSTITUTIONAL LAW 723

Standard Oil Co. v. *United States*	221 U. S. 1	1911
The Daniel Ball	10 Wallace 557	1871
United States v. *American Tobacco Co.*	221 U. S. 106	1911
United States v. *E. C. Knight Co.*	156 U. S. 1	1895
United States v. *Ohio Oil Co.*, et al.	234 U. S. 548	1914
Vance v. *Vandercook*	170 U. S. 438	1898
Wabash, St. L. & Pacific Railway Co. v. *Illinois*	118 U. S. 557	1886
Ward v. *Maryland*	12 Wallace 418	1871
Welton v. *Missouri*	91 U. S. 275	1876
Western Union Telegraph Co. v. *Kansas*	216 U. S. 1	1910

Due Process and Equal Protection of the Law

Allgeyer v. *Louisiana*	165 U. S. 578	1897
Barbier v. *Connolly*	113 U. S. 27	1885
Debs, in re	158 U. S. 564	1895
Hagar v. *Reclamation District*	111 U. S. 701	1884
Hurtado v. *California*	110 U. S. 516	1884
McKane v. *Durston*	153 U. S. 684	1894
Missouri v. *Lewis*	101 U. S. 22	1880
Missouri Pacific Railway Co. v. *Nebraska*	164 U. S. 403	1896
Murray's Lessee v. *The Hoboken Land & Improvement Co.*	18 Howard 272	1856
Pembina Silver Mining Co. v. *Pennsylvania*	125 U. S. 181	1888
Plessy v. *Ferguson*	163 U. S. 537	1896
Smyth v. *Ames*	169 U. S. 466	1898
Strauder v. *West Virginia*	100 U. S. 303	1880
Twining v. *New Jersey*	211 U. S. 78	1908
Yick Wo v. *Hopkins*	118 U. S. 356	1886

Obligation of Contracts

American Smelting & Refining Co. v. *Colorado*	204 U. S. 103	1907
Charles River Bridge Co. v. *The Warren Bridge Co.*	11 Peters 420	1837
Fletcher v. *Peck*	6 Cranch 87	1810
Gelpcke v. *Dubuque*	1 Wallace 175	1864
Lehigh Water Co. v. *Easton*	121 U. S. 388	1887
Long Island Water Supply Co. v. *Brooklyn*	166 U. S. 685	1897
New Jersey v. *Wilson*	7 Cranch 164	1812
Northwestern Fertilizing Co. v. *Hyde Park*	97 U. S. 659	1878
Ogden v. *Saunders*	12 Wheaton 213	1827
Trustees of Dartmouth College v. *Woodward*	4 Wheaton 518	1819

Police Power

Bacon v. *Walker*	204 U. S. 311	1907
Booth v. *Illinois*	184 U. S. 425	1902
Bosley v. *McLaughlin*	236 U. S. 385	1915
Champion v. *Ames* (The Lottery Case)	188 U. S. 321	1903

Chicago, Burlington & Quincy Railway Co. v. *McGuire*	219 U. S. 549	1911
Dent v. *West Virginia*	129 U. S. 114	1889
Escanaba & Lake Michigan Transportation Co. v. *Chicago*	107 U. S. 678	1883
Hennington v. *Georgia*	163 U. S. 299	1896
Hoke v. *United States*	227 U. S. 308	1913
Holden v. *Hardy*	169 U. S. 366	1898
License Cases	5 Howard 504	1847
Miller v. *Wilson*	236 U. S. 373	1915
Mugler v. *Kansas*	123 U. S. 623	1887
Muller v. *Oregon*	208 U. S. 412	1908
Munn v. *Illinois*	94 U. S. 113	1877
Mutual Film Corporation v. *Industrial Commission of Ohio*	236 U. S. 230, 247	1915
Noble State Bank v. *Haskell*	219 U. S. 104, 575	1911
Northwestern Fertilizing Co. v. *Hyde Park*	97 U. S. 659	1878
Plessy v. *Ferguson*	163 U. S. 537	1896
Slaughter House Cases	16 Wallace 36	1873
Smyth v. *Ames*	169 U. S. 466	1898
Stone v. *Mississippi*	101 U. S. 814	1880

TREATY-MAKING POWER AND FOREIGN RELATIONS

Chae Chan Ping v. *United States* (Chinese Exclusion Case)	130 U. S. 581	1889
Cherokee Tobacco Case	11 Wallace 616	1871
De Geofroy v. *Riggs*	133 U. S. 258	1890
Downes v. *Bidwell*	182 U. S. 244	1901
Ex parte Baiz	135 U. S. 403	1890
Fong Yue Ting v. *United States*	149 U. S. 698	1893
Foster v. *Neilson*	2 Peters 253	1829
Head Money Cases	112 U. S. 580	1884
Jones v. *United States*	137 U. S. 202	1890
Terlinden v. *Ames*	184 U. S. 270	1902
United States, ex rel. *Turner* v. *Williams*	194 U. S. 279	1904
United States v. *Lee Yen Tai*	185 U. S. 213	1902
United States v. *Palmer*	3 Wheaton 610	1818
Ware v. *Hylton*	3 Dallas 199	1796
Whitney v. *Robertson*	124 U. S. 190	1888

INDEX

INDEX

Act of Settlement, in England (1701), 425, 428, 525.
Adams, G. B., and Stephens, H. M., *Select Documents*, 428, 434.
Adams, John, addressed Congress, 71, 306; election of, 72; judicial appointments, 235; issues no vetoes, 76.
Adams, John Quincy, issues no vetoes, 76.
Adjournment of Congress, rules for, 121, 122; president's power of, 55.
Administration in United States federal government, 56, 58, 96–114; supervision of, 335, 336; reform needed, 114, 376, 377; in States, 361–377. *See also* Executive power.
Admiralty, jurisdiction in United States federal courts, 233, 251, 252, 253, 254, 261, 264, 265; in England, 530–532; first lord, 436.
Advowsons, legally private property, 520.
Agrarian party, in Germany, 611.
Agriculture, commissioner for, 374; English board president, 436.
Agriculture Committee, of House of Representatives, 159.
Agriculture, department of, in Argentina, 681; France, 567; United States, 48, 91, 97, 106, 108.
Alabama, State constitutions, 344; legislature, 349; on judicial circuit, 244.
Alaska, appeal from courts, 263; in nominating convention, 192; on judicial circuit, 245; resources of, 106.
Alfred, king of England, 414.
Aliens, acquire citizenship, 324, 325; exercise suffrage, 320; status of women, 323; parties to suit, 259, 260, 264.
Allotments Act in England (1885), 534.
Alsace-Lorraine, electoral district of Germany, 603.
Ambassadors, appointed, 59, 61, 64; right to receive, 66; and federal judiciary, 251, 254, 260, 261.
Amendments. *See* Constitution.

American colonies. *See* United States.
American Political Science Association *Proceedings*, 360.
American Political Science Review, cited, 17, 82, 139, 141, 159, 267, 667, 688.
An Analysis of System of Government throughout the British Empire, cited, 549.
Anarchists, in France, 573.
Angles, invade England, 551.
Anglo-Saxon, judicial system, 630; democracies, 580, 582; legislative government system, 375, 694, 697.
Annapolis (Md.), convention at, 18.
Anne, queen of England, 428, 433, 436, 496, 500; veto of, 489.
Anson, Sir William R., *Law and Custom of the Constitution*, 411, 421, 423, 428, 434, 435, 436, 446, 458, 477, 490, 532.
Anti-Masonic Party, nominating convention, 190.
Anti-trust legislation, 112, 300, 301. *See also* Federal Trade Commission.
Appeals:
In Argentina, 682; in colonial courts, 16; in England, 405, 526, 530, 586; France, 571; Switzerland, 625, 626, 628–630, 634, 641; in United States, 107, 234, 236, 239, 241, 248, 249, 253, 260–265; State courts, 381, 382, 390.
APPOINTMENTS:
In Chile, 664.
In France, 565.
In Germany, 607.
In Switzerland, 642.
In United States, president's power of, 58–62, 83, 112; Senate confirms, 34, 138–140, 218, 305, 306; relation to party politics, 304; in the several States, 366–368. *See also* Civil service and Spoils system.
Appropriations, in England, 452, 464, 465; in United States, controlled by Congress, 68, 90, 91, 117; divided responsibility for, 162, 163.

INDEX

Appropriations Committee, of House of Representatives, 159; of Senate, 133.
Arbitration, French courts for, 554; in New Zealand, 545; in Switzerland, 628, 645.
Archives, custodian of, 99, 372.
ARGENTINA:
  Progressive state, 659, 663, 672, 684–686; federal type of government, 668, 672; described, 672–687.
Argentina and Australia:
  progress compared, 684–686.
Argentina and France:
  governments compared, 686, 687.
Argentina and United States:
  development compared, 672, 673; federal systems, 673–674, 679, 680, 682.
Arizona, modifies Constitution, 310.
Arkansas, on judicial circuit, 244.
Army, in France, 565, 575; in United States, under federal control, 7, 55–57, 117. *See also* Military affairs and War department.
Arrondissements, in France, 557, 567, 568, 569.
Arthur, Chester A., vetoes, 76.
Articles of Confederation, in United States, 4, 5; negative influence of, 17; proposed revision, 18; weakness, 18, 255; no judiciary, 232. *See also* Confederation.
Asquith, Henry, English prime minister, 472.
Attainder, forbidden in United States, 8.
Attorney General, in United States, office created, 97; duties, 104, 105; relation to federal courts, 247; succession to presidency, 48; in State administration, 372. *See also* Justice department.
Auditor, in State administration, 372, 373.
AUSTRALIA:
  Constitutional experiments, 501; federation formed, 545, 691; Constitution, 545–547; Parliament, 546, 547; judiciary, 546, 547; interpretation of Constitution, 546, 547; relation to Crown, 485.
Australia and Canada:
  constitutions compared, 545, 546.
Australia and South Africa:
  constitutions compared, 548.
Australia and United States:
  interpretation of Constitution compared, 303; federation, 692. *See also* Argentina and Australia.
Austria, in Charlemagne's empire, 592; ruling dynasty, 593, 595; population, 594, 596; excluded from Germany, 597, 598; European power, 649.
Autocracy in Germany, 599–601, 605–608, 612.

Baden, and the German empire, 602.
Bagehot, Walter, cited, 399, 480, 483, 485, 588; *The English Constitution,* 396, 402, 408, 446, 458, 480, 490.
Balance of powers, in United States Constitution, 5, 6. *See also* Separation of powers.
Baldwin, Simeon E., *American Judiciary,* 280, 391.
Balfour, A. J., position on tariff question, 469; Conservative leader, 442.
Balkan States, origin of, 649, 653.
Ballinger, Richard A., investigation of, 92.
Ballot, the short, advised, 358.
Balloting, in national conventions, 198, 199.
Balmaceda, José Manuel, president of Chile, 668.
Bank of United States, 10, 298, 299.
Banking, in Germany, 605; in United States, 102, 265, 299, 373.
Banking and Currency Committee of House of Representatives, 158, 159.
Bankruptcy, controlled by Congress, 117; in federal courts, 263–265; concurrent jurisdiction in, 8.
Barbarossa, Frederick, German emperor, 593.
Bavaria and the German empire, 602, 605.
Beaconsfield, Benjamin Disraeli, Lord, leader of Conservatives, 442; relation to Crown, 481; prime minister, 496.
Beard, Charles A., *American Government and Politics,* 13, 21, 27, 52, 53, 58, 72, 80, 115, 121, 124, 157, 170, 175, 189, 230, 235, 245, 267, 280, 289, 294, 296, 306, 318, 339, 360, 367, 368, 374, 377, 391; *Readings in American Government and Politics,* 21, 53, 80, 115, 149; *The Supreme Court and the Constitution,* 267, 280.
Becket, Thomas a, opposes Henry II, 517, 523.

INDEX

Belgium, cabinet system, 580; constitutional government, 650, 651; colonial empire, 650; relation to Europe, 649.

Bicameral legislatures in States, 347; proposal to abolish, 354; in England, 644; Switzerland, 627, 641. *See also* the several legislatures.

Bill of Rights, in England, 409, 426; in United States Constitution, 285, 326.

Birmingham Liberal Association, under Chamberlain, 507; plan fails, 512, 513.

Bismarck, Otto, Prince von, German chancellor, 598, 599, 603, 606, 607, 611, 695; dismissed, 607; *Reflections*, 601.

Blaine, James G., defeated, 46.

Blakeslee, George H., editor, 688.

Blockades, president may declare, 57.

Blount, William, impeachment of, 141.

Board of Education. *See* Education.

Board of Trade. *See* Trade.

Bodley, John E., *France*, 581.

Boers, colonize South Africa, 547; relation to English, 485; in South African Union, 695.

Bolln v. Nebraska, cited, 309.

Bonapartists, in France, 580.

Bordeaux, local government, 569.

Boss system, in United States, 202, 229, 383; in South America, 683. *See also* Corruption in politics.

Boston, resistance to tea tax at, 506.

Botha, Louis, prime minister of Union of South Africa, 548; loyal subject, 458.

Boulanger, George E. J., trial of, 577, 578.

Boundaries, disputes concerning, 256; of States, 313.

Bourbons, French dynasty, 552, 553, 555, 563.

Boyne, Battle of the, 522, 536.

Brazil, presidential government, 663; federal type, 668, 669, 672.

Bribery, in nominating conventions, 202; in elections, 229.

British Empire. *See* England and the several colonies.

Brown, Peter H., *History of Scotland*, 539.

Bryan, W. J., speeches printed, 215.

Bryce, James, *Holy Roman Empire*, 591, 595, 601; *Studies in History and Jurisprudence*, 585, 591; *The American Commonwealth*, 13, 19–21, 30, 37, 51, 53, 80, 92, 95, 143, 144, 150, 163, 164, 175, 201, 204, 218, 294, 300, 306, 318, 339, 345, 360, 377, 383, 391, 411, 698.

Buchanan, James, vetoes, 76.

Budget, in England, 476, 477; of 1909, 463, 501.

Buenos Aires, and state of siege, 676.

Bulgarians, war with Greeks, 654.

Bülow, Bernhard von, *Imperial Germany*, 600, 601, 606.

Bundesrath, of German Empire, 602, 603; president, 604, 607; functions, 607, 608.

Burgess, John W., *Political Science and Comparative Constitutional Law*, 323, 328.

Burke, Edmund, *Works*, 408.

Burr, Aaron, vice-president, 40; candidate for president, 286.

Business interests, influence legislation, 228, 354.

Byzantine Empire, decline of, 592; rule of, 653.

Cabal, in reign of Charles II, 427.

CABINET:

As a system of government, 182, 395–402, 639, 663, 687; advantages, 502–504.

In Argentina, 681.

In Chile, 665–668.

In England, 397–408, 432, 437–439, 466, 468; history of, 421–435; relation to Crown, 397, 427, 480–482, 489, 490; to Privy Council, 424, 439; to Parliament, 397, 439, 470, 471, 498, 499, 501–504; to Prime Minister, 442, 443; to executive and judiciary, 435–445; to party system, 400, 401, 412, 439, 513, 514; responsibility of, 397, 438, 439; qualities of, 440, 441, 443, 444, 473, 474, 509, 526, 527, 529.

In France, 562–565; legislative work, 566, 570, 572–581; administrative, 566–571; not a party organ, 580.

In United States, 61, 81–95, 305; administrative duties, 96–114; not responsible to Congress, 93, 94.

Cæsars, temporal head of Roman Empire, 592.

Calendar of bills, in House of Representatives, 167.

California, on judicial circuit, 245.

Cambridge Modern History, cited, 539, 655.

Campaign. *See* Election campaign.

Canada, federation in, 540, 691, 692; relation to England, 484, 485, 521, 544; loyalty to, 484, 693, 694; constitutional system, 501, 540–545; governor general, 541, 542, 544; privy council, 541, 543; Parliament, 541–544; judiciary, 542–544; party system, 541, 542; provinces, 691; civil war of 1837, 540.

Canada and England, constitutional systems compared, 541.

Canada and South Africa, constitutions compared, 548.

Canada and United States, constitutions compared, 540, 541. *See also* Australia and Canada.

Candidate for president, in nominating conventions, 198–200; chooses national committee chairman, 208.

Canon law, relation to modern Roman law, 592.

Canterbury, Archbishop of, 519, 520; in House of Lords, 460; synod of, 519, 520.

Cantons, in France, 567–568; in Switzerland, 614, 615, 619, 621, 622, 695; inherent powers, 618; constitutions, 643; governmental institutions, 622–624, 639; judiciary, 625, 628, 629; legislation, 626, 627, 630; representation in federal legislature, 627, 641, 642.

Caracalla, extended citizenship, 584, 585.

Carnot, Lazare H., French president, 563.

Carson, Hampton L., *History of the Supreme Court of the United States*, 237, 238.

Carter, A. T., *English Legal Institutions*, 532.

Cassimir-Périer, J. P. P., French president, 563.

Caste spirit, and free government, 660.

Catholics, in Canada, 694; Germany, 611; Switzerland, 635, 636, 638, 694.

Caucus, in England, 580; in United States, 159, 305; in legislation, 134–136, 172–174; party machinery, 186–189.

Caudillo, political boss in South America, 683.

Cavaliers, precursors of Tories, 494.

Celtic peoples, habitat, 551.

Censorship, in Germany, 596.

Census, in United States, decennial, 146.

Centralization, in federal governments, 692; in Chile, 668–671; in France, 568–571; in South America, 686, 687; Switzerland, 615, 618, 629, 635, 644; United States, 9–11, 376; opposition to, 4, 5, 9.

Chairman of United States National Committee, 208, 209, 217.

Chamber of Deputies, in French Republic, 556, 557, 558, 564, 570; ministerial access to, 567; responsibility of ministers to, 517; organization, 574–577.

Chamberlain, Joseph, political career, 443, 507, 508, 513; position on tariff, 467; becomes cabinet minister, 507; party organizer, 507–509.

CHANCELLOR:
In England, of the Exchequer, 436, 443, 476, 477; of Duchy of Lancaster, 436. *See also* Lord Chancellor.
In Germany, 604–607, 613; veto rights, 609.
In Switzerland, 633.

Chancery, English court of, 530–532; in States of United States, 382.

Charities and corrections, supervision of, 374.

Charlemagne, founder of empire, 592.

Charles I, king of England, 427, 433, 494, 524; arbitrary rule, 424.

Charles II, king of England, 426, 427, 433, 494.

Charles XIII, king of Sweden, 651.

Charters, for municipalities, 336.

Checks and balances in United States Constitution, 28–30.

Chesterfield, Philip Stanhope, Lord, British statesman, 430, 433.

Chicago, convention of 1860 at, 210; headquarters, 216; strike, 57.

Chief Justice, of United States, 241; duties, 140, 242, 243.

Chief of Staff, in American Army, 103.

Child labor, proposed national law, 300; State laws to regulate, 358, 359.

Chile, government, 663–671.

Chile and England, cabinets compared, 663, 664.

China, United States Court for, 245.

Chinese, in United States, without citizenship, 324, 325.

Chisholm v. *Georgia*, cited, 257.

Christianity, in relation to democracy, 493; to Roman Empire, 583, 592.

Church, as a political power, 580, 592–594; in Canada, 521; in England, 438, 496, 516–523; court for, 435, 527–530; in France, 554; in Scotland, 534;

INDEX

in Switzerland, 621. *See also* Disestablishment.
Churchill, Lord Randolph, English statesman, 513, 514.
Churchill, Winston S., *Life of Lord Randolph Churchill*, 496.
Circuit Court of Appeals, 238, 239, 262–265; procedure, 244, 245; relations to Federal Trade Commission, 111.
Circuit Courts, in United States, 236; reorganized, 238–240.
Circuits, in England, 531; for United States Judges, 244, 245.
Cities. *See* Municipalities.
Citizenship, in federal State, 258; in the Roman Empire, 584, 585; in United States, 287, 322–328.
Civil rights, in federal courts, 265.
Civil service, in England, 440; in United States, 62, 63, 113, 304; in the States, 367. *See also* Appointments and Removals.
Civil Service Commission, in United States, 109, 112, 376; duties, 63, 112–114; in several States, 374.
Civil Service Reform Committee, in House of Representatives, 159.
Claims, court of, 105, 263; established, 240, 247, 248, 255.
Clark, Walter, cited, 268.
Classified service. *See* Civil service.
Clemenceau, Georges, *South America To-day*, 688.
Cleveland, Grover, as president, 32; defeated, 45; elected, 46; cabinet, 87; appointments, 61; removals, 63; vetoes, 75, 76; during railway strike, 57.
Coal, in Alaska, 106.
Code Napoleon (1804), promulgated, 553; importance of, 589, 590; in Germany, 595, 605; Louisiana, 386.
Code of 1912, in Switzerland, 618.
Cohens v. *The State of Virginia*, cited, 252.
Coinage, controlled by federal government, 7, 117; prohibited to States, 8.
Coke, Sir Edward, chief justice of England, 425; position on judiciary, 526.
Collector v. *Day*, cited, 318.
Collectors of Ports, importance of, 101.
Collins, Jesse, land resolution, 473.
Colonial era, in American history. *See* United States.
COLONIES:
British, 437, 540–549; secretary for, 435. *See also* the several colonies.
United States dependencies, 118, 437. *See also* Hawaii, Philippine Islands, and Porto Rico.
Colonies department, in French cabinet, 567.
Colorado, on judicial circuit, 244.
Commerce department, in French cabinet, 567; in United States, 48, 97, 108, 109. *See also* Foreign and Interstate commerce, and Trade.
Commerce, Industry, and Agriculture, Swiss department of, 623.
Commission government in cities, 368.
Commissioner of Internal Revenue, duties, 101.
Commissioner of Works, first, in England, 436.
Commissioning officers, president's power of, 55.
Commissions, in State service, 358, 374–376; in Wisconsin, 342.
Committee system, in England, 452–454, 476; in German legislature, 607, 608; in United States Congress, 94, 133, 134, 305, 452; in State legislatures, 350, 352, 371.
Common Law, in England, 406, 407; growth, 585–588; in United States, 19, 20, 265, 386–388; compared with Roman, 582, 687.
Common Pleas, court of, in England, 523, 524; in States of United States, 382.
Commons, John R., *Proportional Representation*, 150.
Communes, in France, 557, 567–569, 697; history of, 570; officials, 566, 570; in Switzerland, 614, 622, 624, 625, 628, 695.
Compromises of United States Constitution, 33, 128, 146.
Comptroller, in State administration, 373.
Concurrent jurisdiction, of federal and State courts, 8, 9, 261, 262, 386.
Concurrent powers, in Swiss government, 618.
Concurring opinions, in Supreme Court, 243.
Confederation, defined, 3, 4, 689; in Germany, 593, 596, 597, 689; ended, 598; in Switzerland, 615; United States, 11, 689.
Congress, in Argentina, 676–679, 680, 682.

Congress, United States legislature, 116; compared with Parliament, 116, 405; powers, 116–118, 324, 325; implied powers, 298–301; prohibitions, 8; rules of procedure, 121, 122; proposes amendments, 285; relation to executive, 57, 71–74; to Cabinet, 89–93; to treasury department, 100; to judiciary, 233–236, 250, 251, 260–262, 272–274; party leadership of, 172.
See also Continental Congress, House of Representatives, and Senate.

Congressional Campaign Committee, chosen by caucus, 173; organization of, 225–229.

Congressional districts, 148–150; units of representation, 192.

Congressmen, elections and qualifications, 119, 120, 219; compensation and privileges, 122–124; as representatives, 125, 126.

Connecticut, colonial legislature, 15; merges into State, 16, 17; on judicial circuit, 244.

Conservation of resources, investigation of, 92; value, 106, 108; regulated by Congress, 118.

Conservatism, with relation to constitutional readjustment, 281, 282.

Conservative National Union, organized, 511; character, 512, 513.

Conservative party, in Canada, 541; in England, 451, 485; relation to House of Lords, 461, 462, 465, 500, 501; party organization, 510–512, 514; position towards Labor party, 472; tariff, 469; Home Rule, 472; Church of England, 469; propose referendum, 502; Education Act, 440, 441; bid for city vote, 496. *See also* Tory party.

Constantinople, capital of empire, 592, 593.

CONSTITUTION:
Meaning of term, 22, 408, 409; function of, 270.
Australian, 545–548, 692, 693.
Danish, of 1849, 652.
English, 14, 15, 19, 403–411, 560, 561; unwritten, 22, 25; originates in local government, 412–420; relation to religious bodies, 516; contradictions of, 410, 411.
French, 559–561.
German, 602–613, 695.
Prussian, 597, 599, 600, 612.
South African Union, 547, 548.
South American, 656–658, 661, 663, 669, 673–675, 681, 683.
Swedish, 651.
Swiss, 615, 617, 618, 626, 627, 630, 632, 635, 637, 689, 694; amendments, 619, 632, 643, 644.
United States, sources, 14–21; artificiality, 399, 400; framed, 4–6, 9, 12, 14–21, 23, 24, 33–35, 41, 70; framers, 81, 127, 128, 132, 269, 282: principles of, 22–29; reverence for, 282, 290; ratified, 10, 35, 181, 285, 286, 291, 689; distribution of powers, 6–9, 13; executive provisions, 55, 56, 71, 81, 83, 102; judiciary established, 231, 233, 250, 259, 260; on powers of Congress, 116, 118, 119, 129, 139, 324; omissions of, 47, 48, 178, 179; strict construction of, 181, 300, 301; theory of coördinate powers, 266, 267; extra-constitutional features, 43, 50; interpreted by Supreme Court, 12, 252, 267; contravened, 78; modified, 41; readjusted by amendments, 8, 138, 281–293; method of, 284, 285; first ten amendments, *see* Bill of Rights; 11th Amendment, 256, 257, 286; 12th Amendment, 40, 187, 188, 286, 296; 13th Amendment, 287; 14th Amendment, 287, 319, 322, 323, 327, 328; 15th Amendment, 287, 319, 320, 322; 16th Amendment, 287–290; 17th Amendment, 119, 131, 132, 288–290; readjusted otherwise, 295–307; relations to States, 308–310, 313–315, 318, 319, 321, 329, 333; State constitutions, 342–345; imitated by other nations, 591, 693.

Constitutional Convention, origin of, 17, 18; action, 12, 24, 38, 41; discussion in, 35; members, 181, 267, 268. *See also* Compromises.

Constitutional Yearbook, cited, 496.

Consular bureau, in State department, 99.

Consuls, and federal courts, 255.

Contested elections, decided by Congress, 120.

Contested nominations, in nominating conventions, 196, 197, 211.

Continental Congress, failure of, 5, 7, 17; calls Constitutional Convention, 18.

Contract labor cases, in federal courts, 265.

INDEX

Contracts, under State control, 7; obligation may not be impaired, 8, 310.
Conventions, place in politics, 505. *See also* National Convention.
Cooke, George W., *History of Party*, 496.
Cooley, Thomas M., *Constitutional Law*, 318, 328; *Treatise on Constitutional Limitations*, 328, 339.
Coöperation in Swiss government, 632–634.
Copyrights, regulated by Congress, 117; decided by federal courts, 261, 264, 265.
Corn Laws in England, organization to abolish, 506, 507.
Coronation in England, a parliamentary ceremony, 489.
Corporations, relation to state, 372; contributions of, 213, 214; demand for regulation, 105, 111; control of, 11, 300; taxes on, 101; conceded citizenship, 258, 259; and 14th Amendment, 328; for transportation, 110.
Corrupt practices acts, 358.
Corruption, in Congressional elections, 120; in presidential elections, 46; in party politics, 229.
Corwin, Edward S., *The Doctrine of Judicial Review*, 280.
Council of Governor, in States, 384.
Council of Ministers. *See* Cabinet; in France.
Council of State, in Chile, 665, 666; in France, 565, 571.
Council of States, in Switzerland, 621, 627, 641, 642; influence, 628, 633.
Counterfeiting, crime against federal laws, 117.
County, in England, constitutional importance of, 412, 414.
County, in United States. *See* Local Government.
County Central Committee, in party politics, 222–224.
County Councils Act (1888), 528.
County courts, in England, 413–415, 417, 516, 523, 528, 529; in United States, 381, 382.
Court martials, relation to pardons, 64.
Courtney, Leonard Henry, *Working of the Constitution*, 411, 446, 458.
Courts. *See* Judiciary.
Credentials, in nominating conventions, 196, 197, 210.

Criminal Appeal, court of, in England, 531.
Criminal jurisdiction, of federal courts, 265; State courts, 339.
Criminal law, and pardoning power, 366; faults in administering, 389, 390; left to States, 315.
Cromwell, Oliver, in English history, 425, 492.
Crown, in English system, 422, 423, 479, 480, 483; relation to Prime Minister, 447; to Cabinet, 397, 427, 436, 437, 480–482, 489, 490; to Parliament, 425–429, 466, 488, 489; creates peers, 479, 481; relation to judiciary, 424–426, 489, 524, 525; head of church, 518, 519; pardoning power, 489; relation to party leadership, 442, 443; non-partisan, 480–482; relation to democracy, 478–490; to foreign affairs, 482; symbol of unity, 483–485, 489, 490; relation to colonies, 484, 485; reviving power of, 490. *See also* Royal family.
Crown colonies, future government, 549.
Curia regis, in English system, 405, 421, 492, 523, 524.
Currency, created by Congress, 7, 299; issued, 102; taxation of, 10; reform, 73.
Custom, effect on constitutional development, 303, 560.
Customs Appeals, court of, 240, 248, 249.
Customs duties, prohibited to States, 8; controlled by Congress, 116; must be uniform, 117; under Treasury department, 100, 101.

Dallinger, Frederick W., *Nominations for Elective Office*, 190.
Danish Conquest, of England, 404.
Danube River, headwaters, 614.
Davis, Horace A., cited, 267.
Deadlocks, in Senatorial elections, 131.
Dealey, James Q., *Growth of American State Constitution*, 360, 377.
Debate, freedom of, 136.
Decentralization, in States system, 361, 363, 376.
Declaration of Independence, in United States, 690, 691; effect on France, 553; political philosophy, 20.
Defense, in care of Congress, 116, 117.
Delaware, State Senate, 348; on judicial circuit, 244.

Delegated powers, of federal courts, 251.
DEMOCRACY:
Distrust of, 145; development, 407, 408, 493, 550–552; changing character of, 486, 487; relation to federal government, 689–697; effect of, 649; the ultimate problem of government, 655.
In England, 410, 447, 478–490, 529, 539, 644; extended by colonization, 540; in the empire, 549.
In France, 554, 589–591, 644.
In Germany, 611–613, 616.
In Scandinavian countries, 651–653.
In South America, 656–658, 664, 670, 671, 679, 682–684, 687.
In Switzerland, 614–616, 628–632, 639, 644.
In United States, 23, 36, 41, 49; relation to presidency, 34–36, 49, 190; to judiciary, 273, 277, 391; to party systems, 125, 126, 185, 194, 203, 204, 212, 230; to constitutional changes, 281, 290, 292–294; to State policies, 313, 341, 342, 354, 356–358, 376, 377.
Democratic party, principles, 184, 185; attack on Supreme Court, 279; caucus, 135; organization, 217, 226, 227; nominating conventions, 191–193, 195, 199, 210; campaigns, 215, 218; in New York County, 223; gerrymander of, 150.
Democratic-Republican party, principles, 10, 181; party system, 42, 186, 187; leaders, 85, 286.
Denmark, a minor state, 649; government, 652, 653; war with Prussia, 598.
Departmental reports in United States, submitted to Congress, 91. *See also* the several departments.
Departments, as French governmental units, 568–571.
Dependencies, of United States. *See* Colonies.
Dicey, Albert V., *The Law of the Constitution*, 402, 408, 423, 434, 446, 500, 698.
Dickinson, G. Lowes, *Development of Parliament during the Nineteenth Century*, 458, 497.
Diet, in German confederation, 596; in Swiss confederation, 617.
Dillon, John F., *Municipal Corporations*, 334.
Diplomacy, controlled by president, 65; difficulties of, 91.

Diplomatic bureau, in State department, 99.
Direct legislation. *See* Legislation.
Direct primary. *See* Primaries, direct.
Direct taxes, and the Constitution, 283.
Disestablishment, in England, 520, 521; in Ireland, 522; Wales, 522.
Disraeli. *See* Beaconsfield.
Dissent, origin of, 494, 519; influence, 521, 528; political sympathies, 496.
Dissenting opinions, in United States Supreme Court, 243.
Distribution of powers, in United States government, 6–9, 20. *See also* Separation of powers.
District Attorneys, of federal courts, 247.
District Courts, of United States, 236, 237, 245–247; jurisdiction, 246, 247; reorganized, 238–240; appeals from, 262, 264; in the several States, 382.
District of Columbia, citizens of, 258; courts, 240, 249, 263; militia, 124; how governed, 437; committee for, 159.
Divorce, need of uniform laws, 359.
Dodd, Walter F., *Modern Constitutions*, 561, 617, 619, 655, 664, 665, 669, 673, 674, 681.
Domestic relations, under State control, 7, 379.
Domville-Fife, Charles W., *Great States of South America*, 688.
Dougherty, J. Hampden, *The Electoral System of the United States*, 54.
Drafting bureaus, for State legislatures, 353. *See also* Legislative reference libraries.
Dred Scott decision, effect of, 279, 323.
Dublin, capital of Ireland, 537.
Duma, establishment of, 478.
Dupriez, L., *Les Ministres dans les Principaux Pays d'Europe et d'Amérique*, 477.
Durham, Bishop of, sits in House of Lords, 460.
Dutch. *See* Boers and Holland.
Duties. *See* Customs.

Eastern Empire. *See* Byzantine Empire.
Edinburgh Review, cited, 485.
Education, in Argentina, 684; in England, 435, 438; in France, 554; in South America, 659; in Swiss government, 618, 621, 635; in United States,

INDEX

7, 309, 438; national bureau of, 159. *See also* Public Instruction.
Education Act, in England, 440.
Education Committee, in House of Representatives, 159.
Edward I, king of England, 425, 518, 519, 523; attaches Wales to Crown, 484; summons representatives, 404.
Edward II, king of England, 423.
Edward III, importance for parliamentary history, 404, 423.
Edward VII, diplomatic successes of, 482; social welfare interests, 482.
Egerton, Hugh E., and Grant, W. L., *Canadian Constitutional Development*, 549; *Federation and Unions within the British Empire*, 549.
Elections, in Argentina, 684; in England, 464, 514, 515; in France, 558, 562, 577; in United States, for president, 38–53, 209, 212–216, 220–224; of judges, 383, 384; controlled by States, 338, 339; in the States, 219–222, 320–323; districts for, 338.
Electoral college, purpose of, 39–41; failure of, 41–43, 50; present function, 44, 45; abolition suggested, 48.
Electoral commission of 1876, settle dispute, 47.
Elizabeth, queen of England, 493.
Elliot, Jonathan, *Debates*, 291.
Ely, Richard T., *Property and Contract in their Relations to the Distribution of Wealth*, 331, 332, 339.
Engineers, in army, 103.
ENGLAND:
  A European power, 649; insular independence, 550–551; form of government, 3, 4, 395–531; Constitution, 14, 15, 19, 22, 25, 403–420; historical development, 404–409, 412–433, 533; monarchy in, 403, 404, 478, 479 (*See also* Crown); system of law, 19, 582, 585–588 (*see also* Common Law); self-governing colonies, 541, 549, 693. *see also* the several institutions of government, *i.e.* Cabinet, Constitution, Crown, House of Commons, House of Lords, etc.
England and France:
  cabinets compared, 398, 563, 564, 566, 572, 575, 580.
  constitutions compared, 559–561.
  executives compared, 398, 563, 564.
  historical development compared, 550–553, 555, 506.
  judiciary compared, 590, 591.
  legislatures compared, 565, 574, 577.
  party system compared, 573, 574, 580, 581.
England and Germany:
  legislatures compared, 609.
  religious reform compared, 594.
England and Switzerland:
  democracy compared, 616, 631.
  executives compared, 640.
  judiciary compared, 644, 645.
  legislation compared, 644, 645.
England and United States:
  cabinets compared, 396–401.
  colonial systems compared, 437.
  constitutions compared, 14, 15, 19, 22, 29, 399, 400, 405, 409, 412, 501.
  church policy compared, 496.
  democratic progress compared, 485.
  educational system compared, 438.
  effects of custom compared, 303.
  executives compared, 403, 444, 639.
  financial systems compared, 137, 477.
  governmental systems, 444–446, 505, 506.
  judiciary compared, 266, 267, 275, 398, 399, 446, 630; common law systems, 19, 386–388; equity systems, 253, 388.
  legislatures compared, 19, 116, 123, 136, 151, 173, 343.
  local government compared, 336, 419, 420, 437, 438.
  military requirements compared, 487.
  party systems compared, 177, 182, 183, 491, 498, 514, 515.
  patriotism compared, 483, 484.
  public opinion compared, 30.
  speakership compared, 155, 452.
  separation of powers, 29, 526, 527.
Enock, C. Reginald, *Republics of Central and South America*, 669, 688.
Enrolled Bills Committee, of House of Representatives, 169.
Enumerated powers, in United States Constitution, 6.
Episcopal church in United States, 521. *See also* Church; in Canada and England.
Equal Suffrage. *See* Woman's suffrage.
Equity proceedings, in federal courts, 253, 264; in State courts, 388.
Essex, number of electors, 449.
Exchequer court, origin of, 523, 524.

INDEX

Excise. *See* Internal revenue.
Executive, in England, 397, 437; in Swiss Republic, 621–626; in United States, 25–28, 31, 33; in States, 345–347. *See also* Crown, Governors, Kaiser, and President.
Experimentation, in State government, 356–358.
Experts, in administrative offices, 114, 375.
Ex post facto laws, prohibited, 8.
Extra-constitutional rights of president, 70; of party government, 177, 178; of the cabinet, 81, 82.
Extradition, in Argentina, 674; in United States, 98, 99; between the States, 315.

Fairlie, John A., *Local Government in Counties, Towns, and Villages*, 339, 382; *National Administration of the United States*, 59, 80, 107, 115.
Farrand, Max, *The Federal Constitution and the Defects of the Confederation*, 17, 21.
Federal Assembly, in Switzerland, 621, 623, 624, 625, 628, 632, 634, 641, 643.
Federal Council, in Switzerland, 621–626, 628, 633, 634, 638, 642.
Federal Pact, in Switzerland, 615.
Federal system, defined, 3, 4, 7, 649, 689, 696; advantages of, 12, 341; in Australia, 545, 691, 693; in Canada, 540, 541, 691, 692, 694; in South Africa, 692–694; in South America, 668, 671, 672, 684, 687; in Switzerland, 617–619, 621–638, 689, 694, 695, 697; in United Kingdom, 539; in United States, 307, 689–691, 697; relations to States, 316–319.
Federal Trade Commission, organized, 109, 111; duties, 112, 376.
Federal Tribunal, in Switzerland, 621, 625, 628, 629, 630, 634, 641.
Federalist, cited, 24, 39, 41, 54, 75, 76, 80, 128, 141, 178, 268, 280, 283, 284.
Federalist party, in United States, principles, 10, 181, 183; elects president, 42; leader, 85; develops caucus, 187, 188; controls courts, 235; lacks organization, 187; dissolves, 183.
Feudal system, in Europe, 551, 552; decline of, 552, 553, 570, 629.
Fillmore, Millard, uses no vetoes, 76.
Finance, in England, 476; in France, 575; in United States, 99–102; reform needed, 97; in election campaigns, 213–216, 222, 224, 227, 228, 358. *See also* Banking and Treasury.
Finance Committee, in Senate, 133–135.
Finance department, in Argentina, 681; in France, 566, 567. *See also* Treasury department.
Finance, Industry, and Public Works, department in Chile, 665, 667.
Finley, John H., and Sanderson, John F., *The American Executive and Executive Methods*, 76, 77, 80, 95, 115, 378.
Florida, in election of 1876, 47; on judicial circuit, 244.
Follett, M. P., *The Speaker of the House of Representatives*, 175.
Food and dairy commissioners, 374.
Ford, Henry Jones, *The Rise and Growth of American Politics*, 30, 54, 76, 125, 144, 176, 182, 189.
Foreign affairs, in England, 482; secretary for, 436, 439; in United States, 7, 8, 90, 254; president's relations to, 55, 56, 64–69. *See also* State department.
Foreign Affairs and Public Worship department, in Argentina, 681.
Foreign Affairs Committee, in House of Representatives, 159.
Foreign Affairs department, in Chile, 665; in France, 566; in Switzerland, 623.
Foreign commerce, regulations for, 117, 312.
Foreign Relations Committee, in Senate, 68, 133, 134.
Foreign Secretary in England, 436; responsible for diplomacy, 439.
Forests, in national domain, 118; supervised, 106.
Foster v. Neilson, cited, 69.
Fox, Charles James, as party leader, 495.
FRANCE:
European power, 649; form of government, 3, 24, 550, 697; historical outline, 551–556; in Charlemagne's empire, 592; separated from, 593; constitutions in, 22, 553–556; Third Republic, 556–559, 562; alliance with Russia, 565; legal system, 589–591, 631; parties in, 491, 573–576; presidency, 398, 562–571. *See also* the several institutions of government, *i.e.* Cabinet, Constitution.

France and Germany:
  administration compared, 608.
  reform movements, 595.
France and South America:
  cabinet system compared, 663, 666–669.
  progress, 658, 687.
France and Switzerland:
  democracy compared, 616.
  judiciary, 629.
  statutes, 625.
France and United States:
  interrelations, 552, 553.
  cabinets compared, 90.
  constitutions compared, 559–561, 591.
  executives compared, 57.
  judiciary compared, 591.
  legislatures compared, 565, 566.
  local governments compared, 568.
  party systems compared, 578. *See also* Argentina and France; England and France.
Franchise, restrictions on, in England, 482; extension of, 447, 507. *See also* Suffrage.
Francis II, emperor of Austria, titles, 595.
Frankfort, Constitution at, 596, 597.
Franking privilege, of Congressman, 226.
Franks, of German origin, 551.
Frederick, emperor of Germany, 606, 607.
Frederick William III, of Prussia, 595.
Frederick William IV, king of Prussia, 597, 598.
Free debate, restricted in House of Representatives, 165, 166.
Free Silver, in Democratic convention, 197.
Freedom of religion, guaranteed, 285.
Freedom of speech, guaranteed, 285.
Freeman, Edward A., *Growth of the English Constitution*, 404, 623; *Woman Conquest*, 420.
Freemasonry, in France, 579.
French, Burton L., cited, 159.
French, in Switzerland, 614.
French-Canadians, loyalty of, 694.
French Revolution, influence, 594, 595; effects of, 553–555, 561, 568, 579, 629; in Switzerland, 616.
Freund, Ernest, *The Police Power*, 330, 331, 339.

Gallia, under the Roman Empire, 551.
Gambling, State laws against, 337.

Gardiner, Samuel R., *Student's History of England*, 537.
Garfield, James A., uses no vetoes, 76.
General Staff, in American army, 103.
Geographical distribution, of U. S. cabinet, 86, 87.
Geological Survey, duties, 106, 107.
George I, king of England, 429, 430, 433, 519.
George II, king of England, 429, 430, 433.
George III, king of England, 445, 496; attempts to restore royal power, 430, 431, 433; rebellion against, 19, 553; uses no vetoes, 76.
George IV, relation to cabinet, 431.
George V, accession, 464; coronation oath, 489.
Georgia, defies Supreme Court, 257; in judicial circuit, 244.
Germans, in Chile, 670; in Switzerland, 614.
GERMANY:
  European power, 649; historical sketch, 592–599; confederation in, 689; federation, 616, 695, 696; invasion of France, 553; war with Denmark, 652; treaty with France, 556; empire formed, 602; governmental system, 3, 12, 482, 602–613; merchant marine, 650. *See also* Kaiser, Prussia, and the several institutions of government.
Germany and United States:
  administrations compared, 375.
  federation compared, 605.
  See also England and Germany; France and Germany.
Gerry, Elbridge, vice president, 150.
Gerrymandering, term defined, 149, 150.
Gettell, Raymond G., *Introduction to Political Science*, 28.
Gilman v. Philadelphia, cited, 8.
Gladstone, William E., prime minister, 436, 480, 507; cabinet of 1881, 507; civil service, 441; Home Rule policy, 469, 508, 538; party program, 509.
Goodnow, Frank J., *City Government in the United States*, 339; *Politics and Administration*, 189; *The Principles of the Administrative Law of the United States*, 30, 378.
Gorman, A. P., chairman of National Committee, 218.

Governors, in Chile, 669; in United States colonial period, 15, 34; State executive, 89, 99, 361, 363; duties, 362–368; prestige, 311; influence on legislation, 368–371.
Grant, U. S., suspensory power, 63; vetoes, 75, 76.
Great Seal, in State department, 99.
Greece, confederation in ancient, 689, 691; modern war with Bulgaria, 654.
Green, J. R., *History of the English People*, 413, 414, 420, 427; *Making of England*, 522; *Short History of the English People*, 418, 425, 522.
Grévy, Jules, French president, 558; resigns, 563.
Grisons, Swiss canton, 614.
Gully, W. C. (later Viscount Selby), Speaker of the House of Commons, 451.

Habeas Corpus Act, in Great Britain, 19, 409, 675.
Hague Conferences, on federation, 696.
Haines, Charles G., *The American Doctrine of Judicial Supremacy*, 280.
Hall, William E., *International Law*, 655.
Hamilton, Alexander, framer of Constitution, 282; in first cabinet, 85; as a party leader, 10, 180, 181, 186; cited, 39, 41, 74, 268, 269.
Hanna, Marcus, chairman of National Committee, 218.
Hapsburg, House of, 593; in Switzerland, 615.
Harrington, James, political philosopher, 20.
Harris, W., *Radical Party in Parliament*, 497.
Harrison, Benjamin, election of, 45; vetoes, 76.
Harrison, William H., uses no vetoes, 76.
Hart, Albert B., *Actual Government*, 21, 54, 115, 176.
Hartington, Spencer Compton Cavendish, marquis of, political leader, 480.
Hawaii, in nominating convention, 192; appeal from courts 263; on judicial circuit, 245.
Hayes, Rutherford B., election, 47; vetoes, 76.
Health. *See* Public health.
Hearn, William E., *Government of England*, 411, 477, 490.
Henry I, king of England, 405, 415, 416; issues charters, 416, 492.

Henry II, king of England, 405, 415, 417; influence on government, 517, 523, 535.
Henry III, and Magna Charta, 416, 421; influence on growth of government, 518.
Henry IV, a parliamentary king, 423.
Henry VII, absolutist tendencies, 425, 506, 518, 524.
Henry VIII, arbitrary tendencies, 424, 425, 447, 506, 518, 519, 524.
Henry, Patrick, cited, 291, 292.
Hesse, and the German empire, 602.
High Court of Justice, in England, divisions of, 530–532.
Highways. *See* Roads.
Hinds, Asher C., *Precedents*, 124, 148.
Hinsdale, Mary L., *A History of the President's Cabinet*, 82, 83, 95, 100.
Hohenzollern dynasty in Germany, 607.
Holdsworth, William S., *History of English Law*, 532.
Holland, a minor state, 649; colonial empire, 650; constitutional government in, 650, 651.
Holmes, Justice Oliver Wendell, cited, 332.
Holy Roman Empire, history of, 592–594.
Home department, secretary for, 436; controls police, 438, 439, 489; relation to Scotland, 535.
Home Rule for Ireland, 508, 539; a party issue, 469, 472, 474.
Home rule, in United States, in local affairs, 335, 336.
Homestead laws, value of, 106.
Hopkins, Senator Albert J., cited, 121.
HOUSE OF COMMONS:
In British empire, 419, 432; importance of, 410, 447; history, 404, 405, 429, 447; composition, 447–450, 483; dissolution, 449; new election for, 449–451; committee system, 452–454, 476; procedure, 452–458; relation to cabinet, 470, 471, 498, 499; to House of Lords, 462–465; to party system, 412; special functions, 476, 524. *See also* Parliament and Speaker.
House of Deputies, in Argentina, 677–679, 682.
HOUSE OF LORDS:
Origin, 404; history, 459, 463; described, 459, 460; composition of, 460, 461; life peers, 460, 525, 526; representative peers, 460, 534, 537; procedure, 461–463; judicial aspects,

405, 424, 463, 525, 530, 534, 537; relation to cabinet, 499; party sympathies, 496, 500; reform of, 479, 483, 501–503; relation to House of Commons, 447, 462–465.

HOUSE OF REPRESENTATIVES: Colonial prototypes, 16; elections for, 226; membership, 130, 147–151; procedure, 122, 158–176; rules, 122, 164–167; functions, 40, 61, 68, 137, 138, 141, 151–154, 306; leadership in, 173–175; term, 151–154; popular character, 145, 146; compared with Senate, 144, 145, 147. *See also* Congress and Speaker.

Howard, Burt E., *The German Empire*, 601, 603.

Hundred courts, in English judiciary, 523; relation to church, 516.

Hunt, William, *History of the English Church*, 522.

Idaho, on judicial circuit, 245.

Illinois, gerrymander in, 150; senator from, expelled, 120; on judicial circuit, 244; State senate of, 348.

Immigration cases, in federal courts, 265.

Impeachment, in Argentina, 578, 682; in England, 423; not used in Switzerland, 642; in United States, 55, 62, 63, 92, 234, 235; methods, 26, 29, 118, 140, 141, 175; in the several States, 347, 367, 368.

Imperial idea. *See* German Empire and Holy Roman Empire.

Implied powers and the United States Constitution, 6, 10, 269, 298–301.

Imports and Finance, Swiss department of, 623. *See also* Customs.

Income taxation, 101; federal law declared unconstitutional, 243, 278, 288; in Wisconsin, 342.

India, Victoria made Empress of, 484; imperial relations, 436, 437, 453; appeals from, 405; compared with Ireland, 538; future self-government, 549, 697.

Indian Affairs, in United States, commissioner for, 107.

Indiana, gerrymander in, 150; on judicial circuit, 244.

Indians, as national wards, 118; exempt from restriction, 309.

Industrial control, should be uniform, 359.

Industrial development, since the Civil War, 109, 111, 312; causes complexity, 373.

Inherent powers, of Argentine provinces, 673; of Swiss cantons, 618; of States in United States, 251, 262, 307, 308, 342, 379. *See also* Reserved powers.

Initiative, in Switzerland, 619, 626, 632, 643; in United States, 278, 354, 355, 358.

Injunctions, in federal courts, 279; improper use of, 383.

Insurance, in Australia, 685; in Germany, 605; Switzerland, 618; by State authority, 342, 358; supervision of 373.

Intendants, in Chile, 669.

Interior department, in Argentina, 676; in Chile, 665; in French cabinet, 566–569, 571; in Switzerland, 623; in United States, established, 97; duties, 105–108; investigated, 92; secretary's succession to presidency, 48.

Internal improvements, in Argentina, 684; in United States, 103.

Internal navigation, in federal jurisdiction, 253.

Internal revenue, collections of, 101; cases in federal courts, 265.

International law, importance of, 98; offenses against, regulated by Congress, 117; relation to small states, 654, 655.

Interpellation, in French legislature, 576, 577.

Interstate and Foreign Commerce Committee of House of Representatives, 159.

Interstate commerce, under federal control, 7, 8; regulated by Congress, 105, 117, 118, 299, 300; cases in federal courts, 265; conflict of jurisdiction on, 9; aid in centralization, 11.

Interstate Commerce Act of 1887, 109.

Interstate Commerce Commission, organized, 109, 110; duties, 110, 111, 300; importance of, 375.

Interstate Commerce Committee, in Senate, 133.

Intervention, in provincial affairs, in Argentina, 674–676.

Investigations, by Congress, 92.

Iowa, United States District Courts in, 246; on judicial circuit, 244.

Ireland, English rule in, 535–539; executive, 537; chief secretary for, 435;

INDEX

lord lieutenant, 436; relation to cabinet, 436; parliamentary representation, 448-450, 534, 537; representative peers, 460, 537; obstruction tactics, 457; land system, 536-538; judiciary, 524, 537, 582; Home Rule, 469, 472, 508, 539; relation to royal family, 484; church history, 521, 522, 536; government compared with India, 538.

Irish Nationalists, in Parliament, 472.

Irrigation, government aid to, in Argentina, 684; in United States, 106, 107.

Italians, in Switzerland, 614.

Italy, in Charlemagne's empire, 592; independent states in, 593; Roman law, 593; a European power, 649; parties in, 491; compared with South America, 658.

Jackson, Andrew, as president, 32; opposes nullification, 10; vetoes, 74-76.

Jacques, Léon, *Les Partis Politiques sous la IIIe République*, 573, 580.

James I, accession, 534, 536; illegal acts, 425.

James II, despotism of, 425, 426, 524; excluded from throne, 494, 519, 522; attempts to regain Crown, 536.

Japanese, refused United States citizenship, 325.

Jefferson, Thomas, in Washington's cabinet, 82, 85; a party leader, 10 180, 181, 186, 187; chosen president, 40, 286, 287; judiciary under, 235; uses no vetoes, 76; cited, 301, 553; *Manual of Parliamentary Practice*, 164.

John, king of England, 552; arbitrary acts, 416; signs Magna Charta, 423, 492, 517.

Johnson, Andrew, contest with Congress, 62, 225.

Joint Conferences, in United States Congress, 168, 169.

Jones, Chester Lloyd, *Election in the United States*, 189, 195, 201, 218; *Law Making in the United States*, 342, 344, 345, 360.

Judges, appointed by executive, 29, 55, 59, 234, 241, 367, 383, 384; elected, 383; life tenure of, 62; participate in impeachment trials, 368; recall of, 310, 358; terms, 233-235, 241.

Judicature Act of 1873 in England, 531.

Judicial Code of 1912, 236, 240, 244, 296.

JUDICIARY:

In Argentina, 679, 681-683.

In England, differentiated, 523-525; independence, 446, 524, 525; relation to Crown, 489; to Parliament, 406; divisions of, 527-532; compared with American, 398, 399.

In France, 554, 559, 560, 571, 577, 589-591.

In South Africa, 548.

In Switzerland, 619, 621, 625, 628-631, 634.

In United States, in colonial times, 16; federal, 104, 231-240, 250-265, 588, 589; relation to Congress, 117, 266-279, 295; sphere of action, 25, 26, 28, 29, 323, 331, 332; peculiar functions, 275, 276, 380, 384; in the States, 379-391.

Judiciary Act of 1789, in United States, 231, 236, 245, 296.

Judiciary Committee of House of Representatives, 158, 159; of Senate, 133.

Jurisdiction of Argentina federal courts, 682; of Swiss courts, 628; of United States federal courts, 232, 234, 236, 247, 248, 250-265; of State courts, 385, 386; transfer to federal courts, 385, 386.

Jury system, development of, 415; right of trial by, 8, 231, 285; functions, 247, 388, 389; criticized, 390.

Justice, French department of, 566, 567; United States department, 97, 103-105, 110, 112; relation to federal courts, 247. *See also* Attorney General.

Justice and Police, Swiss department of, 623.

Justice and Public Instruction department, in Argentina, 681; in Chile, 665.

Justices of the Peace, in England, 527-529; in Switzerland, 628; in United States, 381.

Justinian, Roman emperor, 592; codifies law, 584, 589.

Juvenile courts, duties, 382; in District of Columbia, 249.

Kaiser, origin of term, 593, 594, 602; office, 604; military powers, 605, 606; other powers, 482, 607-609. *See also* William I and II of Germany.

Kansas, on judicial circuit, 244.

INDEX

Kebbel, Thomas E., *History of Toryism*, 497.

Keith, Arthur B., *Responsible Government in the Dominions*, 549.

Kemble, John M., *Saxons in England*, 420.

Kent, James, cited, 271.

Kentucky, on judicial circuit, 244.

Kilkenny, smallest English constituency, 449.

King. *See* Crown.

King, Joseph, and Rafferty, F. W., *Our Electoral System*, 449.

King's Bench, court of, origin, 523, 524; functions, 530–532.

Knox v. Lee, cited, 275.

Knox, Philander C., secretary of state, 124.

Kruger, Paul, Kaiser's telegram to, 482.

Labor Committee, in House of Representatives, 159.

Labor department, in France, 567; in United States, 48, 97, 108, 109.

Labor disturbances, relation to injunctions, 279.

Labor legislation, in Argentina, 684; in Switzerland, 618, 621; in United States, 575.

Labor party, in England, 472, 515. *See also* Trades unionism.

LaFollette, Robert M., Wisconsin senator, 291.

Landlordism, in England, 483; in Ireland, 536.

Land Office, bureaus, 106; regulations, 57.

Lands, public in United States, under federal control, 118, 251, 259, 265, 309, 310; laws investigated, 97. *See also* Public domain.

Landsgemeinde, in Switzerland, 615, 623, 626.

Land system, and free government, 660, 661; in France, 554; in Ireland, 536–538; in New Zealand, 545.

Language, influence on history, 551.

Larned, Josephus N., *History for Ready Reference*, 599, 600.

Latin America, cited, 638.

La Union, Chilean town, 670.

Laurier, Sir Wilfred, Canadian premier, 694.

Law, Bonar, position on tariff question, 469.

Law, respect for, 104; enforcement, 56, 57, 337, 365; private under state control, 7. *See also* Common Law, Legislation, and Roman Law.

Learned, Henry Barrett, *The President's Cabinet*, 81, 95.

Lecky, W. E. H., *England in the Eighteenth Century*, 497.

Lee, Sir Sidney, *Queen Victoria*, 490.

Legal profession, cabinet members from, 89.

Legislation, movement for direct, 355.

Legislative power, in Switzerland, 626–628; in United States, 25, 26, 33; relation to executive, 27, 70–79. *See also* the several legislative bodies.

Legislative reference libraries, 353.

Legislatures, in France, 565, 566, 570, 572; in United States, colonial era, 15; relation to judiciary, 266–279; in the several States, 129, 131, 132, 340–360; influenced by governors, 368–371. *See also* the several legislative bodies.

Libel action, cannot be brought against Congressmen, 123.

LIBERAL PARTY:
In Canada, 541.
In England, 443, 486, 496; organization, 507–510, 514; relation to House of Lords, 460–461, 500, 501; to Home Rule, 469, 472; to Women's Suffrage, 470; to Labor party, 472; to education, 440, 441.
In Switzerland, 636, 637.

Liberal Unionist party, unites with Conservatives, 472.

Liberal Yearbook, cited, 457–459, 497, 509.

Liberty, essentials of, 24, 29; restrained by police power, 331.

License Cases, cited, 330.

Lieutenant Governor, functions, 349, 371.

Life peers. *See* House of Lords.

Life-saving service, in Treasury department, 102.

Limited powers, of federal government, 251, 270, 307; by constitutions, 342–344, 352; of Congress, 116, 117.

Lincoln, Abraham, nomination, 210; election, 45; chooses cabinet, 86; during the war, 32, 57, 58; vetoes, 76; on Dred Scott decision, 279; reverence for, 484; Gettysburg speech, 691.

INDEX

Liquor traffic, regulated in Switzerland, 621; in United States, 101, 337.
Lloyd, Henry D., *A Sovereign People*, 626.
Lloyd-George, David, English statesman, 443.
Loans, in care of Congress, 116. See also Finance.
LOCAL GOVERNMENT, teaches self-government, 658, 686; transmits governmental forms, 340, 341, 412.
In Chile, 669–671.
In England, 412–420, 436, 526, 529; compared with United States, 437, 438.
In France, 554, 568–571.
In United States, 4, 7, 313, 333–339, 690; dual functions, 336; compared with England, 437, 438.
Local Government Board, in England, 437, 438, 529.
Locke, John, political philosopher, 20.
Log-rolling, in nominating conventions, 202; in State legislatures, 383.
Lollards, rebellion of, 493.
London, representation in Parliament, 449; Bishop of, 460; police force, 438; Court of Appeals sits in, 531.
Long Parliament described, 424, 425, 524.
Lord Chancellor, of England, 437, 459, 489; position, 446; qualifications, 443; functions, 435, 461, 520, 525, 526, 530.
Lorimer, William, expelled from Congress, 120.
Louis XIV, aids Stuart monarchs, 426.
Louis Napoleon. See Napoleon III.
Louisiana, State constitutions, 344; legislature, 349; in election of 1876, 47; judges from, 61; Roman law in, 386, 582; on judicial circuit, 244.
Low, A. Maurice, *The Usurped Powers of the Senate*, 139.
Lowell, A. Lawrence, *Governments and Parties of Europe*, 557, 559, 561, 567, 569, 574, 575, 577, 602, 613, 617, 620; *Public Opinion and Popular Government*, 162; *The Government of England*, 136, 402, 413, 414, 420, 436, 438, 440, 441, 443, 446, 449, 451, 453, 461, 473, 477, 480, 487, 490, 497, 512, 520, 522, 530, 532, 535, 539.
Loyalists, as a political party, 179.
Lyons, local government, 569.

McCall, Samuel, *The Business of Congress*, 154, 176.

McCarthy, Charles R., *The Wisconsin Idea*, 360, 378.
McClain, Emlin, *Constitutional Law in the United States*, 123, 253, 280, 315, 318, 322, 324, 328.
McConachie, Lauros G., *Congressional Committees*, 176.
McCracken, W. D., *The Rise of the Swiss Republic*, 620; *Teutonic Switzerland*, 623.
Machine politics, in nominating conventions, 202.
McCulloch v. Maryland, cited, 6, 10, 298, 317.
McKinley, William, letter of acceptance, 216; vetoes, 76.
MacMahon M. E. P. M., president of France, 556, 557, 562; resigns, 558, 563.
Macy, Jesse, *Party Organization and Party Machinery*, 172, 189, 218, 230; *Political Parties in the United States*, 180, 185, 189; *The English Constitution*, 22, 29, 411, 435.
Madison, James, framer of Constitution, 282, 283, 284; uses term cabinet, 82; employs veto power, 76; cited, 23, 24, 178. See also *Federalist*.
Magna Charta, in English constitutional history, 399, 409, 415, 416, 421, 423, 492, 517, 585, 587, 645; United States heritage in, 19.
Maine, governor's council in, 384; on judicial circuit, 244.
Maitland, Frederick William, *Justice and Police*, 532.
Mann white slave act, 300.
Marbury v. Madison, cited, 269, 270, 272, 297.
Marine department, in Argentina, 681; in French cabinet. See also Navy.
Maritime jurisdiction, distinguished from admiralty, 254.
Marriage, need of uniform laws of, 358, 359.
Marriott, J. A. R., *English Political Institutions*, 532; *Second Chambers*, 581.
Marshall, Chief Justice John, decisions, 10, 12, 269, 270; cited, 271, 272.
Marshals, of United States Courts, 244, 245, 247.
Martial law, in riots, 365.
Mary II, accession, 519.
Maryland, taxes bank notes, 10; on judicial circuit, 244.

Massachusetts, colonial legislature, 15; executive in, 363, 384; on judicial circuit, 244; gerrymander in, 150.
Master of the Rolls, 531.
Matilda, queen of England, 517.
May, Thomas E., *Constitutional History of England*, 431, 434.
Mayors, of French communes, 566, 570; in Swiss communes, 622, 624, 625.
Medley, Dudley J., *English Constitutional History*, 411, 434, 477, 532.
Merchant Marine and Fisheries Committee, of House of Representatives, 159.
Merriam, C. Edward, *American Political Theories*, 30, 220; *Primary Elections*, 230.
Mexico, federal government in, 669.
Meyer, Ernest C., *Nominating Systems*, 189, 201, 202, 204.
Michigan, on judicial circuit, 244.
Mileage, allowed to Congressmen, 123, 127.
Military Affairs, Swiss department of, 623.
Military Affairs Committee, in House of Representatives, 159; in Senate, 133.
Military system, in Germany, 598, 599, 605, 606; in England and United States, 437. *See also* Army, and War department.
Militia, called out by governors, 365; officers, 55, 124; administration, 102.
Minimum wage laws, 358, 359; commission for, 374.
Ministerial responsibility. *See* Cabinet, and Responsibility.
Minnesota, State senate, 348; on judicial circuit, 244.
Minor v. *Happersett*, cited, 321.
Mississippi legislature, 349; gubernatorial election, 362; on judicial circuit, 244.
Missouri, restriction imposed on, 309; county courts in, 381; on judicial circuit, 244.
Model Parliament, summoned, 404, 412.
Monarchy, types of, 3, 478, 479; United States dreads, 5, 34, 35; democratic monarchy a new type, 478, 479, 482, 483; compared with presidency, 488. *See also* Crown.
Money bills. *See* Appropriations.
Monmouth, Duke of, succession, 494.

Monopolies, in Swiss government, 618, 621. *See also* Corporations.
Monroe Doctrine, 691.
Montana, on judicial circuit, 245.
Montesquieu, Charles de Secondat baron de la, political philosopher, 20, 26; influence of, 553; *Spirit of the Laws*, 25.
Montfort, Simon de, place in parliamentary history, 404, 416.
Moon, Reuben O., *The Reorganization of the Federal System*, 238.
Moore, William H., *New Australian Commonwealth*, 549.
Morley, John, *Life of Gladstone*, 480, 539.
Mormons, in Congress, 120, 121.
Morris, Governeur, in Constitutional Convention, 267.
Moses, Bernard, *The Federal Government of Switzerland*, 617, 620.
Mothers' pensions, advocated, 358.
Municipal Councils Act (1835), 529.
Municipal courts, functions, 382.
Municipalities, in Chile, 670; in England, 420, 496, 529; in United States, 229, 334-336; public ownership in, 358; in Europe in general, 334, 335.
Munro, William B., *The Government of American Cities*, 339; *The Government of European Cities*, 550, 571.
Mutiny Act, in English Parliament, 426.

Napoleon I, assumes imperial power, 595; as French emperor, 553-555; institutional measures, 565, 568.
Napoleon III, in France, 556; conquered, 399.
National Assembly in France, elects president, 557, 562; amends constitution, 559.
National Committee, in United States party politics, 191-197, 225, 226; appointment, 199; authority, 196, 197, 207, 212; composition, 206, 207; officials, 208, 209, 213; duties, 207-210, 212-216; permanency, 205, 211, 216-218.
National Convention. *See* Nominating Convention.
National Council, in Switzerland, 621, 625, 641, 644; described, 627, 628.
National Liberal Federation, in England, 507-510, 513.
National Liberal party, in Germany, 610-612.

744 INDEX

National Republican party, in United States, nominating convention of, 191.
Nationalism, in United States, increased power of, 310–314. *See also* Centralization.
Nationalists in England. *See* Irish Nationalists.
Naturalization, under federal control, 117, 324, 325.
Naval Affairs Committee, in House of Representatives, 159.
Navy, in England, represented in cabinet, 436; in United States, under federal control, 7, 55–57, 117. *See also* Marine department.
Navy department, in United States, established, 97; duties, 102, 103; secretary's succession to presidency, 48.
Nebraska, restriction imposed on, 309; impeachment trials, 368; on judicial circuit, 244.
Negroes, protection for, 319, 328; acquire citizenship, 323, 325. *See also* Slavery.
Nevada, population, 284; restriction imposed on, 309; on judicial circuit, 245.
Newcastle Program, in English politics, 509.
New England Confederation of 1643, 690; constitutions of States, 345; judges in, 383. *See also* the several States.
New Hampshire, on judicial circuit, 244; judges in, 384.
New Jersey, State senate, 348; gubernatorial term, 363; on judicial circuit, 244.
New Mexico, State constitution, 345; gubernatorial term, 363.
New York City, customs officers, 101.
New York County, party organization, 223.
New York State, population, 284; State senate, 348; chief justice, 384; courts in, 244, 245; codifies law, 388; impeachment in, 367, 368; importance in presidential campaign, 46; represented in cabinet, 87; congressmen, 124; local rights, 696.
New Zealand, relation to Crown, 485; Constitution, 544, 545; governmental institutions, 544, 545.

Nobility, titles forbidden, in United States, 8.
Noble State Bank v. *Haskell*, cited, 332.
Nominating agencies, 187–189; systems changing, 49, 50, 357.
Nominating Convention, in United States, 43, 49, 505; described, 190–203; temporary, 205; arrangements for, 209, 210; in States, 221; in counties, 223.
Norman Conquest of England, 404, 412, 516; dynasty, 479, 492, 551, 552.
North, Frederick, Lord, advises George III, 431.
North American Act (1868), 540, 545.
North Carolina, and veto power, 370; governor's council in, 384; on judicial circuit, 244.
North Dakota, on judicial circuit, 245.
Norway, a democratic monarchy, 479, 649; merchant marine, 650; church and state in, 496; democracy of, 651, 652.
Notification, of presidential nomination, 199, 200.
Nullification, in South Carolina.
Nullifying power. *See* Judiciary and Supreme Court.

Oaths, importance of, 271.
Office holding. *See* Appointments, Civil service, and Removals.
Ogg, F. A., *Governments of Europe*, 402, 413, 420, 434, 436, 453, 458, 477, 490, 515, 532, 553, 561, 569, 601, 613, 615, 620, 655.
Ohio, restrictions on, 309; on judicial circuit, 244.
Ohio and Mississippi R. R. Company v. *Wheeler*, cited, 259.
Oil carriers, regulations for, 110.
Oklahoma, State constitution, 345; gubernatorial term, 363; on judicial circuit, 245.
Oppenheim, L., *International Law*, 655.
Opposition, party in England, 458, 467, 468; organization, 471; in Parliament, 400, 401, 408, 473, 474; in United States, 171–174.
Orangemen, in Ireland, 522.
Oratory, in nominating conventions, 199.
Ordainers, in reign of Edward II, 423.
Orders in council, authority of, 422.
Ordinance power of president, 56; of cabinet officers, 94, 95.

INDEX

Oregon, in election of 1876, 47; recall of officials, 368; on judicial circuit, 245.

Orleanists, French dynasty, 553, 555, 558.

Osorno, Chilean town, 670.

Ostrogorski, M., *Democracy and the Organization of Political Parties*, 189, 201, 204, 218, 230, 515.

Ottoman Empire. See Turkish.

Panama Canal, constructed, 103.

Paper duties bill (1860), 463.

Parcels post, establishment of, 108.

Pardoning power, in France, 565; in United States, 55, 63, 64; applications for, 105; in the several States, 365, 366; board for, 366.

Paris, Louis Philippe Albert d'Orleans, count of, pretender to French throne, 558.

Paris, Charlemagne's capital, 592; local government of, 569; party organization, 578.

Parish, use of term, 517.

Parish Councils Act (1894), 528.

Parke, Sir James, a life peer, 460.

PARLIAMENT:
Origin of term, 405; history of, 423–434, 552; influence, 19; supremacy, 405, 406; relation to Crown, 488, 489; speech from the throne, 451, 454, 466, 472, 473, 489, 498; relation to Prime Minister, 442, 443; relation to Cabinet, 439; relation to English church, 520; relation to judiciary, 266, 525; has no share in treaty-making, 482; controls local government, 529; controls taxation, 426; money bills, 456; bills classified, 454–457; government bills, 454–456, 467; discussion, 455–458; closure, 457; vote of censure, 472, 473; joint committees, 454; length of session, 451; privileges, 123; party system in, 495, 498–504; whips, 474–476, 499, 513; relation to administration, 526; departmental secretaries, 439, 440. See also Cabinet, House of Commons, House of Lords.

Parliament Act of 1911, 452, 463, 464, 501.

Parliamentary type of government. See Cabinet.

Parnell, Charles, parliamentary leader, 472.

Parole of prisoners, 366.

PARTY POLITICS:
In Canada, 541.

In England, 408, 412, 466, 468–470, 494, 495, 502, 503, 506, 507; defined, 491; history of, 491–496; relation to Crown, 480–482, 487, 488; to Cabinet, 400, 401, 439; to religious bodies, 418, 419, 493, 494, 500; machinery for, 467–477, 498–504; 511–515; whips, 512–514; districts, 450; leaders, 442, 443. See also the several parties, Conservative, Liberal, Whig, etc.

In France, 572–579.

In Germany, 610–613.

In Switzerland, 635, 636.

In United States, 29, 30, 303, 304; relation to executive, 32, 35, 38, 40, 42, 43, 45, 46, 48, 59, 70, 78, 84, 86, 87; and the appointing power, 58, 60–62; relation to Senate, 129, 132, 133; to House of Representatives, 157, 171–174; to the judiciary, 277–279, 383; in the States, 219–229, 350, 351, 357, 369–371; machinery for, 177–190, 201, 202, 205–218; control of, 229, 230; in contested elections, 120; caucus, 134–136; system criticized, 229, 230; dynamic conditions, 281, 302.

Passports, from state department, 98.

Patent office, in Interior department, 57, 107.

Patents, regulated by Congress, 117; commissioner of, 249; cases in federal courts, 261, 264, 265.

Patriotism, in federal governments, 693, 694. See also the several nations.

Patronage, in England, 440; in United States, 61, 217, 218, 225; in post offices, 108; in States, 219, 369. See also Appointments, and Civil service.

Paul v. Virginia, cited, 376.

Pennington, A. Stuart, *The Argentine Republic*, 675, 688.

Pennsylvania, colonial legislature, 15; senator from, 124; on judicial circuit, 244; judges in, 384.

Pension Office, administration of, 57, 107.

Personal rights in State courts, 379.

Petition of Right, source of English constitution, 409.

Petty sessions, courts of, 527, 528.

Philadelphia, customs officers, 101.

Phillip Augustus, king of France, 552.

Philippine Islands, engineering in, 103; represented in nominating convention, 192; appeals from, 263; self-government for, 697.
Pierce, Franklin, vetoes, 76.
Pigeonholing, of legislative proposals, 160.
Pike, Luke Owen, *Constitutional History of the House of Lords*, 458.
Pinckney, Charles, in Constitutional Convention, 81.
Pipe lines, regulations for, 110.
Piracy, crime against federal laws, 117.
Pitt, William, in the House of Commons, 430, 433.
Pitt, William, the younger, as a party leader, 495, 496; ministry of, 431, 433.
Plantagenets, dynasty of, 479, 552.
Platform, adopted by nominating convention, 191, 197, 198, 205; manipulations in framing, 202; relation to Congressional Committee, 228.
Po River, headwaters, 614.
Pocket veto, discussed, 77.
Poincaré, Raymond, French president, 559; *How France is Governed*, 559, 561, 564, 569, 571, 590.
Police power, in United States Constitution, 329-333.
Police system, in England, 438.
Political philosophy, influence of, 20, 553.
Political Science Quarterly, cited, 220, 230, 268, 328.
Polk, James K., responsibility for Mexican War, 65; vetoes, 76.
Polygamy, abolition of, 309. *See also* Mormons.
Pomeroy, John N., *Constitutional Law*, 67.
Pondra and Pierre, *Traité pratique de droit parliamentaire*, 581.
Poole, Reginald L., *Exchequer in Twelfth Century*, 532.
Poor Law Act (1834), 528.
Pope, crowns Charlemagne, 592; relation to English church, 517.
Popular will, source of free government, 3, 23, 24; in United States, 12; relation to presidency, 49, 50, 70, 76, 78, 88, 203; to State legislatures, 343, 351, 352, 354, 357; to State governors, 362, 363, 370. *See also* Public opinion.
Population, in United States, representation based on, 128, 130, 146, 149; growth of, 147.

Porter, Robert P., *The Ten Republics* 688.
Porto Rico, in nominating convention, 192; appeals from, 263.
Portugal, a minor state, 649; colonial empire, 650; becomes a republic, 650.
Postal system, in Germany, 606; in United States, 7, 117; laws for, 56, 265.
Postmaster-General, in England, 436; in United States, 48, 97.
Post Office and Post Roads Committee, in House of Representatives, 159.
Post Office department, in United States, 95, 97, 108.
Posts and Railways, Swiss department, 623.
Prætor, Roman administrative office, 584.
Prayer book of 1549, 520; of 1661, 520.
Prefects, in French administration, 566, 568-571.
Prerogative, theory of royal, 422, 423; defeated, 432.
Presbyterians, settled in Ireland, 536; in Scotland, 521.
PRESIDENT:
In Argentina, 675, 676, 678-682; powers, 683.
In Chile, 664-666, 668-670.
In France, 556, 557, 563; term, 562; powers, 537, 558, 563-565, 570; ordinance power, 566.
In Switzerland, 624, 625, 640; salary, 634.
In United States, prototype, 15; methods of choosing, 14; nomination methods, 190, 194; election, 38-53, 286, 304, 305; eligibility, 50; term, 50, 51; salary, 52; national executive, 26, 99, 346; functions and powers, 31-37, 55-64, 102; veto power, 29, 73-77, 90, 169, 170; guides foreign relations, 64-69; relations to Cabinet, 82-84, 86, 88, 89, 98; to Senate, 88, 138-140; to legislation, 70-79, 93, 94, 118, 175; messages, 71, 72, 306; assent to bills, 169; proclamation, 99; relation to his party, 27, 84, 85, 225; subject to impeachment, 141; responsibility of, 35, 36, 397; relation to popular will, 49, 50, 70, 76, 78, 88, 203; monarchical tendencies, 401; criticism of, 36, 37.
Presidential type of government, 444-505, 639, 663, 668, 687; compared with

Cabinet type, 395–397, 444–446, 505, 506; compared with monarchical type, 488.

Presidential Succession Law, 48.

Press, influence in England, 437; in France, 579; in United States, 215; freedom of, 285.

Primaries, in Prussia, 597; in United States, direct, 192–194, 203, 209, 288, 289; for presidential nomination, 49, 50, 194, 203; criticized, 203, 204; in local nominations, 221, 223.

Prime Minister, in England, 31, 512; creation of office, 429; influence, 442, 443, 466; represents party, 480; popular choice of, 466; relation to Cabinet, 395, 436, 437, 476; to House of Commons, 499; to Church of England, 520; resignation, 436. In France, 563, 564, 567, 575.

Prince consort, prevents war with United States, 482.

Prisons, supervision of, 105.

Private law, in State courts, 379.

Privy Council, beginnings of, 423, 424, 524; composition and functions, 435; judicial functions, 16, 405, 520, 526, 530; veto power, 692; relation to Cabinet, 424, 429; decline of importance, 427–429; lord president, 435.

Privy Seal, lord, position of, 436.

Probate and Divorce, English court of, 530–532.

Progressive party, organized, 209; position on amendments, 290.

Prohibitions, established by Constitution, 8.

Proportional Representation, in Switzerland, 637; on United States senatorial committee, 134.

Property and police power, 331, 332; in State courts, 379.

Protection by tariff, 299.

Protestantism, in England, 518, 519, 552; in Germany, 594. *See also* Church.

Provinces in Argentina, 672–675, 677, 679, 682, 683, 684; in Canada, 691, 692.

Provisions of Oxford, and English constitution, 399, 423, 518.

Prussia, rise of, 594; reform in, 595; Napoleon's relation to, 595, 596; reaction in, 596, 606; constitution granted, 597; king becomes German emperor, 695; relation to Empire, 599, 602–608, 695, 696; opposed by its people, 601. *See also* Germany.

Public debt, administration of, 112. *See also* Finance.

Public domain, in New Zealand, 545; in United States, 106, 373. *See also* Lands.

Public health, in Chile, 670; in United States, 102, 374.

Public hearings, at committee meetings, 161, 162.

Public Instruction, Superintendent of, 373. *See also* Education.

Public Instruction department, in French cabinet, 567.

Public opinion, in free government, 659, 664; influence of, 78, 122, 125, 162, 370; control of, 30, 31. *See also* Popular will.

Public Utilities, control, in Switzerland, 621; in United States, 358; supervision of, 374; state ownership of, 358.

Public Welfare, promoted by police power, 330, 331, 332.

Public Works department, in Argentina, 681; in France, 567.

Publicity, value of, 136; in election campaigns, 214, 215; for committee meetings, 161.

Punic War, in Roman times, 585.

Puritans, rise of, 494; settle in Ireland, 536; a political party, 519.

Quarantine, under police power, 329.

Quarter Sessions, court of, 417, 420, 527, 528.

Quesada, Ernesto, cited, 684–686.

Racial unity and free governments, 659, 660.

RADICAL PARTY:
In England. *See* Liberal party.
In France, 573.
In Switzerland, 636, 637.
See also Social Democrats and Socialists.

Railways, in Argentina, 684, 685; in United States, effect on centralization, 11, 312; on interstate commerce, 299, 300; federal regulation, 109–111; strike on, 57; public ownership of, 635.

Randolph, John, uses term cabinet, 82.

Rates, of public carriers, regulated, 110.

Ray, P. Osman, *An Introduction to Political Parties and Practical Politics*, 195, 204, 216, 218, 230, 360.

Rebates, granted by railways, 109; prohibited, 110.

Recall, of public officers, 358, 368.

Reclamation Service, in Interior Department, 106.

Recorders, duties of, 529.

Redlich, Josef, *Procedure of the House of Commons*, 458.

Reed, Thomas B., speaker, 165, 166.

Referendum, proposed in England, 502; in Switzerland, 619, 626, 632; in United States, 278, 354, 355, 358. *See also* Initiative.

Reform Act of 1832, 479; results of, 432, 433; of 1834, 496.

Reformation, effect on Germany, 594; does not entail disestablishment, 518.

Registration, for suffrage, 224; falsified, 229.

Reichstag, in Germany, 696; composition, 603, 609; powers, 609, 610, 612; parties in, 610–613.

Reinsch, Paul S., *American Legislatures and Legislative Methods*, 144, 150, 176, 357, 360: "Parliamentary Government in Chile," 667, 688; *Readings on American Federal Government*, 66, 80, 115, 117, 118, 144, 176, 280; *On American State Governments*, 360, 379, 389, 391.

Religious bodies in England, relation to parties, 418, 419; economic relations, 493; relations to Constitution, 516–522. *See also* Church.

Religious freedom, in United States, 8.

Religious revivals in England, 493.

Removals, in Chile, 669; in United States, 62, 63, 83; from civil service, 113; from State offices, 368. *See also* Civil service and Spoils system.

Representation, in English Parliament, 448, 449; in United States, 24; theory of, 125, 126; unit of, 147; in State central committee, 220.

Republic, term defined, 23, 24; in France, 3, 556–559, 562; in United States, 1–15, 23–30. *See also* South America.

Republican party, elements, 86; principles, 185; gerrymander, 150; contest with Johnson, 225; in nominating conventions, 192, 193, 195, 197; special conventions, 208, 210, 211; in election campaign, 215, 218; on congressional committee, 226, 227; insurgency among, 228.

Reserved powers, of States, in United States, 6, 7, 333. *See also* Inherent powers.

RESPONSIBILITY:
In presidential system, 27, 35, 36, 639, 640; in cabinet system, 82, 83, 89, 90.
In Argentina, 681.
In Chile, 665, 666.
In England, 422, 438, 439, 467.
In England and Switzerland, compared, 639–641.
In France, 556, 558, 560, 562–564, 566–573, 576.
In Prussia, 599, 600.
In Switzerland, 639–641.
In United States, 35, 36, 397.

Revenue. *See* Customs and Internal revenue.

Revolution of 1688, in England, 427, 478, 552.

Revolution of 1830, in Switzerland, 615.

Revolution of 1848, in Europe, 596, 597, 612; in Switzerland, 615.

Revolution, in France. *See* French Revolution.

Rhine River, headwaters, 614.

Rhode Island, colonial legislature, 15; merges into State, 16, 17; legislative salaries, 349; rights of, 696; judges in, 383, 384; on judicial circuit, 244.

Rhone River, head waters, 614.

Richard II, king of England, 423.

Richman, Julia, *Citizenship of the United States*, 328.

Riksdag, in Sweden, 652.

Riots, executive action against, 57, 365.

Rivers and Harbors Committee, of House of Representatives, 159.

Roads, in Swiss government, 618; in United States, 358, 374.

Robert, Duke of Normandy, 415.

Roberts, Brigham H., representative from Utah, 120.

Roman Empire, component parts, 551; growth, 583; citizenship in, 584, 585; corruption in, 649, 653.

ROMAN LAW:
Origin of, 583, 584; growth, 592–594, 605, 649; compared with Common Law, 585–588.

ROMAN LAW — *Continued*.
Influence on modern governments, 386, 582–591, 687; countries using, 375.
In France, 551, 589–591, 595, 629, 631.
In Switzerland, 625, 629.
Romansch language, in Switzerland, 614.
Rome, conquered by Charlemagne, 592, 593; while a small state, 649.
Romford, largest English constituency, 449.
Roosevelt, Theodore, messages, 72; vetoes, 76; cabinet, 87; candidate for third term, 51.
Rosebery, Archibald, *Lord Randolph Churchill*, 515.
Ross, Edward A., *South of Panama*, 659, 660, 670, 684, 686, 688.
Roundheads, precursors of Whigs, 494.
Rousseau, Jean Jacques, political philosopher, 20, 553.
Rousseau, Waldeck, French leader, 573.
Royal family, in England, 482, 486–488. *See also* Crown.
Royalists, in France, 556–559, 563, 573, 578, 580.
Rules, of nominating conventions, 197; of House of Representatives, 122, 164–167; of State legislatures, 350–352.
Rules Committee, in House of Representatives, 157, 159.
Russia, French alliance with, 565; war with Turkey, 654; constitutional change in, 478; a European power, 649.

St. Bartholomew, massacre of, 552.
"Salary grab," in 1873, 122.
Salisbury, Robert A. T. Gascoyne Cecil, marquis of, leader of Conservatives, 436, 442.
Santiago, Chilian capital, 670.
Savoy, causes trouble between France and Switzerland, 635.
Saxons, invade England, 412, 551; kings, 479. *See also* Anglo-Saxons.
Saxony, and the German Empire, 602.
Schleswig-Holstein, taken from Denmark, 598, 652.
Schwytz, Swiss canton, 615.
Scotland, history, 494, 521, 522, 534; relations to English government, 534, 535, 539; parliamentary representation, 448, 450, 534, 535; peers, 534; secretary for, 436; bills, 455; judiciary, 534, 582; appeals, 530; lord advocate, 535.
Scrutin de liste, in France, 557, 570.
Secession, right of, 11.
Second chamber, types of, 501, 502. *See also* Bicameral legislatures.
Secretaries. *See* the several departments.
Sectional interests, in U. S., 87, 129, 130.
Seignobos, Charles, *A Political History of Contemporary Europe*, 478, 561, 580, 596, 598, 613, 620, 655.
Selby, Viscount. *See* Gully.
SENATE:
In Argentina, 677–679, 682.
In French Republic, 556–559, 570; described, 567, 577, 578; ministerial access to, 567; judicial function, 577, 578.
In United States, prototype, 16; mixed powers, 26; coördinate with president, 88, 137, 138; confirms appointments, 59–62, 112, 305, 306; consents to removals, 63; treaty-making power, 34, 35, 60, 64, 66–69, 138–140; counts electoral votes, 40, 45; relation to Cabinet, 83; composition, 127, 284; organization, 118, 130, 132–134; rules, 122; freedom of debate, 136, 137, 142, 166; president, 52; original function, 128, 130, 138; right of amendment, 168, 170; importance, 141–144, 175, 311.
In States of United States, 367, 368, 371.
Senatorial courtesy, in appointments, 139, 140; described, 60, 61.
Senators, qualifications, 127; election, 119, 125, 131, 219, 284, 288, 289; former election method, 130, 131, 137; in Cabinet, 87, 88; on committee, 227; influence and prestige, 137, 142, 143, 311; expulsion of, 120, 121.
Seniority rule in Senate committees, 133; in House committees, 154.
Separation of powers, theory, 56, 234, 245, 555.
In England, 523.
In United States Constitution, 24–26, 117, 396, 398, 399, 444–446, 477; why established, 526, 527; relation to parties, 181–183; exceptions to, 127; criticism of, 27, 626, 627; in State governments, 369.

Serfs, emancipation of, 599.
Servia, war with Bulgaria, 654.
Seward, William H., candidate for nomination, 210.
Shadow Cabinet, place in constitutional system, 432, 433; changes to Cabinet, 437.
Shaftsbury, Anthony Ashley Cooper, earl of, 494.
Shaw, Albert, *Municipal Government in Continental Europe*, 571.
Shepherd, William R., *Latin America*, 683, 688.
Sherman law of 1890, 300, 301.
Ship money, illegal tax, 424.
Slaughter House Cases, cited, 327.
Slave trade, organizations to abolish, 506.
Slavery, controversy over, 11; compromise in Constitution, 283; abolition, 37, 287, 319, 328.
Slavs, in Austria, 594.
Smith, J. Allen, *The Spirit of American Government*, 30, 189, 280, 291, 293, 294.
Smoot, Reed, Utah Senator, 120, 211.
Smuggling, defined, 101.
Social control of property, 331, 332.
Social Democrats, in Germany, 600, 611, 612; in Switzerland, 636, 637.
Social welfare legislation, in Argentina, 684; in United States, 358, 359.
Socialists, in Argentina, 683, 684; in France, 573, 579, 637; in Germany, 610–612, 637; in Italy, 637; in Switzerland, 636–638.
Sohm, Rudolph, *Institutes of Roman Law*, 583, 585, 591, 601.
Solicitor-General, duties, 104, 105.
South Africa, forms federal union, 547, 548, 692, 693; relation to Crown, 485. *See also* Australia and South Africa; Canada and South Africa.
South America, federal experiments in, 656–658; retardation, 658–661; progress, 661, 662; departure from constitutional forms, 682; system of law, 582. *See also* Argentina, and Chile.
South Carolina, State constitutions, 344; impeachment offenses, 368; nullification in, 10; judges, 383; on judicial circuit, 244; in election of 1876, 47.
South Dakota, on judicial circuit, 245.
Sovereignty, in federal government, 3, 6; under Constitution, 308, 309, 315; divided, 4, 330.
Spain, a minor state, 649; recent developments in, 650; South American relations, 658, 661, 672.
SPEAKER:
In House of Commons, 155, 451, 452.
In House of Representatives, 165, 168, 169; choice of, 153, 154, 173; party alliance, 171; influence, 147, 154–157, 174, 304, 305.
In State legislatures, 350.
Spoils system, in Switzerland, 634, 635; in United States, 113, 114. *See also* Civil service.
Squiarchy, meaning of term, 528.
"Stalwarts," control congressional committee, 228.
Stanwood, Edward, *A History of the Presidency*, 54.
Star Chamber, in English judiciary, 425, 524.
State Central Committee, discussed, 220–222.
State department, in president's cabinet, 65, 89; established, 97; duties, 97–99, 169, 255; secretary of, 48, 65; in several States, 372. *See also* Foreign Affairs.
State of siege, in Argentina, 675, 676, 681.
Staten Island, in Argentina, 676.
STATES:
In Australia, 692.
In United States, emerge from colonies, 16; independence of, 13; rights, 5–7, 9–11, 322; inherent powers, 251, 262, 307, 308, 342, 379; equal senatorial representation, 128, 129; centralization weakens prestige, 11, 310–314, 318; later states artificial, 130; choose presidential electors, 40, 44; vote for president, 45–47; regulate suffrage, 120, 148, 319–322; regulate citizenship, 322–328; regulate elections, 338; congressional districting in, 149, 151; administration in, 377; legislature, 285, 340–360; interpreted by courts, 272, 273; judiciary of, 379–391; criticized, 273, 277; relation to federal judiciary, 257, 258, 260, 263; police power, 329–333; control local government, 333–339; interrelations, 314–316, 321; relation to federal government, 5–7, 307–310, 316–318; decline of prestige, 310–314.
Statesman's Yearbook, cited, 460.
Statutory law, in State courts, 387.

INDEX

Stearns v. *Minnesota*, cited, 310.
Stein, Heinrich Friedrich Karl, baron von, reforms in Germany, 595.
Stephen, influence of church in reign of, 517.
Strict Construction. *See* Constitution: United States.
Strike of railway employees, 57.
Stuarts, English dynasty, 479, 552. *See also* James I, Charles I, Charles II, and James II.
Stubbs, William, *Constitutional History of England*, 412, 414, 420, 421, 424.
Sturges v. *Crowninshield*, cited, 8.
Subcommittees, in legislative work, 159.
Subdelegates, in Chile, 669.
Subprefects, in French administrative system, 568.

SUFFRAGE:
In England, 496.
In France, 554, 557, 568, 569.
In Germany, 616. *See also* Prussia, below.
In Norway, 651.
In Prussia, 597, 599, 605, 612.
In Switzerland, 624, 627.
In United States, 120, 148, 309, 319–328. *See also* Woman's suffrage.

Superior Courts, in States, 382.

SUPREME COURT:
In Argentina, 679, 681–683.
Of Judicature in England, 530, 531.
In United States, established by Constitution, 231, 233, 236, 250; the ultimate authority, 11; interprets the Constitution, 12, 23, 27, 116, 262, 263, 266, 268, 296–298, 300–302; nullifies legislation, 64, 68, 69, 245, 266–270, 276, 278; establishment, 231, 233, 236, 241, 295; changes in, 238–240; procedure, 241–244; original jurisdiction, 254–256, 260, 261; judges, 55, 59, 61; rules, 273–275; appeals to, 111, 248, 262–264; decisions cited, 105, 258, 288, 309, 310, 314, 317, 322, 323, 326, 329, 330; relation to Congress, 117, 260, 261; upholds federal power, 6, 10, 300, 301; criticism of, 237, 244, 271–273, 276, 277, 279, 301, 302; respect for, 244. Of the several States, 381–385.

Sweden, a minor state, 649; government, 651–653.

SWITZERLAND:
A minor state, 649; formerly a confederation, 689; a federal government, 12; Constitution, 545, 614–619, 627; early history, 614–619; federal institutions, 621–631; democracy, 614–616, 628–632, 639, 644; parties, 491, 635–638; patriotism, 483, 484; church policy, 496; direct legislation, 355, 619, 626, 632, 643; public service, 486, 487.

Switzerland and United States:
democracy compared, 616–619, 629–645.
judiciary compared, 630, 631.
legislatures compared, 641–643.
presidency compared, 624, 639, 640.
separation of powers compared, 626, 627, 629.
See also England and Switzerland; France and Switzerland.

Syndicalism, in France, 579.

"Tacking," a parliamentary device, 463.
Taft, William Howard, cabinet, 124; vetoes, 76; cited, 389.
Tariff, for protection, 299; a party issue, 469; in Congress, 10, 135; of 1913, 73; interpreted by courts, 248, 265.

TAXATION:
In Argentina, 678.
In Chile, 670.
In England, 426.
In France, 569.
In Germany, 605.
In United States, under federal control, 7, 9, 317, 318; controlled by Congress, 116, 137; must be uniform, 117; reform, 358; collection of, 337, 338; supervision of, 374; and Supreme Court, 288. *See also* Finance and Income taxation.

Tax Commission, centralizes supervision, 338.
Taylor, Zachary, uses no vetoes, 76.
Temple, Rt. Hon. Sir Richard, *Life in Parliament*, 458.
Temple, Sir William, English statesman, 399.
Temporary chairman, of National Convention, 195, 211.
Tennessee, senator from, 141; on judicial circuit, 244.
Tenure of Office Act, 62.
Territories, under control of Congress, 118, 258, 310.
Texas, on judicial circuit, 244; United States courts in, 245; legislative salaries, 349; local rights, 696.

Teutonic tribes, invasions, 551; conquer Roman Empire, 592. *See also* Germany and Germans.
Tiedeman, C. G., *The Unwritten Constitution of the United States*, 306.
Tierra del Fuego, in Argentina, 676.
Thiers, Adolphe, president of France, 556, 562.
Third term for President, 51.
Thirty-nine Articles, in English church, 520.
Thirty Years' War, in Germany, 594.
Thomas, David Y., "Law of Impeachment in the United States," 141.
Tilden, Samuel, defeat, 47.
Tobacco, tax on, 101.
Todd, Alpheas, *Parliamentary Government in England*, 458; *Parliamentary Government in British Colonies*, 549.
Toleration, in Switzerland, 614.
Tory party in England, 179, 428, 443, 428, 506; origin of term, 494; composition of, 419, 495, 496; and cabinet system, 431; democracy of, 473; local government policy, 420. *See also* Conservative party.
Tout, Thomas F., *Political History of England*, 539.
Trade, Board of, in England, 435. *See also* Commerce and Interstate commerce.
Trades unionism in France, 579. *See also* Labor.
Tradesmarks, under federal jurisdiction, 265.
Transportation, in Australia, 685. *See also* Interstate commerce and Railways.
Treason, punishment for, 231.
Treasurer, lord high, in England, 436; in States of United States, 371, 372, 397.
TREASURY:
  In England, 441, 499; first lord of, 436, 437, 443.
  In United States, secretary, 48; department, 95, 97, 99–102.
TREATIES:
  Franco-German (1871), 556.
  Spanish-American (1898), 124.
  Westphalia (1648), 594.
TREATY-MAKING:
  In Argentina, 682.
  In England, 482.
  In France, 565.
  In Germany, 607.
  In Switzerland, 642.
  In United States, 34, 55, 64–68, 91, 98; confirmation by Senate, 34, 35, 60, 64, 67, 138–140; custodianship, 99; obligations of, 56, 69; enforcement, 251, 252; rights arising from, 233; naturalization regulated by, 325; interpreted by Supreme Court, 262.
Trevelyan, G. M., *England in the Time of Wycliffe*, 522; *England in the Age of Walpole*, 515; *England under the Stuarts*, 522.
Tricolor, in France, 563.
Trimmers, English party, 428.
Trust cases, in federal courts, 265.
Trusts. *See* Corporations.
Tudor dynasty, in England, 413, 479, 484, 492.
Turkish empire, dismembered, 649, 653; despotism in, 653; war with Russia, 654.
Turner, H. G., *First Decade of the Australian Commonwealth*, 547, 549.
Tyler, John, vetoes, 76.

Unanimous verdict, in jury trials, 389.
Underwood-Simmons tariff bill, 135.
Unicameral legislature, proposed, 354, 355.
Uniformity, tendency to, in State legislation, 340–342, 358, 359.
Union of South Africa, *see* South Africa.
Unit rule in German Bundesrath, 602; in Democratic nominating convention, 193, 199.
UNITED STATES:
  Colonial period, 15, 16, 25, 26, 34, 179, 341, 343, 690; severed from England, 3, 431; not a confederation, 11; federal government, 3, 4, 23, 24, 307–310; independent development, 560; influence on South America, 661, 663, 668, 670; patriotic sentiment, in, 489; *Statutes at Large*, cited, 240. *See also* Australia and United States, Canada and United States, England and United States, France and United States, Switzerland and United States, also the several institutions of government, *i.e.* Cabinet, Constitution, etc.
United States v. Wong Kim Ark, cited, 324.
Unterwalden, Swiss canton, 615.
Uri, Swiss canton, 615.

INDEX

Utah, senator from, 120; restrictions imposed on, 245; on judicial circuit, 245.

Van Dyne, Frederick, *Citizenship of the United States*, 328.
Vaud, Swiss canton, 626.
Vermont, judges in, 383–385; legislative salaries, 349; on judicial circuit, 244.
Versailles, National Assembly at, 562; German empire proclaimed at, 599.
VETO POWER:
In Argentina, 678.
In Canada, 542, 543, 692.
In England, 76.
In France, 557, 558.
In Germany, 609.
In United States, in colonial times, 15; uses of, 306; effects, 26, 29; vested in president, 55, 71, 73–77, 90, 169, 170; in governors of States, 370.
Vice president, election of, 39, 40; office, 52, 53; presides in Senate, 132.
Victoria, queen of England, 480, 481; made empress of India, 484; influence during United States Civil War, 482; *Letters*, cited, 490.
Vincent, John M., *Government in Switzerland*, 620, 710.
Virginia, as a colony, 690; state constitutions, 344; judges in, 383; on judicial circuit, 244; and Constitutional Convention, 291.
Virginia v. *Tennessee*, cited, 316.
Voltaire, François M. A., political philosopher, 553.

Wakeman, Henry O., *History of Church of England*, 516, 522.
Wales, Prince of, 533.
Wales, conciliated by Edward I, 454; relation to England, 533, 539; representation in Parliament, 448–450; national characteristics, 533; church history, 521, 522; system of law, 582.
Walpole, Robert, English statesman, 429, 430, 433.
Walpole, Sir Spencer, *England since 1815*, 434, 515.
War, must be declared by Congress, 64, 65, 117; directed by president, 57; secretary for, in England, 436; in United States, 48. *See also* Wars.
War and Marine department in Chile, 665.

WAR DEPARTMENT:
In Argentina, 681.
In France, 567.
In United States, 97, 102, 103.
Ward v. *Maryland*, cited, 327.
WARS:
American Revolution, 4.
Civil, in United States, 10, 11, 64, 107, 311; presidency during, 31, 32; England's relation to, 482; constitutional amendments follow, 287, 319; expansion since, 109.
Franco-Prussian, 599.
Mexican, 65.
Roses (of the), 418, 423, 495.
Spanish-American, 32.
1812 (of), 422.
1914 (of), 612, 613.
Washington, George, in Constitutional Convention, 282; election, 38, 41; administration, 186; addresses Congress, 71, 306; vetoes, 75, 76; declines third term, 180; retires, 42, 51; a symbol of unity, 484; *Farewell Address*, 178, 179, 181, 691.
Washington (D. C.), capital, 40, 45, 112, 113; federal courts at, 248.
Washington (state), on judicial circuit, 245.
Watson, R. Spence, *National Liberal Federation*, 515.
Ways and Means Committee, of House of Commons, 452, 453, 476; of House of Representatives, 157–159, 162, 174.
Webster, Daniel, cited, 271.
Weights and Measures, standards, 117.
Wensleydale case, 460.
Westminster, Palace of, 447.
West Point, military academy at, 102.
West Saxon dynasty, in English history, 404, 516.
West Virginia, county courts in, 381; on judicial circuit, 244.
WHIG PARTY:
In England, origin of term, 494; policy, 179, 419, 428, 439, 506, 552; composition of, 495, 496.
In United States, 185, 191.
White, Edward D., justice of Supreme Court, 61.
White House, expenses of, 52.
White slavery, act to control, 300.
Whitney v. *Robertson*, cited, 69.
Wilkes, John, mob leader, 495.
William I, king of England, 415, 517,

523; separates church from secular courts, 516, 517.
William II, king of England, 414, 415.
William III, accession to throne, 428, 433, 519, 522, 536.
William IV, king of England, 479; creates peers, 500.
William I of Germany, as regent, 598; king of Prussia, 598; Emperor of Germany, 599, 606.
William II of Germany, idea of divine right, 607; telegram to Kruger, 482.
Willoughby, W. W., *Constitutional Law in United States*, 254, 258–260, 271–273, 280, 310, 311, 316; *Supreme Court*, 280; *The American Constitutional System*, 310, 311, 316.
Wilson, Woodrow, president of United States, 13, 194; calls special session of Congress, 135; addresses Congress, 73, 306; cited, 23, 32, 129, 130, 143, 159; *Constitutional Government in the United States*, 7, 10, 13, 32, 54, 79, 130, 149, 156, 159, 160, 166, 167, 176, 189, 275, 276, 280, 303; *The State*, 402, 571, 591, 601, 613, 620.
Winchester, Bishop of, sits in House of Lords, 460.
Winchester, Boyd, *The Swiss Republic*, 620.
Wisconsin, on judicial circuit, 244; new legislature in, 221, 203, 342; commissions, 375; legislative reference library, 353; senator, 291.
Wisconsin v. *Pelican Insurance Company*, cited, 315.
Witan, in relation to *Curia Regis*, 421.
Woman, status of alien, 323.
Woman's suffrage in England, 470, 482; in New Zealand, 545; in Norway, 651; in United States, 320.
Woodburn, James A., *Political Patries and Party Problems in the United States*, 189, 193, 197, 203, 213, 218, 230; *The American Republic*, 13, 30, 54, 75, 80, 144, 176, 181.
Workingmen's Compensation laws, 358, 374.
Worship and Colonization, department in Chile, 665.
Writs of Error, in Supreme Court, 243.
Wyclif, John, religious revival of, 518; political value of, 493.
Wyoming, on judicial circuit, 245.
Würtemburg, and the German empire, 602, 605.

York, Archbishop of, 460, 519; synod, 519.
Young, James T., *The New American Government and its Work*, 80, 115, 144, 176, 280, 339, 379.

Zurich, Socialists in, 637.

THE following pages contain advertisements of Macmillan books of related interest.

Property and Contract in Their Relation to the Distribution of Wealth

By RICHARD T. ELY, Ph.D., LL.D.

Of the University of Wisconsin; Author of "Outlines of Economics," Editor of "The Citizen's Library," etc.

Cloth, 8°, 2 vols., $4.00.
A special law library edition, sheep, $7.50

In this work, which is based upon legal decisions as well as upon economic principles, a leading authority in political economy considers simply and concisely one of the greatest problems now before the American people. Much has been heard and written of late about judicial readjustment and direct government, but few who have discussed the subject have seen the heart of it as clearly as does Professor Ely.

"We are indebted to Professor Ely for an excellent book. His style is clear and perspicuous, and his vocabulary for the most part untechnical. Economists ought to be able to understand his statement of the law, and lawyers his statement of economic theory. A study of the book ought to help bring together two classes who often have the same problems to deal with under different aspects, and often fail to understand each other. It would be an error, however, to give the impression that the book is essentially either a law book or a text book. It really deals in a philosophical way with the concepts of property and contract in their relation to the distribution of wealth.

The book ought to have many readers, and all would find it suggestive and helpful." — *Justice Francis J. Swayze, in the Quarterly Journal of Economics.*

"Our economists, like our legal writers, have for the most part merely carried forward the English tradition with its powerful leaning towards extreme individualism. Professor Ely of the University of Wisconsin was one of the first among American writers upon economic subjects to draw his inspiration from continental sources. His early work in this field set forth ideas drawn from the teachings of distinguished modern German thinkers and writers, and in the present work he has fitted the facts of American economic life into the theories and conclusions of these masters." — *California Law Review.*

"I want to express my great pleasure and profit in reading 'Property and Contract.' This seems to me the strongest of all the author's many able contributions to economic thought. It should be read by all judges, for this book has marked the highroad along which courts must travel if they are to make the law a living science that shall meet the needs of our ever-changing civilization."
— *Judge E. Ray Stevens, Circuit Court, Madison, Wis.*

"The book is one that should be in the hands of every lawyer and I really feel that the author has done the public a service. What we need these days is sanity, and sanity is to be found within the covers of this work."
— *Justice Andrew A. Bruce, Supreme Court, N. D.*

"I do not question that the book will have a wide influence especially on the young people who are breaking away from traditional property concepts, but are not mesmerized by Utopian nonsense." — *Professor Samuel P. Orth, Cornell University.*

THE MACMILLAN COMPANY
Publishers   **64-66 Fifth Avenue**   **New York**

SOCIAL SCIENCE TEXT-BOOKS
Edited by Richard T. Ely

The New American Government and Its Work
By JAMES T. YOUNG
Professor of Public Administration in the University of Pennsylvania

Cloth, 8vo, $2.25

This book, intended for that growing circle of readers who are interested not only in political form and structure, but also more especially in *What the Government Is Doing and Why*, is characterized by the following features:

1. It places greater emphasis than usual on the *work* of the government.

2. It pays more attention to present problems, especially to the *Public Regulation of Business*.

3. It applies to every aspect of government the test of *Results* — whether the subject be the powers of the President, the election laws, or the Sherman act — for the value of a court, a statute, or a political institution should be known by its output.

4. It depicts the *Government As It Is*, and as it has developed. Our system is not a finished crystal, nor an ancient historical manuscript, but a growth. And it is still growing.

5. It includes the interpretation of the Constitution and the chief regulative laws, in the most recent *Decisions of the Supreme Court*. It is this that gives clear, definite meaning to the discussion of government forms and activities.

6. It presents an *Ideal*. It does not hesitate to point out the moral defects, and the social cost of political weakness and inefficiency, but its *Tone* is *Optimistic*.

THE MACMILLAN COMPANY
Publishers　　　64-66 Fifth Avenue　　　**New York**

SOCIAL SCIENCE TEXT-BOOKS

Edited by Richard T. Ely

Outlines of Sociology

By FRANK W. BLACKMAR

Professor of Sociology in the University of Kansas

AND

JOHN L. GILLIN

Associate Professor of Sociology in the University of Wisconsin

8vo, $2.00

This book treats the theory and practice of social science in a series of chapters dealing with social pathology and methods of social investigation. The authors have presented the origin, nature, structure, functions, and abnormal phenomena of society, without controversy, and in a simple direct way, suited to the college undergraduate or the general reader.

Problems of Child Welfare

By GEORGE B. MANGOLD, Ph.D.

Director of the School of Social Economy of Washington University

Cloth, 8vo, $2.00

Although this book is designed especially for use as a text in college courses on philanthropy, it will also appeal to that growing class of men and women who in a systematic way are endeavoring to acquaint themselves with the various aspects of practical sociology.

Much of the constructive philanthropy of to-day must deal directly with the child, the improvement of his conditions being the direct objective. Those problems which affect children in an indirect way, whether in the field of remedial or preventive philanthropy, are not treated. Under each separate problem are discussed the causes and conditions, the machinery of social betterment, and the plans and program of improvement.

THE MACMILLAN COMPANY

Publishers   64-66 Fifth Avenue   New York

SOCIAL SCIENCE TEXT-BOOKS
Edited by Richard T. Ely

History of Economic Thought

A Critical Account of the Origin and Development of the Economic Theories of the Leading Thinkers and the Leading Nations

By LEWIS H. HANEY

Cloth, 8vo, $2.00

"Dr. Haney's work is both complete and exhaustive without being discursive. We shall look far before finding anything of its kind so satisfying."

— *The Argonaut.*

"The book should be of value to English readers and students of economics, for unlike French and German economic writers, who have produced several histories of economic thought, only one has been written previously in English, and that is now out of date. Dr. Haney has made a distinct contribution to economic literature and one reflecting credit on American scholarship." — *The Boston Transcript.*

Business Organization and Combination

An Analysis of the Evolution and Makers of Business Organization in the United States, and a Tentative Solution of the Corporation and Trust Problems

By LEWIS H. HANEY, Ph.D.

Professor of Economics in the University of Texas

Cloth, 8vo, 483 pages, $2.00

EXTRACTS FROM THE PREFACE

This book deals with the organization of business enterprises, chiefly in the United States.

The general scheme of the work is as follows: First comes a series of chapters describing and analyzing the various forms of business organization in such a way as to bring out the centuries-long evolution which has molded them. Then, the corporate form, being clearly dominant, the life history of a corporation is set forth in a series of chapters which describe in some detail the main event; promotion, underwriting, reorganization, and the like. Finally, great evils having appeared in corporate organization, the question of public policy is raised, and an attempt at a comprehensive and scientific solution of that question is made.

THE MACMILLAN COMPANY
Publishers   **64-66 Fifth Avenue**   **New York**

CITIZEN'S LIBRARY OF ECONOMICS, POLITICS, AND SOCIOLOGY

Edited by R. T. Ely

Each volume, 12mo, half leather, $1.25

American City, The. A Problem in Democracy. By D. F. Wilcox.
Child Problems. By George B. Mangold.
Colonial Administration. By Paul S. Reinsch.
Colonial Government. By P. S. Reinsch.
Commission Government in American Cities. By Ernest S. Bradford.
Democracy and Social Ethics. By Jane Addams.
Education and Industrial Evolution. By Frank Tracy Carlton.
Elements of Sociology. By F. W. Blackmar.
Essays in the Monetary History of the United States. By C. J. Bullock.
Foundations of Sociology. By E. A. Ross.
Government in Switzerland. By John M. Vincent.
Great Cities in America : Their Problems and Their Government. By Delos F. Wilcox.
History of Political Parties in the United States. By J. Macy.
International Commercial Policies. By G. M. Fisk.
Introduction to Business Organization. By S. E. Sparling.
Introduction to the Study of Agricultural Economics. By H. C. Taylor.
Irrigation Institutions: A Discussion of the Growth of Irrigated Agriculture in the Arid West. By E. Mead.
Money: A Study of the Theory of the Medium of Exchange. By David Kinley.
Monopolies and Trusts. By R. T. Ely.
Municipal Engineering and Sanitation. By M. N. Baker.
Newer Ideals of Peace. By Jane Addams.
Principles of Anthropology and Sociology, The, in their Relations to Criminal Procedure. By M. Parmelee.
Railway Legislation in the United States. By B. H. Meyer.
Social Control: A Survey of the Foundation of Order. By E. A. Ross.
Some Ethical Gains Through Legislation. By Mrs. Florence Kelley.
Spirit of American Government, The. By J. A. Smith.
Studies in the Evolution of Industrial Society. By R. T. Ely.
Wage-Earning Women. By Annie M. MacLean.
World Politics. By P. S. Reinsch.

CITIZEN'S LIBRARY OF ECONOMICS, POLITICS, AND SOCIOLOGY

New Series

Ellwood, Charles. The Social Problem.		*12mo, $1.25*
DeWitt, Benjamin P. The Progressive Movement.		*12mo, $1.50*
King, Willford I. Wealth and Income of the People of the United States.		*12mo, $1.50*
Zueblin, C. American Municipal Progress. New Edition.		*Preparing*

THE MACMILLAN COMPANY
Publishers   64-66 Fifth Avenue   New York

force
now he has number of plots.

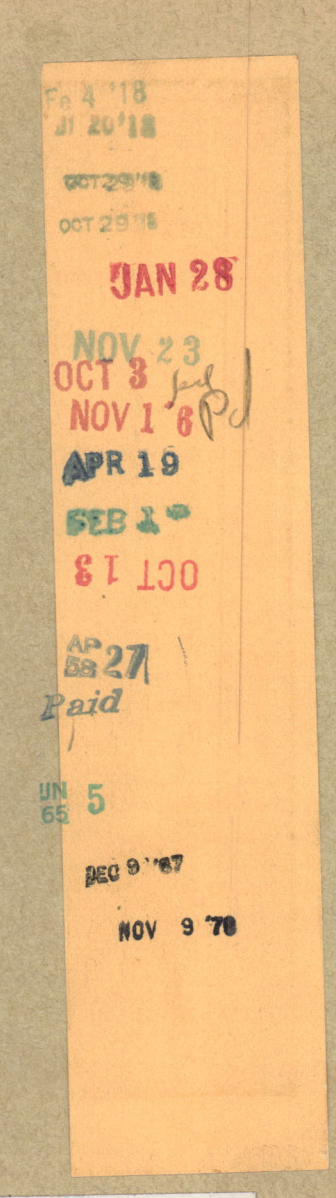